All-Time Nines

ALL-TIME NINES

Baseball's Greatest Teams as Determined by Analytics

DON COX

McFarland & Company, Inc., Publishers
Jefferson, North Carolina

Library of Congress Cataloguing-in-Publication Data

Names: Cox, Don, 1954–
Title: All-time nines : baseball's greatest teams as determined by analytics / Don Cox.
Description: Jefferson, North Carolina : McFarland & Company, Inc., Publishers, 2016 | Includes index.
Identifiers: LCCN 2015044415| ISBN 9781476663289 (softcover : acid free paper) | ISBN 9781476623191 (ebook) ♾
Subjects: LCSH: Baseball teams—United States—History. | Baseball—United States—History. | Baseball—Statistical methods.
Classification: LCC GV875.A1 C69 2016 | DDC 796.357/640973—dc23
LC record available at http://lccn.loc.gov/2015044415

British Library cataloguing data are available

ISBN (print) 978-1-4766-6328-9
ISBN (ebook) 978-1-4766-2319-1

Front cover: (top) baseball glove and bats © 2015 Thinkstock; (bottom) Yankee Stadium in 1923

Printed in the United States of America

McFarland & Company, Inc., Publishers
Box 611, Jefferson, North Carolina 28640
www.mcfarlandpub.com

Table of Contents

Preface

This is a book about major league baseball's best teams. The top 120 team seasons, representing about 5 percent of the total number of team AL and NL seasons from 1901 to 2014, are featured in the first three chapters of this book. Each featured team season has team and individual player valuations for hitting, baserunning, fielding, and pitching compared to league average for that season. The teams from the 1944 and 1945 seasons are not included in any of the rankings because the preponderance of baseball talent was in the military during those years.

How do baseball teams become great? Teams become great by scoring significantly more runs or allowing significantly fewer runs than their opposition. One of the best indicators of team dominance in any given season is run differential per game, which is the difference between runs scored and runs allowed per game. A team that has a run differential of around one run per game is invariably having a dominant season; a team that has a differential of around negative one run per game is invariably having a terrible season. Only one World Series–winning team ever had a negative run differential, the 1987 Twins.

Winning an average of 6 out of 10 regular season games is considered a very successful season and will usually land a team in the postseason. It is a rare team that can win 60 percent of its games for an entire season and even rarer for teams to win at that pace over several consecutive seasons. It is perhaps unsurprising, then, that there is only one manager in the history of major league baseball with a career winning percentage greater than 60 percent, Joe McCarthy, who had a 0.614 winning percentage.

For a team that plays 154 regular-season games, a 60 percent winning percentage translates to a 92-win team, which represents 15 more wins than a team that wins 50 percent of their 154 games. Fifteen more wins equates to about 150 runs above league average.

For a team that plays 162 regular-season games, winning 60 percent translates to a 97-win campaign, which represents 16 more wins than a team that wins 50 percent. Those 16 extra wins are worth about 160 runs above league average. Any combination of hitting, baserunning, fielding, or pitching success equating to at least 150 or 160 runs, respectively, will in most instances propel a team to the postseason; it will also secure that team a spot among the top 10 percent of the 2,216 teams active since 1901.

This book uses analytics to identify major league baseball's best teams of the past and determine which players and what skills (pitching, hitting, fielding, and baserunning) made them great. Each player's skill set for the featured team is translated to a number of runs above or below league average, giving the reader a sense of how effective that player performed for the team. This book also discusses weaknesses in each of the top 120 great teams that, had they been addressed, could have made the team even better. In addition, key statistics are shown for each player on each featured team further helping to explain how that player contributed to the team's success.

Introduction

Ranking Teams—A Methodology

The goal of a baseball team is to win baseball games. In order to win games, a team needs to score more runs than the opposition. A baseball team with a winning record will usually score more runs than they allow, which is otherwise known as a positive run differentiation. There are two primary ways for a team to score runs: hitting and baserunning. There are also two primary ways to prevent the other team from scoring runs: fielding and pitching.

Simple Explanation of the Ranking Method

Teams are ranked based on how the team dominates their opposition during the regular season. Teams were selected to be ranked depending upon their run differentiation per game. Run differentiation is the difference between runs scored and runs allowed. All teams with a run differentiation of at least 0.7 runs per game representing about 500 team seasons were selected to be ranked. World Series winners were also added to the list of teams that were ranked even if the team run differentiation was less than 0.7 runs per game. None of the top 120 greatest teams had a run differentiation less than 0.9 runs per game and the vast majority of these teams had a run differentiation greater than 1.0 runs per game.

Each team's offensive positive outcomes, singles, doubles, triples, home runs, walks, and hit by pitcher, are weighted based on runs per that outcome. Also, the out factor is calculated so that the combined weighted positive outcomes when combined with negative weighted outs for that league season equate to zero. The weight factor for an out depends upon that season's run scoring environment. The team's positive offensive weighted outcomes (hits, walks, and hit by pitcher) are subtracted from its negative weighted outcomes (outs) to come up with hitting runs above or below average. Individual player batting runs are similarly calculated. The team or individual baserunning runs are then added to the batting runs to calculate a team or individual total offense number.

To calculate a team's run allowed, the league average runs allowed per inning pitched is multiplied by the team's inning pitched to obtain the amount of runs allowed if the team is league average. This number is then compared to the actual team's run allowed to obtain the total defense number of runs above average. The individual pitchers are allocated pitching runs in the same fashion. The team's fielding runs above or below league average number is subtracted from the total calculated runs allowed to obtain the number of runs above average attributable to the pitching staff.

Each team's calculated runs scored above league average number is added to the league average runs scored to give a calculated team runs scored. Each team's calculated defensive runs allowed compared to league average is subtracted from the league average runs allowed to give a calculated team runs allowed. Then, the calculated team runs scored and runs allowed numbers are placed into the Pythagenpat formula (see Appendix A) to calculate the winning percentage of each team which is the measure used to rank each team.

Detailed Explanation of the Ranking Method

Batting Runs (Bat >Avg)

Hitters can either get on base or make outs. Studies from Pete Palmer and John Thorn a couple of decades ago in their book titled *The Hidden Game of Baseball* have given accurate weighting to different batting outcomes. Hits, walks, and being hit by pitch contribute to runs scored while outs contribute to fewer runs scored. Extra base hits contribute more than singles and walks. Runs Contributed is the name that Pete Palmer gave to the statistic that is derived from the different hitting events.

Below are the various run weights given to each hitting outcome:

Single (1B): 0.47
Double (2B): 0.78
Triple (3B): 1.09
Homerun (HR): 1.40
Walk (BB): 0.31
Hit by Pitch (HBP): 0.31

Value of an Out: varies around -0.26 runs from year to year depending upon the league's run scoring environment for that season; the exact value of the out constant is calculated using the below formula using regular season league data:

((0.47*1B) + (0.78*2B) + (1.09*3B) + (1.4*HR) + 0.31*(BB + HBP)) / (At Bats—Hits)

The Batting Runs statistic for a team or individual player is calculated using the below formula:

(0.47*1B) + (0.78*2B) + (1.09*3B) + (1.4*HR) + 0.31*(BB + HBP)—(Value of an Out * (At Bats—Hits))

A player with a negative value is hurting his team while a player with a positive value is helping his team win more than an average number of games. Appendices A and B contain additional details and examples of team and player Batting Runs.

Baserunning Runs (BR R>Avg)

Once players are on base, baserunning can contribute or detract from runs scored. The baserunning measurement is calculated using 2 primary criteria, good baserunning resulting in an extra base taken and bad baserunning resulting in an out. Examples of good baserunning are stolen bases, bases taken after a fly out, hitting a triple, reaching base on an error, and extra bases taken as a man on base after your teammate hits a single or double, for example, going from first base to third base on a single or going from first base to home plate on a double. Examples of bad base-running are being picked off base, caught stealing, being thrown out trying to advance a base on a fly out or hit, and grounding into a double play.

It is a rather complex process to total all the good and bad baserunning plays to calculate a number for each team and player. Fortunately, this work has already done by others and is listed on the baseball-reference.com website and in this book as baserunning runs (BR R>Avg). There is limited baserunning data available before 1954. For example, Caught Stealing is not a statistic that was generally available for individual players in both leagues until 1954. So, player baserunning runs shown before 1954 are not as comprehensive as those player baserunning runs in seasons after 1953. A player with a negative baserunning runs value is hurting his team while a player with a positive value is helping his team win more than an average number of games.

Offensive Runs

Player and team offensive effectiveness are measured using two primary statistics: Batting Runs (Bat R>Avg) and Baserunning Runs (BR R>Avg). Each team's baserunning runs (extracted from the baseball-reference web site) and the team's hitting runs are combined and used to calculate the team's offensive runs scored. Below is the formula to calculate a team's Offensive Runs:

Offensive Runs Scored = (Team Bat >Avg) + (Team BR R>Avg) + League Average Runs Scored

A positional player with a negative offensive runs value is hurting his team while a player with a positive value is helping his team win more than an average number of games.

Fielding Runs (Fld >Avg)

On the defensive side, the primary purpose of fielders is to convert balls hit into the field of play into outs. Some ways to measure fielding are: (1) range measured as putouts and assists per 9 innings fielding the position compared to league average, (2) making good plays which are plays that normal fielders do not make, and (3) making bad plays defined as not making plays that fielders normally make at that position. A wonderful team fielding statistic that accurately measures team fielding is BABIP, standing for Batting Average on Balls in Play. The lower the BABIP compared to league average, the better the team fielding. A team's BABIP compared to league average BABIP indicates whether or not fielding is helping this team to be better at fielding than the league average team. Individual players have seasonal Fielding Run numbers based on how well they compared to their peers at their position.

It is another rather complex process to fully consider range, fielding opportunities, BABIP, good fielding plays, and bad fielding plays to calculate a fielding number for each team and player. Fortunately, this work has already done by others and is listed on the baseball-reference.com website and in this book as fielding runs above/below league average (Fld R>Avg). With the advent of new sophisticated video and statistical methods used to evaluate fielding, player fielding runs from 2002 to 2014 are more comprehensive than fielding runs in seasons before

2002. A player with a negative fielding runs value is hurting his team while a player with a positive value is helping his team win more than an average number of games.

Pitching Runs (RAA or Pitching R>Avg)

Pitching effectiveness is measured in this book by Runs Allowed per 9 innings pitched (RAA) compared to league average RAA. Fielders help determine runs allowed by making good and bad plays on balls hit in the field of play. The team fielding measurement of runs above/below average can be apportioned and easily netted from each pitcher's RAA to give a runs allowed below/above league average (RAA) for each pitcher and team. The first step used in this book to calculate a pitcher's net RAA is:

((League Average Runs Allowed per Innings Pitched) × (Pitcher's Innings Pitched))—Pitcher's Actual Runs Allowed

The fielding adjustment is netted from the above calculation to complete the Pitching Runs formula. Since the fielders only effect balls hit into play (BIP), the team's Fielding Runs is apportioned based on the percentage of BIP given up by the pitcher. For example, if Pitcher A is responsible for giving up 10 percent of the team's BIP, then 10 percent of the team's Fielding Runs above league average is netted against the above formula. So, if the team's Fielding Runs is a positive 50, meaning that a team's Fielding Runs is 50 runs better than league average, then, in this example, 5 runs are subtracted from the above formula to calculate the net Pitching Runs above league average for Pitcher A.

A pitcher with a negative RAA value is hurting his team while a player with a positive value is helping his team win more than an average number of games by that number of runs over the course of the season.

Defensive Runs Allowed

Defensive effectiveness is measured using two primary statistics: Fielding Runs (Fld R>Avg) and Pitching Runs (Pitching R>Avg). Each team's fielding runs (extracted from the baseball-reference web site) and the team's calculated pitching runs (RAA) are combined and used to calculate the team's defensive runs scored. Below is the formula to calculate a team's Defensive Runs Allowed:

Defensive Runs Allowed = (League Average Runs Allowed)—(Fld >Avg)—(RAA)

The Defensive Runs Allowed should be close to the Actual Runs Allowed for each team especially if the pitching staff has about the same number of innings pitched as the league average team innings pitched.

Predicted Team Winning Percentage and Team Rankings

Both the calculated runs scored and defensive runs allowed are inserted in a baseball algorithm called the Pythagenpat formula which converts these calculations into a predicted winning percentage used to calculate a team's predicted win-loss record. The predicted team winning percentage is used to rank all the AL and NL teams from 1901 until 2014. Teams from 1901 until 2014 are ranked against each other as well as ranked against teams of its own era. This book defines the different eras as Dead Ball (1901–1919), Live Ball (1920–1960), and Expansion (1961–2014). Appendix A shows the Pythagenpat formula used to calculate winning percentages.

All four measurements of hitting, baserunning, fielding, and pitching in this book are expressed in terms of runs compared to league average. A positive number signifies that the team and individual has had a better than league average season in that category while a negative number signifies that the team or individual has had a worse than league average season in that category. Therefore, it's easy to see a team and individual player's strengths and weaknesses.

For each of the 120 best team seasons listed in Part 1, this book includes detailed statistics of all starting and key bench positional players plus the primary starting and relief pitchers.

The DNA of Great Baseball Teams

Below is a chart listing some key statistics that can be used to draw some conclusions regarding the top 250 greatest baseball teams representing the top 11 percent of all AL and NL team seasons from 1901 to 2014.

	Bat R>Avg	*BR R>Avg*	*Fielding R>Avg*	*Pitching R>Avg*	*Pythag W%*	*R>Avg Total*	*Bat %>Avg*	*BR %>Avg*	*Fldg %>Avg*	*P %>Avg*
Average	81	4	32	69	0.6240	185	43.6%	2.2%	17.0%	37.1%
Max	235	31	119	212	0.7294	398				
Min	-37	-20	-63	-30	0.5943	92				
Median	82	3	31	65	0.6166	179	45.9%	1.7%	17.3%	36.4%

- Defense is slightly more attributable to a top team's success than their offense when defense is defined as both fielding and pitching.
- Pitching is about twice as important to a typical great team's success as fielding.
- Hitting is slightly more important to a typical great team's success than pitching.
- Baserunning is usually not that important for a team's success since most teams do not generate many runs above or below league average via baserunning.
- Considering that positional players also field 8 out of the 9 positions and run the bases, positional players contribute on average about 63 percent to a typical great team's success.
- As shown in the above chart, pitchers contribute an average of 37 percent to a typical great team's success.

Meaningful Hitting Statistics

On Base Percentage

On Base Percentage is the most important hitting statistic because it includes batting average as well as walks and hits by pitcher.

Slugging Percentage and Isolated Power

Slugging Percentage and its more targeted cousin statistic Isolated Power (Slugging Percentage—Batting Average) are the next best hitting statistics because they capture the hitter's ability to hit for power.

Hitting Run Valuations

Singles

Each single is worth approximately 0.47 runs.

Doubles

Each double is worth approximately 0.78 runs equating to the value of a single plus an additional 0.31 runs.

Triples

Each triple is worth approximately 1.09 runs equating to the value of a double plus and additional 0.31 runs.

Home Runs

Each home run is worth approximately 1.40 runs equating to the value of a triple plus and additional 0.31 runs.

Walks and Hit by Pitcher

Each walk and hit by pitcher are both worth 0.31 runs.

Outs

The value of an out varies by season and has a negative effect on runs scored. On average each out is worth approximately -0.26 runs and usually varies from -0.29 to -0.21 runs depending on the league's run scoring environment for that season. A season with a low scoring environment like the AL in 1968 has a low value of an out (-0.22 runs) while a season with a high scoring environment like the AL in 1995 has a high value of an out (-.29).

Meaningful Fielding Statistics

Fielding Runs (Defensive Runs Saved or Fielding Zone Runs)

The most important individual and team fielding statistic is a calculation of how many runs a player saves his team compared to other players at his same position. If a player is better than league average, he has a positive Fielding Runs number. This calculation takes into consideration good plays such as converting double plays and throwing runners out and bad plays such as not making routine plays and throwing and errors.

Batting Average on Balls in Play (BABIP)

A team's opponent BABIP is an important team fielding statistic as it measures the ability of the team to convert balls hit into play into outs.

Range Factor per 9 Innings (RF/9)

Another important fielding statistic is RF/9 or Range Factor per 9 innings played since it measures how many putouts and assists the player makes per 9 innings. When this statistic is compared to other major league players at his position, this statistic is particularly meaningful except at the Catcher and First Base positions. Getting to the ball and making assists and putouts more than the average player at your position, means more than how many errors the player made.

Held+

A measurement of outfield arm strength that calculates the percentage of time that a baserunner does not advance from first base to third base on a single, second base to home on a single, and first base to home on a double. This percentage is then compared to the league average for players at their position. A rating of 100 is league average, a rating of 95 is 5 percent below league average, and a rating of 105 is 5 percent above league average.

Meaningful Pitching Statistics

Runs Allowed (RAA)

The best pitcher statistic is net Runs Allowed above league average (RAA) since it measures pitching effectiveness given the team's defensive fielding. This statistic compares how many runs the pitcher allowed relative to the league average given average team fielding.

Fielding Independent Pitching (FIP)

The next best pitcher statistic since it measures pitching effectiveness given what the pitcher controls and what the fielders cannot control. FIP takes into consideration strikeouts, walks, hit by pitcher, home runs allowed, and innings pitched into the equation. A pitcher's FIP should be compared to the league average FIP which is roughly equivalent to the league ERA.

Meaningful Baserunning Statistics

Stolen Bases and Caught Stealing (SB and CS)

A successful stolen base is similar to a walk or hit by pitcher in its value, about 0.31 run. However, an unsuccessful stolen base is an out plus a removal of a base runner. An out is valued about -0.25 run. Also, the base runner caught stealing is no longer on base so the 0.31 run is eliminated. So, a base runner would need to steal at least 2 bases for every 1 base caught, a steal success rate of 67 percent or better, in order to eliminate the downside of a caught stealing.

Extra Base Taken Percentage (XBT%)

Extra Base Taken Percentage is a measure of baserunning calculating the percentage of opportunities that the base runner advances to first to third on a single, second to home on a single, and first to home on a double. If the player has a higher XBT% than the average for that season, then he could be considered an above average baserunner. The XBT% statistic is available from 1946 to present.

Runs Scored Percentage (RS%)

Runs Scored Percentage is defined as the percentage that the player scores when he reaches base during the season. An average baserunner scores about one third of the time when he is on base. The better base runners will usually score an average of at least 40 percent of the time they reach base. If the player has a higher RS% than the league season average, then he could be considered an above average baserunner.

Team Profile Statistics

Mgr	Joe Torre	
Rk	3	18
Gm	162	
Place	1	
GA	22.0	
Rival	7–5 vs Red Sox; 73 RS, 53 RA	

	W	*L*	*Win%*
Regular Season	114	48	0.704
Runs Record	108	54	0.668
1 Run	21	10	0.677
Extra Innings	9	2	0.818
Blowout	42	13	0.764
RA/G	4.05	5.01	124

	Team	*LgAvg*	*%Avg*	*LgRk*
BABIP	0.280	0.301	108	1
E	98	114	116	3
sOBP	0.309	0.340	110	1
rOBP	0.320	0.337	105	2
R/G	5.96	5.01	119	1
1				

	Tm	*LgAvg*	*>Avg*
RS	965	797	168
RA	656	798	142
DP	146	149	-3

	R/G	*HR*	*K*	*BB*	*SB*	*CS*	*SB%*	*OPS*
Team Offense	5.96	207	1025	653	153	63	71%	0.825
Team Defense	4.05	156	1080	466	102	51	67%	0.699
Difference	1.91	51	55	187	51			118%

	Held+
LF	95
CF	99
RF	106

Mgr: the name of the team's manager when the season completed

Rk: the era rank (1901–1919, 1920–1960, or 1961–2014) and the overall (1901–2014) team rank compared to the other great teams in baseball history; 1901–1919 was the Dead Ball era when the baseball itself had much less bounce which limited home runs; 1920–1960 is the Live Ball era when there were 8 teams in each league; 1961–2014 is the Expansion Era when the number of teams per league gradually expanded from 8 to 15.

Gm: number of games played during the regular season

Place: the position that the team finished in their league or division at the end of the regular season

GA/GB: Games Ahead/Games Behind; the number of games that the team finished ahead of the second place team or behind the first place team in the league or division

Rival: head-to-head record against the league leading team or second place team

Regular Season: the Win-Loss actual record during the regular season

Runs Record: the Win-Loss record resulting from expected runs scored and runs allowed in the regular season; if the Runs Record is much different than the actual regular season record, good or bad luck is probably a factor

1 Run: the Win-Loss record of the team in games decided by 1 run; an indicator of luck especially if the 1 Run Win percentage is higher than 60 percent (good luck) or lower than 40 percent (bad luck); an excellent 1 Run Winning percentage could also indicate excellent late game relief pitching or managerial skill

Extra Innings: the Win-Loss record of the team in games decided in extra innings; another indicator of luck

Blowout: the Win-Loss record of the team in games decided by 5 or more runs; a good indicator of dominance

BABIP: batting average of balls in play allowed by the defense; this statistic when compared to the league BABIP is an excellent comparative fielding measurement

E: errors made

sOBP: the on base percentage allowed by the starting pitching; OBP is calculated as (Hits + Walks + Hit by Pitch) / (At Bats + Walks + Hits by Pitch + Sacrifice Flies)

rOBP: the on base percentage allowed by the relief pitching; OBP is calculated as (Hits + Walks + Hit by Pitch) / (At Bats + Walks + Hits by Pitch + Sacrifice Flies)

R/G: runs per game during the regular season; the difference between the R/G for the offense and the R/G for the defense is run differentiation per game which is a good measure of the dominance of a team; a run differentiation of greater than 0.5 is considered good, a run differentiation of greater than 1.0 is considered great

RA/G: runs allowed per game during the regular season

RS: actual runs scored by the offense during the regular season

RA: actual runs allowed by the defense during the regular season

DP: double plays converted by the fielders

HR: home runs

K: strikeouts

BB: walks

SB: stolen bases

CS: number of times caught stealing

SB%: stolen base percentage; the percentage of successful stolen base attempts; 67 percent is considered good

OPS: on-base percentage + slugging percentage; the team offense and team defense allowed OPS are both shown as well as the ratio of offense OPS to defense OPS; a ratio of 110 percent or better is a good indicator of a great team

Held+: the ratio of the outfielders' ability to prevent the baserunner from advancing the extra base (1B to 3B on a single, 2B to home on a single, or 1B to home on a double) compared to the league average for that outfield position; 100 is league average, 95 is 5 percent worse than league average, and 110 is 10 percent better than league average; the team's LF, CF, and RF overall Held+ is shown; Held+ is an excellent statistic for evaluating a team or player's arm strength in the outfield positions

Positional Player Statistics

Pos	*Rpos*	*PA*	*Age*	*Name*	*BA*	*OBP*	*SLG*	*BB%*	*XBT%*	*Bat R>Avg*	*BR R>Avg*	*Fld R>Avg*	*RAA*	*WAA*
C,DH	5	409	26	Posada, Jorge^	0.268	0.350	0.475	11%	36%	7	-2	7	12	1.1

Pos: most commonly played fielding position(s) listed in the order of most games played

Rpos: positional adjustment runs; run value of the position reflecting the relative scarcity of the position; runs are added to the player's value at some defensive positions such as Catcher and SS and subtracted from other positions such as 1B, LF and RF; it is usually easier for a major league team to find league average or better than average 1B, LF, and RF positional hitters than it is for teams to find higher than league average hitting SS or Catchers; for example, a league average hitting fielding catcher is worth more runs than a league average hitting left fielder; the total of each team's Rpos add to zero; in this book, the pitcher and DH positions are given a 0 Rpos value

PA: plate appearances

Name: the * symbol after the player name signifies a left hand hitter; the ^ symbol after the player name signifies a switch hitter

BA: batting average; the formula is: Hits / At Bats; this statistic ignores walks and hit by pitch in its calculation and assumes every hit, whether it is a single, double, triple, or homerun, is equally weighted in the calculation

OBP: on-base percentage; the formula is (Hits + Walks

+ Hit by Pitch) / (At Bats + Walks + Hit by Pitch + Sacrifice Flies); this statistic is a better indicator of hitting ability than BA since it includes Walks and Hit by Pitch in the calculation; this statistic's main flaw in describing a player's or team's offensive prowess is that every hit, no matter whether it is a single, double, triple, or home run, is equally weighted in the calculation

SLG: slugging percentage; the formula is: (Singles + 2 * Doubles + 3 * Triples + 4 * Homeruns)/At Bats or Total Bases/At Bats; this statistic's main flaw to determine a player's offensive contribution is that it ignores walks and hit by pitch; also it assumes a double is as important as 2 singles, a triple is as important as 3 singles, and a homerun is as important as 4 singles which is not actually the case (see Bat R>Avg definition and discussion)

BB%: walk percentage; calculated as Walks / Plate Appearances; a 5 percent walk percentage is considered poor, a 10 percent walk percentage is considered good, and a 15 percent walk percentage is considered excellent

XBT%: extra base taken percentage; a good measure of baserunning speed that calculates the percentage of when the baserunner takes the extra base after a hit, for example, from first base to third base on a single, from second base to home on a single, and from first base to home on a double; an XBT% of 45 percent or better is considered very good

Bat R>Avg: batting runs above average; the number of runs above or below league average attributed to the hitting skill of the player or team; each offensive event is weighted in the formula; a single is weighted to be 0.47 runs and each extra base is weighted another 0.31 runs while walks and hit by pitch events are weighted as 0.31 runs; making outs are subtracted when calculating each player's Bat R>Avg total; the out value depends on the season run scoring environment but usually averages about 0.26 runs; the formula is: 0.47*1B + .78*2B + 1.09*3B + 1.40*HR + 0.31*(BB + HBP)—value of an out*(AB-Hits); the out value constant formula is: (0.47*lg1B + 0.78*lg2B + 1.09*lg3B + 0.31*(lgBB + lgHBP)) / (lgAB—lgH); a hitter with a negative value is hurting his team while a player with a positive value is helping his team by that number of runs

BR R>Avg: baserunning runs above average; the number of runs above or below league average attributed to the baserunning skill of the player or team; statistics such as GIDP tendency, stolen base attempts, stolen base percentage, extra base taken percentage, runs scored percentage, and triples are used to calculate the BR R>Avg statistic; this statistic is taken from the player and team listings in the baseball-reference.com web site

Fld R>Avg: fielding runs above average; also sometimes called defensive runs saved; the number of runs above or below league position average attributed to the fielding skill of the player or team; the Fld R>Avg is determined using statistics such as fielding range and double play conversion skill for the 2B, SS, and 3B positions, fielding range and arm strength for the outfielders, and caught stealing percentage and passed balls for the catcher position; this statistic is also extracted from the baseball-reference.com web site

RAA: runs above average; the calculation for positional players is Rpos + Bat R>Avg + BR R>Avg + Fld R>avg; the RAA is the total offensive and defensive contribution compared to league average for each positional player

WAA: wins above average; WAA equates to RAA divided by a constant figure which is usually between 9 and 11 depending on the league runs scoring environment for that season; so, in a normal run scoring league environment, then 10 runs above average equates to about 1 win; the exact formula used in this book to convert runs above average to wins is the square root of league total runs divided by half of the league innings pitched multiplied by 10; so a calculation resulting in 10.60 would mean that it would take 10.6 runs for an additional win

% Lg Avg: the ratio of the team totals compared to the league average; for example, a 100 score means that the team is average in that category compared to the league in that category, a 95 score means that the team was 5 percent worse than the league average in that category, and a 110 score means that the profiled team is 10 percent better than the league average.

League Rank: the place that the team finished in the league in that category

Pitching Statistics

GS	*GR*	*IP*	*Age*	*Name*	*W-L*	*GmSc*	*K/9*	*BB/9*	*HR/9*	*FIP*	*ERA*	*RA/9*	*RAA*	*WAA*
32	1	216	26	Petitte, Andy*	16–11	49.8	6.1	3.6	0.83	4.41	4.24	4.58	7	0.7

GS: games started
GR: games in relief
IP: innings pitched
Name: the * symbol appearing after the player name signifies a left-handed pitcher
W-L: the Win-Loss record of the pitcher during the regular season; not a true measure of a pitcher's effectiveness
GmSc: Game Score; a starting pitching statistic developed by Bill James that subtracts points based on negative events such as hits allowed, runs allowed, and walks and adds points based on positive events such as innings pitched, shutout innings, and strikeouts; the league average is usually about 50; a Game Score above league average is a good indicator of starting pitching effectiveness
WHIP (shown in earlier years when the GmSc statistic was not available)**:** walks + hits divided by innings pitched; a good WHIP is less than 1.20
BA (shown in earlier seasons): opposition batting average
K/9: strikeouts per 9 innings pitched
BB/9: walks allowed per 9 innings pitched
HR/9: home runs allowed per 9 innings pitched
FIP: fielding independent pitching; an excellent measure of pitching effectiveness based on those things that pitchers can control such as strikeouts, walks, and hit by pitcher and things that fielders cannot control such as home runs allowed; research has shown that pitchers do not have much control on outcomes of balls in play; whether a ground ball goes for a hit or is turned into an out is mostly outside of a pitcher's control; this statistic measures what a player's ERA would be if the pitcher were to have experienced league average results on balls in play; the formula for FIP is (13*HR + 3*(BB+HBP)—2*K) / IP + constant; the constant is used to adjust the FIP to a number that can be compared to the ERA statistic; the FIP constant is calculated as follows: (13*lgHR + 3*(lgBB + lgHBP) -2*lgK) / lgIP
ERA: earned run average; ERA is calculated as 9* (earned runs/innings pitched); the problem with this statistic is that you don't really know how much the ERA is due to the pitcher alone and how much of the ERA is due to the fielding behind the pitcher
RA/9: runs allowed per 9 innings; similar to ERA except that all runs allowed are counted in the calculation, not just the earned runs; runs allowed statistics are somewhat dependent on the quality of the fielding supporting the pitcher
RAA: runs allowed above/below league average; this calculation subtracts the pitcher's actual runs allowed from the league average runs allowed per inning multiplied by the actual number of innings pitched for that pitcher, then that number is netted for a portion of the team's total Fielding>Avg; the team Fielding R>Avg total is allocated among the pitching staff based on balls in play allowed by each pitcher; for example, if a pitcher allows 15 percent of the entire pitching staff's balls in play, then 15 percent of the team's Fielding>Avg score will be netted during the calculation of the pitcher's RAA score
WAA: wins above average attributed to each pitcher and to the pitching staff overall; the RAA is converted to WAA the same way as it was done in the positional player statistics; the **RAA** and **WAA** statistics are excellent measurements of a pitcher's true effectiveness
% Lg Avg: the ratio of the team totals compared to the league average; for example, a 100 score means that the team is average in that category compared to the league for that category, a 95 score means that the team was 5 percent worse than the league average for that category, and a 110 score means that the profiled team is 10 percent better than the league average in that category
League Rank: the place that the team finished in the league in that category

Other Abbreviations and Statistics

IR stranded: inherited runners stranded; when a relief pitcher enters a game, there may be runners on the bases; if these inherited runners do not score while that pitcher is still on the mound, then the pitcher is credited with stranding the baserunners; for example 40/50/80 percent IR stranded means that the pitcher has prevented scoring of 40 of the 50 baserunners that were on base when the relief pitcher entered the game equating to an IR stranded percentage of 80 percent; an IR stranded percentage of 70 percent or better is considered very good.
Sv: saves; 20/30/67 percent Sv means that the relief pitcher has been credited with 20 Saves out of 30 Save Opportunities implying 10 Blown Saves, and a 67 percent Save percentage; an 80 percent or higher save percentage is considered good for a closer
Hold: means that the pitcher enters the game in a save situation and leaves the game before it is over with

his team still ahead; this is a rather new statistic that became popular over the last twenty years

Lv: Leverage Index; a relief pitcher statistic that indicates the pressure situation when the relief pitcher enters the game; an average (or neutral) Leverage Index is 1, high leverage is 1.5 and above, and lower leverage is below 1; 10 percent of game situations have a Leverage Index greater than 2, while 60 percent of game situations have a Leverage Index less than 1; usually pitchers used in close game situations in the later innings have a Leverage Index greater than 1.1; the Closer usually has the highest team Lv while the set-up pitchers used in close game situations in the 7th and 8th innings have the next highest team Leverage Index

K/BB: strikeout to walk ratio; an important measurement of the effectiveness of a pitcher; a good ratio is 2.0 or better meaning that the pitcher strikes out twice as many batters as he walks

LOB%: left on base percentage; a pitching statistic which is the percentage of baserunners who do not score

RS%: Runs Scored percentage; a baserunning statistic which is the percentage of the time that the player scores when he is on base

1B: First Base position or single dependent on usage

2B: Second Base position or double dependent on usage

3B: Third Base position or triple dependent on usage

HR: Home Run

RoY: Rookie of the Year

K%: percentage of plate appearances that the batter or team had a strikeout

QS%: quality start percentage; in most seasons, the league average quality start percentage is about 50 percent; a quality start is defined as a pitching start when the pitcher completes at least 6 innings and allows 3 or fewer earned runs; a good indicator of starting pitching effectiveness

H/9: hits allowed by the team defense per 9 innings; sometimes used as a measurement of pitcher prowess although this statistic is highly dependent on the team's fielding prowess; better pitcher effectiveness measurements are FIP, RA/9, RAA, GmSc, QS%, K/BB, and ERA

CS%: caught stealing percentage; a CS% of greater than 33 percent is considered good

GIDP: grounded into double plays

OPS: on base percentage + slugging percentage; this statistic adds two flawed statistics but oddly enough the flaws nearly cancel each other out to create a statistic that doesn't mean much by itself, but is a good indicator of hitting contribution especially when compared to league average OPS

ISO: isolated power; calculated using the formula: SLG-BA; a better statistic than the SLG slugging percentage statistic to determine the extra base hitting power of a hitter since it uses a formula that excludes singles in the calculation

PART I

1. The Dead-Ball Era (1901–1919)

1901 Pittsburgh Pirates

The American League began in 1901 with the formation of 8 teams which competed with the established National League for talent and fans. The only team in the NL in 1901 that effectively resisted player defections to the AL was the Pittsburgh Pirates. In fact, the Pirates also had just received some of the best players from the recently defunct Louisville Colonels National League team. Consequently, the 1901 Pirates dominated the other NL teams in 1901 winning nearly 65 percent of their games. The key positional move occurred when RF Lefty Davis was signed as a free agent on June 22, 1901, moving Honus Wagner from RF to the SS position.

Strengths: (1) hitting for average, contact, and power from Wagner (37 2B, 11 3B), Clarke (24 2B, 15 3B), Beaumont, Davis (11 3B), Bransfield (26 2B, 16 3B), and Leach (13 3B), (2) fielding especially from SS Ely (90 Rng+), 3B Leach (109 Rng+), LF Clarke (116 Rng+), 2B Ritchey (104 Rng+), and SS Wagner (116 Rng+), (3) CS% from O'Conner (49%), Zimmer (48%), and Yeager (49%), and (4) pitching featuring excellent control led by the top 3 starters Chesbro, Phillippe, and Tannehill who all had ERAs below 2.40.

Weaknesses: (1) C position, (2) hitting from Ely, (3) team K/9, and (4) pitching from Wiltse (11.9 H/9) and Poole.

Mgr	Fred Clarke	
Rk	15	37
Gm	140	
Place	1	
GA	7.5	
Rival	13–7 vs Phillies, 100 RS & 73 RA	

	W	*L*	*Win%*
Regular Season	90	49	0.647
Runs Record	91	48	0.652
1 Run	17	16	0.515
Blowout	36	11	0.766

	Team	*LgAvg*	*%Avg*	*LgRk*
BABIP	0.278	0.295	106	2
E	285	307	108	4
K%	9.0%	9.9%	110	
RS%	41.2%	37.4%	110	
R/G	5.55	4.63	120	2
RA/G	3.81	4.63	121	1

	Tm	*LgAvg*	*>Avg*
RS	777	650	127
RA	534	650	116
DP	97	91	6

	R/G	*HR*	*K*	*BB*	*SB*	*CS*	*SB%*	*OBP*
Team Offense	5.55	29	493	386	203			0.345
Team Defense	3.81	20	505	244	133	124	52%	0.296
Difference	1.74	9	12	142	70			116%

Pos	*Rpos*	*PA*	*Age*	*Name*	*BA*	*OBP*	*SLG*	*BB%*	*SB*	*Bat R>Avg*	*BR R>Avg*	*Fld R>Avg*	*RAA*	*WAA*
C	4	267	40	Zimmer, Chief	0.220	0.292	0.275	7%	6	-8	0	2	-2	-0.2
1B	-3	609	26	Bransfield, Kitty	0.295	0.335	0.398	5%	23	12	0	-1	8	0.7
2B	1	611	27	Ritchey, Claude^	0.296	0.358	0.354	8%	15	10	-1	7	17	1.7
3B,SS	5	408	23	Leach, Tommy	0.305	0.347	0.422	5%	16	12	0	5	22	2.2
SS	4	253	38	Ely, Bones	0.208	0.234	0.258	2%	5	-16	0	9	-3	-0.3
LF	-7	601	28	Clarke, Fred*	0.324	0.395	0.461	8%	23	36	-1	8	36	3.6
CF	-4	616	24	Beaumont, Ginger*	0.332	0.382	0.418	7%	36	27	0	0	23	2.2
RF	-5	401	26	Davis, Lefty*	0.313	0.415	0.421	14%	22	23	0	4	22	2.2
SS,RF	2	619	27	Wagner, Honus	0.353	0.417	0.494	9%	49	49	3	4	58	5.7
C	4	220	35	O'Conner, Jack	0.193	0.238	0.257	5%	2	-13	0	1	-8	-0.8
C	1	100	28	Yeager, George	0.264	0.302	0.308	4%	1	-2	0	0	-1	-0.1

Pos	Rpos	PA	Age	Name	BA	OBP	SLG	BB%	SB	Bat R>Avg	BR R>Avg	Fld R>Avg	RAA	WAA
SS	1	32	28	Carr, Lew	0.250	0.344	0.357	6%	0	0	0	0	1	0.1
P,LF	0	144	26	Tannehill, Jesse^	0.244	0.277	0.333	4%	0	-3	0	0	-3	-0.3
	-3	587		Others	0.199	0.260	0.256	6%	5	-29	-1	3	-30	-3.0
	0		28.9	Team Total	0.286	0.345	0.379	7.1%	203	99	0	42	141	13.8
				League Average	0.267	0.321	0.348	6.3%	175					
				% Lg Avg	107	107	109	113	116					
				League Rank	2	1	3	2	2		2	1		

GS	GR	IP	Age	Name	W–L	WHIP	BA	K/9	BB/9	FIP	ERA	R/9	RAA	WAA
32	5	296	29	Phillippe, Deacon	22–12	1.05	0.244	3.1	1.2	3.03	2.22	3.50	29	2.8
28	8	288	27	Chesbro, Jack	21–10	1.09	0.240	4.0	1.6	2.91	2.38	3.25	36	3.6
30	2	252	26	Tannehill, Jesse*	18–10	1.09	0.249	4.2	1.3	2.60	2.18	3.35	29	2.8
20	1	176	29	Leever, Sam	14–5	1.26	0.265	4.2	2.0	2.94	2.86	4.19	4	0.4
10	2	80	26	Poole, Ed	5–4	1.35	0.254	2.9	3.4	4.12	3.60	5.06	-6	-0.6
10	1	77	27	Doheny, Ed*	6–2	1.17	0.236	3.3	2.6	3.43	1.99	4.22	1	0.1
5	2	44	29	Wiltse, Snake*	1–4	1.58	0.310	2.0	2.6	4.29	4.27	5.69	-7	-0.7
3	0	24	21	Merritt, George	3–0	1.38	0.289	1.9	1.9	3.39	4.88	6.75	-6	-0.6
2	0	8	24	Waddell, Rube*	0–2	2.47	0.313	4.7	10.5	5.79	9.35	14.03	-8	-0.8
140	21		26.4	Team Total		1.16	0.251	3.65	1.76	3.07	2.58	3.86	72	7.1
				League Average		1.31	0.267	3.83	2.42	3.32	3.32	4.68		
				% Lg Avg		113	106	95	137	108	129	121		
				League Rank		1	2	6	1	1	1			

1902 Pittsburgh Pirates

The Pirates led their league in most runs scored per game and least runs allowed per game becoming one of the few truly great teams in baseball history winning an incredible 74 percent of their games. The 1902 Pirate team was the best of the early Pirate teams that featured Honus Wagner and player manager Fred Clarke who both came over from the Louisville Colonels in 1900. This team never lost more than two consecutive games during the season. However, the Pirates were raided after the 1902 season losing starter Jack Chesbro to the AL New York Highlanders.

Strengths: (1) hitting for average, contact, and power especially from Wagner (30 2B, 16 3B), Beaumont (166 1B, 21 2B), Clarke (14 3B), and Leach (22 3B), (2) fielding led by 3B Leach (106 Rng+), SS Conroy (102 Rng+), 2B Ritchey (101 Rng+), and SS/OF Wagner (99 Rng+ at SS, 110 Rng+ in the OF), (3) CS% from O'Conner (53%), Zimmer (51%), and Smith (47%), and (4) pitching led by Chesbro, Phillippe, Leever, Tannehill, and Doheny.

Weaknesses: (1) hitting from Harry Smith, (2) pitching from Cushman (10.5 H/9), and (3) hit batters by Chesbro (21) and Doheny (15).

Mgr	Fred Clarke	
Rk	2	4
Gm	142	
Place	1	
GA	28	
Rival	14–6 vs Dodgers, 119 RS & 65 RA	

	W	L	Win%
Regular Season	103	36	0.741
Runs Record	99	40	0.713
1 Run	15	12	0.556
Blowout	43	8	0.843

	Team	LgAvg	%Avg	LgRk
BABIP	0.273	0.286	105	1
E	247	299	121	2
K%	8.0%	9.3%	115	
RS%	41.4%	34.3%	121	
R/G	5.45	3.98	137	1
RA/G	3.10	3.98	128	1

	Tm	LgAvg	>Avg
RS	774	561	213
RA	440	561	121
DP	87	98	-11

	R/G	HR	K	BB	SB	CS	SB%	OBP
Team Offense	5.45	18	441	372	222			0.344
Team Defense	3.10	4	564	250	117	116	50%	0.288
Difference	2.35	14	123	122	105			120%

Pos	Rpos	PA	Age	Name	BA	OBP	SLG	BB%	SB	Bat R>Avg	BR R>Avg	Fld R>Avg	RAA	WAA
C	3	196	27	Smith, Harry	0.189	0.211	0.222	2%	4	-13	0	1	-9	-1.0
1B	-3	442	27	Bransfield, Kitty	0.305	0.336	0.397	4%	23	13	1	3	14	1.5
2B	0	483	28	Ritchey, Claude^	0.277	0.370	0.328	11%	10	13	-1	9	21	2.2

Pos	Rpos	PA	Age	Name	BA	OBP	SLG	BB%	SB	Bat R>Avg	BR R>Avg	Fld R>Avg	RAA	WAA
3B	4	576	24	Leach, Tommy	0.278	0.341	0.426	8%	25	24	0	12	40	4.2
SS	6	404	25	Conroy, Wid	0.244	0.299	0.312	6%	10	-3	0	8	11	1.2
LF	-6	530	29	Clarke, Fred*	0.316	0.401	0.449	10%	29	38	0	4	36	3.8
CF	-4	599	25	Beaumont, Ginger*	0.357	0.404	0.418	7%	33	37	-1	2	34	3.6
RF	-3	274	27	Davis, Lefty*	0.280	0.377	0.336	13%	19	9	1	0	7	0.7
SS,OF	-1	599	28	Wagner, Honus	0.330	0.394	0.463	7%	42	43	2	10	54	5.7
2B,OF	0	227	27	Burke, Jimmy	0.296	0.359	0.374	7%	9	8	0	0	8	0.8
C,1B	3	176	33	O'Conner, Jack	0.294	0.306	0.341	2%	2	0	0	0	3	0.3
C	3	163	41	Zimmer, Chief	0.268	0.338	0.324	7%	4	2	0	2	7	0.7
RF	-1	86	20	Sebring, Jimmy*	0.325	0.365	0.475	6%	2	6	0	2	7	0.7
	-1	725		Others	0.223	0.255	0.288	3%	10	-23	-1	-1	-26	-2.8
	0		27.8	Team Total	0.286	0.344	0.374	6.8%	222	152	1	52	205	21.7
				League Average	0.259	0.313	0.318	6.2%	171					
				% Lg Avg	111	110	117	109	130					
				League Rank	1	1	1	3	2		3	1		

GS	GR	IP	Age	Name	W–L	WHIP	BA	K/9	BB/9	FIP	ERA	R/9	RAA	WAA
33	2	286	28	Chesbro, Jack	28–6	1.06	0.229	4.3	1.9	2.49	2.17	2.55	36	3.8
30	1	272	30	Phillippe, Deacon	20–9	1.07	0.255	4.0	0.9	2.01	2.05	2.98	21	2.2
24	2	231	27	Tannehill, Jesse*	20–6	0.99	0.236	3.9	1.0	2.12	1.95	3.04	16	1.7
26	2	222	30	Leever, Sam	15–7	1.05	0.243	3.5	1.3	2.40	2.39	2.96	18	1.8
21	1	188	28	Doheny, Ed*	16–4	1.18	0.231	4.2	2.9	2.80	2.53	3.25	9	1.0
3	0	26	26	McLaughlin, Warren*	3–0	1.38	0.267	4.5	3.1	2.68	2.77	4.50	-2	-0.3
4	0	26	24	Cushman, Harvey*	0–4	2.38	0.291	4.2	10.9	5.45	7.36	10.87	-21	-2.2
0	2	13		Others	1–0	1.20	0.224	4.7	3.4	2.60	0.68	4.05	-1	-0.1
141	10		27.6	Team Total		1.10	0.241	4.01	1.78	2.41	2.30	3.13	77	8.1
				League Average		1.25	0.258	3.52	2.37	2.77	2.78	4.05		
				% Lg Avg		114	107	114	133	115	121	129		
				League Rank		1	2	1	1	1	2			

1903 Boston Americans

Pitching from Cy Young and Bill Dinneen as well as outstanding hitting and fielding from Freddy Parent, Jimmy Collins, and Patsy Dougherty led the Boston Red Sox to the pennant. The 1903 Americans became the winner of the first World Series defeating a powerful Pirate team that had recently been weakened by AL defections.

Strengths: (1) pitching from Young, Dinneen, and Hughes, (2) hitting for average and power from Freeman (39 2B, 20 3B, 13 HR), Dougherty (19 2B, 12 3B), Collins (33 2B, 17 3B), and Parent (31 2B, 17 3B), (3) infield fielding from SS Parent (103 Rng+), 2B Ferris (107 Rng+), and 3B Collins (109 Rng+), and (4) CS% from Criger (53%), Farrell (52%), and Stahl (46%). This team also gained wins from good hitting pitchers and easily led the league with 113 team triples showing off their power and speed.

Weaknesses: (1) 1B and CF positions, (2) drawing walks, (3) hitting from Criger and O'Brien, and (4) pitching from number 4 and 5 starters Gibson and Winter.

Mgr	Jimmy Collins	
Rk	23	75
Gm	141	
Place	1	
GA	14.5	
Rival	13–6 vs A's, 98 RS & 69 RA	

	W	L	Win%
Regular Season	91	47	0.659
Runs Record	87	51	0.630
1 Run	19	16	0.543
Blowout	39	13	0.750

	Team	LgAvg	%Avg	LgRk
BABIP	0.272	0.289	106	1
E	239	269	113	2
K%	10.4%	10.2%	98	
RS%	41.6%	36.5%	114	
R/G	5.02	4.10	122	1
RA/G	3.58	4.10	114	1

	Tm	LgAvg	>Avg
RS	708	568	140
RA	505	568	63
DP	86	86	0

	R/G	HR	K	BB	SB	CS	SB%	OBP
Team Offense	5.02	48	559	262	141			0.313
Team Defense	3.58	23	579	269	122	131	48%	0.288
Difference	1.44	25	20	-7	19			109%

Pos	Rpos	PA	Age	Name	BA	OBP	SLG	BB%	SB	Bat R>Avg	BR R>Avg	Fld R>Avg	RAA	WAA
C	6	358	31	Criger, Lou	0.192	0.256	0.306	7%	5	-10	0	2	-2	-0.2
1B	-5	579	33	LaChance, Candy^	0.257	0.303	0.328	5%	12	-3	-1	3	-6	-0.6
2B	0	566	28	Ferris, Hobe	0.251	0.287	0.366	4%	11	0	-1	14	13	1.3
3B	4	579	33	Collins, Jimmy	0.296	0.329	0.448	4%	23	22	0	9	35	3.7
SS	9	592	27	Parent, Freddy	0.304	0.326	0.441	2%	24	21	0	14	44	4.6
LF	-7	647	26	Dougherty, Patsy*	0.331	0.372	0.424	5%	35	31	0	4	28	2.9
CF	-2	332	30	Stahl, Chick*	0.274	0.338	0.375	8%	10	8	0	-2	4	0.4
RF	-8	611	31	Freeman, Buck*	0.287	0.328	0.496	5%	5	32	0	0	24	2.5
CF,3B	-2	376	30	O'Brien, Jack*	0.210	0.262	0.302	6%	10	-10	0	-3	-15	-1.6
C	-2	98	24	Stahl, Jake	0.239	0.286	0.446	4%	1	2	-1	-2	-3	-0.3
C	1	62	36	Farrell, Duke^	0.404	0.466	0.538	8%	1	7	0	-1	7	0.7
P	0	146	36	Young, Cy	0.321	0.340	0.431	3%	2	5	0	0	5	0.6
P	0	100	24	Hughes, Long Tom	0.280	0.309	0.398	3%	1	2	0	0	2	0.2
	6	319		Others	0.192	0.242	0.240	6%	1	-17	1	-1	-11	-1.1
	0		29.9	Team Total	0.272	0.313	0.392	4.9%	141	91	-2	37	126	13.1
				League Average	0.255	0.303	0.344	5.5%	147					
				% Lg Avg	106	103	114	88	96					
				League Rank	1	2	1	8	5		6	1		

GS	GR	IP	Age	Name	W–L	WHIP	BA	K/9	BB/9	FIP	ERA	R/9	RAA	WAA
35	5	342	36	Young, Cy	28–9	0.97	0.232	4.6	1.0	2.38	2.08	3.03	34	3.5
34	3	299	27	Dinneen, Bill	21–13	1.07	0.230	4.5	2.0	2.75	2.26	2.95	32	3.4
31	2	245	24	Hughes, Long Tom	20–7	1.19	0.249	4.1	2.2	2.97	2.57	3.49	11	1.2
21	3	183	26	Gibson, Norwood	13–9	1.26	0.241	3.7	3.2	3.27	3.19	4.66	-15	-1.6
19	5	178	25	Winter, George	9–8	1.23	0.263	3.2	1.9	3.09	3.08	4.64	-15	-1.5
1	0	8	26	Altrock, Nick*	0–1	2.13	0.361	3.4	4.5	3.53	9.00	11.25	-7	-0.7
141	18		27.3	Team Total		1.12	0.242	4.15	1.93	2.82	2.57	3.62	41	4.2
				League Average		1.21	0.255	3.86	2.08	2.96	2.96	4.18		
				% Lg Avg		107	105	107	108	105	115	115		
				League Rank		1	1	2	3	2	1			

1904 New York Giants

The Giants led the NL in scoring and fewest runs allowed. Superstar seasons from McGinnity and Mathewson plus solid hitting and excellent fielding from SS Dahlen carried this team. OF Mike Donlin, who was obtained in a trade with the Reds in early August, added additional punch. The Giants had an impressive 283 stolen bases.

Strengths: (1) hitting for average, contact, and power led by Bresnahan (22 2B), McGann (22 2B), Mertes (28 2B, 11 3B), Devlin (8 3B), and Browne (144 1B), (2) hitting from the bench, (3) drawing walks featuring Devlin (62) and Bresnahan (58), (4) baserunning featuring Dahlen and Mertes, (5) fielding from infielders SS Dahlen (106 Rng+), rookie 3B Devlin (99 Rng+), 2B Gilbert (101 Rng+), and 1B McGann, (6) CS% from Warner (56%) and Bowerman (54%), and (7) pitching from McGinnity (9 shutouts, 5 Sv), Mathewson (212 K), and Taylor.

Weaknesses: (1) C position, (2) hitting from Warner, (3) pitching from Milligan (13.0 H/9), and (4) pitching depth beyond the top 3 hurlers.

Mgr	John McGraw	
Rk	5	12
Gm	158	
Place	1	
GA	13.0	
Rival	11–11 vs Cubs, 85 RS & 73 RA	

	W	L	Win%
Regular Season	106	47	0.693
Runs Record	104	49	0.680
1 Run	22	18	0.550
Blowout	31	9	0.775

	Team	LgAvg	%Avg	LgRk
BABIP	0.251	0.276	110	1
E	294	324	110	2
K%	7.8%	9.4%	120	
RS%	39.0%	35.0%	111	
R/G	4.71	3.91	120	1
RA/G	3.01	3.91	130	1

	Tm	LgAvg	>Avg
RS	744	609	135
RA	476	609	133
DP	93	89	4

	R/G	HR	K	BB	SB	CS	SB%	OBP
Team Offense	4.71	31	454	434	283			0.328
Team Defense	3.01	36	707	349	134	167	45%	0.276
Difference	1.70	-5	253	85	149			119%

Pos	*Rpos*	*PA*	*Age*	*Name*	*BA*	*OBP*	*SLG*	*BB%*	*SB*	*Bat R>Avg*	*BR R>Avg*	*Fld R>Avg*	*RAA*	*WAA*
C	5	315	31	Warner, Jack*	0.199	0.253	0.233	4%	7	-14	0	3	-6	-0.7
1B	-5	593	32	McGann, Dan^	0.286	0.354	0.387	6%	42	21	2	7	25	2.7
2B	0	557	28	Gilbert, Billy	0.253	0.340	0.299	8%	33	5	0	12	17	1.8
3B	4	562	24	Devlin, Art	0.281	0.371	0.354	11%	33	19	0	9	32	3.4
SS	10	579	34	Dahlen, Bill	0.268	0.326	0.337	8%	47	7	4	17	38	4.0
LF,CF	-7	611	31	Mertes, Sam	0.276	0.346	0.393	9%	47	21	4	6	24	2.6
CF,1B	-3	468	25	Bresnahan, Roger	0.284	0.381	0.410	12%	13	26	-1	2	24	2.5
RF	-8	661	28	Browne, George*	0.284	0.332	0.347	6%	24	11	-1	3	5	0.5
C,1B	5	319	35	Bowerman, Frank	0.232	0.288	0.318	5%	7	-2	0	2	5	0.5
CF	-2	220	23	McCormick, Moose*	0.266	0.323	0.374	6%	13	5	1	0	4	0.4
3B,SS	2	199	31	Dunn, Jack	0.309	0.356	0.414	6%	11	9	0	1	12	1.2
LF,CF	-2	145	26	Donlin, Mike*	0.280	0.340	0.424	7%	1	6	0	-2	2	0.2
C	0	18	28	Marshall, Doc	0.353	0.389	0.412	6%	0	1	0	0	1	0.1
	1	581		Others	0.189	0.237	0.252	5%	5	-26	1	0	-24	-2.5
	0		28.9	Team Total	0.262	0.328	0.344	7.4%	283	87	10	60	157	16.6
				League Average	0.249	0.306	0.322	6.5%	197					
				% Lg Avg	105	107	107	114	144					
				League Rank	1	1	1	2	1		1	1		

GS	*GR*	*IP*	*Age*	*Name*	*W–L*	*WHIP*	*BA*	*K/9*	*BB/9*	*FIP*	*ERA*	*R/9*	*RAA*	*WAA*
44	7	408	33	McGinnity, Joe	35–8	0.96	0.206	3.2	1.9	2.61	1.61	2.27	61	6.4
46	2	368	25	Mathewson, Christy	33–12	1.04	0.226	5.2	1.9	2.10	2.03	2.94	29	3.0
36	1	296	29	Taylor, Dummy	21–15	1.03	0.214	4.2	2.3	2.51	2.34	3.04	20	2.1
16	8	165	23	Wiltse, Hooks*	13–3	1.28	0.240	5.7	3.3	2.89	2.84	3.61	1	0.1
13	3	115	21	Ames, Red	4–6	1.15	0.222	7.3	3.0	2.01	2.27	3.44	3	0.3
1	4	25	25	Milligan, Billy*	0–1	1.60	0.310	2.2	1.4	3.49	5.40	7.92	-12	-1.3
1	2	15	24	Elliott, Claude	0–2	1.60	0.328	4.8	1.8	3.60	3.00	7.80	-7	-0.7
0	0	5		Others	0–0	2.00	0.240	1.8	7.2	6.93	5.40	14.40	-6	-0.6
157	27		25.7	Team Total		1.07	0.222	4.56	2.25	2.48	2.17	3.07	87	9.2
				League Average		1.22	0.250	3.53	2.58	2.73	2.73	4.02		
				% Lg Avg		114	113	129	115	110	126	131		
				League Rank		1	1	1	3	1	1			

1905 Chicago White Sox

The 1905 White Sox were actually a better team than their 1906 world championship team featuring a terrific team 1.99 ERA and super fielding. Unfortunately for them, they lost a close pennant race to a nearly equally strong Philadelphia Athletic team. The White Sox actually won the same number of games as the A's but lost 4 more games than the A's finishing 2 full games behind. The White Sox led the league in fewest average runs allowed per game.

Strengths: (1) P, 1B, SS, and CF positions, (1) hitting for contact and getting on base especially from Davis (29 2B), Donahue (22 2B), and Jones (12 3B), (2) drawing walks especially from Green and Jones, (3) fielding from 3B Tannehill (119 Rng+), SS Davis (106 Rng+), CF Jones (128 Rng+), 1B Donahue (114 assists), and 2B Dundon (105 Rng+, 9 E in 523 chances), (4) CS% from Sullivan (49%) and McFarland (50%), and (5) starting pitching from White (7.1 H/9), Altrock (7.8 H/9), Owen (7.4 H/9), and Smith (171 K, 6.6 H/9).

Weaknesses: (1) LF position, (2) hitting for average and power especially from Dundon, Tannehill, Sullivan, and Holmes and (2) fielding from RF Green (66 Rng+).

Mgr	Fielder Jones
Rk	30 117
Gm	158
Place	2
GB	2.0
Rival	9–12 vs A's; 57 RS & 74 RA

	W	*L*	*Win%*
Regular Season	92	60	0.605
Runs Record	94	58	0.619
1 Run	31	20	0.608
Blowout	28	7	0.800

	Team	*LgAvg*	*%Avg*	*LgRk*
BABIP	0.253	0.271	107	1
E	218	273	125	1
K%	10.5%	11.2%	107	
RS%	35.5%	33.8%	105	
R/G	3.89	3.68	105	2
RA/G	2.85	3.68	129	1

	Tm	*LgAvg*	*>Avg*
RS	614	568	46
RA	450	568	118
DP	95	80	15

	R/G	*HR*	*K*	*BB*	*SB*	*CS*	*SB%*	*OBP*
Team Offense	3.89	11	613	439	194			0.305
Team Defense	2.85	11	613	329	132	126	51%	0.275
Difference	1.04	0	0	110	62			111%

Pos	*Rpos*	*PA*	*Age*	*Name*	*BA*	*OBP*	*SLG*	*BB%*	*SB*	*Bat R>Avg*	*BR R>Avg*	*Fld R>Avg*	*RAA*	*WAA*
C	6	349	30	Sullivan, Billy	0.201	0.239	0.269	4%	14	-13	1	1	-5	-0.5
1B	-5	608	25	Donahue, Jiggs*	0.287	0.346	0.349	7%	32	16	0	11	22	2.4
2B,SS	0	406	30	Dundon, Gus	0.192	0.248	0.228	6%	14	-17	0	10	-7	-0.8
3B	5	549	24	Tannehill, Lee	0.200	0.274	0.244	8%	8	-15	-1	19	8	0.9
SS	10	654	34	Davis, George^	0.278	0.353	0.340	9%	31	18	0	14	42	4.6
LF,RF	-5	388	31	Callahan, Jimmy	0.272	0.336	0.368	7%	26	11	2	-2	6	0.7
CF	-4	661	33	Jones, Fielder*	0.245	0.335	0.327	11%	20	12	-1	14	21	2.4
RF	-6	454	28	Green, Danny*	0.243	0.345	0.309	12%	11	8	-1	-4	-3	-0.3
2B,RF	-2	389	29	Isbell, Frank*	0.296	0.335	0.440	4%	15	18	0	5	21	2.3
LF	-5	382	36	Holmes, Ducky*	0.201	0.258	0.259	5%	11	-11	0	0	-16	-1.8
C	5	281	30	McFarland, Ed	0.280	0.345	0.364	8%	5	9	0	2	16	1.7
3B,2B	1	133	30	Rohe, George	0.212	0.310	0.248	9%	2	-1	0	1	1	0.1
P	0	118	25	Smith, Frank	0.226	0.299	0.311	6%	2	0	0	0	0	0.0
	0	480		Others	0.152	0.202	0.182	5%	3	-35	0	0	-35	-3.8
	0		29.6	Team Total	0.237	0.305	0.304	7.5%	194	0	0	71	71	7.8
				League Average	0.241	0.299	0.314	6.6%	168					
				% Lg Avg	98	102	97	114	115					
				League Rank	5	3	6	2	2		4	1		

GS	*GR*	*IP*	*Age*	*Name*	*W–L*	*WHIP*	*BA*	*K/9*	*BB/9*	*FIP*	*ERA*	*R/9*	*RAA*	*WAA*
38	4	334	25	Owen, Frank	21–13	0.99	0.227	3.4	1.5	2.52	2.10	2.96	11	1.2
34	4	316	28	Altrock, Nick*	23–12	1.07	0.236	2.8	1.8	2.58	1.88	2.54	25	2.8
31	8	292	25	Smith, Frank	19–13	1.10	0.208	5.3	3.3	2.47	2.13	2.99	10	1.1
33	3	260	26	White, Doc*	17–13	1.01	0.218	4.1	2.0	2.41	1.76	2.32	28	3.1
13	9	137	24	Walsh, Ed	8–3	1.10	0.239	4.7	1.9	2.12	2.17	3.49	-3	-0.3
9	4	89	28	Patterson, Roy	4–6	1.00	0.226	2.9	1.6	2.34	1.83	3.45	-2	-0.2
158	32		26.0	Team Total		1.05	0.224	3.87	2.07	2.45	1.99	2.84	70	7.7
				League Average		1.16	0.240	4.18	2.44	2.64	2.65	3.73		
				% Lg Avg		111	107	93	118	107	133	131		
				League Rank		1	1	5	2	2	1			

1905 New York Giants

The legendary Giants manager John McGraw correctly called this team the best team he ever managed. The Giants, led by the hitting from Mike Donlin, easily led the NL in runs scored. The pitching, led by Christy Mathewson, enabled the Giants to have the second fewest average runs allowed per game, just behind the Chicago Cubs. In the World Series, the rested Giants beat the pennant weary A's in 5 games where every game featured a shutout with the A's only scoring a total of 3 runs. Christy Mathewson pitched 3 of the 4 Giant shutouts in the World Series!

Strengths: (1) P, C, 1B, 3B, SS, LF, and CF positions, (2) hitting for average, contact, and power especially from Donlin (31 2B, 16 3B), McGann (14 3B), Mertes (17 3B), Browne (16 3B), and Bresnahan, (3) drawing walks, (4) baserunning featuring Devlin (35% RS) and Mertes (36% RS), (5) infield fielding featuring SS Dahlen (102 Rng+), 3B Devlin (94 Rng+), and 2B Gilbert (104 Rng+), (6) league leading CS% from Bresnahan (55%) and Bowerman (50%), and (7) pitching from Mathewson who won the Triple Crown for pitchers (1.28 ERA, 31 wins, and 206 K) and Wiltse.

Weaknesses: (1) control from Ames (30 WP, 105 BB) and (2) pitching from Elliott (9.7 H/9).

Mgr	John McGraw	
AT Rk	3	5
Gm	15	
Place	1	
GA	9.0	
Rival	12–10 vs Pirates, 106 RS & 96 RA	

	W	*L*	*Win%*
Regular Season	105	48	0.686
Runs Record	106	47	0.692
1 Run	29	18	0.617
Blowout	41	12	0.774

	Team	*LgAvg*	*%Avg*	*LgRk*
BABIP	0.265	0.282	107	2
E	258	294	114	3
K%	8.5%	9.8%	114	
RS%	37.7%	35.1%	107	
R/G	5.02	4.10	122	1
RA/G	3.26	4.10	126	2

	Tm	*LgAvg*	*>Avg*
RS	778	636	142
RA	505	636	131
DP	93	100	-7

	R/G	*HR*	*K*	*BB*	*SB*	*CS*	*SB%*	*OBP*
Team Offense	5.02	39	499	517	291			0.351
Team Defense	3.26	25	760	364	123	138	47%	0.284
Difference	1.76	14	261	153	168			123%

Pos	*Rpos*	*PA*	*Age*	*Name*	*BA*	*OBP*	*SLG*	*BB%*	*SB*	*Bat R>Avg*	*BR R>Avg*	*Fld R>Avg*	*RAA*	*WAA*
C,OF	6	399	26	Bresnahan, Roger	0.302	0.411	0.375	13%	11	20	-1	1	26	2.7
1B	-4	584	33	McGann, Dan^	0.299	0.391	0.434	9%	22	34	-1	5	34	3.5
2B	0	437	29	Gilbert, Billy	0.247	0.331	0.293	9%	11	-1	-1	10	8	0.8
3B	5	616	25	Devlin, Art	0.246	0.344	0.310	11%	59	5	7	8	25	2.6
SS	10	601	35	Dahlen, Bill	0.242	0.337	0.337	10%	37	7	2	18	37	3.8
LF	-8	627	32	Mertes, Sam	0.279	0.351	0.417	9%	52	24	6	-2	20	2.1
CF	-4	676	27	Donlin, Mike*	0.356	0.413	0.495	8%	33	56	-1	-2	49	5.1
RF	-7	569	29	Browne, George*	0.293	0.321	0.397	4%	26	11	0	2	6	0.6
2B,OF	-1	369	28	Strang, Sammy^	0.259	0.389	0.347	16%	23	13	0	3	15	1.6
C,1B	4	327	36	Bowerman, Frank	0.269	0.322	0.333	4%	6	1	-1	2	6	0.6
1B	0	56	0	Clarke, Boileryard	0.180	0.241	0.240	7%	1	-3	0	-1	-4	-0.4
P	0	87	25	Wiltse, Hooks	0.278	0.388	0.306	14%	2	2	0	0	2	0.2
P	0	141	24	Mathewson, Christy	0.236	0.307	0.323	7%	2	-1	-1	0	-2	-0.2
-1	350			Others	0.173	0.210	0.226	4%	6	-25	1	0	-25	-2.6
	0		26.8	Team Total	0.273	0.351	0.368	8.9%	291	143	10	44	197	20.5
				League Average	0.255	0.315	0.332	7.0%	200					
				% Lg Avg	107	111	111	127	146					
				League Rank	1	1	1	1	1		1	1	2	

GS	*GR*	*IP*	*Age*	*Name*	*W–L*	*WHIP*	*BA*	*K/9*	*BB/9*	*FIP*	*ERA*	*R/9*	*RAA*	*WAA*
37	6	339	24	Mathewson, Christy	31–9	0.93	0.205	5.5	1.7	2.10	1.28	2.26	61	6.4
38	8	320	34	McGinnity, Joe	21–15	1.12	0.240	3.5	2.0	2.85	2.87	3.68	6	0.7
31	3	263	22	Ames, Red	22–8	1.24	0.230	6.8	3.6	2.41	2.74	3.87	1	0.1
28	4	213	30	Taylor, Dummy	16–9	1.18	0.247	3.8	2.2	2.87	2.66	3.59	7	0.7
19	13	197	25	Wiltse, Hooks*	15–6	1.11	0.219	5.5	2.8	2.69	2.47	3.24	14	1.5
2	8	38	28	Elliott, Claude	0–1	1.39	0.270	4.7	2.8	3.59	4.03	4.74	-4	-0.4
155	42		27.2	Team Total		1.11	0.229	4.99	2.39	2.58	2.39	3.32	86	8.9
				League Average		1.25	0.255	3.65	2.67	3.00	2.99	4.17		
				% Lg Avg		113	112	137	112	116	125	126		
				League Rank		2	2	1	1	1	2			

1905 Chicago Cubs

The 1905 Cubs led the NL in fewest runs allowed. This team finished strong when their star player Frank Chance assumed the managerial reigns from Frank Selee who had to leave the team due to a serious illness. This team won 17 out of their last 20 games portending even better things to come in 1906. The starting pitchers completed 133 out of 153 games and had 23 complete game shutouts. This team was rather unlucky losing over 60 percent of their games by only one run, winning less than half of their one run games, and having a losing record against the first place Giants despite outscoring them.

Strengths: (1) P, 1B, and SS positions, (2) hitting for contact, (3) individual hitting from Chance (12 3B) and Slagle (19 2B), (4) drawing walks especially from Slagle (97 BB) and Chance (78 BB), (5) baserunning from Maloney (14 3B), (6) fielding from SS Tinker (108 Rng+), 3B Casey (91 Rng+), and CF/RF Slagle (111 Rng+, 27 assists), (7) CS% from Kling (47%) and O'Neill (47%), and (8) pitching with the entire staff having better than league average seasons especially Reulbach (5 shutouts, 6.4 H/9).

Weaknesses: (1) C position, (2) hitting for average and power especially from Kling, Tinker, O'Neill, and Casey, (3) hitting from the pitchers especially Reulbach and Briggs, and (4) injuries to Evers, Chance, and Brown limiting their play.

Mgr	Frank Chance	
Rk	14	36
Gm	155	
Place	3	
GB	13.0	
Rival	10–12 vs Giants, 72 RS & 55 RA	

	W	*L*	*Win%*
Regular Season	92	61	0.601
Runs Record	100	53	0.653
1 Run	30	32	0.484
Blowout	30	7	0.811

	Team	*LgAvg*	*%Avg*	*LgRk*
BABIP	0.253	0.282	111	1
E	248	294	119	1
K%	8.8%	9.8%	111	
RS%	37.5%	35.1%	107	
R/G	4.30	4.10	105	5
RA/G	2.85	4.10	144	1

	Tm	*LgAvg*	*>Avg*
RS	667	636	31
RA	442	636	194
DP	99	100	-1

	R/G	*HR*	*K*	*BB*	*SB*	*CS*	*SB%*	*OBP*
Team Offense	4.30	12	510	448	267			0.313
Team Defense	2.85	14	627	385	168	150	53%	0.286
Difference	1.45	-2	117	63	99			110%

Pos	*Rpos*	*PA*	*Age*	*Name*	*BA*	*OBP*	*SLG*	*BB%*	*SB*	*Bat R>Avg*	*BR R>Avg*	*Fld R>Avg*	*RAA*	*WAA*
C,RF	425	7	29	Kling, Johnny	0.218	0.272	0.279	7%	13	-13	0	1	-12	-1.3
1B	502	-4	28	Chance, Frank	0.316	0.450	0.434	16%	38	41	1	5	47	4.8
2B	389	0	23	Evers, Johnny*	0.276	0.333	0.329	7%	19	2	0	5	7	0.8
SS	611	10	24	Tinker, Joe	0.247	0.292	0.320	6%	31	-8	1	22	15	1.6
3B	594	5	35	Casey, Doc^	0.232	0.295	0.316	7%	22	-7	0	6	-1	-0.1
LF,RF	549	-7	22	Schulte, Wildfire*	0.274	0.326	0.367	6%	16	7	-1	2	8	0.9
CF,LF	681	-5	31	Slagle, Jimmy*	0.269	0.379	0.317	14%	27	16	-2	6	20	2.1
RF,CF	627	-8	27	Maloney, Billy*	0.260	0.325	0.351	7%	59	6	8	8	22	2.3
2B,SS	316	0	22	Hofman, Solly	0.237	0.289	0.324	6%	15	-4	1	6	3	0.3
C	197	3	32	O'Neill, Jack	0.198	0.277	0.244	4%	6	-7	0	2	-5	-0.6
CF,LF	186	-2	36	McCarthy, Jack*	0.276	0.320	0.335	5%	8	0	0	0	0	0.0
1B	111	-1	26	Barry, Shad	0.212	0.255	0.231	5%	5	-6	0	1	-5	-0.5
	622	2		Others	0.152	0.189	0.182	4%	8	-57	1	0	-56	-5.8
		0	27.9	Team Total	0.245	0.313	0.314	7.7%	267	-30	9	64	43	4.5
				League Average	0.255	0.315	0.332	7.0%	200					
				% Lg Avg	96	99	95	111	134					
				League Rank	7	5	7	2	2	2	2	1		

GS	*GR*	*IP*	*Age*	*Name*	*W–L*	*WHIP*	*BA*	*K/9*	*BB/9*	*FIP*	*ERA*	*R/9*	*RAA*	*WAA*
29	5	292	22	Reulbach, Ed	18–14	0.96	0.201	4.7	2.3	2.53	1.42	2.19	51	5.3
30	3	250	31	Weimer, Jake*	18–12	1.17	0.229	3.8	2.9	2.89	2.27	3.02	20	2.1
24	6	249	28	Brown, Mordecai	18–12	1.06	0.235	3.2	1.6	2.57	2.17	3.22	14	1.5
22	0	178	27	Wicker, Bob	13–6	1.04	0.221	4.3	2.4	2.65	2.02	2.33	29	3.0
19	4	169	25	Lundgren, Carl	13–5	1.09	0.220	3.7	2.8	3.10	2.23	3.08	13	1.3
20	0	168	29	Briggs, Button	8–8	1.15	0.237	3.6	2.8	2.89	2.14	3.11	12	1.3
11	4	101	23	Pfeffer, Big Jeff	4–4	1.19	0.240	5.0	3.2	2.92	2.50	3.21	7	0.7
155	22		26.4	Team Total		1.08	0.224	4.01	2.46	2.76	2.04	2.83	146	15.2
				League Average		1.25	0.255	3.65	2.67	3.00	2.99	4.17		
				% Lg Avg		116	114	110	108	109	147	148		
				League Rank		1	1	2	4	2	1			

1906 Cleveland Naps

The 1906 Cleveland Naps, named after their best player and manager, Nap Lajoie, was easily the best team in the AL outscoring the pennant winner White Sox by nearly 100 runs, but finished third. This unlucky team statistically should have won 10 more games. Also, this team had a mediocre 21–25 W–L record in 1 run games while New York was 30–16 and Chicago was 29–19 in 1 run games. The unlucky Naps had losing records against both the Highlanders and White Sox despite outscoring them.

Strengths: (1) hitting for average, contact, and power featuring Lajoie (48 2B, 9 3B), Flick (33 2B, 22 3B, 39 SB), Congalton, Turner (27 2B), and Clarke, (2) infield fielding from SS Turner (108 Rng+), 2B Lajoie (114 Rng+, 76 DP), 3B Bradley (110 Rng+), and 1B Stovall, and (3) pitching led by Joss (9 shutouts, 7.0 H/9), Rhoads (7 shutouts), and Hess (7 shutouts).

Weaknesses: (1) LF position, (2) drawing walks, (3) Jackson's hitting, (4) pitching K/9, (5) hitting from the pitching staff, and (6) Townsend's pitching (8.9 H/9).

Mgr	Nap Lajoie	
Rk	10	27
Gm	157	
Place	3	
GB	5.0	
Rival	10–12 vs White Sox, 107 RS, 89 RA; 10–11 vs Yankees, 69 RS, 61 RA	

	W	*L*	*Win%*
Regular Season	89	64	0.582
Runs Record	101	52	0.660
1 Run	21	25	0.457
Blowout	31	7	0.816

	Team	*LgAvg*	*%Avg*	*LgRk*
BABIP	0.257	0.276	108	2
E	217	270	124	1
K%	9.4%	10.2%	108	
RS%	34.8%	33.3%	105	
R/G	4.23	3.66	116	1
RA/G	3.07	3.66	119	2

	Tm	*LgAvg*	*>Avg*
RS	664	561	103
RA	482	561	79
DP	111	84	27

	R/G	*HR*	*K*	*BB*	*SB*	*CS*	*SB%*	*OBP*
Team Offense	4.23	12	562	330	203			0.325
Team Defense	3.07	16	530	365	170	140	55%	0.290
Difference	1.16	-4	-32	-35	33			112%

Pos	*Rpos*	*PA*	*Age*	*Name*	*BA*	*OBP*	*SLG*	*BB%*	*SB*	*Bat R>Avg*	*BR R>Avg*	*Fld R>Avg*	*RAA*	*WAA*
C	5	318	32	Bemis, Harry	0.276	0.311	0.374	4%	8	6	0	1	7	0.7
1B	-4	431	25	Rossman, Claude*	0.308	0.338	0.359	4%	11	10	-1	-1	8	0.9
2B,3B	1	655	31	Lajoie, Nap	0.355	0.392	0.465	5%	20	48	-2	20	66	7.3
3B	3	340	28	Bradley, Bill	0.275	0.324	0.358	5%	13	6	0	6	12	1.3
SS	10	643	25	Turner, Terry	0.291	0.338	0.372	5%	27	18	-1	34	51	5.6
LF	-6	428	28	Jackson, Jim	0.214	0.290	0.259	9%	25	-8	2	2	-4	-0.5
CF,RF	-6	700	30	Flick, Elmer*	0.311	0.372	0.439	8%	39	42	1	2	45	4.9
RF,LF	-6	470	31	Congalton, Bunk*	0.320	0.361	0.396	5%	12	20	-1	2	21	2.3
1B,3B	-1	469	28	Stovall, George	0.273	0.288	0.339	2%	15	-1	0	8	7	0.8
CF	-2	321	28	Bay, Harry*	0.275	0.337	0.325	8%	17	5	0	0	5	0.5
C	3	195	23	Clarke, Nig*	0.358	0.404	0.486	7%	3	17	0	3	20	2.2
3B	2	143	24	Barbeau, Jap	0.194	0.257	0.279	6%	5	-4	0	-3	-7	-0.8
LF	0	41	21	Birmingham, Joe	0.325	0.341	0.425	2%	2	2	0	1	3	0.3
	1	833		Others	0.179	0.230	0.212	5%	6	-48	-1	-4	-53	-5.8
	0		27.2	Team Total	0.279	0.325	0.357	5.5%	203	111	-3	71	179	19.6
				League Average	0.249	0.303	0.318	6.2%	192					
				% Lg Avg	112	107	112	88	106					
				League Rank	1	2	3	7	5		6	1		

GS	*GR*	*IP*	*Age*	*Name*	*W–L*	*WHIP*	*BA*	*K/9*	*BB/9*	*FIP*	*ERA*	*R/9*	*RAA*	*WAA*
36	7	334	27	Hess, Otto*	20–17	1.08	0.227	4.5	2.3	2.61	1.83	2.81	18	2.0
34	4	315	26	Rhoads, Bob	22–10	1.11	0.227	2.5	2.6	3.04	1.80	2.71	19	2.1
31	3	282	26	Joss, Addie	21–9	0.93	0.218	3.4	1.4	2.35	1.72	2.59	22	2.4
30	1	255	35	Bernhard, Bill	16–15	1.10	0.248	3.0	1.7	2.47	2.54	3.49	-7	-0.7
12	5	93	27	Townsend, Jack	3–7	1.33	0.262	3.0	3.0	3.14	2.91	4.37	-12	-1.3
4	1	30	28	Moore, Earl	1–1	1.52	0.245	2.4	5.5	4.40	3.94	4.55	-4	-0.5
2	0	18	23	Liebhardt, Glenn	2–0	0.78	0.206	4.5	0.5	1.64	1.50	2.00	3	0.3
8	6	86	26	Eells, Harry	4–5	1.45	0.242	3.6	5.0	3.59	2.61	4.07	-8	-0.8
157	27		27.3	Team Total		1.11	0.233	3.38	2.33	2.75	2.09	3.07	32	3.5
				League Average		1.18	0.248	3.78	2.35	2.69	2.69	3.73		
				% Lg Avg		107	106	89	101	98	129	121		
				League Rank		3	2	7	5	5	1			

1906 Chicago Cubs

The 1906 season featured the best team of the Dead-ball era. These Cubs were victims of one of the biggest upsets in World Series history when the cross-town White Sox beat them 4 games to 2. The Cubs won 116 games to establish the NL record that has never been eclipsed. This team had a winning percentage of .682 or better against every team (another NL record) and had a 60–12 W–L record in the second half of the season. Also, this team won a record 80 percent of their games that were played on the road. Management made key trades to improve the team obtaining positional players Steinfeldt, Moran, and Sheckard in the off-season and pitchers Orval Overall in June and Jack Taylor in July.

Strengths: (1) hitting for average, contact, and power featuring Steinfeldt (10 3B), Chance (10 3B), Schulte (13 3B), and Kling, (2) baserunning especially from Evers (37% RS) and Chance (43% RS), (3) SB differentiation, (4) fielding led by SS Tinker (97 Rng+), 2B Evers (103 Rng+), and 1B Chance, (5) CS% from Kling (58%) and Moran (56%), and (6) team pitching (28 shutouts) especially ERA and K/9 featuring Brown (9 shutouts, 6.4 H/9), Reulbach (6 shutouts, 5.3 H/9), and rookie southpaw Pfiester (6.2 H/9).

Weaknesses: (1) hitting from Tinker, (2) pitching control, (3) hitting from the pitchers, and (4) pitching from Wicker (8.7 H/9).

Mgr	Frank Chance	
Rk	1	3
Gm	155	
Place	1	
GA	20.0	
Rival	15–7 vs Giants, 121 RS & 79 RA	

	W	*L*	*Win%*
Regular Season	116	36	0.763
Runs Record	110	42	0.720
1 Run	27	13	0.675
Blowout	33	6	0.846

	Team	*LgAvg*	*%Avg*	*LgRk*
BABIP	0.239	0.273	115	1
E	194	260	134	1
K%	9.0%	10.1%	113	
RS%	38.2%	32.0%	119	
R/G	4.54	3.57	127	1
RA/G	2.46	3.57	145	1

	Tm	*LgAvg*	*>Avg*
RS	704	549	155
RA	381	549	168
DP	100	93	7

	R/G	*HR*	*K*	*BB*	*SB*	*CS*	*SB%*	*OBP*
Team Offense	4.54	20	515	448	283			0.328
Team Defense	2.46	12	702	446	107	143	43%	0.280
Difference	2.08	8	187	2	176			117%

Pos	*Rpos*	*PA*	*Age*	*Name*	*BA*	*OBP*	*SLG*	*BB%*	*SB*	*Bat R>Avg*	*BR R>Avg*	*Fld R>Avg*	*RAA*	*WAA*
C,RF	6	375	30	Kling, Johnny	0.312	0.357	0.420	6%	14	18	-1	3	26	2.9
1B	-4	574	29	Chance, Frank	0.319	0.419	0.430	12%	57	42	5	11	54	6.1
2B	0	595	24	Evers, Johnny*	0.255	0.305	0.315	6%	49	-1	6	15	20	2.2
3B	5	625	28	Steinfeldt, Harry	0.327	0.395	0.430	8%	29	40	-1	6	50	5.6
SS	10	603	25	Tinker, Joe	0.233	0.293	0.289	7%	30	-7	1	20	24	2.6
LF	-8	662	27	Sheckard, Jimmy*	0.262	0.349	0.353	10%	30	18	0	8	18	2.0
CF,LF	-4	571	32	Slagle, Jimmy*	0.239	0.324	0.279	11%	25	-1	-1	9	3	0.3
RF	-8	630	23	Schulte, Wildfire*	0.281	0.324	0.396	5%	25	17	0	8	17	1.9
C	4	243	30	Moran, Pat	0.252	0.281	0.319	3%	6	-3	0	1	2	0.3
CF,1B	-1	221	23	Hofman, Solly	0.256	0.326	0.328	9%	13	2	0	3	4	0.5
CF	-1	99	25	Gessler, Doc*	0.253	0.354	0.289	12%	4	1	0	-1	-1	-0.1
	1	544		Others	0.152	0.201	0.171	5%	1	-43	0	0	-42	-4.7
	0		26.9	Team Total	0.262	0.328	0.339	7.8%	283	84	9	83	176	19.5
				League Average	0.244	0.310	0.310	7.5%	183					
				% Lg Avg	107	106	109	104	155					
				League Rank	1	2	1	3	2			1	1	

GS	*GR*	*IP*	*Age*	*Name*	*W–L*	*WHIP*	*BA*	*K/9*	*BB/9*	*FIP*	*ERA*	*R/9*	*RAA*	*WAA*
32	4	277	29	Brown, Mordecai	26–6	0.93	0.202	4.7	2.0	1.97	1.04	1.82	40	4.4
29	2	251	28	Pfiester, Jack*	20–8	0.94	0.194	5.5	2.3	2.10	1.51	2.26	24	2.7
24	9	218	23	Reulbach, Ed	19–4	1.01	0.175	3.9	3.8	2.96	1.65	2.11	25	2.7
24	3	208	26	Lundgren, Carl	17–6	1.20	0.221	4.5	3.9	2.85	2.21	2.73	9	1.0
16	1	147	32	Taylor, Jack	12–3	1.05	0.223	2.1	2.4	2.80	1.83	2.57	8	0.9
14	4	144	25	Overall, Orval	12–3	1.16	0.217	5.9	3.2	2.19	1.88	2.69	7	0.7
8	2	72	28	Wicker, Bob	3–5	1.23	0.257	3.1	2.4	2.35	2.99	4.48	-12	-1.3
6	8	70	26	Beebe, Frank	7–1	1.26	0.210	7.1	4.1	2.46	2.70	3.47	-3	-0.3
1	0	1	28	Harper, Jack	0–0	0.00	0.000	0.0	0.0	2.26	0.00	0.00	0	0.0
154	33		27.2	Team Total		1.05	0.207	4.55	2.89	2.44	1.75	2.47	98	10.9
				League Average		1.20	0.244	3.76	2.80	2.61	2.62	3.64		
				% Lg Avg		114	118	121	97	107	150	148		
				League Rank		1	1	1	5	3	1			

1907 Chicago Cubs

Despite scoring a hundred fewer runs than they did in 1906, the Cubs made a mockery of the pennant race winning 107 games and beating the second place Pirates by 17 games. They won primarily with pitching and infield fielding featuring a team ERA of 1.73, the lowest in MLB history. The top 5 starting pitchers each had an ERA below 2.00 representing 4 of the top 5 league leading ERA seasons. In the World Series, the Cubs swept the Tigers in 4 straight games after the first game was called because of darkness.

Strengths: (1) P, C, 1B, 2B, 3B, and SS positions, (2) hitting for average led by Chance (19 2B, 13 HBP), Sheckard (23 2B, 76 BB), Kling (8 3B), and Schulte (7 3B), (3) fielding featuring 2B Evers (109 Rng+), SS Tinker (107 Rng+), 3B Steinfeldt (93 Rng+), 1B Chance, and OF Hofman (112 Rng+), (4) CS% from Kling (46%) and Moran (50%), (5) baserunning especially from Evers (38% RS) and Chance (33% RS), and (6) pitching anchored by Lundgren (7 shutouts, 0 HR allowed, 5.7 H/9), Overall (8 shutouts, 6.7 H/9), Brown (6 shutouts, 7.0 H/9), and Reulbach (4 shutouts, 6.9 H/9).

Weaknesses: (1) isolated power, (2) hitting from Tinker and Moran, (3) bench strength beyond Hofman, (4) hitting from the pitchers, and (5) pitching from Taylor (9.3 H/9).

Mgr	Frank Chance	
Rk	16	40
Gm	155	
Place	1	
GA	17.0	
Rival	12–10 vs Pirates, 72 RS & 63 RA	

	W	*L*	*Win%*
Regular Season	107	45	0.704
Runs Record	99	53	0.651
1 Run	37	16	0.698
Blowout	27	14	0.659

	Team	*LgAvg*	*%Avg*	*LgRk*
BABIP	0.244	0.270	111	1
E	194	260	134	1
K%	8.0%	9.4%	118	
RS%	32.9%	30.9%	107	
R/G	3.68	3.40	108	3
RA/G	2.52	3.40	135	1

	Tm	*LgAvg*	*>Avg*
RS	571	523	48
RA	390	523	133
DP	110	101	9

	R/G	*HR*	*K*	*BB*	*SB*	*CS*	*SB%*	*OBP*
Team Offense	3.68	13	445	435	235			0.318
Team Defense	2.52	11	586	402	148	133	53%	0.281
Difference	1.17	2	141	33	87			113%

Pos	*Rpos*	*PA*	*Age*	*Name*	*BA*	*OBP*	*SLG*	*BB%*	*SB*	*Bat R>Avg*	*BR R>Avg*	*Fld R>Avg*	*RAA*	*WAA*
C	6	367	31	Kling, Johnny	0.284	0.342	0.386	7%	9	13	-1	5	23	2.6
1B	-4	451	30	Chance, Frank	0.293	0.395	0.361	11%	35	22	2	12	32	3.7
2B	0	565	25	Evers, Johnny*	0.250	0.309	0.313	7%	46	1	5	26	32	3.6
3B	5	613	29	Steinfeldt, Harry	0.266	0.323	0.336	6%	19	8	-1	15	27	3.0
SS	7	444	26	Tinker, Joe	0.221	0.269	0.271	6%	20	-11	1	15	12	1.3
LF	-8	601	28	Sheckard, Jimmy*	0.267	0.373	0.324	13%	31	18	0	0	10	1.1
CF	-4	575	33	Slagle, Jimmy*	0.258	0.359	0.294	13%	28	10	-1	-1	4	0.5
RF	-5	389	24	Schulte, Wildfire*	0.287	0.339	0.386	6%	7	12	-1	4	10	1.2
OF,SS	-1	536	24	Hofman, Solly	0.268	0.328	0.311	8%	29	4	0	8	11	1.3
C	4	214	31	Moran, Pat	0.227	0.271	0.278	5%	5	-5	0	1	0	0.0
1B,OF	-2	157	29	Howard, Del*	0.230	0.269	0.270	4%	3	-4	0	0	-6	-0.7
RF	-1	88	27	Randall, Newt	0.205	0.279	0.308	9%	2	-1	0	2	0	0.0
P	0	105	26	Overall, Orval^	0.213	0.237	0.298	3%	0	-3	0	0	-3	-0.4
	3	465		Others	0.150	0.181	0.185	3%	1	-38	2	-2	-35	-4.0
	0		27.9	Team Total	0.250	0.318	0.311	7.8%	235	25	6	85	116	13.2
				League Average	0.243	0.308	0.309	7.4%	173					
				% Lg Avg	103	103	101	106	136					
				League Rank	3	3	4	4	2		2	1		

GS	*GR*	*IP*	*Age*	*Name*	*W–L*	*WHIP*	*BA*	*K/9*	*BB/9*	*FIP*	*ERA*	*R/9*	*RAA*	*WAA*
30	6	268	26	Overall, Orval	23–8	1.01	0.208	4.7	2.3	2.00	1.68	2.08	26	2.9
27	7	233	30	Brown, Mordecai	20–6	0.94	0.221	4.1	1.5	1.80	1.39	1.97	25	2.9
25	3	207	27	Lundgren, Carl	18–7	1.07	0.185	3.7	4.0	2.56	1.17	1.83	26	2.9
22	8	195	29	Pfiester, Jack*	14–9	0.98	0.207	4.2	2.2	1.97	1.15	2.82	3	0.3
22	5	192	24	Reulbach, Ed	17–4	1.10	0.217	4.5	3.0	2.22	1.69	2.25	15	1.7
15	7	138	33	Fraser, Chick	8–5	1.14	0.229	2.7	3.0	2.58	2.28	3.32	-6	-0.7
13	5	123	33	Taylor, Jack	7–5	1.30	0.268	1.6	2.4	2.80	3.29	4.54	-23	-2.6
1	4	17	20	Durbin, Kid	0–1	1.44	0.233	2.7	5.4	3.39	5.40	7.02	-8	-0.9

GS	GR	IP	Age	Name	W–L	WHIP	BA	K/9	BB/9	FIP	ERA	R/9	RAA	WAA
155	45		27.8	Team Total		1.06	0.216	3.84	2.63	2.23	1.73	2.56	57	6.5
				League Average		1.20	0.243	3.51	2.85	2.46	2.46	3.49		
				% Lg Avg		113	112	109	108	111	142	136		
				League Rank		1	1	3	3	2	1			

1908 New York Giants

The 1908 Giants were one of three teams involved in the greatest pennant race in MLB history. Unfortunately for the Giants, when the regular season ended, they had tied with the Cubs but lost in the make-up game to decide the pennant. This team underperformed while the Cubs were pretty lucky. For example, the Giants split their 22 games with the Cubs despite outscoring them by 16 runs.

Strengths: (1) hitting for average led by Donlin (26 2B, 13 3B), Bresnahan (25 2B), and Doyle (9 3B), (2) hitting for contact easily leading the league in fewest strikeouts, (3) drawing walks especially from Bresnahan (83 BB) and Tenney (72 BB), (4) fielding from SS Bridwell (100 Rng+), 3B Devlin (104 Rng+), and 1B Tenney (117 assists), (5) CS% from Needham (51%) and Bresnahan (47%), (6) terrific pitching control especially from Mathewson, and (7) pitching from Mathewson who won the pitching Triple Crown (37 wins, 1.43 ERA, and 259 K as well as throwing 11 shutouts, 6.5 H/9), Wiltse (7 shutouts, 7.3 H/9), and Ames (7.6 H/9).

Weaknesses: (1) LF position, (2) baserunning, (3) fielding from LF/RF McCormick (78 Rng+), and (4) pitching from Taylor (9.0 H/9).

Mgr	John McGraw	
Rk	13	34
Gm	157	
Place	2	
GB	1.0	
Rival	11–11 vs Cubs, 85 RS & 69 RA	

	W	L	Win%
Regular Season	98	56	0.636
Runs Record	101	53	0.654
1 Run	26	20	0.565
Blowout	27	6	0.818

	Team	LgAvg	%Avg	LgRk
BABIP	0.264	0.264	100	7
E	250	253	101	5
K%	6.5%	9.2%	142	
RS%	33.5%	31.0%	108	
R/G	4.15	3.33	125	1
RA/G	2.90	3.33	115	2

	Tm	LgAvg	RAA
RS	652	517	135
RA	455	517	62
DP	79	75	4

	R/G	HR	K	BB	SB	CS	SB%	OBP
Team Offense	4.15	20	378	494	181			0.342
Team Defense	2.90	26	656	288	135	125	52%	0.279
Difference	1.25	-6	278	206	46			123%

Pos	Rpos	PA	Age	Name	BA	OBP	SLG	BB%	SB	Bat R>Avg	BR R>Avg	Fld R>Avg	RAA	WAA
C	9	562	29	Bresnahan, Roger	0.283	0.401	0.359	15%	14	30	-1	1	39	4.6
1B	-5	684	36	Tenney, Fred*	0.256	0.344	0.304	11%	17	12	-1	9	15	1.7
2B	0	429	21	Doyle, Larry*	0.308	0.354	0.398	5%	17	19	0	-3	16	1.8
3B	5	629	28	Devlin, Art	0.253	0.346	0.313	10%	19	13	-1	6	23	2.7
SS	9	545	24	Bridwell, Al*	0.285	0.364	0.319	10%	20	15	-1	4	27	3.2
LF,RF	-4	313	30	Shannon, Spike^	0.224	0.314	0.250	9%	13	-2	0	-2	-8	-1.0
CF	-4	653	35	Seymour, Cy*	0.267	0.306	0.339	5%	18	7	-1	0	2	0.2
RF,LF	-8	654	30	Donlin, Mike*	0.334	0.364	0.452	4%	30	40	0	6	38	4.5
LF,RF	-4	263	27	McCormick, Moose*	0.302	0.315	0.389	2%	6	7	0	-4	-1	-0.1
2B,SS	1	213	22	Herzog, Buck	0.300	0.448	0.363	17%	16	15	0	-1	15	1.8
C	2	115	29	Needham, Tom	0.209	0.339	0.242	10%	0	0	0	-1	1	0.2
1B,OF	-1	47	19	Merkle, Fred	0.268	0.333	0.439	9%	0	2	0	0	1	0.1
2B,OF	0	80	31	Strang, Sammy^	0.094	0.385	0.094	29%	5	0	0	-3	-3	-0.3
P	0	83	20	Crandall, Doc	0.222	0.273	0.361	5%	0	0	0	0	0	0.0
	0	556		Others	0.186	0.256	0.213	7%	6	-22	-2	-4	-28	-3.3
	0		27.2	Team Total	0.267	0.342	0.333	8.5%	181	138	-7	8	139	16.1
				League Average	0.239	0.299	0.306	6.8%	172					
				% League Average	112	114	109	125	105					
				League Rank	1	1	1	1	5		8	5		

GS	GR	IP	Age	Name	W–L	WHIP	BA	K/9	BB/9	FIP	ERA	R/9	RAA	WAA
44	12	391	27	Mathewson, Christy	37–11	0.83	0.202	6.0	1.0	1.14	1.43	1.96	57	6.7
38	6	330	28	Wiltse, Hooks*	23–14	1.03	0.224	3.2	2.0	2.14	2.24	2.59	25	2.9
24	8	215	20	Crandall, Doc	12–12	1.20	0.248	3.2	2.5	2.37	2.93	3.48	-5	-0.6
20	17	186	37	McGinnity, Joe	11–7	1.23	0.275	2.7	1.8	2.63	2.27	3.53	-5	-0.6
15	12	128	33	Taylor, Dummy	8–5	1.26	0.253	3.5	2.4	2.57	2.33	3.95	-10	-1.1
15	3	114	25	Ames, Red	7–4	1.08	0.232	6.4	2.1	1.27	1.81	2.76	7	0.8
0	15	35	29	Malarkey, Bill	0–2	1.17	0.242	3.1	2.6	2.58	2.57	4.11	-3	-0.4
1	3	13		Others	0–1	1.97	0.365	2.8	4.3	2.98	6.40	8.53	-7	-0.9
157	76		28.4	Team Total		1.06	0.234	4.18	1.84	1.95	2.14	2.90	58	6.8
				League Average		1.13	0.239	3.35	2.46	2.31	2.35	3.33		
				% League Average		107	102	125	134	118	109	115		
				League Rank		1	5	1	1	1	3			

1909 Detroit Tigers

The 1909 Tigers won their third straight AL pennant beating a young and talented A's team only to lose the World Series for the third straight season. The A's had better pitching than the Tigers, but Ty Cobb put this team on his back and led them to the pennant. Coincidently, 3 of this team's top 4 starting pitchers were all named Ed. They lost the World Series in 7 games to an excellent Pirate team.

Strengths: (1) hitting for average and power led by Triple Crown winner Cobb (.377 BA, 9 HR, 107 RBI, 33 2B, 10 3B), Sam Crawford (35 2B, 14 3B), and rookie SS Bush who had his career best season (18 2B), (2) team baserunning featuring Cobb (41% RS) and Bush (48% RS), (3) fielding led by SS Bush (108 Rng+), 3B Moriarty (105 Rng+), and 2B Schaefer (109 Rng+), (4) CS% from Schmidt (48%), and (5) pitching featuring Killian (7.8 H/9), Mullin (7.6 H/9), and Summers (7.8 H/9).

Weaknesses: (1) hitting from O'Leary and Schmidt, (2) double plays made, (3) pitching K/9, and (4) pitching from Speer (10.4 H/9).

Mgr	Hughie Jennings	
Rk	24	83
Gm	158	
Place	1	
GA	3.5	
Rival	8–14 vs A's; 66 RS & 90 RA	

	W	L	Win%
Regular Season	98	54	0.645
Runs Record	95	57	0.628
1 Run	26	15	0.634
Blowout	30	11	0.732

	Team	LgAvg	%Avg	LgRk
BABIP	0.262	0.276	105	3
E	275	277	101	4
K%	10.8%	10.9%	101	
RS%	36.4%	32.0%	114	
R/G	4.22	3.44	123	1
RA/G	3.12	3.44	110	3

	Tm	LgAvg	>Avg
RS	666	534	132
RA	493	534	41
DP	87	98	-11

	R/G	HR	K	BB	SB	CS	SB%	OBP
Team Offense	4.22	19	625	397	280			0.325
Team Defense	3.12	16	528	359	190	156	55%	0.293
Difference	1.09	3	-97	38	90			111%

Pos	Rpos	PA	Age	Name	BA	OBP	SLG	BB%	SB	Bat R>Avg	BR R>Avg	Fld R>Avg	RAA	WAA
C	5	285	28	Schmidt, Boss^	0.209	0.240	0.269	2%	7	-10	0	0	-5	-0.6
1B	-2	310	28	Rossman, Claude*	0.261	0.293	0.310	4%	10	-2	0	-1	-5	-0.5
2B	0	308	33	Schaefer, Germany	0.250	0.286	0.293	5%	12	-4	0	6	2	0.3
3B,1B	3	515	29	Moriarty, George	0.273	0.309	0.338	5%	34	5	2	9	19	2.1
SS	10	676	21	Bush, Donie^	0.273	0.380	0.314	13%	53	21	3	8	42	4.8
LF	-6	542	29	McIntyre, Matty*	0.244	0.325	0.326	10%	13	8	-1	3	4	0.4
CF,1B	-4	662	29	Crawford, Sam*	0.314	0.366	0.452	7%	30	41	0	-2	35	4.0
RF	-8	651	22	Cobb, Ty*	0.377	0.431	0.517	7%	76	67	9	4	72	8.2
3B,2B	2	278	33	O'Leary, Charley	0.203	0.224	0.241	2%	9	-14	0	2	-10	-1.1
C	5	269	26	Stanage, Oscar	0.262	0.298	0.341	4%	2	2	0	2	9	1.0
LF,CF	-3	239	29	Jones, Davy*	0.279	0.369	0.309	12%	12	6	0	0	3	0.4
2B	0	185	30	Delahanty, Jim	0.253	0.364	0.333	9%	9	6	0	1	7	0.8
1B	-1	172	32	Jones, Tom	0.281	0.317	0.340	3%	9	2	0	3	4	0.5

Pos	Rpos	PA	Age	Name	BA	OBP	SLG	BB%	SB	Bat R>Avg	BR R>Avg	Fld R>Avg	RAA	WAA
2B	0	68	24	Killefer, Red	0.279	0.343	0.426	4%	2	3	0	1	4	0.5
	-1	603		Others	0.176	0.224	0.216	5%	2	-34	-1	1	-35	-3.9
	0		28.1	Team Total	0.267	0.325	0.342	6.9%	280	98	12	37	147	16.7
				League Average	0.244	0.303	0.309	6.5%	192					
				% Lg Avg	109	107	111	106	146					
				League Rank	1	1	2	4	1		1	2		

GS	GR	IP	Age	Name	W–L	WHIP	BA	K/9	BB/9	FIP	ERA	R/9	RAA	WAA
35	5	304	28	Mullin, George	29–8	1.11	0.234	3.7	2.3	2.36	2.22	2.85	14	1.6
34	7	293	25	Willett, Ed	21–10	1.08	0.221	2.7	2.3	2.83	2.34	3.44	-6	-0.7
32	3	282	24	Summers, Ed	19–9	1.05	0.227	3.4	1.7	2.37	2.24	2.91	11	1.2
19	6	173	32	Killian, Ed*	11–9	1.15	0.236	2.8	2.5	2.69	1.71	2.34	18	2.0
17	4	140	32	Donovan, Wild Bill	8–7	1.29	0.235	4.9	3.8	2.62	2.31	3.21	1	0.1
4	12	64	21	Works, Ralph	4–1	1.23	0.261	4.4	2.4	2.16	1.97	2.67	4	0.5
4	5	44	26	Suggs, George	1–3	0.99	0.228	3.7	2.0	2.65	2.03	2.44	4	0.5
8	4	76	23	Speer, Kid*	4–4	1.32	0.293	1.4	1.5	2.98	2.83	4.60	-12	-1.3
2	0	10	27	Jones, Elijah	1–1	1.00	0.278	1.8	0.0	1.89	2.70	2.70	1	0.1
3	4	34		Others	0–2	1.56	0.333	4.0	1.1	2.61	4.24	6.88	-14	-1.6
158	50		26.4	Team Total		1.14	0.238	3.35	2.27	2.56	2.26	3.12	20	2.3
				League Average		1.16	0.245	4.01	2.49	2.47	2.47	3.49		
				% Lg Avg		102	103	83	109	96	109	112		
				League Rank		3	3	8	3	6	3			

1909 Philadelphia Athletics

The 1909 A's team had a statistically better team than the 1909 Detroit Tigers. This team would subsequently dominate the league winning the pennant four of the next five seasons.

Strengths: (1) hitting for average and power led by Collins (30 2B, 10 3B), Baker (27 2B, 19 3B), Murphy (28 2B, 14 3B), and Davis (11 3B), (2) baserunning especially from Collins (38.4% RS), (3) fielding led by 2B Collins (106 Rng+) and CF Ganley (140 Rng+), (4) CS% from Livingston (56%) and Thomas (49%), and (5) pitching anchored by rookie 20-year-old Harry Krause (6 shutouts, 6.4 H/9), Morgan (6.0 H/9), Bender (161 K, 7.1 H/9), Plank (7.3 H/9), and Coombs (6 shutouts, 6.8 H/9).

Weaknesses: (1) C, 2B, and CF positions, (2) hitting from Ganley and Barry, (3) double plays made, and (4) pitching from Vickers (9.7 H/9) and Dygert.

Mgr	Connie Mack	
Rk	7	17
Gm	153	
Place	2	
GB	3.5	
Rival	14–8 vs Tigers, 90 RS & 66 RA	

	W	L	Win%
Regular Season	95	58	0.621
Runs Record	102	51	0.670
1 Run	29	28	0.509
Blowout	30	5	0.857

	Team	LgAvg	%Avg	LgRk
BABIP	0.255	0.276	108	1
E	245	277	113	1
K%	10.2%	10.9%	107	
RS%	34%	32%	107	
R/G	3.93	3.44	114	3
RA/G	2.72	3.44	127	1

	Tm	LgAvg	>Avg
RS	601	534	67
RA	416	534	118
DP	92	98	-6

	R/G	HR	K	BB	SB	CS	SB%	OBP
Team Offense	3.93	21	576	403	201			0.321
Team Defense	2.72	9	728	386	152	163	48%	0.284
Difference	1.21	12	152	17	49			113%

Pos	Rpos	PA	Age	Name	BA	OBP	SLG	BB%	SB	Bat R>Avg	BR R>Avg	Fld R>Avg	RAA	WAA
C	5	286	28	Thomas, Ira	0.223	0.292	0.281	6%	4	-3	0	2	4	0.4
1B	-5	603	35	Davis, Harry	0.268	0.338	0.374	8%	20	17	-1	1	12	1.4
2B	0	660	22	Collins, Eddie*	0.347	0.416	0.450	9%	63	53	5	11	69	7.8
3B	5	606	23	Baker, Home Run*	0.305	0.343	0.447	4%	20	31	-1	-1	34	3.9
SS	8	491	22	Barry, Jack	0.215	0.307	0.259	9%	17	-5	-1	5	7	0.8

Pos	Rpos	PA	Age	Name	BA	OBP	SLG	BB%	SB	Bat R>Avg	BR R>Avg	Fld R>Avg	RAA	WAA
LF	-4	323	35	Hartsel, Topsy*	0.270	0.381	0.326	15%	3	12	0	4	12	1.3
CF	-2	338	34	Ganley, Bob*	0.197	0.272	0.226	8%	16	-10	1	8	-3	-0.4
RF	-8	616	32	Murphy, Danny	0.281	0.332	0.412	6%	19	23	-1	0	14	1.6
CF,LF	-3	367	25	Oldring, Rube	0.230	0.287	0.328	5%	17	0	1	3	1	0.1
LF,CF	-3	239	26	Heitmuller, Heine	0.286	0.351	0.405	8%	7	11	0	2	10	1.1
C	3	207	29	Livingston, Paddy	0.234	0.323	0.314	7%	4	2	0	0	5	0.6
C	1	62	24	Lapp, Jack*	0.339	0.373	0.429	5%	1	4	0	-2	3	0.3
SS	1	50	18	McInnis, Stuffy	0.239	0.286	0.304	4%	0	0	0	-2	-1	-0.2
	2	772		Others	0.175	0.219	0.213	4%	10	-45	-1	-3	-47	-5.3
	0		27.2	Team Total	0.256	0.321	0.343	7.2%	201	91	2	28	121	13.5
				League Average	0.244	0.303	0.309	6.5%	192					
				% Lg Avg	105	106	111	110	105					
				League Rank	3	3	1	3	4		2	2		

GS	GR	IP	Age	Name	W–L	WHIP	BA	K/9	BB/9	FIP	ERA	R/9	RAA	WAA
33	1	265	33	Plank, Eddie*	19–10	1.04	0.232	4.5	2.1	2.13	1.76	2.51	23	2.7
29	5	250	25	Bender, Chief	18–8	0.96	0.214	5.8	1.6	1.65	1.66	2.45	24	2.7
26	2	229	30	Morgan, Cy	16–11	0.98	0.191	3.2	2.8	2.89	1.65	2.20	28	3.2
21	11	213	20	Krause, Harry*	18–8	0.94	0.204	5.9	2.1	1.98	1.39	2.07	29	3.3
24	6	206	26	Coombs, Jack	12–11	1.11	0.213	4.2	3.2	2.56	2.32	2.76	12	1.4
13	19	137	24	Dygert, Jimmy	9–5	1.22	0.242	5.2	3.3	2.56	2.43	3.93	-10	-1.1
3	15	56	31	Vickers, Rube	2–2	1.42	0.282	4.0	3.1	2.52	3.39	5.17	-12	-1.3
3	1	13	24	Schlitzer, Biff	0–3	1.50	0.245	4.1	4.7	3.64	5.41	6.09	-4	-0.5
1	0	6	21	Atkins, Tommy*	0–0	1.83	0.261	6.0	7.5	3.45	4.50	6.00	-2	-0.2
0	1	3	27	Kull, John*	1–0	2.67	0.250	12.0	15.0	5.62	3.00	3.00	0	0.0
153	61		26.1	Team Total		1.06	0.218	4.75	2.52	2.30	1.93	2.72	90	10.2
				League Average		1.16	0.245	4.01	2.49	2.47	2.47	3.49		
				% Lg Avg		110	112	118	99	108	128	128		
				League Rank		1	1	1	6	2	1			

1909 Pittsburgh Pirates

The 1909 Pirates head-to-head W–L record versus the pitching rich Cubs helped the Pirates capture the pennant. Wagner had a MVP worthy season. The World Series featured a match-up of two of baseball's greatest players, Ty Cobb and Honus Wagner. Wagner and team pitching, especially from Adams who won 3 games in the World Series, enabled the Pirates to beat the Tigers in 7 games.

Strengths: (1) hitting led by Wagner (39 2B, 10 3B), Clarke (11 3B), Miller (31 2B, 13 3B), Leach (29 2B), and Wilson (12 3B), (2) fielding anchored by SS Wagner (109 Rng+), 2B Miller (97 Rng+), C Gibson (53% CS), LF Clarke (123 Rng+, 17 assists), and RF Wilson (100 Rng+, 19 assists), (3) stolen base differentiation, and (4) team pitching led by Camnitz (6.6 H/9), Willis (7.6 H/9), and 27-year-old rookie starter/reliever and World Series hero Babe Adams (6.1 H/9).

Weaknesses: (1) 1B position, (2) hitting and fielding from 3B Barbeau (87 Rng+), and (3) hitting from the pitchers.

Mgr	Fred Clarke	
Rk	8	20
Gm	154	
Place	1	
GA	6.5	
Rival	13–9 vs Cubs, 78 RS & 68 RA	

	W	L	Win%
Regular Season	110	42	0.724
Runs Record	101	51	0.667
1 Run	33	13	0.717
Blowout	34	9	0.791

	Team	LgAvg	%Avg	LgRk
BABIP	0.254	0.270	106	2
E	227	284	125	1
K%	8.7%	9.7%	112	
RS%	37.1%	32.1%	116	
R/G	4.55	3.65	125	1
RA/G	2.91	3.65	125	2

	Tm	LgAvg	>Avg
RS	701	566	135

	R/G	HR	K	BB	SB	CS	SB%	OBP
Team Offense	4.55	25	507	479	185			0.327

	Tm	LgAvg	>Avg
RA	448	566	118
DP	100	99	1

	R/G	HR	K	BB	SB	CS	SB%	OBP
Team Defense	2.91	12	490	320	129	143	47%	0.284
Difference	1.64	13	-17	159	56			115%

Pos	Rpos	PA	Age	Name	BA	OBP	SLG	BB%	SB	Bat R>Avg	BR R>Avg	Fld R>Avg	RAA	WAA
C	10	571	28	Gibson, George	0.265	0.326	0.361	8%	9	12	-1	3	24	2.7
1B	-4	570	26	Abstein, Bill	0.260	0.302	0.344	5%	16	5	-1	-1	-1	-0.1
2B	0	631	22	Miller, Dots	0.279	0.329	0.396	6%	14	20	-1	9	28	3.1
3B	3	399	27	Barbeau, Jap	0.220	0.302	0.283	9%	19	-3	0	-6	-6	-0.7
SS	9	591	35	Wagner, Honus	0.339	0.420	0.489	11%	35	52	1	7	69	7.7
LF	-8	660	36	Clarke, Fred*	0.287	0.384	0.373	12%	31	23	-1	12	26	2.9
CF,3B	-3	682	31	Leach, Tommy	0.261	0.337	0.368	10%	27	16	0	4	17	1.9
RF	-8	614	25	Wilson, Chief*	0.272	0.303	0.374	3%	17	13	-1	8	12	1.4
3B	2	206	24	Byrne, Bobby	0.272	0.407	0.335	16%	8	4	0	5	11	1.3
1B,3B	0	131	24	Storke, Alan	0.265	0.314	0.345	5%	1	1	0	1	2	0.3
SS,2B	1	107	32	Abbaticchio, Ed	0.230	0.368	0.264	18%	2	0	0	1	2	0.2
LF,1B	0	71	24	Hyatt, Ham*	0.299	0.329	0.463	4%	1	4	0	1	5	0.6
C	0	16	29	O'Conner, Paddy	0.313	0.313	0.375	0%	0	1	0	0	1	0.1
	-2	611		Others	0.143	0.202	0.181	7%	5	-31	0	-2	-35	-3.9
	0		27.9	Team Total	0.260	0.327	0.353	8.2%	185	118	-4	42	156	17.3
				League Average	0.244	0.310	0.314	7.8%	190					
				% Lg Avg	107	106	112	105	97					
				League Rank	1	2	1	4	4		6	1		

GS	GR	IP	Age	Name	W–L	WHIP	BA	K/9	BB/9	FIP	ERA	R/9	RAA	WAA
35	4	290	33	Willis, Vic	22–11	1.13	0.231	3.0	2.6	2.52	2.24	2.61	25	2.8
30	11	283	27	Camnitz, Howie	25–6	0.97	0.211	4.2	2.2	2.04	1.62	2.39	32	3.6
27	4	203	22	Maddox, Nick	13–8	1.04	0.232	2.5	1.7	2.52	2.21	3.19	4	0.5
27	5	202	25	Leifield, Lefty*	19–8	1.12	0.229	1.9	2.4	2.87	2.37	3.39	-1	-0.1
12	10	132	37	Phillippe, Deacon	8–3	1.03	0.253	2.6	1.0	2.17	2.32	2.80	8	0.9
12	13	130	27	Adams, Babe	12–3	0.85	0.196	4.5	1.6	1.74	1.11	1.73	24	2.7
4	15	70	37	Leever, Sam	8–1	1.26	0.276	3.0	1.8	2.26	2.83	3.86	-4	-0.4
2	11	41	22	Brandom, Chick	1–0	1.06	0.239	4.6	2.2	1.92	1.11	2.66	3	0.4
4	4	36	26	Frock, Sam	2–1	1.32	0.299	2.7	1.0	2.12	2.48	4.71	-6	-0.6
1	5	15		Others	0–1	1.96	0.333	2.9	6.5	3.84	5.28	8.22	-8	-0.9
154	82		28.4	Team Total		1.07	0.232	3.15	2.05	2.34	2.07	2.88	79	8.8
				League Average		1.21	0.243	3.57	2.91	2.58	2.59	3.65		
				% Lg Avg		113	105	88	142	110	125	127		
				League Rank		2	2	5	1	3	2			

1909 CHICAGO CUBS

The 1909 Cubs 9–13 Win-Loss record vs the Pirates was the primary factor for their second place finish. In addition, the contract holdout of standout C Johnny Kling for the entire season also probably cost this team at least a couple wins since catchers Archer and Moran had below average seasons. The top three Wins Above Average (WAA) players on this team were all pitchers.

Strengths: (1) hitting for power from Hofman (21 2B) and Evers (73 BB), (2) fielding from SS Tinker (106 Rng+), 3B Steinfeldt (99 Rng+), 2B Evers (104 Rng+), and CF Hofman (117 Rng+, 16 assists), (3) CS% from Moran (51%) and Archer (49%), and (4) pitching (32 shutouts) led by Brown (8 shutouts, 7 saves, 6.5 H/9), Overall (205 K, 9 shutouts, 6.4 H/9), Reulbach (6 shutouts, 6.6 H/9), and Kroh (7.3 H/9).

Weaknesses: (1) C and RF positions, (2) hitting from the catcher and pitcher positions, (3) hitting from 1B Howard, (4) weak bench, and (5) fielding from 2B Zimmerman (83 Rng+) and RF Schulte (65 Rng+).

			W	L	Win%		Team	LgAvg	%Avg	LgRk
Mgr	Frank Chance	**Regular Season**	104	49	0.68	**BABIP**	0.250	0.270	108	1

Rk	9	25
Gm	155	
Place	2	
GB	6.5	
Rival	9–13 vs Pirates, 68 RS & 78 RA	

	W	*L*	*Win%*
Runs Record	101	52	0.663
1 Run	25	15	0.625
Blowout	35	4	0.897

	Team	*LgAvg*	*%Avg*	*LgRk*
E	244	280	115	3
K%	9.6%	9.7%	100	
RS%	36.9%	32.1%	115	
R/G	4.08	3.65	112	2
RA/G	2.51	3.65	145	1

	Tm	*LgAvg*	*>Avg*
RS	632	566	66
RA	389	566	177
DP	95	99	-4

	R/G	*HR*	*K*	*BB*	*SB*	*CS*	*SB%*	*OBP*
Team Offense	4.08	20	549	420	187			0.308
Team Defense	2.51	6	680	364	149	146	51%	0.275
Difference	1.57	14	131	56	38			112%

Pos	*Rpos*	*PA*	*Age*	*Name*	*BA*	*OBP*	*SLG*	*BB%*	*SB*	*Bat R>Avg*	*BR R>Avg*	*Fld R>Avg*	*RAA*	*WAA*
C	5	286	26	Archer, Jimmy	0.230	0.266	0.291	4%	5	-7	0	-1	-3	-0.3
1B	-3	370	32	Chance, Frank	0.272	0.341	0.346	8%	29	8	3	3	11	1.2
2B	0	552	27	Evers, Johnny*	0.263	0.369	0.337	13%	28	17	0	7	24	2.7
3B	5	621	31	Steinfeldt, Harry	0.252	0.331	0.337	9%	22	9	-1	6	19	2.1
SS	9	555	28	Tinker, Joe	0.256	0.280	0.372	3%	23	2	1	15	27	3.0
LF	-8	644	30	Sheckard, Jimmy*	0.255	0.346	0.335	11%	15	13	-1	2	6	0.6
CF,RF	-4	613	26	Hofman, Solly	0.285	0.351	0.351	9%	20	15	-1	10	20	2.3
RF	-8	591	26	Schulte, Wildfire*	0.264	0.298	0.357	4%	23	3	0	-4	-9	-1.0
C	4	269	33	Moran, Pat	0.220	0.278	0.285	6%	2	-6	0	2	0	0.0
1B	-4	241	31	Howard, Del*	0.197	0.282	0.251	7%	6	-6	0	0	-10	-1.1
2B,SS	1	190	22	Zimmerman, Heinie	0.273	0.285	0.344	2%	7	-1	0	-5	-5	-0.5
1B	0	43	23	Luderus, Fred*	0.297	0.366	0.459	7%	0	3	0	-1	2	0.2
P	0	107	28	Overall, Orval^	0.229	0.282	0.375	7%	0	1	0	0	1	0.1
	3	614		Others	0.161	0.214	0.192	6%	7	-43	-1	-1	-42	-4.7
	0		27.9	Team Total	0.245	0.308	0.322	7.4%	187	7	0	33	40	4.5
				League Average	0.244	0.310	0.314	7.8%	190					
				% Lg Avg	101	99	103	95	98					
				League Rank	4	5	4	5	3		6	2		

GS	*GR*	*IP*	*Age*	*Name*	*W–L*	*WHIP*	*BA*	*K/9*	*BB/9*	*FIP*	*ERA*	*R/9*	*RAA*	*WAA*
34	16	343	32	Brown, Mordecai	27–9	0.87	0.205	4.5	1.4	1.70	1.31	2.05	53	5.9
32	6	285	28	Overall, Orval	20–11	1.00	0.198	6.5	2.5	1.68	1.42	2.08	43	4.8
32	3	263	26	Reulbach, Ed	19–10	1.05	0.220	3.6	2.8	2.46	1.78	2.36	32	3.5
25	4	197	31	Pfiester, Jack*	17–6	1.16	0.240	3.3	2.2	2.29	2.43	3.07	8	0.9
13	4	120	22	Kroh, Rube*	9–4	1.06	0.224	3.8	2.2	2.28	1.65	1.94	20	2.2
7	6	79	23	Hagerman, Rip	4–4	1.16	0.225	3.6	3.2	2.47	1.82	3.30	1	0.1
6	13	78	27	Higginbotham, Irv	5–2	1.08	0.213	3.7	2.3	2.21	2.19	3.69	-2	-0.3
1	0	9	20	Brown, Ray	1–0	1.00	0.172	2.0	4.0	3.03	2.00	3.00	0	0.0
1	0	9	23	Cole, King	1–0	1.00	0.194	1.0	3.0	2.92	0.00	0.00	3	0.4
2	1	14	25	Schwenck, Rudy*	1–1	1.36	0.308	1.9	1.9	2.57	3.86	4.50	-2	-0.2
2	4	13		Others	0–2	2.38	0.365	2.8	8.3	4.30	4.85	8.31	-7	-0.8
155	57		25.7	Team Total		1.03	0.217	4.34	2.32	2.09	1.74	2.48	150	16.7
				League Average		1.21	0.243	3.57	2.91	2.58	2.59	3.65		
				% Lg Avg		117	112	122	125	124	149	147		
				League Rank		1	1	2	2	1	1			

1910 Philadelphia Athletics

The 1910 A's had their franchise best season easily winning the AL pennant becoming the AL's first 100+ victory team. The 1910 Philadelphia A's were the lesser known of the two back-to-back A's world championship teams. The A's mortgaged their long-term future to win in 1910 by trading for 26-year-old Bris Lord from Cleveland in exchange for 2 young future superstars who couldn't quite crack the A's starting line-up: 22-year-old Shoeless Joe Jackson and 23-year-old Morrie Rath. The A's beat the Cubs in 5 games in the World Series.

Strengths: (1) hitting for average and power led by Collins (15 3B), Murphy (18 3B), Oldring (14 3B), and Baker (15 3B), (2) baserunning from Collins (33% RS), (3) fielding featuring 2B Collins (114 Rng+), (4) CS% from

Livingston (50%), Thomas (47%), and Lapp (45%), and (5) team pitching especially Coombs (224 K, 13 shutouts, 6.3 H/9), Bender (6.6 H/9), Morgan (6.6 H/9), and Plank (7.8 H/9).

Weaknesses: (1) pitching from Atkins (8.4 H/9), Dygert, and Krause, (2) pitching BB/9, and (3) drawing walks.

				W	L	Win%		Team	LgAvg	%Avg	LgRk
Mgr	Connie Mack		**Regular Season**	102	48	0.680	**BABIP**	0.265	0.279	105	1
Rk	4	8	**Runs Record**	103	47	0.684	**E**	230	277	120	1
Gm	155		**1 Run**	23	19	0.548	**K%**	9.9%	11.4%	116	
Place	1		**Blowout**	29	9	0.763	**RS%**	36.0%	32.5%	111	
GA	14.5						**R/G**	4.33	3.65	119	2
Rival	12–9 vs Yankees, 94 RS & 65 RA						**RA/G**	2.85	3.65	128	1

	Tm	LgAvg	>Avg
RS	671	572	99
RA	441	572	131
DP	117	99	18

	R/G	HR	K	BB	SB	CS	SB%	OBP
Team Offense	4.33	19	573	409	207			0.326
Team Defense	2.85	8	789	450	186	168	53%	0.296
Difference	1.48	11	216	-41	21			110%

Pos	Rpos	PA	Age	Name	BA	OBP	SLG	BB%	SB	Bat R>Avg	BR R>Avg	Fld R>Avg	RAA	WAA
C	4	219	25	Lapp, Jack*	0.234	0.310	0.286	9%	0	-1	0	2	5	0.5
1B	-5	573	36	Davis, Harry	0.248	0.332	0.309	9%	17	5	-1	1	0	0.0
2B	0	660	23	Collins, Eddie*	0.322	0.381	0.417	7%	81	36	10	24	70	7.8
3B	5	620	24	Baker, Home Run*	0.283	0.329	0.392	5%	21	18	-1	4	26	2.9
SS	9	566	23	Barry, Jack	0.259	0.336	0.337	9%	14	10	-2	4	21	2.3
LF	-4	351	36	Hartsel, Topsy*	0.221	0.353	0.277	17%	11	4	-1	-1	-2	-0.2
CF	-4	594	26	Oldring, Rube	0.308	0.340	0.430	4%	17	26	-1	1	22	2.4
RF	-8	613	33	Murphy, Danny	0.300	0.338	0.436	5%	18	27	-1	2	20	2.2
LF	-4	326	26	Lord, Bris	0.278	0.333	0.427	7%	6	13	-1	6	14	1.6
C	4	189	29	Thomas, Ira	0.278	0.301	0.361	3%	2	2	0	1	7	0.7
C	2	133	30	Livingston, Paddy	0.208	0.264	0.292	5%	2	-3	0	0	-1	-0.1
LF,CF	-1	121	27	Heitmuller, Heine	0.243	0.288	0.297	6%	6	-2	0	0	-3	-0.3
SS	1	81	19	McInnis, Stuffy	0.301	0.363	0.438	9%	3	4	0	0	5	0.6
	1	763		Others	0.192	0.251	0.223	5%	9	-35	-1	4	-31	-3.4
	0		27.5	Team Total	0.266	0.326	0.355	7.0%	207	105	1	48	154	17.1
				League Average	0.243	0.308	0.313	7.3%	209					
				% Lg Avg	110	106	113	96	99					
				League Rank	1	2	1	7	3		4	1		

GS	GR	IP	Age	Name	W–L	WHIP	BA	K/9	BB/9	FIP	ERA	R/9	RAA	WAA
38	7	353	27	Coombs, Jack	31–9	1.03	0.207	5.7	2.9	2.02	1.30	1.89	58	6.4
34	2	291	31	Morgan, Cy	18–12	1.14	0.216	4.1	3.6	2.72	1.55	2.85	16	1.8
32	6	250	34	Plank, Eddie*	16–10	1.09	0.244	4.4	2.0	2.18	2.01	3.20	4	0.4
28	2	250	26	Bender, Chief	23–5	0.92	0.207	5.6	1.7	1.74	1.58	2.27	30	3.3
11	5	112	21	Krause, Harry*	6–6	1.26	0.254	4.8	3.4	2.98	2.89	3.69	-4	-0.5
8	11	99	25	Dygert, Jimmy	4–4	1.31	0.231	5.3	4.4	2.63	2.54	3.99	-7	-0.8
3	12	57	22	Atkins, Tommy*	3–2	1.33	0.254	4.6	3.6	2.49	2.68	5.21	-12	-1.3
1	0	9	19	Russell, Lefty*	1–0	1.11	0.258	5.0	2.0	1.80	0.00	0.00	3	0.4
155	45			Team Total		1.09	0.223	5.00	2.85	2.28	1.79	2.79	88	9.8
			25.6	League Average		1.19	0.243	4.21	2.76	2.52	2.52	3.65		
				% Lg Avg		109	109	119	97	111	141	131		
				League Rank		2	1	2	5	2	1			

1910 Chicago Cubs

The Cubs continued their run as one of baseball's perennial best teams easily winning the NL pennant, its fourth pennant in 5 years. The Cubs also earned 100 or more victories for the fourth time in 5 years. Only the great 1909 Pirate team was able to break the streak of Cub pennant winning teams. Serious injuries dogged this team: (1) Reulbach had diphtheria, (2) Evers had a broken ankle causing him to miss the pennant stretch and the World Series, (3) Overall had a lame arm much of the season, (4) Brown started the season out of shape spending considerable time in the bullpen, and (5) Pfiester had a broken wrist. On the plus side, Kling returned to the team as the starting catcher after his 1909 season long holdout due to a contract dispute.

Strengths: (1) hitting for average and power led by Hofman (29 2B, 16 3B), Schulte (29 2B, 15 3B), Chance, and Tinker (25 2B, 9 3B), (2) drawing walks led by Evers (108 BB) and Sheckard (83 BB), (3) fielding anchored by SS Tinker (104 Rng+) and LF Sheckard (110 Rng+, 21 assists), (4) CS% from Archer (54%) and Kling (49%), and (5) pitching featuring Cole (6.5 H/9), Brown (7 saves, 7.8 H/9), Overall (6.6 H/9, and Pfiester (7.4 H/9).

Weaknesses: (1) hitting from Steinfeldt and Needham, (2) Zimmerman's infield fielding (90 Rng+ at 2B, 106 Rng+ at 3B, 88 Rng+ at SS), (3) Pfeffer's pitching (9.4 H/9), and (4) injuries to key players including Chance, Kling, and Tinker on this veteran but aging club.

Mgr	Frank Chance	
Rk	17	46
Gm	154	
Place	1	
GA	13.0	
Rival	14–8 vs Giants, 110 RS & 102 RA	

	W	*L*	*Win%*
Regular Season	104	50	0.675
Runs Record	99	55	0.645
1 Run	32	18	0.640
Blowout	28	12	0.700

	Team	*LgAvg*	*%Avg*	*LgRk*
BABIP	0.265	0.283	107	1
E	229	264	115	1
K%	8.6%	9.5%	110	2
RS%	36.0%	32.9%	109	
R/G	4.62	4.03	115	1
RA/G	3.24	4.03	124	1

	Tm	*LgAvg*	*>Avg*
RS	711	626	85
RA	499	626	127
DP	110	117	-7

	R/G	*HR*	*K*	*BB*	*SB*	*CS*	*SB%*	*OBP*
Team Offense	4.62	34	501	542	173			0.344
Team Defense	3.24	18	609	474	145	148	49%	0.307
Difference	1.38	16	108	68	28			112%

Pos	*Rpos*	*PA*	*Age*	*Name*	*BA*	*OBP*	*SLG*	*BB%*	*SB*	*Bat R>Avg*	*BR R>Avg*	*Fld R>Avg*	*RAA*	*WAA*
C	6	343	34	Kling, Johnny	0.269	0.354	0.360	11%	3	6	0	1	13	1.3
1B	-3	348	33	Chance, Frank	0.298	0.395	0.393	11%	16	15	-1	3	14	1.4
2B	0	556	28	Evers, Johnny*	0.263	0.413	0.321	19%	28	19	-1	4	22	2.3
3B	4	526	32	Steinfeldt, Harry	0.252	0.323	0.317	7%	10	-4	-1	4	3	0.3
SS	9	515	29	Tinker, Joe	0.288	0.322	0.397	5%	20	6	0	9	24	2.6
LF	-8	626	31	Sheckard, Jimmy*	0.256	0.366	0.363	13%	22	14	-1	9	14	1.5
CF,1B	-4	572	27	Hofman, Solly	0.325	0.406	0.461	11%	29	36	0	3	35	3.6
RF	-8	628	27	Schulte, Wildfire*	0.301	0.349	0.460	6%	22	25	-1	0	16	1.7
2B,SS	2	363	23	Zimmerman, Heinie	0.284	0.326	0.394	6%	7	5	-1	-5	1	0.1
C,1B	2	344	27	Archer, Jimmy	0.259	0.293	0.371	4%	6	-2	0	-2	-2	-0.2
CF,LF	-2	209	33	Beaumont, Ginger*	0.267	0.373	0.343	13%	4	4	0	0	2	0.2
C	2	92	31	Needham, Tom	0.184	0.287	0.250	11%	1	-3	0	0	-1	-0.1
LF,CF	0	74	27	Kane, John	0.242	0.338	0.290	12%	2	-1	0	-2	-3	-0.3
	0	596		Others	0.185	0.234	0.236	5%	3	-39	-1	-1	-41	-4.3
	0		29.4	Team Total	0.268	0.344	0.366	9.4%	173	81	-7	23	97	10.2
				League Average	0.256	0.328	0.338	8.6%	199					
				% Lg Avg	105	105	108	108	87					
				League Rank	2	3	2	3	5		7	1		

GS	*GR*	*IP*	*Age*	*Name*	*W–L*	*WHIP*	*BA*	*K/9*	*BB/9*	*FIP*	*ERA*	*R/9*	*RAA*	*WAA*
31	15	295	33	Brown, Mordecai	25–14	1.08	0.232	4.4	2.0	2.25	1.86	2.90	33	3.5
29	4	240	34	Cole, King	20–4	1.27	0.211	4.3	4.9	3.29	1.80	2.40	40	4.2
19	9	176	31	McIntire, Harry	13–9	1.15	0.240	3.3	2.6	3.05	3.07	3.58	6	0.7
23	1	173	27	Reulbach, Ed	12–8	1.21	0.250	2.9	2.5	2.84	3.12	3.95	-1	-0.1
21	2	145	29	Overall, Orval	12–6	1.11	0.212	5.7	3.4	2.44	2.68	2.74	19	2.0
13	1	100	32	Pfiester, Jack*	6–3	1.08	0.225	3.0	2.3	2.53	1.79	2.51	16	1.6
11	19	130	26	Richie, Lew	11–4	1.29	0.257	3.7	3.5	2.93	2.70	3.12	12	1.2
7	19	119		Others	0–0	1.45	0.271	4.0	3.8	3.30	4.00	5.81	-25	-2.7
154	48		30.3	Team Total		1.19	0.235	3.98	3.09	2.80	2.51	3.26	100	10.5
				League Average		1.30	0.256	3.66	3.26	3.02	3.02	4.06		
				% Lg Avg		109	109	109	105	108	121	125		
				League Rank		1	1	3	3	2	1			

1910 New York Giants

The Giants had another superb season in 1910. However, the Cubs also had an excellent season, and the Giants finished behind them by 13 games. Their 8–14 W–L record in head-to-head competition versus the Cubs contributed to their second place finish.

Strengths: (1) P, C, 1B, 2B, SS, and RF positions, (2) hitting for average and power led by Snodgrass (22 2B), Doyle (21 2B, 14 3B), Merkle (35 2B, 14 3B), Devore (10 3B), Murray (27 2B), and Bridwell, (3) drawing walks especially from Bridwell (73 BB), Doyle (71 BB), and Snodgrass (71 BB), (4) team baserunning (83 more SB than league average) especially from Murray (57 SB), and (5) deep pitching anchored by top 5 starters Mathewson, Drucke, Wiltse, Crandall (5 Sv), and Ames. The defensive standout was RF Murray (26 assists, 88 Rng+).

Weaknesses: (1) team fielding especially from LF Devore (77 Rng+), 2B Doyle (92 Rng+), and CF Seymour (91 Rng+), (2) hitting from Fletcher and Schlei, and (3) pitching from Raymond (9.6 H/9).

Mgr	John McGraw	
Rk	27	109
Gm	155	
Place	2	
Gm	13.0	
Rival	8–14 vs Cubs, 102 RS & 110 RA	

	W	*L*	*Win%*
Regular Season	91	63	0.591
Runs Record	96	58	0.621
1 Run	28	21	0.571
Blowout	30	14	0.682

	Team	*LgAvg*	*%Avg*	*LgRk*
BABIP	0.288	0.283	99	7
E	291	264	91	6
K%	8.3%	9.5%	114	
RS%	34.6%	32.9%	105	
R/G	4.61	4.03	114	2
RA/G	3.67	4.03	110	2

	Tm	*LgAvg*	*>Avg*
RS	715	626	89
RA	569	626	57
DP	117	117	0

	R/G	*HR*	*K*	*BB*	*SB*	*CS*	*SB%*	*OBP*
Team Offense	4.61	31	489	562	282		100%	0.354
Team Defense	3.67	30	717	397	192	153	56%	0.310
Difference	0.94	1	228	165	90			114%

Pos	*Rpos*	*PA*	*Age*	*Name*	*BA*	*OBP*	*SLG*	*BB%*	*SB*	*Bat R>Avg*	*BR R>Avg*	*Fld R>Avg*	*RAA*	*WAA*
C	7	422	29	Meyers, Chief	0.285	0.362	0.342	9%	5	6	0	-2	11	1.2
1B	-5	572	21	Merkle, Fred	0.292	0.353	0.441	8%	23	21	0	-1	15	1.6
2B	0	670	23	Doyle, Larry*	0.285	0.369	0.412	11%	39	24	1	-7	18	1.9
3B	5	592	30	Devlin, Art	0.260	0.353	0.327	10%	28	5	0	-2	8	0.8
SS	9	589	26	Bridwell, Al*	0.276	0.374	0.335	12%	14	11	-2	2	20	2.1
LF,RF	-7	549	22	Devore, Josh*	0.304	0.371	0.380	8%	43	16	2	-8	3	0.3
CF,OF	-5	493	22	Snodgrass, Fred	0.321	0.440	0.432	14%	33	35	0	2	32	3.3
RF,LF	-8	634	26	Murray, Red	0.277	0.345	0.376	8%	57	11	7	5	15	1.5
CF	-2	322	37	Seymour, Cy*	0.265	0.324	0.334	7%	10	-1	-1	-6	-10	-1.1
CF,RF	-2	143	23	Becker, Beals*	0.286	0.357	0.437	10%	11	5	1	-2	2	0.3
SS,2B	2	132	25	Fletcher, Art	0.224	0.248	0.256	3%	9	-8	1	-3	-8	-0.8
C	2	120	32	Schlei, Admiral	0.192	0.304	0.232	12%	4	-4	0	1	-1	-0.1
C	1	65	24	Wilson, Art	0.269	0.387	0.385	14%	2	2	0	0	3	0.4
P	0	81	22	Crandall, Doc	0.342	0.385	0.521	6%	0	6	0	0	6	0.6
	3	489		Others	0.196	0.258	0.266	7%	4	-23	0	0	-20	-2.1
	0		25.9	Team Total	0.275	0.354	0.366	9.6%	282	106	9	-21	94	9.9
				League Average	0.256	0.328	0.338	8.6%	199					
				% Lg Avg	108	108	108	111	142					
				League Rank	1	1	1	2	2		2	6		

GS	*GR*	*IP*	*Age*	*Name*	*W–L*	*WHIP*	*BA*	*K/9*	*BB/9*	*FIP*	*ERA*	*R/9*	*RAA*	*WAA*
35	3	318	29	Mathewson, Christy	27–9	1.11	0.254	5.2	1.7	2.04	1.89	2.83	48	5.1
30	6	235	30	Wiltse, Hooks*	14–12	1.21	0.261	3.4	2.0	2.56	2.72	3.67	14	1.5
27	7	215	21	Drucke, Louis	12–10	1.19	0.228	6.3	3.4	2.47	2.47	3.05	27	2.8
23	10	190	27	Ames, Red	12–11	1.18	0.237	4.4	3.0	2.70	2.22	3.69	11	1.1
18	24	208	22	Crandall, Doc	17–4	1.14	0.246	3.2	1.9	3.00	2.56	3.73	11	1.2
11	8	99	28	Raymond, Bugs	4–11	1.47	0.280	5.0	3.6	3.00	3.81	5.71	-17	-1.8
1	11	30	31	Dickson, Walt	1–0	1.35	0.272	2.7	2.7	3.14	5.46	5.76	-5	-0.5
8	5	71	23	Marquard, Rube*	4–4	1.49	0.254	6.6	5.1	3.16	4.46	4.46	-2	-0.2
2	6	25		Others	0–2	1.72	0.315	4.0	2.9	2.48	5.76	6.84	-7	-0.8
155	80		26.4	Team Total		1.21	0.252	4.64	2.57	2.58	2.68	3.68	80	8.4
				League Average		1.30	0.256	3.66	3.26	3.02	3.02	4.06		

GS	GR	IP	Age	Name	W–L	WHIP	BA	K/9	BB/9	FIP	ERA	R/9	RAA	WAA
				% Lg Avg		107	102	127	127	117	113	110		
				League Rank		3	4	1	1	1	2			

1911 Philadelphia Athletics

The 1911 A's easily won their second straight pennant in the AL beating a strong hitting Tigers team with even stronger hitting and much better pitching team. The A's continued their dynasty as this team was easily the best team in the AL enjoying a relatively injury free season. They outscored and enjoyed a winning record against every team they played in the AL except the Tigers. Then, this team won the World Series in 6 games over a tough Giant team.

Strengths: (1) hitting for average, contact, and power led by Collins (13 3B), Baker (42 2B, 14 3B, 11 HR, 301 TB), Murphy (27 2B, 11 3B), Lord (37 2B, 11 3B), McInnis (10 3B), and Lapp, (2) fielding from LF/RF Lord (113 Rng+, 17 assists), (3) CS% from Thomas (51%), and (4) pitching led by all 5 starters: Plank (6 shutouts), Bender, Krause, Morgan (7.8 H/9, 0 HR allowed), and Coombs (185 K). Also, RF Murphy sacrificed range (70 Rng+) for assists (34) in the outfield.

Weaknesses: (1) CF position, (2) fielding from 1B/SS McInnis (55 assists at 1B, 79 Rng+ at SS) and CF Oldring (only 2.00 range per game), (3) hitting from reserves Davis Derrick, (4) drawing walks, (5) pitching control, and (6) pitching from Russell (12.8 H/9).

Mgr	Connie Mack	
Rk	19	55
Gm	152	
Place	1	
GA	14	
Rival	10–12 vs Tigers, 138 RS & 141 RA	

	W	L	Win%
Regular Season	101	50	0.669
Runs Record	96	55	0.639
1 Run	21	20	0.512
Blowout	35	11	0.761

	Team	LgAvg	%Avg	LgRk
BABIP	0.306	0.298	97	4
E	228	302	132	1
K%	8.7%	10.9%	125	2
RS%	41.4%	36.2%	114	
R/G	5.66	4.60	123	1
RA/G	3.96	4.60	116	1

	Tm	LgAvg	>Avg
RS	861	707	154
RA	602	707	105
DP	100	96	4

	R/G	HR	K	BB	SB	CS	SB%	OBP
Team Offense	5.66	35	517	424	226			0.357
Team Defense	3.96	17	739	487	185	170	52%	0.338
Difference	1.70	18	222	-63	41			106

Pos	Rpos	PA	Age	Name	BA	OBP	SLG	BB%	SB	Bat R>Avg	BR R>Avg	Fld R>Avg	RAA	WAA
C	6	337	30	Thomas, Ira	0.273	0.341	0.340	7%	4	-1	0	2	7	0.7
1B,SS	-2	518	20	McInnis, Stuffy	0.321	0.361	0.425	5%	23	14	-1	-9	2	0.2
2B	0	588	24	Collins, Eddie*	0.365	0.451	0.481	11%	38	46	-1	-1	44	4.4
3B	5	659	25	Baker, Home Run*	0.334	0.379	0.508	6%	38	38	1	-3	41	4.0
SS	8	514	24	Barry, Jack	0.265	0.333	0.344	7%	30	-3	1	2	8	0.8
LF,RF	-7	631	27	Lord, Bris	0.310	0.355	0.429	6%	15	16	-1	9	17	1.7
CF	-3	547	27	Oldring, Rube	0.297	0.332	0.394	4%	21	3	-1	-5	-6	-0.5
RF	-7	593	34	Murphy, Danny	0.329	0.398	0.461	8%	22	30	-2	-3	18	1.8
CF,LF	-2	269	22	Strunk, Amos*	0.256	0.363	0.321	13%	13	1	0	-1	-2	-0.2
1B	-2	214	37	Davis, Harry	0.197	0.297	0.273	11%	2	-8	0	1	-9	-0.9
C	3	196	26	Lapp, Jack*	0.353	0.435	0.467	12%	4	14	0	3	20	1.9
2B,SS	0	116	25	Derrick, Claud	0.230	0.294	0.280	6%	7	-4	0	0	-4	-0.4
C	1	80	31	Livingston, Paddy	0.239	0.316	0.296	9%	1	-2	0	1	0	0.0
P	0	152	28	Coombs, Jack^	0.319	0.356	0.418	5%	5	4	0	0	4	0.3
	0	506		Others	0.192	0.241	0.216	5%	3	-40	-1	1	-40	-3.9
	0		27.1	Team Total	0.296	0.357	0.398	7.2%	226	108	-5	-3	100	9.8
				League Average	0.273	0.338	0.358	7.6%	214					
				% Lg Avg	108	106	111	94	106					
				League Rank	1	1	1	7	3		6	3		

GS	GR	IP	Age	Name	W–L	WHIP	BA	K/9	BB/9	FIP	ERA	R/9	RAA	WAA
40	7	337	28	Coombs, Jack	28–12	1.42	0.280	4.9	3.2	3.33	3.53	4.44	9	0.9
30	10	257	35	Plank, Eddie*	23–8	1.22	0.255	5.2	2.7	2.92	2.10	2.98	48	4.7
30	8	250	32	Morgan, Cy	15–7	1.32	0.243	4.9	4.1	3.43	2.70	3.93	21	2.0
24	7	216	27	Bender, Chief	17–5	1.18	0.252	4.7	2.4	2.84	2.16	2.75	46	4.5
19	8	169	22	Krause, Harry*	11–8	1.20	0.251	4.5	2.5	3.06	3.04	3.46	23	2.2
3	8	38	23	Martin, Doc	1–1	1.50	0.272	5.0	4.0	3.89	4.50	6.16	-6	-0.6
2	12	34	21	Danforth, Dave*	4–1	1.36	0.240	5.6	4.5	3.83	3.74	4.81	-1	-0.1
2	5	32	20	Russell, Lefty*	0–3	1.99	0.357	2.0	5.1	5.06	7.67	9.09	-16	-1.5
1	4	19	22	Leonard, Elmer	2–2	1.89	0.329	4.7	4.7	3.76	2.84	5.21	-1	-0.1
1	8	25	0	Others	0–3	1.88	0.350	4.0	4.0	3.59	6.48	8.64	-11	-1.1
152	77		25.6	Team Total		1.33	0.264	4.83	3.19	3.24	3.01	3.94	112	11.0
				League Average		1.36	0.273	4.19	2.99	3.34	3.34	4.65		

1911 New York Giants

The 1911 Giants featured strong pitching and speed on the base-paths stealing 347 bases. The Giants were the first of two straight pennant winning Giant teams. Bidwell was traded in mid-season to the Boston Rustlers (Braves) in exchange for Buck Herzog. McGraw's offense had faltered by mid-season but the team jelled and marched to the pennant when he made a lineup change to insert Herzog at third base and Art Fletcher at shortstop. The Giants outscored every team during the regular season and had a winning record against every team except the second place Cubs. This team had 201 more stolen bases and 161 more walks than they allowed.

Strengths: (1) hitting for average, contact, and power anchored by Doyle (25 2B, 25 3B, 13 HR), Meyers (9 3B), Murray (27 2B, 15 3B), Fletcher (8 3B), and Merkle (24 2B, 10 3B, 12 HR), (2) baserunning led by Murray (36% RS), Devore (38% RS), Merkle (36% RS), Snodgrass (51 SB), and Doyle (38 SB), (3) fielding from 1B Merkle (117 assists), (4) CS% from Meyers (44% CS), and (5) pitching especially control and strikeouts led by Mathewson (3.7 K/BB), Marquard (237 K, 7.2 H/9), Ames, and Crandall.

Weaknesses: (1) below average team BABIP, (2) individual fielding from 2B Doyle (86 Rng+), RF/LF Murray (77 Rng+), and RF/LF Becker (70 Rng+), and (3) double plays made.

Mgr	John McGraw	
Rk	6	16
Gm	154	
Place	1	
GA	7.5	
Rival	11–11 vs Cubs, 102 RS & 91 RA	

	W	L	Win%
Regular Season	99	54	0.647
Runs Record	103	50	0.676
1 Run	25	15	0.625
Extra Innings	5	3	0.625
Blowout	31	8	0.795

	Team	LgAvg	%Avg	LgRk
BABIP	0.287	0.280	98	7
E	255	266	104	4
K%	8.8%	10.2%	116	1
RS%	36.2%	34.6%	105	
R/G	4.91	4.42	111	1
RA/G	3.52	4.42	126	1

	Tm	LgAvg	>Avg
RS	756	688	68
RA	542	688	146
DP	86	110	-24

	R/G	HR	K	BB	SB	CS	SB%	OBP
Team Offense	4.91	41	506	530	347			0.358
Team Defense	3.52	33	771	369	146	117	56%	0.303
Difference	1.39	8	265	161	201			118%

Pos	Rpos	PA	Age	Name	BA	OBP	SLG	BB%	SB	Bat R>Avg	BR R>Avg	Fld R>Avg	RAA	WAA
C	7	439	30	Meyers, Chief	0.332	0.392	0.432	6%	7	19	-1	2	27	2.7
1B	-5	604	22	Merkle, Fred	0.283	0.342	0.431	7%	49	14	5	11	25	2.5
2B	0	622	24	Doyle, Larry*	0.310	0.397	0.527	11%	38	44	1	-6	39	3.9
3B	3	319	31	Devlin, Art	0.273	0.386	0.350	13%	9	7	-1	3	12	1.2
SS	5	310	27	Bridwell, Al*	0.270	0.358	0.316	11%	8	0	-1	2	6	0.6
LF,RF	-8	661	23	Devore, Josh*	0.280	0.376	0.365	12%	61	13	5	-1	9	0.9
CF	-4	647	23	Snodgrass, Fred	0.294	0.393	0.388	11%	51	21	3	1	21	2.1
RF,LF	-7	547	27	Murray, Red	0.291	0.354	0.426	8%	48	15	6	-3	11	1.1
SS,3B	6	377	26	Fletcher, Art	0.319	0.400	0.429	8%	20	18	-1	3	26	2.6
3B	2	279	25	Herzog, Buck	0.267	0.325	0.368	5%	22	0	2	2	6	0.6

Pos	Rpos	PA	Age	Name	BA	OBP	SLG	BB%	SB	Bat R>Avg	BR R>Avg	Fld R>Avg	RAA	WAA
RF,LF	-3	200	24	Becker, Beals*	0.262	0.359	0.355	13%	19	2	2	-3	-2	-0.2
C	2	134	25	Wilson, Art	0.303	0.411	0.431	14%	6	7	0	-1	8	0.8
P	0	127	23	Crandall, Doc	0.239	0.295	0.372	6%	2	-2	0	0	-2	-0.2
	2	515		Others	0.168	0.211	0.208	4%	7	-48	2	-1	-45	-4.5
	0		25.4	Team Total	0.279	0.358	0.390	9.2%	347	109	22	9	140	14.0
				League Average	0.260	0.335	0.356	9.1%	212					
				% Lg Avg	108	107	110	101	164					
				League Rank	1	1	1	4	1		1	5		

GS	GR	IP	Age	Name	W–L	WHIP	BA	K/9	BB/9	FIP	ERA	R/9	RAA	WAA
37	8	307	30	Mathewson, Christy	26–13	1.11	0.266	4.1	1.1	2.30	1.99	2.99	48	4.8
33	12	278	24	Marquard, Rube*	24–7	1.18	0.223	7.7	3.4	2.53	2.50	3.18	38	3.8
23	11	205	28	Ames, Red	11–10	1.09	0.223	5.2	2.4	2.32	2.68	3.51	20	2.0
24	6	187	31	Wiltse, Hooks*	12–9	1.15	0.251	4.4	1.9	2.78	3.27	3.99	9	0.9
10	5	76	22	Drucke, Louis	4–4	1.64	0.281	5.0	4.9	3.63	4.04	4.64	-2	-0.2
15	26	199	23	Crandall, Doc	15–5	1.26	0.256	4.3	2.3	3.19	2.63	3.71	15	1.5
9	8	82	29	Raymond, Bugs	6–4	1.30	0.248	4.3	3.6	3.11	3.31	4.41	0	0.0
3	1	31	24	Maxwell, Bert	1–2	1.42	0.311	2.3	2.0	2.98	2.90	4.35	0	0.0
0	3	4		Others	0–0	1.00	0.250	0.0	0.0	2.62	6.75	6.75	-1	-0.1
154	80		26.4	Team Total		1.20	0.248	5.07	2.43	2.68	2.69	3.57	127	12.8
				League Average		1.35	0.260	3.89	3.47	3.39	3.39	4.46		
				% Lg Avg		113	105	130	143	126	126	125		
				League Rank		2	4	1	1	1	1			

1912 Boston Red Sox

The 1912 Red Sox opened Fenway Park, a more intimate park than the spacious Huntington Avenue Grounds. They went from a fifth place finish in 1911 to a first place finish and a league record 105 victories under new manager Jake Stahl. The 1912 Boston Red Sox team featured one of Tris Speaker's finest seasons and a tremendous overall performance from Smoky Joe Wood.

Strengths: (1) hitting led by MVP Speaker (53 2B, 12 3B), Gardner (18 3B), Lewis (36 2B, 9 3B), and Stahl, (2) drawing walks especially by Speaker (82), (3) good hitting pitchers, (4) fielding featuring 3B Gardner (99 Rng+) and CF Speaker (134 Rng+, 35 assists), (5) CS% from Cady (45%) and Carrigan (44%), and (6) pitching anchored by Wood (258 K), Collins, O'Brien, and Bedient.

Weaknesses: (1) 2B and RF positions, (2) hitting from Yerkes, Bradley, and Hooper, (3) team baserunning (50% team SB%) especially from Stahl (13 SB, 22 CS), Yerkes (4 SB, 16 CS), and Lewis (9 SB, 19 CS), (4) double plays made, (5) fielding from SS Heinie Wagner (98 Rng+), and (6) pitching from Pape (13.7 H/9) and Cicotte (11.3 H/9).

Mgr	Jake Stahl	
Rk	12	32
Gm	154	
Place	1	
GA	14.0	
Rival	12–10 vs Senators, 104 RS & 91 RA	

	W	L	Win%
Regular Season	105	47	0.691
Runs Record	100	52	0.656
1 Run	30	19	0.612
Blowout	32	10	0.762

	Team	LgAvg	%Avg	LgRk
BABIP	0.288	0.300	104	3
E	267	308	115	2
K%	10.4%	11.0%	106	
BB%	9.6%	8.2%	118	1
R/G	5.19	4.45	117	1
RA/G	3.53	4.45	126	1

	Tm	LgAvg	>Avg
RS	799	688	111
RA	544	687	143
DP	88	102	-14

	R/G	HR	K	BB	SB	CS	SB%	OBP
Team Offense	5.19	29	612	565	185	182	50%	0.355
Team Defense	3.53	18	712	385	202	155	57%	0.308
Difference	1.66	11	100	180	-17			115%

Pos	Rpos	PA	Age	Name	BA	OBP	SLG	BB%	SB	Bat R>Avg	BR R>Avg	Fld R>Avg	RAA	WAA
C	5	314	28	Carrigan, Bill	0.263	0.359	0.297	12%	7	0	-2	0	3	0.3
1B	-3	380	33	Stahl, Jake	0.301	0.372	0.429	8%	13	14	-5	1	7	0.7
2B	0	593	24	Yerkes, Steve	0.252	0.312	0.317	7%	4	-10	-4	-3	-17	-1.7
3B	5	590	26	Gardner, Larry*	0.315	0.383	0.449	9%	25	28	-2	7	38	3.8
SS	10	584	31	Wagner, Heinie	0.274	0.358	0.359	11%	21	8	-2	-5	11	1.1
LF	-8	667	24	Lewis, Duffy	0.284	0.346	0.408	8%	9	14	-4	4	6	0.6
CF	-4	675	24	Speaker, Tris*	0.383	0.464	0.567	12%	52	76	2	8	82	8.2
RF	-8	684	24	Hooper, Harry*	0.242	0.326	0.327	10%	29	-5	0	3	-10	-1.0
1B,2B	0	207	28	Engle, Clyde	0.234	0.348	0.298	14%	12	-1	0	-2	-3	-0.3
1B	-1	160	27	Bradley, Hugh	0.190	0.275	0.307	9%	3	-5	0	1	-5	-0.5
C	2	155	26	Cady, Hick	0.259	0.324	0.385	6%	0	1	0	3	6	0.6
C	2	115	23	Nunamaker, Les	0.252	0.313	0.340	5%	2	-1	0	0	1	0.1
RF	-1	72	24	Henriksen, Olaf*	0.321	0.457	0.411	19%	0	5	0	-2	2	0.2
P	0	141	22	Wood, Smoky Joe	0.290	0.348	0.435	8%	0	4	0	0	4	0.4
	1	535		Others	0.201	0.288	0.249	10%	8	-23	2	0	-20	-2.0
	0		26.0	Team Total	0.277	0.355	0.380	9.6%	185	104	-15	15	104	10.4
				League Average	0.265	0.333	0.348	8.2%	228					
				% Lg Avg	105	106	109	118	81					
				League Rank	2	1	1	1	7		8	3		

GS	GR	IP	Age	Name	W–L	WHIP	BA	K/9	BB/9	FIP	ERA	R/9	RAA	WAA
38	5	344	22	Wood, Smoky Joe	34–5	1.01	0.223	6.8	2.1	2.35	1.91	2.72	66	6.5
34	3	276	30	O'Brien, Buck	20–13	1.19	0.237	3.8	2.9	3.35	2.58	3.49	28	2.8
28	13	231	22	Bedient, Hugh	20–9	1.13	0.240	4.8	2.1	2.99	2.92	3.62	21	2.0
24	3	199	25	Collins, Ray*	13–8	1.17	0.256	3.7	1.9	3.05	2.53	2.94	33	3.3
20	14	191	27	Hall, Sea Lion	15–8	1.30	0.257	3.9	3.3	3.45	3.02	4.01	9	0.9
6	3	46	28	Cicotte, Eddie	1–3	1.59	0.319	3.9	2.9	3.12	5.67	6.65	-11	-1.1
2	11	49	26	Pape, Larry	1–1	1.85	0.366	3.1	3.0	3.36	4.99	6.65	-12	-1.2
2	7	26		Others	1–0	1.75	0.301	5.1	5.1	3.63	4.79	6.84	-7	-0.7
154	59		25.7	Team Total		1.20	0.249	4.70	2.54	3.00	2.76	3.59	126	12.5
				League Average		1.33	0.266	4.25	3.11	3.34	3.34	4.52		
				% Lg Avg		112	107	111	122	111	121	126		
				League Rank		1	2	2	1	1	2			

1912 NEW YORK GIANTS

The 1912 Giants repeated their league championship by dominating the pennant race finishing with the top offense and the best pitching in the NL. Also, this team had a whopping league leading 319 SB. Twelve positional players and seven pitchers had above league average seasons. Also, about one third of this team's victories were won in blowouts (5 or more runs). The exciting 7 game World Series between two equally matched dominant teams featured one tie game called by darkness and four 1-run games including the 3–2 finale won by the Red Sox when the Giants Fred Merkle muffed a fly ball in the 10th inning.

Strengths: (1) hitting for average, contact, and power featuring MVP Doyle (33 2B), Meyers, and Merkle (22 SB, 11 HR), (2) drawing walks, (3) baserunning, (4) fielding anchored by SS Fletcher (107 Rng+), 3B Herzog (111 Rng+), and RF Murray (20 assists, 7 DP), and (5) pitching led by Mathewson, Marquard (175 K), and rookie spitballer Jeff Tesreau.

Weaknesses: (1) fielding from 1B Merkle (27 errors) and LF Devore (82 Rng+, 15 errors in 184 chances) and (2) pitching from Crandall (10.1 H/9).

Mgr	John McGraw	
Rk	11	28
Gm	154	
Place	1	
GA	10.0	
Rival	12–8 vs Pirates, 71 RS & 76 RA	

	W	L	Win%
Regular Season	103	48	0.682
Runs Record	99	52	0.659
1 Run	32	14	0.696
Blowout	34	10	0.773

	Team	LgAvg	%Avg	LgRk
BABIP	0.291	0.300	103	3
E	280	250	89	7
K%	8.6%	9.9%	116	2
RS%	39.1%	35.5%	110	
R/G	5.34	4.62	116	1
RA/G	3.71	4.62	125	1

	Tm	LgAvg	>Avg
RS	823	707	116
RA	571	707	136
DP	123	114	9

	R/G	HR	K	BB	SB	CS	SB%	OBP
Team Offense	5.34	47	497	514	319			0.360
Team Defense	3.71	35	652	338	141	114	55%	0.307
Difference	1.64	12	155	176	178			117%

Pos	Rpos	PA	Age	Name	BA	OBP	SLG	BB%	SB	Bat R>Avg	BR R>Avg	Fld R>Avg	RAA	WAA
C	7	435	31	Meyers, Chief	0.358	0.441	0.477	11%	8	31	-1	-1	36	3.5
1B	-4	537	23	Merkle, Fred	0.309	0.374	0.449	8%	37	19	2	-4	13	1.3
2B	0	629	25	Doyle, Larry*	0.330	0.393	0.471	9%	36	31	0	5	36	3.6
3B	5	563	26	Herzog, Buck	0.263	0.350	0.355	10%	37	1	2	10	18	1.7
SS	8	463	27	Fletcher, Art	0.282	0.330	0.372	3%	16	-2	-1	12	17	1.7
LF	-5	390	24	Devore, Josh*	0.275	0.381	0.373	13%	27	8	1	-4	0	0.0
CF	-4	469	25	Becker, Beals*	0.264	0.354	0.393	12%	30	6	2	0	4	0.4
RF	-8	603	28	Murray, Red	0.277	0.320	0.413	4%	38	2	3	9	6	0.6
CF,LF	-6	634	24	Snodgrass, Fred	0.269	0.362	0.364	11%	43	6	2	-2	0	0.0
SS,3B	3	203	23	Shafer, Tillie^	0.288	0.408	0.325	15%	22	4	2	0	9	0.9
C	2	140	26	Wilson, Art	0.289	0.358	0.413	9%	2	3	0	0	5	0.5
2B,SS	1	56	22	Groh, Heinie	0.271	0.375	0.354	14%	6	1	1	-1	2	0.2
LF,OF	-1	60	22	Burns, George	0.294	0.400	0.373	13%	7	2	1	-2	0	0.0
LF,CF	0	45	31	McCormick, Moose*	0.622	0.682	0.703	16%	1	10	0	-1	9	0.9
P	0	89	24	Crandall, Doc	0.313	0.360	0.438	7%	0	2	0	0	2	0.2
	2	486		Others	0.204	0.247	0.263	5%	9	-34	1	-1	-32	-3.1
	0		25.4	Team Total	0.286	0.360	0.395	8.9%	319	89	15	20	124	12.2
				League Average	0.272	0.340	0.369	8.3%	197					
				% Lg Avg	105	106	107	106	162					
				League Rank	1	1	2	2	1		1	3		

GS	GR	IP	Age	Name	W–L	WHIP	BA	K/9	BB/9	FIP	ERA	R/9	RAA	WAA
34	9	310	33	Mathewson, Christy	23–12	1.11	0.260	3.9	1.0	2.44	2.12	3.11	48	4.8
38	5	295	22	Marquard, Rube*	26–11	1.24	0.255	5.3	2.4	2.80	2.57	3.42	36	3.5
28	8	243	23	Tesreau, Jeff	17–7	1.16	0.204	4.4	3.9	3.31	1.96	3.33	32	3.2
22	11	179	29	Ames, Red	11–5	1.28	0.281	4.2	1.8	2.69	2.46	4.12	8	0.8
17	11	134	31	Wiltse, Hooks*	9–6	1.25	0.273	3.9	1.9	3.21	3.16	4.23	4	0.4
10	27	162	24	Crandall, Doc	13–7	1.33	0.286	3.3	1.9	3.25	3.61	4.72	-4	-0.4
2	0	16	27	Demaree, Al	1–0	1.19	0.288	6.2	1.1	1.75	1.69	1.69	5	0.5
1	1	10	24	Bader, King	2–0	1.50	0.250	2.7	5.4	4.25	0.90	1.80	3	0.3
2	4	21		Others	1–0	2.33	0.378	3.9	5.1	4.98	7.71	11.57	-17	-1.6
154	76		26.6	Team Total		1.23	0.259	4.28	2.22	2.92	2.58	3.75	116	11.4
				League Average		1.38	0.271	3.81	3.19	3.40	3.40	4.65		
				% Lg Avg		111	105	113	144	116	132	124		
				League Rank		1	3	1	1	1	1			

1912 Pittsburgh Pirates

The Giants, Pirates, and Cubs finished as the top 3 teams in the NL for the fifth consecutive year in 1912. The 1912 Pirates were an impressive balanced team that underperformed. For example, they lost 12 out of the 20 games they played against the pennant winning Giants despite outscoring them by 5 runs.

Strengths: (1) batting for average, contact, and power featuring Wagner (35 2B, 20 3B) and Wilson who hit a phenomenal 36 triples which still is the highest total in MLB history, (2) good hitting from the pitchers, (3) fielding led by SS Wagner (114 Rng+, 74 DP), 2B McCarthy (105 Rng+), LF Carey (120 Rng+, 19 assists), and CF/RF Wilson (105 Rng+, 20 assists), (4) CS% from Simon (52%) and Gibson (48%), and (5) pitching depth anchored by Robinson, Hendrix, Camnitz, and O'Toole (6 shutouts).

Weaknesses: (1) 1B position, (2) hitting from Gibson, (3) fielding from 3B Byrne (85 Rng+), (4) pitching from Cole (11.2 H/9), and (5) drawing walks.

				W	L	Win%
Mgr	Fred Clarke		Regular Season	93	58	0.616
Rk	22	64	Runs Record	96	55	0.634
Gm	152		1 Run	28	23	0.549
Place	2		Blowout	32	12	0.727
GB	10.0					
Rival	8–12 vs Giants, 76 RS & 71 RA					

	Team	LgAvg	%Avg	LgRk
BABIP	0.284	0.300	106	1
E	169	250	148	1
K%	8.7%	9.9%	113	3
RS%	37.5%	35.5%	106	
R/G	4.94	4.62	107	3
RA/G	3.72	4.62	124	2

	Tm	LgAvg	>Avg
RS	751	707	44
RA	565	707	142
DP	125	114	11

	R/G	HR	K	BB	SB	CS	SB%	OBP
Team Offense	4.94	39	514	420	177			0.340
Team Defense	3.72	28	664	497	154	137	53%	0.324
Difference	1.22	11	150	-77	23			105

Pos	Rpos	PA	Age	Name	BA	OBP	SLG	BB%	SB	Bat R>Avg	BR R>Avg	Fld R>Avg	RAA	WAA
C	6	331	31	Gibson, George	0.240	0.290	0.327	6%	0	-11	1	2	-2	-0.2
1B	-5	628	25	Miller, Dots	0.275	0.324	0.397	6%	18	0	-1	3	-3	-0.3
2B,3B	0	450	23	McCarthy, Alex	0.277	0.332	0.334	7%	8	-6	-1	9	2	0.2
3B	4	598	27	Byrne, Bobby	0.288	0.358	0.405	9%	20	10	-1	-5	8	0.8
SS	10	634	38	Wagner, Honus	0.324	0.395	0.496	9%	26	37	-1	20	66	6.5
LF	-8	690	22	Carey, Max^	0.302	0.372	0.394	9%	45	13	2	9	16	1.6
CF,RF	-6	643	28	Wilson, Chief*	0.300	0.342	0.513	5%	16	26	-1	7	26	2.5
RF,CF	-3	275	34	Donlin, Mike*	0.316	0.370	0.443	7%	8	9	-1	1	6	0.6
2B	0	173	24	Butler, Art	0.273	0.337	0.344	9%	2	-1	0	3	2	0.2
C	2	141	26	Kelly, Billy	0.318	0.328	0.394	1%	8	0	0	0	2	0.2
C	2	118	29	Simon, Mike	0.301	0.331	0.336	4%	1	-2	0	1	1	0.1
CF	-1	110	34	Leach, Tommy	0.299	0.376	0.381	11%	6	2	0	2	3	0.3
CF,RF	-1	122	26	Mensor, Ed^	0.263	0.402	0.333	19%	10	2	0	0	1	0.1
	0	966		Others	0.246	0.284	0.327	5%	9	-35	2	4	-29	-2.9
	0		28.2	Team Total	0.284	0.340	0.398	7.1%	177	44	-1	56	99	9.7
				League Average	0.272	0.340	0.369	8.3%	197					
				% Lg Avg	104	100	108	86	90					
				League Rank	2	3	1	8	5		3	1		

GS	GR	IP	Age	Name	W–L	WHIP	BA	K/9	BB/9	FIP	ERA	R/9	RAA	WAA
32	7	289	23	Hendrix, Claude	24–9	1.25	0.246	5.5	3.3	2.98	2.59	3.43	28	2.8
32	9	277	30	Camnitz, Howie	22–12	1.22	0.251	3.9	2.7	3.28	2.83	3.38	27	2.7
36	1	275	23	O'Toole, Marty	15–17	1.44	0.241	4.9	5.2	3.60	2.71	3.60	22	2.1
20	8	170	30	Adams, Babe	11–8	1.20	0.262	3.3	1.8	2.98	2.91	3.86	8	0.7
16	17	175	24	Robinson, Hank*	12–7	1.01	0.237	4.1	1.5	2.75	2.26	2.78	30	2.9
5	7	49	26	Cole, King	2–2	1.61	0.330	2.0	3.3	3.79	6.43	7.71	-19	-1.9
3	8	45	23	Warner, Ed*	1–1	1.29	0.242	2.6	3.6	3.57	3.60	4.00	1	0.1
3	8	39	25	Ferry, Jack	2–0	1.44	0.234	2.3	5.3	4.41	3.00	4.85	-3	-0.2
4	2	38	20	Cooper, Wilbur*	3–0	1.24	0.227	7.1	3.6	2.69	1.66	1.66	11	1.1
1	5	24	28	Leifield, Lefty*	1–2	1.65	0.302	3.0	3.8	3.59	4.18	5.70	-4	-0.4
0	0	4		Others	0–0	2.56	0.563	6.3	4.2	2.75	6.28	18.84	-7	-0.7
152	72		25.2	Team Total		1.27	0.251	4.31	3.23	3.22	2.85	3.67	94	9.3
				League Average		1.38	0.271	3.81	3.19	3.40	3.40	4.65		
				% Lg Avg		108	108	113	99	105	119	127		
				League Rank		2	1	2	3	2	2			

1913 New York Giants

The 1913 Giants became the third straight Giant team to capture the pennant. The Giants were not quite as good as they were in 1911 and 1912 but still allowed the fewest runs per game. The Giants won with excellent pitching from screwball pitcher Mathewson who had an ERA of 1.14, fifth best in MLB history. The Giants, depleted by injuries to positional players Merkle, Snodgrass, and Meyers, once again lost the World Series to the A's primarily due to wonderful A's pitching from Bender, Plank, and Bush.

Strengths: (1) hitting for average and contact led by Doyle (25 2B), Meyers (18 2B), Snodgrass (21 2B), Shafer (12 3B), and Fletcher (20 2B, 9 3B), (2) baserunning especially from Doyle (38 SB, 14 CS), (3) fielding featuring SS Fletcher (101 Rng+), OF Burns (110 Rng+, 22 assists), and OF Murray (99 Rng+, 24 assists), (4) CS% from Meyers (48%) and Wilson (45%), and (5) starting pitching.

Weaknesses: (1) 1B position, (2) isolated power, (3) hitting from starting OF Murray and backup catcher Wilson, (4) fielding from 1B Merkle, and (5) pitching from Fromme obtained May 22, 1913, from the Reds for Ames, Devore, Groh, and $20,000 in a poor trade.

Mgr	John McGraw	
Rk	18	51
Gm	156	
Place	1	
GA	12.5	
Rival	14–8 vs Phillies, 14–7 vs Cubs	

	W	*L*	*Win%*
Regular Season	101	51	0.664
Runs Record	97	55	0.640
1 Run	31	18	0.633
Blowout	26	12	0.684

	Team	*LgAvg*	*%Avg*	*LgRk*
BABIP	0.272	0.289	106	1
E	254	242	95	6
K%	8.6%	9.9%	116	1
RS%	34.3%	33.7%	102	
R/G	4.38	4.15	106	2
RA/G	3.30	4.15	126	1

	Tm	*LgAvg*	*>Avg*
RS	684	643	41
RA	515	643	128
DP	107	105	2

	R/G	*HR*	*K*	*BB*	*SB*	*CS*	*SB%*	*OBP*
Team Offense	4.38	31	501	444	296	195	60%	0.338
Team Defense	3.30	38	651	315	158	135	54%	0.289
Difference	1.08	-7	150	129	138			117%

Pos	*Rpos*	*PA*	*Age*	*Name*	*BA*	*OBP*	*SLG*	*BB%*	*SB*	*Bat R>Avg*	*BR R>Avg*	*Fld R>Avg*	*RAA*	*WAA*
C	7	428	32	Meyers, Chief	0.312	0.387	0.410	9%	7	18	-1	0	24	2.5
1B	-5	617	24	Merkle, Fred	0.261	0.315	0.373	7%	35	0	2	-4	-7	-0.7
2B	0	558	26	Doyle, Larry*	0.280	0.364	0.388	11%	38	15	4	0	19	1.9
3B	3	324	27	Herzog, Buck	0.286	0.349	0.390	7%	23	6	0	2	11	1.2
SS	9	594	28	Fletcher, Art	0.297	0.345	0.390	4%	32	10	2	8	29	3.1
LF,RF	-8	676	23	Burns, George	0.286	0.352	0.370	9%	40	11	-3	8	8	0.8
CF	-4	526	25	Snodgrass, Fred	0.291	0.373	0.383	10%	27	15	0	4	15	1.5
RF,LF	-8	578	29	Murray, Red	0.267	0.320	0.331	6%	35	-5	0	9	-4	-0.4
3B,2B	3	584	24	Shafer, Tillie^	0.287	0.369	0.398	10%	32	18	-2	-3	16	1.7
C	2	91	27	Wilson, Art	0.190	0.289	0.215	12%	1	-5	-1	0	-4	-0.4
RF,CF	-1	86	32	McCormick, Moose*	0.275	0.318	0.375	6%	0	0	0	-1	-2	-0.2
C	1	79	31	McLean, Larry	0.320	0.354	0.373	5%	1	1	0	-1	1	0.1
CF,LF	0	22	21	Cooper, Claude*	0.200	0.273	0.250	9%	1	-1	0	-3	-4	-0.4
C	0	21	24	Hartley, Grover	0.316	0.350	0.316	5%	4	0	1	-1	0	0.0
P	0	50	25	Crandall, Doc	0.319	0.360	0.447	6%	0	2	0	0	2	0.2
	1	603		Others	0.192	0.236	0.235	5%	20	-42	4	-1	-38	-4.0
	0		26.5	Team Total	0.273	0.338	0.361	7.6%	296	43	6	17	66	6.8
				League Average	0.262	0.325	0.354	7.6%	197					
				% Lg Avg	104	104	102	100	150					
				League Rank	1	1	4	5	1		2	1		

GS	*GR*	*IP*	*Age*	*Name*	*W–L*	*WHIP*	*BA*	*K/9*	*BB/9*	*FIP*	*ERA*	*R/9*	*RAA*	*WAA*
38	3	282	25	Tesreau, Jeff	22–13	1.21	0.220	5.3	3.8	3.10	2.17	3.13	29	3.0
35	5	306	32	Mathewson, Christy	25–11	1.02	0.252	2.7	0.6	2.56	2.06	2.76	43	4.5
33	9	288	26	Marquard, Rube*	23–10	1.03	0.237	4.7	1.5	2.57	2.50	3.13	30	3.1
25	6	200	28	Demaree, Al	13–4	1.07	0.243	3.4	1.7	2.77	2.21	2.93	25	2.6
12	14	112	29	Fromme, Art	11–6	1.26	0.260	4.0	2.3	3.14	4.01	4.65	-7	-0.8
5	3	42	30	Ames, Red	2–1	1.03	0.241	6.5	1.7	1.83	2.16	2.38	8	0.8
2	33	98	25	Crandall, Doc	4–4	1.29	0.273	3.9	2.2	2.93	2.86	4.15	-1	-0.1
2	15	58	33	Wiltse, Hooks*	0–0	1.06	0.237	3.9	1.2	2.45	1.56	3.75	2	0.2
1	4	12	22	Schupp, Ferdie*	0–0	1.08	0.244	1.5	2.3	3.04	0.75	2.25	2	0.2
2	0	13	22	Hearn, Bunny*	1–1	1.54	0.277	5.5	4.8	3.01	2.77	4.15	0	0.0
1	2	12		Schauer, Rube	0–1	1.92	0.292	5.3	6.8	3.71	7.50	8.25	-6	-0.6
156	94		27.2	Team Total		1.12	0.243	4.12	1.99	2.76	2.42	3.26	125	13.0
				League Average		1.29	0.262	3.72	2.85	3.20	3.20	4.16		
				% Lg Avg		115	108	111	143	116	132	128		
				League Rank		1	1	1	1	1	1			

1915 Boston Red Sox

This was an intriguing year for baseball since this would be the last year of the Federal League which folded after the season due to low attendance. The 1915 Red Sox team was engaged in a thrilling pennant race with the White Sox and Tigers never more than 4.5 games in front. Babe Ruth and Carl Mays had their first full pitching seasons. The team's head-to-head W–L records versus the White Sox and Tigers helped capture the pennant. The Red Sox counted on lady luck winning 7 more games than expected given their offense and defense performance. Although they would still win 2 more pennants over the next 3 seasons, the Red Sox, led by Tris Speaker and outstanding starting pitching, had their last great season until after World War II beating the Phillies in the Series.

Strengths: (1) hitting for average and contact featuring Speaker (12 3B, 81 BB) and Lewis (31 2B), (2) hitting from the pitchers especially Ruth, (3) fielding anchored by SS Scott (99 Rng+), CF Speaker (135 Rng+, 21 assists), and RF Hooper (95 Rng+, 23 assists), (4) CS% from Carrigan (49%), Thomas (44%), and Cady (42%), and (5) starting pitching depth.

Weaknesses: (1) SS position, (2) hitting from Scott and Thomas, (3) fielding from 2B Wagner (93 Rng+), and (4) pitching from Collins.

Mgr	Bill Carrigan	
Rk	29	116
Gm	155	
Place	1	
GA	2.5	
Rival	14–8 vs Tigers, 12–10 vs White Sox	

	W	*L*	*Win%*
Regular Season	101	50	0.669
Runs Record	94	57	0.620
1 Run	29	21	0.580
Extra Innings	7	4	0.636
Blowout	23	8	0.742

	Team	*LgAvg*	*%Avg*	*LgRk*
BABIP	0.262	0.279	107	1
E	226	263	116	3
K%	8.1%	10.5%	129	1
RS%	35.0%	33.0%	106	
R/G	4.31	3.96	109	3
RA/G	3.22	3.96	123	2

	Tm	*LgAvg*	*>Avg*
RS	668	615	53
RA	499	615	116
DP	95	108	-13

	R/G	*HR*	*K*	*BB*	*SB*	*CS*	*SB%*	*OBP*
Team Offense	4.31	14	476	527	118	117	50%	0.336
Team Defense	3.22	18	634	446	157	126	55%	0.300
Difference	1.09	-4	158	81	-39			112%

Pos	*Rpos*	*PA*	*Age*	*Name*	*BA*	*OBP*	*SLG*	*BB%*	*SB*	*Bat R>Avg*	*BR R>Avg*	*Fld R>Avg*	*RAA*	*WAA*
C	4	224	27	Thomas, Pinch*	0.236	0.286	0.296	6%	3	-6	0	2	0	0.0
1B	-4	469	26	Hoblitzell, Doc	0.283	0.351	0.396	8%	9	13	-3	4	10	1.1
2B	0	321	34	Wagner, Heinie	0.240	0.339	0.296	12%	8	0	1	-4	-3	-0.4
3B	4	500	29	Gardner, Larry*	0.258	0.327	0.326	8%	11	0	-1	0	3	0.3
SS	7	399	22	Scott, Everett	0.201	0.237	0.231	4%	4	-25	-1	6	-13	-1.3
LF	-8	634	27	Lewis, Duffy	0.291	0.348	0.382	7%	14	15	2	0	9	0.9
CF	-4	652	27	Speaker, Tris*	0.322	0.416	0.411	12%	29	38	-2	10	42	4.5
RF	-8	675	27	Hooper, Harry*	0.235	0.342	0.327	13%	22	6	-2	10	6	0.6
SS,3B	5	357	22	Janvrin, Hal	0.269	0.317	0.304	4%	8	-4	-3	-1	-3	-0.3
2B	0	302	28	Barry, Jack	0.262	0.342	0.331	8%	0	2	0	4	6	0.7
1B,CF	-2	240	28	Gainer, Del	0.295	0.371	0.415	9%	7	10	1	2	11	1.1
C	4	231	29	Cady, Hick	0.278	0.342	0.346	8%	0	3	0	2	9	0.9
C	2	119	31	Carrigan, Bill	0.200	0.321	0.232	13%	0	-3	0	0	-1	-0.1
P	0	103	20	Ruth, Babe*	0.315	0.376	0.576	9%	0	9	0	0	9	1.0
	0	639		Others	0.213	0.301	0.285	10%	3	-12	0	-2	-14	-1.5
	0		26.9	Team Total	0.260	0.336	0.339	9.0%	118	46	-8	33	71	7.5
				League Average	0.248	0.325	0.326	9.1%	180					
				% Lg Avg	105	103	104	99	66					
				League Rank	2	3	3	4	8		7	1		

GS	*GR*	*IP*	*Age*	*Name*	*W–L*	*WHIP*	*BA*	*K/9*	*BB/9*	*FIP*	*ERA*	*R/9*	*RAA*	*WAA*
33	4	255	27	Foster, Rube	19–8	1.19	0.237	2.9	3.0	3.02	2.11	2.93	24	2.5
32	6	247	24	Shore, Ernie	19–8	1.11	0.228	3.7	2.4	2.56	1.64	2.73	28	3.0
28	4	218	20	Ruth, Babe*	18–8	1.15	0.212	4.6	3.5	2.78	2.44	3.31	11	1.2
21	11	183	23	Leonard, Dutch*	15–7	1.07	0.208	5.7	3.3	2.65	2.36	2.80	20	2.2
16	9	157	25	Wood, Smoky Joe	15–5	1.04	0.216	3.6	2.5	2.52	1.49	1.83	34	3.6
6	32	132	23	Mays, Carl	6–5	1.06	0.244	4.4	1.4	1.98	2.60	3.69	1	0.1
9	16	105	28	Collins, Ray*	4–7	1.26	0.261	3.7	2.7	2.60	4.30	5.33	-18	-1.9

GS	GR	IP	Age	Name	W–L	WHIP	BA	K/9	BB/9	FIP	ERA	R/9	RAA	WAA
9	9	75	30	Gregg, Vean*	4–2	1.37	0.260	5.2	3.8	3.06	3.36	4.44	-6	-0.6
0	3	9	24	Comstock, Ralph	1–0	1.33	0.294	1.0	2.0	5.71	2.00	3.00	1	0.1
1	5	16		Others	0–0	2.19	0.359	3.9	6.8	3.75	8.44	9.00	-9	-1.0
155	99		24.9	Team Total		1.15	0.231	4.08	2.87	2.69	2.39	3.21	87	9.2
				League Average		1.28	0.248	3.94	3.42	2.93	2.93	3.99		
				% Lg Avg		111	107	104	119	109	123	124		
				League Rank		2	1	3	3	3	2			

1915 Chicago White Sox

The 1915 White Sox showed signs of even better things to come when they won the last 11 games of the season. The White Sox would become a powerhouse with the purchase during the pre-season of Eddie Collins from the A's and the late season trade to obtain "Shoeless Joe" Jackson from the Indians. However, in 1915, this was an underachieving team with plenty of talent but with a below .500 record in 1 run games and a losing record against both teams ahead of them in the standings.

Strengths: (1) hitting for average, contact, and power featuring Collins (22 2B, 10 3B), Fournier (20 2B, 18 3B), and Eddie Murphy who was purchased mid-season from the A's, (2) drawing walks led by Collins (119 BB), (3) fielding led by SS Weaver (101 Rng+), C Schalk (52% CS), and Eddie Collins (110 Rng+), and (4) pitching anchored by Scott (7 shutouts), Benz, and Faber (182 K).

Weaknesses: (1) 3B position, (2) hitting from 3B Blackburne, (3) team SB%, (4) fielding from 22-year-old 3B/LF Braggo Roth (73 Rng+ at 3B, 85 Rng+ in the OF) who was traded to the Indians as part of the August 21, 1915, deal for "Shoeless Joe" Jackson, and (5) turning DP.

				W	L	Win%
Mgr	Pants Rowland		Regular Season	93	61	0.604
Rk	21	57	Runs Record	98	56	0.637
Gm	155		1 Run	23	26	0.469
Place	3		Extra Innings	6	4	0.600
GB	9.5		Blowout	28	7	0.800
Rival	10–12 vs Red Sox, 60 RS, 63 RA; 7–15 vs Tigers, 97 RS, 110 RA					

	Team	LgAvg	%Avg	LgRk
BABIP	0.276	0.279	101	6
E	222	263	118	2
K%	9.8%	10.5%	106	4
RS%	36.5%	33.0%	111	
R/G	4.63	3.96	117	2
RA/G	3.28	3.96	121	3

	Tm	LgAvg	>Avg
RS	717	615	102
RA	509	615	106
DP	95	108	-13

	R/G	HR	K	BB	SB	CS	SB%	OBP
Team Offense	4.63	25	575	583	233	183	56%	0.345
Team Defense	3.28	14	635	350	100	102	50%	0.296
Difference	1.34	11	60	233	133			117%

Pos	Rpos	PA	Age	Name	BA	OBP	SLG	BB%	SB	Bat R>Avg	BR R>Avg	Fld R>Avg	RAA	WAA
C	8	495	22	Schalk, Ray	0.266	0.366	0.327	13%	15	9	-3	4	18	1.9
1B,OF	-5	514	25	Fournier, Jack*	0.322	0.429	0.491	12%	21	43	0	2	40	4.3
2B	0	680	28	Collins, Eddie*	0.332	0.460	0.436	18%	46	55	0	12	67	7.1
3B,SS	3	342	28	Blackburne, Lena	0.216	0.304	0.240	10%	13	-10	-1	-3	-11	-1.2
SS	10	644	24	Weaver, Buck	0.268	0.316	0.355	5%	24	2	-1	5	16	1.7
OF,1B	-7	650	29	Collins, Shano	0.257	0.298	0.368	4%	38	0	2	4	-1	-0.1
CF,LF	-4	496	23	Felsch, Happy	0.248	0.334	0.363	10%	16	7	-2	-2	-1	-0.1
RF	-4	321	23	Murphy, Eddie*	0.315	0.410	0.392	12%	20	17	0	1	14	1.5
3B,LF	0	277	22	Roth, Braggo	0.250	0.338	0.396	10%	12	7	1	-6	2	0.2
CF,LF	-2	193	25	Jackson, Joe*	0.272	0.378	0.399	12%	6	8	-2	-2	2	0.2
1B	-2	182	22	Brief, Bunny	0.214	0.305	0.318	9%	8	-2	0	1	-3	-0.3
RF,OF	-1	131	27	Quinlan, Finners*	0.193	0.270	0.219	3%	3	-7	-1	-1	-10	-1.0
3B	1	111	27	Johns, Pete	0.210	0.275	0.250	7%	2	-5	-2	-1	-7	-0.7
CF,LF	-1	97	23	Leibold, Nemo*	0.230	0.360	0.243	15%	1	0	-1	3	1	0.1
C	1	63	24	Mayer, Wally	0.222	0.288	0.315	8%	0	-1	-1	0	-1	-0.1
	3	642		Others	0.166	0.247	0.199	8%	8	-40	3	-3	-37	-3.9
	0		24.8	Team Total	0.258	0.345	0.348	10.0%	233	83	-8	14	89	9.4
				League Average	0.248	0.325	0.326	9.1%	180					

Pos	Rpos	PA	Age	Name	BA	OBP	SLG	BB%	SB	Bat R>Avg	BR R>Avg	Fld R>Avg	RAA	WAA
				% Lg Avg	104	106	107	110	129					
				League Rank	3	2	2	2	2		7	4		

GS	GR	IP	Age	Name	W–L	WHIP	BA	K/9	BB/9	FIP	ERA	R/9	RAA	WAA
32	18	300	26	Faber, Red	24–14	1.21	0.248	5.5	3.0	2.39	2.55	3.54	12	1.3
35	13	296	27	Scott, Jim	24–11	1.13	0.238	3.6	2.4	2.54	2.03	2.98	30	3.2
28	11	238	29	Benz, Joe	15–11	1.06	0.238	3.1	1.6	2.49	2.11	2.95	25	2.7
25	16	229	26	Russell, Reb*	11–10	1.14	0.249	3.5	1.8	2.29	2.59	3.53	9	1.0
26	13	223	31	Cicotte, Eddie	13–12	1.18	0.261	4.3	1.9	2.27	3.02	3.59	8	0.8
2	15	54	25	Wolfgang, Mellie	2–2	0.95	0.211	3.5	2.0	2.32	1.84	3.02	5	0.6
3	0	27	34	Walsh, Ed	3–0	0.96	0.216	4.0	2.3	2.27	1.33	1.33	8	0.8
2	1	13	27	Klepfer, Ed	1–0	1.23	0.234	2.1	3.5	3.07	2.77	2.77	2	0.2
2	-2	20		Others	0–1	1.18	0.191	8.8	4.9	3.46	4.42	4.42	-1	-0.1
155	85		28.1	Team Total		1.14	0.244	4.08	2.25	2.42	2.43	3.27	97	10.4
				League Average		1.28	0.248	3.94	3.42	2.93	2.93	3.99		
				% Lg Avg		113	102	103	152	121	121	122		
				League Rank		1	3	2	1	1	3			

1917 Chicago White Sox

The 1917 season featured the ascendance of the White Sox to the pennant after their 2 previous years of contending and arguably having the AL's strongest team. The White Sox led or were second in the AL in most offense, fielding, and pitching categories. The White Sox put it all together in 1917 to win their first pennant since 1906 and then went on to win the World Series against a strong Giant team. All 8 of the Black Sox players that were banished in September 1920 for participating in the fix of the 1919 World Series played for the '17 White Sox—Gandil, Weaver, Risberg, McMullin, Cicotte, Felsch, Shoeless Joe Jackson, and Lefty Williams. Walk differential and OBP differential helped this team win games in another weak year for offensive production.

Strengths: (1) hitting for average and contact featuring Shoeless Joe Jackson (20 2B, 17 3B), Eddie Collins (12 3B), and Felsch (10 3B), (2) drawing walks led by Collins (89 BB) and Leibold (74 BB), (3) baserunning featuring the mercurial Eddie Collins (53 SB, 36% RS), (4) CS% from Schalk (52%), and (5) pitching anchored by Cicotte (7 shutouts), Russell, Scott, and Faber.

Weaknesses: (1) 1B and SS positions, (2) hitting from Risberg and Shano Collins, (3) double plays made, and (4) fielding from rookie SS Risberg (61 errors in 704 chances, 88 Rng+). Risberg starting at SS enabled Weaver to move to his more natural 3B position.

Mgr	Pants Rowland	
Rk	28	113
Gm	156	
Place	1	
GA	9.0	
Rival	12–10 vs Red Sox, 90 RS & 60 RA	

	W	L	Win%
Regular Season	100	54	0.649
Runs Record	95	59	0.620
1 Run	31	24	0.564
Extra Innings	12	7	0.632
Blowout	25	5	0.833

	Team	LgAvg	%Avg	LgRk
BABIP	0.261	0.273	105	2
E	204	234	115	2
sOBP	0.296	0.311	105	2
rOBP	0.309	0.324	105	3
R/G	4.21	3.65	115	1
RA/G	2.96	3.65	123	2

	Tm	LgAvg	>Avg
RS	657	568	89
RA	462	565	103
DP	117	121	-4

	R/G	HR	K	BB	SB	CS	SB%	OBP
Team Offense	4.21	18	479	522	219			0.329
Team Defense	2.96	10	517	413	108	110	50%	0.297
Difference	1.25	8	38	109	111			111%

Pos	Rpos	PA	Age	Name	BA	OBP	SLG	BB%	SB	Bat R>Avg	BR R>Avg	Fld R>Avg	RAA	WAA
C	8	507	24	Schalk, Ray	0.226	0.331	0.292	12%	19	0	0	4	12	1.3
1B	-6	601	30	Gandil, Chick	0.273	0.316	0.315	5%	16	-2	-1	3	-6	-0.7
2B	0	689	30	Collins, Eddie*	0.289	0.389	0.363	13%	53	27	4	-5	26	2.9

Pos	Rpos	PA	Age	Name	BA	OBP	SLG	BB%	SB	Bat R>Avg	BR R>Avg	Fld R>Avg	RAA	WAA
3B,SS	4	514	26	Weaver, Buck	0.284	0.332	0.362	5%	19	8	0	-1	11	1.2
SS	9	563	22	Risberg, Swede	0.203	0.297	0.285	10%	16	-9	0	-17	-17	-1.9
LF,RF	-8	621	27	Jackson, Joe*	0.301	0.375	0.429	9%	13	32	-1	9	32	3.6
CF	-4	632	25	Felsch, Happy	0.308	0.352	0.403	5%	26	22	-1	6	23	2.6
RF,LF	-6	509	25	Leibold, Nemo*	0.236	0.350	0.292	15%	27	4	0	0	-2	-0.2
RF,LF	-4	270	31	Collins, Shano	0.234	0.269	0.321	4%	14	-5	1	1	-7	-0.8
3B	2	245	25	McMullin, Fred	0.237	0.339	0.258	11%	9	-1	0	-2	-1	-0.2
C	1	84	28	Lynn, Byrd	0.222	0.300	0.250	8%	1	-2	0	0	-1	-0.1
RF	0	60	25	Murphy, Eddie*	0.314	0.386	0.392	8%	4	3	0	-2	1	0.1
1B	0	35	21	Jourdan, Ted*	0.147	0.171	0.206	3%	0	-3	0	0	-3	-0.4
P	5	74	28	Russell, Reb*	0.279	0.300	0.412	3%	0	1	0	0	6	0.7
	-1	457		Others	0.123	0.211	0.149	9%	2	-38	0	0	-39	-4.3
	0		26.2	Team Total	0.253	0.329	0.326	8.9%	219	36	2	-4	34	3.8
				League Average	0.248	0.318	0.320	8.3%	159					
				% Lg Avg	102	104	102	108	138					
				League Rank	3	1	2	2	1		2	5		

GS	GR	IP	Age	Name	W–L	WHIP	BA	K/9	BB/9	FIP	ERA	R/9	RAA	WAA
35	14	347	33	Cicotte, Eddie	28–12	0.91	0.202	3.9	1.8	1.98	1.53	1.97	65	7.2
29	12	248	28	Faber, Red	16–13	1.25	0.245	3.0	3.1	2.66	1.92	3.34	9	1.0
29	16	230	24	Williams, Lefty*	17–8	1.31	0.251	3.3	3.2	2.74	2.97	3.68	0	0.0
24	11	189	28	Russell, Reb*	15–5	1.07	0.244	2.6	1.5	2.16	1.95	2.90	16	1.8
17	7	125	29	Scott, Jim	6–7	1.34	0.269	2.7	3.0	2.70	1.87	2.66	14	1.5
13	6	95	31	Benz, Joe	7–3	1.05	0.220	2.4	2.2	2.54	2.47	3.42	3	0.3
9	41	173	27	Danforth, Dave*	11–6	1.32	0.243	4.1	3.8	2.64	2.65	2.91	14	1.6
0	5	18	27	Wolfgang, Mellie	0–0	1.36	0.305	1.5	3.1	3.73	5.09	5.09	-3	-0.3
156	112			Team Total		1.16	0.237	3.27	2.61	2.45	2.16	2.92	118	13.1
			28.4	League Average		1.24	0.247	3.32	3.07	2.66	2.66	3.64		
				% Lg Avg		107	104	98	118	109	123	125		
				League Rank		2	2	4	1	1	1			

1917 New York Giants

The 1917 Giants dominated the other NL teams leading the league in both runs scored and fewest runs allowed per game. There were no real superstar seasons other than an outstanding fielding season from SS Fletcher, but there were no player seasons that were much below league average either.

Strengths: (1) C, 3B, SS, LF, and CF positions, (2) hitting for average, contact, and power compared to league average featuring Burns (25 2B, 13 3B), Kauff (22 2B), and Zimmerman (22 2B, 9 3B), (3) fielding led by SS Fletcher (109 Rng+) and 3B Zimmerman (108 Rng+), and (4) pitching anchored by Schupp, Anderson, and Perritt.

Weaknesses: (1) 1B position, (2) drawing walks, (3) fielding from 1B Holke, and (4) CS% from Rariden (31%) and McCarty (32%).

Mgr	John McGraw	
Rk	26	98
Gm	158	
Place	1	
GA	10.0	
Rival	14–8 vs Phillies, 85 RS & 65 RA	

	W	L	Win%
Regular Season	98	56	0.636
Runs Record	96	58	0.623
1 Run	28	22	0.560
Extra Innings	7	7	0.500
Blowout	27	9	0.750

	Team	LgAvg	%Avg	LgRk
BABIP	0.257	0.275	107	1
E	208	234	113	1
sOBP	0.277	0.303	109	1
rOBP	0.311	0.315	101	3
R/G	4.02	3.53	114	1
RA/G	2.89	3.53	122	1

	Tm	LgAvg	>Avg
RS	635	551	84
RA	457	552	95
DP	122	121	1

	R/G	HR	K	BB	SB	CS	SB%	OBP
Team Offense	4.02	39	533	373	162			0.317
Team Defense	2.89	29	551	327	137	64	68%	0.283
Difference	1.13	10	18	46	25			112%

Pos	Rpos	PA	Age	Name	BA	OBP	SLG	BB%	SB	Bat R>Avg	BR R>Avg	Fld R>Avg	RAA	WAA
C	5	314	29	Rariden, Bill	0.271	0.372	0.316	13%	3	8	0	0	13	1.5
1B	-5	583	24	Holke, Walter^	0.277	0.327	0.338	6%	13	6	-1	-5	-5	-0.5
2B	0	477	31	Herzog, Buck	0.235	0.308	0.312	6%	12	-1	0	2	1	0.1
3B	5	620	30	Zimmerman, Heinie	0.297	0.317	0.391	3%	13	13	-1	11	28	3.2
SS	10	608	32	Fletcher, Art	0.260	0.312	0.343	4%	12	4	-1	30	43	4.9
LF	-8	678	27	Burns, George	0.302	0.380	0.412	11%	40	36	1	9	38	4.3
CF	-4	644	27	Kauff, Benny*	0.308	0.379	0.388	9%	30	29	0	1	26	2.9
RF	-8	560	27	Robertson, Dave*	0.259	0.276	0.391	2%	17	3	0	6	1	0.1
C	3	181	28	McCarty, Lew	0.247	0.311	0.327	8%	1	0	0	0	3	0.4
2B,SS	1	109	22	Smith, Jimmy^	0.229	0.295	0.302	8%	6	-1	0	3	3	0.3
RF,CF	-1	59	31	Wilhoit, Joe*	0.340	0.431	0.460	14%	0	5	0	0	4	0.5
CF	0	29	20	Youngs, Ross*	0.346	0.370	0.654	3%	1	3	0	0	3	0.4
RF,LF	-1	68	30	Thorpe, Jim	0.193	0.303	0.316	12%	1	0	0	0	-1	-0.1
	3	857		Others	0.174	0.220	0.213	5%	13	-55	3	2	-47	-5.3
	0		27.5	Team Total	0.261	0.317	0.343	6.4%	162	50	1	59	110	12.5
				League Average	0.249	0.305	0.328	6.6%	143					
				% Lg Avg	105	104	105	97	113					
				League Rank	2	1	2	5	1		2	1		

GS	GR	IP	Age	Name	W–L	WHIP	BA	K/9	BB/9	FIP	ERA	R/9	RAA	WAA
18	20	272	26	Schupp, Ferdie*	21–7	1.00	0.209	4.9	2.3	2.45	1.95	2.28	27	3.1
32	4	216	32	Sallee, Slim*	18–7	1.08	0.249	2.3	1.4	2.61	2.17	2.92	5	0.6
26	9	215	25	Perritt, Pol	17–7	1.07	0.237	3.0	1.9	2.62	1.88	2.55	14	1.6
24	10	215	27	Benton, Rube*	15–9	1.07	0.238	2.9	1.7	2.70	2.72	3.27	-3	-0.3
25	10	184	29	Tesreau, Jeff	13–8	1.23	0.249	4.2	2.8	2.88	3.09	3.48	-6	-0.7
11	4	78	32	Demaree, Al	4–5	1.11	0.239	2.6	2.0	2.65	2.64	3.79	-6	-0.6
20	13	162	31	Anderson, Fred	8–8	0.96	0.209	3.8	1.9	2.28	1.44	2.22	17	1.9
1	0	38	25	Smith, George	0–3	1.29	0.270	3.8	2.6	2.83	2.84	3.08	0	0.0
0	13	36	28	Middleton, Jim	1–1	1.19	0.255	2.3	2.0	2.99	2.75	4.50	-6	-0.6
1	13	6	21	Swigler, Ad	0–1	2.50	0.333	6.0	12.0	5.05	6.00	6.00	-2	-0.2
0	0	5	21	Kelly, High Pockets	1–0	1.00	0.211	3.6	1.8	2.18	0.00	0.00	2	0.2
158	96		27.0	Team Total		1.09	0.234	3.48	2.06	2.62	2.27	2.88	43	4.8
				League Average		1.19	0.249	3.59	2.44	2.70	2.70	3.53		
				% Lg Avg		109	106	97	118	103	119	122		
				League Rank		1	1	5	2	3	1			

1918 Chicago Cubs

The Cubs won their first pennant since 1910 easily beating the second place Giants by 10.5 games. The Cubs outscored and allowed fewer runs than any of their NL competition. Rumors still swirl that some Cubs players were involved in throwing the 1918 World Series to the less statistically talented Red Sox. Two transactions before the season began helped this team win the pennant: (1) the acquisition of SS Charlie Hollocher from the minor leagues and (2) the trade to obtain Lefty Tyler from the Boston Braves in exchange for veterans Larry Doyle, Art Wilson, and $15,000.

Strengths: (1) hitting for average, contact, and power compared to league average led by rookie Hollocher (23 2B) who had his career best season, Paskert (24 2B) who was obtained in a trade in the offseason from the Phillies, Merkle (25 2B), Mann (27 2B), and Flack (10 3B), (2) CS% from Killefer (45%) and O'Farrell (45%), and (3) pitching by the two top pitchers in the league, Hippo Vaughn (Triple Crown with 22 wins, 1.74 ERA, and 148 K plus 7 shutouts) and Lefty Tyler (6 shutouts).

Weaknesses: (1) 2B and 3B positions, (2) hitting from starters Deal and Killefer, and (3) pitching from seldom used Roy Walker.

				W	L	Win%		Team	LgAvg	%Avg	LgRk
Mgr	Fred Mitchell		**Regular Season**	84	45	0.651	**BABIP**	0.266	0.274	103	3
Rk	25	84	**Runs Record**	81	48	0.628	**E**	188	190	101	4

Gm	131
Place	1
GA	10.5
Rival	14–6 vs Giants, 100 RS & 59 RA

	W	*L*	*Win%*
1 Run	26	17	0.605
Extra Innings	6	3	0.667
Blowout	22	9	0.710

	Team	*LgAvg*	*%Avg*	*LgRk*
sOBP	0.286	0.308	108	2
rOBP	0.324	0.332	102	2
R/G	4.11	3.62	113	2
RA/G	3.00	3.62	121	1

	Tm	*LgAvg*	*>Avg*
RS	538	460	78
RA	393	460	67
DP	94	100	-6

	R/G	*HR*	*K*	*BB*	*SB*	*CS*	*SB%*	*OBP*
Team Offense	4.11	21	343	358	159			0.325
Team Defense	3.00	13	472	296	121	100	55%	0.291
Difference	1.11	8	129	62	38			112%

Pos	*Rpos*	*PA*	*Age*	*Name*	*BA*	*OBP*	*SLG*	*BB%*	*SB*	*Bat R>Avg*	*BR R>Avg*	*Fld R>Avg*	*RAA*	*WAA*
C	5	364	30	Killefer, Bill	0.233	0.276	0.281	5%	5	-10	0	1	-4	-0.4
1B	-5	541	29	Merkle, Fred	0.297	0.349	0.388	6%	21	17	0	6	18	2.0
2B	1	288	34	Zeider, Rollie	0.223	0.288	0.251	8%	16	-8	1	1	-5	-0.6
3B	4	459	26	Deal, Charlie	0.239	0.279	0.290	5%	11	-11	-1	-2	-10	-1.1
SS	9	586	22	Hollocher, Charlie*	0.316	0.379	0.397	8%	26	26	0	-1	34	3.8
LF	-6	555	25	Mann, Les	0.288	0.342	0.384	7%	21	15	0	-2	7	0.8
CF	-3	539	36	Paskert, Dode	0.286	0.362	0.369	10%	20	17	-1	0	13	1.4
RF	-6	552	28	Flack, Max*	0.257	0.343	0.360	10%	17	12	-1	1	6	0.7
CF,RF	-2	135	24	Barber, Turner*	0.236	0.293	0.293	7%	3	-2	0	-1	-5	-0.6
C	2	125	21	O'Farrell, Bob	0.283	0.347	0.425	8%	0	5	0	-1	6	0.7
2B,3B	0	108	30	Pick, Charlie*	0.326	0.417	0.393	13%	7	6	0	1	7	0.8
2B	0	109	25	Kilduff, Pete	0.204	0.267	0.269	6%	1	-3	0	-3	-6	-0.7
P	0	101	29	Hendrix, Claude	0.264	0.302	0.462	4%	1	3	0	0	3	0.4
	1	440		Others	0.204	0.249	0.247	5%	10	-20	0	0	-19	-2.2
	0		27.6	Team Total	0.265	0.325	0.342	7.3%	159	48	-2	0	46	5.1
				League Average	0.254	0.311	0.328	7.7%	129					
				% Lg Avg	104	105	104	94	123					
				League Rank	2	2	2	4	2		5	4		

GS	*GR*	*IP*	*Age*	*Name*	*W–L*	*WHIP*	*BA*	*K/9*	*BB/9*	*FIP*	*ERA*	*R/9*	*RAA*	*WAA*
33	2	290	30	Vaughn, Hippo*	22–10	1.01	0.208	4.6	2.4	2.32	1.74	2.32	41	4.6
30	3	269	28	Tyler, Lefty*	19–8	1.06	0.226	3.4	2.2	2.39	2.00	2.41	36	4.0
27	5	233	29	Hendrix, Claude	20–7	1.21	0.259	3.3	2.1	2.43	2.78	3.36	6	0.7
19	6	157	28	Douglas, Phil	10–9	1.12	0.246	2.9	1.8	2.43	2.13	3.27	6	0.6
4	17	73	24	Carter, Paul	3–2	1.33	0.290	1.6	2.3	3.12	2.71	3.58	0	0.0
7	6	43	25	Walker, Roy	1–3	1.50	0.298	4.2	3.1	2.78	2.70	5.61	-10	-1.1
3	5	33	26	Weaver, Harry	2–2	1.04	0.227	2.5	1.9	2.79	2.20	3.58	0	0.0
5	4	54	24	Martin, Speed	5–2	1.14	0.246	2.7	2.3	2.54	1.84	3.19	3	0.3
3	0	26	31	Alexander, Pete	2–1	0.85	0.207	5.2	1.0	1.61	1.73	2.42	3	0.4
0	3	12	24	Aldridge, Vic	0–1	1.38	0.275	7.3	4.4	2.14	1.46	2.19	2	0.2
0	1	7		Napier, Buddy	0–0	2.10	0.357	2.7	5.4	3.50	5.40	5.40	-1	-0.1
131	52		26.9	Team Total		1.12	0.239	3.55	2.23	2.45	2.18	2.95	87	9.7
				League Average		1.21	0.254	2.87	2.49	2.76	2.76	3.61		
				% Lg Avg		108	106	124	112	113	127	122		
				League Rank		2	1	1	3	1	1			

1919 Cincinnati Reds

The 1919 Reds won the pennant for the first time in their franchise history as the defense allowed the fewest runs in the major leagues. This team upset the favored Giants and the prior year winner Cubs with a franchise best winning percentage. The Reds were the statistically better team in 1919 but did not have the postseason experience of the White Sox who were heavily favored to win the World Series based on their performance against the Giants in 1917 and the recent dominance of American League teams in the World Series. Several players on the pennant winning Chicago White Sox conspired to throw the World Series to the Reds.

Strengths: (1) hitting for average and contact led by Roush (12 3B) and Groh (11 3B), (2) drawing walks especially from Rath (64 BB) and Groh (56 BB), (3) fielding featuring 2B Rath (113 Rng+) and CF Roush (109 Rng+, 22 assists), (4) CS% from Wingo (47%) and Rariden (45%), and (5) pitching anchored by all 5 starters: Ruether (7.2 H/9), Sallee, Ring (7.4 H/9), Eller (7 shutouts, 2.7 K/BB, 7.8 H/9), and Fisher (5 shutouts, 7.3 H/9). Eller, Ruether, and Fisher all had good hitting seasons for pitchers.

Weaknesses: (1) RF position, (2) hitting from Rariden, (3) pitching K/9, and (4) double plays made.

Mgr	Pat Moran	
Rk	20	56
Gm	140	
Place	1	
GA	9.0	
Rival	12–8 vs Giants, 61 RS & 63 RA	

	W	*L*	*Win%*
Regular Season	96	44	0.686
Runs Record	89	51	0.638
1 Run	29	18	0.617
Extra Innings	7	7	0.500
Blowout	23	13	0.639

	Team	*LgAvg*	*%Avg*	*LgRk*
BABIP	0.258	0.278	108	1
E	152	197	130	1
sOBP	0.288	0.308	107	2
rOBP	0.292	0.324	111	3
R/G	4.13	3.65	113	2
RA/G	2.86	3.65	127	1

	Tm	*LgAvg*	*>Avg*
RS	578	509	69
RA	401	509	108
DP	98	99	-1

	R/G	*HR*	*K*	*BB*	*SB*	*CS*	*SB%*	*OBP*
Team Offense	4.13	20	368	405	143			0.327
Team Defense	2.86	21	407	298	130	114	53%	0.288
Difference	1.26	-1	39	107	13			114%

Pos	*Rpos*	*PA*	*Age*	*Name*	*BA*	*OBP*	*SLG*	*BB%*	*SB*	*Bat R>Avg*	*BR R>Avg*	*Fld R>Avg*	*RAA*	*WAA*
C	3	271	28	Wingo, Ivy*	0.273	0.336	0.371	8%	4	5	0	-2	6	0.7
1B	-6	613	35	Daubert, Jake*	0.276	0.322	0.350	6%	11	5	-1	3	1	0.1
2B	2	624	32	Rath, Morrie*	0.264	0.343	0.298	10%	17	2	-1	17	20	2.2
3B	4	523	29	Groh, Heinie	0.310	0.392	0.431	11%	21	30	-1	2	35	3.9
SS	9	545	28	Kopf, Larry^	0.270	0.313	0.326	5%	18	-2	0	4	11	1.3
LF,RF	1	197	24	Bressler, Rube	0.206	0.311	0.309	12%	2	-1	0	2	2	0.2
CF	-4	572	26	Roush, Edd*	0.321	0.380	0.431	7%	20	30	-1	6	31	3.4
RF,LF	-7	585	27	Neale, Greasy*	0.242	0.316	0.316	8%	28	-1	1	4	-3	-0.4
C	3	242	31	Rariden, Bill	0.216	0.275	0.284	7%	4	-7	0	1	-3	-0.3
LF	-2	201	34	Magee, Sherry	0.215	0.337	0.264	13%	4	-1	0	2	-1	-0.1
RF,LF	-1	105	27	Cueto, Manuel	0.250	0.340	0.273	10%	5	0	0	1	0	0.0
LF	-1	103	25	Duncan, Pat	0.244	0.306	0.411	8%	2	2	0	1	2	0.2
3B,SS	0	48	24	Smith, Jimmy^	0.275	0.341	0.525	8%	1	3	0	-1	2	0.2
	-1	585		Others	0.219	0.252	0.289	4%	6	-21	-1	3	-20	-2.3
	0		28.5	Team Total	0.263	0.327	0.342	7.8%	143	43	-4	43	82	9.1
				League Average	0.258	0.311	0.337	6.3%	146					
				% Lg Avg	102	105	101	123	98					
				League Rank	3	1	2	1	6		8	2		

GS	*GR*	*IP*	*Age*	*Name*	*W–L*	*WHIP*	*BA*	*K/9*	*BB/9*	*FIP*	*ERA*	*R/9*	*RAA*	*WAA*
30	8	248	24	Eller, Hod	19–9	1.07	0.238	5.0	1.8	2.36	2.39	2.90	13	1.4
29	4	243	25	Ruether, Dutch*	19–6	1.15	0.223	2.9	3.1	2.97	1.82	2.56	21	2.3
28	1	228	34	Sallee, Slim*	21–7	1.06	0.258	0.9	0.8	2.74	2.06	2.49	21	2.3
18	14	183	24	Ring, Jimmy	10–9	1.10	0.232	3.0	2.5	2.80	2.26	2.61	15	1.7
20	6	174	31	Fisher, Ray	14–5	1.03	0.226	2.1	2.0	2.94	2.17	2.84	10	1.1
4	9	42	24	Bressler, Rube*	2–4	1.08	0.248	2.8	1.7	2.71	3.46	4.10	-4	-0.4
9	21	106	28	Luque, Dolf	10–3	1.18	0.237	3.4	3.1	3.01	2.63	2.97	4	0.5
1	6	31	34	Mitchell, Roy	0–1	1.32	0.276	2.9	2.6	2.67	2.32	4.65	-5	-0.5
1	4	17	21	Gerner, Ed*	1–0	1.47	0.333	1.1	1.6	3.09	3.18	5.29	-4	-0.4
0	1	2	31	Regan, Mike	0–0	0.43	0.143	3.9	0.0	1.58	0.00	3.86	0	0.0
140	74		27.6	Team Total		1.10	0.239	2.88	2.11	2.77	2.23	2.83	71	7.9
				League Average		1.21	0.258	2.95	2.34	2.91	2.91	3.64		
				% Lg Avg		110	108	98	111	105	130	129		
				League Rank		1	1	4	4	3	2			

2. *The Live Ball Era (1920–1960)*

1920 Cleveland Indians

The 1920 Indians won their first pennant in a tight race against the Ruth led Yankees and the defending champion White Sox team that lost 8 key players the last 10 days of the season due to the commissioner's suspension for the 1919 World Series fix allegations. Indians SS Ray Chapman was beaned and tragically killed by a Carl Mays fastball in late August. Late season replacements SS Joe Sewell and P Duster Mails helped win crucial games down the stretch. This team won the World Series over the Brooklyn Robins.

Strengths: (1) hitting for average, contact, and power led by Speaker (50 2B, 11 3B), Elmer Smith (37 2B, 12 3B), and O'Neill (39 2B), (2) drawing walks especially by Speaker (97 BB) and O'Neill (69 BB), (3) fielding anchored by 3B Gardner (97 Rng+, 37 DP) and SS Chapman (111 Rng+), and (4) starting pitching featuring Bagby, Coveleski (8.1 H/9), and Mails.

Weaknesses: (1) RP, 1B, and 2B positions, (2) hitting from Wambsganss, (3) team SB% especially from Gardner (3 SB, 20 CS) and Wambsganss (9 SB, 18 CS), and (4) pitching from Myers (11.7 H/9), Caldwell (10.8 H/9), and Morton.

Mgr	Tris Speaker	
Rk	30	79
Gm	154	
Place	1	
GA	2.0	
Rival	12–10 vs WS, 9–13 vs Yankees	

	W	*L*	*Win%*
Regular Season	98	56	0.636
Runs Record	97	57	0.629
1 Run	23	23	0.500
Extra Innings	5	6	0.455
Blowout	41	14	0.745

	Team	*LgAvg*	*%Avg*	*LgRk*
BABIP	0.297	0.297	100	5
E	185	215	116	2
sOBP	0.322	0.342	106	1
rOBP	0.369	0.369	100	5
R/G	5.56	4.76	117	1
RA/G	4.17	4.76	114	2

	Tm	*LgAvg*	*>Avg*
RS	856	734	122
RA	642	734	92
DP	124	120	4

	R/G	*HR*	*K*	*BB*	*SB*	*CS*	*SB%*	*OBP*
Team Offense	5.56	35	376	574	73	93	44%	0.376
Team Defense	4.17	31	472	406	84	70	55%	0.330
Difference	1.39	4	96	168	-11			114%

Pos	*Rpos*	*PA*	*Age*	*Name*	*BA*	*OBP*	*SLG*	*BB%*	*RS%*	*Bat R>Avg*	*BR R>Avg*	*Fld R>Avg*	*RAA*	*WAA*
C	7	576	28	O'Neill, Steve	0.321	0.408	0.440	12%	27%	23	0	2	32	3.1
1B	-6	593	32	Johnston, Doc*	0.292	0.333	0.385	5%	35%	-4	2	-1	-9	-0.9
2B	3	664	26	Wambsganss, Bill	0.244	0.316	0.317	8%	42%	-21	-4	-1	-23	-2.2
3B	5	683	34	Gardner, Larry*	0.310	0.367	0.414	8%	29%	10	-6	12	21	2.1
SS	7	530	29	Chapman, Ray	0.303	0.380	0.423	10%	51%	12	0	6	25	2.4
LF,1B	-5	425	27	Jamieson, Charlie*	0.319	0.388	0.411	10%	43%	10	-2	2	5	0.5
CF	-4	674	32	Speaker, Tris*	0.388	0.483	0.562	14%	42%	70	-1	3	68	6.6
RF	-6	525	27	Smith, Elmer*	0.316	0.391	0.520	10%	37%	29	1	4	28	2.7
LF,SS	-2	189	25	Evans, Joe	0.349	0.404	0.506	8%	42%	11	1	0	10	1.0
LF	-2	191	34	Graney, Jack*	0.296	0.412	0.382	14%	41%	5	1	-2	2	0.2
RF	-2	176	30	Wood, Smoky Joe	0.270	0.390	0.401	14%	38%	4	0	-2	0	0.0
SS	1	83	21	Sewell, Joe*	0.329	0.413	0.414	11%	42%	3	0	-1	3	0.3

Pos	Rpos	PA	Age	Name	BA	OBP	SLG	BB%	RS%	Bat R>Avg	BR R>Avg	Fld R>Avg	RAA	WAA
C,1B	0	59	31	Nunamaker, Les	0.333	0.379	0.500	7%	45%	3	0	0	3	0.3
	4	699		Others	0.239	0.297	0.299	7%	36%	-32	1	3	-24	-2.3
	0		28.9	Team Total	0.303	0.376	0.417	9.5%	38.2%	123	-7	25	141	13.7
				League Average	0.283	0.347	0.387	8.0%	35.2%					
				% Lg Avg	107	108	108	119	109					
				League Rank	2	1	3	1			7	3		

GS	GR	IP	Age	Name	W–L	WHIP	K/9	BB/9	HR/9	FIP	ERA	R/9	RAA	WAA
38	10	340	30	Bagby, Jim	31–12	1.24	2.0	2.2	0.2	3.57	2.89	3.23	52	5.1
38	3	315	30	Coveleski, Stan	24–14	1.11	3.8	1.9	0.2	2.96	2.49	3.14	52	5.1
33	1	238	32	Caldwell, Ray	20–10	1.47	3.0	2.4	0.3	3.58	3.86	5.11	-13	-1.3
17	12	137	27	Morton, Guy	8–6	1.45	4.7	3.8	0.1	3.35	4.47	5.26	-9	-0.9
8	1	63	25	Mails, Duster*	7–0	1.14	3.7	2.6	0.1	3.14	1.85	2.56	15	1.4
6	21	85	21	Uhle, George	4–5	1.50	2.9	3.1	0.3	4.03	5.21	5.53	-9	-0.8
7	9	72	26	Myers, Elmer	2–4	1.63	2.0	3.0	0.1	3.81	4.77	6.53	-15	-1.5
3	16	40	27	Niehaus, Dick*	1–2	1.45	2.7	3.6	0.0	3.57	3.60	4.73	0	0.0
2	9	42	22	Clark, Bob	1–2	1.33	1.9	2.8	0.0	3.47	3.43	3.64	5	0.4
0	13	25	26	Faeth, Tony	0–0	2.04	6.1	7.2	0.0	4.06	4.32	6.84	-6	-0.6
2	-2	21		Others	0–1	1.95	2.6	7.7	0.0	4.90	5.14	6.86	-5	-0.5
154	93		26.6	Team Total		1.34	3.08	2.65	0.20	3.46	3.41	4.20	65	6.3
				League Average		1.42	2.96	3.10	0.30	3.79	3.79	4.79		
				% Lg Avg		107	104	117	148	110	111	114		
				League Rank		1	4	1	1	1	2			

1921 NEW YORK YANKEES

The 1921 Yankees earned their first of many pennants in a close race against the defending world champion Indians as these two teams dominated the other six teams in the pennant race. Babe Ruth had perhaps his finest season. Another significant offseason transaction with the Red Sox solidified this team when the Yankees traded Del Pratt, Muddy Ruel, Hank Thormahlen, and Sammy Vick to the Red Sox for Harry Harper, Waite Hoyt, Mike McNally, and Wally Schang. The Yankees lost to the Giants in the Series.

Strengths: (1) hitting for average and power led by Ruth (44 2B, 16 3B, 59 HR, 457 TB), Meusel (40 2B, 16 3B, 24 HR), and Schang (30 2B), (2) drawing walks led by Ruth (145 BB), Peckinpaugh (84 BB), and Schang (78 BB), (3) fielding led by 2B/3B Ward (101 Rng+ at 2B, 119 Rng+ at 3B), 3B Baker (11 errors in 268 chances, 95 Rng+), 3B McNally (116 Rng+, 5 errors in 190 chances), 1B Pipp (89 assists), and LF/CF Ruth (109 Rng+, 17 assists), and (4) starting pitching anchored by Mays (7 saves) and Hoyt.

Weaknesses: (1) RP position, (2) hitting for contact, (3) hitting from McNally, (4) CS% from Schang (40%), and (5) pitching from Collins (10.4 H/9), Ferguson (10.2 H/9), and Sheehan (11.7 H/9).

Mgr	Miller Huggins	
Rk	34	89
Gm	153	
Place	1	
GA	4.5	
Rival	14–8 vs Indians, 128 RS & 127 RA	

	W	L	Win%
Regular Season	98	55	0.641
Runs Record	96	57	0.626
1 Run	15	19	0.441
Extra Innings	4	3	0.571
Blowout	42	15	0.737

	Team	LgAvg	%Avg	LgRk
BABIP	0.298	0.310	104	1
E	220	218	99	4
sOBP	0.330	0.351	106	1
rOBP	0.399	0.380	95	7
R/G	6.20	5.10	121	1
RA/G	4.61	5.10	111	3

	Tm	LgAvg	>Avg
RS	948	787	161
RA	706	787	81
DP	138	137	1

	R/G	HR	K	BB	SB	CS	SB%	OBP
Team Offense	6.20	134	571	575	89	64	58%	0.374
Team Defense	4.61	51	481	470	82	57	59%	0.342
Difference	1.58	83	-90	105	7			109%

Pos	Rpos	PA	Age	Name	BA	OBP	SLG	BB%	RS%	Bat R>Avg	BR R>Avg	Fld R>Avg	RAA	WAA
C	6	513	31	Schang, Wally^	0.316	0.428	0.453	15%	34%	23	1	0	30	2.8
1B	-7	667	28	Pipp, Wally*	0.296	0.347	0.427	7%	42%	0	0	8	1	0.1
2B	4	635	24	Ward, Aaron	0.306	0.363	0.423	7%	33%	4	-1	12	19	1.8
3B	3	369	35	Baker, Home Run*	0.294	0.353	0.436	7%	31%	2	0	8	13	1.2
SS	10	696	30	Peckinpaugh, Roger	0.288	0.380	0.397	12%	49%	6	1	-4	13	1.2
LF,CF	-6	693	26	Ruth, Babe*	0.378	0.512	0.846	21%	40%	124	-1	6	123	11.5
CF	-2	270	30	Miller, Elmer	0.298	0.356	0.450	7%	41%	3	0	1	2	0.2
RF,LF	-7	646	24	Meusel, Bob	0.318	0.356	0.559	5%	40%	27	2	4	26	2.5
CF,LF	-1	248	25	Fewster, Chick	0.280	0.382	0.386	11%	47%	2	0	-4	-3	-0.3
3B,2B	2	240	27	McNally, Mike	0.260	0.306	0.312	6%	51%	-12	-1	8	-3	-0.3
CF,RF	-1	176	28	Roth, Braggo	0.283	0.370	0.408	11%	44%	1	0	-1	-1	-0.1
CF,LF	0	79	25	Hawks, Chicken*	0.288	0.333	0.479	6%	58%	1	0	0	1	0.1
P	0	156	29	Mays, Carl*	0.343	0.365	0.434	3%	31%	1	0	0	1	0.1
	-1	668		Others	0.235	0.277	0.296	5%	32%	-45	2	-5	-49	-4.5
	0		27.8	Team Total	0.300	0.374	0.464	9.5%	39.6%	138	3	33	174	16.3
				League Average	0.292	0.356	0.408	8.1%	35.7%					
				% Lg Avg	103	105	114	117	111					
				League Rank	4	3	1	2			3	2		

GS	GR	IP	Age	Name	W–L	WHIP	K/9	BB/9	HR/9	FIP	ERA	R/9	RAA	WAA
38	11	337	29	Mays, Carl	27–9	1.21	1.9	2.0	0.3	3.98	3.05	3.88	39	3.6
32	11	282	21	Hoyt, Waite	19–13	1.35	3.3	2.6	0.1	3.54	3.09	3.86	33	3.1
31	7	245	30	Shawkey, Bob	18–12	1.35	4.6	3.2	0.6	4.12	4.08	4.81	3	0.3
16	12	137	25	Collins, Rip	11–5	1.72	4.2	5.1	0.4	4.77	5.44	6.75	-28	-2.6
10	4	82	25	Piercy, Bill	5–4	1.35	3.9	3.1	0.4	4.28	2.97	4.41	5	0.4
13	20	119	37	Quinn, Jack	8–7	1.60	3.3	2.4	0.2	3.63	3.78	4.61	4	0.4
4	13	56	24	Ferguson, Alex	3–1	1.62	1.4	4.3	0.6	5.47	5.91	6.39	-9	-0.9
1	11	33	27	Sheehan, Tom	1–0	1.88	1.9	5.2	0.3	5.00	5.45	6.27	-5	-0.5
0	5	11	29	Rogers, Tom	0–1	1.91	0.0	7.4	0.8	7.12	7.36	7.36	-3	-0.3
7	1	53	26	Harper, Harry*	4–3	1.46	3.8	4.3	0.5	4.66	3.76	3.93	6	0.5
1	1	9		Ruth, Babe	2–0	2.56	2.0	9.0	1.0	7.21	9.00	10.00	-5	-0.5
153	96		27.3	Team Total		1.42	3.17	3.10	0.34	4.14	3.82	4.66	39	3.7
				League Average		1.49	2.95	3.22	0.39	4.28	4.28	5.14		
				% Lg Avg		105	108	104	116	103	112	110		
				League Rank		1	1	4	5	3	1			

1922 St. Louis Browns

The 1922 Browns had its best team in the history of its franchise, yet still came in second place to a rather lucky Yankee team and could not win the crucial head-to-head games versus the defending pennant winner Yankees. Looking at run differential alone, the Browns should have easily won the pennant by 9 games instead of losing it by 1 game. The Browns never again came this close to winning the pennant until 1944 when most of the major league talent was serving in the military.

Strengths: (1) SP, RP, C, 1B, 2B, LF, and CF positions, (2) hitting for average, contact, and power featuring George Sisler (42 SB, 18 3B), Ken Williams (74 BB, 34 2B, 39 HR, 41 game hitting streak), Tobin (34 2B), Jacobson (16 3B), and McManus (34 2B), (3) baserunning featuring Sisler (51 SB, 19 CS) and Williams (37 SB, 19 CS) who was the first member of the 30 HR & 30 SB club, (4) fielding led by SS Gerber (103 Rng+), 2B McManus (103 Rng+), and 3B Ellerbe (124 Rng+), (5) double plays made, (6) CS% from Severeid (57%), and (7) pitching anchored by innings eater Shocker, Vangilder, who also had a terrific hitting season, starter/reliever Wright, and reliever/occasional starter Pruett.

Weaknesses: (1) 3B and SS positions, (2) hitting from starting infielders Gerber and Ellerbe, and (3) fielding from RF Tobin (91 Rng+).

Mgr	Lee Fohl	
Rk	13	31
Gm	154	
Place	2	
GB	1.0	
Rival	8–14 vs Yankees, 105 RS & 100 RA	

	W	*L*	*Win%*
Regular Season	93	61	0.604
Runs Record	101	53	0.658
1 Run	22	26	0.458
Extra Innings	7	9	0.438
Blowout	31	14	0.689

	Team	*LgAvg*	*%Avg*	*LgRk*
BABIP	0.291	0.301	104	2
E	197	192	97	4
sOBP	0.327	0.343	105	2
rOBP	0.346	0.370	107	1
R/G	5.64	4.74	119	1
RA/G	4.12	4.74	115	2

	Tm	*LgAvg*	*>Avg*
RS	868	733	135
RA	634	731	97
DP	158	142	16

	R/G	*HR*	*K*	*BB*	*SB*	*CS*	*SB%*	*OBP*
Team Offense	5.64	98	380	471	136	75	64%	0.369
Team Defense	4.12	71	534	419	70	79	47%	0.330
Difference	1.52	27	154	52	66			112%

Pos	*Rpos*	*PA*	*Age*	*Name*	*BA*	*OBP*	*SLG*	*BB%*	*RS%*	*Bat R>Avg*	*BR R>Avg*	*Fld R>Avg*	*RAA*	*WAA*
C	4	559	31	Severeid, Hank	0.321	0.356	0.427	5%	24%	6	-1	1	10	1.0
1B	-6	654	29	Sisler, George*	0.420	0.467	0.594	7%	43%	69	4	6	73	7.1
2B	5	665	22	McManus, Marty	0.312	0.358	0.459	6%	35%	14	0	8	27	2.6
3B	3	390	26	Ellerbe, Frank	0.246	0.303	0.319	6%	37%	-16	0	8	-5	-0.5
SS	10	689	30	Gerber, Wally	0.267	0.326	0.334	8%	38%	-18	1	7	0	0.0
LF,CF	-7	678	32	Williams, Ken*	0.332	0.413	0.627	11%	38%	61	0	8	62	6.0
CF,LF	-4	629	31	Jacobson, Baby Doll	0.317	0.379	0.463	7%	36%	19	2	5	22	2.2
RF	-7	699	30	Tobin, Jack*	0.331	0.388	0.474	8%	43%	27	-1	-6	13	1.2
3B	1	170	35	Foster, Eddie	0.306	0.394	0.333	12%	45%	1	0	2	4	0.4
CF,OF	-1	152	30	Shorten, Chick*	0.275	0.354	0.489	11%	40%	4	0	0	3	0.3
C,1B	1	149	25	Collins, Pat	0.307	0.405	0.543	14%	12%	10	0	1	12	1.1
P	0	110	26	Vangilder, Elam	0.344	0.396	0.559	5%	37%	7	0	0	7	0.7
P	0	71	27	Kolp, Ray	0.298	0.333	0.439	4%	35%	0	0	0	0	0.0
	1	515		Others	0.205	0.267	0.269	7%	36%	-36	2	-1	-34	-3.3
	0		28.8	Team Total	0.310	0.369	0.453	7.7%	36.8%	148	7	39	194	18.8
				League Average	0.285	0.348	0.398	7.9%	34.1%					
				% Lg Avg	109	106	114	97	108					
				League Rank	1	2	1	6			1	2		

GS	*GR*	*IP*	*Age*	*Name*	*W–L*	*WHIP*	*K/9*	*BB/9*	*HR/9*	*FIP*	*ERA*	*R/9*	*RAA*	*WAA*
38	10	348	31	Shocker, Urban	24–17	1.21	3.9	1.5	0.57	3.32	2.97	3.65	34	3.3
30	13	245	26	Vangilder, Elam	19–13	1.21	2.3	1.8	0.48	3.67	3.42	4.00	14	1.3
25	0	174	31	Davis, Dixie	11–6	1.43	3.4	4.5	0.52	4.51	4.08	4.70	-3	-0.3
18	14	170	27	Kolp, Ray	14–4	1.39	2.9	1.9	0.53	3.75	3.93	4.72	-4	-0.4
16	15	154	26	Wright, Rasty	9–7	1.29	2.6	2.9	0.41	3.78	2.92	3.74	13	1.3
10	10	80	32	Danforth, Dave*	5–2	1.66	5.4	4.3	0.11	3.30	3.28	4.18	3	0.3
8	31	120	21	Pruett, Hub*	7–7	1.32	5.3	4.4	0.15	3.32	2.33	3.61	13	1.2
9	17	93	23	Bayne, Bill*	4–5	1.41	3.7	3.6	0.49	4.19	4.56	4.76	-2	-0.2
0	5	9		Others	0–0	2.78	3.0	7.0	1.00	5.06	5.00	6.00	-2	-0.1
154	115		27.1	Team Total		1.33	3.45	2.71	0.46	3.70	3.38	4.10	65	6.3
				League Average		1.43	2.92	3.11	0.43	4.04	4.03	4.77		
				% Lg Avg		108	118	115	93	109	119	116		
				League Rank		2	1	1	7	1	1			

1922 NEW YORK GIANTS

The 1922 Giants were the second of the four straight pennant winning Giants teams from 1921 through 1924 continuing their run of finishing first or second every year since 1917. This would be the last Giant world championship team for manager McGraw. Late in the season, Commissioner Kenesaw Mountain Landis banned Phil Douglas from professional baseball for life after he wrote a letter to another team soliciting throwing games for profit. Another pitcher, Fred Toney, was a holdout throughout much of the season.

Strengths: (1) SP, C, 1B, 1B, 2B, SS, LF, CF, and RF positions, (2) hitting for average and power led by Irish Meusel (17 3B, 16 HR), Kelly (33 2B, 17 HR), Stengel, Youngs (34 2B, 10 3B), Snyder, Bancroft (41 2B), and Frisch (13 3B), (3) fielding featuring SS Bancroft (116 Rng+), 2B/3B Frisch (98 Rng+ at 2B, 109 Rng+ at 3B), 2B Rawlings

(97 Rng+ at 2B, only 7 errors in 425 chances), and 3B Groh (95 Rng+), and (4) consistently good pitching anchored by Phil Douglas and Art Nehf. The Giants had a .305 team BA featuring 7 everyday positional players that had a batting average of better than .300.

Weaknesses: (1) hitting from Groh and Shinners and (2) team pitching K/9.

Mgr	John McGraw	
Rk	31	80
Gm	156	
Place	1	
GA	7.0	
Rival	12–10 vs Reds, 91 RS & 81 RA	

	W	*L*	*Win%*
Regular Season	93	61	0.604
Runs Record	97	57	0.629
1 Run	30	23	0.566
Extra Innings	6	9	0.400
Blowout	36	10	0.783

	Team	*LgAvg*	*%Avg*	*LgRk*
BABIP	0.283	0.307	109	1
E	194	210	108	2
sOBP	0.325	0.343	106	2
rOBP	0.327	0.367	112	1
R/G	5.46	5.00	109	3
RA/G	4.22	5.00	119	1

	Tm	*LgAvg*	*>Avg*
RS	852	774	78
RA	658	774	116
DP	145	138	7

	R/G	*HR*	*K*	*BB*	*SB*	*CS*	*SB%*	*OBP*
Team Offense	5.46	80	421	448	116	83	58%	0.363
Team Defense	4.22	71	388	393	76	58	57%	0.324
Difference	1.24	9	-33	55	40			112%

Pos	*Rpos*	*PA*	*Age*	*Name*	*BA*	*OBP*	*SLG*	*BB%*	*RS%*	*Bat R>Avg*	*BR R>Avg*	*Fld R>Avg*	*RAA*	*WAA*
C	3	354	28	Snyder, Frank	0.343	0.387	0.487	6%	23%	14	-1	1	17	1.6
1B	-7	640	26	Kelly, George	0.328	0.363	0.497	5%	38%	21	3	10	27	2.5
2B,3B	4	582	23	Frisch, Frankie^	0.327	0.387	0.438	8%	45%	15	1	12	32	3.0
3B	4	497	32	Groh, Heinie	0.265	0.353	0.350	11%	36%	-6	0	5	3	0.3
SS	10	745	31	Bancroft, Dave^	0.321	0.397	0.418	11%	39%	19	0	17	46	4.3
LF	-7	676	29	Meusel, Irish	0.331	0.369	0.509	5%	37%	25	0	1	19	1.8
CF	-2	283	31	Stengel, Casey*	0.368	0.436	0.564	7%	36%	23	1	3	25	2.4
RF	-7	642	25	Youngs, Ross*	0.331	0.398	0.465	9%	41%	24	1	6	24	2.3
2B,3B	2	346	29	Rawlings, Johnny	0.282	0.342	0.386	7%	39%	-3	0	10	9	0.9
C	3	275	25	Smith, Earl*	0.278	0.383	0.474	13%	21%	10	0	-2	11	1.0
CF	-2	243	27	Cunningham, Bill	0.328	0.350	0.437	3%	43%	2	-1	2	1	0.1
CF,RF	-1	151	26	Shinners, Ralph	0.252	0.308	0.311	3%	36%	-7	-1	0	-9	-0.8
CF	0	50	32	Robertson, Dave*	0.277	0.320	0.383	6%	27%	-1	0	-1	-2	-0.2
	0	625		Others	0.197	0.238	0.233	5%	37%	-60	0	1	-59	-5.6
	0		28.0	Team Total	0.305	0.363	0.428	7.3%	37.2%	77	3	65	145	13.7
				League Average	0.292	0.348	0.404	7.2%	35.9%					
				% Lg Avg	104	104	106	102	103					
				League Rank	2	1	2	4	4		3	1		

GS	*GR*	*IP*	*Age*	*Name*	*W–L*	*WHIP*	*K/9*	*BB/9*	*HR/9*	*FIP*	*ERA*	*R/9*	*RAA*	*WAA*
35	2	268	29	Nehf, Art*	19–13	1.30	2.0	2.1	0.5	4.11	3.29	4.09	16	1.5
30	7	213	29	Barnes, Jesse	13–8	1.29	2.2	1.6	0.4	3.77	3.51	4.57	1	0.1
21	3	158	32	Douglas, Phil	11–4	1.20	1.9	2.0	0.3	3.89	2.63	3.20	25	2.4
13	2	94	26	McQuillan, Hugh	6–5	1.54	2.3	3.2	0.7	4.61	3.82	4.58	0	0.0
12	1	86	33	Toney, Fred	5–6	1.41	1.0	3.2	0.5	4.74	4.17	4.59	0	0.0
10	7	80	30	Scott, Jack	8–2	1.33	4.2	2.6	0.8	4.23	4.41	4.74	-1	-0.1
0	33	96	24	Jonnard, Claude	6–1	1.29	4.1	2.6	0.7	4.07	3.84	4.22	5	0.5
20	26	192	24	Ryan, Rosy	17–12	1.40	3.5	3.5	0.2	3.82	3.01	4.09	12	1.1
2	22	71	28	Causey, Red	4–3	1.46	1.7	4.3	0.3	4.52	3.18	4.33	2	0.2
2	20	52	25	Barnes, Virgil	1–0	1.10	2.8	1.9	0.2	3.34	3.48	4.70	0	0.0
11	12	87		Others	3–7	1.25	2.5	2.2	0.6	4.17	4.12	4.64	0	0.0
156	135		28.0	Team Total		1.32	2.50	2.53	0.46	4.07	3.45	4.24	61	5.7
				League Average		1.45	2.74	2.80	0.43	4.10	4.10	5.05		
				% Lg Avg		110	91	111	94	101	119	119		

1923 New York Yankees

The 1923 season ended with the Ruth-led Yankees easily leading the AL in fewest runs allowed per game, capturing their third straight AL pennant in dominant fashion by 16 games over the Tigers, and winning their first World Series. The third time was the charm as it was the third straight Giants–Yankees World Series. The famous Yankee Stadium opened on opening day 1923. Backup C Fred Hoffman filled in admirably for Schang when he was out due to a groin injury.

Strengths: (1) hitting for average and power led by Ruth who had another monster season (45 2B, 13 3B, 41 HR, 170 BB), Meusel (29 2B, 10 3B), and Witt (10 3B), (2) fielding featuring 2B Ward (108 Rng+), SS Scott (91 Rng+), 3B Dugan (95 Rng+), and Ruth (127 Rng+ in RF, 126 Rng+ in LF, 20 assists), and (3) starting pitching depth anchored by all 5 primary starters having better than league average seasons led by recently acquired Pennock, Bush, Hoyt, and Shawkey.

Weaknesses: (1) RP and SS positions, (2) hitting from Scott and Dugan, (3) hitting for contact, (4) SB% especially from Ruth (17 SB, 21 CS), Pipp (6 SB, 13 CS), and Meusel (13 SB, 15 CS), (5) CS% from Hofmann (35%), and (6) pitching from Mays (9.6 H/9) who would play his last season with the Yankees in 1923.

Mgr	Miller Huggins	
Rk	47	114
Gm	152	
Place	1	
GA	16.0	
Rival	12–10 vs Tigers, 124 RS & 117 RA	

	W	*L*	*Win%*
Regular Season	98	54	0.645
Runs Record	94	58	0.620
1 Run	26	15	0.634
Extra Innings	9	4	0.692
Blowout	33	12	0.733

	Team	*LgAvg*	*%Avg*	*LgRk*
BABIP	0.281	0.300	107	1
E	144	200	139	1
sOBP	0.325	0.344	106	1
rOBP	0.382	0.378	99	6
R/G	5.42	4.85	112	2
RA/G	4.09	4.85	119	1

	Team	*LgAvg*	*RAA*
RS	824	736	88
RA	622	735	113
DP	131	137	-6

	R/G	*HR*	*K*	*BB*	*SB*	*CS*	*SB%*	*OBP*
Team Offense	5.42	105	515	511	69	74	48%	0.357
Team Defense	4.09	68	506	491	78	57	58%	0.330
Difference	1.33	37	-9	20	-9			108%

Pos	*Rpos*	*PA*	*Age*	*Name*	*BA*	*OBP*	*SLG*	*BB%*	*RS%*	*Bat R>Avg*	*BR R>Avg*	*Fld R>Avg*	*RAA*	*WAA*
C	3	315	33	Schang, Wally^	0.276	0.360	0.342	9%	34%	-2	1	-1	1	0.1
1B	-7	634	30	Pipp, Wally*	0.304	0.352	0.397	6%	35%	1	-3	8	-1	-0.1
2B	5	640	26	Ward, Aaron	0.284	0.351	0.422	9%	33%	6	0	16	27	2.6
3B	5	684	26	Dugan, Joe	0.283	0.311	0.384	4%	51%	-14	1	9	1	0.1
SS	10	568	30	Scott, Everett	0.246	0.266	0.325	2%	30%	-32	0	6	-16	-1.5
LF,RF	-6	503	26	Meusel, Bob	0.313	0.359	0.478	6%	30%	14	-3	-2	3	0.3
CF	-4	685	27	Witt, Whitey*	0.314	0.386	0.408	10%	43%	14	-1	4	13	1.3
RF,LF	-7	699	28	Ruth, Babe*	0.393	0.545	0.764	24%	33%	123	-4	19	131	12.7
C	2	263	29	Hofmann, Fred	0.290	0.350	0.403	7%	24%	1	1	-1	3	0.3
RF	-2	208	30	Smith, Elmer*	0.306	0.377	0.475	10%	33%	7	1	1	7	0.7
LF	-1	69	25	Hendrick,Harvey*	0.273	0.294	0.485	3%	35%	0	1	-1	-1	-0.1
SS	1	40	35	Johnson, Ernie*	0.447	0.462	0.605	3%	29%	4	0	-1	4	0.4
1B	0	29	20	Gehrig, Lou*	0.423	0.464	0.769	7%	42%	4	0	-1	3	0.3
C	0	58	24	Bengough, Benny	0.132	0.193	0.170	7%	9%	-8	0	0	-8	-0.7
P	0	116	30	Bush, Bullet Joe	0.274	0.293	0.425	3%	31%	-2	0	0	-2	-0.2
	1	537		Others	0.189	0.246	0.228	7%	46%	-46	2	0	-43	-4.2
	0		27.9	Team Total	0.291	0.357	0.423	8.4%	36.0%	73	-4	56	125	12.1
				League Average	0.283	0.351	0.388	8.4%	34.4%					
				% Lg Avg	103	102	109	100	105					
				League Rank	3	3	1	5	2		6	1		

GS	*GR*	*IP*	*Age*	*Name*	*W–L*	*WHIP*	*K/9*	*BB/9*	*HR/9*	*FIP*	*ERA*	*R/9*	*RAA*	*WAA*
30	7	276	30	Bush, Joe	19–15	1.38	4.1	3.8	0.23	3.66	3.43	3.75	21	2.1
31	5	259	32	Shawkey, Bob	16–11	1.29	4.3	3.5	0.59	4.02	3.51	3.97	14	1.4
27	12	243	30	Jones, Sad Sam	21–8	1.27	2.5	2.6	0.41	3.86	3.63	4.22	5	0.5
28	9	239	23	Hoyt, Waite	17–9	1.23	2.3	2.5	0.34	3.77	3.02	3.66	20	2.0
27	8	238	29	Pennock, Herb*	19–6	1.27	3.5	2.6	0.42	3.61	3.13	3.25	31	3.0
7	16	81	31	Mays, Carl	5–2	1.86	1.8	3.5	0.89	5.12	6.20	6.53	-19	-1.9
2	6	33	23	Pipgras, George	1–3	1.77	3.2	6.8	0.54	5.31	5.95	5.95	-6	-0.5
0	5	12	23	Roettger, Oscar	0–0	2.39	5.4	9.2	2.31	8.38	8.46	11.54	-9	-0.9
152	68		27.6	Team Total		1.34	3.3	3.2	0.44	3.94	3.62	4.05	59	5.7
				League Average		1.45	2.9	3.4	0.36	3.98	3.98	4.80		
				% Lg Avg		108	112	105	82	101	110	118		
				League Rank		1	1	3	8	4	1			

1924 New York Giants

The 1924 Giants were the last of the history making 4 consecutive pennant winning Giant teams. However, losing the World Series to the underdog Senators signaled the end of their domination. John McGraw, manager of the Giants through the 1932 season, would never again manage the team to another pennant despite managing several more good Giant teams.

Strengths: (1) C, 1B, 2B, 3B, SS, and RF positions, (2) hitting for average and power led by Youngs (33 2B, 12 3B, 77 BB), Kelly (37 2B, 9 3B, 21 HR), Frisch (33 2B, 15 3B), Wilson (12 3B), Meusel (26 2B, 9 3B), Jackson (26 2B, 8 3B), and Gowdy, (3) drawing walks featuring Youngs (77 BB), (4) baserunning especially Frisch (22 SB, 9 CS), (5) infield fielding featuring 2B Frisch (116 Rng+, 101 DP), SS Jackson (106 Rng+, 101 DP), and 3B Groh (100 Rng+, only 7 errors in 414 chances), and (6) pitching anchored by Barnes, McQuillan, and Jonnard.

Weaknesses: (1) RP position, (2) hitting from reserve OF Southworth, (3) CS% from Snyder (40%), (4) pitching from starter Wayland Dean, and (5) team pitching K/9, HR/9, and FIP.

Mgr	John McGraw	
Rk	43	102
Gm	154	
Place	1	
GA	1.5	
Rival	14–8 vs Dodgers, 109 RS & 79 RA	

	W	*L*	*Win%*
Regular Season	93	60	0.608
Runs Record	95	58	0.622
1 Run	18	19	0.486
Extra Innings	5	9	0.357
Blowout	31	10	0.756

	Team	*LgAvg*	*%Avg*	*LgRk*
BABIP	0.287	0.298	104	3
E	186	192	103	4
sOBP	0.326	0.336	103	4
rOBP	0.331	0.339	102	3
R/G	5.56	4.54	123	1
RA/G	4.16	4.54	109	3

	Tm	*LgAvg*	*>Avg*
RS	857	698	159
RA	641	698	57
DP	160	153	7

	R/G	*HR*	*K*	*BB*	*SB*	*CS*	*SB%*	*OBP*
Team Offense	5.56	95	479	467	82	53	61%	0.358
Team Defense	4.16	77	406	392	96	75	56%	0.327
Difference	1.40	18	-73	75	-14			110%

Pos	*Rpos*	*PA*	*Age*	*Name*	*BA*	*OBP*	*SLG*	*BB%*	*RS%*	*Bat R>Avg*	*BR R>Avg*	*Fld R>Avg*	*RAA*	*WAA*
C	3	390	30	Snyder, Frank	0.302	0.357	0.412	8%	24%	6	2	1	12	1.2
1B,2B	-6	627	28	Kelly, High Pockets	0.324	0.371	0.531	6%	34%	34	2	2	32	3.1
2B,SS	6	675	25	Frisch, Frankie^	0.328	0.387	0.468	8%	46%	29	3	20	58	5.7
3B	5	635	34	Groh, Heinie	0.281	0.354	0.360	8%	37%	-1	1	11	16	1.6
SS	10	633	20	Jackson, Travis	0.302	0.326	0.428	3%	37%	3	0	10	23	2.3
LF	-6	603	31	Meusel, Irish	0.310	0.351	0.423	5%	35%	9	1	1	5	0.5
CF,LF	-3	434	24	Wilson, Hack	0.295	0.369	0.486	10%	35%	17	1	-2	13	1.3
RF	-6	612	27	Youngs, Ross*	0.356	0.441	0.521	13%	40%	49	0	1	44	4.4
CF,RF	-2	325	31	Southworth, Billy*	0.256	0.332	0.335	10%	37%	-5	-2	-2	-11	-1.1
C	2	219	34	Gowdy, Hank	0.325	0.411	0.445	12%	24%	10	1	1	14	1.4
1B	-2	180	25	Terry, Bill*	0.239	0.311	0.399	9%	41%	-2	0	-1	-5	-0.4
CF,RF	-1	118	23	O'Connell, Jimmy*	0.317	0.388	0.452	9%	51%	5	0	-4	0	0.0
2B,3B	1	88	18	Lindstrom, Freddie	0.253	0.314	0.316	7%	70%	-3	0	0	-2	-0.2
	-1	528		Others	0.228	0.265	0.319	5%	42%	-27	1	0	-27	-2.7
	0		26.9	Team Total	0.300	0.358	0.432	7.7%	37.5%	124	10	38	172	17.0
				League Average	0.283	0.337	0.392	6.8%	34.0%					
				% Lg Avg	106	106	110	113	110					
				League Rank	1	1	1	2	1		2	2		

GS	*GR*	*IP*	*Age*	*Name*	*W–L*	*WHIP*	*K/9*	*BB/9*	*HR/9*	*FIP*	*ERA*	*R/9*	*RAA*	*WAA*
29	6	229	27	Barnes, Virgil	16–10	1.29	2.3	2.2	0.4	3.75	3.06	3.41	23	2.3
24	4	188	29	Bentley, Jack*	16–5	1.34	2.9	2.7	0.5	4.03	3.78	4.07	5	0.5
23	4	184	28	McQuillan, Hugh	14–8	1.21	2.4	2.1	0.4	3.72	2.69	3.33	20	2.0
20	10	172	31	Nehf, Art*	14–4	1.22	3.8	2.2	0.7	3.94	3.62	3.93	8	0.8
20	6	126	22	Dean, Wayland	6–12	1.46	2.8	3.2	0.6	4.46	5.01	5.73	-20	-2.0
16	6	100	27	Watson, Mule	7–4	1.46	1.6	2.2	0.6	4.26	3.79	4.87	-6	-0.6
9	28	125	26	Ryan, Rosy	8–6	1.40	2.6	2.7	0.1	3.42	4.26	4.62	-4	-0.4
3	31	90	26	Jonnard, Claude	3–5	1.16	4.0	2.4	0.2	3.22	2.41	3.31	10	1.0
2	8	34	24	Baldwin, Harry	3–1	1.57	1.3	2.9	1.3	5.56	4.27	4.81	-2	-0.2
3	3	29	26	Gearin, Dinty*	1–2	1.59	1.2	5.0	0.9	5.68	2.48	2.79	5	0.5
5	42	102		Others	5–3	1.68	2.1	3.3	0.6	4.49	4.76	5.99	-19	-1.9

GS	GR	IP	Age	Name	W–L	WHIP	K/9	BB/9	HR/9	FIP	ERA	R/9	RAA	WAA
154	148			Team Total		1.35	2.65	2.56	0.50	3.99	3.62	4.19	20	2.0
			26.6	League Average		1.38	2.77	2.62	0.41	3.87	3.87	4.56		
				% Lg Avg		102	96	102	81	97	107	109		
				League Rank		4	3	4	6	5	3			

1927 New York Yankees

The 1927 season will be forever remembered as the year that the Yankees put it all together becoming the best team in baseball history. They supplemented an awesome offensive attack with great pitching and fielding. This team completely dominated their competition easily leading the league in most runs scored per game, allowing the fewest runs per game, winning the pennant by 19 games over a solid A's team, and sweeping a good Pirate team in the World Series. No team has ever had 2 players with stronger seasons in the same year as those by Ruth and Gehrig in 1927.

Strengths: (1) hitting led by Ruth (29 2B, 60 HR, 417 TB), MVP Gehrig (52 2B, 18 3B, 47 HR, 447 TB), Combs (36 2B, 23 3B), Meusel (47 2B, 9 3B), and Lazzeri (29 2B, 8 3B, 18 HR), (2) drawing walks from Ruth (138 BB) and Gehrig (109 BB), (3) fielding from 2B/SS Lazzeri (102 Rng+ at 2B, 93 Rng+ at SS), SS Koenig (115 Rng+), LF/RF Ruth (115 Rng+ in RF, 113 Rng+ in LF, 14 OF assists), and CF Combs (102 Rng+), and (4) pitching anchored by Hoyt, Moore (13 Sv), Pennock, and Shocker.

Weaknesses: (1) 3B position, (2) hitting for contact, (3) hitting from Koenig, Dugan, Morehart, Bengough, and Grabowski, (4) pitching from Thomas and Giard, (5) double plays made, and (6) CS% from C Pat Collins (28%) and Grabowski (32%).

Mgr	Miller Huggins	
Rk	1	1
Gm	155	
Place	1	
GA	19.0	
Rival	14–8 vs A's, 157 RS & 106 RA	

	W	L	Win%
Regular Season	110	44	0.714
Runs Record	112	42	0.729
1 Run	24	19	0.558
Extra Innings	4	4	0.500
Blowout	43	8	0.843

	Team	LgAvg	%Avg	LgRk
BABIP	0.284	0.303	107	1
E	196	207	106	2
sOBP	0.318	0.349	110	1
rOBP	0.329	0.362	110	2
R/G	6.30	4.92	128	1
RA/G	3.90	4.92	126	1

	Tm	LgAvg	>Avg
RS	976	762	214
RA	605	762	157
DP	123	144	-21

	R/G	HR	K	BB	SB	CS	SB%	OBP
Team Offense	6.30	158	610	642	90	64	58%	0.384
Team Defense	3.90	42	431	409	94	44	68%	0.321
Difference	2.39	116	-179	233	-4			119%

Pos	Rpos	PA	Age	Name	BA	OBP	SLG	BB%	RS%	Bat R>Avg	BR R>Avg	Fld R>Avg	RAA	WAA
C	3	311	30	Collins, Pat	0.275	0.407	0.418	17%	26%	10	0	-1	12	1.1
1B	-7	717	24	Gehrig, Lou*	0.373	0.474	0.765	15%	36%	105	0	5	103	9.8
2B,SS	7	660	23	Lazzeri, Tony	0.309	0.383	0.482	10%	33%	24	-1	14	44	4.2
3B	3	429	30	Dugan, Joe	0.269	0.321	0.362	6%	32%	-10	-1	0	-8	-0.8
SS	7	568	22	Koenig, Mark^	0.285	0.320	0.382	4%	55%	-11	0	7	3	0.3
LF,RF	-6	584	30	Meusel, Bob	0.337	0.393	0.510	8%	31%	28	1	1	24	2.2
CF	-4	724	28	Combs, Earle*	0.356	0.414	0.511	9%	45%	42	1	8	47	4.5
LF,RF	-7	692	32	Ruth, Babe*	0.356	0.487	0.772	20%	36%	105	0	12	110	10.4
2B	2	230	27	Morehart, Ray*	0.256	0.353	0.328	13%	56%	-4	-1	1	-2	-0.2
C	2	223	27	Grabowski, Johnny	0.277	0.350	0.328	9%	38%	-4	0	0	-2	-0.2
3B	2	148	30	Gazella, Mike	0.278	0.403	0.417	16%	30%	4	1	-1	6	0.6
LF,OF	-1	87	31	Paschal, Ben	0.317	0.349	0.549	5%	50%	4	-1	-1	1	0.1
C	1	90	28	Bengough, Benny	0.247	0.281	0.353	4%	24%	-4	-1	0	-4	-0.4
	-2	759		Others	0.223	0.265	0.280	4%	37%	-52	0	-4	-58	-5.5
	0		27.8	Team Total	0.307	0.384	0.488	10.3%	38.0%	235	-2	41	274	26.0
				League Average	0.286	0.352	0.399	8.4%	35.6%					
				% Lg Avg	108	109	122	123	107					
				League Rank	1	1	1	1	1		5	1		

GS	GR	IP	Age	Name	W–L	WHIP	K/9	BB/9	HR/9	FIP	ERA	R/9	RAA	WAA
32	4	256	27	Hoyt, Waite	22–7	1.15	3.0	1.9	0.4	3.58	2.63	3.16	44	4.2
26	8	210	33	Pennock, Herb*	19–8	1.30	2.2	2.1	0.2	3.60	3.00	3.82	21	2.0
27	4	200	36	Shocker, Urban	18–6	1.24	1.6	1.8	0.4	3.86	2.84	3.87	19	1.8
26	1	184	33	Ruether, Dutch*	13–6	1.38	2.2	2.5	0.4	4.17	3.38	4.30	8	0.8
21	8	166	27	Pipgras, George	10–3	1.35	4.4	4.2	0.1	3.65	4.11	4.38	7	0.6
9	12	89	29	Thomas, Myles	7–4	1.74	2.5	4.4	0.4	4.57	4.87	5.89	-12	-1.1
12	38	213	30	Moore, Wilcy	19–7	1.15	3.2	2.5	0.1	3.32	2.28	2.87	44	4.2
2	17	44	36	Shawkey, Bob	2–3	1.37	4.7	3.3	0.2	3.47	2.89	3.92	4	0.4
0	16	27	28	Giard, Joe*	0–0	2.11	3.3	6.3	0.3	4.91	8.00	8.33	-11	-1.0
0	1	1	27	Beall, Walter	0–0	1.00	0.0	0.0	0.0	3.06	9.00	9.00	0	0.0
155	109			Team Total		1.30	2.79	2.65	0.27	3.75	3.20	3.92	124	11.7
			30.6	League Average		1.46	2.78	3.30	0.36	4.13	4.14	4.98		
				% Lg Avg		112	100	124	132	110	129	127		
				League Rank		1	3	1	3	1	1			

1928 Philadelphia Athletics

The Yankees came back to earth in 1928 but still won the pennant for the third straight season over an improved A's squad. The Yankees led the league in offense (runs scored per game) and the A's led the league in defense (runs allowed per game). The 1928 A's were a talented bunch with good slugging and excellent pitching. Their head-to-head W–L record of 6–16 against the Yankees was their undoing. This team became the nucleus for 3 consecutive pennant winning teams beginning in 1929. Twenty-year-old Foxx showed everyone a preview of his Hall of Fame career with his .328/.416/.548 season in 1928.

Strengths: (1) SP, RP, C, 1B, 2B, 3B, and LF positions, (2) hitting for average and power led by Simmons (33 2B, 9 3B), Foxx (29 2B, 10 3B), Miller (34 2B), Bishop, and Cochrane (26 2B, 12 3B), (3) depth with 10 everyday players and 6 pitchers having above league average seasons, (4) drawing walks featuring Bishop (100 BB) and Cochrane (76 BB), (5) fielding led by 3B Hale (114 Rng+) and 2B Bishop (99 Rng+), and (6) pitching anchored by Grove (183 K, 4 Sv), Rommel (4 Sv), Quinn, and Walberg.

Weaknesses: (1) SS position, (2) hitting and fielding from SS Boley (90 Rng+), (3) DP made, (4) SB%, and (5) 32 CS% from Cochrane.

Mgr	Connie Mack	
Rk	19	47
Gm	153	
Place	2	
GB	2.5	
Rival	6–16 vs Yankees, 93 RS & 138 RA	

	W	L	Win%
Regular Season	98	55	0.641
Runs Record	99	54	0.644
1 Run	30	13	0.698
Extra Innings	8	0	1.000
Blowout	35	17	0.673

	Team	LgAvg	%Avg	LgRk
BABIP	0.283	0.299	105	1
E	183	193	105	3
sOBP	0.311	0.342	110	1
rOBP	0.349	0.354	101	3
R/G	5.41	4.77	113	2
RA/G	4.02	4.77	119	1

	Tm	LgAvg	>Avg
RS	828	735	93
RA	615	733	118
DP	124	146	-22

	R/G	HR	K	BB	SB	CS	SB%	OBP
Team Offense	5.41	89	435	532	59	54	52%	0.363
Team Defense	4.02	66	607	424	83	40	67%	0.318
Difference	1.39	23	172	108	-24			114%

Pos	Rpos	PA	Age	Name	BA	OBP	SLG	BB%	RS%	Bat R>Avg	BR R>Avg	Fld R>Avg	RAA	WAA
C	4	568	25	Cochrane, Mickey*	0.293	0.395	0.464	13%	40%	23	0	-3	24	2.3
1B	-4	366	29	Hauser, Joe*	0.260	0.369	0.517	14%	39%	16	0	0	12	1.1
2B	4	589	28	Bishop, Max*	0.316	0.438	0.432	17%	40%	30	-2	3	35	3.4
3B	2	336	31	Hale, Sammy	0.309	0.334	0.468	3%	32%	5	1	5	13	1.3
SS	8	479	31	Boley, Joe	0.264	0.317	0.325	7%	34%	-15	1	-5	-11	-1.1
LF	-5	509	26	Simmons, Al	0.351	0.396	0.558	6%	35%	34	-1	4	32	3.1
RF,CF	-5	564	33	Miller, Bing	0.329	0.372	0.471	5%	35%	18	0	6	19	1.8
RF	-4	393	41	Cobb, Ty*	0.323	0.389	0.431	9%	35%	11	-2	2	7	0.7
3B,1B	1	473	20	Foxx, Jimmie	0.328	0.416	0.548	13%	40%	34	-3	3	35	3.4
CF	-2	365	24	Haas, Mule*	0.280	0.331	0.422	6%	31%	0	0	-2	-4	-0.4

Pos	Rpos	PA	Age	Name	BA	OBP	SLG	BB%	RS%	Bat R>Avg	BR R>Avg	Fld R>Avg	RAA	WAA
2B,SS	3	286	31	Dykes, Jimmy	0.277	0.361	0.384	9%	36%	1	0	0	4	0.4
CF	-1	212	40	Speaker, Tris*	0.267	0.310	0.450	5%	42%	0	1	-1	-1	-0.1
1B,P	0	191	27	Orwoll, Ossie*	0.306	0.366	0.406	8%	41%	2	0	1	3	0.3
	-1	675		Others	0.215	0.261	0.275	5%	32%	-46	2	-2	-47	-4.6
	0		29.7	Team Total	0.294	0.363	0.436	8.9%	36.6%	114	-3	11	122	11.8
				League Average	0.281	0.344	0.397	8.0%	35.0%					
				% Lg Avg	105	106	110	111	104					
				League Rank	2	2	2	3			6	2		

GS	GR	IP	Age	Name	W–L	WHIP	K/9	BB/9	HR/9	FIP	ERA	RAA	RAA	WAA
31	8	262	28	Grove, Lefty*	24–8	1.12	6.3	2.2	0.3	2.87	2.58	3.20	45	4.3
30	8	236	31	Walberg, Rube*	17–12	1.27	4.3	2.4	0.7	3.98	3.55	4.24	13	1.3
28	3	211	44	Quinn, Jack	18–7	1.29	1.8	1.4	0.1	3.39	2.90	3.92	19	1.8
22	4	158	28	Earnshaw, George	7–7	1.53	6.7	5.7	0.4	4.04	3.81	4.60	2	0.2
18	5	139	34	Ehmke, Howard	9–8	1.28	2.2	2.8	0.4	4.14	3.62	4.20	8	0.8
11	32	174	30	Rommel, Eddie	13–5	1.17	1.9	1.3	0.6	3.91	3.06	3.63	21	2.1
8	19	106	27	Orwoll, Ossie*	6–5	1.51	4.5	4.2	0.6	4.36	4.58	5.01	-3	-0.3
2	9	35	35	Bush, Joe	2–1	1.61	3.8	4.6	0.3	4.16	5.09	5.35	-2	-0.2
2	1	14	24	Shores, Bill	1–1	1.43	3.2	4.5	0.0	3.82	3.21	4.50	0	0.0
0	9	12	22	Powers, Ike	1–0	1.50	3.0	7.5	0.8	6.20	4.50	4.50	0	0.0
1	5	20		Others	0–1	1.38	1.8	3.1	0.4	4.31	3.54	4.43	1	0.1
153	103		30.3	Team Total		1.30	3.99	2.79	0.43	3.75	3.36	4.05	104	10.1
				League Average		1.43	3.04	3.14	0.40	4.04	4.04	4.81		
				% Lg Avg		110	132	112	91	108	120	119		
				League Rank		1	1	1	7	1	1			

1929 Philadelphia Athletics

Connie Mack had meticulously reconstructed the Philadelphia Athletics, the team he dismantled after the 1914 season. It took him 15 years of re-building to once again repeat as the pennant winner. The A's led the AL in fewest runs allowed per game and nearly led the league in most runs per game absolutely dominating the competition and winning the pennant by 18 games over the former world champion Yankees and beating the Cubs in 5 games in the World Series.

Strengths: (1) hitting for average and power featuring Foxx (33 HR), Simmons (41 2B, 34 HR), Dykes (34 2B), Miller (16 3B), Cochrane (37 2B), and Haas (41 2B), (2) drawing walks led by Bishop (128 BB), Foxx (103 BB), and Cochrane (68 BB), (3) fielding from LF Simmons (117 Rng+, 19 assists, and four errors in 372 chances), and (4) pitching anchored by Grove (170K), Walberg, Earnshaw, Shores, and Rommel. The stolen base leader was Miller (24 SB, 9 CS).

Weaknesses: (1) hitting from Hale, Boley, and Perkins, (2) double plays made, (3) fielding from SS/3B Dykes (96 Rng+ at SS, 100 Rng+ at 3B with 11 errors in 150 chances), and (4) CS% from Perkins (25%) and Cochrane (35%).

Mgr	Connie Mack	
Rk	19	47
Gm	153	
Place	2	
GB	2.5	
Rival	6–16 vs Yankees, 93 RS & 138 RA	

	W	L	Win%
Regular Season	98	55	0.641
Runs Record	99	54	0.644
1 Run	30	13	0.698
Extra Innings	8	0	1.000
Blowout	35	17	0.673

	Team	LgAvg	%Avg	LgRk
BABIP	0.283	0.299	105	1
E	183	193	105	3
sOBP	0.311	0.342	110	1
rOBP	0.349	0.354	101	3
R/G	5.41	4.77	113	2
RA/G	4.02	4.77	119	1

	Tm	LgAvg	>Avg
RS	828	735	93
RA	615	733	118
DP	124	146	-22

	R/G	HR	K	BB	SB	CS	SB%	OBP
Team Offense	5.41	89	435	532	59	54	52%	0.363
Team Defense	4.02	66	607	424	83	40	67%	0.318
Difference	1.39	23	172	108	-24			114%

Pos	Rpos	PA	Age	Name	BA	OBP	SLG	BB%	RS%	Bat R>Avg	BR R>Avg	Fld R>Avg	RAA	WAA
C	4	568	25	Cochrane, Mickey*	0.293	0.395	0.464	13%	40%	23	0	-3	24	2.3
1B	-4	366	29	Hauser, Joe*	0.260	0.369	0.517	14%	39%	16	0	0	12	1.1
2B	4	589	28	Bishop, Max*	0.316	0.438	0.432	17%	40%	30	-2	3	35	3.4
3B	2	336	31	Hale, Sammy	0.309	0.334	0.468	3%	32%	5	1	5	13	1.3
SS	8	479	31	Boley, Joe	0.264	0.317	0.325	7%	34%	-15	1	-5	-11	-1.1
LF	-5	509	26	Simmons, Al	0.351	0.396	0.558	6%	35%	34	-1	4	32	3.1
RF,CF	-5	564	33	Miller, Bing	0.329	0.372	0.471	5%	35%	18	0	6	19	1.8
RF	-4	393	41	Cobb, Ty*	0.323	0.389	0.431	9%	35%	11	-2	2	7	0.7
3B,1B	1	473	20	Foxx, Jimmie	0.328	0.416	0.548	13%	40%	34	-3	3	35	3.4
CF	-2	365	24	Haas, Mule*	0.280	0.331	0.422	6%	31%	0	0	-2	-4	-0.4
2B,SS	3	286	31	Dykes, Jimmy	0.277	0.361	0.384	9%	36%	1	0	0	4	0.4
CF	-1	212	40	Speaker, Tris*	0.267	0.310	0.450	5%	42%	0	1	-1	-1	-0.1
1B,P	0	191	27	Orwoll, Ossie*	0.306	0.366	0.406	8%	41%	2	0	1	3	0.3
	-1	675		Others	0.215	0.261	0.275	5%	32%	-46	2	-2	-47	-4.6
	0		29.7	Team Total	0.294	0.363	0.436	8.9%	36.6%	114	-3	11	122	11.8
				League Average	0.281	0.344	0.397	8.0%	35.0%					
				% Lg Avg	105	106	110	111	104					
				League Rank	2	2	2	3			6	2		

GS	GR	IP	Age	Name	W–L	WHIP	K/9	BB/9	HR/9	FIP	ERA	RAA	RAA	WAA
31	8	262	28	Grove, Lefty*	24–8	1.12	6.3	2.2	0.3	2.87	2.58	3.20	45	4.3
30	8	236	31	Walberg, Rube*	17–12	1.27	4.3	2.4	0.7	3.98	3.55	4.24	13	1.3
28	3	211	44	Quinn, Jack	18–7	1.29	1.8	1.4	0.1	3.39	2.90	3.92	19	1.8
22	4	158	28	Earnshaw, George	7–7	1.53	6.7	5.7	0.4	4.04	3.81	4.60	2	0.2
18	5	139	34	Ehmke, Howard	9–8	1.28	2.2	2.8	0.4	4.14	3.62	4.20	8	0.8
11	32	174	30	Rommel, Eddie	13–5	1.17	1.9	1.3	0.6	3.91	3.06	3.63	21	2.1
8	19	106	27	Orwoll, Ossie*	6–5	1.51	4.5	4.2	0.6	4.36	4.58	5.01	-3	-0.3
2	9	35	35	Bush, Joe	2–1	1.61	3.8	4.6	0.3	4.16	5.09	5.35	-2	-0.2
2	1	14	24	Shores, Bill	1–1	1.43	3.2	4.5	0.0	3.82	3.21	4.50	0	0.0
0	9	12	22	Powers, Ike	1–0	1.50	3.0	7.5	0.8	6.20	4.50	4.50	0	0.0
1	5	20		Others	0–1	1.38	1.8	3.1	0.4	4.31	3.54	4.43	1	0.1
153	103		30.3	Team Total		1.30	3.99	2.79	0.43	3.75	3.36	4.05	104	10.1
				League Average		1.43	3.04	3.14	0.40	4.04	4.04	4.81		
				% Lg Avg		110	132	112	91	108	120	119		
				League Rank		1	1	1	7	1	1			

1930 Washington Senators

The 1930 Senators were a strong second place team that had impressive winning records against the first place A's and the third place Yankees but struggled against the sixth place Browns. This team improved by 29 games from their finish in 1929. Goslin got off to a slow start and was traded in mid–June to the Browns for LF Manush and starting pitcher Crowder who both had effective seasons. Goslin would return to the Senators in time for their pennant winning 1933 season. The team 3.96 ERA was the highest league leading ERA to date.

Strengths: (1) hitting led by Cronin (41 2B, 9 3B, 13 HR), Judge (29 2B, 11 3B), Manush (33 2B), Rice (35 2B, 13 3B), West (10 3B), and Harris, (2) fielding featuring SS Cronin (121 Rng+, 95 DP), 3B Bluege (104 Rng+), 2B Myer (97 Rng+), CF West (100 Rng+, 8 assists), and RF Rice (116 Rng+, 13 assists), (3) CS% from Spencer (56% CS), and (4) starting pitching depth.

Weaknesses: (1) C position, (2) hitting from Spencer and Ruel, and (3) ballpark effects limiting home-runs and isolated power.

				W	L	Win%		Team	LgAvg	%Avg	LgRk
Mgr	Walter Johnson		**Regular Season**	94	60	0.610	**BABIP**	0.285	0.306	107	1
Rk	39	95	**Runs Record**	96	58	0.624	**E**	155	194	125	2
Gm	154		**1 Run**	23	21	0.523	**sOBP**	0.329	0.345	105	1

			W	L	Win%
Place	2	Extra Innings	6	5	0.545
GB	8.0	Blowout	32	12	0.727
Rival	12–10 vs A's, 17–5 vs NY, 10–12 vs Browns				

	Team	LgAvg	%Avg	LgRk
rOBP	0.344	0.372	108	1
R/G	5.79	5.41	107	3
RA/G	4.46	5.41	121	1

	Tm	LgAvg	>Avg
RS	892	834	58
RA	687	833	146
DP	150	146	4

	R/G	HR	K	BB	SB	CS	SB%	OBP
Team Offense	5.79	57	438	533	101	68	60%	0.369
Team Defense	4.46	52	524	504	58	53	52%	0.332
Difference	1.33	5	86	29	43			111%

Pos	Rpos	PA	Age	Name	BA	OBP	SLG	BB%	RS%	Bat R>Avg	BR R>Avg	Fld R>Avg	RAA	WAA
C	3	350	30	Spencer, Roy	0.255	0.303	0.315	5%	31%	-18	1	0	-14	-1.3
1B	-5	515	36	Judge, Joe*	0.326	0.410	0.509	12%	37%	26	1	4	26	2.3
2B	4	617	26	Myer, Buddy*	0.303	0.373	0.377	9%	43%	-1	-1	5	7	0.6
3B	3	562	29	Bluege, Ossie	0.290	0.368	0.395	9%	31%	1	0	9	13	1.1
SS	10	686	23	Cronin, Joe	0.346	0.422	0.513	10%	43%	38	0	20	68	6.2
LF	-4	393	28	Manush, Heinie*	0.362	0.406	0.559	7%	45%	25	0	3	24	2.1
CF	-2	458	25	West, Sammy*	0.328	0.385	0.474	8%	41%	14	-1	9	20	1.8
RF,CF	-6	668	40	Rice, Sam*	0.349	0.407	0.457	8%	45%	23	0	11	28	2.6
RF,OF	-2	242	29	Harris, Dave	0.317	0.399	0.546	12%	40%	13	0	2	13	1.2
C	2	229	34	Ruel, Muddy	0.253	0.342	0.308	10%	23%	-8	1	1	-4	-0.3
LF	-2	214	29	Goslin, Goose*	0.271	0.344	0.495	9%	42%	4	0	-2	0	0.0
2B,3B	1	178	23	Hayes, Jackie	0.283	0.312	0.367	4%	45%	-6	-1	4	-2	-0.2
CF,LF	-1	160	28	Loepp, George	0.276	0.382	0.343	13%	38%	-1	-2	-2	-6	-0.5
1B	-1	91	23	Shires, Art*	0.369	0.404	0.464	5%	29%	3	-1	0	1	0.1
	0	754		Others	0.204	0.266	0.280	7%	34%	-57	1	0	-56	-5.1
	0		28.8	Team Total	0.302	0.369	0.425	8.7%	39.1%	56	-2	64	118	10.7
				League Average	0.288	0.351	0.421	8.2%	37.9%					
				% Lg Avg	105	105	101	106	103					
				League Rank	3	2	4	3			5	1		

GS	GR	IP	Age	Name	W–L	WHIP	K/9	BB/9	HR/9	FIP	ERA	R/9	RAA	WAA
34	8	260	25	Hadley, Bump	15–11	1.33	5.6	3.6	0.2	3.78	3.73	4.25	25	2.2
25	2	202	31	Crowder, General	15–9	1.29	2.9	3.1	0.3	4.23	3.60	4.00	24	2.2
22	16	197	25	Brown, Lloyd*	16–12	1.45	2.7	3.0	0.3	4.31	4.25	4.52	12	1.1
22	11	185	31	Marberry, Firpo	15–5	1.31	2.7	2.6	0.7	4.76	4.09	4.48	12	1.1
25	0	183	37	Jones, Sad Sam	15–7	1.40	2.9	3.0	0.2	4.13	4.08	4.66	8	0.7
16	16	151	23	Liska, Ad	9–7	1.40	2.4	4.2	0.4	4.95	3.28	4.12	16	1.4
0	15	27	30	Braxton, Garland*	3–2	1.14	2.3	3.0	1.0	5.35	3.30	3.63	4	0.4
4	20	74	23	Burke, Bobby*	3–4	1.22	4.2	3.5	0.2	4.15	3.63	4.97	1	0.1
4	4	33	24	Fischer, Carl*	1–1	1.65	5.7	4.9	0.0	3.99	4.86	5.95	-3	-0.3
0	4	12	23	Moore, Carlos	0–0	1.11	1.5	3.1	0.0	4.13	2.31	2.31	4	0.3
2	15	44		Others	2–2	1.80	3.5	4.1	0.8	5.23	7.81	8.63	-17	-1.6
154	111		27.2	Team Total		1.37	3.44	3.31	0.34	4.34	3.96	4.52	86	7.8
				League Average		1.50	3.38	3.28	0.56	4.65	4.65	5.50		
				% Lg Avg		109	102	99	162	107	117	122		
				League Rank		1	4	5	1	1	1			

1931 PHILADELPHIA ATHLETICS

The 1931 A's were the last of the consecutive trio of pennant winning A's teams. They featured 3 of the top 10 league positional seasons and 3 of the top 10 AL pitching seasons including one of the best performances of all time by MVP Lefty Grove to beat a talented second place Yankee team by a whopping 13.5 games. The Cardinals upset the A's in 7 games in the Series.

Strengths: (1) hitting for average and power led by Simmons (37 2B, 13 3B, 22 HR), Cochrane (31 2B, 17 HR), Foxx (32 2B, 10 3B, 30 HR), Bishop, and Haas (29 2B), (3) drawing walks especially from Bishop (112 BB) and Foxx (73 BB), (4) fielding featuring 2B Bishop (102 Rng+, only 12 errors in 740 chances), SS Williams (106 Rng+), RF Bing Miller (118 Rng+), and LF Simmons (115 Rng+, 10 assists), (5) CS% from Heving (48%) and Cochrane

(42%), and (6) pitching anchored by Triple Crown winner Grove (175 K, 5 Sv), Walberg, Earnshaw (6 Sv), and starter/reliever Rommel.

Weaknesses: (1) SS position, (2) hitting from Boley, Cramer, McNair, Heving, Todt, and Williams, (3) positional bench depth, (4) hitting for contact, (5) team speed especially SB and SB%, and (6) control from Shores and McDonald.

				W	L	Win%		Team	LgAvg	%Avg	LgRk
Mgr	Connie Mack		**Regular Season**	107	45	0.704	**BABIP**	0.276	0.296	107	1
Rk	12	30	**Runs Record**	100	52	0.659	**E**	140	196	140	1
Gm	153		**1 Run**	19	14	0.576	**sOBP**	0.312	0.340	109	1
Place	1		**Extra Innings**	7	4	0.636	**rOBP**	0.342	0.359	105	2
GA	13.5		**Blowout**	31	14	0.689	**R/G**	5.61	5.14	109	3
Rival	11–11 vs Yankees, 97 RS & 124 RA						**RA/G**	4.09	5.14	126	1

	Tm	LgAvg	>Avg
RS	858	794	64
RA	626	794	168
DP	151	141	10

	R/G	HR	K	BB	SB	CS	SB%	OBP
Team Offense	5.61	118	543	528	25	23	52%	0.355
Team Defense	4.09	73	574	457	66	51	56%	0.316
Difference	1.52	45	31	71	-41			112%

Pos	Rpos	PA	Age	Name	BA	OBP	SLG	BB%	RS%	Bat R>Avg	BR R>Avg	Fld R>Avg	RAA	WAA
C	4	521	28	Cochrane, Mickey*	0.349	0.423	0.553	11%	35%	40	0	0	44	4.6
1B,3B	-5	593	23	Foxx, Jimmie	0.291	0.380	0.567	12%	32%	37	0	4	36	3.8
2B	4	614	31	Bishop, Max*	0.294	0.426	0.400	18%	43%	24	1	18	47	4.9
3B,SS	3	414	34	Dykes, Jimmy	0.273	0.371	0.389	12%	30%	4	0	2	9	1.0
SS,2B	5	315	21	Williams, Dib	0.269	0.313	0.384	6%	38%	-6	1	3	3	0.4
LF	-6	563	29	Simmons, Al	0.390	0.444	0.641	8%	36%	63	0	9	66	6.9
CF	-2	489	27	Haas, Mule*	0.323	0.366	0.475	6%	45%	15	1	2	16	1.7
RF	-6	585	36	Miller, Bing	0.281	0.338	0.425	6%	36%	3	1	11	9	1.0
3B,2B	2	299	22	McNair, Eric	0.271	0.306	0.368	4%	44%	-8	-1	2	-5	-0.5
SS	4	244	34	Boley, Joe	0.228	0.282	0.295	6%	38%	-14	0	3	-7	-0.7
CF,RF	-1	242	25	Cramer, Doc*	0.260	0.301	0.341	5%	51%	-8	0	0	-9	-1.0
1B	-2	207	29	Todt, Phil*	0.244	0.273	0.411	4%	35%	-6	0	0	-8	-0.8
C	1	121	35	Heving, Johnny	0.239	0.277	0.327	5%	22%	-6	0	-1	-6	-0.6
LF,RF	0	32	20	Finney, Lou*	0.375	0.516	0.458	19%	44%	3	0	1	4	0.4
	-1	781		Others	0.213	0.266	0.285	6%	32%	-51	1	0	-51	-5.3
	0		28.1	Team Total	0.287	0.355	0.435	8.8%	37.2%	93	4	54	151	15.8
				League Average	0.279	0.344	0.396	8.6%	36.2%					
				% Lg Avg	103	103	110	102	103					
				League Rank	3	3	2	3	3		3	1		

GS	GR	IP	Age	Name	W–L	WHIP	K/9	BB/9	HR/9	FIP	ERA	R/9	RAA	WAA
35	9	291	34	Walberg, Rube*	20–12	1.40	3.3	3.4	0.5	4.36	3.74	4.11	23	2.4
30	11	289	31	Grove, Lefty*	31–4	1.08	5.5	1.9	0.3	3.15	2.06	2.62	72	7.5
30	13	282	31	Earnshaw, George	21–7	1.17	4.9	2.4	0.5	3.74	3.67	4.15	22	2.3
20	10	162	28	Mahaffey, Roy	15–4	1.50	3.3	4.5	0.5	4.82	4.21	4.82	0	0.0
14	2	111	31	Hoyt, Waite	10–5	1.50	2.4	3.0	0.7	4.77	4.22	4.86	-1	-0.1
10	9	70	20	McDonald, Hank	2–4	1.46	2.9	5.2	0.4	4.95	3.71	5.50	-5	-0.5
10	15	118	33	Rommel, Eddie	7–5	1.38	1.4	2.1	0.4	4.21	2.97	3.81	13	1.3
2	4	16	27	Shores, Bill	0–3	2.25	1.1	5.6	1.7	7.32	5.06	10.13	-10	-1.0
1	2	11	19	Krausse, Lew	1–0	1.09	0.8	4.9	1.6	7.07	4.09	4.91	0	0.0
1	7	15		Others	0–1	1.76	4.7	4.7	0.0	3.78	8.22	8.81	-7	-0.7
153	82		28.2	Team Total		1.32	3.78	3.01	0.48	4.13	3.47	4.13	107	11.1
				League Average		1.48	3.30	3.40	0.47	4.38	4.38	5.19		
				% Lg Avg		112	115	113	98	106	126	126		
				League Rank		1	2	2	7	2	1			

1931 New York Yankees

The Yankees had a terrific run differential of 2.0 runs per game and were one of the best second place teams of all-time. Even though they lost the pennant by 13.5 games, this Yankee team had a half run larger run differential per game than the first place A's. Their 11–11 W–L versus against the A's despite outscoring them by 27 runs was prototypical of their unlucky season. This Yankee team easily led the AL in offense but had below league average fielding and pitching.

Strengths: (1) hitting featuring great seasons from Ruth (31 2B, 46 HR, 374 TB, 199 H), Gehrig (31 2B, 15 3B, 46 HR, 410 TB, 211 H), Chapman (28 2B, 11 3B, 17 HR), Combs (31 2B, 13 3B), Lary (35 2B, 9 3B), and Dickey (10 3B), (2) drawing walks led by Ruth (128 BB), Gehrig (117 BB), and Lazzeri (79 BB), (3) baserunning especially from Chapman (61 SB, 23 CS), (4) fielding from LF/RF Chapman (123 Rng+ in LF, 14 assists), (5) CS% from Dickey (46%), and (6) pitching from Gomez and Pennock.

Weaknesses: (1) SP and RP positions, (2) hitting from Reese, (3) bench hitting, (4) fielding from 1B Gehrig and OF Byrd (76 Rng+ in the OF), (5) double plays made, (6) team relief pitching, and (7) pitching from Sherid.

Mgr	Joe McCarthy	
Rk	14	33
Gm	155	
Place	2	
GB	13.5	
Rival	11–11 vs A's, 124 RS & 97 RA	

	W	*L*	*Win%*
Regular Season	94	59	0.614
Runs Record	100	53	0.655
1 Run	19	20	0.487
Extra Innings	5	11	0.313
Blowout	44	9	0.830

	Team	*LgAvg*	*%Avg*	*LgRk*
BABIP	0.294	0.296	101	3
E	167	196	117	3
sOBP	0.328	0.340	104	2
rOBP	0.365	0.359	98	4
R/G	6.88	5.14	134	1
RA/G	4.90	5.14	105	3

	Tm	*LgAvg*	*>Avg*
RS	1067	794	273
RA	760	794	34
DP	131	141	-10

	R/G	*HR*	*K*	*BB*	*SB*	*CS*	*SB%*	*OBP*
Team Offense	6.88	155	554	750	139	68	67%	0.383
Team Defense	4.90	67	686	543	71	54	57%	0.335
Difference	1.98	88	132	207	68			114%

Pos	*Rpos*	*PA*	*Age*	*Name*	*BA*	*OBP*	*SLG*	*BB%*	*RS%*	*Bat R>Avg*	*BR R>Avg*	*Fld R>Avg*	*RAA*	*WAA*
C	4	523	24	Dickey, Bill*	0.327	0.378	0.442	7%	31%	14	1	3	22	2.1
1B	-7	738	28	Gehrig, Lou*	0.341	0.446	0.662	16%	41%	85	-1	-8	69	6.4
2B,3B	4	568	27	Lazzeri, Tony	0.267	0.371	0.401	14%	29%	8	0	1	13	1.2
3B	2	571	32	Sewell, Joe*	0.302	0.390	0.388	11%	46%	10	1	0	13	1.3
SS	10	712	25	Lary, Lyn	0.280	0.376	0.416	12%	35%	15	-1	1	25	2.3
LF,RF	-6	686	22	Chapman, Ben	0.315	0.396	0.483	11%	41%	32	3	10	39	3.6
CF	-2	636	32	Combs, Earle*	0.318	0.394	0.446	11%	47%	23	2	-2	21	2.0
RF,LF	-6	663	36	Ruth, Babe*	0.373	0.495	0.700	19%	37%	96	0	-2	88	8.2
CF,OF	-3	281	24	Byrd, Sammy	0.270	0.349	0.395	10%	51%	1	2	-5	-5	-0.5
2B	2	265	29	Reese, Jimmie*	0.241	0.293	0.335	6%	51%	-11	0	-2	-11	-1.0
C	1	111	26	Jorgens, Art	0.270	0.330	0.320	8%	33%	-3	0	-1	-3	-0.3
LF,RF	-1	47	24	Cooke, Dusty*	0.333	0.447	0.436	17%	45%	3	0	0	2	0.2
P	0	116	26	Ruffing, Red	0.330	0.336	0.505	1%	32%	3	0	0	3	0.3
	2	556	0	Others	0.171	0.222	0.218	6%	45%	-56	1	-4	-57	-5.3
	0			Team Total	0.297	0.383	0.457	11.6%	39.8%	220	8	-9	219	20.4
				League Average	0.279	0.344	0.396	8.6%	36.2%					
				% Lg Avg	107	111	116	135	110					
				League Rank	1	1	1	1			2	4		

GS	*GR*	*IP*	*Age*	*Name*	*W–L*	*WHIP*	*K/9*	*BB/9*	*HR/9*	*FIP*	*ERA*	*R/9*	*RAA*	*WAA*
26	14	243	22	Gomez, Lefty*	21–9	1.20	5.6	3.1	0.3	3.49	2.67	3.26	53	5.0
30	7	237	26	Ruffing, Red	16–14	1.38	5.0	3.3	0.4	3.92	4.41	4.94	8	0.7
23	17	196	25	Johnson, Hank	13–8	1.42	4.9	4.7	0.6	4.61	4.72	5.23	0	0.0
25	0	189	37	Pennock, Herb*	11–6	1.46	3.1	1.4	0.3	3.54	4.28	4.56	14	1.3
11	7	87	23	Rhodes, Gordon	6–3	1.54	3.7	5.4	0.3	4.67	3.41	5.07	2	0.2
14	22	138	31	Pipgras, George	7–6	1.39	3.9	3.8	0.5	4.46	3.79	4.77	7	0.7
10	17	117	31	Wells, Ed*	9–5	1.43	2.6	2.9	0.5	4.43	4.32	5.24	0	0.0
8	9	74	24	Sherid, Roy	5–5	1.59	4.7	2.9	0.5	3.99	5.69	6.30	-9	-0.8
5	12	58	27	Weaver, Jim	2–1	1.65	4.4	4.5	0.2	4.07	5.30	5.77	-3	-0.3
3	4	34	24	Andrews, Ivy	2–0	1.28	2.6	2.1	0.8	4.51	4.20	4.46	3	0.3
0	23	37		Others	2–2	2.19	6.6	7.5	0.7	5.85	8.03	8.76	-14	-1.3

GS	GR	IP	Age	Name	W–L	WHIP	K/9	BB/9	HR/9	FIP	ERA	R/9	RAA	WAA
155	132			Team Total		1.42	4.38	3.47	0.43	4.11	4.20	4.85	62	5.7
				League Average		1.48	3.32	3.40	0.47	4.38	4.38	5.19		
				% Lg Avg		104	132	98	110	107	104	107		
				League Rank		3	1	5	3	1	3			

1932 New York Yankees

The 1932 Yankees led the league in most runs scored per game and least runs allowed per game. Despite another super season, Babe Ruth was less fit at 37 years old with nagging aches and pains limiting his games played and plate appearances. Dickey was suspended 30 days for punching out Senators OF Carl Reynolds and breaking his jaw. This offensive powerhouse team did not get shut out all season. This powerful team swept the Cubs in the World Series.

Strengths: (1) SP, 1B, 2B, LF, CF, and RF positions, (2) hitting for average and power led by Gehrig (42 2B, 9 3B, 34 HR), Ruth (41 HR), Lazzeri (28 2B, 16 3B, 15 HR), Combs (32 2B, 10 3B), Chapman (41 2B, 15 3B), and Dickey (15 HR), (3) drawing walks featuring Ruth (130 BB), Gehrig (108 BB), Lazzeri (82 BB), and Combs (81 BB), and (4) starting pitching especially K/9 anchored by Ruffing (190 K), Allen, and Gomez (176 K). The stolen base leader was Chapman (38 SB, 18 CS).

Weaknesses: (1) hitting from Jorgens and Crosetti, (2) fielding especially from CF Byrd (64 Rng+) and LF Hoag (35 Rng+), (3) CS% from Dickey (38%) and Jorgens (29%), and (4) DP made.

Mgr	Joe McCarthy	
Rk	15	35
Gm	156	
Place	1	
GA	13.0	
Rival	14–8 vs A's, 168 RS & 125 RA	

	W	L	Win%
Regular Season	107	47	0.695
Runs Record	101	53	0.653
1 Run	32	19	0.627
Extra Innings	9	7	0.563
Blowout	39	11	0.780

	Team	LgAvg	%Avg	LgRk
BABIP	0.290	0.292	101	5
E	190	187	98	5
sOBP	0.326	0.341	105	2
rOBP	0.372	0.365	98	6
R/G	6.42	5.23	123	1
RA/G	4.64	5.23	113	1

	Tm	LgAvg	>Avg
RS	1002	804	198
RA	724	804	80
DP	124	150	-26

	R/G	HR	K	BB	SB	CS	SB%	OBP
Team Offense	6.42	160	526	765	77	66	54%	0.376
Team Defense	4.64	93	780	561	66	39	63%	0.332
Difference	1.78	67	254	204	11			113%

Pos	Rpos	PA	Age	Name	BA	OBP	SLG	BB%	RS%	Bat R>Avg	BR R>Avg	Fld R>Avg	RAA	WAA
C	4	459	25	Dickey, Bill*	0.310	0.361	0.482	7%	34%	13	-1	-1	15	1.4
1B	-7	708	29	Gehrig, Lou*	0.349	0.451	0.621	15%	36%	74	-3	-4	60	5.5
2B	5	601	28	Lazzeri, Tony	0.300	0.399	0.506	14%	29%	31	-2	1	35	3.2
3B	2	576	33	Sewell, Joe*	0.272	0.349	0.392	10%	45%	-1	0	4	5	0.5
SS,3B	6	461	21	Crosetti, Frankie	0.241	0.335	0.374	11%	29%	-6	0	-4	-4	-0.3
LF,RF	-8	662	23	Chapman, Ben	0.299	0.381	0.473	11%	38%	23	1	7	23	2.1
CF,LF	-4	675	33	Combs, Earle*	0.321	0.405	0.455	12%	51%	27	-2	4	25	2.3
RF,LF	-6	589	37	Ruth, Babe*	0.341	0.489	0.661	22%	32%	75	0	0	69	6.4
SS	5	339	26	Lary, Lyn	0.232	0.358	0.343	15%	45%	-3	1	-3	0	0.0
CF,OF	-2	243	24	Byrd, Sammy	0.297	0.385	0.478	12%	49%	9	0	-14	-7	-0.6
C	1	166	27	Jorgens, Art	0.219	0.285	0.318	8%	24%	-9	0	-1	-9	-0.8
LF,RF	-1	61	24	Hoag, Myril	0.370	0.443	0.519	11%	65%	5	0	-6	-2	-0.2
P	0	132	28	Ruffing, Red	0.306	0.338	0.444	5%	41%	1	0	0	1	0.1
	5	672		Others	0.169	0.227	0.227	6%	38%	-67	2	-1	-61	-5.6
	0		27.5	Team Total	0.286	0.376	0.454	12.1%	38.3%	172	-4	-18	150	13.9
				League Average	0.277	0.346	0.404	9.0%	36.1%					
				% Lg Avg	103	109	112	133	106					
				League Rank	2	1	2	1			7	6		

GS	GR	IP	Age	Name	W–L	WHIP	K/9	BB/9	HR/9	FIP	ERA	R/9	RAA	WAA
31	6	265	23	Gomez, Lefty*	24–7	1.40	6.0	3.6	0.8	4.14	4.21	4.75	18	1.7
29	6	259	28	Ruffing, Red	18–7	1.29	6.6	4.0	0.6	3.83	3.09	3.54	52	4.8

GS	GR	IP	Age	Name	W–L	WHIP	K/9	BB/9	HR/9	FIP	ERA	R/9	RAA	WAA
27	5	219	32	Pipgras, George	16–9	1.47	4.6	3.6	0.6	4.28	4.19	4.93	11	1.0
21	12	192	26	Allen, Johnny	17–4	1.24	5.1	3.6	0.5	3.93	3.70	4.03	28	2.6
21	1	147	38	Pennock, Herb*	9–5	1.56	3.3	2.3	0.5	3.88	4.60	5.77	-6	-0.6
15	2	121	27	MacFayden, Danny	7–5	1.43	2.4	2.7	0.8	4.73	3.93	5.12	4	0.3
3	16	56	25	Brown, Jumbo	5–2	1.58	5.0	4.9	0.2	3.97	4.53	4.85	3	0.3
0	22	32	32	Wells, Ed*	3–3	1.58	3.7	3.4	0.3	3.85	4.26	5.40	0	0.0
1	9	25	35	Moore, Wilcy	2–0	1.32	2.9	2.2	0.4	3.73	2.52	2.88	7	0.6
1	3	25	25	Andrews, Ivy	2–1	1.18	2.6	3.3	0.0	3.65	1.82	2.92	7	0.6
7	11	68		Others	4–4	1.74	6.4	6.1	0.9	5.09	6.12	6.38	-8	-0.7
156	93		29.1	Team Total		1.41	4.99	3.59	0.59	4.12	3.98	4.63	117	10.8
				League Average		1.49	3.28	3.60	0.58	4.48	4.48	5.26		
				% Lg Avg		106	152	100	97	109	112	114		
				League Rank		1	1	4	6	1	1			

1932 Philadelphia Athletics

The Philadelphia A's had their last great season in 1932 although the pitching was no longer the best in the league. Facing ever improving competition from the Yankees and Senators and experiencing declining attendance due to the Great Depression, Connie Mack, who needed money to pay bank loans needed to ride out the depressed economy, decided for the second time to dismantle his team by selling Simmons, Dykes, and Haas to the White Sox for $100,000.

Strengths: (1) hitting for average and power led by MVP Foxx (33 2B, 9 3B, 58 HR, 213 H, 438 TB), Simmons (28 2B, 9 3B, 35 HR, 216 H, 367 TB), Cochrane (35 2B, 23 HR), Cramer (27 2B), Haas (28 2B), and SS McNair (18 HR), (2) drawing walks especially by Foxx (116 BB), Bishop (110 BB), and Cochrane (100 BB), (3) fielding from 2B Bishop (95 Rng+) and CF/RF Cramer (118 Rng+ in CF, 109 Rng+ in RF, 7 assists), and (4) starting pitching anchored by Lefty Grove (188 K) and Tony Freitas.

Weaknesses: (1) RP position, (2) hitting for contact, (3) hitting from the pitchers except Earnshaw, (4) pitching depth, (5) relief pitching, (6) last in the AL in team HR/9, (7) lack of any baserunning threats, and (8) HR/9 from Mahaffey and Earnshaw.

Mgr	Connie Mack	
Rk	41	99
Gm	154	
Place	2	
GB	13.0	
Rival	8–14 vs Yankees, 125 RS & 168 RA	

	W	L	Win%
Regular Season	94	60	0.610
Runs Record	96	58	0.623
1 Run	25	22	0.532
Extra Innings	6	9	0.400
Blowout	38	14	0.731

	Team	LgAvg	%Avg	LgRk
BABIP	0.288	0.292	101	3
E	123	187	152	1
sOBP	0.328	0.341	104	3
rOBP	0.377	0.365	97	8
R/G	6.37	5.23	122	2
RA/G	4.88	5.23	107	4

	Tm	LgAvg	>Avg
RS	981	804	177
RA	751	804	53
DP	142	150	-8

	R/G	HR	K	BB	SB	CS	SB%	OBP
Team Offense	6.37	172	629	650	37	24	61%	0.367
Team Defense	4.88	112	595	511	68	50	58%	0.336
Difference	1.49	60	-34	139	-31			109%

Pos	Rpos	PA	Age	Name	BA	OBP	SLG	BB%	RS%	Bat R>Avg	BR R>Avg	Fld R>Avg	RAA	WAA
C	4	625	29	Cochrane, Mickey*	0.293	0.412	0.510	16%	41%	36	0	1	41	3.8
1B,3B	-6	701	24	Foxx, Jimmie	0.364	0.469	0.749	17%	34%	102	-2	5	99	9.1
2B	3	522	32	Bishop, Max*	0.254	0.412	0.359	21%	40%	11	0	9	23	2.1
3B,SS	3	647	35	Dykes, Jimmy	0.265	0.358	0.373	12%	29%	-1	2	2	6	0.5
SS	9	591	23	McNair, Eric	0.285	0.323	0.478	5%	40%	6	1	-3	13	1.2
LF	-7	718	30	Simmons, Al	0.322	0.368	0.548	7%	48%	36	1	-1	29	2.7
CF,RF	-2	407	26	Cramer, Doc*	0.336	0.367	0.461	4%	48%	10	1	7	16	1.5
CF,RF	-3	649	28	Haas, Mule*	0.305	0.376	0.405	10%	37%	9	1	4	11	1.0
RF	-4	330	37	Miller, Bing	0.295	0.343	0.446	6%	31%	3	1	4	4	0.4
2B	2	241	22	Williams, Dib	0.251	0.329	0.363	9%	35%	-4	0	0	-2	-0.2
C	1	85	36	Heving, Johnny	0.273	0.333	0.377	8%	50%	-1	0	0	0	0.0

Pos	Rpos	PA	Age	Name	BA	OBP	SLG	BB%	RS%	Bat R>Avg	BR R>Avg	Fld R>Avg	RAA	WAA
RF	-1	74	30	Coleman, Ed*	0.342	0.351	0.507	1%	48%	2	0	0	1	0.1
C	0	38	23	Madjeski, Ed	0.229	0.289	0.229	8%	36%	-3	0	1	-2	-0.2
1B	-1	66	32	Roettger, Oscar	0.233	0.292	0.250	8%	37%	-4	0	-1	-6	-0.6
P	0	102	32	Earnshaw, George	0.286	0.286	0.352	0%	38%	-4	0	0	-4	-0.4
	2	504		Others	0.176	0.236	0.230	7%	31%	-47	1	0	-44	-4.1
	0		29.3	Team Total	0.290	0.367	0.457	10.3%	38.4%	150	6	28	184	17.0
				League Average	0.277	0.346	0.404	9.0%	36.1%					
				% Lg Avg	105	106	113	114	107					
				League Rank	1	2	1	2			2	2		

GS	GR	IP	Age	Name	W–L	WHIP	K/9	BB/9	HR/9	FIP	ERA	RAA	RAA	WAA
30	14	292	32	Grove, Lefty*	25–10	1.19	5.8	2.4	0.4	3.24	2.84	3.12	64	5.9
34	7	272	35	Walberg, Rube*	17–10	1.50	3.2	3.4	0.5	4.32	4.73	5.26	-6	-0.5
33	3	245	32	Earnshaw, George	19–13	1.45	4.0	3.4	1.0	4.92	4.77	5.39	-9	-0.8
28	9	223	28	Mahaffey, Roy	13–13	1.53	4.3	3.9	1.1	5.11	5.09	5.50	-10	-1.0
18	5	150	24	Freitas, Tony*	12–5	1.32	1.9	2.9	0.7	4.70	3.83	4.07	17	1.5
6	4	45	25	Cane, Sugar	3–4	1.56	4.8	5.6	0.2	4.22	5.00	5.40	-2	-0.1
0	17	65	34	Rommel, Eddie	1–2	1.56	2.2	2.5	0.8	4.66	5.51	5.92	-6	-0.6
3	17	57	20	Krausse, Lew	4–1	1.54	2.5	3.8	0.5	4.51	4.58	4.89	1	0.1
2	16	37		Others	0–2	2.10	2.2	5.2	1.7	7.16	9.08	9.57	-18	-1.7
154	92		28.8	Team Total		1.43	3.86	3.32	0.73	4.46	4.45	4.88	31	2.8
				League Average		1.49	3.28	3.60	0.58	4.48	4.48	5.26		
				% Lg Avg		104	118	108	80	100	101	108		
				League Rank		3	2	2	8	4	5			

1934 Detroit Tigers

The Detroit Tigers improved from 5th place in 1933 to the pennant in 1934 by improving their offense from 4.7 to 6.2 runs per game. The acquisition of player-manager Mickey Cochrane from the A's and Goose Goslin from the Senators improved their team's competitiveness which was also led by 2B Gehringer and 1B Greenberg. The Tigers won their first pennant since 1909 helped by having a 23–6 W–L record in August. Every starting positional player had a batting average of .285 or better with 6 starters hitting over .300. The team scored 958 runs which is still a franchise record. This team lost the World Series to the Cardinals in 7 games.

Strengths: (1) hitting from MVP runner-up Gehringer (50 2B), Greenberg (63 2B, 26 HR), MVP Cochrane (32 2B), Owen (34 2B, 9 3B), Goslin (38 2B), and White, (2) drawing walks from Gehringer (99 BB), Cochrane (78 BB), and White (69 BB), (3) baserunning led by White (28 SB, 6 CS), (4) infield fielding led by SS Rogell (100 Rng+, 99 DP) and 2B Gehringer (101 Rng+, 100 DP), (5) CS% from Cochrane (53%) and Hayworth (48%), and (6) pitching anchored by Rowe, Bridges, and submariner starter/reliever Auker.

Weaknesses: (1) hitting for power from outfielders Fox and Doljack, (2) fielding from 3B Owen (100 Rng+), and (3) pitching depth.

Mgr	Mickey Cochrane	
Rk	48	115
Gm	154	
Place	1	
GA	7.0	
Rival	12–10 vs Yankees, 101 RS & 108 RA	

	W	L	Win%
Regular Season	101	53	0.656
Runs Record	95	59	0.620
1 Run	26	18	0.591
Extra Innings	12	2	0.857
Blowout	33	12	0.733

	Team	LgAvg	%Avg	LgRk
BABIP	0.297	0.297	100	4
E	156	178	114	1
sOBP	0.334	0.348	104	2
rOBP	0.339	0.360	106	1
R/G	6.21	5.13	121	1
RA/G	4.60	5.13	112	2

	Team	LgAvg	RAA
RS	957	788	169
RA	708	788	80
DP	150	153	-3

	R/G	HR	K	BB	SB	CS	SB%	OBP
Team Offense	6.21	74	526	636	125	55	69%	0.376
Team Defense	4.60	86	640	488	41	43	49%	0.335
Difference	1.62	-12	114	148	84			112%

Pos	Rpos	PA	Age	Name	BA	OBP	SLG	BB%	RS%	Bat R>Avg	BR R>Avg	Fld R>Avg	RAA	WAA
C	4	524	31	Cochrane, Mickey*	0.320	0.428	0.412	15%	33%	20	0	1	25	2.3
1B	-7	667	23	Greenberg, Hank	0.339	0.404	0.600	9%	38%	53	0	3	49	4.5
2B	5	708	31	Gehringer, Charlie*	0.356	0.450	0.517	14%	40%	54	-1	11	69	6.4
3B	3	637	28	Owen, Marv	0.317	0.385	0.451	9%	30%	19	0	-6	16	1.5
SS	10	679	29	Rogell, Billy^	0.296	0.374	0.392	11%	45%	6	2	13	31	2.9
LF	-7	686	33	Goslin, Goose*	0.305	0.373	0.453	9%	39%	17	0	-1	9	0.8
CF,RF	-2	460	25	White, Jo-Jo*	0.313	0.419	0.385	15%	51%	13	3	-2	12	1.1
RF,CF	-5	579	25	Fox, Pete	0.285	0.351	0.364	8%	50%	-5	1	4	-5	-0.5
CF,RF	-2	373	26	Walker, Gee	0.300	0.340	0.418	5%	40%	0	0	2	0	0.0
C	2	183	30	Hayworth, Ray	0.293	0.355	0.347	9%	31%	-2	-1	0	-1	-0.1
RF,CF	-1	136	26	Doljack, Frank	0.233	0.313	0.333	10%	34%	-5	0	-2	-8	-0.7
P	0	119	24	Rowe, Schoolboy	0.303	0.339	0.450	5%	35%	1	0	0	1	0.1
	0	480		Others	0.155	0.206	0.188	5%	32%	-57	1	0	-56	-5.2
	0		27.6	Team Total	0.300	0.376	0.424	10.2%	39.6%	111	5	23	139	13.0
				League Average	0.279	0.351	0.399	9.5%	35.0%					
				% Lg Avg	108	107	106	107	88					
				League Rank	1	1	2	2	3		2	3		

GS	GR	IP	Age	Name	W–L	WHIP	K/9	BB/9	HR/9	FIP	ERA	R/9	RAA	WAA
35	1	275	27	Bridges, Tommy	22–11	1.28	4.9	3.4	0.52	3.98	3.67	3.83	38	3.5
30	15	266	24	Rowe, Schoolboy	24–8	1.28	5.0	2.7	0.41	3.55	3.45	3.72	40	3.7
19	9	130	33	Sorrell, Vic	6–9	1.47	3.2	3.1	0.90	4.86	4.79	5.27	-3	-0.3
19	19	156	35	Marberry, Firpo	15–5	1.43	3.7	2.8	0.69	4.26	4.57	5.32	-5	-0.4
15	5	95	28	Fischer, Carl*	6–4	1.53	3.7	3.6	0.47	4.25	4.36	4.74	3	0.3
18	25	205	23	Auker, Eldon	15–7	1.41	3.8	2.5	0.40	3.75	3.42	4.52	12	1.1
5	15	75	29	Hamlin, Luke	2–3	1.74	3.6	5.3	1.31	6.01	5.38	5.73	-6	-0.5
0	26	50	30	Hogsett, Chief*	3–2	1.59	4.1	3.4	0.72	4.47	4.29	6.08	-6	-0.5
9	0	67	35	Crowder, General	5–1	1.51	4.0	2.7	0.40	3.74	4.18	4.72	2	0.2
1	6	23	25	Phillips, Red	2–0	2.01	1.2	6.2	0.39	5.51	6.17	6.56	-4	-0.4
1	1	6	23	Larkin, Steve	0–0	2.17	12.0	7.5	0.00	2.99	1.50	10.50	-4	-0.3
2	6	23		Frasier, Vic	1–3	1.85	4.4	4.8	0.00	3.90	5.96	7.54	-6	-0.6
154	128		28.4	Team Total		1.43	4.20	3.20	0.56	4.13	4.06	4.65	62	5.7
				League Average		1.52	3.54	3.81	0.57	4.50	4.50	5.20		
				% Lg Avg		107	119	119	101	109	111	112		
				League Rank		2	2	1	7	2	2			

1934 New York Yankees

The 1934 Yankees lost the pennant to a strong Tiger team despite having the Triple Crown winner on both offense with Gehrig (.363 BA, 49 HR, 165 RBI) and pitching with Lefty Gomez (26 wins, 2.33 ERA, 158 K). Significant injuries that happened during the season that hurt the Yankees pennant chances were Dickey's broken finger, Combs' fractured skull, and Allen's sore pitching arm. This was a very good team that should have finished first or a much closer second.

Strengths: (1) hitting for power featuring Gehrig (40 2B, 49 HR), 39-year-old Ruth in his last year with the Yankees (22 HR), Dickey (24 2B), and Chapman (13 3B), (3) drawing walks especially from Gehrig (109 BB), Ruth (104 BB), and Lazzeri (71 BB), (4) fielding led by SS Crosetti (99 Rng+, 77 DP in 119 G) and CF/LF Chapman (109 Rng+ in CF, 118 Rng+ in LF, 12 OF assists), and (5) pitching anchored by Gomez and Murphy.

Weaknesses: (1) RP position, (2) hitting by Jorgens, Heffner, Byrd, and Hoag, (3) CS% from Dickey (31%) and Jorgens (31%), and (4) pitching from Van Atta (10.9 H/9).

Mgr	Joe McCarthy	
Rk	36	92
Gm	154	
Place	2	

	W	L	Win%
Regular Season	94	60	0.610
Runs Record	96	58	0.624
1 Run	26	14	0.650
Extra Innings	9	3	0.750

	Team	LgAvg	%Avg	LgRk
BABIP	0.279	0.297	107	1
E	160	178	111	2
sOBP	0.320	0.348	109	1
rOBP	0.346	0.360	104	2

			W	L	Win%		Team	LgAvg	%Avg	LgRk
GB	7.0	**Blowout**	33	13	0.717	**R/G**	5.47	5.13	107	2
Rival	10–12 vs Tigers, 108 RS & 101 RS					**RA/G**	4.34	5.13	118	1

	Tm	LgAvg	>Avg
RS	842	788	54
RA	669	788	119
DP	151	153	-2

	R/G	HR	K	BB	SB	CS	SB%	OBP
Team Offense	5.47	135	602	700	71	46	61%	0.364
Team Defense	4.34	71	656	542	68	31	69%	0.324
Difference	1.12	64	54	158	3			112%

Pos	Rpos	PA	Age	Name	BA	OBP	SLG	BB%	RS%	Bat R>Avg	BR R>Avg	Fld R>Avg	RAA	WAA
C	4	438	27	Dickey, Bill*	0.322	0.384	0.494	9%	28%	18	-1	1	22	2.0
1B	-7	690	31	Gehrig, Lou*	0.363	0.465	0.706	16%	29%	91	0	3	87	8.1
2B,3B	4	514	30	Lazzeri, Tony	0.267	0.369	0.445	14%	26%	11	2	3	20	1.9
3B	2	406	31	Saltzgaver, Jack*	0.271	0.359	0.351	12%	42%	-3	2	1	2	0.1
SS,3B	8	632	23	Crosetti, Frankie	0.265	0.344	0.401	10%	37%	-2	-1	5	10	1.0
LF,OF	-4	218	27	Byrd, Sammy	0.246	0.318	0.335	8%	45%	-7	-1	0	-12	-1.1
CF,OF	-4	666	25	Chapman, Ben	0.308	0.381	0.413	10%	31%	12	-2	12	18	1.6
RF,LF	-5	471	39	Ruth, Babe*	0.288	0.448	0.537	22%	30%	37	-1	6	37	3.5
SS,3B	-2	309	25	Rolfe, Red*	0.287	0.348	0.348	8%	51%	-5	-1	0	-8	-0.7
CF,LF	-1	295	35	Combs, Earle*	0.319	0.412	0.434	14%	38%	11	0	1	11	1.0
RF,OF	-4	275	26	Hoag, Myril	0.267	0.324	0.351	8%	49%	-7	-1	0	-12	-1.1
2B	2	270	23	Heffner, Don	0.261	0.331	0.320	9%	33%	-8	0	2	-4	-0.4
LF,RF	-2	192	0	Selkirk, George*	0.313	0.370	0.449	8%	27%	4	0	3	5	0.5
C	2	207	29	Jorgens, Art	0.208	0.296	0.251	11%	23%	-13	1	1	-9	-0.9
	7	595		Others	0.156	0.211	0.199	6%	37%	-68	1	0	-60	-5.6
	0		26.5	Team Total	0.278	0.364	0.419	11.3%	34.0%	71	-2	38	107	9.9
				League Average	0.279	0.351	0.399	9.5%	35.0%					
				% Lg Avg	100	104	105	119	97					
				League Rank	4	2	4	1			6	1		

GS	GR	IP	Age	Name	W–L	WHIP	K/9	BB/9	HR/9	FIP	ERA	R/9	RAA	WAA
33	5	282	25	Gomez, Lefty*	26–5	1.13	5.0	3.1	0.4	3.61	2.33	2.75	70	6.5
31	5	256	29	Ruffing, Red	19–11	1.31	5.2	3.7	0.6	4.13	3.93	4.71	7	0.7
24	2	177	24	Broaca, Johnny	12–9	1.51	3.8	3.3	0.5	4.10	4.16	4.77	3	0.3
10	3	72	29	Allen, Johnny	5–2	1.31	6.8	4.0	0.4	3.62	2.89	3.77	10	0.9
20	20	208	25	Murphy, Johnny	14–10	1.30	3.0	3.3	0.5	4.27	3.12	3.42	35	3.3
12	19	134	24	DeShong, Jimmie	6–7	1.36	2.7	3.8	0.4	4.44	4.11	4.78	2	0.2
11	11	96	29	MacFayden, Danny	4–3	1.47	3.8	2.9	0.5	4.01	4.50	5.34	-4	-0.4
9	19	88	28	Van Atta, Russ*	3–5	1.74	4.0	4.7	0.3	4.35	6.34	7.06	-21	-1.9
4	27	70		Others	5–8	1.83	4.0	4.6	0.5	4.59	5.63	6.27	-10	-1.0
154	111		26.6	Team Total		1.37	4.27	3.53	0.46	4.07	3.76	4.35	92	8.6
				League Average		1.52	3.54	3.81	0.57	4.50	4.50	5.20		
				% Lg Avg		111	121	108	123	110	120	120		
				League Rank		1	1	3	4	1	1			

1935 Detroit Tigers

The 1935 season was a wonderful year for baseball featuring 2 strong teams in each league and 2 exciting pennant races. Major League Baseball was played at night for the first time in 1935. The Tigers led the majors in runs scored per game and repeated as pennant winners but had to hold off a strong Yankee team who allowed the fewest runs per game in the AL and finished in second place for the third consecutive season. The Tigers won their first world championship over the Cubs in their 5th World Series.

Strengths: (1) hitting for average, contact, and power led by MVP Greenberg (46 2B, 16 3B, 36 HR), Gehringer (32 2B, 8 3B, 19 HR), Cochrane (33 2B), and Fox (38 2B, 8 3B, 15 HR), (2) drawing walks featuring Cochrane (96 BB), Greenberg (87 BB), Rogell (80 BB), Gehringer (79 BB), and White (68 BB), (3) fielding especially from the double play combo of SS Rogell (101 Rng+, 104 DP) and 2B Gehringer (100 Rng+, 99 DP, only 13 errors in

851 chances), (4) CS% from Hayworth (63%) and Cochrane (41%), and (5) starting pitching anchored by Rowe who also contributed with his hitting, submariner Auker, and Bridges.

Weaknesses: (1) RP, 3B, and CF positions, (2) hitting from Owen, White, and Clifton, and (3) winning 1 run games.

Mgr	Mickey Cochrane	
Rk	32	82
Gm	152	
Place	1	
GA	3.0	
Rival	11–11 vs Yankees, 105 RS & 85 RA	

	W	*L*	*Win%*
Regular Season	93	58	0.616
Runs Record	95	56	0.629
1 Run	19	27	0.413
Extra Innings	8	6	0.571
Blowout	38	14	0.731

	Team	*LgAvg*	*%Avg*	*LgRk*
BABIP	0.292	0.296	101	3
E	126	145	87	2
sOBP	0.331	0.345	104	3
rOBP	0.375	0.371	99	6
R/G	6.05	5.09	119	1
RA/G	4.38	5.09	116	2

	Tm	*LgAvg*	*>Avg*
RS	919	778	141
RA	665	777	112
DP	154	145	9

	R/G	*HR*	*K*	*BB*	*SB*	*CS*	*SB%*	*OBP*
Team Offense	6.05	106	453	628	70	45	61%	0.366
Team Defense	4.38	78	584	522	44	41	52%	0.339
Difference	1.67	28	131	106	26			108%

Pos	*Rpos*	*PA*	*Age*	*Name*	*BA*	*OBP*	*SLG*	*BB%*	*RS%*	*Bat R>Avg*	*BR R>Avg*	*Fld R>Avg*	*RAA*	*WAA*
C	4	522	32	Cochrane, Mickey*	0.319	0.452	0.450	18%	39%	30	-1	0	33	3.1
1B	-7	710	24	Greenberg, Hank	0.328	0.411	0.628	12%	33%	63	0	5	61	5.7
2B	5	709	32	Gehringer, Charlie*	0.330	0.409	0.502	11%	39%	37	1	14	57	5.3
3B	3	544	29	Owen, Marv	0.263	0.326	0.346	8%	29%	-15	-1	-2	-15	-1.4
SS	10	648	30	Rogell, Billy^	0.275	0.367	0.388	12%	36%	2	-1	19	30	2.8
LF,RF	-7	651	34	Goslin, Goose*	0.292	0.355	0.415	9%	36%	3	0	6	2	0.2
CF	-1	483	26	White, Jo-Jo*	0.240	0.348	0.345	14%	48%	-7	0	-2	-10	-1.0
RF,CF	-6	581	26	Fox, Pete	0.321	0.382	0.513	8%	50%	25	2	0	21	2.0
CF,LF	-2	385	27	Walker, Gee	0.301	0.329	0.453	4%	38%	1	0	0	-1	0.0
C	2	190	31	Hayworth, Ray	0.309	0.342	0.411	5%	35%	0	0	1	3	0.2
3B,2B	1	120	25	Clifton, Flea	0.255	0.293	0.300	4%	44%	-7	0	0	-6	-0.5
P	0	124	25	Rowe, Schoolboy	0.312	0.380	0.459	10%	37%	3	0	0	3	0.3
P	0	119	28	Bridges, Tommy	0.239	0.278	0.303	5%	28%	-7	0	0	-7	-0.7
	-2	396		Others	0.194	0.251	0.253	7%	39%	-34	0	0	-36	-3.3
	0		28.4	Team Total	0.290	0.366	0.435	10.2%	38.5%	96	0	41	137	12.8
				League Average	0.280	0.351	0.402	9.4%	34.5%					
				% Lg Avg	104	104	108	108	111					
				League Rank	1	1	1	2			4	2		

GS	*GR*	*IP*	*Age*	*Name*	*W–L*	*WHIP*	*K/9*	*BB/9*	*HR/9*	*FIP*	*ERA*	*R/9*	*RAA*	*WAA*
34	8	276	25	Rowe, Schoolboy	19–13	1.23	4.6	2.2	0.4	3.36	3.69	3.95	28	2.6
34	2	274	28	Bridges, Tommy	21–10	1.42	5.3	3.7	0.7	4.21	3.51	4.23	20	1.8
32	1	241	36	Crowder, General	16–10	1.39	2.2	2.5	0.6	4.35	4.26	4.74	3	0.3
25	11	195	24	Auker, Eldon	18–7	1.41	2.9	2.8	0.6	4.39	3.83	3.97	19	1.8
12	13	126	24	Sullivan, Joe*	6–6	1.51	3.8	5.1	0.3	4.43	3.51	4.73	2	0.2
6	6	51	34	Sorrell, Vic	4–3	1.75	3.9	4.4	0.4	4.32	4.03	4.91	0	0.0
0	40	97	31	Hogsett, Chief*	6–6	1.63	3.6	4.6	0.1	4.09	3.54	4.19	7	0.7
4	3	40	29	Lawson, Roxie	3–1	1.45	3.6	5.4	0.7	5.07	1.58	2.48	11	1.0
2	3	19	36	Marberry, Firpo	0–1	1.63	3.3	4.3	0.9	5.14	4.26	5.21	-1	-0.1
3	8	45		Others	0–1	2.10	4.4	6.9	0.8	5.72	7.15	8.14	-17	-1.6
152	95		29.7	Team Total		1.44	3.85	3.44	0.51	4.19	3.82	4.39	71	6.7
				League Average		1.52	3.25	3.75	0.55	4.46	4.46	5.13		
				% Lg Avg		106	119	109	106	106	117	117		
				League Rank		3	2	3	4	2	2			

1935 Chicago Cubs

The Cubs surprised the Giants and Cardinals with 100 wins including 21 straight wins to capture the pennant by 4 games over the defending world champion Cardinals. The Cubs put it all together in 1935 leading the NL in most runs scored and fewest runs allowed per game finishing with an impressive 1.63 runs per game differential. This team won 21 straight games in September capping off a sizzling 60–22 W–L record in the second half of the season. Curiously, the Cubs released veteran 36-year-old Cuyler in early July. Cuyler bounced back with a fine season with the Reds in 1936.

Strengths: (1) hitting for average, contact, and power led by Galan (41 2B, 11 3B), MVP Hartnett (32 2B), Herman (57 2B), Hack (23 2B, 9 3B), and Klein (21 HR), (3) drawing walks led by Galan (87 BB) and Hack (65 BB), (4) fielding featuring SS Jurges (112 Rng+, 99 DP), 2B Herman (113 Rng+, 109 DP), and 3B Hack (108 Rng+), (5) double plays made, (6) CS% from Hartnett (61%), and (7) pitching anchored by Warneke, French, Lee, and Root.

Weaknesses: (1) 1B position and (2) hitting from Billy Jurges and Freddy Lindstrom.

Mgr	Charlie Grimm	
Rk	18	44
Gm	154	
Place	1	
GA	4.0	
Rival	8–14 vs Cardinals; 80 RS & 98 RA	

	W	*L*	*Win%*
Regular Season	100	54	0.649
Runs Record	100	54	0.646
1 Run	25	23	0.521
Extra Innings	11	10	0.524
Blowout	34	8	0.810

	Team	*LgAvg*	*%Avg*	*LgRk*
BABIP	0.283	0.294	104	2
E	186	191	103	3
sOBP	0.314	0.326	104	3
rOBP	0.330	0.346	105	3
R/G	5.50	4.71	117	1
RA/G	3.87	4.71	122	1

	Tm	*LgAvg*	*>Avg*
RS	847	726	121
RA	596	726	130
DP	163	131	32

	R/G	*HR*	*K*	*BB*	*SB*	*CS*	*SB%*	*OBP*
Team Offense	5.50	88	471	464	66			0.347
Team Defense	3.87	85	589	400	45	50	47%	0.316
Difference	1.63	3	118	64	21			110%

Pos	*Rpos*	*PA*	*Age*	*Name*	*BA*	*OBP*	*SLG*	*BB%*	*RS%*	*Bat R>Avg*	*BR R>Avg*	*Fld R>Avg*	*RAA*	*WAA*
C	4	461	34	Hartnett, Gabby	0.344	0.404	0.545	9%	32%	34	0	2	40	3.9
1B	-7	636	18	Cavarretta, Phil*	0.275	0.322	0.404	6%	39%	0	0	1	-6	-0.6
2B	5	735	25	Herman, Billy	0.341	0.383	0.476	6%	40%	33	0	15	53	5.1
3B,1B	2	504	25	Hack, Stan*	0.311	0.406	0.436	13%	36%	22	0	8	32	3.2
SS	10	584	27	Jurges, Billy	0.241	0.304	0.314	7%	40%	-19	0	20	11	1.1
LF	-7	748	23	Galan, Augie^	0.314	0.399	0.467	12%	43%	37	0	6	36	3.5
CF,RF	-2	420	25	Demaree, Frank	0.325	0.369	0.410	6%	39%	9	-1	0	6	0.6
RF	-5	485	30	Klein, Chuck*	0.293	0.355	0.488	8%	34%	18	0	4	17	1.7
CF,3B	0	363	29	Lindstrom, Freddie	0.275	0.297	0.389	3%	45%	-6	0	2	-4	-0.4
C	2	231	22	O'Dea, Ken*	0.257	0.345	0.431	11%	33%	4	0	-2	4	0.4
CF	-1	177	36	Cuyler, Kiki	0.268	0.331	0.389	6%	34%	0	0	0	-1	-0.1
3B,SS	1	109	29	English, Woody	0.202	0.368	0.298	18%	24%	0	0	1	2	0.2
RF	-1	97	23	Stainback, Tuck	0.255	0.271	0.394	0%	57%	-3	0	-2	-6	-0.5
	-1	583		Others	0.205	0.229	0.242	3%	36%	-49	-1	0	-51	-4.9
	0			Team Total	0.288	0.347	0.414	7.6%	38.1%	81	-2	55	134	13.1
				League Average	0.277	0.331	0.391	6.9%	34.6%					
				% Lg Avg	104	105	106	110	110					
				League Rank	1	1	2	2			6	1		

GS	*GR*	*IP*	*Age*	*Name*	*W–L*	*WHIP*	*K/9*	*BB/9*	*HR/9*	*FIP*	*ERA*	*R/9*	*RAA*	*WAA*
30	12	262	26	Warneke, Lon	20–13	1.17	4.1	1.7	0.7	3.66	3.06	3.51	27	2.6
32	7	252	25	Lee, Bill	20–6	1.29	3.6	3.0	0.4	3.85	2.96	3.79	18	1.7
30	12	246	27	French, Larry*	17–10	1.31	3.3	1.6	0.4	3.38	2.96	3.43	26	2.6
22	9	171	28	Carleton, Tex	11–8	1.34	4.4	3.2	0.9	4.44	3.89	4.32	2	0.2
18	13	143	23	Henshaw, Roy*	13–5	1.42	3.3	4.3	0.4	4.34	3.28	3.78	10	1.0
18	20	201	36	Root, Charlie	15–8	1.19	4.2	2.1	0.7	3.80	3.08	3.80	14	1.4
2	18	55	27	Kowalik, Fabian	2–2	1.44	3.3	3.1	0.3	3.80	4.42	5.07	-4	-0.4
0	13	26	21	Casey, Hugh	0–0	1.68	3.5	4.9	0.7	4.89	3.86	4.56	0	0.0
1	8	23	23	Bryant, Clay	1–2	1.81	5.2	2.8	0.4	3.37	5.16	5.96	-4	-0.4
1	4	13	23	Shoun, Clyde*	1–0	1.50	3.6	3.6	1.4	5.47	2.84	2.84	2	0.2
0	2	3		Joiner, Roy*	0–0	2.40	0.0	5.4	0.0	4.82	5.41	10.81	-2	-0.2
154	118			Team Total		1.30	3.80	2.58	0.55	3.87	3.26	3.85	88	8.5
				League Average		1.40	3.34	2.69	0.54	4.02	4.02	4.77		
				% Lg Avg		107	114	104	99	104	123	124		
				League Rank		2	2	4	5	3	1			

1936 New York Yankees

The Yankees hit on all cylinders beginning in 1936 when they began their 4 year domination leading the AL in most runs scored, fewest runs allowed, most games won, and winning the World Series. The 1936 Yankees, led by rookie Joe DiMaggio, were primarily responsible for raising the AL average runs per game per team from 5.1 in 1935 to 5.7 as they scored 1065 runs which is still a franchise record. This team overpowered everyone including the second place former world champion Detroit Tigers.

Strengths: (1) hitting led by MVP Gehrig (37 2B, 49 HR, 205 H, 403 TB), Dickey (26 2B, 8 3B, 22 HR), Selkirk (28 2B, 9 3B, 18 HR), rookie DiMaggio (44 2B, 15 3B, 29 HR, 367 TB, 206 H), Rolfe (39 3B, 15 3B), Lazzeri (29 2B, 14 HR), and Crosetti (35 2B, 15 HR), (2) drawing walks from Gehrig (130 BB), Lazzeri (97 BB), Selkirk (94 BB), and Crosetti (90 BB), (3) fielding featuring SS Crosetti (99 Rng+, 95 DP), Rolfe (106 Rng+), and LF/CF DiMaggio (125 Rng+ in LF, 95 Rng+ in CF, 22 assists), (4) CS% from Dickey (54%), and (5) pitching depth anchored by Pearson, Ruffing, Broaca, Gomez, Hadley, Malone (9 saves) and Murphy (5 saves).

Weaknesses: (1) hitting for contact, (2) team pitching control (BB/9), (3) fielding from 2B Lazzeri (92 Rng+), and (4) bullpen depth.

Mgr	Joe McCarthy	
Rk	4	10
Gm	155	
Place	1	
GA	19.5	
Rival	14–8 vs Tigers, 173 RS & 117 RA	

	W	*L*	*Win%*
Regular Season	102	51	0.667
Runs Record	104	49	0.682
1 Run	22	17	0.564
Extra Innings	9	3	0.750
Blowout	47	19	0.712

	Team	*LgAvg*	*%Avg*	*LgRk*
BABIP	0.294	0.305	104	1
E	163	176	108	2
sOBP	0.349	0.358	103	2
rOBP	0.357	0.377	106	2
R/G	6.87	5.67	121	1
RA/G	4.72	5.67	120	1

	Tm	*LgAvg*	*>Avg*
RS	1065	876	189
RA	731	876	145
DP	148	154	-6

	R/G	*HR*	*K*	*BB*	*SB*	*CS*	*SB%*	*OBP*
Team Offense	6.87	182	593	700	77	40	66%	0.381
Team Defense	4.72	79	624	663	47	44	52%	0.351
Difference	2.15	103	31	37	30			109%

Pos	*Rpos*	*PA*	*Age*	*Name*	*BA*	*OBP*	*SLG*	*BB%*	*RS%*	*Bat R>Avg*	*BR R>Avg*	*Fld R>Avg*	*RAA*	*WAA*
C	3	472	29	Dickey, Bill*	0.362	0.428	0.617	10%	43%	40	-1	0	42	3.7
1B	-7	719	33	Gehrig, Lou*	0.354	0.478	0.696	18%	40%	88	-1	0	80	7.1
2B	5	638	32	Lazzeri, Tony	0.287	0.397	0.441	15%	29%	14	0	-7	12	1.1
3B	3	646	27	Rolfe, Red*	0.319	0.392	0.493	11%	44%	21	1	9	34	3.0
SS	10	740	25	Crosetti, Frankie	0.288	0.387	0.437	12%	45%	12	1	2	25	2.2
LF,CF	-2	360	27	Powell, Jake	0.306	0.370	0.429	9%	44%	2	0	2	2	0.2
LF,CF	-5	668	21	DiMaggio, Joe	0.323	0.352	0.576	4%	50%	26	1	11	33	3.0
RF,LF	-6	592	28	Selkirk, George*	0.308	0.420	0.511	16%	33%	30	0	6	30	2.6
LF,RF	-1	170	33	Johnson, Roy*	0.265	0.361	0.367	12%	33%	-3	0	0	-4	-0.3
CF,RF	-1	169	28	Hoag, Myril	0.301	0.343	0.468	4%	37%	1	0	-2	-2	-0.2
CF	0	156	27	Chapman, Ben	0.266	0.338	0.432	10%	35%	-1	-1	2	0	0.0
C	1	150	27	Glenn, Joe	0.271	0.373	0.349	13%	36%	-2	0	0	-1	-0.1
P	0	140	31	Ruffing, Red	0.291	0.348	0.449	8%	21%	0	0	0	0	0.0
	0	771		Others	0.213	0.259	0.284	6%	39%	-66	2	2	-62	-5.4
	0		28.3	Team Total	0.300	0.381	0.483	11.0%	39.6%	162	2	25	189	16.7
				League Average	0.289	0.363	0.421	9.8%	36.9%					
				% Lg Avg	104	105	115	112	107					
				League Rank	2	1	1	1				4	2	

GS	*GR*	*IP*	*Age*	*Name*	*W–L*	*WHIP*	*K/9*	*BB/9*	*HR/9*	*FIP*	*ERA*	*R/9*	*RAA*	*WAA*
33	0	271	31	Ruffing, Red	20–12	1.34	3.4	3.0	0.73	4.82	3.85	4.42	36	3.2
31	2	223	27	Pearson, Monte	19–7	1.46	4.8	5.4	0.52	5.04	3.71	4.00	40	3.6
27	10	206	26	Broaca, Johnny	12–7	1.46	3.7	2.9	0.70	4.64	4.24	4.81	18	1.6
30	1	189	27	Gomez, Lefty*	13–7	1.62	5.0	5.8	0.29	4.75	4.39	4.96	14	1.2
17	14	174	31	Hadley, Bump	14–4	1.63	3.8	4.6	0.62	5.09	4.35	5.03	11	1.0
9	26	135	33	Malone, Pat	12–4	1.51	4.8	4.0	0.27	4.23	3.81	4.01	24	2.1
5	22	88	27	Murphy, Johnny	9–3	1.43	3.5	3.7	0.00	3.98	3.38	3.89	17	1.5
3	17	64	29	Brown, Jumbo	1–4	1.91	2.7	4.1	0.56	5.07	5.91	6.61	-7	-0.6

GS	GR	IP	Age	Name	W–L	WHIP	K/9	BB/9	HR/9	FIP	ERA	R/9	RAA	WAA
0	19	29	37	Kleinhans, Ted*	1–1	2.01	3.1	7.1	0.00	5.16	5.83	7.67	-7	-0.6
0	7	20	29	Wicker, Kemp*	1–2	2.10	2.3	5.0	0.90	5.94	7.65	8.10	-6	-0.5
0	1	2	26	Sundra, Steve	0–0	2.00	4.5	9.0	0.00	5.49	0.00	0.00	1	0.1
155	119		29.7	Team Total		1.53	4.01	4.26	0.51	4.78	4.17	4.70	142	12.5
				League Average		1.60	3.32	4.00	0.62	5.04	5.04	5.77		
				% Lg Avg		105	121	94	123	105	121	123		
				League Rank		2	2	7	3	3	1			

1937 New York Yankees

The 1937 Yankees won 102 games and easily won the pennant over the Tigers who nearly outscored the Yankees but couldn't match their pitching. The 1937 Yankees averaged more than 6 runs per game and were led by DiMaggio, Gehrig in his last great season, and Dickey. Except for DiMaggio, the outfielders were rather injury prone which provided valuable playing time for Tommy Henrich who enjoyed an impressive rookie season. This team beat the Giants in 5 games in the World Series.

Strengths: (1) hitting for average and power led by Gehrig (37 2B, 9 3B, 37 HR, 200 H, 366 TB), MVP runner-up DiMaggio (35 2B, 15 3B, 46 HR, 410 TB), Dickey (35 2B, 29 HR, 302 TB), Selkirk (18 HR), and Henrich, (2) drawing walks featuring Gehrig (127 BB), Rolfe (90 BB), and Crosetti (86 BB), (3) fielding from SS Crosetti (105 Rng+), 3B Rolfe (107 Rng+), and 2B Lazzeri (96 Rng+), (4) CS% from Dickey (48%), and (5) starting pitching anchored by Gomez (194 K, 6 shutouts), Ruffing, Pearson, and Chandler.

Weaknesses: (1) RP, SS, and LF positions, (2) hitting from Crosetti, Powell, and Heffner, (3) fielding from 1B Gehrig, (4) double plays made, (5) league average relief pitching, and (6) individual pitching from Hadley, Malone (10.7 H/9), and Makosky.

Mgr	Joe McCarthy	
Rk	11	26
Gm	157	
Place	1	
GA	13.0	
Rival	13–9 vs Tigers, 132 RS & 107 RA	

	W	L	Win%
Regular Season	102	52	0.662
Runs Record	102	52	0.661
1 Run	23	20	0.535
Extra Innings	7	4	0.636
Blowout	39	13	0.750

	Team	LgAvg	%Avg	LgRk
BABIP	0.283	0.299	106	1
E	170	171	101	3
sOBP	0.318	0.352	111	1
rOBP	0.364	0.366	101	5
R/G	6.24	5.23	119	1
RA/G	4.27	5.23	122	1

	Tm	LgAvg	>Avg
RS	979	813	166
RA	671	813	142
DP	134	156	-22

	R/G	HR	K	BB	OBP	SB	CS	SB%
Team Offense	6.24	174	607	712	0.369	60	36	63%
Team Defense	4.27	92	652	506	0.326	51	41	55%
Difference	1.96	82	45	206	113	9		

Pos	Rpos	PA	Age	Name	BA	OBP	SLG	BB%	RS%	Bat R>Avg	BR R>Avg	Fld R>Avg	RAA	WAA
C	4	608	30	Dickey, Bill*	0.332	0.417	0.570	12%	26%	43	0	3	50	4.6
1B	-7	700	34	Gehrig, Lou*	0.351	0.473	0.643	18%	34%	79	0	-6	66	6.0
2B	4	518	33	Lazzeri, Tony	0.244	0.348	0.399	14%	25%	-3	1	5	7	0.6
3B	3	740	28	Rolfe, Red*	0.276	0.365	0.378	12%	52%	-4	0	7	6	0.6
SS	10	721	26	Crosetti, Frankie	0.234	0.340	0.352	12%	50%	-16	0	3	-3	-0.3
LF	-4	400	28	Powell, Jake	0.263	0.314	0.364	6%	43%	-13	-1	4	-14	-1.3
CF	-2	692	22	DiMaggio, Joe	0.346	0.412	0.673	9%	44%	67	1	6	72	6.6
RF,LF	-4	404	29	Hoag, Myril	0.301	0.364	0.423	8%	32%	2	-2	0	-4	-0.3
RF	-3	293	29	Selkirk, George*	0.328	0.411	0.629	12%	30%	24	1	5	27	2.5
LF,RF	-3	242	24	Henrich, Tommy*	0.320	0.419	0.553	14%	33%	16	1	-2	12	1.1
2B,SS	2	221	26	Heffner, Don	0.249	0.314	0.328	9%	33%	-10	-2	-2	-12	-1.1
C	1	64	28	Glenn, Joe	0.283	0.397	0.396	16%	24%	1	0	0	2	0.2
LF	-1	54	34	Johnson, Roy*	0.294	0.333	0.353	6%	28%	-2	0	-2	-5	-0.4
	0	637		Others	0.171	0.229	0.201	7%	37%	-73	2	0	-71	-6.5
	0		28.5	Team Total	0.283	0.369	0.456	11.3%	37.9%	113	1	21	135	12.3
				League Average	0.281	0.355	0.415	9.8%	34.9%					

Pos	Rpos	PA	Age	Name	BA	OBP	SLG	BB%	RS%	Bat R>Avg	BR R>Avg	Fld R>Avg	RAA	WAA
				% Lg Avg	101	104	110	116	108					
				League Rank	3	2	1	1			5	3		

GS	GR	IP	Age	Name	W–L	WHIP	K/9	BB/9	HR/9	FIP	ERA	R/9	RAA	WAA
34	0	278	28	Gomez, Lefty*	21–11	1.17	6.3	3.0	0.3	3.21	2.33	2.85	73	6.7
31	0	256	32	Ruffing, Red	20–7	1.21	4.6	2.4	0.6	3.77	2.98	3.55	47	4.4
25	4	178	32	Hadley, Bump	11–8	1.58	3.5	4.2	0.8	4.95	5.30	6.16	-19	-1.7
20	2	145	28	Pearson, Monte	9–3	1.44	4.4	4.0	0.4	4.03	3.17	3.73	24	2.2
10	6	88	30	Wicker, Kemp*	7–3	1.51	1.4	2.7	0.8	4.88	4.40	5.32	-1	-0.1
10	2	82	29	Chandler, Spud	7–4	1.20	3.4	2.2	0.9	4.40	2.84	3.39	17	1.5
4	35	110	28	Murphy, Johnny	13–4	1.55	2.9	4.1	0.6	4.69	4.17	4.83	5	0.4
9	19	92	34	Malone, Pat	4–4	1.57	4.8	3.4	0.5	4.04	5.48	6.36	-12	-1.1
1	25	58	27	Makosky, Frank	5–2	1.52	4.2	3.7	0.9	4.78	4.97	6.52	-8	-0.8
5	6	49	30	Andrews, Ivy	3–2	1.35	3.1	3.1	0.4	4.00	3.12	3.49	9	0.9
8	1	59		Others	2–4	1.61	1.8	4.0	1.1	5.58	4.27	4.88	2	0.2
157	100		29.8	Team Total		1.38	4.20	3.26	0.59	4.16	3.65	4.33	137	12.5
				League Average		1.55	3.66	3.93	0.66	4.62	4.62	5.34		
				% Lg Avg		112	115	120	112	111	127	124		
				League Rank		1	2	1	3	2	1			

1938 New York Yankees

The 1938 Yankees were the third of the four straight world championship teams who led their league in both R/G and RA/G. They were a great example of a team that hit for a below league average batting average but dominated the league in isolated power and were patient enough to draw enough walks to nearly lead the league in OBP. Gordon assumed the starting 2B position from Lazzeri.

Strengths: (1) isolated power led by DiMaggio (32 2B, 13 3B, 32 HR), Gehrig (32 2B, 29 HR), MVP runner-up Dickey (27 HR), Henrich (24 2B, 22 HR), Rolfe (36 2B), and Gordon (25 HR), (2) drawing walks especially from Gehrig (107 BB), Crosetti (106 BB), and Henrich (92 BB), (3) baserunning led by Rolfe (13 SB, 1 CS), (4) fielding led by SS Crosetti (109 Rng+, 120 DP) and rookie 2B Gordon (110 Rng+, 98 DP), (5) CS% from Dickey (47% CS), and (6) pitching depth anchored by all 5 starting pitchers: Ruffing (61% QS, 8.0 IP/S), Gomez (63% QS), Hadley (35% QS), Chandler (52% QS), and Pearson (44% QS).

Weaknesses: (1) LF position, (2) team hitting for average and contact, (3) hitting from Hoag, Powell, and Glenn, and (4) pitching from Ferrell (0% QS), Beggs (22% QS), and Sundra (25% QS).

Mgr	Joe McCarthy	
Rk	25	66
Gm	157	
Place	1	
GA	9.5	
Rival	11–11 vs Red Sox, 117 RS & 114 RA	

	W	L	Win%
Regular Season	99	53	0.651
Runs Record	96	56	0.633
1 Run	16	15	0.516
Extra Innings	5	2	0.714
Blowout	33	14	0.702

	Team	LgAvg	%Avg	LgRk
BABIP	0.287	0.296	103	1
E	169	173	102	4
sOBP	0.339	0.355	105	1
rOBP	0.338	0.369	109	1
R/G	6.15	5.37	115	1
RA/G	4.53	5.37	119	1

	Tm	LgAvg	>Avg
RS	966	823	143
RA	711	823	112
DP	177	160	17

	R/G	HR	K	BB	SB	CS	SB%	OBP
Team Offense	6.15	174	617	749	91	28	76%	0.366
Team Defense	4.53	85	567	566	54	37	59%	0.339
Difference	1.62	89	-50	183	37			108%

Pos	Rpos	PA	Age	Name	BA	OBP	SLG	BB%	RS%	Bat R>Avg	BR R>Avg	Fld R>Avg	RAA	WAA
C	4	532	31	Dickey, Bill*	0.313	0.412	0.568	14%	30%	35	1	0	40	3.6
1B	-7	689	35	Gehrig, Lou*	0.295	0.410	0.523	16%	34%	36	1	-2	28	2.6
2B	5	520	23	Gordon, Joe	0.255	0.340	0.502	11%	38%	8	1	9	23	2.1
3B	2	714	29	Rolfe, Red*	0.311	0.386	0.441	10%	46%	14	3	3	22	2.0

Pos	Rpos	PA	Age	Name	BA	OBP	SLG	BB%	RS%	Bat R>Avg	BR R>Avg	Fld R>Avg	RAA	WAA
SS	10	757	27	Crosetti, Frankie	0.263	0.382	0.371	14%	37%	0	0	8	18	1.7
LF	-4	407	30	Selkirk, George*	0.254	0.384	0.409	17%	33%	5	0	0	1	0.1
CF	-1	660	23	DiMaggio, Joe	0.324	0.386	0.581	9%	43%	39	1	2	41	3.7
RF	-6	575	25	Henrich, Tommy*	0.270	0.391	0.490	16%	44%	20	1	4	19	1.7
LF,RF	-3	298	30	Hoag, Myril	0.277	0.344	0.352	8%	28%	-7	0	0	-10	-0.9
LF,RF	-2	183	29	Powell, Jake	0.256	0.326	0.378	8%	44%	-5	0	0	-7	-0.6
2B,SS	1	143	26	Knickerbocker, Bill	0.250	0.309	0.383	8%	33%	-4	0	0	-3	-0.3
C	1	133	29	Glenn, Joe	0.260	0.316	0.350	8%	24%	-5	0	-1	-5	-0.5
P	0	125	33	Ruffing, Red	0.224	0.331	0.364	14%	24%	-3	0	0	-3	-0.3
	0	523		Others	0.170	0.226	0.230	7%	43%	-57	3	-2	-56	-5.1
	0		28.5	Team Total	0.274	0.366	0.446	12.0%	37.8%	77	11	21	109	9.9
				League Average	0.281	0.358	0.415	10.2%	35.4%					
				% Lg Avg	97	102	107	117	107					
				League Rank	6	2	1	1	2		1	1		

GS	GR	IP	Age	Name	W–L	GmSc	K/9	BB/9	HR/9	FIP	ERA	R/9	RAA	WAA
31	0	247	33	Ruffing, Red	21–7	54.9	4.6	3.0	0.6	3.92	3.31	3.78	44	4.0
32	0	239	29	Gomez, Lefty*	18–12	52.9	4.9	3.7	0.3	3.67	3.35	4.14	33	3.0
27	1	202	29	Pearson, Monte	16–7	49.4	4.4	5.0	0.5	4.60	3.97	4.77	14	1.2
23	0	172	30	Chandler, Spud	14–5	49.1	1.9	2.5	0.4	4.08	4.03	4.50	17	1.5
17	12	167	33	Hadley, Bump	9–8	52.1	3.3	3.5	0.7	4.63	3.60	4.25	21	1.9
9	5	58	27	Beggs, Joe	3–2	42.3	1.2	3.1	1.1	5.43	5.40	6.33	-6	-0.6
2	30	91	29	Murphy, Johnny	8–2	43.5	4.2	4.0	0.5	4.27	4.24	4.63	8	0.7
8	17	94	28	Sundra, Steve	6–4	34.8	3.2	4.1	0.7	4.76	4.80	5.86	-5	-0.5
1	18	48	31	Andrews, Ivy	1–3	64.0	2.4	3.2	0.6	4.45	3.00	4.69	4	0.3
4	1	30	30	Ferrell, Wes	2–2	20.0	2.1	5.4	1.8	7.05	8.10	9.90	-15	-1.4
3	7	33		Others	1–1	—	3.3	5.5	0.5	5.08	4.63	4.91	2	0.2
157	91		29.9	Team Total		49	3.69	3.69	0.55	4.34	3.91	4.63	115	10.4
				League Average		45	3.56	4.12	0.72	4.79	4.79	5.51		
				% Lg Avg		109	104	112	131	110	122	119		
				League Rank		1	3	2	2	1	1			

1939 New York Yankees

The Yankees once again ran over the rest of the AL with one of the most dominating teams of all time ending the season by sweeping the Reds in the Series. This team had an historic 2.7 run per game differential. Joe DiMaggio had one of his best seasons and won the AL MVP award even though he was only able to play 120 games. This was the season when the consecutive game streak of Lou Gehrig was broken as he unexpectedly was unable to play most of the season due to his crippling illness.

Strengths: (1) hitting led by DiMaggio (32 2B, 30 HR), Selkirk (21 HR), Rolfe (46 2B, 10 3B), rookie Keller (21 2B), Dickey (24 HR), and Gordon (32 2B, 28 HR), (2) drawing walks especially from Selkirk (103 BB), Rolfe (81 BB), Keller (81 BB), Dickey (77 BB), and Gordon (75 BB), (3) fielding featuring SS Crosetti (110 Rng+, 118 DP), 2B Gordon (107 Rng+, 116 DP), CF DiMaggio (105 Rng+, 13 assists), 3B Rolfe (94 Rng+, 19 E in 452 chances), and RF/CF Henrich (105 Rng+ in RF, 103 Rng+ in CF), (4) CS% from Dickey (43%), and (5) deep pitching staff anchored by Ruffing, Gomez, Russo, Hildebrand, Sundra, and Hadley.

Weaknesses: (1) 1B position, (2) hitting from Crosetti and Dahlgren, and (3) CS% from reserve catcher Rosar (29%).

Mgr	Joe McCarthy
Rk	2 2
Gm	152
Place	1
GA	17.0
Rival	8–11 vs Red Sox, 97 RS & 93 RA

	W	L	Win%
Regular Season	106	45	0.702
Runs Record	110	41	0.727
1 Run	22	15	0.595
Extra Innings	3	4	0.429
Blowout	41	6	0.872

	Team	LgAvg	%Avg	LgRk
BABIP	0.257	0.295	115	1
E	126	183	145	4
sOBP	0.317	0.348	110	1
rOBP	0.332	0.365	110	1
R/G	6.36	5.21	122	1
RA/G	3.66	5.21	142	1

	Tm	LgAvg	>Avg
RS	967	801	166
RA	556	801	245
DP	159	148	11

	R/G	HR	K	BB	SB	CS	SB%	OBP
Team Offense	6.36	166	543	701	72	37	66%	0.374
Team Defense	3.66	85	565	567	49	32	60%	0.319
Difference	2.70	81	22	134	23			117%

Pos	Rpos	PA	Age	Name	BA	OBP	SLG	BB%	RS%	Bat R>Avg	BR R>Avg	Fld R>Avg	RAA	WAA
C	4	565	32	Dickey, Bill*	0.302	0.403	0.513	14%	37%	29	2	2	37	3.4
1B	-7	603	27	Dahlgren, Babe	0.235	0.312	0.377	9%	33%	-16	0	2	-21	-1.9
2B	6	648	24	Gordon, Joe	0.284	0.370	0.506	12%	30%	23	-2	21	48	4.4
3B	2	731	30	Rolfe, Red*	0.329	0.404	0.495	11%	44%	35	-1	7	43	4.0
SS	10	743	28	Crosetti, Frankie	0.233	0.315	0.332	9%	45%	-27	0	22	5	0.4
LF,RF	-6	537	31	Selkirk, George*	0.306	0.452	0.517	19%	38%	39	1	7	41	3.8
CF	-1	524	24	DiMaggio, Joe	0.381	0.448	0.671	10%	39%	60	1	11	71	6.5
RF,LF	-5	490	22	Keller, Charlie*	0.334	0.447	0.500	17%	37%	32	0	6	33	3.1
RF,CF	-3	406	26	Henrich, Tommy*	0.277	0.371	0.429	13%	40%	6	2	7	12	1.1
C	1	121	24	Rosar, Buddy	0.276	0.356	0.343	11%	43%	-2	1	0	0	0.0
LF	-1	91	30	Powell, Jake	0.244	0.270	0.349	3%	48%	-5	-1	2	-5	-0.5
RF	0	47	25	Gallagher, Joe	0.244	0.311	0.439	6%	50%	0	0	0	0	0.0
P	0	124	35	Ruffing, Red	0.307	0.347	0.342	6%	27%	-3	0	0	-3	-0.2
	0	499		Others	0.215	0.269	0.266	7%	36%	-38	0	1	-37	-3.4
	0		27.5	Team Total	0.287	0.374	0.451	11.4%	38.3%	134	3	88	225	20.7
				League Average	0.279	0.352	0.407	9.6%	35.3%					
				% Lg Avg	103	106	111	119	108					
				League Rank	2	1	1	1	2		2	1		

GS	GR	IP	Age	Name	W–L	GmSc	K/9	BB/9	HR/9	FIP	ERA	R/9	RAA	WAA
28	0	233	35	Ruffing, Red	21–7	57.6	3.7	2.9	0.6	4.15	2.93	3.39	34	3.1
26	0	198	30	Gomez, Lefty*	12–8	55.8	4.6	3.8	0.5	4.15	3.41	3.64	24	2.2
18	8	154	34	Hadley, Bump	12–6	54.1	3.8	5.0	0.6	4.85	2.98	3.62	19	1.7
20	4	153	28	Donald, Atley	13–3	50.6	3.2	3.5	0.7	4.61	3.71	4.35	6	0.5
20	2	146	29	Pearson, Monte	12–5	49.0	4.7	4.3	0.6	4.35	4.49	4.74	0	0.0
15	6	127	32	Hildebrand, Oral	10–4	55.1	3.6	2.9	0.8	4.47	3.06	3.13	22	2.1
0	38	61	30	Murphy, Johnny	3–6	—	4.4	4.1	0.0	3.53	4.40	4.84	-1	-0.1
11	13	121	29	Sundra, Steve	11–1	52.5	2.0	4.2	0.5	4.84	2.76	3.21	19	1.8
11	10	116	24	Russo, Marius*	8–3	64.0	4.3	3.2	0.5	3.95	2.41	2.87	24	2.2
0	11	19	31	Chandler, Spud	3–0	—	1.9	4.3	0.0	4.14	2.84	3.32	3	0.2
3	1	20		Others	1–2	—	2.7	8.0	1.8	7.76	4.87	4.87	0	0.0
152	93		30.2	Team Total		54	3.77	3.78	0.57	4.40	3.31	3.71	150	13.8
				League Average		47	3.57	3.86	0.66	4.62	4.62	5.30		
				% Lg Avg		115	105	102	116	105	140	143		
				League Rank		1	3	4	4	4	1			

1940 CINCINNATI REDS

The 1940 Reds repeated as NL pennant winners with excellent fielding and pitching leading the majors with only 3.4 runs allowed per game. It would be more than 20 years before the Reds would play again in the postseason and 35 years before the Reds were able to win another world championship. All-star catcher Ernie Lombardi started only 97 games due to injuries which included a severe ankle sprain. In the World Series, the Reds won 4 games to 3 over the Tigers to become world champions for the first time since 1919.

Strengths: (1) hitting for average, contact, and power led by Frank McCormick (44 2B, 19 HR), Lombardi (22 2B, 14 HR), and Werber (35 2B), (2) fielding led by 2B Frey (114 Rng+, 111 DP), SS Myers (97 Rng+, 62 DP), SS Joost (99 Rng+, 48 DP), 3B Werber (106 Rng+, 24 DP), and 1B Frank McCormick, and (3) pitching anchored by Reds ace Bucky Walters (69% QS, 8.5 IP/S), Derringer (70% QS, 8.0 IPS/S), and closer Beggs (7 Sv, 4 BSv, 12/18 IR stranded, 1.885 Lv).

Weaknesses: (1) CF and RF positions, (2) hitting from Craft, Joost, and Myers, (3) pitching from Shoffner, and (4) drawing walks.

Mgr	Bill McKechnie	
Rk	40	97
Gm	155	
Place	1	
GA	12.0	
Rival	14–8 vs Dodgers, 125 RS & 83 RA	

	W	*L*	*Win%*
Regular Season	100	53	0.654
Runs Record	95	58	0.623
1 Run	41	17	0.707
Extra Innings	8	8	0.500
Blowout	28	10	0.737

	Team	*LgAvg*	*%Avg*	*LgRk*
BABIP	0.257	0.280	109	1
E	117	174	149	1
sOBP	0.299	0.321	107	2
rOBP	0.317	0.342	108	1
R/G	4.56	4.40	104	3
RA/G	3.41	4.40	129	1

	Tm	*LgAvg*	*>Avg*
RS	707	678	29
RA	528	678	150
DP	158	143	15

	R/G	*HR*	*K*	*BB*	*SB*	*CS*	*SB%*	*OBP*
Team Offense	4.56	89	503	453	72			0.327
Team Defense	3.41	73	557	445	51	29	64%	0.302
Difference	1.15	16	54	8	21			108%

Pos	*Rpos*	*PA*	*Age*	*Name*	*BA*	*OBP*	*SLG*	*BB%*	*RS%*	*Bat R>Avg*	*BR R>Avg*	*Fld R>Avg*	*RAA*	*WAA*
C	3	414	32	Lombardi, Ernie	0.319	0.382	0.489	7%	25%	23	0	0	26	2.6
1B	-7	676	29	McCormick, Frank	0.309	0.367	0.482	8%	32%	32	0	13	38	3.8
2B	6	663	29	Frey, Lonny*	0.266	0.361	0.371	12%	42%	9	0	25	40	4.1
3B	1	663	32	Werber, Bill	0.277	0.361	0.416	10%	41%	17	0	10	28	2.9
SS	5	323	29	Myers, Billy	0.202	0.283	0.319	9%	33%	-10	0	14	9	0.9
CF,LF	-3	453	23	McCormick, Mike	0.300	0.326	0.355	3%	34%	-3	0	8	2	0.2
CF	-1	452	25	Craft, Harry	0.244	0.277	0.353	4%	35%	-13	0	6	-8	-0.8
RF	-6	594	31	Goodman, Ival*	0.258	0.335	0.389	10%	36%	5	0	4	3	0.3
SS,2B	6	323	24	Joost, Eddie	0.216	0.301	0.266	10%	25%	-12	0	13	7	0.7
LF	-3	226	29	Arnovich, Morrie	0.284	0.326	0.351	6%	23%	-2	0	4	-1	-0.1
C	1	133	30	Hershberger, Will	0.309	0.351	0.374	5%	13%	1	0	0	2	0.2
LF	-1	124	27	Rizzo, Johnny	0.282	0.363	0.445	11%	32%	4	0	2	5	0.5
LF,RF	-1	119	30	Ripple, Jimmy*	0.307	0.397	0.525	11%	26%	8	0	-1	6	0.6
3B	0	74	30	Riggs, Lew*	0.292	0.311	0.458	3%	32%	1	0	1	2	0.2
	0	749		Others	0.207	0.231	0.261	3%	38%	-54	1	0	-53	-5.4
	0		28.6	Team Total	0.266	0.327	0.379	7.6%	33.8%	6	1	99	106	10.8
				League Average	0.264	0.326	0.376	7.9%	32.4%					
				% Lg Avg	101	100	101	95	105					
				League Rank	5	5	5	4	3			1	1	

GS	*GR*	*IP*	*Age*	*Name*	*W–L*	*GmSc*	*K/9*	*BB/9*	*HR/9*	*FIP*	*ERA*	*R/9*	*RAA*	*WAA*
36	0	305	31	Walters, Bucky	22–10	61.7	3.4	2.7	0.6	3.76	2.48	2.80	34	3.4
37	0	297	33	Derringer, Paul	20–12	57.3	3.5	1.5	0.5	3.20	3.06	3.34	13	1.4
31	2	225	23	Thompson, Junior	16–9	54.1	4.1	3.8	0.4	3.72	3.32	3.59	4	0.5
23	1	187	36	Turner, Jim	14–7	55.6	2.6	1.5	0.4	3.32	2.89	3.37	8	0.8
15	10	117	28	Moore, Whitey	8–8	53.5	4.6	4.2	0.6	4.20	3.63	3.70	1	0.1
7	3	48	25	VanderMeer, John*	3–1	52.9	7.7	7.7	0.6	4.48	3.75	4.50	-3	-0.3
1	36	77	29	Beggs, Joe	12–3	27.0	2.9	2.5	0.1	3.13	2.00	2.23	13	1.3
0	20	54	34	Shoffner, Milt*	1–0	—	2.8	3.0	0.5	3.83	5.63	5.80	-13	-1.3
4	15	54	24	Hutchings, Johnny	2–1	40.5	3.0	3.0	0.5	3.86	3.50	3.50	1	0.1
1	14	34	25	Riddle, Elmer	1–2	51.0	2.4	4.5	0.0	3.73	1.87	3.21	2	0.2
0	5	10		Others	1–0	—	0.9	6.1	0.0	4.88	2.61	3.48	0	0.0
155	106		28.8	Team Total		56	3.56	2.85	0.47	3.62	3.05	3.38	61	6.2
				League Average		51	3.51	3.06	0.56	3.85	3.85	4.40		
				% Lg Avg		110	101	107	120	106	126	130		
				League Rank		1	4	3	2	2	1			

1941 Brooklyn Dodgers

The team with the largest run differentiation in the major leagues in 1941 was the Dodgers. The Dodgers jelled into a very impressive pre-war team who won the pennant for the first time since 1920, but ran into a talented, better rested, and post-season experienced Yankee team in the World Series. The Dodgers became an instant pennant contender when they obtained 2B Billy Herman from the Cubs to replace the struggling Coscarart.

Strengths: (1) hitting for average, contact, and power led by MVP Camilli (29 2B, 34 HR), MVP runner-up Reiser (39 2B, 17 3B) who actually had a better season than Camilli, Medwick (33 2B, 10 3B), and Walker (32 2B), (3) drawing walks especially from Camilli (104 BB), Lavagetto (80 BB), and Walker (70 BB), (4) GIDP, (5) fielding featuring SS Reese (112 Rng+), CF Reiser (113 Rng+, 14 assists), 2B Herman (94 Rng+), and RF Walker (109 Rng+, 19 assists), (6) CS% from Franks (77%), and Owen (52%), and (7) pitching anchored by Wyatt (176 K, 77% QS, 8.0 IP/S) and Davis (75% QS, 8.0 IP/S).

Weaknesses: (1) C position, (2) hitting from Reese, Owen, and Franks, (3) double plays made, and (4) pitching from Hamlin and Casey.

Mgr	Leo Durocher	
Rk	17	43
Gm	157	
Place	1	
GA	2.5	
Rival	11–11 vs Cardinals, 101 RS & 94 RA	

	W	*L*	*Win%*
Regular Season	100	54	0.648
Runs Record	100	54	0.648
1 Run	28	16	0.636
Extra Innings	8	4	0.667
Blowout	35	11	0.761

	Team	*LgAvg*	*LgRk*	*%Avg*
BABIP	0.249	0.277	111	1
E	162	174	107	3
sOBP	0.297	0.323	109	1
rOBP	0.310	0.335	108	1
R/G	5.10	4.23	120	1
RA/G	3.70	4.23	114	2

	Tm	*LgAvg*	*>Avg*
RS	800	658	142
RA	581	659	78
DP	125	144	-19

	R/G	*HR*	*K*	*BB*	*SB*	*CS*	*SB%*	*OBP*
Team Offense	5.10	101	535	600	36			0.347
Team Defense	3.70	81	603	495	33	39	46%	0.300
Difference	1.39	20	68	105	3			116%

Pos	*Rpos*	*PA*	*Age*	*Name*	*BA*	*OBP*	*SLG*	*BB%*	*RS%*	*Bat R>Avg*	*BR R>Avg*	*Fld R>Avg*	*RAA*	*WAA*
C	4	437	25	Owen, Mickey	0.231	0.296	0.288	8%	25%	-14	0	2	-8	-0.8
1B	-7	641	34	Camilli, Dolph*	0.285	0.407	0.556	16%	26%	55	0	6	54	5.5
2B	6	604	31	Herman, Billy	0.291	0.361	0.379	10%	35%	12	0	5	23	2.3
3B	0	523	28	Lavagetto, Cookie	0.277	0.388	0.370	15%	37%	15	-1	0	14	1.5
SS	10	674	22	Reese, Pee Wee	0.229	0.311	0.294	10%	36%	-16	-1	13	6	0.6
LF	-6	579	29	Medwick, Joe	0.318	0.364	0.517	7%	43%	34	0	4	32	3.3
CF	-1	601	22	Reiser, Pete*	0.343	0.406	0.558	8%	45%	52	0	10	61	6.3
RF	-6	606	30	Walker, Dixie*	0.311	0.391	0.452	12%	35%	31	0	14	39	4.0
RF	-3	287	27	Wasdell, Jimmy*	0.298	0.345	0.419	6%	37%	7	0	0	4	0.4
3B	0	220	31	Riggs, Lew*	0.305	0.357	0.487	7%	31%	10	0	-1	9	0.9
C	1	156	27	Franks, Herman*	0.201	0.275	0.273	9%	22%	-7	0	1	-5	-0.5
2B	1	65	28	Kampouris, Alex	0.314	0.444	0.588	17%	23%	7	0	2	10	1.0
P	0	122	33	Wyatt, Whit	0.239	0.272	0.367	3%	25%	-3	0	0	-3	-0.3
	1	703		Others	0.176	0.226	0.226	6%	30%	-55	2	0	-52	-5.3
	0		28.2	Team Total	0.272	0.347	0.405	9.6%	34.6%	128	0	56	184	18.9
				League Average	0.258	0.326	0.361	8.7%	31.7%					
				% Lg Avg	105	106	112	111	109					
				League Rank	1	1	1	1	1		2	1		

GS	*GR*	*IP*	*Age*	*Name*	*W–L*	*GmSc*	*K/9*	*BB/9*	*HR/9*	*FIP*	*ERA*	*R/9*	*RAA*	*WAA*
39	9	298	26	Higbe, Kirby	22–9	55.8	3.7	4.0	0.5	3.84	3.14	3.71	7	0.7
35	3	288	33	Wyatt, Whit	22–10	63.9	5.5	2.6	0.3	2.67	2.34	2.78	37	3.8
16	12	154	37	Davis, Curt	13–7	62.1	2.9	1.6	0.4	3.07	2.98	3.39	9	0.9
20	10	136	36	Hamlin, Luke	8–8	49.8	3.8	2.7	0.9	4.00	4.24	4.96	-16	-1.7
12	1	83	39	Fitzsimmons, Fred	6–1	53.4	2.1	2.8	0.3	3.59	2.07	3.59	3	0.3
4	7	57	35	Allen, Johnny	3–0	66.0	3.3	1.9	0.9	3.83	2.53	2.84	7	0.7
18	27	162	27	Casey, Hugh	14–11	45.6	3.4	3.2	0.4	3.53	3.89	4.50	-11	-1.1
5	10	52	26	Kimball, Newt	3–1	48.2	2.9	5.0	0.0	3.58	3.63	3.81	1	0.1
0	24	43	32	Brown, Mace	3–2	—	4.6	5.4	0.6	4.33	3.14	3.56	2	0.2
0	9	22	33	Swift, Bill	3–0	—	3.7	2.9	1.6	5.07	3.27	3.68	1	0.1
8	45	126		Others	3–5	—	3.5	4.0	0.7	4.18	3.79	4.00	-1	-0.1
157	157		32.4	Team Total		55	3.82	3.14	0.51	3.54	3.14	3.68	37	3.8
				League Average		51	3.57	3.36	0.48	3.63	3.63	4.27		
				% Lg Avg		108	107	107	94	103	116	116		
				League Rank		2	3	2	6	4	1			

1942 New York Yankees

The Yankees led the league in most runs scored and fewest runs allowed becoming one of the best teams in baseball history featuring a great outfield consisting of DiMaggio, Keller, and Henrich and wonderful seasons from Rizzuto and Gordon. However, they were defeated 4–1 in the World Series by an equally dominating Cardinal team. Heinrich was called to military service late in the season providing playing time for Roy Cullenbinet. This team kept winning despite injuries and illnesses to Rolfe, Dickey, and Russo.

Strengths: (1) hitting for average and power led by Keller (24 2B, 26 HR), MVP Joe Gordon (29 2B, 18 HR), DiMaggio (29 2B, 13 3B, 21 HR), and Henrich (30 2B), (2) drawing walks especially from Keller (114 BB) and Gordon (79 BB), (3) baserunning especially from Rizzuto (22 SB, 6 CS, 37% RS) and Keller (14 SB, 2 CS, 5 GIDP), (4) fielding especially making double plays featuring SS Rizzuto (113 Rng+, 114 DP) and 2B Gordon (100 Rng+, 121 DP), (5) CS% from Rosar (61%) and Dickey (59%), and (6) pitching anchored by starters Bonham (78% QS, 8.3 IP/S), Chandler (79% QS, 8.4 IP/S), Borowy (67% QS), and Ruffing (58% QS, 8.1 IP/S).

Weaknesses: (1) RP, (2) hitting from Rosar and Rolfe, (3) hitting for contact from Gordon and Priddy, and (4) control from Gomez.

Mgr	Joe McCarthy	
Rk	5	11
Gm	154	
Place	1	
GA	9.0	
Rival	10–12 vs Red Sox, 93 RS & 88 RA	

	W	L	Win%
Regular Season	103	51	0.669
Runs Record	105	49	0.681
1 Run	22	22	0.500
Extra Innings	9	7	0.563
Blowout	34	5	0.872

	Team	LgAvg	%Avg	LgRk
BABIP	0.263	0.275	105	2
E	142	176	124	1
sOBP	0.302	0.327	108	1
rOBP	0.324	0.338	104	2
R/G	5.20	4.26	122	1
RA/G	3.29	4.26	129	1

	Tm	LgAvg	>Avg
RS	801	651	150
RA	507	651	144
DP	190	151	39

	R/G	HR	K	BB	SB	CS	SB%	OBP
Team Offense	5.20	108	556	591	69	33	68%	0.346
Team Defense	3.29	71	558	431	37	49	43%	0.305
Difference	1.91	37	2	160	32			113%

Pos	Rpos	PA	Age	Name	BA	OBP	SLG	BB%	RS%	Bat R>Avg	BR R>Avg	Fld R>Avg	RAA	WAA
C	3	295	35	Dickey, Bill*	0.295	0.359	0.373	9%	25%	5	0	1	9	0.9
1B	-6	581	30	Hassett, Buddy*	0.284	0.325	0.364	6%	42%	-1	0	7	0	0.0
2B	7	625	27	Gordon, Joe	0.322	0.409	0.491	13%	30%	43	1	16	67	6.9
3B	1	328	31	Crosetti, Frankie	0.242	0.335	0.337	9%	44%	-1	0	1	1	0.1
SS	9	613	24	Rizzuto, Phil	0.284	0.343	0.374	7%	37%	6	3	21	39	4.0
LF	-7	661	25	Keller, Charlie*	0.292	0.417	0.513	17%	32%	52	3	3	51	5.2
CF	-1	680	27	DiMaggio, Joe	0.305	0.376	0.498	10%	43%	40	1	4	44	4.5
RF,1B	-6	555	29	Henrich, Tommy*	0.267	0.352	0.431	10%	36%	17	0	3	14	1.4
3B	0	291	33	Rolfe, Red*	0.219	0.281	0.355	8%	47%	-6	0	4	-2	-0.2
C	2	226	27	Rosar, Buddy	0.230	0.288	0.306	8%	25%	-7	0	2	-3	-0.3
3B,1B	0	222	22	Priddy, Jerry	0.280	0.385	0.381	14%	25%	7	0	4	11	1.1
RF	-1	97	28	Cullenbine, Roy^	0.364	0.484	0.532	19%	32%	11	0	2	12	1.2
C	1	92	35	Hemsley, Rollie	0.294	0.333	0.353	5%	40%	0	0	1	2	0.2
	-2	743		Others	0.169	0.225	0.204	6%	37%	-62	-1	1	-64	-6.6
	0			Team Total	0.269	0.346	0.394	9.8%	35.7%	104	7	70	181	18.5
				League Average	0.257	0.329	0.357	9.2%	31.8%					
				% Lg Avg	105	105	110	107	112					
				League Rank	2	2	2	3	1		2	1		

GS	GR	IP	Age	Name	W–L	GmSc	K/9	BB/9	HR/9	FIP	ERA	R/9	RAA	WAA
27	1	226	28	Bonham, Tiny	21–5	61.7	2.8	1.0	0.4	2.89	2.27	2.59	31	3.2
24	0	201	34	Chandler, Spud	16–5	59.3	3.3	3.3	0.6	3.82	2.38	2.87	21	2.2
24	0	194	38	Ruffing, Red	14–7	56.8	3.7	1.9	0.5	3.08	3.21	3.35	10	1.1
21	4	178	26	Borowy, Hank	15–4	56.3	4.3	3.3	0.3	3.14	2.52	2.83	20	2.1
19	8	164	28	Breuer, Marv	8–9	54.1	3.9	2.0	0.6	3.24	3.07	3.67	3	0.3
19	1	148	31	Donald, Atley	11–3	54.7	3.2	2.7	0.4	3.27	3.11	3.53	5	0.5
13	0	80	33	Gomez, Lefty*	6–4	48.5	4.6	7.3	0.5	4.69	4.28	4.73	-8	-0.8
5	4	45	27	Russo, Marius*	4–1	56.0	3.0	2.8	0.4	3.45	2.78	2.98	4	0.4

GS	GR	IP	Age	Name	W–L	GmSc	K/9	BB/9	HR/9	FIP	ERA	R/9	RAA	WAA
0	31	58	33	Murphy, Johnny	4–10	—	3.7	3.6	0.3	3.46	3.41	4.19	-2	-0.2
2	21	53	25	Lindell, Johnny	2–1	35.5	4.8	3.8	0.5	3.54	3.76	4.27	-3	-0.3
0	19	28		Others	2–2	—	4.8	6.4	1.0	5.20	3.81	5.08	-4	-0.4
154	89			Team Total		56	3.65	2.82	0.46	3.39	2.91	3.32	78	8.0
				League Average		51	3.41	3.55	0.44	3.66	3.66	4.29		
				% Lg Avg		110	107	126	94	108	126	129		
				League Rank		1	2	1	6	1	1			

1942 Boston Red Sox

The Red Sox had a very impressive offense led by Triple Crown winner Ted Williams. Williams was the best player in the majors in both 1941 and 1942 but did not win the MVP in either season as he finished second to Yankee Joe DiMaggio in 1941 and to Yankee Joe Gordon in 1942. The 1942 Red Sox had the top AL positional and pitcher players with Williams and Hughson. The release of 34-year-old Hall of Famer Jimmie Foxx on June 1, 1942, hurt this team as Foxx was having a better offensive season than Lupien.

Strengths: (1) hitting led by MVP runner-up and Triple Crown winner Ted Williams (.356 BA, 36 HR, 137 RBI, 34 2B), Doerr (35 2B, 15 HR), Dom DiMaggio (36 2B), and Pesky (29 2B, 9 3B), (2) drawing walks especially from Williams (145 BB), (3) GIDP, (4) fielding from SS Pesky (113 Rng+, 94 DP), 2B Doerr (108 Rng+, 105 DP), and CF Dom DiMaggio (112 Rng+, 19 assists), (5) CS% from Peacock (47% CS), and (6) pitching anchored by Hughson (67% QS), Butland (60% QS), and Dobson (61% QS).

Weaknesses: (1) C and 3B positions, (2) hitting from the catcher position (Conroy and Peacock), (3) hitting and fielding from 3B Tabor (97 Rng+, 33 errors in 437 chances) as 35-year-old player-manager Cronin should have probably inserted himself in the lineup at 3B more often, (4) baserunning from Tabor (6 SB, 13 CS), and (5) pitching from Newsome (39% QS) and Terry (45% QS).

Mgr	Joe Cronin	
Rk	44	104
Gm	152	
Place	2	
GB	9.0	
Rival	12–10 vs Yankees, 88 RS & 93 RA	

	W	L	Win%
Regular Season	93	59	0.612
Runs Record	94	58	0.621
1 Run	30	23	0.566
Extra Innings	10	6	0.625
Blowout	26	8	0.765

	Team	LgAvg	%Avg	LgRk
BABIP	0.263	0.275	105	1
E	157	176	112	2
sOBP	0.319	0.327	103	2
rOBP	0.335	0.338	101	4
R/G	5.01	4.26	118	2
RA/G	3.91	4.26	109	3

	Tm	LgAvg	RAA
RS	761	651	110
RA	594	651	57
DP	156	151	5

	R/G	HR	K	BB	SB	CS	SB%	OBP
Team Offense	5.01	103	508	591	68	61	53%	0.352
Team Defense	3.91	65	500	553	62	48	56%	0.322
Difference	1.10	38	-8	38	6			109%

Pos	Rpos	PA	Age	Name	BA	OBP	SLG	BB%	RS%	Bat R>Avg	BR R>Avg	Fld R>Avg	RAA	WAA
C	2	298	27	Conroy, Bill	0.200	0.315	0.280	13%	20%	-7	1	0	-4	-0.4
1B	-6	525	25	Lupien, Tony*	0.281	0.351	0.384	10%	34%	9	-2	-4	-3	-0.3
2B	6	625	24	Doerr, Bobby	0.290	0.369	0.455	11%	27%	27	0	10	43	4.4
3B	0	554	25	Tabor, Jim	0.252	0.303	0.366	7%	29%	-5	-3	-5	-13	-1.3
SS	10	686	22	Pesky, Johnny*	0.331	0.375	0.416	6%	42%	23	0	10	43	4.4
LF	-7	671	23	Williams, Ted*	0.356	0.499	0.648	22%	35%	97	0	5	95	9.7
CF	-1	702	25	DiMaggio, Dom	0.286	0.364	0.437	10%	40%	26	0	14	39	4.0
RF	-4	431	31	Finney, Lou*	0.285	0.335	0.383	7%	39%	4	0	5	5	0.5
C	3	309	32	Peacock, Johnny*	0.266	0.316	0.311	7%	18%	-6	0	1	-2	-0.2
RF,LF	-3	286	33	Fox, Pete	0.262	0.323	0.395	7%	45%	2	-1	-4	-6	-0.6
1B	-1	120	34	Foxx, Jimmie	0.270	0.392	0.460	15%	31%	7	0	3	9	0.9
3B,1B	0	95	35	Cronin, Joe	0.304	0.415	0.494	16%	9%	7	0	0	7	0.7
3B,2B	1	105	31	Newsome, Skeeter	0.274	0.337	0.337	9%	20%	0	0	0	1	0.1
	0	577		Others	0.164	0.210	0.208	5%	38%	-50	0	-3	-53	-5.5

Pos	Rpos	PA	Age	Name	BA	OBP	SLG	BB%	RS%	Bat R>Avg	BR R>Avg	Fld R>Avg	RAA	WAA
	0		28.2	Team Total	0.276	0.352	0.403	9.9%	33.6%	132	-5	32	159	16.3
				League Average	0.257	0.329	0.357	9.2%	31.8%					
				% Lg Avg	108	107	113	108	106					
				League Rank	1	1	1	2	3		7	2		

GS	GR	IP	Age	Name	W–L	GmSc	K/9	BB/9	HR/9	FIP	ERA	R/9	RAA	WAA
30	8	281	26	Hughson, Tex	22–6	59.8	3.6	2.4	0.3	3.02	2.59	2.95	35	3.6
26	3	205	29	Wagner, Charlie	14–11	53.6	2.3	4.2	0.2	3.82	3.29	3.81	6	0.6
23	7	183	25	Dobson, Joe	11–9	55.2	3.5	3.4	0.4	3.55	3.30	3.60	10	1.0
23	1	158	32	Newsome, Dick	8–10	44.7	2.3	3.8	0.6	4.22	5.01	5.58	-27	-2.7
19	12	150	34	Judd, Oscar*	8–10	50.8	4.2	5.4	0.2	3.71	3.89	4.31	-4	-0.4
11	9	85	31	Terry, Yank	6–5	48.1	3.9	4.6	0.5	4.03	3.92	5.08	-10	-1.0
0	34	60	33	Brown, Mace	9–3	—	3.0	4.2	0.6	4.14	3.43	4.03	0	0.0
10	13	111	24	Butland, Bill*	7–1	59.5	3.7	2.7	0.6	3.63	2.51	2.83	16	1.6
0	18	44	39	Ryba, Mike	3–3	—	3.2	2.6	1.0	4.24	3.86	5.08	-5	-0.5
10	3	80	28	Chase, Ken*	5–1	51.5	3.8	4.6	0.6	4.04	3.81	4.15	-1	-0.1
152	108		30.1	Team Total		53	3.31	3.66	0.43	3.69	3.44	3.93	21	2.2
				League Average		51	3.41	3.55	0.44	3.66	3.66	4.29		
				% Lg Avg		104	97	97	102	99	106	109		
				League Rank		3	5	6	4	6	3			

1942 St. Louis Cardinals

The 1942 Cardinals peaked as a dominant team in the war years due to Branch Rickey's superior minor league system that kept promoting players from the minors when the major league players got called to military service. Other teams would begin soon to copy this system of owning minor league teams and cheaply grooming and promoting players. The Cardinals also had the advantage of having their 6 best players still on their roster in 1942: Musial, Slaughter, Marion, Moore, and Walker and Mort Cooper. This team would have been even better if Branch Rickey had not traded all-star Johnny Mize prior to the 1942 season due to Mize's refusal to play for the salary offered by Rickey. The deep Cardinals became much better with the first full season of Stan Musial.

Strengths: (1) hitting for average, contact, and power led by Slaughter (31 2B, 17 3B) and Musial (32 2B, 10 3B), (2) bench depth, (3) GIDP, (4) fielding from SS Marion (104 Rng+), (5) CS% from Cooper (59% CS) and O'Dea (58% CS), and (6) pitching depth anchored by Cooper (80% QS), Beazley (83% QS), Krist (50% QS), Lanier (60% QS), and Dickson (1.461 Lv).

Weaknesses: (1) 1B and 2B positions, (2) hitting from the 2B position (Crespi and Brown), and (3) fielding from the 1B position.

Mgr	Billy Southworth	
Rk	7	14
Gm	156	
Place	1	
GA	2.0	
Rival	13–9 vs Dodgers, 102 RS &78 RA	

	W	L	Win%
Regular Season	106	48	0.688
Runs Record	104	50	0.673
1 Run	25	24	0.510
Extra Innings	12	5	0.706
Blowout	34	8	0.810

	Team	LgAvg	%Avg	LgRk
BABIP	0.252	0.266	105	2
E	169	163	96	4
sOBP	0.299	0.316	106	2
rOBP	0.280	0.324	116	1
R/G	4.84	3.90	124	1
RA/G	3.08	3.90	127	1

	Team	LgAvg	>Avg
RS	755	598	157
RA	480	598	118
DP	137	140	-3

	R/G	HR	K	BB	SB	CS	SB%	OBP
Team Offense	4.84	60	505	551	71			0.338
Team Defense	3.08	49	651	473	34	48	41%	0.294
Difference	1.76	11	146	78	37			115%

Pos	Rpos	PA	Age	Name	BA	OBP	SLG	BB%	RS%	Bat R>Avg	BR R>Avg	Fld R>Avg	RAA	WAA
C	4	474	27	Cooper, Walker	0.281	0.327	0.434	6%	35%	13	0	-3	14	1.5
1B	-4	354	25	Hopp, Johnny*	0.258	0.334	0.382	10%	33%	6	1	-4	-1	-0.1

Pos	Rpos	PA	Age	Name	BA	OBP	SLG	BB%	RS%	Bat R>Avg	BR R>Avg	Fld R>Avg	RAA	WAA
2B,SS	4	334	24	Crespi, Creepy	0.243	0.309	0.271	8%	33%	-8	0	-2	-6	-0.6
3B	0	418	24	Kurowski, Whitey	0.254	0.326	0.391	8%	34%	7	0	4	11	1.2
SS	10	554	24	Marion, Marty	0.276	0.343	0.375	9%	36%	10	0	15	35	3.8
LF	-6	536	21	Musial, Stan*	0.315	0.397	0.490	12%	38%	39	0	8	41	4.4
CF	-1	559	30	Moore, Terry	0.288	0.364	0.391	10%	38%	17	0	-1	15	1.7
RF	-7	687	26	Slaughter, Enos*	0.318	0.412	0.494	13%	32%	54	-1	2	48	5.2
2B,3B	5	668	32	Brown, Jimmy^	0.256	0.315	0.320	8%	36%	-6	0	2	1	0.1
1B	-4	328	25	Sanders, Ray*	0.252	0.351	0.379	13%	29%	8	0	-2	2	0.2
C	2	211	29	O'Dea, Ken*	0.234	0.297	0.359	8%	30%	-1	0	0	1	0.1
CF	-1	209	25	Walker, Harry*	0.314	0.355	0.398	5%	53%	6	0	0	5	0.5
LF	-2	171	30	Triplett, Coaker	0.273	0.345	0.390	10%	29%	4	0	0	2	0.2
	0	622		Others	0.186	0.233	0.220	5%	36%	-42	-1	1	-42	-4.5
	0			Team Total	0.268	0.338	0.379	9.0%	35.3%	109	-1	20	128	13.7
				League Average	0.249	0.318	0.343	8.7%	30.1%					
				% Lg Avg	108	106	110	103	117					
				League Rank	1	1	1	4	2		5	4		

GS	GR	IP	Age	Name	W–L	GmSc	K/9	BB/9	HR/9	FIP	ERA	R/9	RAA	WAA
35	2	279	29	Cooper, Mort	22–7	65.1	4.9	2.2	0.3	2.40	1.78	2.36	44	4.8
23	20	215	24	Beazley, Johnny	21–6	58.7	3.8	3.1	0.2	2.74	2.13	2.80	23	2.5
20	14	161	26	Lanier, Max*	13–8	53.5	5.2	3.4	0.2	2.61	2.96	3.07	13	1.4
19	7	128	25	White, Ernie*	7–5	52.7	4.7	2.9	0.8	3.36	2.52	4.00	-3	-0.3
12	0	82	33	Warneke, Lon	6–4	54.3	3.4	1.6	0.9	3.35	3.29	3.73	0	0.0
19	19	163	32	Gumbert, Harry	9–5	48.9	2.9	3.3	0.2	2.99	3.26	3.70	1	0.1
7	29	121	25	Dickson, Murry	6–3	46.4	4.9	4.5	0.1	2.84	2.91	3.06	10	1.1
8	26	118	26	Krist, Howie	13–3	48.4	3.6	3.3	0.2	2.85	2.51	2.59	16	1.7
13	14	109	21	Pollet, Howie*	7–5	54.2	3.5	3.2	0.6	3.47	2.88	3.54	3	0.3
0	5	13	29	Lohrman, Bill	1–1	—	4.3	1.4	0.0	1.81	1.42	2.13	2	0.3
0	13	21		Others	1–1	—	1.7	5.1	0.0	3.74	2.53	2.53	3	0.3
156	149			Team Total		56	4.15	3.02	0.31	2.86	2.55	3.06	113	12.1
				League Average		53	3.43	3.32	0.44	3.31	3.31	3.91		
				% Lg Avg		106	121	110	141	116	130	128		
				League Rank		2	1	2	2	1	1			

1942 Brooklyn Dodgers

Although a great team in its own right, the 1942 Dodgers couldn't stop the second half surge of the Cardinals who had an incredible 63–19 W–L record in the last 82 regular season games allowing them to come from behind and beat the Dodgers by 2 games. The Dodgers 9–13 W–L record against the Cardinals was their own undoing. Also, Reiser's head injury, limiting him to 125 games played, contributed to the Dodgers second place finish despite winning 104 games. Although there were few weaknesses on this team, there were no real superstar seasons either.

Strengths: (1) SP, RP, 1B, SS, and CF positions, (2) hitting for average, contact, and power led by Camilli (26 HR), Reiser (33 2B), Walker (28 2B), and Medwick (37 2B), (3) drawing walks especially from Camilli (97 BB), Reese (82 BB), and Herman (72), (4) GIDP, (5) fielding led by SS Reese (111 Rng+, 99 DP) and 2B Herman (99 Rng+, 97 DP), (6) CS% from Owen (56%), and (7) pitching anchored by Davis (58% QS), French (57% QS), Casey (13 Sv, 3 BSv, 36/51 IR stranded, 1.318 Lv), and Macon (100% QS).

Weaknesses: (1) HR/9 from pitchers Allen, Higbe, and Head which contributed to a negative team homerun differential.

Mgr	Leo Durocher	
Rk	28	77
Gm	155	
Place	2	

	W	L	Win%
Regular Season	104	50	0.675
Runs Record	97	57	0.629
1 Run	27	17	0.614
Extra Innings	13	7	0.650

	Team	LgAvg	%Avg	LgRk
BABIP	0.251	0.266	106	1
E	138	163	118	2
sOBP	0.298	0.316	106	1
rOBP	0.317	0.324	102	4

			W	L	Win%		Team	LgAvg	%Avg	LgRk
GB	2.0	**Blowout**	29	8	0.784	**R/G**	4.79	3.90	123	2
Rival	9–13 vs Cardinals, 78 RS & 102 RA					**RA/G**	3.30	3.90	118	2

	Tm	LgAvg	>Avg
RS	742	598	144
RA	512	598	86
DP	150	140	10

	R/G	HR	K	BB	SB	CS	SB%	OBP
Team Offense	4.79	62	485	572	81			0.338
Team Defense	3.30	73	612	493	35	38	48%	0.302
Difference	1.48	-11	127	79	46			112%

Pos	Rpos	PA	Age	Name	BA	OBP	SLG	BB%	RS%	Bat R>Avg	BR R>Avg	Fld R>Avg	RAA	WAA
C	4	484	26	Owen, Mickey	0.259	0.330	0.311	9%	34%	-2	0	2	4	0.5
1B	-7	625	35	Camilli, Dolph*	0.252	0.372	0.471	16%	31%	36	0	4	33	3.5
2B	6	647	32	Herman, Billy	0.256	0.339	0.333	11%	34%	4	0	5	15	1.6
3B,SS	1	558	30	Vaughan, Arky*	0.277	0.348	0.341	9%	42%	6	-1	3	9	1.0
SS	10	655	23	Reese, Pee Wee	0.255	0.350	0.332	13%	38%	7	0	21	38	4.1
LF	-6	587	30	Medwick, Joe	0.300	0.338	0.403	5%	34%	14	0	4	12	1.3
CF	-1	537	23	Reiser, Pete*	0.310	0.375	0.463	9%	42%	30	1	-2	28	3.0
RF	-5	451	31	Walker, Dixie*	0.290	0.367	0.412	10%	33%	17	0	4	16	1.8
RF,LF	-3	244	29	Rizzo, Johnny	0.230	0.307	0.323	10%	39%	-2	0	2	-3	-0.4
CF,OF	-2	234	30	Galan, Augie^	0.263	0.339	0.340	10%	30%	2	0	0	0	0.0
3B	0	199	32	Riggs, Lew*	0.278	0.333	0.356	7%	27%	2	0	0	2	0.2
C	1	115	31	Sullivan, Billy*	0.267	0.345	0.337	10%	26%	1	0	0	2	0.2
CF,RF	0	62	32	Bordagaray, Frenchy	0.241	0.279	0.276	5%	65%	-2	0	-3	-5	-0.6
	2	594		Others	0.202	0.238	0.248	4%	33%	-34	-1	0	-33	-3.5
	0			Team Total	0.264	0.338	0.362	9.5%	35.4%	79	-1	40	118	12.7
				League Average	0.249	0.318	0.343	8.7%	30.1%					
				% Lg Avg	106	106	106	110	118					
				League Rank	2	2	2	1	1		5	1		

GS	GR	IP	Age	Name	W–L	GmSc	K/9	BB/9	HR/9	FIP	ERA	R/9	RAA	WAA
32	6	222	27	Higbe, Kirby	16–11	55.8	4.7	4.3	0.7	3.71	3.25	3.61	1	0.1
30	1	217	34	Wyatt, Whit	19–7	57.5	4.3	2.6	0.4	2.83	2.73	3.40	6	0.7
26	6	206	38	Davis, Curt	15–6	56.5	2.6	2.2	0.4	3.18	2.36	2.71	21	2.3
15	12	118	37	Allen, Johnny	10–6	55.9	3.8	3.0	0.8	3.69	3.20	4.04	-5	-0.6
15	21	137	24	Head, Ed	10–6	55.6	5.1	3.1	0.7	3.29	3.56	3.95	-4	-0.5
14	24	148	34	French, Larry*	15–4	59.7	3.8	2.2	0.1	2.37	1.83	2.38	21	2.2
2	48	112	28	Casey, Hugh	6–3	48.0	4.3	3.5	0.2	2.90	2.25	2.57	14	1.5
8	6	84	26	Macon, Max*	5–3	57.8	2.9	3.5	0.3	3.36	1.93	2.36	12	1.3
3	16	52	27	Webber, Les	3–2	55.7	4.0	3.8	0.3	3.18	2.96	2.96	4	0.4
5	1	32	34	Newsom, Bobo	2–2	54.2	5.9	3.9	0.3	2.79	3.38	3.66	0	0.0
5	24	72		Others	3–0	—	2.3	4.8	0.6	4.36	5.15	5.40	-14	-1.5
155	165			Team Total		56	3.94	3.17	0.47	3.22	2.84	3.29	55	5.9
				League Average		53	3.43	3.32	0.44	3.31	3.31	3.91		
				% Lg Avg		106	115	105	94	103	116	119		
				League Rank		1	2	4	6	3	3			

1943 St. Louis Cardinals

The Cardinals had a winning record against every NL club and had a margin of pennant victory (18 games) that was the league's largest victory margin since 1902. Due to injuries, only 2 pitchers started 20 or more games. Sixty-two Cardinal games were decided by one run, and more than half of the Cardinal losses were decided by one run. The Cardinals had the top position player (Musial) and the top pitcher (Cooper) in the NL in 1943. This time the Cardinals lost the World Series in 5 games to the Yankees.

Strengths: (1) SP, C, 2B, SS, and RF positions, (2) hitting for average, contact, and power led by MVP Musial (48 2B, 20 3B, 347 TB, 220 H), Sanders (77 BB), MVP runner-up Walker Cooper (30 2B), Kurowski, and rookie Klein (28 2B, 14 3B), (3) GIDP, (4) fielding featuring SS Marion (103 Rng+, 93 DP), 2B Klein (96 Rng+, 99 DP), and RF Musial (120 Rng+, 15 assists), (5) CS% from O'Dea (59% allowing only 9 SB) and Cooper (49% limiting the opposition to 20 SB), and (6) deep pitching anchored by Cooper (6 shutouts, 75% QS, 8.4 IP/S), Lanier (80% QS), Pollet (79% QS, 5 shutouts), and rookies Brazle (100% QS) and Brecheen (62% QS).

Weaknesses: (1) hitting from Brown, Hopp, Garms, and Fallon, (2) drawing walks, and (3) BB/9 from Munger and White.

Mgr	Billy Southworth	
Rk	6	13
Gm	157	
Place	1	
GA	18.0	
Rival	12–10 vs Reds, 62 RS & 67 RA	

	W	*L*	*Win%*
Regular Season	105	49	0.682
Runs Record	105	49	0.679
1 Run	35	27	0.565
Extra Innings	10	14	0.417
Blowout	27	8	0.771

	Team	*LgAvg*	*%Avg*	*LgRk*
BABIP	0.265	0.276	104	1
E	151	164	109	2
sOBP	0.303	0.319	105	2
rOBP	0.303	0.343	113	1
R/G	4.32	3.94	110	2
RA/G	3.01	3.92	130	1

	Tm	*LgAvg*	*>Avg*
RS	679	612	67
RA	473	612	139
DP	183	154	29

	R/G	*HR*	*K*	*BB*	*SB*	*CS*	*SB%*	*OBP*
Team Offense	4.32	70	437	428	40			0.334
Team Defense	3.01	33	639	477	30	33	48%	0.303
Difference	1.31	37	202	-49	10			110%

Pos	*Rpos*	*PA*	*Age*	*Name*	*BA*	*OBP*	*SLG*	*BB%*	*RS%*	*Bat R>Avg*	*BR R>Avg*	*Fld R>Avg*	*RAA*	*WAA*
C	4	476	28	Cooper, Walker	0.318	0.349	0.463	4%	28%	20	0	-3	21	2.2
1B	-6	571	26	Sanders, Ray*	0.280	0.381	0.414	13%	29%	24	0	-1	17	1.8
2B,SS	9	694	24	Klein, Lou	0.287	0.342	0.410	7%	37%	17	0	17	43	4.5
3B	0	565	25	Kurowski, Whitey	0.287	0.330	0.439	5%	33%	15	0	-1	14	1.5
SS	8	463	25	Marion, Marty	0.280	0.334	0.337	7%	25%	0	0	22	30	3.2
LF	-3	283	26	Litwhiler, Danny	0.279	0.333	0.438	7%	38%	8	0	4	9	1.0
CF	-1	640	26	Walker, Harry*	0.294	0.341	0.376	6%	36%	8	0	-2	5	0.6
RF,LF	-7	701	22	Musial, Stan*	0.357	0.425	0.562	10%	34%	70	-1	13	75	8.0
LF,1B	-3	272	26	Hopp, Johnny*	0.224	0.297	0.307	9%	40%	-6	0	0	-9	-0.9
RF,3B	-2	268	35	Garms, Debs*	0.257	0.299	0.313	5%	33%	-6	0	-2	-10	-1.0
C	2	227	30	O'Dea, Ken*	0.281	0.345	0.399	8%	16%	5	0	1	8	0.9
2B,3B	1	120	33	Brown, Jimmy^	0.182	0.224	0.255	5%	23%	-8	0	2	-5	-0.5
2B	2	87	26	Fallon, George	0.231	0.259	0.244	2%	29%	-5	0	4	1	0.1
	-4	688		Others	0.193	0.224	0.230	3%	34%	-50	1	-1	-54	-5.8
	0			Team Total	0.279	0.334	0.392	7.1%	32%	93	0	53	146	15.6
				League Average	0.258	0.324	0.347	8.5%	30%					
				% Lg Avg	108	103	113	83	106					
				League Rank	1	4	1	8	3		3	1		

GS	*GR*	*IP*	*Age*	*Name*	*W–L*	*GmSc*	*K/9*	*BB/9*	*HR/9*	*FIP*	*ERA*	*R/9*	*RAA*	*WAA*
32	5	274	30	Cooper, Mort	21–8	62.5	4.6	2.6	0.2	2.60	2.30	2.66	29	3.0
25	7	213	27	Lanier, Max*	15–7	60.5	5.2	3.2	0.1	2.58	1.90	2.62	23	2.5
19	2	133	33	Gumbert, Harry	10–5	56.5	2.7	2.2	0.3	2.98	2.84	3.11	7	0.7
14	2	118	22	Pollet, Howie*	8–4	66.9	4.6	2.4	0.2	2.52	1.75	1.98	22	2.3
10	4	79	26	White, Ernie*	5–5	52.2	3.2	3.8	0.5	3.72	3.78	4.35	-7	-0.7
17	17	164	27	Krist, Howie	11–5	56.2	3.1	3.4	0.3	3.38	2.90	3.12	8	0.9
13	16	135	28	Brecheen, Harry*	9–6	57.0	4.5	2.6	0.3	2.78	2.26	2.73	13	1.4
7	24	116	26	Dickson, Murry	8–2	47.7	3.4	3.8	0.3	3.46	3.58	3.97	-5	-0.5
9	23	93	24	Munger, Red	9–5	47.1	4.3	4.1	0.2	3.14	3.95	4.53	-10	-1.1
9	4	88	29	Brazle, Al*	8–2	63.7	2.7	3.0	0.0	2.87	1.53	1.84	17	1.8
2	0	13	22	Byerly, Bud	1–0	50.0	4.2	3.5	0.0	2.70	3.46	4.15	-1	-0.1
157	104			Team Total		58	4.03	3.01	0.21	2.92	2.57	2.98	96	10.3
				League Average		53	3.27	3.24	0.35	3.37	3.38	3.92		
				% Lg Avg		109	123	108	167	116	132	132		
				League Rank		1	1	5	1	1	1			

1946 Boston Red Sox

Everyone was back from World War II military service as teams brought back their veterans. MVP Ted Williams had a terrific season leading the 1946 Red Sox to its first pennant since 1918. The Red Sox easily led the major league in runs scored per game. This team outscored and had a winning record against every team they played during the regular season.

Strengths: (1) hitting led by MVP Ted Williams (37 2B, 8 3B, 38 HR, 343 TB), Pesky (43 2B), Dom DiMaggio (24 2B, 7 3B), York (30 2B, 6 3B, 17 HR), and Doerr (34 2B, 9 3B, 18 HR), (3) drawing walks especially from Williams (156 BB) and York (86 BB), (4) fielding featuring 2B Doerr (115 Rng+, 13 errors in 916 chances, 129 DP), SS Pesky (109 Rng+, 96 DP), CF Dom DiMaggio (108 Rng+, 9 assists), and LF Ted Williams (113 Held+), (5) excellent pitching control, and (6) individual pitching from Hughson (69% QS, 7.8 IP/S), Ferriss (57% QS, 7.7 IP/S) who was purchased as a free agent in May 1946, and closer Klinger (9/9/100% Sv, 1.902 Lv).

Weaknesses: (1) 3B and RF positions, (2) pitching from Bagby (45% QS, 9.9 H/9) and Harris (9.5 H/9), (3) hitting from 3B Russell and RF Moses, (4) GIDP especially from Doerr (18), (5) fielding from RF Metkovich (79 Rng+), and (6) Held+ from RF Moses (54).

Mgr	Joe Cronin	
Rk	46	110
Gm	156	
Place	1	
GA	12.0	
Rival	15–7 vs Tigers, 124 RS &101 RA	

	W	*L*	*Win%*
Regular Season	104	50	0.675
Runs Record	96	58	0.621
1 Run	27	17	0.614
Extra Innings	7	6	0.538
Blowout	29	14	0.674

	Team	*LgAvg*	*%Avg*	*LgRk*
BABIP	0.277	0.279	101	5
E	139	163	117	1
sOBP	0.313	0.322	103	3
rOBP	0.346	0.347	100	3
R/G	5.08	4.06	125	1
RA/G	3.81	4.06	107	3

	Tm	*LgAvg*	*>Avg*
RS	792	630	162
RA	594	630	36
DP	163	157	6

	R/G	*HR*	*K*	*BB*	*SB*	*CS*	*SB%*	*OBP*	*Held+*	
Team Offense	5.08	109	661	687	45	36	56%	0.356	LF	112
Team Defense	3.81	89	667	501	39	28	58%	0.320	**CF**	108
Difference	1.27	20	6	186	6			111%	**RF**	90

Pos	*Rpos*	*PA*	*Age*	*Name*	*BA*	*OBP*	*SLG*	*BB%*	*XBT*	*Bat R>Avg*	*BR R>Avg*	*Fld R>Avg*	*RAA*	*WAA*
C	4	445	30	Wagner, Hal*	0.230	0.354	0.322	16%	23%	1	1	1	7	0.7
1B	-7	669	32	York, Rudy	0.276	0.371	0.437	13%	38%	26	0	-1	18	1.9
2B	7	659	28	Doerr, Bobby	0.271	0.346	0.453	10%	38%	21	-1	14	41	4.3
3B	0	295	31	Russell, Rip	0.208	0.247	0.318	4%	50%	-14	0	1	-13	-1.4
SS	10	703	26	Pesky, Johnny*	0.335	0.401	0.427	9%	67%	33	0	9	52	5.4
LF	-7	672	27	Williams, Ted*	0.342	0.497	0.667	23%	40%	99	1	4	97	10.1
CF	-1	610	29	DiMaggio, Dom	0.316	0.393	0.427	11%	63%	27	0	6	32	3.3
RF	-4	320	25	Metkovich, Catfish*	0.246	0.333	0.356	11%	43%	0	1	-4	-7	-0.7
3B	0	227	37	Higgins, Pinky	0.275	0.356	0.370	11%	75%	3	0	0	3	0.3
RF,CF	-2	204	26	Culberson, Leon	0.313	0.369	0.430	8%	20%	7	0	-3	2	0.2
RF	-2	191	35	Moses, Wally*	0.206	0.268	0.337	7%	25%	-6	-1	2	-7	-0.8
RF	-2	165	31	McBride, Tom	0.301	0.340	0.359	5%	0%	0	0	-2	-4	-0.4
C	1	128	28	Partee, Roy	0.315	0.387	0.396	10%	50%	4	0	-1	4	0.4
	3	838		Others	0.176	0.233	0.226	6%	43%	-64	0	-1	-62	-6.5
	0		29.6	Team Total	0.271	0.356	0.402	11.2%	44%	136	1	25	162	17.0
				League Average	0.256	0.328	0.364	9.3%	44%					
				% Lg Avg	106	109	110	121	101					
				League Rank	1	1	1	1	3		4	2		

GS	*GR*	*IP*	*Age*	*Name*	*W–L*	*GmSc*	*K/9*	*BB/9*	*HR/9*	*FIP*	*ERA*	*R/9*	*RAA*	*WAA*
35	4	278	30	Hughson, Tex	20–11	60.2	5.6	1.7	0.5	2.48	2.75	2.88	33	3.4
35	5	274	24	Ferriss, Dave (Boo)	25–6	54.7	3.5	2.3	0.5	3.15	3.25	3.58	11	1.1
30	4	223	29	Harris, Mickey*	17–9	53.2	5.3	3.1	0.7	3.39	3.64	4.24	-8	-0.8
24	8	167	29	Dobson, Joe	13–7	53.1	4.9	3.7	0.6	3.46	3.24	3.89	1	0.1
11	10	107	29	Bagby, Jim	7–6	49.0	1.3	4.1	0.3	4.04	3.71	4.64	-9	-0.9
7	8	57	33	Zuber, Bill	5–1	53.7	4.6	6.2	0.6	4.41	2.54	3.18	5	0.5
1	27	57	38	Klinger, Bob	3–2	48.0	2.5	3.9	0.2	3.48	2.37	2.53	9	0.9
5	24	80	27	Johnson, Earl*	5–4	39.8	4.5	4.4	0.6	3.80	3.71	4.39	-4	-0.4
1	19	47	30	Dreisewerd, Clem*	4–1	37.0	3.6	2.9	0.6	3.42	4.18	4.18	-1	-0.1
0	18	26	37	Brown, Mace	3–1	0.0	3.4	5.5	0.7	4.50	2.05	2.39	5	0.5
7	24	81		Others	2–2	0.0	4.1	5.8	1.3	5.41	6.09	6.64	-24	-2.6
156	151		30.6	Team Total		54	4.30	3.23	0.57	3.43	3.38	3.83	17	1.8
				League Average		52	4.25	3.58	0.53	3.50	3.50	4.10		
				% Lg Avg		104	101	111	93	102	104	107		
				League Rank		3	3	1	7	3	4			

1947 New York Yankees

The 1947 Yankees dominated the AL competition winning the pennant by 12 games over the Tigers and won the World Series in 7 games over the Dodgers. Dodger GM Branch Rickey integrated baseball by bringing in Jackie Robinson, the first black baseball player to play in the major leagues. Baseball thus began including a whole segment of the U.S. population that had been excluded until now. The Yankees led the AL in most runs per games and led the majors in fewest runs allowed per game.

Strengths: (1) hitting from MVP DiMaggio (31 2B, 10 3B, 20 HR), Henrich (35 2B, 13 3B, 16 HR, 71 BB), McQuinn (24 2B), Keller, and Johnson, (2) fielding featuring LF Lindell (119 Rng+), SS Rizzuto (106 Rng+, 111 DP) and 2B Stirnweiss (96 Rng+, 107 DP), (3) Held+ from LF Lindell (108), CF DiMaggio (121), and RF Henrich (121), and (4) pitching anchored by closer Page (17/21/81% Sv, 41/55/75% IR stranded, 1.357 Lv), Shea (65% QS), Chandler (75% QS), Reynolds (53% QS), and Newsom (80% QS).

Weaknesses: (1) fielding from hobbled CF DiMaggio (82 Rng+) and 3B Johnson (89 Rng+), (2) CS% from Robinson (32%) and Berra (36%), (3) team BB/9 and HR/9, and (4) starting pitching from Drews (20% QS, 9.0 H/9) and Bevens (35% QS, 9.1 H/9).

Mgr	Bucky Harris	
Rk	33	87
Gm	155	
Place	1	
GA	12.0	
Rival	14–8 vs Tigers, 123 RS & 102 RA	

	W	L	Win%
Regular Season	97	57	0.630
Runs Record	96	58	0.626
1 Run	22	29	0.431
Extra Innings	5	6	0.455
Blowout	33	11	0.750

	Team	LgAvg	%Avg	LgRk
BABIP	0.259	0.274	106	2
E	109	135	124	2
sOBP	0.318	0.329	103	1
rOBP	0.339	0.347	102	3
R/G	5.12	4.14	124	1
RA/G	3.66	4.14	113	1

	Tm	LgAvg	>Avg
RS	794	645	149
RA	568	645	77
DP	151	163	-12

	R/G	HR	K	BB	SB	CS	SB%	OBP	Held+	
Team Offense	5.12	115	581	610	27	23	54%	0.349	LF	115
Team Defense	3.66	95	691	628	61	31	66%	0.323	CF	122
Difference	1.46	20	110	-18	-34			108%	RF	113

Pos	Rpos	PA	Age	Name	BA	OBP	SLG	BB%	XBT	Bat R>Avg	BR R>Avg	Fld R>Avg	RAA	WAA
C	2	292	32	Robinson, Aaron*	0.270	0.370	0.413	14%	22%	9	0	0	11	1.1
1B	-7	609	37	McQuinn, George*	0.304	0.395	0.437	13%	47%	28	0	8	29	3.0
2B	7	673	28	Stirnweiss, Snuffy	0.256	0.358	0.342	13%	52%	4	0	7	18	1.8
3B	0	547	28	Johnson, Billy	0.285	0.351	0.417	8%	59%	12	0	-5	7	0.7
SS	10	623	29	Rizzuto, Phil	0.273	0.350	0.364	9%	61%	4	1	9	24	2.5
LF,OF	-5	513	30	Lindell, Johnny	0.275	0.322	0.412	6%	39%	4	0	10	9	0.9
CF	-1	601	32	DiMaggio, Joe	0.315	0.391	0.522	11%	45%	41	1	-8	33	3.4
RF,CF	-6	629	34	Henrich, Tommy*	0.287	0.372	0.485	11%	59%	31	0	5	30	3.1
C,OF	0	306	22	Berra, Yogi*	0.280	0.310	0.464	4%	68%	5	0	-1	4	0.5
LF	-2	193	30	Keller, Charlie*	0.238	0.404	0.550	21%	26%	15	0	0	13	1.4
3B,SS	1	175	22	Brown, Bobby*	0.300	0.390	0.373	12%	32%	5	-1	-1	4	0.4
C	1	104	27	Houk, Ralph	0.272	0.356	0.326	11%	43%	0	0	-1	0	0.0
RF,LF	-1	73	24	Clark, Allie	0.373	0.417	0.493	7%	60%	5	0	0	4	0.4
	1	693		Others	0.175	0.231	0.240	6%	35%	-52	2	-1	-50	-5.2
	0		28.8	Team Total	0.271	0.349	0.407	10.1%	47%	110	3	22	135	14.0
				League Average	0.256	0.333	0.364	10.0%	46%					
				% Lg Avg	106	105	112	101	103					
				League Rank	1	2	1	4	3		1	3		

GS	GR	IP	Age	Name	W–L	GmSc	K/9	BB/9	HR/9	FIP	ERA	R/9	RAA	WAA
30	4	242	30	Reynolds, Allie	19–8	56.0	4.8	4.6	0.86	4.17	3.20	3.50	15	1.5
23	4	179	26	Shea, Spec	14–5	59.7	4.5	4.5	0.50	3.72	3.07	3.17	18	1.8
23	5	165	30	Bevens, Bill	7–13	49.7	4.2	4.2	0.71	3.93	3.82	4.31	-5	-0.5
16	1	128	39	Chandler, Spud	9–5	62.0	4.8	2.9	0.28	2.73	2.46	2.88	17	1.7
15	2	116	39	Newsom, Bobo	7–5	55.7	3.3	2.3	0.62	3.43	2.80	2.96	14	1.4
14	1	105	28	Raschi, Vic	7–2	54.4	4.4	3.3	0.95	3.93	3.87	4.04	0	0.0
2	54	141	29	Page, Joe*	14–8	38.5	7.4	4.6	0.32	2.79	2.48	2.61	23	2.4
10	20	92	27	Drews, Karl	6–6	37.7	4.4	5.4	0.59	4.26	4.91	5.60	-16	-1.6

GS	GR	IP	Age	Name	W–L	GmSc	K/9	BB/9	HR/9	FIP	ERA	R/9	RAA	WAA
8	7	54	20	Johnson, Don	4–3	46.8	2.7	3.8	0.33	3.64	3.64	4.31	-2	-0.2
5	6	52	31	Wensloff, Butch	3–1	51.2	3.1	3.8	0.52	3.76	2.61	2.96	6	0.6
9	36	102		Others	7–1	—	3.5	5.1	0.89	4.66	5.22	5.75	-19	-2.0
			29.9	Team Total		54	4.53	4.11	0.62	3.73	3.39	3.72	50	5.2
				League Average		52	3.76	3.86	0.55	3.71	3.71	4.19		
				% Lg Avg		104	120	94	89	99	109	113		
				League Rank		1	1	8	7	4	1			

1948 Cleveland Indians

For the first time in the history of the AL, 2 teams tied for first place when the regular season ended. The pitching rich 1948 Indians beat the Red Sox in a one game winner-take-all playoff game. The 1948 Indians were the best Cleveland Indian team ever, but almost lost the pennant to a weaker Red Sox team,

Strengths: (1) hitting led by MVP Boudreau (98 BB, 34 2B, 18 HR), Keltner (89 BB, 31 HR), Mitchell (30 2B), and Doby (9 3B), (2) fielding featuring SS Boudreau (107 Rng+, 119 DP), 2B Gordon (99 Rng+, 97 DP), 3B Keltner (97 Rng+), and rookie RF/CF Doby (96 Rng+ in CF, 114 Rng+ in RF, 12 assists), (3) CS% from Hegan (52%), (4) Held+ from Clark (116 in LF, 121 in RF), LF Mitchell (107), Doby (133 in CF, 97 in RF), and CF Tucker (108), and (5) pitching from Lemon (65% QS), RoY runner-up Bearden (76% QS), Feller (58% QS), Klieman (27/46/59% IR stranded, 1.013 Lv), Christopher (47/72/65% IR stranded, 1.593 Lv), and Paige (1.159 Lv).

Weaknesses: (1) 1B position, (2) hitting from Robinson and Berardino, (3) baserunning from Keltner (23 GIDP) and Mitchell (13 SB, 18 CS), and (4) pitching from Black (30% QS, 4.0 IP/S).

				W	L	Win%		Team	LgAvg	%Avg	LgRk
Mgr	Lou Boudreau		**Regular Season**	97	58	0.626	**BABIP**	0.257	0.283	110	1
Rk	3	7	**Runs Record**	107	48	0.689	**E**	114	138	121	2
Gm	156		**1 Run**	10	20	0.333	**sOBP**	0.314	0.346	110	1
Place	1		**Extra Innings**	8	4	0.667	**rOBP**	0.350	0.359	103	3
GA	1.0		**Blowout**	43	13	0.768	**R/G**	5.38	4.72	114	3
Rival	12–11 vs Red Sox, 147 RS, 118 RA; 10–12 vs Yankees, 104 RS, 114 RA						**RA/G**	3.63	4.72	130	
1											

	Tm	LgAvg	>Avg		R/G	HR	K	BB	SB	CS	SB%	OBP	Held+	
RS	840	730	110	Team Offense	5.38	155	575	646	54	44	55%	0.360	LF	108
RA	567	730	163	Team Defense	3.63	82	593	625	30	32	48%	0.323	CF	113
DP	183	169	14	Difference	1.75	73	18	21	24			112%	RF	115

Pos	Rpos	PA	Age	Name	BA	OBP	SLG	BB%	XBT	Bat R>Avg	BR R>Avg	Fld R>Avg	RAA	WAA
C	5	524	27	Hegan, Jim	0.248	0.317	0.407	9%	47%	-4	0	2	3	0.3
1B	-6	540	27	Robinson, Eddie*	0.254	0.307	0.408	7%	35%	-6	0	5	-7	-0.7
2B	7	633	33	Gordon, Joe	0.280	0.371	0.507	12%	52%	28	0	16	51	4.9
3B	0	656	31	Keltner, Ken	0.297	0.395	0.522	14%	46%	38	-5	12	45	4.3
SS	10	676	30	Boudreau, Lou	0.355	0.453	0.534	14%	48%	57	0	20	87	8.4
LF	-6	656	26	Mitchell, Dale*	0.336	0.383	0.431	7%	44%	18	-5	7	14	1.4
RF,CF	-3	500	23	Doby, Larry*	0.301	0.384	0.490	11%	57%	22	4	11	34	3.3
CF	0	274	30	Tucker, Thurman*	0.260	0.347	0.343	11%	57%	-3	4	4	5	0.5
RF,LF	-3	298	25	Clark, Allie	0.310	0.364	0.443	8%	54%	7	-2	2	4	0.4
CF,1B	-2	281	31	Judnich, Wally*	0.257	0.411	0.372	20%	41%	7	-1	-1	3	0.3
RF	-2	179	29	Edwards, Hank*	0.269	0.346	0.406	10%	57%	1	2	4	5	0.5
C	1	97	26	Tipton, Joe	0.289	0.333	0.356	4%	50%	-2	0	0	-1	-0.1
2B,1B	1	179	31	Berardino, Johnny	0.190	0.328	0.279	15%	40%	-6	-2	3	-4	-0.4
	-2	708		Others	0.215	0.262	0.295	6%	36%	-44	1	-5	-50	-4.8
	0		28.4	Team Total	0.282	0.360	0.431	10.4%	46%	112	-4	80	188	18.2
				League Average	0.266	0.349	0.382	10.8%	45%					

Pos	Rpos	PA	Age	Name	BA	OBP	SLG	BB%	XBT	Bat R>Avg	BR R>Avg	Fld R>Avg	RAA	WAA
				% Lg Avg	106	103	113	96	103					
				League Rank	1	2	2	4	2		4	1		

GS	GR	IP	Age	Name	W–L	GmSc	K/9	BB/9	HR/9	FIP	ERA	R/9	RAA	WAA
37	6	294	27	Lemon, Bob	20–14	58.7	4.5	4.0	0.4	3.63	2.82	3.19	36	3.5
38	6	280	29	Feller, Bob	19–15	54.9	5.3	3.7	0.6	3.77	3.56	3.95	11	1.0
29	8	230	27	Bearden, Gene*	20–7	58.2	3.1	4.2	0.4	3.98	2.43	2.82	37	3.6
12	11	106	29	Zoldak, Sam*	9–6	52.8	1.4	2.0	0.5	3.85	2.81	3.15	13	1.2
10	8	52	31	Black, Don	2–2	44.5	2.8	6.9	0.9	5.75	5.37	5.71	-9	-0.8
9	29	130	28	Gromek, Steve	9–3	60.4	3.5	3.5	0.7	4.29	2.84	3.60	10	0.9
7	14	73	41	Paige, Satchel	6–1	57.9	5.6	3.1	0.2	2.94	2.48	2.60	14	1.3
9	12	72	32	Muncrief, Bob	5–4	44.1	3.0	3.9	1.0	4.81	3.98	4.60	-3	-0.3
0	45	59	30	Christopher, Russ	3–2	—	2.1	4.1	0.5	4.31	2.90	3.20	7	0.7
0	44	80	30	Klieman, Ed	3–2	—	2.0	5.2	0.3	4.59	2.60	2.94	12	1.2
5	13	34		Others	1–2	—	4.7	7.9	1.0	5.92	10.75	10.75	-25	-2.4
156	196		30.4	Team Total		55	3.79	3.99	0.52	4.03	3.22	3.62	103	9.9
				League Average		48	3.53	4.29	0.58	4.28	4.29	4.79		
				% Lg Avg		115	107	107	111	106	133	132		
				League Rank		1	3	3	3	2	1			

1948 New York Yankees

The 1948 Yankees had another statistically impressive year with solid performances from most everyone on the team. Yankee skipper Bucky Harris was replaced after this season by Casey Stengel who immediately made Berra his starting catcher and went on to win 5 straight world championships in his first 5 years as Yankee manager. Keller was injured with a broken hand limiting his playing time during the 1948 season. The Yankees were second in the AL in both runs scored and runs allowed per game.

Strengths: (1) SP, C, LF, CF, and RF positions, (2) hitting for average, contact, and power led by DiMaggio (26 2B, 11 3B, 39 HR), Henrich (42 2B, 14 3B, 25 HR), Lindell, Berra (10 3B), and Johnson (20 2B, 12 HR), (3) fielding from 2B Stirnweiss (94 Rng+, 103 DP, 5 errors in 715 chances), (4) CS% from Niarhos (65%), and (5) pitching depth anchored by Reynolds (45% QS), Shea (64% QS), Byrne (55% QS, 7.2 IP/S), Raschi (6 shutouts, 52% QS), and Lopat (48% QS).

Weaknesses: (1) hitting from Rizzuto and Souchock, (2) CS% from 23-year-old C Berra (38%), and (3) Held+ from RF Berra (79).

Mgr	Bucky Harris	
Rk	38	94
Gm	154	
Place	3	
GB	2.5	
Rival	12–10 vs Indians, 8–14 vs Red Sox	

	W	L	Win%
Regular Season	94	60	0.610
Runs Record	96	58	0.624
1 Run	19	17	0.528
Extra Innings	6	6	0.500
Blowout	33	9	0.786

	Team	LgAvg	%Avg	LgRk
BABIP	0.272	0.283	104	2
E	120	138	115	4
sOBP	0.334	0.346	104	3
rOBP	0.344	0.359	104	2
R/G	5.56	4.72	118	2
RA/G	4.11	4.72	115	2

	Tm	LgAvg	>Avg
RS	857	730	127
RA	633	730	97
DP	161	169	-8

	R/G	HR	K	BB	SB	CS	SB%	OBP
Team Offense	5.56	139	478	623	24	24	50%	0.356
Team Defense	4.11	94	654	641	49	42	54%	0.336
Difference	1.45	45	176	-18	-25			106%

Held+	
LF	101
CF	97
RF	91

Pos	Rpos	PA	Age	Name	BA	OBP	SLG	BB%	XBT	Bat R>Avg	BR R>Avg	Fld R>Avg	RAA	WAA
C	2	285	27	Niarhos, Gus	0.268	0.404	0.338	18%	45%	4	1	0	7	0.7
1B	-4	346	38	McQuinn, George*	0.248	0.336	0.421	12%	25%	2	-2	2	-2	-0.2
2B	7	610	29	Stirnweiss, Snuffy	0.252	0.360	0.336	14%	52%	-4	1	8	12	1.2

Pos	Rpos	PA	Age	Name	BA	OBP	SLG	BB%	XBT	Bat R>Avg	BR R>Avg	Fld R>Avg	RAA	WAA
3B	0	492	29	Johnson, Billy	0.294	0.358	0.446	8%	43%	11	-2	-2	7	0.6
SS	8	539	31	Rizzuto, Phil	0.252	0.340	0.328	11%	63%	-10	2	1	1	0.1
LF	-4	345	31	Lindell, Johnny	0.317	0.387	0.511	10%	55%	18	-1	2	15	1.4
CF	-1	669	33	DiMaggio, Joe	0.320	0.396	0.598	10%	46%	53	1	2	55	5.4
RF,1B	-7	673	35	Henrich, Tommy*	0.308	0.391	0.554	11%	57%	44	2	2	41	3.9
C,RF	0	497	23	Berra, Yogi*	0.305	0.341	0.488	5%	50%	13	2	-2	13	1.2
3B,SS	2	416	23	Brown, Bobby*	0.300	0.383	0.405	12%	40%	9	-3	-2	6	0.6
LF	0	289	31	Keller, Charlie*	0.267	0.372	0.417	14%	30%	6	1	0	7	0.7
1B	-2	126	29	Souchock, Steve	0.203	0.248	0.322	6%	25%	-8	1	0	-9	-0.9
OF	-1	94	26	Mapes, Cliff*	0.250	0.298	0.432	6%	20%	-1	0	0	-2	-0.2
	0	667		Others	0.224	0.274	0.297	6%	30%	-37	-1	0	-38	-3.7
	0		29.6	Team Total	0.278	0.356	0.432	10.3%	46%	99	2	11	112	10.8
				League Average	0.266	0.349	0.382	10.8%	45%					
				% Lg Avg	105	102	113	95	103					
				League Rank	2	3	1	5	4		3	3		

GS	GR	IP	Age	Name	W–L	GmSc	K/9	BB/9	HR/9	FIP	ERA	RA/9	RAA	WAA
31	8	236	31	Reynolds, Allie	16–7	48.8	3.8	4.2	0.6	4.29	3.77	4.11	16	1.5
31	2	227	30	Lopat, Ed*	17–11	50.8	3.3	2.6	0.6	3.83	3.65	4.21	13	1.2
31	5	223	29	Raschi, Vic	19–8	54.4	5.0	3.0	0.6	3.55	3.84	4.16	14	1.3
22	6	156	27	Shea, Spec	9–10	54.2	4.1	5.0	0.6	4.38	3.40	3.81	16	1.5
12	4	78	24	Porterfield, Bob	5–3	44.8	3.5	3.9	0.6	4.12	4.50	4.85	-1	-0.1
11	20	134	28	Byrne, Tommy*	8–5	55.7	6.2	6.8	0.5	4.50	3.29	3.69	15	1.5
8	12	77	30	Embree, Red	5–3	50.1	2.9	3.5	0.7	4.33	3.75	4.34	3	0.3
1	54	108	30	Page, Joe*	7–8	32.0	6.4	5.5	0.5	3.91	4.26	4.93	-3	-0.2
5	17	62	27	Hiller, Frank	5–2	52.0	3.6	4.3	1.2	5.11	4.04	4.19	4	0.4
2	17	38	28	Drews, Karl	2–3	50.0	2.6	7.3	0.7	5.64	3.79	4.03	3	0.3
0	17	27		Others	1–0	—	4.6	3.6	0.3	3.52	2.97	3.63	3	0.3
28.4Team Total			51	4.31	4.22	0.62	4.15	3.75	4.17	82	8.0			
				League Average		48	3.52	4.29	0.58	4.28	4.29	4.79		
				% Lg Avg		106	122	101	94	103	114	115		
				League Rank		2	2	5	6	4	2			

1948 Boston Braves

The Boston Braves broke through and won the pennant for the first time since 1914. The Braves won it with pitching and fielding allowing the fewest runs per game. Despite a rather deep above average starting staff, this team inspired the phrase "Spahn and Sain and 2 days of rain" when the Braves won 14 out of 15 games with Spahn and Sain winning 9 of them. The Braves had a great walk differential of 247. Three positional starters had an OBP of over .400. During the season, both Stanky and Heath broke their ankles.

Strengths: (1) hitting for average, contact, and power featuring Elliott (23 HR), Heath (26 2B, 20 HR), Holmes (35 2B), Stanky, and Dark (39 2B), (2) drawing walks led by Elliott (131 BB), Torgeson (81 BB), and Stanky (61 BB), (3) fielding especially from SS Dark (106 Rng+), 2B Stanky (117 Rng+), and CF Russell (114 Rng+), and (4) pitching anchored by MVP runner-up Sain (7.8 IP/S, 74% QS, 7.8 IP/S), Voiselle (57% QS), Bickford (55% QS), Potter (57% QS), and Spahn (49% QS).

Weaknesses: (1) hitting from Sisti & Ryan, (2) CS% from Salkeld (34%), and (3) fielding from CF Conatser (87 Rng+, 78 Held+).

Mgr	Billy Southworth	
Rk	21	51
Gm	154	
Place	1	
GA	6.5	

	W	L	Win%
Regular Season	91	62	0.595
Runs Record	98	55	0.640
1 Run	28	20	0.583
Extra Innings	3	6	0.333
Blowout	28	11	0.718

	Team	LgAvg	%Avg	LgRk
BABIP	0.270	0.277	103	2
E	143	157	110	3
sOBP	0.309	0.328	106	1
rOBP	0.317	0.345	109	1
R/G	4.80	4.42	109	3

	W	L	Win%		Team	LgAvg	%Avg	LgRk
Rival 11–11 vs Cardinals, 113 RS & 98 RA				RA/G	3.78	4.42	117	1

	Tm	LgAvg	>Avg
RS	739	686	53
RA	582	686	104
DP	132	140	-8

	R/G	HR	K	BB	SB	CS	SB%	OBP	Held+
Team Offense	4.80	95	537	677	43		100%	0.359	LF 107
Team Defense	3.78	93	579	430	64	35	65%	0.310	CF 91
Difference	1.02	2	42	247	-21			116%	RF 92

Pos	Rpos	PA	Age	Name	BA	OBP	SLG	BB%	XBT	Bat R>Avg	BR R>Avg	Fld R>Avg	RAA	WAA
C	4	423	32	Masi, Phil	0.253	0.318	0.343	8%	39%	-7	-2	2	-3	-0.3
1B	-6	531	24	Torgeson, Earl*	0.253	0.372	0.397	15%	61%	12	3	5	14	1.4
2B	3	312	32	Stanky, Eddie	0.320	0.455	0.417	20%	48%	19	0	4	26	2.6
3B	0	675	31	Elliott, Bob	0.283	0.423	0.474	19%	53%	43	-1	1	43	4.3
SS	9	579	26	Dark, Al	0.322	0.353	0.433	4%	63%	12	3	0	24	2.4
LF	-5	419	33	Heath, Jeff*	0.319	0.404	0.582	12%	29%	35	-1	4	33	3.3
CF	-1	374	29	Russell, Jim^	0.264	0.361	0.410	12%	55%	8	1	6	14	1.4
RF	-6	639	31	Holmes, Tommy*	0.325	0.375	0.439	7%	29%	21	0	3	18	1.8
LF,OF	-4	383	31	McCormick, Mike	0.303	0.363	0.417	8%	36%	8	-1	-3	0	0.0
2B,SS	4	261	27	Sisti, Sibby	0.244	0.340	0.290	12%	63%	-5	2	-1	0	0.0
CF,LF	-1	259	26	Conatser, Clint	0.277	0.370	0.384	12%	47%	4	0	-5	-2	-0.2
C	2	250	31	Salkeld, Bill*	0.242	0.378	0.414	17%	45%	7	0	1	10	1.0
1B	-2	194	37	McCormick, Frank	0.250	0.289	0.389	5%	0%	-3	-1	2	-4	-0.4
2B	2	148	28	Ryan, Connie	0.213	0.333	0.238	14%	30%	-5	0	1	-2	-0.2
	1	683		Others	0.194	0.241	0.238	5%	15%	-52	-1	1	-51	-5.1
	0		29.9	Team Total	0.275	0.359	0.399	11.0%	43%	97	2	21	120	12.0
				League Average	0.261	0.333	0.383	9.3%	44%					
				% Lg Avg	106	108	104	119	98					
				League Rank	1	1	2	1	4		4	2		

GS	GR	IP	Age	Name	W–L	GmSc	K/9	BB/9	HR/9	FIP	ERA	RA/9	RAA	WAA
39	3	315	30	Sain, Johnny	24–15	58.3	3.9	2.4	0.5	3.32	2.60	3.00	47	4.7
35	1	257	27	Spahn, Warren*	15–12	53.5	4.0	2.7	0.7	3.55	3.71	4.03	10	1.0
30	7	216	29	Voiselle, Bill	13–13	49.8	3.7	3.8	0.8	4.12	3.63	3.88	12	1.2
22	11	146	27	Bickford, Vern	11–5	53.6	3.7	3.9	0.6	3.90	3.27	3.64	12	1.2
13	21	128	33	Barrett, Red	7–8	48.1	2.8	1.8	0.6	3.46	3.65	3.93	6	0.6
7	11	85	36	Potter, Nels	5–2	55.9	5.0	0.8	0.4	2.35	2.33	2.86	14	1.4
1	39	86	27	Hogue, Bobby	8–2	40.0	4.5	2.0	0.4	2.90	3.23	3.54	8	0.8
2	34	74	36	Shoun, Clyde*	5–1	47.5	3.0	2.4	0.9	3.93	4.01	4.50	-1	-0.1
0	15	23	31	White, Ernie*	0–2	—	3.1	6.7	0.0	4.09	1.96	2.74	4	0.4
0	4	4	18	Antonelli, Johnny*	0–0	—	0.0	6.8	0.0	4.82	2.25	2.25	1	0.1
5	21	55		Others	3–2	—	2.6	3.9	0.7	4.23	6.51	7.81	-21	-2.1
154	167		29.4	Team Total		53	3.75	2.79	0.60	3.56	3.38	3.77	91	9.1
				League Average		50	3.87	3.61	0.69	3.95	3.95	4.50		
				% Lg Avg		106	97	130	115	111	117	119		
				League Rank		2	5	1	2	2	1			

1949 Boston Red Sox

The Curse of the Bambino raised its ugly head in 1949 as a more talented Red Sox team, who led the majors in scoring, lost the pennant to the Yankees and the magical managing of Casey Stengel. The Red Sox featured the best 2 positional players (Williams and Stephens) and the best pitcher (Parnell) in the league. This team had a 9–13 record versus the Yankees despite outscoring them.

Strengths: (1) hitting led by MVP Ted Williams (39 2B, 43 HR, 368 TB), Stephens (31 2B, 39 HR, 329 TB), Doerr (30 2B, 18 HR), Dom DiMaggio (34 2B), and Pesky (27 2B), (2) drawing walks especially from Williams (162 BB), Stephens (101 BB), Pesky (100 BB), and DiMaggio (96 BB), (3) baserunning from Pesky (38% RS) and Zarilla (34% RS), (4) infield fielding especially making double plays featuring SS Stephens (103 Rng+, 128 DP) and 2B Doerr (117 Rng+, 134 DP), (5) CS% from Tebbetts (49% CS), (6) Held+ from CF Dom DiMaggio (119), and (7) pitching from starters Parnell (67% QS, 8.7 IP/S) and Kinder (50% QS, 6 shutouts, 7.6 IP/S).

Weaknesses: (1) RP, 1B, and RF positions, (2) hitting from Hitchcock, (3) hitting from the bench, (4) GIDP especially Doerr (31), (5) Held+ from RF Zarilla (91), and (6) pitching from Johnson (0.922 Lv) and Kramer (39% QS).

				W	L	Win%
Mgr	Joe McCarthy		**Regular Season**	96	58	0.623
Rk	27	71	**Runs Record**	97	57	0.631
Gm	155		**1 Run**	19	21	0.475
Place	2		**Extra Innings**	7	6	0.538
GB	1.0		**Blowout**	33	14	0.702
Rival	9–13 vs Yankees, 102 RS & 101 RA					

	Team	LgAvg	%Avg	LgRk
BABIP	0.283	0.279	98	6
E	120	137	114	2
sOBP	0.340	0.349	103	3
rOBP	0.378	0.366	97	6
R/G	5.78	4.67	124	1
RA/G	4.30	4.67	109	4

	Tm	LgAvg	>Avg
RS	896	722	174
RA	667	722	55
DP	207	186	21

	R/G	HR	K	BB	SB	CS	SB%	OBP	Held%	
Team Offense	5.78	131	510	835	43	25	63%	0.381	LF	104
Team Defense	4.30	82	598	661	35	28	56%	0.347	CF	117
Difference	1.48	49	88	174	8	-3	8%	110%	RF	87

Pos	Rpos	PA	Age	Name	BA	OBP	SLG	BB%	XBT	Bat R>Avg	BR R>Avg	Fld R>Avg	RAA	WAA
C	4	472	36	Tebbetts, Birdie	0.270	0.369	0.342	13%	23%	-1	-4	1	0	0.0
1B	-5	509	23	Goodman, Billy*	0.298	0.382	0.363	11%	43%	4	0	2	1	0.1
2B	7	623	31	Doerr, Bobby	0.309	0.393	0.497	12%	37%	31	-2	11	47	4.5
3B	0	713	29	Pesky, Johnny*	0.306	0.408	0.384	14%	59%	19	8	5	32	3.1
SS	10	711	28	Stephens, Vern	0.290	0.391	0.539	14%	43%	43	-1	10	62	6.0
LF	-7	730	30	Williams, Ted*	0.343	0.490	0.650	22%	33%	94	1	-1	87	8.4
CF	-1	706	32	DiMaggio, Dom	0.307	0.404	0.420	14%	45%	24	2	3	28	2.7
RF	-6	527	30	Zarilla, Al*	0.281	0.352	0.422	9%	45%	6	4	-2	2	0.2
C	2	183	27	Batts, Matt	0.242	0.350	0.369	14%	43%	-1	0	-1	0	0.0
1B,2B	-1	170	32	Hitchcock, Billy	0.204	0.291	0.259	10%	29%	-10	-1	-1	-13	-1.3
RF,CF	-1	149	30	O'Brien, Tommy	0.224	0.336	0.336	14%	45%	-3	0	-2	-6	-0.6
2B	0	46	32	Stringer, Lou	0.268	0.348	0.439	11%	63%	1	0	0	1	0.1
3B	0	34	29	Combs, Merl*	0.208	0.424	0.250	26%	50%	0	-1	-1	-2	-0.2
	-2	677		Others	0.181	0.253	0.214	8%	23%	-58	0	0	-60	-5.8
	0		29.9	Team Total	0.282	0.381	0.420	13.4%	41%	147	6	24	177	17.2
				League Average	0.263	0.353	0.379	11.7%	43%					
				% Lg Avg	107	108	111	115	94					
				League Rank	1	1	1	1	7		2	3		

GS	GR	IP	Age	Name	W–L	GmSc	K/9	BB/9	HR/9	FIP	ERA	RA/9	RAA	WAA
33	6	295	27	Parnell, Mel*	25–7	59.2	3.7	4.1	0.2	3.43	2.77	3.11	49	4.8
30	13	252	34	Kinder, Ellis	23–6	53.8	4.9	3.5	0.8	3.68	3.36	3.68	26	2.5
27	6	213	32	Dobson, Joe	14–12	48.9	3.7	4.1	0.5	3.80	3.85	4.36	6	0.5
19	7	152	19	Stobbs, Chuck*	11–6	52.5	4.1	4.4	0.6	3.95	4.03	4.26	6	0.6
18	3	112	31	Kramer, Jack	6–8	43.9	1.9	3.9	0.6	4.34	5.16	5.64	-13	-1.3
12	0	80	20	McDermott, Mick*	5–4	53.0	5.6	5.9	0.6	4.12	4.05	4.16	4	0.4
6	1	38	32	Harris, Mickey*	2–3	40.0	3.3	4.8	0.7	4.46	5.02	6.21	-7	-0.7
2	27	78	33	Hughson, Tex	4–2	35.0	4.1	4.8	0.6	4.05	5.33	5.68	-9	-0.9
5	13	55	29	Masterson, Walt	3–4	47.0	3.1	5.7	0.3	4.18	4.25	4.91	-2	-0.2
3	16	49	30	Johnson, Earl*	3–6	36.0	3.6	5.3	0.2	3.95	7.48	8.21	-20	-1.9
0	28	54		Others	0–0	—	3.2	5.0	1.2	5.32	5.03	5.03	-3	-0.3
155	120		28.7	Team Total		51	3.91	4.32	0.54	3.89	3.97	4.36	36	3.5
				League Average		49	3.59	4.63	0.63	4.20	4.20	4.75		
				% Lg Avg		104	109	107	118	108	106	109		
				League Rank		3	3	3	3	2	4			

1949 Brooklyn Dodgers

Branch Rickey put together a youthful and talented 1949 Dodger team that won the pennant by 1 game over an experienced Cardinal team by winning 21 of their final 29 games. The Dodgers won 43 percent of their games by 5 or more runs.

Strengths: (1) hitting led by 7 starters including MVP Jackie Robinson (38 2B, 12 3B, 16 HR), Furillo (27 2B, 10 3B, 18 HR), Snider (28 2B, 7 3B, 23 HR), Campanella (22 2B, 22 HR), Reese (27 2B, 16 HR), Hodges (23 2B, 23 HR), and Hermanski, (2) drawing walks from Reese (116 BB) and Robinson (86 BB), (3) baserunning led by Robinson (37 SB, 10 ROE) and Reese (26 SB, 14 ROE), (4) fielding anchored by SS Reese (106 Rng+, 93 DP), 2B Robinson (103 Rng+, 119 DP), CF Snider (98 Rng+, 12 assists), and 3B Cox (106 Rng+), (5) CS% from Campanella (57%, 20 SB allowed), (6) Held+ from RF Furillo (115), LF Hermanski (113), and LF Rackley (133), and (7) pitching featuring Rookie of the Year Newcombe (58% QS, 7.7 IP/S) and Roe (74% QS, 7.6 IP/S).

Weaknesses: (1) 3B and LF positions, (2) hitting from Cox, (3) hitting from the pitchers, (4) Held+ from CF Snider (92), (5) pitching team BB/9, (6) pitching from Hatten (45% QS), Branca (37% QS), and Martin (50% QS), and (7) starting pitching depth.

Mgr	Burt Shotton	
Rk	37	93
Gm	156	
Place	1	
GA	1.0	
Rival	10–12 vs Cards, 118 RS & 118 RA	

	W	*L*	*Win%*
Regular Season	97	57	0.630
Runs Record	96	58	0.624
1 Run	16	12	0.571
Extra Innings	7	8	0.467
Blowout	42	11	0.792

	Team	*LgAvg*	*%Avg*	*LgRk*
BABIP	0.266	0.275	103	2
E	124	150	121	1
sOBP	0.320	0.330	103	1
rOBP	0.338	0.345	102	3
R/G	5.63	4.54	124	1
RA/G	4.17	4.54	109	2

	Tm	*LgAvg*	*>Avg*
RS	879	706	173
RA	651	706	55
DP	162	152	10

	R/G	*HR*	*K*	*BB*	*SB*	*CS*	*SB%*	*OBP*	*Held+*	
Team Offense	5.63	152	570	638	117			0.354	LF	106
Team Defense	4.17	132	743	582	25	30	45%	0.325	CF	89
Difference	1.46	20	173	56	92			109%	RF	114

Pos	*Rpos*	*PA*	*Age*	*Name*	*BA*	*OBP*	*SLG*	*BB%*	*XBT*	*Bat R>Avg*	*BR R>Avg*	*Fld R>Avg*	*RAA*	*WAA*
C	4	507	27	Campanella, Roy	0.287	0.385	0.498	13%	45%	26	-2	1	29	2.9
1B	-7	676	25	Hodges, Gil	0.285	0.360	0.453	10%	48%	19	1	1	14	1.4
2B	7	704	30	Robinson, Jackie	0.342	0.432	0.528	12%	73%	55	5	10	77	7.6
3B	0	426	29	Cox, Billy	0.233	0.290	0.351	7%	54%	-13	2	5	-6	-0.6
SS	10	743	30	Reese, Pee Wee	0.279	0.396	0.410	16%	49%	25	5	12	52	5.1
LF,RF	-4	282	29	Hermanski, Gene*	0.299	0.431	0.487	17%	51%	19	3	0	18	1.8
CF	-1	615	22	Snider, Duke*	0.292	0.361	0.493	9%	66%	25	2	10	36	3.5
RF	-6	596	27	Furillo, Carl	0.322	0.368	0.506	6%	43%	28	4	5	31	3.1
LF	-2	166	27	Rackley, Marv*	0.300	0.360	0.367	8%	58%	1	3	-2	0	0.0
C	1	173	25	Edwards, Bruce	0.209	0.324	0.392	14%	33%	0	0	0	1	0.1
3B	0	160	29	Jorgensen, Spider*	0.269	0.376	0.343	14%	47%	1	3	1	5	0.5
LF,CF	-1	111	29	Olmo, Luis	0.305	0.336	0.390	5%	53%	0	-1	-2	-4	-0.4
LF	-1	95	21	Brown, Tommy	0.303	0.347	0.427	6%	44%	1	0	0	0	0.0
	0	919		Others	0.171	0.229	0.215	7%	38%	-84	1	0	-83	-8.2
	0		26.9	Team Total	0.274	0.354	0.419	10.3%	51%	103	26	41	170	16.9
				League Average	0.262	0.334	0.389	9.2%	45%					
				% Lg Avg	104	106	108	113	114					
				League Rank	2	1	1	2	1		1	1		

GS	*GR*	*IP*	*Age*	*Name*	*W–L*	*GmSc*	*K/9*	*BB/9*	*HR/9*	*FIP*	*ERA*	*RA/9*	*RAA*	*WAA*
31	7	244	23	Newcombe, Don	17–8	59.2	5.5	2.7	0.6	3.15	3.17	3.28	28	2.8
27	3	213	33	Roe, Preacher*	15–6	58.7	4.6	1.9	1.1	3.68	2.79	2.92	33	3.3
29	8	187	32	Hatten, Joe*	12–8	48.6	2.8	3.3	0.7	4.09	4.18	4.90	-13	-1.3
27	7	187	23	Branca, Ralph	13–5	49.8	5.3	4.4	1.0	4.32	4.39	4.82	-11	-1.0
20	18	141	24	Barney, Rex	9–8	52.2	5.1	5.7	1.0	4.74	4.41	4.80	-7	-0.7
1	48	97	21	Palica, Erv	8–9	38.0	4.1	4.5	0.6	3.97	3.62	3.99	3	0.3
12	36	152	24	Banta, Jack	10–6	47.9	5.7	4.0	0.7	3.74	3.37	3.72	10	1.0
3	19	80	22	Erskine, Carl	8–1	57.0	5.5	5.8	0.7	4.27	4.63	4.97	-6	-0.6
1	26	47	25	Minner, Paul*	3–1	37.0	3.2	3.4	1.3	4.94	3.80	4.18	1	0.1
4	6	31	26	Martin, Morrie*	1–3	47.5	4.4	4.4	1.5	5.33	7.04	7.34	-10	-1.0
1	15	30		Others	1–2	—	4.8	4.5	0.9	4.36	4.50	5.70	-5	-0.5
156	193		25.3	Team Total		53	4.75	3.72	0.84	3.99	3.80	4.16	25	2.4
				League Average		50	3.71	3.56	0.76	4.04	4.04	4.58		
				% Lg Avg		106	128	96	90	101	106	110		
				League Rank		1	1	7	6	4	2			

1952 New York Yankees

The 1952 Yankees allowed the fewest runs in the AL and won their 4th straight pennant and world championship over the Dodgers. They were chased by a very good Indian team who led the AL in scoring and would finish only 2 games behind the powerful Yankees by season end. The Yankees won 50 of their last 80 games to finish the season strongly.

Strengths: (1) hitting led by Mantle (37 2B, 23 HR, 75 BB), Woodling (19 2B), Berra (30 HR), Collins (8 3B, 18 HR), and Bauer (31 2B), (2) grounded into the fewest double plays (93) and completed the most double plays in the majors (199), (3) fielding from SS Rizzuto (118 Rng+, 116 DP), 2B Martin (104 Rng+, 92 DP), and 3B McDougald (113 Rng+, 38 DP) who formed one of the best infield combinations in baseball history, (4) Held+ from CF Mantle (113) and RF Bauer (109), and (5) starting pitching anchored by Allie Reynolds (79% QS, 8.1 IP/S, 6 shutouts, 6 Sv), Lopat (74% QS, 7.8 IP/S), and Rashi (68% QS). Rizzuto (40% RS) was the team baserunning leader.

Weaknesses: (1) pitching control, (2) HR/9 from Hogue and Gorman (33% QS), (3) hitting from Martin and Noren, and (4) drawing BB.

Mgr	Casey Stengel	
Rk	35	91
Gm	154	
Place	1	
GA	2.0	
Rival	12–10 vs Indians, 105 RS & 100 RA	

	W	*L*	*Win%*
Regular Season	95	59	0.617
Runs Record	96	58	0.624
1 Run	22	19	0.537
Extra Innings	6	6	0.500
Blowout	30	16	0.652

	Team	*LgAvg*	*%Avg*	*LgRk*
BABIP	0.263	0.272	103	2
E	127	141	111	2
sOBP	0.317	0.326	103	3
rOBP	0.348	0.342	98	6
R/G	4.72	4.18	113	2
RA/G	3.62	4.18	116	1

	Tm	*LgAvg*	*>Avg*
RS	727	649	78
RA	557	649	92
DP	199	163	36

	R/G	*HR*	*K*	*BB*	*SB*	*CS*	*SB%*	*OBP*	*Held+*	
Team Offense	4.72	129	652	565	52	42	55%	0.341	LF	100
Team Defense	3.62	94	666	581	49	37	57%	0.324	CF	111
Difference	1.10	35	14	-16	3			105%	RF	107

Pos	*Rpos*	*PA*	*Age*	*Name*	*BA*	*OBP*	*SLG*	*BB%*	*XBT*	*Bat R>Avg*	*BR R>Avg*	*Fld R>Avg*	*RAA*	*WAA*
C	5	605	27	Berra, Yogi*	0.273	0.358	0.478	11%	50%	26	1	2	34	3.5
1B	-5	489	29	Collins, Joe*	0.280	0.364	0.481	11%	32%	22	1	1	19	2.0
2B	5	401	24	Martin, Billy	0.267	0.323	0.344	5%	44%	-4	-3	15	13	1.4
3B,2B	2	632	24	McDougald, Gil	0.263	0.336	0.369	9%	48%	2	1	13	18	1.9
SS	10	673	35	Rizzuto, Phil	0.254	0.337	0.341	10%	48%	-2	4	19	31	3.2
LF	-5	471	29	Woodling, Gene*	0.309	0.397	0.473	13%	49%	27	0	3	25	2.6
CF,RF	-2	626	20	Mantle, Mickey^	0.311	0.394	0.530	12%	64%	45	2	0	45	4.7
RF,LF	-6	615	29	Bauer, Hank	0.293	0.355	0.463	8%	43%	23	2	4	23	2.3
CF,1B	-3	306	27	Noren, Irv*	0.235	0.316	0.353	8%	42%	-3	2	-3	-7	-0.7
1B	-1	150	39	Mize, Johnny*	0.263	0.327	0.416	7%	22%	2	-2	1	0	0.0
LF,CF	-1	96	26	Cerv, Bob	0.241	0.313	0.356	9%	40%	-1	-1	0	-3	-0.3
C	1	60	27	Silvera, Charlie	0.327	0.383	0.382	8%	75%	2	-1	0	2	0.2
2B	0	47	27	Coleman, Jerry	0.405	0.468	0.500	11%	56%	4	0	1	5	0.6
	0	818		Others	0.191	0.252	0.241	7%	36%	-54	1	1	-52	-5.4
	0			Team Total	0.267	0.341	0.403	9.4%	45%	88	7	57	152	15.8
				League Average	0.253	0.330	0.365	9.7%	44%					
				% Lg Avg	106	103	110	98	103					
				League Rank	1	3	2	5	4		3	1		

GS	*GR*	*IP*	*Age*	*Name*	*W–L*	*GmSc*	*K/9*	*BB/9*	*HR/9*	*FIP*	*ERA*	*RA/9*	*RAA*	*WAA*
29	6	244	35	Reynolds, Allie	20–8	63.3	5.9	3.6	0.4	2.86	2.06	2.58	34	3.5
31	0	223	33	Raschi, Vic	16–6	58.7	5.1	3.7	0.5	3.23	2.78	3.15	17	1.7
19	1	149	34	Lopat, Ed*	10–5	58.8	3.4	3.2	0.7	3.72	2.53	2.83	16	1.7
12	4	94	22	Morgan, Tom	5–4	54.0	3.4	3.2	0.8	3.91	3.07	3.27	6	0.6
13	8	88	24	Miller, Bill*	4–6	53.9	4.6	5.0	0.5	3.82	3.48	4.40	-6	-0.6
16	19	148	34	Sain, Johnny	11–6	48.2	3.5	2.3	0.9	3.72	3.46	4.25	-8	-0.8
12	16	133	29	Kuzava, Bob*	8–8	53.5	4.5	4.3	0.5	3.48	3.45	3.59	3	0.4
6	6	61	27	Gorman, Tom	6–2	46.5	4.6	3.3	1.2	4.24	4.60	5.04	-8	-0.9
5	21	69	25	McDonald, Jim	3–4	40.2	2.6	5.2	0.1	3.79	3.50	4.02	-2	-0.2

GS	GR	IP	Age	Name	W–L	GmSc	K/9	BB/9	HR/9	FIP	ERA	RA/9	RAA	WAA
0	27	47	31	Hogue, Bobby	3–5	—	2.3	4.8	1.1	5.15	5.32	5.70	-10	-1.0
11	35	124		Others	9–5	—	4.1	5.1	0.8	4.38	3.99	4.86	-15	-1.5
				Team Total		56	4.34	3.79	0.61	3.62	3.14	3.63	27	2.8
				League Average		52	4.15	3.73	0.64	3.67	3.67	4.18		
				% Lg Avg		108	105	98	104	101	117	115		
				League Rank		1	4	7	3	4	1			

1953 NEW YORK YANKEES

The 1953 Yankees led the AL in both most runs scored and fewest runs allowed and was Stengel's best Yankee team culminating with another World Series victory over a strong Dodger team. This team's real strength was its lack of weakness with 13 positional players and 9 pitchers having above league average seasons.

Strengths: (1) hitting led by Mantle (21 HR), Woodling (26 2B), MVP runner-up Berra (27 HR), Bauer, McDougald (27 2B), and Collins, (2) drawing walks featuring Woodling (82 BB) and Mantle (79 BB), (3) baserunning led by Mantle (43% RS, 2 GIDP), (4) fielding from SS Rizzuto (105 Rng+, 100 DP), RF Bauer (104 Rng+, 12 assists), and OF Noren (106 Rng+, 11 assists), (5) Held+ from RF Bauer (132), Noren (134 in RF, 123 in CF, 127 in LF), CF Mantle (114), and LF Woodling (110), (6) CS% from Silvera (75%) and Berra (51%), and (7) pitching from Lopat (75% QS), Ford (70% QS), Sain (53% QS), and Raschi (62% QS).

Weaknesses: (1) hitting and baserunning from Martin (6 SB, 7 CS, and 19 GIDP) and (2) hitting for contact.

Mgr	Casey Stengel	
Rk	9	21
Gm	151	
Place	1	
GA	8.5	
Rival	11–11 vs Indians, 93 RS & 84 RA	

	W	L	Win%
Regular Season	99	52	0.656
Runs Record	101	50	0.666
1 Run	18	18	0.500
Extra Innings	9	4	0.692
Blowout	32	13	0.711

	Team	LgAvg	%Avg	LgRk
BABIP	0.269	0.280	104	3
E	126	134	106	3
sOBP	0.315	0.332	105	1
rOBP	0.341	0.350	103	4
R/G	5.30	4.46	119	1
RA/G	3.62	4.46	123	1

	Tm	LgAvg	>Avg
RS	801	689	112
RA	547	689	142
DP	182	168	14

	R/G	HR	K	BB	SB	CS	SB%	OBP
Team Offense	5.30	139	643	655	34	44	44%	0.358
Team Defense	3.62	94	604	500	33	37	47%	0.321
Difference	1.68	45	-39	155	1			112%

Pos	Rpos	PA	Age	Name	BA	OBP	SLG	BB%	XBT	Bat R>Avg	BR R>Avg	Fld R>Avg	RAA	WAA
C	4	557	28	Berra, Yogi*	0.296	0.363	0.523	9%	44%	28	2	2	36	3.6
1B	-5	450	30	Collins, Joe*	0.269	0.365	0.439	13%	56%	13	2	-2	8	0.8
2B,SS	7	645	25	Martin, Billy	0.257	0.314	0.395	7%	48%	-4	-5	-2	-4	-0.4
3B,2B	2	614	25	McDougald, Gil	0.285	0.361	0.416	10%	51%	12	3	2	19	1.9
SS	8	506	35	Rizzuto, Phil	0.271	0.383	0.351	14%	56%	6	-2	9	21	2.1
LF	-5	482	30	Woodling, Gene*	0.306	0.429	0.468	17%	42%	30	-2	3	26	2.7
CF,RF	-1	540	21	Mantle, Mickey^	0.295	0.398	0.497	15%	56%	31	6	1	37	3.7
RF	-5	503	30	Bauer, Hank	0.304	0.394	0.446	12%	48%	21	4	7	27	2.7
RF,CF	-3	391	28	Noren, Irv*	0.267	0.350	0.388	11%	53%	3	2	6	8	0.8
1B	-2	178	32	Bollweg, Don*	0.297	0.384	0.503	12%	50%	9	1	-1	7	0.8
LF	-2	137	28	Renna, Bill	0.314	0.385	0.463	9%	31%	6	-1	-1	2	0.2
1B	0	118	40	Mize, Johnny*	0.250	0.339	0.394	10%	29%	1	0	0	1	0.1
3B	0	91	21	Carey, Andy	0.321	0.389	0.531	10%	60%	6	1	1	8	0.8
C	1	94	28	Silvera, Charlie	0.280	0.352	0.341	10%	33%	0	0	4	5	0.5
	1	655		Others	0.187	0.248	0.245	7%	42%	-49	-5	6	-47	-4.7
	0		28.6	Team Total	0.273	0.358	0.417	11.0%	48%	113	6	35	154	15.4
				League Average	0.262	0.336	0.383	9.3%	44%					
				% Lg Avg	104	107	109	118	110					
				League Rank	1	1	1	1	2		3	3		

GS	GR	IP	Age	Name	W–L	GmSc	K/9	BB/9	HR/9	FIP	ERA	RA/9	RAA	WAA
30	2	207	26	Ford, Whitey*	18–6	54.1	4.8	4.8	0.6	3.97	3.00	3.35	21	2.1
26	2	181	34	Raschi, Vic	13–6	55.2	3.8	2.7	0.5	3.45	3.33	3.68	12	1.2
24	1	178	35	Lopat, Ed*	16–4	56.8	2.5	1.6	0.7	3.56	2.42	2.93	26	2.6
18	9	130	26	McDonald, Jim	9–7	53.4	3.0	2.7	0.3	3.23	3.82	4.44	-3	-0.3
19	21	189	35	Sain, Johnny	14–7	53.1	4.0	2.1	0.8	3.54	3.00	3.24	21	2.1
15	26	145	38	Reynolds, Allie	13–7	50.6	5.3	3.8	0.6	3.55	3.41	3.97	5	0.5
3	2	25	24	Kraly, Steve*	0–2	53.0	2.9	5.8	0.7	5.13	3.24	3.60	2	0.2
6	27	92	30	Kuzava, Bob*	6–5	57.8	4.7	3.3	0.9	3.90	3.31	3.41	9	0.9
1	39	77	28	Gorman, Tom	4–5	23.0	4.4	3.7	0.6	3.90	3.39	3.74	4	0.4
1	24	55	35	Scarborough, Ray	2–2	55.0	3.3	4.3	0.7	4.43	3.29	3.79	3	0.3
8	23	79		Others	4–1	0.0	4.7	5.7	0.9	4.85	3.86	4.76	-5	-0.5
151	176		31.1	Team Total		54	4.00	3.31	0.62	3.75	3.20	3.62	95	9.5
				League Average		49	4.00	3.64	0.72	4.00	3.99	4.49		
				% Lg Avg		110	100	110	115	106	125	124		
				League Rank		1	5	2	2	1	1			

1953 Brooklyn Dodgers

The 1953 Dodgers had their best hitting team since World War II while their pitching and fielding were also solid despite Newcombe serving in the military. This Dodger team was wonderfully portrayed in the book *The Boys of Summer* by Roger Kahn.

Strengths: (1) hitting led by Snider (38 2B, 42 HR), MVP Campanella (26 2B, 41 HR), Furillo (38 2B, 21 HR), Hodges (31 HR), Robinson (34 2B), RoY Gilliam (31 2B, 17 3B), and Reese (25 2B), (2) drawing walks featuring Gilliam (100), Reese (82), Snider (82), Hodges (75), and Robinson (74), (3) baserunning featuring Reese (22 SB, 6 CS, 44% RS), Robinson (17 SB, 4 CS, 43% RS), and Snider (10 GIDP), (4) fielding especially from SS Reese (103 Rng+), C Campanella (54% CS, only 19 SB allowed), 2B Gilliam (105 Rng+, 102 DP), LF Robinson (114 Rng+, 9 assists), 3B Cox (96 Rng+, only 6 errors in 234 chances), and CF Snider (98 Rng+, 9 assists), and (5) pitching anchored by Erskine (187 K, 45% QS), Labine (1.413 Lv), and Hughes (26/40/65% IR stranded, 1.154 Lv).

Weaknesses: (1) starting pitching, (2) hitting from Thompson, (3) Held+ from CF Snider (89), (4) pitching from Meyer (28% QS, 9.5 H/9), Loes (32% QS, 9.1 H/9), and Black (5 Sv, 3 BSv, 11/21/52% IR stranded, 0.863 Lv, 9.2 H/9), and (5) team HR/9.

Mgr	Charlie Dressen	
Rk	16	39
Gm	155	
Place	1	
GA	13.0	
Rival	13–9 vs Braves, 110 RS & 96 RA	

	W	L	Win%
Regular Season	105	49	0.682
Runs Record	100	54	0.652
1 Run	31	17	0.646
Extra Innings	8	8	0.500
Blowout	35	19	0.648

	Team	LgAvg	%Avg	LgRk
BABIP	0.271	0.281	103	2
E	118	148	125	3
sOBP	0.322	0.330	102	4
rOBP	0.318	0.350	110	1
R/G	6.16	4.75	130	1
RA/G	4.45	4.75	107	3

	Tm	LgAvg	>Avg
RS	955	739	216
RA	689	739	50
DP	161	157	4

	R/G	HR	K	BB	SB	CS	SB%	OBP	Held%	
Team Offense	6.16	208	686	655	90	47	66%	0.366	LF	100
Team Defense	4.45	169	817	509	22	25	47%	0.320	CF	91
Difference	1.72	39	131	146	68			114%	RF	100

Pos	Rpos	PA	Age	Name	BA	OBP	SLG	BB%	XBT	Bat R>Avg	BR R>Avg	Fld R>Avg	RAA	WAA
C	5	590	31	Campanella, Roy	0.312	0.395	0.611	11%	47%	48	-1	7	59	5.7
1B,LF	-7	598	29	Hodges, Gil	0.302	0.393	0.550	13%	52%	38	1	3	35	3.4
2B	6	710	24	Gilliam, Jim^	0.278	0.383	0.415	14%	60%	16	1	4	27	2.6
3B	1	371	33	Cox, Billy	0.291	0.363	0.443	10%	38%	8	-2	6	13	1.2
SS	8	625	34	Reese, Pee Wee	0.271	0.374	0.420	13%	56%	12	9	7	36	3.5
LF,3B	-3	574	34	Robinson, Jackie	0.329	0.425	0.502	13%	66%	36	7	12	52	5.0

Pos	Rpos	PA	Age	Name	BA	OBP	SLG	BB%	XBT	Bat R>Avg	BR R>Avg	Fld R>Avg	RAA	WAA
CF	-1	680	26	Snider, Duke*	0.336	0.419	0.627	12%	47%	65	4	8	76	7.3
RF	-6	518	31	Furillo, Carl	0.344	0.393	0.580	7%	49%	38	1	2	35	3.4
3B,SS	2	232	27	Morgan, Bobby	0.260	0.370	0.418	14%	64%	4	-1	0	5	0.5
LF	-2	189	28	Shuba, George*	0.254	0.326	0.426	9%	67%	0	0	2	0	0.0
1B	-2	180	22	Belardi, Wayne*	0.239	0.311	0.485	9%	20%	2	0	0	0	0.0
LF,RF	-3	169	29	Thompson, Don*	0.242	0.310	0.294	8%	38%	-7	-1	2	-9	-0.9
C	1	103	27	Walker, Rube*	0.242	0.301	0.400	7%	0%	-2	-1	0	-2	-0.2
	1	599		Others	0.164	0.192	0.217	3%	30%	-69	-1	-3	-72	-7.0
	0		28.8	Team Total	0.285	0.366	0.474	10.7%	50%	188	16	50	254	24.4
				League Average	0.266	0.335	0.411	8.9%	45%					
				% Lg Avg	107	109	115	121	112					
				League Rank	1	1	1	1	2		1	1		

GS	GR	IP	Age	Name	W–L	GmSc	K/9	BB/9	HR/9	FIP	ERA	RA/9	RAA	WAA
33	6	247	26	Erskine, Carl	20–6	56.4	6.8	3.5	0.8	3.40	3.54	3.87	19	1.8
32	2	191	29	Meyer, Russ	15–5	48.8	5.0	3.0	1.2	4.21	4.56	5.13	-13	-1.3
25	7	163	23	Loes, Billy	14–8	47.3	4.1	2.9	1.2	4.40	4.54	5.09	-11	-1.0
24	1	157	38	Roe, Preacher*	11–3	49.5	4.9	2.3	1.5	4.55	4.36	4.47	1	0.1
18	15	115	20	Podres, Johnny*	9–4	48.1	6.4	5.0	0.9	4.24	4.23	4.85	-4	-0.4
10	27	118	26	Milliken, Bob	8–4	51.1	5.0	3.2	1.0	4.02	3.37	3.98	7	0.7
0	48	86	30	Hughes, Jim	4–3	—	5.1	4.3	0.6	3.85	3.47	3.47	10	1.0
7	30	110	26	Labine, Clem	11–6	53.4	3.6	2.4	0.7	3.69	2.77	3.18	16	1.6
0	32	90	30	Wade, Ben	7–5	—	6.5	3.3	1.5	4.56	3.79	3.99	6	0.5
3	31	73	29	Black, Joe	6–3	47.0	5.2	3.3	1.5	4.76	5.33	5.70	-10	-0.9
3	13	31		Others	0–2	—	4.9	6.0	2.3	7.05	8.91	9.19	-16	-1.6
155	212		27.7	Team Total		50	5.33	3.32	1.10	4.17	4.10	4.49	5	0.5
				League Average		49	4.35	3.46	0.98	4.28	4.29	4.85		
				% Lg Avg		102	122	104	89	103	105	108		
				League Rank		4	1	3	7	4	3			

1954 Cleveland Indians

After finishing in second place for the last 3 seasons, the 1954 Indians broke through with a magnificent year and recaptured the pennant they held in 1948 beating powerful Yankee and White Sox teams. The Indians allowed fewer runs than any full season AL team since 1917. The 1954 Indians won a season franchise record 111 games breaking the AL season wins record held by the 1927 Yankees. Being swept by the Giants was the most surprising World Series sweep since the 1914 Braves swept the A's.

Strengths: (1) hitting led by Avila (27 2B), Rosen (24 HR), Doby (32 HR), Smith (29 2B), and Wertz, (2) drawing walks from Smith (88 BB), Doby (85 BB), and Rosen (85 BB), (3) fielding from SS Strickland (95 Rng+), SS Dente (87 Rng+), 2B Avila (104 Rng+, 100 DP), and CF Doby (99 Rng+, 14 assists, 2 errors in 427 chances), (4) CS% from Hegan (51%), and (5) pitching from Garcia (71% QS), Wynn (69% QS), Lemon (73% QS), Feller (74% QS), Newhouser, Mossi, and Narleski.

Weaknesses: (1) C and RF positions, (2) hitting from Hegan, Strickland, and Philley, (3) DP made, and (4) Held+ from RF Philley (87).

Mgr	Al Lopez	
Rk	8	15
Gm	156	
Place	1	
GA	8.0	
Rival	11–11 vs Yankees, 99 RS & 95 RA	

	W	L	Win%
Regular Season	111	43	0.721
Runs Record	105	49	0.680
1 Run	32	13	0.711
Extra Innings	13	6	0.684
Blowout	30	9	0.769

	Team	LgAvg	%Avg	LgRk
BABIP	0.250	0.274	110	1
E	128	140	109	3
sOBP	0.298	0.329	110	1
rOBP	0.293	0.339	116	1
R/G	4.78	4.19	114	2
RA/G	3.23	4.19	130	1

	Tm	*LgAvg*	*>Avg*
RS	746	650	96
RA	504	650	146
DP	148	160	-12

	R/G	*HR*	*K*	*BB*	*SB*	*CS*	*SB%*	*OPS*	*Held+*	
Team Offense	4.78	156	668	637	30	33	48%	0.744	LF	101
Team Defense	3.23	89	678	486	43	40	52%	0.626	CF	101
Difference	1.55	67	10	151	-13			119%	RF	86

Pos	*Rpos*	*PA*	*Age*	*Name*	*BA*	*OBP*	*SLG*	*BB%*	*XBT*	*Bat R>Avg*	*BR R>Avg*	*Fld R>Avg*	*RAA*	*WAA*
C	5	468	33	Hegan, Jim	0.234	0.289	0.374	7%	48%	-9	0	3	-1	-0.1
1B	-4	335	29	Wertz, Vic*	0.275	0.344	0.478	10%	52%	12	1	1	10	1.0
2B	6	638	30	Avila, Bobby	0.341	0.402	0.477	9%	57%	36	5	4	51	5.3
3B,1B	-2	566	30	Rosen, Al	0.300	0.404	0.506	15%	52%	38	0	-5	31	3.2
SS	6	433	28	Strickland, George	0.213	0.314	0.313	13%	53%	-9	1	5	3	0.3
LF,3B	-5	583	26	Smith, Al	0.281	0.398	0.435	15%	62%	26	3	5	29	3.0
CF	-1	675	29	Doby, Larry*	0.272	0.364	0.484	13%	57%	30	3	10	42	4.3
RF	-6	522	34	Philley, Dave^	0.226	0.308	0.347	11%	56%	-8	0	4	-10	-1.0
LF,RF	-3	274	33	Westlake, Wally	0.263	0.337	0.454	9%	42%	7	-1	-1	2	0.2
3B	0	208	24	Regalado, Rudy	0.250	0.333	0.311	9%	60%	-3	0	1	-2	-0.2
SS,2B	3	194	32	Dente, Sam	0.266	0.319	0.337	7%	12%	-3	0	7	7	0.7
1B	-2	185	28	Glynn, Bill*	0.251	0.297	0.380	6%	48%	-2	-1	2	-3	-0.4
LF,RF	-1	114	29	Pope, Dave*	0.294	0.354	0.451	9%	60%	4	1	0	4	0.4
2B,3B	1	129	37	Majeski, Hank	0.281	0.320	0.388	5%	36%	0	-1	0	0	0.0
C	1	113	25	Naragon, Hal*	0.238	0.300	0.297	8%	43%	-4	0	1	-2	-0.2
	2	612		Others	0.197	0.258	0.253	7%	34%	-38	-1	-4	-41	-4.2
	0		29.8	Team Total	0.262	0.341	0.402	10.5%	51%	76	10	33	119	12.3
				League Average	0.257	0.331	0.373	9.7%	45%					
				% Lg Avg	102	103	108	109	114					
				League Rank	4	4	2	3	1		1	2		

GS	*GR*	*IP*	*Age*	*Name*	*W–L*	*GmSc*	*K/9*	*BB/9*	*HR/9*	*FIP*	*ERA*	*RA/9*	*RAA*	*WAA*
36	4	271	34	Wynn, Early	23–11	59.5	5.2	2.8	0.7	3.16	2.73	3.09	28	2.9
34	11	259	30	Garcia, Mike	19–8	57.9	4.5	2.5	0.2	2.53	2.64	2.96	30	3.1
33	3	258	33	Lemon, Bob	23–7	57.2	3.8	3.2	0.4	3.25	2.72	3.31	20	2.0
25	7	188	26	Houtteman, Art	15–7	51.9	3.3	2.8	0.7	3.61	3.35	3.83	3	0.3
19	0	140	35	Feller, Bob	13–3	56.0	3.8	2.5	0.8	3.64	3.09	3.41	9	1.0
2	40	89	25	Narleski, Ray	3–3	46.0	5.3	4.4	0.8	3.93	2.22	2.53	15	1.5
5	35	93	25	Mossi, Don*	6–1	65.0	5.3	3.8	0.5	3.18	1.94	2.13	20	2.0
1	25	47	33	Newhouser, Hal*	7–2	38.0	4.8	3.5	0.6	3.30	2.51	3.09	5	0.5
0	17	35	32	Hooper, Bob	0–0	—	3.1	4.2	0.8	4.28	4.93	5.71	-7	-0.7
1	13	27	28	Hoskins, Dave	0–1	37.0	3.0	3.4	1.0	4.29	3.04	3.37	2	0.2
0	5	14		Others	2–0	—	2.6	9.9	0.7	6.04	1.32	1.98	3	0.3
156	160		30.1	Team Total		57	4.30	3.08	0.56	3.30	2.78	3.20	128	13.2
				League Average		51	4.16	3.74	0.67	3.72	3.72	4.22		
				% Lg Avg		112	103	121	118	113	134	132		
				League Rank		1	4	1	3	1	1			

1954 New York Yankees

The 1954 Yankees put up the good fight winning 103 games which bettered the victory totals of any of the previous 5 Yankee pennant winning teams. Woodling suffered a hand injury during the season which opened playing time for Irv Noren who shined. Nine positional players and eight pitchers had better than league average seasons. The Yankees led the majors in runs per game.

Strengths: (1) hitting for average and power led by Mantle (12 3B, 27 HR), MVP Berra (28 2B, 22 HR), Noren, and Skowron (9 3B), (2) drawing walks featuring Mantle (102 BB), (3) baserunning led by Mantle (3 GIDP, 43% RS), Bauer (44% RS), and Collins (42% RS), (4) fielding from 2B McDougald (104 Rng+, 84 DP in 92 games), SS Rizzuto (104 Rng+), and 3B Carey (112 Rng+), (5) CS% from Berra (56%), (6) Held+ from CF Mantle (116) and RF Bauer (113), and (7) pitching from Ford (61% QS) and AL RoY Bob Grim (60% QS, 7.5 IP/S),

Weaknesses: (1) SS position, (2) hitting from Rizzuto and Coleman, and (3) LF Woodling's Held+ (92).

			W	L	Win%		Team	LgAvg	%Avg	LgRk
Mgr	Casey Stengel	**Regular Season**	103	51	0.669	**BABIP**	0.271	0.274	101	3
Rk	26 69	**Runs Record**	98	56	0.636	**E**	127	140	110	2
Gm	155	**1 Run**	25	19	0.568	**sOBP**	0.328	0.329	100	4
Place	2	**Extra Innings**	5	7	0.417	**rOBP**	0.319	0.339	106	2
GB	8.0	**Blowout**	35	11	0.761	**R/G**	5.19	4.19	124	1
Rival	11–11 vs Indians, 95 RS & 99 RA					**RA/G**	3.63	4.19	115	3

	Tm	LgAvg	>Avg
RS	805	650	155
RA	563	650	87
DP	198	160	38

	R/G	HR	K	BB	SB	CS	SB%	OPS	Held+	
Team Offense	5.19	133	632	650	34	41	45%	0.756	LF	94
Team Defense	3.63	86	655	552	34	37	48%	0.673	CF	110
Difference	1.56	47	23	98	0			112%	RF	101

Pos	Rpos	PA	Age	Name	BA	OBP	SLG	BB%	XBT	Bat R>Avg	BR R>Avg	Fld R>Avg	RAA	WAA
C	6	652	29	Berra, Yogi*	0.307	0.367	0.488	9%	42%	31	2	-1	38	3.9
1B	-4	398	31	Collins, Joe*	0.271	0.365	0.446	13%	63%	13	3	2	14	1.5
2B,3B	4	473	26	McDougald, Gil	0.259	0.364	0.416	13%	41%	12	0	9	25	2.6
3B	0	471	22	Carey, Andy	0.302	0.373	0.423	9%	45%	15	-3	6	18	1.9
SS	6	369	36	Rizzuto, Phil	0.195	0.291	0.251	11%	61%	-18	0	3	-9	-0.9
LF	-4	360	31	Woodling, Gene*	0.250	0.358	0.352	15%	36%	3	1	-2	-2	-0.2
CF	-1	651	22	Mantle, Mickey^	0.300	0.408	0.525	16%	62%	48	7	-1	53	5.4
RF	-5	423	31	Bauer, Hank	0.294	0.360	0.459	9%	70%	15	4	4	18	1.8
LF,OF	-5	480	29	Noren, Irv*	0.319	0.377	0.481	9%	44%	24	-2	7	24	2.5
2B,SS	5	332	29	Coleman, Jerry	0.217	0.278	0.277	8%	49%	-17	0	0	-12	-1.2
1B	-2	237	23	Skowron, Bill	0.340	0.392	0.577	8%	52%	20	0	-3	15	1.5
1B	-1	163	33	Robinson, Eddie*	0.261	0.344	0.387	12%	67%	2	0	4	5	0.5
LF	-1	112	28	Cerv, Bob	0.260	0.330	0.470	10%	18%	3	-1	-3	-2	-0.2
RF	-1	154	38	Slaughter, Enos*	0.248	0.386	0.336	18%	37%	2	0	-5	-4	-0.4
SS	3	129	28	Miranda, Willy^	0.254	0.305	0.351	8%	53%	-2	0	-3	-2	-0.2
	0	624		Others	0.175	0.240	0.218	7%	30%	-49	-2	1	-50	-5.2
	0		29.1	Team Total	0.268	0.348	0.408	10.8%	49%	101	9	18	128	13.2
				League Average	0.257	0.331	0.373	9.7%	45%					
				% Lg Avg	104	105	109	112	109					
				League Rank	1	1	1	1	2		2	3		

GS	GR	IP	Age	Name	W–L	GmSc	K/9	BB/9	HR/9	FIP	ERA	RA/9	RAA	WAA
28	6	211	25	Ford, Whitey*	16–8	57.4	5.3	4.3	0.4	3.26	2.82	3.08	24	2.5
20	17	199	24	Grim, Bob	20–6	54.0	4.9	3.8	0.4	3.21	3.26	3.53	13	1.3
23	3	170	36	Lopat, Ed*	12–4	50.3	2.9	1.7	0.7	3.50	3.55	3.92	3	0.3
18	18	157	37	Reynolds, Allie	13–4	52.6	5.7	3.8	0.7	3.50	3.32	3.72	7	0.7
17	15	143	24	Morgan, Tom	11–5	54.2	2.1	2.5	0.5	3.57	3.34	3.65	7	0.7
21	4	132	29	Byrd, Harry	9–7	52.2	3.5	2.9	0.7	3.71	2.99	3.81	4	0.4
10	6	71	27	McDonald, Jim	4–1	54.8	2.5	5.7	0.4	4.31	3.17	3.55	4	0.4
5	0	40	34	Byrne, Tommy*	3–2	58.6	5.4	4.3	0.2	2.93	2.70	2.93	5	0.5
0	45	77	36	Sain, Johnny	6–6	—	3.9	1.8	1.3	3.96	3.16	3.16	8	0.8
0	23	37	29	Gorman, Tom	0–0	—	7.6	3.4	0.2	2.27	2.21	3.44	3	0.3
13	45	142		Others	9–8	—	4.7	5.8	0.4	3.85	4.24	4.93	-13	-1.4
155	182			Team Total		53	4.27	3.60	0.56	3.50	3.26	3.67	65	6.7
			30.1	League Average		52	4.16	3.74	0.67	3.72	3.72	4.22		
				% Lg Avg		102	103	104	119	106	114	115		
				League Rank		3	5	4	3	3	3			

1954 CHICAGO WHITE SOX

Unfortunately for this strong 1954 White Sox team, they competed against excellent Indian and Yankee teams. So, winning 94 games was only good enough for a third place finish in the AL. The 1954 White Sox were actually in first place for 34 days in the first half of the season winning 54 out of their first 85 games played. Their 7–15 W–L record versus the Yankees contributed to their third place finish.

Strengths: (1) hitting led by Minoso (29 2B, 18 3B, 19 HR, 16 HBP), Fox (24 2B), and Rivera (8 3B), (3) fielding from SS Carrasquel (101 Rng+, 102 DP, 20 errors in 792 chances), 2B Fox (100 Rng+, 103 DP, 9 errors in 801 chances) and LF Minoso (112 Rng+, 14 assists), (4) CS% from Lollar (68%) and Sawatski (59%), (5) Held+ from LF Minoso (114) and RF Rivera (115), and (6) pitching anchored by ace Trucks (70% QS), Dorish (6/7/86% Sv, 20/28/71% IR stranded), and Martin (23/24/96% IR stranded).

Weaknesses: (1) C position, (2) team isolated power, (3) hitting from the catcher position, and (4) baserunning from Groth (3 SB, 9 CS, 22% RS, 19 GIDP, 3 ROE).

Mgr	Paul Richards	
Rk	29	78
Gm	155	
Place	3	
GB	17.0	
Rival	11–11 vs Indians; 7–15 vs Yankees	

	W	*L*	*Win%*
Regular Season	94	60	0.610
Runs Record	97	57	0.633
1 Run	21	25	0.457
Extra Innings	4	5	0.444
Blowout	31	10	0.756

	Team	*LgAvg*	*%Avg*	*LgRk*
BABIP	0.265	0.274	103	2
E	108	140	130	1
sOBP	0.310	0.329	106	2
rOBP	0.323	0.339	105	3
R/G	4.59	4.19	109	3
RA/G	3.36	4.19	125	2

	Tm	*LgAvg*	*>Avg*
RS	711	650	61
RA	521	650	129
DP	149	160	-11

	R/G	*HR*	*K*	*BB*	*SB*	*CS*	*SB%*	*OPS*	*Held+*	
Team Offense	4.59	94	536	604	98	58	63%	0.726	LF	114
Team Defense	3.36	94	701	517	33	41	45%	0.666	CF	101
Difference	1.23	0	165	87	65			109%	RF	114

Pos	*Rpos*	*PA*	*Age*	*Name*	*BA*	*OBP*	*SLG*	*BB%*	*XBT*	*Bat R>Avg*	*BR R>Avg*	*Fld R>Avg*	*RAA*	*WAA*
C	3	365	29	Lollar, Sherm	0.244	0.334	0.351	10%	32%	-2	-1	2	2	0.3
1B	-3	281	33	Fain, Ferris*	0.303	0.400	0.419	14%	34%	12	3	0	12	1.3
2B	6	706	26	Fox, Nellie*	0.319	0.372	0.391	7%	50%	15	4	11	36	3.7
3B	0	345	28	Michaels, Cass	0.261	0.391	0.396	16%	54%	11	2	5	18	1.9
SS	9	718	28	Carrasquel, Chico	0.255	0.348	0.368	12%	46%	4	2	20	35	3.6
LF,RF	-6	676	28	Minoso, Minnie	0.320	0.410	0.534	11%	61%	52	2	16	64	6.6
CF,LF	-1	477	27	Groth, Johnny	0.275	0.341	0.372	9%	50%	2	-7	6	0	0.0
RF,CF	-6	552	32	Rivera, Jim*	0.286	0.356	0.431	9%	50%	14	1	-2	7	0.7
1B,3B	-2	261	31	Kell, George	0.283	0.323	0.391	7%	21%	1	-1	-3	-5	-0.5
1B,RF	-2	188	37	Cavarretta, Phil*	0.316	0.417	0.411	14%	42%	9	2	-3	6	0.6
C	2	179	32	Batts, Matt	0.228	0.299	0.342	9%	38%	-4	-2	-2	-6	-0.6
3B	0	109	30	Marsh, Fred	0.306	0.364	0.398	8%	35%	2	-2	8	8	0.8
1B	-1	107	20	Jackson, Ron	0.280	0.333	0.452	6%	63%	2	0	2	3	0.3
C	1	127	26	Sawatski, Carl*	0.183	0.276	0.294	12%	33%	-5	0	1	-3	-0.3
	0	881		Others	0.179	0.252	0.225	9%	35%	-62	-3	11	-54	-5.6
	0		29.1	Team Total	0.267	0.347	0.379	10.1%	45%	51	0	72	123	12.7
				League Average	0.257	0.331	0.373	9.7%	45%					
				% Lg Avg	104	105	102	105	100					

GS	*GR*	*IP*	*Age*	*Name*	*W–L*	*GmSc*	*K/9*	*BB/9*	*HR/9*	*FIP*	*ERA*	*RA/9*	*RAA*	*WAA*
33	7	265	37	Trucks, Virgil	19–12	58.2	5.2	3.2	0.4	2.96	2.79	2.96	24	2.4
27	4	210	33	Keegan, Bob	16–9	53.2	2.6	3.5	0.7	3.98	3.09	3.61	2	0.2
26	10	189	27	Pierce, Billy*	9–10	54.0	7.1	4.1	0.7	3.26	3.48	4.10	-7	-0.7
21	14	177	26	Harshman, Jack*	14–8	59.5	6.8	4.9	0.4	3.09	2.95	3.10	13	1.4
17	22	154	33	Consuegra, Sandy	16–3	54.2	1.8	2.0	0.5	3.42	2.69	3.04	11	1.2
6	9	42	22	Fornieles, Mike	1–2	48.7	3.9	3.0	0.9	3.76	4.29	5.14	-7	-0.7
16	30	144	27	Johnson, Don	8–7	52.8	4.3	2.7	0.9	3.59	3.13	3.31	7	0.7
6	31	109	32	Dorish, Fritz	6–4	64.2	4.0	2.4	0.7	3.40	2.72	2.89	11	1.1
2	33	70	31	Martin, Morrie*	5–4	76.0	4.0	3.1	0.6	3.49	2.06	2.31	11	1.2
0	9	14	30	Strahs, Dick	0–0	—	5.0	5.0	0.0	2.94	5.65	6.28	-4	-0.4
1	7	10		Others	0–1	—	1.9	4.7	1.9	6.21	9.32	10.25	-7	-0.7
155	176		29.8	Team Total		56	4.56	3.36	0.61	3.40	3.05	3.39	55	5.7
				League Average		51	4.16	3.74	0.67	3.72	3.72	4.22		
				% Lg Avg		110	110	111	109	110	122	124		
				League Rank		2	1	3	5	2	2			

1954 New York Giants

The 1954 Giants got back Willie Mays from military service and recaptured the pennant they held in 1951. In the World Series, the NL team beat the AL team for the first time since 1946.

Strengths: (1) hitting led by MVP Mays (33 2B, 13 3B, 41 HR, 377 TB), Thompson (26 HR, 90 BB), Rhodes (15 HR), Mueller (35 2B), and Irvin (19 HR, 70 BB), (2) baserunning, (3) fielding from CF Mays (110 Rng+, 13 assists), 2B Williams (97 Rng+, 112 DP), SS Dark (99 Rng+, 105 DP), and LF Irvin (109 Rng+), (4) Held+ from CF Mays (122) and LF Irvin (120), (5) CS% from Katt (67%) and Westrum (59%), and (6) pitching from Antonelli (62% QS), Maglie (59% QS), Gomez (56% QS), Liddle, Wilhelm (31/46/67% IR stranded, 1.160 Lv) and Grissom (34/50/68% IR stranded, 1.522 Lv).

Weaknesses: (1) C, 1B, and 2B positions, (2) hitting from Williams, Westrum, and Lockman, (3) drawing walks, (4) defense from 1B Lockman, (5) team pitching BB/9, and (6) pitching from Jansen (14% QS, 12.6 H/9) and Hearn (50% QS, 9.5 H/9).

Mgr	Leo Durocher	
Rk	24	64
Gm	154	
Place	1	
GA	5.0	
Rival	13–9 vs Dodgers, 124 RS, 88 RA	

	W	*L*	*Win%*
Regular Season	97	57	0.630
Runs Record	98	56	0.637
1 Run	29	23	0.558
Extra Innings	10	6	0.625
Blowout	26	11	0.703

	Team	*LgAvg*	*%Avg*	*LgRk*
BABIP	0.260	0.277	106	1
E	154	144	94	6
sOBP	0.321	0.330	103	3
rOBP	0.337	0.349	104	3
R/G	4.75	4.56	104	3
RA/G	3.57	4.56	128	1

	Tm	*LgAvg*	*>Avg*
RS	732	703	29
RA	550	703	153
DP	172	161	11

	R/G	*HR*	*K*	*BB*	*SB*	*CS*	*SB%*	*OPS*	*Held+*	
Team Offense	4.75	186	561	522	30	23	57%	0.755	LF	113
Team Defense	3.57	113	692	613	29	34	46%	0.676	CF	124
Difference	1.18	73	131	-91	1			112%	RF	104

Pos	*Rpos*	*PA*	*Age*	*Name*	*BA*	*OBP*	*SLG*	*BB%*	*XBT*	*Bat R>Avg*	*BR R>Avg*	*Fld R>Avg*	*RAA*	*WAA*
C	3	299	31	Westrum, Wes	0.187	0.315	0.305	15%	59%	-10	0	3	-4	-0.4
1B	-7	639	27	Lockman, Whitey*	0.251	0.318	0.375	9%	50%	-10	4	-6	-19	-1.9
2B	6	601	26	Williams, Davey	0.222	0.284	0.316	7%	53%	-29	2	10	-11	-1.1
3B	0	557	28	Thompson, Hank*	0.263	0.389	0.482	16%	56%	24	4	4	32	3.2
SS	9	693	32	Dark, Al	0.293	0.325	0.446	4%	61%	4	4	5	22	2.1
LF	-6	512	35	Irvin, Monte	0.262	0.363	0.438	14%	60%	11	-2	13	16	1.6
CF	-1	640	23	Mays, Willie	0.345	0.411	0.667	10%	73%	67	3	21	90	8.9
RF	-7	658	27	Mueller, Don*	0.342	0.363	0.444	3%	61%	14	2	1	10	1.0
C	2	227	27	Katt, Ray	0.255	0.314	0.435	8%	33%	0	0	-1	1	0.1
LF	-2	186	27	Rhodes, Dusty*	0.341	0.410	0.695	10%	40%	20	1	-1	18	1.8
1B,2B	-1	148	28	Hofman, Bobby	0.224	0.317	0.456	11%	30%	1	-1	-2	-3	-0.3
3B,2B	1	115	26	Gardner, Billy	0.213	0.261	0.287	5%	44%	-8	0	5	-2	-0.2
C	0	55	32	St. Claire, Ebba^	0.262	0.436	0.429	22%	50%	3	0	-2	1	0.1
C	0	13	28	Garagiola, Joe*	0.273	0.308	0.455	8%	100%	0	0	0	0	0.0
	3	593		Others	0.146	0.195	0.199	5%	36%	-69	-3	0	-69	-6.9
	0		28.4	Team Total	0.264	0.332	0.424	8.8%	55%	17	14	50	81	8.1
				League Average	0.265	0.335	0.407	9.2%	45%					
				% Lg Avg	100	99	104	95	122					
				League Rank	5	5	2	6	2		1	1		

GS	*GR*	*IP*	*Age*	*Name*	*W–L*	*GmSc*	*K/9*	*BB/9*	*HR/9*	*FIP*	*ERA*	*RA/9*	*RAA*	*WAA*
37	2	259	24	Antonelli, Johnny*	21–7	59.6	5.3	3.3	0.8	3.50	2.30	2.71	45	4.5
32	5	222	26	Gomez, Ruben	17–9	55.2	4.3	4.4	0.8	4.20	2.88	3.45	20	2.0
32	2	218	37	Maglie, Sal	14–6	53.5	4.8	2.9	0.9	3.60	3.26	3.42	20	2.0
18	11	130	33	Hearn, Jim	8–8	48.0	3.1	4.6	0.7	4.29	4.15	4.92	-10	-1.0
19	9	127	29	Liddle, Don*	9–4	53.5	3.1	3.9	0.4	3.61	3.05	3.41	12	1.2
7	6	41	33	Jansen, Larry	2–2	37.1	3.3	3.3	1.1	4.46	5.97	7.08	-13	-1.3
3	53	122	36	Grissom, Marv	10–7	60.3	4.7	3.7	1.0	4.15	2.35	2.72	21	2.1
0	57	111	31	Wilhelm, Hoyt	12–4	—	5.2	4.2	0.4	3.39	2.10	2.59	21	2.1
4	29	61	28	McCall, Windy*	2–5	42.8	5.6	4.3	0.7	3.81	3.25	3.84	3	0.3
0	20	31	27	Corwin, Al	1–3	—	4.0	4.0	1.2	4.53	4.03	5.46	-4	-0.4

GS	GR	IP	Age	Name	W–L	GmSc	K/9	BB/9	HR/9	FIP	ERA	RA/9	RAA	WAA
2	41	68		Others	1–2	—	4.4	7.8	0.4	4.62	5.03	5.16	-7	-0.7
154	235		30.4	Team Total		54	4.48	3.97	0.73	3.88	3.09	3.56	109	10.8
				League Average		50	4.15	3.60	0.91	4.07	4.07	4.59		
				% Lg Avg		108	108	91	124	105	132	129		
				League Rank		2	3	7	1	2	1			

1955 New York Yankees

The 1955 Yankees won the pennant in a close race with the defending pennant winner Indians and the White Sox. One of the lesser hyped Yankee teams due to their loss in game seven to the Dodgers in the World Series, the 1955 Yankees were a very strong team finishing first in the AL by three games over the 1954 pennant winner Indians. Berra won the MVP award even though Mantle was clearly the best player in the entire AL.

Strengths: (1) hitting for power led by Mantle (11 3B, 37 HR, 113 BB), Berra (27 HR), Bauer (20 2B, 20 HR), and Skowron, (2) positional depth with above league average contributions from 13 positional players, (3) fielding from 2B/3B McDougald (110 Rng+, 119 DP in 126 games), SS Hunter (93 Rng+), RF Bauer (104 Rng+, 113 Held+), CF Mantle (94 Rng+), and C Berra (52% CS), (4) team GIDP led by Mantle (4 GIDP) and Bauer (4 GIDP), and (5) pitching from Ford (76% QS) and Turley (68% QS, 210 K).

Weaknesses: (1) team pitching BB/9 leading to a negative BB differential, (2) hitting from SS Hunter, and (3) hitting from the pitchers.

Mgr	Casey Stengel	
Rk	22	54
Gm	154	
Place	1	
GA	3.0	
Rival	9–13 vs Indians, 80 RS & 94 RA	

	W	L	Win%
Regular Season	96	58	0.623
Runs Record	99	55	0.639
1 Run	26	21	0.553
Extra Innings	7	6	0.538
Blowout	34	13	0.723

	Team	LgAvg	%Avg	LgRk
BABIP	0.251	0.275	110	1
E	128	136	106	3
sOBP	0.330	0.335	102	4
rOBP	0.317	0.338	107	2
R/G	4.94	4.44	111	2
RA/G	3.69	4.44	120	2

	Tm	LgAvg	>Avg
RS	761	686	75
RA	569	686	117
DP	180	160	20

	R/G	HR	K	BB	SB	CS	SB%	OPS	Held+	
Team Offense	4.94	175	655	607	55	25	69%	0.758	LF	101
Team Defense	3.69	108	732	688	27	34	44%	0.664	CF	105
Difference	1.25	67	77	-81	28			114%	RF	112

Pos	Rpos	PA	Age	Name	BA	OBP	SLG	BB%	XBT	Bat R>Avg	BR R>Avg	Fld R>Avg	RAA	WAA
C	6	615	30	Berra, Yogi*	0.272	0.349	0.470	10%	46%	18	2	3	29	2.9
1B	-3	314	24	Skowron, Bill	0.319	0.369	0.524	7%	39%	17	-1	-2	11	1.1
2B,3B	4	615	27	McDougald, Gil	0.285	0.361	0.407	11%	48%	11	4	15	34	3.4
3B	0	570	23	Carey, Andy	0.257	0.313	0.378	8%	53%	-6	1	8	3	0.3
SS	5	279	27	Hunter, Billy	0.227	0.269	0.298	5%	54%	-15	-1	10	-1	-0.1
LF,CF	-5	423	30	Noren, Irv*	0.253	0.331	0.375	10%	41%	-1	2	12	8	0.8
CF	-1	638	23	Mantle, Mickey^	0.306	0.431	0.611	18%	64%	64	6	10	79	7.9
RF,LF	-6	563	32	Bauer, Hank	0.278	0.360	0.461	10%	52%	18	6	16	34	3.4
1B,RF	-5	330	32	Collins, Joe*	0.234	0.339	0.414	13%	64%	4	3	5	7	0.7
1B	-2	215	34	Robinson, Eddie*	0.208	0.358	0.491	17%	25%	8	-1	3	8	0.8
LF,RF	-3	305	26	Howard, Elston	0.290	0.336	0.477	7%	48%	8	0	4	9	0.9
SS	3	181	38	Rizzuto, Phil	0.259	0.369	0.322	12%	53%	0	3	-3	3	0.3
LF,CF	-1	96	29	Cerv, Bob	0.341	0.411	0.541	7%	46%	7	1	1	8	0.8
2B	1	80	27	Martin, Billy	0.300	0.354	0.371	9%	88%	1	0	2	4	0.4
	7	719		Others	0.166	0.236	0.211	8%	31%	-63	-4	-12	-72	-7.2
	0		28.7	Team Total	0.260	0.340	0.418	10.2%	49%	71	21	72	164	16.4
				League Average	0.258	0.336	0.381	10.0%	44%					
				% Lg Avg	101	101	110	102	112					
				League Rank	5	5	1	4	1		2	1		

GS	GR	IP	Age	Name	W–L	GmSc	K/9	BB/9	HR/9	FIP	ERA	RA/9	RAA	WAA
33	6	254	26	Ford, Whitey*	18–7	60.4	4.9	4.0	0.7	3.72	2.63	2.94	31	3.1
34	2	247	24	Turley, Bob	17–13	59.1	7.7	6.5	0.6	3.84	3.06	3.36	20	2.0
22	5	160	35	Byrne, Tommy*	16–5	54.0	4.3	4.9	0.7	4.25	3.15	3.88	2	0.2
13	6	97	25	Larsen, Don	9–2	52.9	4.1	4.7	0.7	4.23	3.06	3.53	5	0.5
12	4	87	37	Lopat, Ed*	4–8	48.2	2.5	1.7	1.2	4.24	3.74	4.67	-7	-0.7
13	16	127	21	Kucks, Johnny	8–7	49.4	3.5	3.1	0.6	3.51	3.41	3.84	2	0.2
11	15	92	25	Grim, Bob	7–5	47.6	6.1	4.1	0.9	3.81	4.19	4.78	-8	-0.8
0	45	74	38	Konstanty, Jim	7–2	—	2.3	2.9	0.6	3.78	2.32	3.42	4	0.4
1	39	72	25	Morgan, Tom	7–3	31.0	2.1	3.0	0.4	3.63	3.25	3.63	3	0.3
1	32	68	25	Sturdivant, Tom	1–3	58.0	6.3	5.5	0.8	4.14	3.16	3.16	7	0.7
14	20	95		Others	2–3	—	4.2	6.4	0.8	5.00	4.72	5.48	-16	-1.6
154	190		28.1	Team Total		54	4.80	4.51	0.71	3.97	3.23	3.73	42	4.2
				League Average		49	4.41	3.92	0.78	3.96	3.96	4.48		
				% Lg Avg		110	109	87	111	100	123	120		
				League Rank		1	2	7	4	4	1			

1955 Brooklyn Dodgers

The Dodgers led by Campanella and Snider were an offensive juggernaut scoring over a run more per game than the league average. Above average fielding at every position greatly contributed to the pitching success. This team dominated the pennant race and beat the preseason favorite Braves by 13.5 games. The Dodgers finally won the World Series and their first championship in franchise history beating the Yankees which was climaxed by a 2–0 win in Game 7. These two same teams previously met in World Series match-ups in 1941, 1947, 1949, 1952, and 1953 which were all won by the Yankees.

Strengths: (1) hitting from MVP runner-up Snider (34 2B, 42 HR), MVP Campanella (32 HR), Hodges (27 HR), and Furillo (26 HR), (2) drawing walks from Snider (104 BB), (3) baserunning led by Robinson, Snider (37% RS, 9 GIDP), and Gilliam (16 ROE, 51% RS), (4) fielding from 3B Hoak (118 Rng+), SS Reese (92 Rng+), 2B/LF Gilliam (95 Rng+ at 2B, 116 Rng+ in LF), RF Furillo (104 Rng+, 10 assists), CF Snider (96 Rng+, 10 assists), and 3B Robinson (102 Rng+), and (5) Held+ from LF Gilliam (123) and RF Furillo (117).

Weaknesses: (1) hitting from Gilliam and Robinson, (2) GIDP, (3) allowing HR, and (4) pitching from Meyer (9% QS) and Roebuck.

Mgr	Walter Alston	
Rk	23	61
Gm	154	
Place	1	
GA	13.5	
Rival	15–7 vs Braves, 132 RS & 113 RA	

	W	L	Win%
Regular Season	98	55	0.641
Runs Record	97	56	0.635
1 Run	21	19	0.525
Extra Innings	7	9	0.438
Blowout	32	14	0.696

	Team	LgAvg	%Avg	LgRk
BABIP	0.262	0.269	103	3
E	133	142	107	2
sOBP	0.311	0.322	104	2
rOBP	0.318	0.342	108	1
R/G	5.56	4.53	123	1
RA/G	4.22	4.53	107	1

	Tm	LgAvg	>Avg
RS	857	697	160
RA	650	697	47
DP	156	155	1

	R/G	HR	K	BB	SB	CS	SB%	OPS
Team Offense	5.56	201	718	674	79	56	59%	0.804
Team Defense	4.22	168	773	483	34	28	55%	0.717
Difference	1.34	33	55	191	45			112%

Held+	
LF	103
CF	105
RF	113

Pos	Rpos	PA	Age	Name	BA	OBP	SLG	BB%	XBT	Bat R>Avg	BR R>Avg	Fld R>Avg	RAA	WAA
C	5	522	33	Campanella, Roy	0.308	0.383	0.564	11%	28%	36	-2	2	41	4.1
1B,RF	-8	642	31	Hodges, Gil	0.292	0.380	0.504	12%	43%	32	1	7	32	3.1
2B,LF	1	627	26	Gilliam, Jim^	0.236	0.325	0.336	11%	75%	-14	5	12	4	0.4
3B,LF	0	390	36	Robinson, Jackie	0.226	0.341	0.321	16%	55%	-7	7	5	5	0.5
SS	8	652	36	Reese, Pee Wee	0.271	0.359	0.388	12%	58%	6	1	7	22	2.2
LF,CF	-5	455	25	Amoros, Sandy*	0.242	0.340	0.393	12%	45%	1	4	4	4	0.4
CF	-1	653	28	Snider, Duke*	0.306	0.415	0.624	16%	52%	62	7	6	74	7.3
RF	-7	578	33	Furillo, Carl	0.314	0.372	0.521	7%	44%	29	2	11	35	3.5
3B	0	332	27	Hoak, Don	0.244	0.354	0.367	14%	63%	0	-1	15	14	1.4

Pos	Rpos	PA	Age	Name	BA	OBP	SLG	BB%	XBT	Bat R>Avg	BR R>Avg	Fld R>Avg	RAA	WAA
2B,SS	4	309	24	Zimmer, Don	0.289	0.342	0.534	6%	65%	11	0	-2	13	1.3
C	1	120	29	Walker, Rube*	0.248	0.336	0.352	13%	25%	-1	-2	-1	-3	-0.3
1B	-1	91	30	Kellert, Frank	0.321	0.380	0.568	10%	44%	6	-1	1	5	0.5
P	0	125	29	Newcombe, Don*	0.400	0.438	0.705	5%	40%	15	1	0	16	1.6
	3	541		Others	0.215	0.278	0.310	6%	42%	-20	2	-1	-16	-1.6
	0		29.8	Team Total	0.271	0.356	0.448	11.2%	51%	142	24	66	232	24.5
				League Average	0.259	0.328	0.407	9.0%	43%					
				% Lg Avg	105	108	110	124	119					
				League Rank	1	1	1	1	1		1	1		

GS	GR	IP	Age	Name	W–L	GmSc	K/9	BB/9	HR/9	FIP	ERA	RA/9	RAA	WAA
31	3	234	29	Newcombe, Don	20–5	56.5	5.5	1.5	1.3	3.63	3.20	3.97	5	0.5
29	2	195	28	Erskine, Carl	11–8	51.7	3.9	3.0	1.3	4.44	3.79	4.11	0	0.0
24	3	159	22	Podres, Johnny*	9–10	51.7	6.4	3.2	0.8	3.33	3.95	4.52	-7	-0.7
19	3	128	25	Loes, Billy	10–4	55.8	6.0	3.2	1.1	3.82	3.59	4.15	0	0.0
11	7	73	31	Meyer, Russ	6–2	45.9	3.2	3.8	1.0	4.16	5.42	5.67	-13	-1.3
14	15	99	24	Spooner, Karl*	8–6	46.3	7.1	3.7	0.7	3.26	3.65	4.56	-4	-0.4
10	11	91	25	Craig, Roger	5–3	54.2	4.8	4.3	0.8	3.77	2.78	3.67	5	0.5
0	47	84	23	Roebuck, Ed	5–6	—	3.5	2.6	1.5	4.59	4.71	5.46	-13	-1.3
8	52	144	28	Labine, Clem	13–5	46.9	4.2	3.4	0.7	3.64	3.24	3.80	5	0.5
2	22	63	24	Bessent, Don	8–1	58.0	4.1	3.0	1.0	3.84	2.70	2.70	10	1.0
6	44	108		Others	3–5	—	5.5	5.2	1.3	4.87	4.24	4.57	-5	-0.5
154	209		25.9	Team Total		53	5.05	3.15	1.10	3.90	3.68	4.25	-16	-1.6
				League Average		50	4.44	3.47	1.03	4.04	4.04	4.57		
				% Lg Avg		106	114	110	94	103	110	108		
				League Rank		1	1	3	7	1	1			

1956 New York Yankees

Only the Yankees had a greater than 1.0 run per game differential in either league. This time the Yankees turned the tables on the defending world champion Dodgers by defeating them in a 7 game World Series.

Strengths: (1) hitting led by MVP and Triple Crown winner Mantle (52 HR, 112 BB), Berra (30 HR), Skowron (23 HR), and McDougald (13 HR, 68 BB), (2) hitting from the pitchers, (3) baserunning especially GIDP from Mantle (4 GIDP, 10 SB, 1 CS), Berra (8 GIDP), and Martin (46% RS), (4) fielding featuring SS/2B McDougald (105 DP, 106 Rng+ at SS, 101 Rng+ at 2B), and 1B/OF Collins (0 errors in 281 chances at 1B, 132 Rng+ in RF), (5) Held+ from CF Mantle (111), RF Bauer (118), and RF Collins (176), and (6) pitching from Ford (67% QS, 15 pickoffs, allowed 1 SB), Sturdivant (65% QS), and Larsen (45% QS).

Weaknesses: (1) RP, 3B, and LF positions, (2) hitting from Carey, Coleman, Howard, Siebern, and Martin, (3) pitching control and drawing walks causing a negative BB differential, and (4) pitching from Turley (38% QS).

Mgr	Casey Stengel	
Rk	45	107
Gm	154	
Place	1	
GA	9.0	
Rival	12–10 vs Indians, 103 RS & 92 RA	

	W	L	Win%
Regular Season	97	57	0.630
Runs Record	96	58	0.624
1 Run	18	19	0.486
Extra Innings	6	6	0.500
Blowout	34	12	0.739

	Team	LgAvg	%Avg	LgRk
BABIP	0.269	0.278	103	2
E	136	146	107	3
sOBP	0.332	0.336	101	5
rOBP	0.343	0.353	103	3
R/G	5.56	4.66	119	1
RA/G	4.10	4.66	114	2

	Tm	LgAvg	>Avg
RS	857	720	137
RA	631	720	89
DP	214	166	48

	R/G	HR	K	BB	SB	CS	SB%	OPS	Held+	
Team Offense	5.56	190	755	615	51	37	58%	0.781	LF	101
Team Defense	4.10	114	732	652	33	33	50%	0.700	CF	109
Difference	1.47	76	-23	-37	18			112%	RF	123

Pos	Rpos	PA	Age	Name	BA	OBP	SLG	BB%	XBT	Bat R>Avg	BR R>Avg	Fld R>Avg	RAA	WAA
C	6	597	31	Berra, Yogi*	0.298	0.378	0.534	11%	49%	32	6	5	49	4.8
1B	-6	523	25	Skowron, Bill	0.308	0.382	0.528	10%	48%	28	-1	2	23	2.3
2B,3B	4	504	28	Martin, Billy	0.264	0.310	0.397	6%	53%	-6	5	-4	-1	-0.1
3B	1	480	24	Carey, Andy	0.237	0.310	0.339	9%	46%	-13	0	2	-10	-1.0
SS,2B	7	518	28	McDougald, Gil	0.311	0.405	0.443	13%	47%	21	-2	7	33	3.2
LF	-1	316	27	Howard, Elston	0.262	0.312	0.362	7%	31%	-7	-2	-1	-11	-1.1
CF	-1	652	24	Mantle, Mickey^	0.353	0.464	0.705	17%	60%	87	8	5	99	9.7
RF	-6	612	33	Bauer, Hank	0.241	0.316	0.445	10%	65%	2	4	4	4	0.4
1B,OF	-5	301	33	Collins, Joe*	0.225	0.313	0.347	11%	42%	-7	0	13	1	0.1
2B,SS	3	203	31	Coleman, Jerry	0.257	0.305	0.295	6%	43%	-9	-1	-2	-9	-0.9
LF	-2	184	22	Siebern, Norm*	0.204	0.286	0.333	10%	58%	-7	-1	6	-4	-0.4
LF,CF	-1	135	30	Cerv, Bob	0.304	0.396	0.530	13%	33%	8	-1	-4	2	0.2
1B	-1	62	35	Robinson, Eddie*	0.222	0.323	0.519	8%	0%	2	-1	1	1	0.1
	2	988		Others	0.227	0.291	0.293	8%	40%	-50	3	-5	-50	-4.9
	0		28.5	Team Total	0.270	0.347	0.434	10.1%	49%	80	17	29	126	12.4
				League Average	0.260	0.341	0.394	10.4%	46%					
				% Lg Avg	104	102	110	97	106					
				League Rank	3	4	1	5	2		1	2		

GS	GR	IP	Age	Name	W–L	GmSc	K/9	BB/9	HR/9	FIP	ERA	RA/9	RAA	WAA
30	1	226	27	Ford, Whitey*	19–6	60.5	5.6	3.3	0.5	3.21	2.47	2.79	43	4.2
31	3	224	22	Kucks, Johnny	18–9	50.2	2.7	2.9	0.8	4.18	3.85	4.53	-1	-0.1
20	18	180	26	Larsen, Don	11–5	55.0	5.4	4.8	1.0	4.48	3.26	3.61	18	1.8
17	15	158	26	Sturdivant, Tom	16–8	57.6	6.3	3.0	0.9	3.41	3.30	3.58	16	1.6
21	6	132	25	Turley, Bob	8–4	47.0	6.2	7.0	0.9	4.91	5.05	5.18	-10	-1.0
9	14	87	27	McDermott, Mick*	2–6	43.1	3.9	4.9	1.0	4.75	4.24	4.76	-2	-0.2
0	41	71	26	Morgan, Tom	6–7	—	2.5	3.4	0.3	3.48	4.17	5.18	-5	-0.5
8	29	110	36	Byrne, Tommy*	7–3	39.5	4.3	5.9	0.7	4.59	3.36	4.10	5	0.5
9	20	88	24	Coleman, Rip*	3–5	47.6	4.3	4.3	0.6	3.94	3.67	4.28	2	0.2
6	20	75	26	Grim, Bob	6–1	54.3	5.8	3.7	0.4	3.14	2.77	3.25	10	1.0
3	14	31		Others	1–3	—	4.6	7.5	1.5	6.16	8.13	9.00	-16	-1.5
154	181		26.5	Team Total		52	4.77	4.25	0.74	4.05	3.63	4.11	61	6.0
				League Average		49	4.74	4.09	0.88	4.16	4.16	4.70		
				% Lg Avg		106	101	96	118	103	115	114		
				League Rank		3	3	4	2	4	2			

1957 NEW YORK YANKEES

The 1957 Yankees once again dominated the AL leading the league in runs scored and least runs allowed per game. MVP Mickey Mantle had another terrific season with over a .500 OBP and 1.177 OPS to help carry this team to yet another pennant. Whitey Ford was hampered by a shoulder injury. Stengel kept fresh arms available by not starting anybody on the pitching staff more than 28 games. The Braves, who were led by 3 complete game victories from Lew Burdette, overcame the Yankees in 7 games.

Strengths: (1) hitting for average and power led by Mantle (28 2B, 34 HR, 146 BB) and Berra (24 HR), (2) fielding especially from SS McDougald (104 DP, 107 Rng+), 2B Richardson (98 Rng+), and RoY 3B/SS/OF Kubek (90 Rng+ at 3B, 108 Rng+ at SS, 98 Rng+ in LF), (3) CS% from Howard (60%) and Berra (56%), (4) Held+ from CF Mantle (114), and (5) pitching anchored by Turley (70% QS), Sturdivant (75% QS), Shantz (81% QS, 7.5 IP/S), and Ford (59% QS). Baserunning leaders were Mantle (5 GIDP) and Bauer.

Weaknesses: (1) 2B and LF positions, (2) team pitching control contributing to a negative BB differential, (3) hitting from Richardson and Howard, (4) Held+ from RF Bauer (87), and (5) pitching control from Larsen (45% QS).

Mgr	Casey Stengel	
Rk	20	48

	W	L	Win%
Regular Season	98	56	0.636
Runs Record	99	55	0.644

	Team	LgAvg	%Avg	LgRk
BABIP	0.256	0.273	106	1
E	123	127	103	4

			W	L	Win%		Team	LgAvg	%Avg	LgRk
Gm	154	**1 Run**	30	21	0.588	**sOBP**	0.317	0.323	102	4
Place	1	**Extra Innings**	13	5	0.722	**rOBP**	0.306	0.333	109	1
GA	8.0	**Blowout**	24	9	0.727	**R/G**	4.69	4.23	111	1
Rival	14–8 vs White Sox, 99 RS & 83 RA					**RA/G**	3.47	4.23	122	1

	Tm	LgAvg	>Avg
RS	723	651	72
RA	534	651	117
DP	183	165	18

	R/G	HR	K	BB	SB	CS	SB%	OPS	Held+	
Team Offense	4.69	145	707	561	49	38	56%	0.747	LF	102
Team Defense	3.47	110	810	580	41	50	45%	0.657	CF	117
Difference	1.23	35	103	-19	8			114%	RF	83

Pos	Rpos	PA	Age	Name	BA	OBP	SLG	BB%	XBT	Bat R>Avg	BR R>Avg	Fld R>Avg	RAA	WAA
C,LF	6	545	32	Berra, Yogi*	0.251	0.329	0.438	10%	41%	9	2	3	20	2.1
1B	-6	501	26	Skowron, Bill	0.304	0.347	0.470	6%	50%	17	-2	8	17	1.8
2B	3	320	21	Richardson, Bobby	0.256	0.274	0.298	3%	57%	-15	-1	8	-5	-0.6
3B	1	273	25	Carey, Andy	0.255	0.309	0.393	5%	35%	-1	-1	4	3	0.3
SS,2B	8	624	29	McDougald, Gil	0.289	0.362	0.442	9%	51%	19	0	14	41	4.2
LF,C	-2	380	28	Howard, Elston	0.253	0.283	0.379	4%	47%	-8	-4	-1	-15	-1.5
CF	-1	623	25	Mantle, Mickey^	0.365	0.512	0.665	23%	55%	93	7	1	100	10.3
RF	-6	535	34	Bauer, Hank	0.259	0.321	0.455	8%	65%	10	4	-3	5	0.5
3B,SS	1	475	21	Kubek, Tony*	0.297	0.335	0.381	5%	53%	1	3	7	12	1.3
LF	-3	256	41	Slaughter, Enos*	0.254	0.369	0.368	16%	28%	4	-1	6	6	0.7
RF,LF	-3	247	31	Simpson, Harry*	0.250	0.307	0.402	8%	65%	-1	1	-1	-4	-0.4
2B,3B	2	180	32	Coleman, Jerry	0.268	0.354	0.376	11%	50%	2	-1	-3	0	0.0
3B	1	113	24	Lumpe, Jerry*	0.340	0.389	0.437	8%	50%	5	0	1	7	0.7
	-1	920		Others	0.191	0.259	0.248	8%	52%	-59	2	2	-56	-5.8
	0		28.4	Team Total	0.268	0.339	0.409	9.4%	50%	75	9	46	130	13.5
				League Average	0.255	0.326	0.382	9.1%	47%					
				% Lg Avg	105	104	107	103	107					
				League Rank	1	3	1	4	3		2	3		

GS	GR	IP	Age	Name	W–L	GmSc	K/9	BB/9	HR/9	FIP	ERA	RA/9	RAA	WAA
28	0	202	27	Sturdivant, Tom	16–6	58.6	5.3	3.6	0.6	3.45	2.54	2.90	23	2.4
23	14	179	23	Kucks, Johnny	8–10	50.1	3.9	3.0	0.7	3.66	3.56	4.12	-4	-0.5
23	9	176	26	Turley, Bob	13–6	61.7	7.8	4.3	0.9	3.61	2.71	3.01	19	1.9
21	9	173	31	Shantz, Bobby*	11–5	57.9	3.7	2.1	0.8	3.57	2.45	3.02	17	1.7
20	7	140	27	Larsen, Don	10–4	50.8	5.2	5.6	0.8	4.32	3.74	4.38	-7	-0.7
17	7	129	28	Ford, Whitey*	11–5	55.4	5.8	3.7	0.7	3.38	2.58	3.20	10	1.1
0	46	72	27	Grim, Bob	12–8	—	6.5	4.5	0.6	3.25	2.63	2.75	10	1.0
11	35	127	28	Ditmar, Art	8–3	41.1	4.5	2.5	0.6	3.26	3.25	3.89	0	0.0
4	26	85	37	Byrne, Tommy*	4–6	47.0	6.1	6.4	0.9	4.68	4.36	4.36	-4	-0.4
2	18	65	27	Cicotte, Al	2–2	39.0	5.0	4.1	0.7	3.77	3.03	3.45	3	0.4
5	8	47		Others	3–1	—	3.1	2.9	0.4	3.33	2.31	2.51	7	0.7
154	179		28.1	Team Total		55	5.22	3.74	0.71	3.65	3.00	3.44	73	7.6
				League Average		50	4.70	3.48	0.83	3.78	3.79	4.21		
				% Lg Avg		110	111	93	117	104	1	122		
				League Rank		1	2	5	2	2	126			

1958 New York Yankees

The 1958 season was virtually a repeat of the 1957 season with the Yankees and Braves repeating as league champions, but this time the Yankees won the Series in 7 games instead of the Braves. Only the Yankees won more than 82 games in the AL as 6 teams finished right around the .500 winning percentage. This team was led by another MVP-like performance from Mickey Mantle.

Strengths: (1) hitting for average and power led by Mantle (42 HR, 129 BB), Carey (19 2B), Howard (19 2B), and Berra (22 HR), (2) baserunning led by Mantle (18 SB, 3 CS) and Kubek (37% RS), (3) led AL in fewest GIDP and most DP made, (4) fielding especially from SS Kubek (98 DP, 108 Rng+), 2B McDougald (97 DP, 97 Rng+),

LF Siebern (107 Rng+), and 1 error at the C position, (5) Held+ from CF Mantle (112) and RF Bauer (109), (6) CS% from Berra (55%) and Howard (49%), and (7) pitching anchored by Ford (72% QS), Cy Young winner and MVP runner-up Turley (71% QS), and Duren (20/23/87% Sv, 25/33/76% IR stranded, 1.506 Lv).

Weaknesses: (1) SP and RP positions, (2) hitting by Kubek and Richardson, (3) fielding by CF Mantle (85 Rng+) whose range was hampered by his aching legs, (4) pitching from Kucks (53% QS) and Sturdivant (40% QS), and (5) team pitching BB/9.

Mgr	Casey Stengel	
Rk	42	101
Gm	155	
Place	1	
GA	10.0	
Rival	15–7 vs White Sox, 105 RS & 63 RA	

	W	*L*	*Win%*
Regular Season	92	62	0.597
Runs Record	96	58	0.626
1 Run	19	17	0.528
Extra Innings	5	3	0.625
Blowout	39	19	0.672

	Team	*LgAvg*	*%Avg*	*LgRk*
BABIP	0.256	0.273	107	1
E	128	125	98	6
sOBP	0.311	0.320	103	4
rOBP	0.322	0.328	102	2
R/G	4.90	4.17	118	1
RA/G	3.72	4.17	112	1

	Tm	*LgAvg*	*>Avg*
RS	759	645	114
RA	577	645	68
DP	182	164	18

	R/G	*HR*	*K*	*BB*	*SB*	*CS*	*SB%*	*OPS*	*Held+*	
Team Offense	4.90	164	818	537	48	32	60%	0.751	LF	105
Team Defense	3.72	116	796	557	42	48	47%	0.665	CF	113
Difference	1.17	48	-22	-20	6			113%	RF	100

Pos	*Rpos*	*PA*	*Age*	*Name*	*BA*	*OBP*	*SLG*	*BB%*	*XBT*	*Bat R>Avg*	*BR R>Avg*	*Fld R>Avg*	*RAA*	*WAA*
C,RF	4	476	33	Berra, Yogi*	0.266	0.319	0.471	7%	35%	11	1	4	20	2.1
1B	-6	503	27	Skowron, Bill	0.273	0.317	0.424	6%	47%	5	0	6	5	0.5
2B,SS	5	578	30	McDougald, Gil	0.250	0.329	0.376	10%	49%	1	2	5	13	1.4
3B	1	365	26	Carey, Andy	0.286	0.363	0.486	9%	39%	16	0	5	22	2.3
SS	8	597	22	Kubek, Tony*	0.265	0.295	0.317	4%	64%	-19	5	14	8	0.8
LF	-6	533	24	Siebern, Norm*	0.300	0.388	0.454	12%	60%	25	2	12	33	3.4
CF	-1	654	26	Mantle, Mickey^	0.304	0.443	0.592	20%	53%	68	7	-5	69	7.2
RF	-5	490	35	Bauer, Hank	0.268	0.316	0.423	7%	43%	4	2	8	9	0.9
C,LF	2	406	29	Howard, Elston	0.314	0.348	0.479	5%	40%	15	-1	4	20	2.1
3B	1	262	25	Lumpe, Jerry*	0.254	0.319	0.362	9%	74%	-2	4	6	9	1.0
2B,3B	2	195	22	Richardson, Bobby	0.247	0.276	0.302	4%	58%	-8	1	3	-2	-0.3
1B	-2	172	24	Throneberry, Marv*	0.227	0.316	0.427	11%	36%	2	0	-2	-2	-0.2
LF,RF	-2	160	42	Slaughter, Enos*	0.304	0.396	0.435	13%	52%	7	1	-2	4	0.4
	-1	580		Others	0.190	0.249	0.255	6%	29%	-38	-1	0	-40	-4.1
	0		28.1	Team Total	0.268	0.336	0.416	9.0%	48%	88	23	58	169	17.5
				League Average	0.254	0.322	0.383	8.7%	47%					
				% Lg Avg	105	104	108	104	102					
				League Rank	1	2	1	2	4				1	1

GS	*GR*	*IP*	*Age*	*Name*	*W–L*	*GmSc*	*K/9*	*BB/9*	*HR/9*	*FIP*	*ERA*	*RA/9*	*RAA*	*WAA*
31	2	245	27	Turley, Bob	21–7	61.0	6.2	4.7	0.9	4.06	2.97	3.01	23	2.4
29	1	219	29	Ford, Whitey*	14–7	63.1	6.0	2.5	0.6	2.87	2.01	2.54	32	3.3
19	0	114	28	Larsen, Don	9–6	53.5	4.3	4.1	0.3	3.40	3.07	3.39	5	0.6
13	9	101	29	Maas, Duke	7–3	53.5	4.4	3.2	0.8	3.81	3.82	4.53	-8	-0.8
10	5	71	28	Sturdivant, Tom	3–6	44.8	5.2	4.8	0.8	4.20	4.20	4.71	-7	-0.7
13	25	140	29	Ditmar, Art	9–8	53.2	3.4	2.4	0.9	3.95	3.41	4.57	-12	-1.2
15	19	126	24	Kucks, Johnny	8–8	47.3	3.3	2.8	1.0	4.25	3.93	4.79	-14	-1.4
13	20	126	32	Shantz, Bobby*	7–6	55.2	5.7	2.5	0.6	2.78	3.36	3.71	1	0.2
1	43	76	29	Duren, Ryne	6–4	62.0	10.3	5.1	0.5	2.84	2.02	2.38	13	1.4
6	15	58	26	Monroe, Zack	4–2	48.3	2.8	4.2	1.2	5.03	3.26	4.50	-4	-0.5
5	45	103		Others	4–5	—	4.7	5.2	1.0	4.64	4.82	5.52	-19	-2.0
155	184		28.1	Team Total		55	5.20	3.64	0.76	3.71	3.22	3.77	10	1.1
				League Average		50	4.93	3.32	0.86	3.77	3.77	4.21		
				% Lg Avg		110	105	91	114	102	117	112		
				League Rank		1	2	7	4	3	1			

3. The Expansion Era (1961–2014)

1961 New York Yankees

Expansion occurred for the first time since 1901 when the Los Angeles Angels and the Washington Senators were added to the AL. Games also expanded from 154 to 162 in the AL to accommodate the larger number of teams. The 1961 Yankees repeated as pennant winners despite tough competition from the surprising Tigers who led the AL in offense. Maris beat Babe Ruth's season record of 60 HR by hitting 61 HR. Mantle also stood a good chance of beating the record but was hurt the last 2 weeks of the season and finished with 54 HR, his career high. This team finished things off with a 5 game victory over the Reds in the World Series.

Strengths: (1) hitting HR led by MVP Maris (61), MVP runner-up Mantle (54), Skowron (28), Berra (22), and Blanchard (21), (2) baserunning led by Mantle (12 SB, 1 CS, 2 GIDP), (3) fielding especially from 3B Boyer (120 Rng+, 36 DP) and SS Kubek (105 Rng+, 107 DP), (4) Held+ from RF Maris (116), (5) pitching from Cy Young winner Ford (62% QS, 209 K), Stafford (72% QS), Terry (59% QS), and Arroyo (29/39/74% Sv, 33/65/51% IR stranded, 1.802 Lv), and (6) injury free seasons from most of the roster.

Weaknesses: (1) 2B position, (2) drawing walks, (3) hitting from Richardson, Boyer, and Lopez, and (4) pitching from Turley (33% QS).

Mgr	Ralph Houk	
Rk	15	58
Gm	163	
Place	1	
GA	8.0	
Rival	10–8 vs Tigers, 104 RS & 85 RA	

	W	*L*	*Win%*
Regular Season	109	53	0.673
Runs Record	103	59	0.637
1 Run	29	21	0.580
Extra Innings	11	2	0.846
Blowout	26	10	0.722

	Team	*LgAvg*	*%Avg*	*LgRk*
BABIP	0.261	0.275	105	2
E	124	151	122	1
sOBP	0.308	0.327	106	2
rOBP	0.317	0.334	105	2
R/G	5.07	4.53	112	2
RA/G	3.75	4.53	121	2

	Tm	*LgAvg*	*>Avg*
RS	827	734	93
RA	612	734	122
DP	180	159	21

	R/G	*HR*	*K*	*BB*	*SB*	*CS*	*SB%*	*OPS*	*Held+*	
Team Offense	5.07	240	785	543	28	18	61%	0.771	LF	96
Team Defense	3.75	137	866	542	44	31	59%	0.681	CF	104
Difference	1.32	103	81	1	-16			113%	RF	119

Pos	*Rpos*	*PA*	*Age*	*Name*	*BA*	*OBP*	*SLG*	*BB%*	*XBT*	*Bat R>Avg*	*BR R>Avg*	*Fld R>Avg*	*RAA*	*WAA*
C,1B	6	482	32	Howard, Elston	0.348	0.387	0.549	6%	33%	33	-2	3	40	3.9
1B	-8	607	30	Skowron, Bill	0.267	0.318	0.472	6%	42%	10	-2	8	8	0.8
2B	4	706	25	Richardson, Bobby	0.261	0.295	0.316	4%	54%	-28	2	-7	-29	-2.9
3B,SS	4	578	24	Boyer, Clete	0.224	0.308	0.347	11%	51%	-12	-3	30	19	1.9
SS	9	658	24	Kubek, Tony*	0.276	0.306	0.395	4%	63%	-8	3	14	18	1.8
LF,C	-4	437	36	Berra, Yogi*	0.271	0.330	0.466	8%	43%	9	3	4	12	1.2
CF	-1	646	29	Mantle, Mickey^	0.317	0.448	0.687	20%	56%	81	8	1	89	8.8
RF,CF	-7	698	26	Maris, Roger*	0.269	0.372	0.620	13%	55%	55	2	1	51	5.1
C,LF	2	275	28	Blanchard, Johnny*	0.305	0.382	0.613	10%	35%	23	-3	0	22	2.1
LF,RF	-4	273	31	Lopez, Hector	0.222	0.292	0.305	9%	53%	-11	2	4	-9	-0.9
LF	-2	131	35	Cerv, Bob	0.271	0.344	0.483	9%	58%	4	0	6	8	0.8

Pos	Rpos	PA	Age	Name	BA	OBP	SLG	BB%	XBT	Bat R>Avg	BR R>Avg	Fld R>Avg	RAA	WAA
3B	1	109	33	Gardner, Billy	0.212	0.278	0.293	6%	33%	-6	-1	3	-3	-0.3
	0	639		Others	0.159	0.209	0.185	6%	37%	-69	-3	6	-66	-6.5
	0		29.4	Team Total	0.263	0.330	0.442	8.7%	49%	82	6	73	161	15.9
				League Average	0.256	0.329	0.395	9.5%	47%					
				% Lg Avg	103	100	112	92	104					
				League Rank	4	5	1	9	5		2	1		

GS	GR	IP	Age	Name	W–L	GmSc	K/9	BB/9	HR/9	FIP	ERA	RA/9	RAA	WAA
39	0	283	34	Ford, Whitey*	25–4	58.1	6.6	2.9	0.7	3.10	3.21	3.43	22	2.2
25	11	195	21	Stafford, Bill	14–9	57.7	4.7	2.7	0.6	3.32	2.68	3.00	24	2.4
27	4	188	25	Terry, Ralph	16–3	55.9	4.1	2.0	0.9	3.65	3.15	3.54	12	1.2
21	14	163	24	Sheldon, Rollie	11–5	52.1	4.6	3.0	0.9	3.90	3.60	3.87	4	0.4
17	6	130	28	Daley, Bud*	8–9	50.7	5.8	3.5	1.2	4.12	3.96	4.37	-4	-0.4
12	3	72	30	Turley, Bob	3–5	44.2	6.0	6.4	1.4	5.51	5.75	5.88	-14	-1.4
8	4	55	32	Ditmar, Art	2–3	46.8	3.9	2.3	1.5	4.70	4.61	5.43	-8	-0.8
0	65	119	34	Arroyo, Luis*	15–5	—	6.6	3.7	0.4	2.76	2.19	2.57	21	2.1
11	32	141	28	Coates, Jim	11–5	50.5	5.1	3.4	1.0	4.09	3.44	3.82	5	0.5
0	25	45	22	Reniff, Hal	2–0	—	4.2	6.2	0.2	3.78	2.58	2.78	7	0.7
0	21	32	28	Clevenger, Tex	1–1	—	4.0	6.0	0.9	4.90	4.83	5.68	-6	-0.6
3	16	28		Others	1–4	—	9.2	7.6	1.3	5.11	7.63	7.63	-11	-1.1
163	201		27.8	Team Total		54	5.37	3.36	0.85	3.73	3.46	3.80	53	5.3
				League Average		50	5.20	3.68	0.96	4.02	4.02	4.58		
				% Lg Avg		108	103	110	113	108	116	121		
				League Rank		3	4	3	3	2	2			

1968 Detroit Tigers

The 1968 season became the Year of the Pitcher with both leagues falling below 3.5 runs scored per team per game. Outstanding pitching performances were highlighted by AL MVP and Cy Young winner Denny McClain's 31 win performance for the Tigers, the first (and last) 30 game winner in the major leagues since Dizzy Dean's 1934 season and NL MVP and Cy Young winner Bob Gibson's 1.12 ERA for the Cardinals, the lowest major league ERA since the 1920 live ball. The average AL team batting average of 0.230 was the lowest ever in the AL. After the season, mound heights were lowered and the strike zone was narrowed to try to increase run production and lessen pitching domination. Neither the Tigers nor the Cardinals had much trouble capturing their respective league pennants. This was the first Tiger pennant since 1945. The Tigers led the AL in most runs scored per game and fewest runs allowed per game. The 1968 World Series was a classic with Mickey Lolich for the Tigers and Gibson for the Cardinals both engaged in epic duels with the Tigers winning in 7 games.

Strengths: (1) hitting for power led by Horton (36 HR), MVP runner-up Freehan (25 HR), Cash (25 HR), McAuliffe (10 3B, 82 BB), Northrup (29 2B, 21 HR), and Kaline, (3) fielding especially from RF/CF Northrup (120 Rng+ in RF & 87 Rng+ in CF), CF Stanley (98 Rng+, 0 errors in 308 chances), 3B Wert (93 Rng+, only 15 errors in 441 chances), 2B McAuliffe (88 Rng+, only 9 errors in 645 chances), and SS Tracewski (93 Rng+), (4) Held+ from RF/CF Northrup (138 in RF & 126 in CF), CF Stanley (138), LF Horton (115), and RF Kaline (107), and (5) pitching anchored by MVP & Cy Young winner McLain (280 K, 6 shutouts, 85% QS, 8.2 IP/S, 6.5 H/9).

Weaknesses: (1) 3B and SS positions, (2) GIDP especially from Stanley (22), (3) hitting from Oyler, Wert, Tracewski, Matchick, and Price, (4) CS% from Price (13%), and (5) pitching from Sparma (42% QS).

Mgr	Mayo Smith	
Rk	28	85
Gm	164	
Place	1	
GA	12.0	
Rival	10–8 vs Orioles, 69 RS & 57 RA	

	W	L	Win%
Regular Season	103	59	0.636
Runs Record	102	60	0.628
1 Run	35	23	0.603
Extra Innings	10	5	0.667
Blowout	22	7	0.759

	Team	LgAvg	%Avg	LgRk
BABIP	0.250	0.260	104	3
E	105	137	130	1
sOBP	0.285	0.296	104	4
rOBP	0.283	0.302	107	2
R/G	4.09	3.41	120	1
RA/G	3.00	3.41	114	1

	Tm	LgAvg	>Avg
RS	671	553	118
RA	492	553	61
DP	133	139	-6

	R/G	HR	K	BB	SB	CS	SB%	OPS	Held+	
Team Offense	4.09	185	964	521	26	32	45%	0.692	LF	114
Team Defense	3.00	129	1115	486	80	40	67%	0.611	CF	135
Difference	1.09	56	151	35	-54			113%	RF	126

Pos	Rpos	PA	Age	Name	BA	OBP	SLG	BB%	XBT	Bat R>Avg	BR R>Avg	Fld R>Avg	RAA	WAA
C,1B	7	635	26	Freehan, Bill	0.263	0.366	0.454	10%	35%	37	-2	5	47	5.4
1B	-6	458	33	Cash, Norm*	0.263	0.329	0.487	9%	38%	24	-1	5	22	2.6
2B	4	658	28	McAuliffe, Dick*	0.249	0.344	0.411	12%	60%	25	2	7	38	4.4
3B	3	589	29	Wert, Don	0.200	0.258	0.299	6%	44%	-16	0	7	-6	-0.7
SS	5	247	29	Oyler, Ray	0.135	0.213	0.186	8%	47%	-18	-2	3	-12	-1.4
LF	-7	578	25	Horton, Willie	0.285	0.352	0.543	8%	41%	45	-2	-2	34	3.9
CF,1B	-1	641	25	Stanley, Mickey	0.259	0.311	0.364	7%	64%	7	1	10	17	2.0
RF,CF	-6	643	28	Northrup, Jim*	0.264	0.324	0.447	8%	60%	26	0	18	38	4.3
RF,1B	-5	389	33	Kaline, Al	0.287	0.392	0.428	14%	58%	24	0	4	23	2.7
SS,2B	3	244	24	Matchick, Tommy*	0.203	0.248	0.286	4%	46%	-9	-1	2	-5	-0.5
SS,3B	4	240	33	Tracewski, Dick	0.156	0.239	0.236	10%	62%	-12	2	6	0	0.0
C	2	146	26	Price, Jim	0.174	0.253	0.273	9%	44%	-5	1	-2	-4	-0.5
LF	-1	104	29	Brown, Gates*	0.370	0.442	0.685	12%	33%	16	-1	1	15	1.7
P	0	92	33	Wilson, Earl	0.227	0.253	0.489	2%	50%	2	0	0	2	0.3
	-2	515		Others	0.138	0.175	0.194	4%	38%	-45	-4	-1	-52	-6.0
	0		28.6	Team Total	0.235	0.307	0.385	8.4%	51%	102	-7	63	158	18.1
				League Average	0.230	0.297	0.339	8.1%	48%					
				% Lg Avg	102	103	114	104	105					
				League Rank	4	2	1	4	2		10	2		

GS	GR	IP	Age	Name	W–L	GmSc	K/9	BB/9	HR/9	FIP	ERA	RA/9	RAA	WAA
41	0	336	24	McLain, Denny	31–6	68.8	7.5	1.7	0.83	2.46	1.96	2.30	28	3.2
33	1	224	33	Wilson, Earl	13–12	58.3	6.7	2.6	0.80	2.81	2.85	3.09	-1	-0.2
32	7	220	27	Lolich, Mickey*	17–9	57.4	8.1	2.7	0.94	2.88	3.19	3.44	-9	-1.1
31	3	182	26	Sparma, Joe	10–10	51.0	5.4	3.8	0.69	3.46	3.70	4.00	-20	-2.3
10	37	125	26	Dobson, Pat	5–8	54.8	6.7	3.5	0.94	3.25	2.66	2.81	3	0.4
12	27	128	25	Hiller, John*	9–6	58.2	5.5	3.6	0.63	3.13	2.39	2.60	6	0.7
1	37	68	24	Patterson, Daryl	2–3	44.0	6.5	3.6	0.40	2.79	2.12	2.51	4	0.4
0	34	49	26	Lasher, Fred	5–1	—	5.9	4.1	0.92	3.28	3.33	3.51	-3	-0.3
0	28	37	21	Warden, John*	4–1	—	6.0	3.6	1.21	3.78	3.62	3.62	-2	-0.3
0	20	36	38	McMahon, Don	3–1	—	8.3	2.5	0.50	1.97	2.02	2.02	4	0.5
4	44	84		Others	4–2	—	5.3	4.6	0.43	3.15	2.56	2.88	1	0.1
164	238		27.0	Team Total		59	6.74	2.94	0.78	2.92	2.71	2.97	11	1.3
				League Average		56	5.96	3.02	0.68	2.98	2.98	3.42		
				% Lg Avg		105	113	103	88	102	110	115		
				League Rank		3	2	4	9	5	3			

1969 Baltimore Orioles

The 1969 Orioles broke out from the competition winning 18 more games than they had won in 1968 and became one of the greatest teams in baseball history despite being the victim of the biggest World Series upset since the 1906 White Sox beat the Cubs. Both leagues improved their run production by over 20% as the mound height was lowered and the strike zone shrunk. Expansion, always a boost for hitting, occurred in both leagues as the Seattle Pilots and the Kansas City Royals joined the AL and the San Diego Padres and the Montreal Expos joined the NL. Each league divided itself into 2 divisions with a playoff between the 2 divisional champs to determine each league's World Series representative. Cy Young award co-winner Mike Cuellar was obtained in the off-season in a trade with the Astros for Curt Blefary. This team had above league seasons at every position and led the majors in fewest runs allowed per game. The Orioles swept the Twins in the first AL divisional playoff but lost to the Mets in 5 games in the World Series.

Strengths: (1) hitting for average, contact, and power led by Frank Robinson (32 HR), MVP runner-up Powell (25 2B, 37 HR), Buford (31 2B), and Blair (32 2B, 26 HR), (3) drawing walks featuring Buford (96 BB), Frank

Robinson (88 BB), and Powell (72 BB), (4) fielding featuring 3B Brooks Robinson (109 Rng+, 37 DP, only 13 E in 546 chances), CF Blair (112 Rng+, 14 assists, 5 DP), SS Mark Belanger (99 Rng+), 2B Davey Johnson (99 Rng+), 1B Powell, and LF Buford (93 Rng+), (5) Held+ from CF Blair (111) and LF Buford (112), (6) CS% from Hendricks (46%,), Etchebarren (59%), and Dalrymple (55%), and (7) pitching anchored by Cuellar (72% QS, 7.5 IP/S), Palmer (74% QS), Hall (20/33/61% IR stranded, 1.525 Lv), Watt (16/21/76% Sv, 32/47/68% IR stranded, 1.520 Lv), and Richert (12/15/80% Sv, 40/54/74% IR stranded, 1.741 Lv).

Weaknesses: (1) baserunning from Johnson (23% RS) and Powell (23% RS, 18 GIDP) and (2) HR/9 from Phoebus and Hardin.

				W	*L*	*Win%*		*Team*	*LgAvg*	*%Avg*	*LgRk*
Mgr	Earl Weaver		**Regular Season**	109	53	0.673	**BABIP**	0.246	0.270	110	1
Rk	1	6	**Runs Record**	112	50	0.691	**E**	101	139	138	1
Gm	162		**1 Run**	35	21	0.625	**sOBP**	0.293	0.319	109	1
Place	1		**Extra Innings**	13	7	0.650	**rOBP**	0.281	0.325	116	1
GA	19.0		**Blowout**	30	8	0.789	**R/G**	4.81	4.09	118	2
Rival	8–4 vs Twins, 52 RS, 40 RA; 11–7 vs Tigers, 70 RS, 58 RA						**RA/G**	3.19	4.09	128	1

	Tm	*LgAvg*	*>Avg*		*R/G*	*HR*	*K*	*BB*	*SB*	*CS*	*SB%*	*OPS*	*Held+*	
RS	779	663	116	Team Offense	4.81	175	806	634	82	45	65%	0.756	LF	109
RA	517	663	146	Team Defense	3.19	117	897	498	48	51	48%	0.620	CF	107
DP	145	154	-9	Difference	1.62	58	91	136	34			122%	RF	91

Pos	*Rpos*	*PA*	*Age*	*Name*	*BA*	*OBP*	*SLG*	*BB%*	*XBT*	*Bat R>Avg*	*BR R>Avg*	*Fld R>Avg*	*RAA*	*WAA*
C	5	339	28	Hendricks, Ellie*	0.244	0.333	0.383	12%	35%	3	-1	7	14	1.5
1B	-8	615	27	Powell, Boog*	0.304	0.383	0.559	12%	33%	48	-3	8	45	4.7
2B	4	580	26	Johnson, Davey	0.280	0.351	0.391	10%	44%	11	-4	8	19	2.0
3B	3	670	32	Robinson, Brooks	0.234	0.298	0.395	8%	52%	-1	-1	23	24	2.5
SS	9	594	25	Belanger, Mark	0.287	0.351	0.345	9%	56%	3	3	12	27	2.9
LF,2B	-6	663	32	Buford, Don^	0.291	0.397	0.417	14%	53%	30	-1	10	33	3.5
CF	-1	685	25	Blair, Paul	0.285	0.327	0.477	6%	71%	22	5	26	52	5.4
RF,1B	-7	643	33	Robinson, Frank	0.308	0.415	0.540	14%	58%	54	5	7	59	6.2
C	4	255	26	Etchebarren, Andy	0.249	0.350	0.350	11%	35%	2	-2	6	10	1.1
LF,OF	-3	226	26	Rettenmund, Merv	0.247	0.338	0.395	12%	44%	4	-1	0	0	0.0
2B,SS	0	104	28	Salmon, Chico	0.297	0.375	0.451	10%	69%	5	0	-2	3	0.3
LF,RF	-1	104	28	Motton, Curt	0.303	0.398	0.573	13%	58%	9	1	-1	8	0.8
C	1	94	32	Dalrymple, Clay*	0.238	0.340	0.388	14%	25%	1	-1	5	6	0.7
RF	-1	131	25	May, Dave*	0.242	0.305	0.367	7%	33%	-1	0	2	0	0.0
	1	625		Others	0.161	0.206	0.209	5%	40%	-56	-3	3	-55	-5.7
	0		28.1	Team Total	0.265	0.343	0.414	10.0%	49%	135	-3	114	246	25.8
				League Average	0.246	0.321	0.369	9.5%	48%					
				% Lg Avg	108	107	112	103	103					
				League Rank	2	1	2	4	2		5	1		

GS	*GR*	*IP*	*Age*	*Name*	*W–L*	*GmSc*	*K/9*	*BB/9*	*HR/9*	*FIP*	*ERA*	*RA/9*	*RAA*	*WAA*
39	0	291	32	Cuellar, Mike*	23–11	62.5	5.6	2.4	0.56	2.78	2.38	2.91	16	1.7
40	1	269	26	McNally, Dave*	20–7	56.0	5.6	2.8	0.70	3.18	3.22	3.45	-2	-0.2
33	2	202	27	Phoebus, Tom	14–7	52.4	5.2	3.9	1.02	4.08	3.52	3.97	-13	-1.4
23	3	181	23	Palmer, Jim	16–4	64.0	6.1	3.2	0.55	2.97	2.34	2.39	21	2.2
20	10	138	25	Hardin, Jim	6–7	51.5	4.2	2.8	1.18	4.16	3.60	4.05	-11	-1.1
0	56	71	28	Watt, Eddie	5–2	—	5.8	3.3	0.38	2.70	1.65	2.28	9	0.9
3	34	94	28	Leonhard, Dave	7–4	46.0	3.5	3.6	0.77	3.75	2.49	2.68	7	0.7
4	23	69	25	Lopez, Marcelino*	5–3	45.0	7.4	4.4	0.39	2.78	4.41	4.41	-8	-0.8
0	39	66	38	Hall, Dick	5–2	—	4.2	1.2	0.41	2.31	1.92	1.92	11	1.1
0	44	57	29	Richert, Pete*	7–4	—	8.5	2.2	1.10	2.81	2.20	2.67	5	0.5
0	23	36		Others	1–2	—	5.0	5.0	0.50	3.41	1.98	2.48	4	0.4
162	235	28.1		Team Total		57	5.48	3.04	0.71	3.24	2.83	3.16	39	4.1
				League Average		52	5.58	3.62	0.85	3.63	3.62	4.09		
				% Lg Avg		110	98	119	119	112	128	130		
				League Rank		1	5	1	3	1	1			

1970 Baltimore Orioles

The Orioles had another terrific season leading the AL in both runs scored and fewest runs allowed. For the second straight season, the Orioles swept the Twins in the AL playoffs. Blair suffered a severe beaning which opened up significant playing time for Rettenmund who had a terrific season. The walk differential of +248 is one of the highest ever. The O's beat a tough Red team in 5 games in the World Series.

Strengths: (1) SP, 1B, 2B, 3B, LF, CF, and RF positions, (2) hitting for average and power led by MVP Powell (28 2B, 35 HR), Frank Robinson (25 HR), Rettenmund (18 HR), Buford (17 HR), Blair (24 2B, 18 HR), Brooks Robinson (31 2B, 18 HR), and Davey Johnson (27 2B), (3) drawing walks featuring Buford (109 BB) and Powell (104 BB), (4) baserunning from Belanger (13 SB, 2 CS, 4 GIDP), (5) fielding especially from CF Blair (119 Rng+, 10 assists), SS Belanger (99 Rng+, 78 DP in 128 GS), 2B Johnson (101 Rng+, 101 DP), C Hendricks (48% CS, 2.97 ERA), and 3B Brooks Robinson (100 Rng+, 30 DP), (6) Held+ from CF Blair (124), and (7) pitching anchored by Palmer (64% QS, 7.8 IP/S, 5 shutouts, 199 K), McNally (68% QS, 7.4 IP/S, 185 K), and co-closer Richert (13/17/76% Sv, 2.209 Lv, 33/54/61% IR stranded).

Weaknesses: (1) hitting from Belanger, (2) baserunning from Brooks Robinson (18 GIDP), (3) team IR% stranded, and (4) blown saves.

Mgr	Earl Weaver	
Rk	11	45
Gm	162	
Place	1	
GA	15.0	
Rival	11–7 vs Yankees, 5–7 vs Twins	

	W	*L*	*Win%*
Regular Season	108	54	0.667
Runs Record	105	57	0.648
1 Run	40	15	0.727
Extra Innings	16	9	0.640
Blowout	25	5	0.833

	Team	*LgAvg*	*%Avg*	*LgRk*
BABIP	0.264	0.274	104	3
E	117	136	116	2
sOBP	0.296	0.321	108	1
rOBP	0.314	0.325	104	5
R/G	4.89	4.17	117	1
RA/G	3.54	4.17	118	1

	Tm	*LgAvg*	*>Avg*
RS	792	676	116
RA	574	676	102
DP	148	154	-6

	R/G	*HR*	*K*	*BB*	*SB*	*CS*	*SB%*	*OPS*
Team Offense	4.89	179	952	717	84	39	68%	0.745
Team Defense	3.54	139	941	469	55	43	56%	0.665
Difference	1.35	40	-11	248	29			112%

Held+	
LF	102
CF	116
RF	103

Pos	*Rpos*	*PA*	*Age*	*Name*	*BA*	*OBP*	*SLG*	*BB%*	*XBT*	*Bat R>Avg*	*BR R>Avg*	*Fld R>Avg*	*RAA*	*WAA*
C	5	365	29	Hendricks, Ellie*	0.242	0.317	0.382	9%	39%	0	1	3	9	0.9
1B	-8	643	28	Powell, Boog*	0.297	0.412	0.549	16%	38%	54	-2	-2	42	4.3
2B	4	600	27	Johnson, Davey	0.281	0.360	0.392	11%	53%	12	-1	6	21	2.1
3B	3	673	33	Robinson, Brooks	0.276	0.335	0.429	8%	43%	13	-4	5	17	1.8
SS	8	527	26	Belanger, Mark	0.218	0.303	0.259	10%	54%	-21	6	9	2	0.2
LF	-7	629	33	Buford, Don^	0.272	0.406	0.411	17%	42%	29	2	4	28	2.9
CF	-1	548	26	Blair, Paul	0.267	0.344	0.438	10%	58%	14	2	26	41	4.3
RF,1B	-6	553	34	Robinson, Frank	0.306	0.398	0.520	12%	50%	39	2	0	35	3.6
CF,OF	-3	385	27	Rettenmund, Merv	0.322	0.394	0.544	10%	57%	29	-1	10	35	3.6
C	4	256	27	Etchebarren, Andy	0.243	0.313	0.348	8%	25%	-3	-3	-1	-3	-0.3
RF,1B	-3	190	23	Crowley, Terry*	0.257	0.394	0.388	18%	44%	7	0	-3	1	0.1
SS,2B	2	184	29	Salmon, Chico	0.250	0.287	0.395	4%	53%	-2	0	-4	-4	-0.4
LF	-1	105	29	Motton, Curt	0.226	0.369	0.393	17%	57%	3	0	0	2	0.2
	3	758		Others	0.146	0.210	0.206	7%	43%	-70	2	6	-59	-6.1
	0		28.5	Team Total	0.257	0.344	0.401	11.2%	46%	101	4	59	164	17.0
				League Average	0.250	0.322	0.379	9.2%	46%					
				% Lg Avg	103	107	106	122	101					
				League Rank	3	1	3	1	8		4	1		

GS	*GR*	*IP*	*Age*	*Name*	*W–L*	*GmSc*	*K/9*	*BB/9*	*HR/9*	*FIP*	*ERA*	*RA/9*	*RAA*	*WAA*
39	0	305	24	Palmer, Jim	20–10	60.2	5.9	3.0	0.6	3.08	2.71	2.89	32	3.3
40	0	298	33	Cuellar, Mike*	24–8	56.7	5.7	2.1	1.0	3.40	3.48	3.81	0	0.0
40	0	296	27	McNally, Dave*	24–9	57.0	5.6	2.4	0.9	3.39	3.22	3.47	12	1.2
19	17	145	26	Hardin, Jim	6–5	53.2	4.8	1.6	0.8	3.12	3.53	3.72	1	0.1
21	6	135	28	Phoebus, Tom	5–5	53.9	4.8	4.1	0.7	4.00	3.07	3.87	-1	-0.1
0	50	55	30	Richert, Pete*	7–2	—	10.9	4.0	0.8	2.52	1.98	2.30	10	1.0
0	32	61	39	Hall, Dick	10–5	—	4.4	0.9	1.2	3.45	3.08	3.67	1	0.1

GS	GR	IP	Age	Name	W–L	GmSc	K/9	BB/9	HR/9	FIP	ERA	RA/9	RAA	WAA
3	22	61	26	Lopez, Marcelino*	1–1	54.0	7.3	5.5	0.3	3.03	2.08	2.82	7	0.7
0	53	55	29	Watt, Eddie	7–7	—	5.4	4.7	0.5	3.62	3.25	3.25	4	0.4
0	21	33	34	Drabowsky, Moe	4–2	—	5.7	4.1	1.9	5.18	3.78	4.59	-3	-0.3
0	27	34		Others	0–0	—	4.7	6.0	1.6	5.15	5.23	6.01	-8	-0.9
			29.6	Team Total		57.0	5.73	2.85	0.85	3.40	3.15	3.49	54	5.6
				League Average		51.0	5.65	3.51	0.90	3.72	3.71	4.18		
				League Rank		1	5	2	4	2	1			
				% Lg Avg		112	101	123	106	109	118	120		

1971 Baltimore Orioles

Baltimore won its third straight pennant winning the division by double digits and sweeping the AL West division winner Oakland who would go on to win the next 3 pennants. For the second consecutive season, the Orioles led the league in most runs scored and fewest runs allowed. The 1971 Orioles were known as a wonderful pitching team due to having twenty game win seasons from all 4 primary starters (Cuellar, McNally, Palmer, and Dobson). Superb fielding and timely hitting helped to prop up these 4 individual pitching seasons. Pinpoint control and selective hitting grew the walk differential to the highest total in major league history. The Pirates beat the O's in the World Series in 7 games.

Strengths: (1) hitting for average and power led by Rettenmund (23 2B), Buford (19 HR), Frank Robinson (28 HR), Powell (22 HR), Johnson (26 2B, 18 HR), and Brooks Robinson (21 2B, 20 HR), (2) drawing walks featuring Buford (89 BB), Rettenmund (87 BB), Powell (82 BB), Belanger (73 BB), and F Robinson (72 BB), (3) depth featuring 12 positional players that had above league average seasons, (4) fielding especially from 3B Brooks Robinson (105 Rng+, 35 DP), SS Belanger (104 Rng+), and CF Blair (99 Rng+), (5) Held+ from Blair (123), (6) CS% by Dalrymple (60%), Etchebarren (55%), and Hendricks (41%), and (7) pitching anchored by Palmer (59% QS), Dobson (70% QS), Cuellar (63% QS), and McNally (73% QS).

Weaknesses: (1) RP position, (2) fielding from RF/1B Frank Robinson (95 Held% in RF), (3) baserunning from F Robinson (21 GIDP) and Etchebarren (18% RS), (4) team %IR stranded, (5) team pitching K/9, and (6) 10.8 H/9 from reliever Dick Hall.

Mgr	Earl Weaver	
Rk	10	42
Gm	158	
Place	1	
GA	12.0	
Rival	8–10 vs Tigers, 90 RS, 81 RA; 7–4 vs A's, 37 RS, 29 RA	

	W	L	Win%
Regular Season	101	57	0.639
Runs Record	103	55	0.651
1 Run	27	21	0.563
Extra Innings	7	7	0.500
Blowout	33	11	0.750

	Team	LgAvg	%Avg	LgRk
BABIP	0.258	0.272	105	3
E	112	126	113	2
sOBP	0.288	0.314	109	1
rOBP	0.325	0.327	101	5
R/G	4.70	3.87	121	1
RA/G	3.35	3.87	115	1

	Tm	LgAvg	>Avg
RS	742	623	119
RA	530	623	93
DP	148	154	-6

	R/G	HR	K	BB	SB	CS	SB%	OPS
Team Offense	4.70	158	844	672	66	38	63%	0.745
Team Defense	3.35	125	793	416	56	52	52%	0.649
Difference	1.34	33	-51	256	10			115%

	Held+
LF	106
CF	117
RF	94

Pos	Rpos	PA	Age	Name	BA	OBP	SLG	BB%	XBT	Bat R>Avg	BR R>Avg	Fld R>Avg	RAA	WAA
C	5	361	30	Hendricks, Ellie*	0.250	0.334	0.386	11%	45%	5	0	1	11	1.2
1B	-7	509	29	Powell, Boog*	0.256	0.379	0.459	16%	38%	27	1	5	26	2.8
2B	4	574	28	Johnson, Davey	0.282	0.351	0.443	9%	30%	20	-1	2	25	2.7
3B	3	663	34	Robinson, Brooks	0.272	0.341	0.413	10%	43%	16	-1	20	38	4.1
SS	9	590	27	Belanger, Mark	0.266	0.365	0.320	12%	49%	5	1	13	28	3.0
LF	-6	549	34	Buford, Don^	0.290	0.413	0.477	16%	52%	38	3	2	37	4.0
CF	-1	555	27	Blair, Paul	0.262	0.306	0.397	6%	56%	2	0	8	9	0.9
RF,1B	-6	545	35	Robinson, Frank	0.281	0.384	0.510	13%	52%	37	-3	-9	19	2.0
RF,OF	-6	589	28	Rettenmund, Merv	0.318	0.422	0.448	15%	59%	39	3	5	41	4.4
C	4	243	28	Etchebarren, Andy	0.270	0.321	0.428	7%	35%	4	-3	5	10	1.1
2B,SS	1	94	25	Davanon, Jerry	0.235	0.340	0.296	13%	80%	-1	1	1	2	0.2

Pos	Rpos	PA	Age	Name	BA	OBP	SLG	BB%	XBT	Bat R>Avg	BR R>Avg	Fld R>Avg	RAA	WAA
C	1	67	23	Dalrymple, Clay*	0.204	0.409	0.286	24%	40%	2	0	0	3	0.3
LF,RF	-1	65	30	Motton, Curt	0.189	0.317	0.434	15%	57%	1	1	0	1	0.1
	0	739		Others	0.170	0.207	0.219	4%	41%	-62	0	1	-61	-6.6
	0		29.1	Team Total	0.261	0.347	0.398	10.9%	47%	133	2	54	189	20.3
				League Average	0.247	0.317	0.364	8.9%	47%					
				% Lg Avg	106	109	109	123	100					
				League Rank	1	1	2	1	5		5	1		

GS	GR	IP	Age	Name	W–L	GmSc	K/9	BB/9	HR/9	FIP	ERA	RA/9	RAA	WAA
38	0	292	34	Cuellar, Mike*	20–9	57.5	3.8	2.4	0.92	3.76	3.08	3.42	13	1.4
37	1	282	29	Dobson, Pat	20–8	59.3	6.0	2.0	0.77	2.92	2.90	3.32	16	1.7
37	0	282	25	Palmer, Jim	20–9	60.0	5.9	3.4	0.61	3.15	2.68	3.00	16	1.7
30	0	224	28	McNally, Dave*	21–5	58.1	3.7	2.3	0.96	3.87	2.89	3.01	6	0.6
6	6	54	30	Leonhard, Dave	2–3	49.7	3.0	3.2	0.83	4.12	2.83	3.00	-1	-0.2
0	35	40	30	Watt, Eddie	3–1	—	5.9	1.8	0.23	2.02	1.81	2.72	2	0.2
9	20	78	28	Jackson, Grant*	4–3	53.9	5.9	2.3	0.81	2.99	3.13	3.59	-1	-0.2
0	27	43	40	Hall, Dick	6–6	—	5.4	2.3	0.83	2.68	4.98	5.61	-8	-0.9
0	28	38	28	Dukes, Tom	1–5	—	7.0	1.9	0.94	2.81	3.52	3.52	0	0.0
0	35	36	31	Richert, Pete*	3–5	—	8.7	5.5	0.74	3.02	3.47	3.72	1	0.1
1	25	45		Others	1–3	50.0	4.2	4.6	0.80	4.03	3.60	5.60	-12	-1.3
158	177		30.3	Team Total		58	5.04	2.65	0.79	3.34	2.99	3.37	29	3.1
				League Average		53	5.42	3.37	0.77	3.47	3.46	3.89		
				% Lg Avg		109	93	127	97	104	116	115		
				League Rank		1	9	2	6	4	1	2		

1972 Pittsburgh Pirates

The Pirates repeated as divisional winners while the Reds with the addition of Joe Morgan rebounded to win the NL West. The Pirates led the NL East in most runs scored per game and fewest runs allowed per game. The Reds and Pirates slugged it out in the NLCS with the Reds winning in the final fifth game. The season ended with a loss to the A's in 7 games in the Series.

Strengths: (1) hitting for led by Stargell (28 2B, 33 HR), Hebner (19 HR), Oliver (27 2B), Clemente, Clines, and Davalillo, (2) baserunning especially from Davalillo (14 SB, 1 CS, 39% RS, 3 GIDP) and Clemente (42% RS), (3) fielding featuring 2B Cash (116 Rng+), RF Clemente (112 Rng+, 124 Held+), C Sanguillen, and 2B/LF Stennett (115 Rng+ at 2B, 113 Rng+ in LF), (4) CS% from May (50%) and Sanguillen (41%), and (5) pitching anchored by CY Young runner-up Blass (78% QS), Moose (73% QS), Ellis (68% QS), Hernandez (14/15/93% Sv, 34/43/79% IR stranded, 1.179 Lv), and Giusti (22/27/81% Sv, 31/43/72% IR stranded, 1.725 Lv).

Weaknesses: (1) SS position, (2) drawing walks, (3) hitting from Hernandez, and (4) fielding from 1B/LF Stargell (86 Rng+ in LF, 89 Held+ in LF), CF Oliver (96 Rng+, 90 Held+), 3B Pagan (78 Rng+), and RF Clines (99 Rng+, 66 Held+).

				W	L	Win%
Mgr	Bill Virdon		**Regular Season**	96	59	0.619
Rk	19	65	**Runs Record**	98	57	0.634
Gm	155		**1 Run**	23	21	0.523
Place	1		**Extra Innings**	12	5	0.706
GA	11.0		**Blowout**	25	9	0.735
Rival	12–3 vs Cubs, 73 RS, 41 RA; 4–8 vs Reds, 50 RS, 58 RA					

	Team	LgAvg	%Avg	LgRk
BABIP	0.272	0.277	102	4
E	136	135	99	7
sOBP	0.305	0.310	102	5
rOBP	0.293	0.329	112	1
R/G	4.46	3.91	114	3
RA/G	3.30	3.91	118	1

	Tm	LgAvg	>Avg
RS	691	605	86
RA	512	605	93
DP	171	142	29

	R/G	HR	K	BB	SB	CS	SB%	OPS
Team Offense	4.46	110	871	404	49	30	62%	0.721
Team Defense	3.30	90	838	433	54	41	57%	0.637
Difference	1.15	20	-33	-29	-5			113%

	Held+
LF	101
CF	91
RF	101

Pos	Rpos	PA	Age	Name	BA	OBP	SLG	BB%	XBT	Bat R>Avg	BR R>Avg	Fld R>Avg	RAA	WAA
C	8	547	28	Sanguillen, Manny	0.298	0.322	0.404	4%	40%	7	-1	6	20	2.2
1B,LF	-8	569	32	Stargell, Willie*	0.293	0.373	0.558	11%	27%	44	-1	-9	26	2.8
2B	3	452	24	Cash, Dave	0.282	0.316	0.374	5%	51%	1	0	12	16	1.7
3B	2	492	24	Hebner, Richie*	0.300	0.378	0.508	11%	44%	33	1	2	38	4.0
SS	6	389	31	Alley, Gene	0.248	0.321	0.320	10%	41%	-4	2	0	4	0.4
LF,RF	-5	403	35	Davalillo, Vic*	0.318	0.367	0.413	6%	51%	13	5	4	17	1.9
CF	-1	612	25	Oliver, Al*	0.312	0.352	0.437	6%	33%	22	3	-8	16	1.7
RF	-4	413	37	Clemente, Roberto	0.312	0.356	0.479	7%	65%	20	3	11	30	3.3
2B,LF	0	381	21	Stennett, Rennie	0.286	0.307	0.376	2%	50%	-1	-2	6	3	0.3
1B,LF	-6	354	25	Robertson, Bob	0.193	0.291	0.346	12%	26%	-5	-1	5	-7	-0.7
RF,OF	-4	334	25	Clines, Gene	0.334	0.369	0.421	5%	56%	12	1	-4	5	0.6
C	2	151	21	May, Milt*	0.281	0.325	0.353	7%	21%	0	-1	4	5	0.5
3B	1	137	37	Pagan, Jose	0.252	0.284	0.394	4%	33%	-1	1	-4	-3	-0.3
SS	3	186	31	Hernandez, Jackie	0.188	0.227	0.256	5%	31%	-13	-1	-5	-16	-1.7
	3	603		Others	0.162	0.202	0.199	4%	47%	-55	-2	-3	-57	-6.1
	0		28.3	Team Total	0.274	0.324	0.397	6.7%	45%	74	7	17	98	10.5
				League Average	0.248	0.315	0.365	8.5%	44%					
				% Lg Avg	110	103	109	79	102					
				League Rank	1	5	1	12	5		6	3		

GS	GR	IP	Age	Name	W–L	GmSc	K/9	BB/9	HR/9	FIP	ERA	RA/9	RAA	WAA
32	1	250	30	Blass, Steve	19–8	58.4	4.2	3.0	0.65	3.62	2.49	2.88	25	2.7
30	1	226	24	Moose, Bob	13–10	57.6	5.7	1.9	0.44	2.57	2.91	3.35	11	1.2
27	1	196	28	Briles, Nelson	14–11	55.7	5.5	2.0	0.64	2.91	3.08	3.82	-1	-0.1
25	0	163	27	Ellis, Dock	15–7	56.1	5.3	1.8	0.33	2.55	2.70	3.31	9	0.9
18	14	152	22	Kison, Bruce	9–7	55.9	6.0	4.1	0.65	3.76	3.26	3.61	3	0.3
12	14	93	28	Walker, Luke*	4–6	47.2	4.7	3.3	0.39	3.15	3.40	3.98	-2	-0.2
0	54	75	32	Giusti, Dave	7–4	—	6.5	2.4	0.36	2.30	1.93	2.17	13	1.4
11	20	116	29	Johnson, Bob	4–4	51.0	6.1	3.6	1.09	3.95	2.96	3.11	9	0.9
0	53	70	31	Hernandez, Ramon*	5–0	—	6.0	2.8	0.39	2.86	1.67	1.80	15	1.7
0	36	54	33	Miller, Bob	5–2	—	3.0	4.0	0.50	3.71	2.65	3.15	4	0.4
0	11	20		Others	1–0	—	5.8	4.9	1.33	4.63	4.43	5.31	-3	-0.4
			28.4	Team Total		56	5.33	2.76	0.57	3.15	2.81	3.26	83	8.9
				League Average		54	5.65	3.21	0.73	3.46	3.45	3.89		
				% Lg Avg		104	94	116	127	110	123	119		
				League Rank		2	9	3	2	2	2			

1973 Baltimore Orioles

Because of the new AL Designated Hitter (DH) rule, most AL managers left their starting pitchers in the game longer resulting in more wins and more innings pitched for the starting pitchers. The 1973 Orioles easily led the AL in fewest runs allowed and were a close third to the A's and Royals in scoring. Before the 1973 began, the Orioles traded veterans Davey Johnson and Pat Dobson to the Braves for C Earl Williams who had a solid season in 1973. The top 4 starting pitchers rarely missed starts. Their season terminated with a 3 games to 2 loss to the A's in the ALCS.

Strengths: (1) hitting for average and contact led by Bumbry (11 3B), Powell, Coggins (9 3B), Grich (29 2B), Baylor (20 2B), and Rettenmund, (2) drawing walks from Grich (107) and Powell (85), (3) baserunning led by Rettenmund (11 SB, 2 CS, 37% RS), (4) fielding from SS Belanger (104 Rng+, 100 DP), 2B Grich (110 Rng+, 130 DP), 3B Robinson (108 Rng+), CF Blair (108 Rng+, 14 assists), and RF Rettenmund (121 Rng+), (5) Held+ from CF Blair (111) and RF Rettenmund (106), and (6) pitching from Cy Young winner and MVP runner-up Palmer (73% QS), Reynolds (9/12/75% Sv, 34/60/57% IR stranded, 1.105 Lv), and Jackson (9/11/82% Sv, 41/57/72% IR stranded, 1.181 Lv).

Weaknesses: (1) SP position, (2) hitting from Belanger, Brooks Robinson, Hendricks, and Crowley, (3) baserunning from Williams (23% RS), and (4) pitching K/9 and HR/9 from starters Cuellar, Jefferson, and Alexander.

Mgr	Earl Weaver	
Rk	12	49
Gm	162	
Place	1	
GA	8.0	

Rival 7–11 vs Red Sox, 75 RS, 72 RA; 5–7 vs A's, 51 RS, 46 RA

	W	*L*	*Win%*
Regular Season	97	65	0.599
Runs Record	104	58	0.643
1 Run	23	24	0.489
Extra Innings	11	9	0.550
Blowout	31	9	0.775

	Team	*LgAvg*	*%Avg*	*LgRk*
BABIP	0.255	0.282	111	1
E	119	142	119	2
sOBP	0.310	0.327	105	2
rOBP	0.273	0.332	122	1
R/G	4.65	4.28	109	3
RA/G	3.46	4.28	123	1

	Tm	*LgAvg*	*>Avg*
RS	754	693	61
RA	561	693	132
DP	184	166	18

	R/G	*HR*	*K*	*BB*	*SB*	*CS*	*SB%*	*OPS*
Team Offense	4.65	119	752	648	146	64	70%	0.734
Team Defense	3.46	124	715	475	70	54	56%	0.660
Difference	1.19	-5	-37	173	76			111%

Held+	
LF	102
CF	111
RF	99

Pos	*Rpos*	*PA*	*Age*	*Name*	*BA*	*OBP*	*SLG*	*BB%*	*XBT*	*Bat R>Avg*	*BR R>Avg*	*Fld R>Avg*	*RAA*	*WAA*
C,1B	3	536	24	Williams, Earl	0.237	0.333	0.425	12%	31%	8	-6	4	9	0.9
1B	-6	464	31	Powell, Boog*	0.265	0.398	0.395	18%	37%	17	-2	-2	7	0.7
2B	5	700	24	Grich, Bobby	0.251	0.373	0.387	15%	51%	15	2	29	51	5.2
3B	4	619	36	Robinson, Brooks	0.257	0.326	0.344	9%	31%	-7	-2	18	13	1.3
SS	10	544	29	Belanger, Mark	0.226	0.302	0.262	9%	46%	-23	1	26	14	1.4
LF	-5	459	24	Baylor, Don	0.286	0.357	0.437	8%	69%	13	1	5	14	1.4
CF	0	554	29	Blair, Paul	0.280	0.334	0.402	8%	52%	4	4	19	27	2.8
RF	-4	390	30	Rettenmund, Merv	0.262	0.378	0.411	15%	53%	12	5	13	26	2.6
DH,1B	-2	590	34	Davis, Tommy	0.306	0.341	0.391	5%	34%	4	1	0	3	0.3
RF,CF	-3	426	22	Coggins, Rich*	0.319	0.363	0.468	7%	58%	16	3	5	21	2.1
LF,RF	-5	395	26	Bumbry, Al*	0.337	0.398	0.500	9%	43%	24	0	-2	17	1.8
C	3	168	30	Etchebarren, Andy	0.257	0.317	0.368	7%	38%	-1	-2	4	4	0.4
C	2	114	32	Hendricks, Ellie*	0.178	0.257	0.337	9%	40%	-5	1	0	-2	-0.2
DH,RF	-2	148	26	Crowley, Terry*	0.206	0.297	0.305	11%	35%	-5	0	-1	-8	-0.8
	0	228		Others	0.184	0.257	0.308	9%	62%	-11	3	1	-7	-0.7
	0		28.4	Team Total	0.266	0.345	0.389	10.2%	45%	61	9	119	189	19.4
				League Average	0.259	0.328	0.381	8.9%	46%					
				% Lg Avg	103	105	102	115	98					
				League Rank	3	1	4	2	9		1	1		

GS	*GR*	*IP*	*Age*	*Name*	*W–L*	*GmSc*	*K/9*	*BB/9*	*HR/9*	*FIP*	*ERA*	*RA/9*	*RAA*	*WAA*
37	1	296	27	Palmer, Jim	22–9	62.1	4.8	3.4	0.49	3.43	2.40	2.61	32	3.3
38	0	267	36	Cuellar, Mike*	18–13	53.6	4.7	2.8	0.98	3.95	3.27	4.04	-15	-1.5
38	0	266	30	McNally, Dave*	17–17	54.1	2.9	2.7	0.54	3.70	3.21	3.38	4	0.4
26	3	175	22	Alexander, Doyle	12–8	50.2	3.2	2.7	0.98	4.29	3.86	4.38	-16	-1.7
15	3	101	24	Jefferson, Jesse	6–5	47.7	4.6	4.1	1.34	4.91	4.11	4.74	-13	-1.4
4	4	32	23	Hood, Don*	3–2	44.8	5.0	1.7	0.28	2.60	3.90	4.74	-4	-0.4
1	41	111	26	Reynolds, Bob	7–5	51.0	6.2	2.5	0.24	2.31	1.95	2.19	18	1.8
0	45	80	30	Jackson, Grant*	8–0	—	5.3	2.7	0.56	3.05	1.91	2.02	15	1.5
0	30	71	32	Watt, Eddie	3–4	—	4.8	2.7	1.01	3.82	3.30	3.30	2	0.2
2	9	45	39	Pena, Orlando	1–1	57.5	4.6	1.6	2.01	5.15	4.03	4.03	-2	-0.2
1	4	18		Others	0–1	—	6.1	4.6	1.02	4.30	4.07	4.58	-2	-0.2
162	140		28.9	Team Total		54	4.40	2.92	0.76	3.73	3.08	3.45	19	1.9
				League Average		51	5.10	3.44	0.80	3.82	3.82	4.30		
				% Lg Avg		106	86	118	105	102	124	125		
				League Rank		2	11	2	7	5	1			

1974 Los Angeles Dodgers

The Dodgers and Reds had the two best teams in the NL in 1974 with the powerful Dodgers winning the NL West division by 4 games over the Reds but losing to the A's in 5 games in the World Series. The Dodgers led the NL in runs scored per game and were a close second to the Braves in fewest runs allowed per game. The Dodgers were an extremely well-balanced team that could hit, field, throw, run, and pitch with the best teams in baseball history. Wynn and Marshall were received in trades in December 1973 helping this team recapture the NL West crown from the Reds.

Strengths: (1) hitting for average and power led by Wynn (108 BB, 32 HR), MVP Garvey (32 2B, 21 HR), Crawford (23 2B), Ferguson (16 HR), Buckner (30 2B), and Cey (20 2B, 18 HR), (2) baserunning featuring Lopes (59 SB, 18 CS, 42% RS) and Garvey (15 ROE), (3) fielding especially from 3B Cey (109 Rng+), CF Wynn (96 Rng+, 10 assists), SS Russell (90 Rng+), and C Yeager (38% CS, 2.70 ERA), (4) Held+ from RF Crawford (119), and (5) pitching anchored by Cy Young runner-up Messersmith (221 K, 67% QS), Cy Young winner Marshall (9 Holds, 21/33/64% Sv, 44/75/59% IR, 1.477 Lv), Tommy John (73% QS) who had his now famous elbow injury after 22 starts, and Sutton (65% QS, 5 shutouts).

Weaknesses: (1) hitting from reserve outfielders Joshua and Paciorek, (2) making DP, and (3) pitching from Downing (44% QS).

Mgr	Walter Alston	
Rk	9	41
Gm	162	
Place	1	
GA	4.0	
Rival	12–6 vs Reds,79 RS, 57 RA; 4–8 vs Pirates, 40 RS, 47 RA	

	W	*L*	*Win%*
Regular Season	102	60	0.630
Runs Record	105	57	0.649
1 Run	29	23	0.558
Extra Innings	11	7	0.611
Blowout	32	7	0.821

	Team	*LgAvg*	*%Avg*	*LgRk*
BABIP	0.262	0.282	108	1
E	157	154	98	7
sOBP	0.293	0.323	110	1
rOBP	0.297	0.332	112	1
R/G	4.93	4.15	119	1
RA/G	3.46	4.15	120	2

	Tm	*LgAvg*	*>Avg*
RS	798	673	125
RA	561	673	112
DP	122	153	-31

	R/G	*HR*	*K*	*BB*	*SB*	*CS*	*SB%*	*OPS*	*Held+*	
Team Offense	4.93	139	820	597	149	75	67%	0.743	**LF**	107
Team Defense	3.46	112	943	464	76	47	62%	0.634	**CF**	106
Difference	1.46	27	123	133	73			117%	**RF**	115

Pos	*Rpos*	*PA*	*Age*	*Name*	*BA*	*OBP*	*SLG*	*BB%*	*XBT*	*Bat R>Avg*	*BR R>Avg*	*Fld R>Avg*	*RAA*	*WAA*
C	6	354	25	Yeager, Steve	0.266	0.334	0.437	9%	48%	8	-3	6	17	1.8
1B	-9	685	25	Garvey, Steve	0.312	0.342	0.469	5%	45%	24	4	0	19	2.0
2B	4	613	29	Lopes, Davey	0.266	0.350	0.383	11%	57%	9	8	-3	18	1.9
3B	4	673	26	Cey, Ron	0.262	0.349	0.397	11%	51%	13	-1	12	28	2.9
SS	10	625	25	Russell, Bill	0.269	0.336	0.351	8%	45%	0	0	6	16	1.6
LF,1B	-6	620	24	Buckner, Bill*	0.314	0.351	0.412	5%	54%	13	2	5	14	1.5
CF	0	656	32	Wynn, Jimmy	0.271	0.387	0.497	16%	46%	41	0	14	55	5.7
RF	-5	540	27	Crawford, Willie*	0.295	0.376	0.432	12%	47%	21	-1	3	18	1.9
C,RF	4	430	27	Ferguson, Joe	0.252	0.380	0.436	17%	53%	18	-2	2	22	2.3
LF,RF	-3	189	27	Paciorek, Tom	0.240	0.282	0.371	5%	57%	-3	0	1	-5	-0.6
CF,LF	-1	134	26	Joshua, Von*	0.234	0.276	0.315	5%	33%	-5	-1	-3	-10	-1.0
2B	1	83	26	Lacy, Lee	0.282	0.293	0.359	2%	45%	-1	2	-1	1	0.1
2B,SS	2	82	24	Auerbach, Rick	0.342	0.407	0.384	10%	24%	3	-1	-5	-1	-0.1
	-7	648		Others	0.206	0.253	0.257	5%	36%	-38	1	0	-44	-4.5
	0		26.4	Team Total	0.272	0.342	0.401	9.4%	47%	103	8	37	148	15.4
				League Average	0.255	0.326	0.367	9.1%	43%					
				% Lg Avg	106	105	109	103	110					
				League Rank	2	2	1	5	2		3	3		

GS	*GR*	*IP*	*Age*	*Name*	*W–L*	*GmSc*	*K/9*	*BB/9*	*HR/9*	*FIP*	*ERA*	*RA/9*	*RAA*	*WAA*
39	0	292	28	Messersmith, Andy	20–6	61.9	6.8	2.9	0.74	3.28	2.59	2.86	35	3.6
40	0	276	29	Sutton, Don	19–9	56.5	5.8	2.6	0.75	3.43	3.23	3.62	9	1.0
35	1	198	25	Rau, Doug*	13–11	51.3	5.7	3.2	0.91	3.87	3.72	4.08	-4	-0.4
22	0	153	31	John, Tommy*	13–3	57.7	4.6	2.5	0.24	2.89	2.59	3.00	16	1.6
16	5	98	33	Downing, Al*	5–6	49.9	5.8	4.1	0.64	3.84	3.66	4.76	-9	-1.0
10	11	80	28	Zahn, Geoff*	3–5	56.5	3.7	1.8	0.34	3.03	2.03	3.16	6	0.7
0	106	208	31	Marshall, Mike	15–12	—	6.2	2.4	0.39	2.72	2.42	2.85	25	2.6
0	49	96	26	Hough, Charlie	9–4	—	5.9	3.8	1.13	4.35	3.75	4.22	-3	-0.3
0	24	39	36	Brewer, Jim*	4–4	—	5.9	2.3	1.14	3.75	2.52	3.20	3	0.3
0	4	9	21	Rhoden, Rick	1–0	—	7.0	4.0	1.00	3.62	2.00	2.00	2	0.2
0	9	15		Others	0–0	—	2.4	4.2	2.40	7.06	4.80	5.40	-3	-0.3
			28.8	Team Total		56	5.79	2.85	0.69	3.42	2.97	3.45	78	8.1
				League Average		52	5.13	3.51	0.66	3.63	3.62	4.15		
				% Lg Avg		108	113	123	96	106	122	120		
				League Rank		1	1	1	10	1	1			

1975 Cincinnati Reds

In 1975, the Big Red Machine obliterated the second place Dodgers by 20 games in the NL West and easily led the NL in runs scored and won 108 games, 10 more games than they had won in 1974. This team turned the season around in early May when Pete Rose moved from LF and began playing at 3B filling a glaring offensive hole and opening up playing time in LF for slugger and slick fielder George Foster. The Reds swept the Pirates in the NLCS and won perhaps the greatest World Series ever played against a gritty Red Sox team in 7 games.

Strengths: (1) hitting led by MVP Morgan (27 2B, 17 HR), Rose (47 2B), Bench (39 2B, 28 HR), Foster (23 HR), Perez (28 2B, 20 HR), and Griffey, (2) drawing walks led by Morgan (132 BB) and Rose (89 BB), (3) baserunning from Morgan (67 SB, 10 CS, 3 GIDP), Griffey (44% RS, 10 GIDP), and Concepcion (33 SB, 6 CS, 7 GIDP), (4) fielding led by CF Geronimo (115 Rng+, 11 assists, 131 Held+), SS Concepcion (110 Rng+, 102 DP), 2B Morgan (105 Rng+, 96 DP), C Bench (46% CS), and LF Foster (116 Rng+, 9 assists, 108 Held+), and (5) pitching from Gullett (59% QS), Nolan (59% QS), Eastwick (22/25/85% Sv, 40/46/87% IR stranded), Clay Carroll (26/38/68% IR stranded), and McEnaney (15/19/79% Sv).

Weaknesses: (1) SP position, (2) hitting from Plummer and Chaney, (3) 8% CS from Plummer, (4) fielding from 3B Rose (89 Rng+), RF Griffey (90 Rng+, 96 Held+), and 1B/LF Driessen (80 Rng+ in LF), and (5) pitching from Kirby (37% QS) and Billingham (9.6 H/9).

			W	L	Win%
Mgr	Sparky Anderson	**Regular Season**	108	54	0.667
Rk	8 38	**Runs Record**	105	57	0.650
Gm	162	**1 Run**	32	20	0.615
Place	1	**Extra Innings**	11	4	0.733
GA	20.0	**Blowout**	35	5	0.875
Rival	8–10 vs Dodgers, 69 RS, 64 RA; 6–6 vs Pirates, 55 RS, 55 RA				

	Team	LgAvg	%Avg	LgRk
BABIP	0.274	0.284	104	3
E	102	155	152	1
sOBP	0.320	0.323	101	4
rOBP	0.316	0.337	107	3
R/G	5.19	4.13	126	1
RA/G	3.62	4.13	114	3

	Tm	LgAvg	>Avg
RS	840	668	172
RA	586	668	82
DP	173	153	20

	R/G	HR	K	BB	SB	CS	SB%	OPS
Team Offense	5.19	124	916	691	168	36	82%	0.754
Team Defense	3.62	112	663	487	61	29	68%	0.690
Difference	1.57	12	-253	204	107			109%

	Held+
LF	114
CF	126
RF	95

Pos	Rpos	PA	Age	Name	BA	OBP	SLG	BB%	XBT	Bat R>Avg	BR R>Avg	Fld R>Avg	RAA	WAA
C,LF	7	605	27	Bench, Johnny	0.283	0.359	0.519	11%	44%	33	2	10	45	4.7
1B	-7	574	33	Perez, Tony	0.282	0.350	0.466	9%	32%	21	-3	7	25	2.6
2B	4	639	31	Morgan, Joe*	0.327	0.466	0.508	21%	52%	61	12	14	87	9.1
3B,LF	2	764	34	Rose, Pete^	0.317	0.406	0.432	12%	49%	38	0	-12	26	2.7
SS	8	558	27	Concepcion, Dave	0.274	0.326	0.353	7%	54%	-3	3	15	15	1.6
LF,CF	-5	511	26	Foster, George	0.300	0.356	0.518	8%	50%	28	0	15	43	4.4
CF	0	557	27	Geronimo, Cesar*	0.257	0.327	0.363	9%	53%	-1	2	24	25	2.6
RF	-5	540	25	Griffey Sr., Ken*	0.305	0.391	0.402	12%	54%	19	5	-6	18	1.9
1B,LF	-3	249	23	Driessen, Dan*	0.281	0.386	0.429	14%	52%	10	-1	-5	4	0.5
RF,LF	-2	226	32	Rettenmund, Merv	0.239	0.356	0.314	15%	44%	0	0	2	2	0.2
C	3	189	28	Plummer, Bill	0.182	0.291	0.245	13%	62%	-8	1	-4	-11	-1.2
SS,2B	3	175	27	Chaney, Darrel^	0.219	0.280	0.294	8%	44%	-7	0	2	-5	-0.6
3B,2B	3	143	24	Flynn, Doug	0.268	0.324	0.346	8%	41%	-1	1	4	4	0.4
LF,1B	0	78	28	Crowley, Terry*	0.268	0.333	0.394	9%	80%	1	0	1	2	0.2
	-8	611		Others	0.148	0.198	0.175	5%	36%	-63	2	-6	-67	-7.0
	0		28.0	Team Total	0.271	0.353	0.401	10.8%	48%	128	24	61	213	22.2
				League Average	0.257	0.327	0.369	9.0%	43%					
				% Lg Avg	106	108	109	120	111					
				League Rank	2	1	3	1	1		1	2		

GS	GR	IP	Age	Name	W–L	GmSc	K/9	BB/9	HR/9	FIP	ERA	RA/9	RAA	WAA
32	0	211	27	Nolan, Gary	15–9	54.5	3.2	1.2	0.8	3.52	3.16	3.20	13	1.3
32	1	208	32	Billingham, Jack	15–10	48.0	3.4	3.3	1.0	4.42	4.11	4.33	-13	-1.4
26	8	188	32	Norman, Fred*	12–4	52.3	5.7	4.0	1.1	4.34	3.73	4.07	-6	-0.6
22	0	160	24	Gullett, Don*	15–4	60.0	5.5	3.2	0.6	3.44	2.42	2.76	18	1.9
22	5	131	25	Darcy, Pat	11–5	49.2	3.2	4.1	0.3	3.60	3.58	3.72	0	0.0

GS	GR	IP	Age	Name	W–L	GmSc	K/9	BB/9	HR/9	FIP	ERA	RA/9	RAA	WAA
19	7	111	27	Kirby, Clay	10–6	46.3	3.9	4.4	1.1	4.93	4.72	5.12	-17	-1.8
0	58	90	24	Eastwick, Rawly	5–3	—	6.1	2.5	0.6	3.03	2.60	2.60	12	1.2
0	67	125	28	Borbon, Pedro	9–5	—	2.1	1.5	0.4	3.35	2.95	3.38	5	0.5
2	54	96	34	Carroll, Clay	7–5	50.5	4.1	3.0	0.2	2.95	2.62	2.80	10	1.1
0	70	91	23	McEnaney, Will*	5–2	—	4.7	2.3	0.6	3.15	2.47	2.87	9	0.9
7	7	49		Others	4–1	—	3.1	5.1	0.2	4.16	4.78	5.14	-8	-0.8
162	277		27.6	Team Total		51	4.09	3.00	0.69	3.77	3.37	3.61	23	2.4
				League Average		52	5.05	3.47	0.64	3.63	3.62	4.13		
				% Lg Avg		98	81	116	92	96	107			
				League Rank		6	12	2	9	8	3			

1976 CINCINNATI REDS

The Reds won 6 fewer games than in 1975 but still won the division by 10 games over the Dodgers leading the division in runs scored and finishing second to the Dodgers in fewest runs allowed. The Big Red Machine swept the talented Phillies in the NLCS and then swept the Yankees in the World Series limiting the Yankees to 8 runs scored over the four games. The 1976 Reds were the first NL team since the 1923–1924 Giants to win back-to-back world championships.

Strengths: (1) hitting featuring MVP Morgan (30 2B, 27 HR), Rose (42 2B), MVP runner-up Foster (21 2B, 9 3B, 29 HR), Griffey (28 2B, 9 3B), Geronimo (24 2B, 11 3B), Perez (32 2B, 19 HR), and Bench (24 2B), (2) drawing walks led by Morgan (114 BB), Rose (86 BB), and Bench (81 BB), (3) baserunning especially from Morgan (60 SB, 9 CS, 36% RS, 2 GIDP), Griffey (34 SB, 11 CS, 44% RS, 3 GIDP), Rose (40% RS), Geronimo (22 SB, 5 CS, 6 GIDP), and Driessen (14 SB, 1 CS), (4) fielding led by SS Concepcion (110 Rng+, 93 DP), C Bench (42% CS, 3.54 ERA), and LF Foster (110 Rng+, 9 assists), (5) Held+ from LF Foster (116), and (6) pitching anchored by Rookie of the Year Zachry (71% QS) and Eastwick (26/35/74% Sv).

Weaknesses: (1) RP, (2) baserunning from Plummer (25% RS), (3) fielding from RF Griffey (86 Held+, 96 Rng+), (4) CS% by Plummer (20% CS), and (5) pitching from Billingham (48% QS), Alcala (48% QS), and McEnaney (12.1 H/9, 24/36/67% IR stranded).

Mgr	Sparky Anderson	
Rk	7	29
Gm	162	
Place	1	
GA	10.0	
Rival	5–7 vs Phillies, 60 RS, 62 RA; 13–5 vs Dodgers, 77 RS, 57 RA	

	W	L	Win%
Regular Season	102	60	0.630
Runs Record	106	56	0.657
1 Run	31	24	0.564
Extra Innings	10	4	0.714
Blowout	34	12	0.739

	Team	LgAvg	%Avg	LgRk
BABIP	0.283	0.281	99	8
E	102	145	142	1
sOBP	0.315	0.316	100	5
rOBP	0.325	0.330	102	4
R/G	5.29	3.98	133	1
RA/G	3.91	3.98	102	5

	Tm	LgAvg	>Avg
RS	857	645	212
RA	633	645	12
DP	157	151	6

	R/G	HR	K	BB	SB	CS	SB%	OPS
Team Offense	5.29	141	902	681	210	57	79%	0.781
Team Defense	3.91	100	790	491	94	51	65%	0.688
Difference	1.38	41	-112	190	116			113%

Held+	
LF	117
CF	103
RF	93

Pos	Rpos	PA	Age	Name	BA	OBP	SLG	BB%	XBT	Bat R>Avg	BR R>Avg	Fld R>Avg	RAA	WAA
C	8	552	28	Bench, Johnny	0.234	0.348	0.394	15%	44%	12	0	10	30	3.2
1B	-7	586	34	Perez, Tony	0.260	0.328	0.452	9%	52%	17	1	4	15	1.6
2B	4	599	32	Morgan, Joe*	0.320	0.444	0.576	19%	54%	65	12	-1	80	8.5
3B	4	759	35	Rose, Pete^	0.323	0.404	0.450	11%	54%	45	4	2	55	5.8
SS	10	636	28	Concepcion, Dave	0.281	0.335	0.401	8%	47%	11	0	9	30	3.2
LF,OF	-6	627	27	Foster, George	0.306	0.364	0.530	8%	55%	41	2	7	44	4.7
CF	0	555	28	Geronimo, Cesar*	0.307	0.382	0.414	10%	36%	22	3	-6	19	2.0
RF	-5	628	26	Griffey Sr., Ken*	0.336	0.401	0.450	10%	55%	36	9	-11	29	3.1
1B,LF	-3	268	24	Driessen, Dan*	0.247	0.362	0.402	16%	50%	9	0	0	6	0.6
2B,SS	4	235	25	Flynn, Doug	0.283	0.312	0.338	4%	38%	-3	0	1	2	0.2

Pos	Rpos	PA	Age	Name	BA	OBP	SLG	BB%	XBT	Bat R>Avg	BR R>Avg	Fld R>Avg	RAA	WAA
C	3	168	29	Plummer, Bill	0.248	0.311	0.379	8%	9%	0	-3	-4	-4	-0.4
RF,LF	-1	90	27	Armbrister, Ed	0.295	0.341	0.462	7%	40%	3	1	3	6	0.7
LF,3B	-1	141	33	Bailey, Bob	0.298	0.376	0.508	11%	58%	9	-1	-4	3	0.3
LF	-1	164	30	Lum, Mike	0.228	0.331	0.346	13%	57%	1	-1	-2	-3	-0.3
	-9	530		Others	0.153	0.190	0.170	4%	29%	-54	0	-1	-64	-6.8
	0		29.0	Team Total	0.280	0.357	0.424	10.4%	48%	214	27	7	248	26.3
				League Average	0.255	0.320	0.361	8.5%	44%					
				% Lg Avg	110	111	117	123	109					
				League Rank	1	1	1	1	1		1	6		

GS	GR	IP	Age	Name	W–L	GmSc	K/9	BB/9	HR/9	FIP	ERA	RA/9	RAA	WAA
34	0	239	28	Nolan, Gary	15–9	54.9	4.2	1.0	1.05	3.66	3.46	3.61	9	0.9
28	10	204	24	Zachry, Pat	14–7	56.2	6.3	3.7	0.35	3.06	2.74	3.09	20	2.1
24	9	180	33	Norman, Fred*	12–7	57.3	6.3	3.5	0.50	3.22	3.09	3.54	8	0.9
29	5	177	33	Billingham, Jack	12–10	47.6	3.9	3.2	0.86	4.19	4.32	4.88	-18	-2.0
21	9	132	23	Alcala, Santo	11–4	48.6	4.6	4.6	0.82	4.45	4.70	4.91	-14	-1.5
20	3	126	25	Gullett, Don*	11–3	52.6	4.6	3.4	0.57	3.65	3.00	3.43	7	0.8
0	71	108	25	Eastwick, Rawly	11–5	—	5.8	2.3	0.25	2.55	2.09	2.51	17	1.8
1	68	121	29	Borbon, Pedro	4–3	29.0	3.9	2.3	0.30	2.91	3.35	3.64	4	0.4
0	55	72	24	McEnaney, Will*	2–6	—	3.5	2.9	0.37	3.19	4.85	5.48	-12	-1.3
0	22	44	20	Sarmiento, Manny	5–1	—	4.1	2.5	0.21	2.83	2.06	2.88	5	0.5
5	22	68		Others	5–5	—	4.0	5.5	0.80	4.49	5.58	5.72	-13	-1.4
162	274		26.4	Team Total		52	4.83	3.00	0.61	3.50	3.51	3.87	12	1.3
				League Average		52	4.95	3.23	0.57	3.51	3.50	3.99		
				% Lg Avg		100	98	107	94	100	100	103		
				League Rank		5	7	6	8	5	5			

1976 Philadelphia Phillies

The 1976 Phillies led the division by 9 games over the second place Pirates leading the division in runs scored. The 1976 Phillies were the first of 3 consecutive division winning Phillies teams. Unfortunately for the Phillies, the West Division Reds won their second of their two consecutive world championship seasons. The Phillies outscored every team they played.

Strengths: (1) hitting for average and power led by Schmidt (31 2B, 38 HR, 100 BB), Luzinski (28 2B, 21 HR), Maddox (37 2B), Johnstone (38 2B), and Allen (15 HR), (2) fielding featuring CF Maddox (115 Rng+, 10 assists), SS Bowa (88 Rng+, 90 DP), 3B Schmidt (111 Rng+), and RF Johnstone (117 Rng+), (3) Held+ by RF Johnstone (118) and CF Maddox (103), and (4) pitching anchored by Carlton (63% QS, 195 K) and Reed (14/23/61% Sv, 25/35/71% IR stranded, 1.359 Lv). The baserunning standouts were Bowa (30 SB, 8 CS, 38% RS) and Maddox (29 SB, 12 CS, 32% RS).

Weaknesses: (1) 1B position, (2) hitting from Bowa and Tolan, (3) baserunning from Luzinski (26% RS), (4) fielding from LF Luzinski (85 Rng+, 82 Held+), 1B/CF Tolan (13 assists at 1B in 335 innings played), and 1B Allen, (5) CS% from McCarver (21%) and Boone (28%), and (6) pitching from Christenson (48% QS, 10.6 H/9).

Mgr	Danny Ozark	
Rk	23	72
Gm	162	
Place	1	
GA	9.0	
Rival	7–5 vs Reds, 62 RS, 60 RA; 8–10 vs Pirates, 89 RS, 86 RA	

	W	L	Win%
Regular Season	101	61	0.623
Runs Record	102	60	0.629
1 Run	26	24	0.520
Extra Innings	7	7	0.500
Blowout	34	9	0.791

	Team	LgAvg	%Avg	LgRk
BABIP	0.282	0.281	100	7
E	115	145	126	2
sOBP	0.305	0.316	104	4
rOBP	0.289	0.330	114	1
R/G	4.75	3.98	119	2
RA/G	3.44	3.98	116	3

	Tm	LgAvg	>Avg
RS	770	645	125
RA	557	645	88
DP	148	151	-3

	R/G	HR	K	BB	SB	CS	SB%	OPS
Team Offense	4.75	110	793	542	127	70	64%	0.733
Team Defense	3.44	98	918	397	103	38	73%	0.668
Difference	1.31	12	125	145	24			110%

Held%	
LF	88
CF	106
RF	112

Pos	Rpos	PA	Age	Name	BA	OBP	SLG	BB%	XBT	Bat R>Avg	BR R>Avg	Fld R>Avg	RAA	WAA
C,1B	7	418	28	Boone, Bob	0.271	0.348	0.366	11%	31%	6	-3	2	12	1.3
1B	-4	339	34	Allen, Dick	0.268	0.346	0.480	11%	38%	15	-2	-6	3	0.3
2B	5	727	28	Cash, Dave	0.284	0.337	0.345	7%	39%	1	-2	0	4	0.5
3B	4	705	26	Schmidt, Mike	0.262	0.376	0.524	14%	51%	47	0	10	61	6.5
SS	10	672	30	Bowa, Larry^	0.248	0.283	0.301	5%	46%	-23	6	6	-1	-0.1
LF	-5	605	25	Luzinski, Greg	0.304	0.369	0.478	8%	24%	32	-4	-15	8	0.9
CF	0	586	26	Maddox, Garry	0.330	0.377	0.456	7%	45%	30	2	20	52	5.5
RF,1B	-5	491	30	Johnstone, Jay*	0.318	0.373	0.457	8%	44%	24	-1	13	31	3.3
1B,CF	-4	290	30	Tolan, Bobby*	0.261	0.285	0.342	2%	34%	-6	-1	-7	-18	-1.9
RF,LF	-2	247	32	Brown, Ollie	0.254	0.350	0.383	13%	32%	5	1	1	5	0.5
C	2	194	34	McCarver, Tim*	0.277	0.409	0.432	18%	57%	11	1	-3	11	1.2
CF,LF	-2	129	27	Martin, Jerry	0.248	0.287	0.355	5%	44%	-2	-1	5	0	0.0
1B	-2	153	30	Hutton, Tom*	0.202	0.342	0.282	18%	26%	-1	-2	1	-4	-0.4
C	2	107	30	Oates, Johnny*	0.253	0.308	0.273	7%	56%	-3	-1	1	-1	-0.1
	-6	574		Others	0.207	0.248	0.277	4%	31%	-30	2	1	-33	-3.6
	0		29.3	Team Total	0.272	0.338	0.395	8.7%	39%	106	-5	29	130	13.8
				League Average	0.255	0.320	0.361	8.5%	44%					
				% Lg Avg	107	106	109	103	89					
				League Rank	2	2	2	5	11		9	2		

GS	GR	IP	Age	Name	W–L	GmSc	K/9	BB/9	HR/9	FIP	ERA	RA/9	RAA	WAA
35	0	253	31	Carlton, Steve*	20–7	58.5	6.9	2.6	0.68	3.02	3.13	3.35	13	1.4
35	3	228	37	Kaat, Jim*	12–14	51.7	3.3	1.3	0.83	3.62	3.48	3.76	1	0.1
32	1	222	34	Lonborg, Jim	18–10	55.5	4.8	2.0	0.73	3.45	3.08	3.45	9	0.9
29	3	169	22	Christenson, Larry	13–8	48.0	2.9	2.2	0.43	3.44	3.68	4.11	-6	-0.7
25	8	156	22	Underwood, Tom*	10–5	51.9	5.4	3.6	0.52	3.54	3.53	3.64	3	0.3
4	55	128	33	Reed, Ron	8–7	55.2	6.8	2.3	0.56	2.71	2.46	2.74	15	1.6
0	58	97	31	McGraw, Tug*	7–6	—	7.0	3.9	0.37	2.72	2.50	3.14	7	0.8
0	59	93	28	Garber, Gene	9–3	—	8.9	2.9	0.39	2.18	2.82	3.20	6	0.7
2	24	62	28	Twitchell, Wayne	3–1	59.0	9.8	2.6	0.44	2.20	1.75	2.63	8	0.9
0	35	50	28	Schueler, Ron	1–0	—	7.8	2.9	0.72	3.05	2.90	3.26	3	0.3
0	1	3		Lerch, Randy*	0–0	—	0.0	0.0	0.00	2.77	3.00	3.00	0	0.0
162	247		29.4	Team Total		53	5.66	2.45	0.60	3.15	3.10	3.44	61	6.5
				League Average		52	4.95	3.23	0.57	3.51	3.50	3.99		
				% Lg Avg		102	114	132	95	112	113	116		
				League Rank		4	2	1	10	2	3			

1977 New York Yankees

Expansion from 12 to 14 teams occurred in the AL as the Toronto Blue Jays were added in the AL East and the Seattle Mariners were added in the AL West. The Yankees led the AL East in fewest runs allowed. The Yankees repeated as AL champs by beating the Royals in game 5 of the ALCS for the second year in a row, this time overcoming a 3–1 deficit in the final game of the ALCS then beating the Dodgers in 6 games in the World Series. The Yankees exercised their financial might by signing free agents Don Gullett and Reggie Jackson before the season. Paul Blair was obtained from the Orioles providing solid OF support. The SS position was upgraded by trading RF Gamble and cash to the White Sox for SS Bucky Dent. Also, during the mid-season, the Yankees obtained Cliff Johnson and Dave Kingman for the DH.

Strengths: (1) SP, C, 2B, 3B, LF, CF, and RF positions, (2) hitting led by Jackson (39 2B, 32 HR, 74 BB), Nettles (23 2B, 37 HR), Piniella, Munson (28 2B), Johnson, and Chambliss (32 2B), (3) baserunning featuring Rivers (2 GIDP, 35% RS), (4) fielding featuring SS Dent (97 Rng+, 90 DP), 2B Randolph (105 Rng+, 108 DP), CF Rivers (112 Rng+), and 3B Nettles (100 Rng+, 31 DP), and (5) pitching anchored by Guidry (68% QS), Figueroa (56%), Gullett (59% QS), Cy Young winner Sparky Lyle (26/34/76% Sv, 61/99/62% IR stranded, 1.714 Lv), and Tidrow (26/41/63% IR, 0.843 Lv).

Weaknesses: (1) %IR stranded, (2) hitting from Dent and May, (3) fielding from RF Jackson (98 Rng+, 95 Held+) and OF Piniella (92 Rng+ in RF, 70 Rng+ in LF), and (4) pitching from Holtzman (27% QS, 13.2 H/9) and Hunter (45% QS, 1.8 HR/9).

Mgr	Billy Martin	
Rk	34	103
Gm	162	
Place	1	
GA	2.5	
Rival	7–8 vs O's, 79 RS, 66 RA; 7–8 vs Red Sox, 54 RS, 76 RA	

	W	*L*	*Win%*
Regular Season	100	62	0.617
Runs Record	101	61	0.625
1 Run	24	19	0.558
Extra Innings	6	4	0.600
Blowout	32	12	0.727

	Team	*LgAvg*	*%Avg*	*LgRk*
BABIP	0.271	0.287	106	1
E	132	142	108	4
sOBP	0.313	0.328	105	2
rOBP	0.324	0.336	104	2
R/G	5.13	4.53	113	4
RA/G	4.02	4.53	113	1

	Tm	*LgAvg*	*>Avg*
RS	831	732	99
RA	651	732	81
DP	151	153	-2

	R/G	*HR*	*K*	*BB*	*SB*	*CS*	*SB%*	*OPS*
Team Offense	5.13	184	681	533	93	57	62%	0.788
Team Defense	4.02	139	758	486	89	60	60%	0.704
Difference	1.11	45	77	47	4			112%

Held+	
LF	99
CF	101
RF	102

Pos	*Rpos*	*PA*	*Age*	*Name*	*BA*	*OBP*	*SLG*	*BB%*	*XBT*	*Bat R>Avg*	*BR R>Avg*	*Fld R>Avg*	*RAA*	*WAA*
C,DH	8	638	30	Munson, Thurman	0.308	0.351	0.462	6%	55%	15	0	-2	21	2.1
1B	-9	652	28	Chambliss, Chris*	0.287	0.336	0.445	7%	38%	9	-1	2	1	0.1
2B	5	624	22	Randolph, Willie	0.274	0.347	0.387	10%	55%	2	3	12	22	2.2
3B	4	664	32	Nettles, Graig*	0.255	0.333	0.496	10%	41%	17	1	9	31	3.1
SS	10	540	25	Dent, Bucky	0.247	0.300	0.352	7%	40%	-14	-2	12	6	0.6
LF	-6	606	33	White, Roy^	0.268	0.358	0.405	12%	52%	7	3	7	11	1.1
CF	0	594	28	Rivers, Mickey*	0.326	0.350	0.439	3%	58%	10	6	14	30	3.0
RF,DH	-6	606	31	Jackson, Reggie*	0.286	0.375	0.550	12%	46%	36	2	-6	26	2.6
OF,DH	-5	369	33	Piniella, Lou	0.330	0.365	0.510	5%	55%	16	-2	-6	3	0.3
CF,RF	-2	183	33	Blair, Paul	0.262	0.303	0.396	5%	42%	-2	-1	5	0	0.0
DH,C	0	168	29	Johnson, Cliff	0.296	0.405	0.606	12%	20%	14	-1	2	15	1.5
2B	1	75	26	Zeber, George^	0.323	0.405	0.508	12%	25%	4	-2	-1	2	0.2
DH	0	27	28	Kingman, Dave	0.250	0.333	0.833	7%	0%	3	-1	0	2	0.2
DH	0	203	29	May, Carlos*	0.227	0.292	0.309	8%	32%	-8	-1	0	-9	-0.9
	0	312		Others	0.237	0.322	0.348	11%	49%	-6	4	-4	-6	-0.6
	0		29.1	Team Total	0.281	0.344	0.444	8.5%	46%	104	8	44	156	15.5
				League Average	0.266	0.330	0.405	8.4%	47%					
				% Lg Avg	106	104	110	101	99					
				League Rank	3	3	2	9	9		4	2		

GS	*GR*	*IP*	*Age*	*Name*	*W–L*	*GmSc*	*K/9*	*BB/9*	*HR/9*	*FIP*	*ERA*	*RA/9*	*RAA*	*WAA*
32	0	239	28	Figueroa, Ed	16–11	53.5	3.9	2.8	0.71	3.95	3.57	3.84	12	1.2
31	0	217	30	Torrez, Mike	14–12	51.5	3.7	3.1	0.83	4.30	3.82	4.11	4	0.4
25	6	211	26	Guidry, Ron*	16–7	62.2	7.5	2.8	0.51	2.79	2.82	3.08	29	2.9
22	0	158	26	Gullett, Don	14–4	55.5	6.6	3.9	0.80	3.81	3.58	3.81	9	0.9
22	0	143	31	Hunter, Catfish	9–9	48.6	3.3	3.0	1.82	5.71	4.71	5.21	-15	-1.5
11	7	72	31	Holtzman, Ken*	2–3	39.7	1.8	3.0	0.88	4.66	5.77	6.90	-21	-2.1
0	72	137	32	Lyle, Sparky*	13–5	—	4.5	2.2	0.46	3.13	2.17	2.69	24	2.4
7	42	151	30	Tidrow, Dick	11–4	59.4	4.9	2.4	1.19	4.08	3.16	3.40	15	1.5
3	18	56	23	Clay, Ken	2–3	41.3	3.2	3.9	0.97	4.69	4.36	5.17	-6	-0.6
6	4	33	21	Patterson, Gil	1–2	44.8	7.8	5.4	0.81	4.23	5.41	5.41	-4	-0.4
3	0	20	32	Ellis, Dock	1–1	52.7	2.3	3.7	0.46	4.19	1.83	4.11	0	0.0
0	5	12		Others	1–1	—	0.7	3.7	0.73	4.94	5.12	10.24	-8	-0.8
162	154		28.2	Team Total		53.0	4.71	3.02	0.86	4.01	3.61	4.04	39	3.9
				League Average		49.0	5.00	3.24	0.90	4.07	4.06	4.56		
				% Lg Avg		108	94	107	104	102	112	113		
				League Rank		3	11	4	8	8	3			

1977 Los Angeles Dodgers

The Dodgers had another terrific team easily leading the NL in fewest runs allowed. The Reds won 14 fewer games than their 1976 championship team finishing second to the Dodgers in the NL West.

Strengths: (1) hitting featuring four players who each hit 30 or more HR: Reggie Smith (32), Baker (30), Garvey (33), and Cey (30), (2) drawing walks especially from Smith (104 BB) and Cey (93 BB), (3) baserunning led by

Lopes (47 SB, 12 CS, 3 GIDP), (4) infield fielding led by SS Russell (103 Rng+, 102 DP), 2B Lopes (105 Rng+), 3B Cey (108 Rng+), and C Yeager (39% CS, 3.28 ERA), (5) Held+ by RF Smith (104), and (6) pitching anchored by Hooton (77% QS), Cy Young runner-up John (74% QS), Sutton (64%), Rau (56% QS), Sosa (28/35/80% IR stranded), Garman (12/17/71% Sv, 25/36/69% IR stranded, 1.694 Lv), and Hough (22/27/81% Sv, 16/31/52% IR stranded, 1.782 Lv).

Weaknesses: (1) CF position, (2) hitting from Russell and Burke, (3) bench hitting except Mota, (4) baserunning from Cey (23% RS), and (5) fielding from CF Monday (75 Rng+) and reserve CF Burke (75 Rng+, 89 Held+).

				W	L	Win%
Mgr	Tommy Lasorda		**Regular Season**	98	64	0.605
Rk	16	59	**Runs Record**	103	59	0.635
Gm	162		**1 Run**	32	31	0.508
Place	1		**Extra Innings**	9	11	0.450
GA	10.0		**Blowout**	27	5	0.844
Rival	8–10 vs Reds, 75 RS, 73 RA; 6–6 vs Phillies, 50 RS, 52 RA					

	Team	LgAvg	%Avg	LgRk
BABIP	0.282	0.287	102	5
E	124	144	116	3
sOBP	0.305	0.329	108	1
rOBP	0.317	0.325	103	7
R/G	4.75	4.40	108	3
RA/G	3.59	4.40	123	1

	Tm	LgAvg	>Avg
RS	769	713	56
RA	582	713	131
DP	160	145	15

	R/G	HR	K	BB	SB	CS	SB%	OPS		Held+
Team Offense	4.75	191	896	588	114	62	65%	0.753	**LF**	101
Team Defense	3.59	119	930	438	108	59	65%	0.676	**CF**	101
Difference	1.15	72	34	150	6			112%	**RF**	110

Pos	Rpos	PA	Age	Name	BA	OBP	SLG	BB%	XBT	Bat R>Avg	BR R>Avg	Fld R>Avg	RAA	WAA
C	7	438	28	Yeager, Steve	0.256	0.334	0.444	10%	48%	7	1	6	21	2.1
1B	-9	696	28	Garvey, Steve	0.297	0.335	0.498	5%	58%	22	2	6	21	2.1
2B	4	589	32	Lopes, Davey	0.283	0.372	0.406	12%	50%	13	6	9	32	3.3
3B	4	669	29	Cey, Ron	0.241	0.347	0.450	14%	42%	16	-4	4	20	2.0
SS	10	673	28	Russell, Bill	0.278	0.304	0.360	4%	62%	-15	1	15	11	1.1
LF	-6	604	28	Baker, Dusty	0.291	0.364	0.512	10%	47%	29	0	-2	21	2.1
CF	0	456	31	Monday, Rick*	0.230	0.330	0.383	13%	47%	-1	1	-10	-10	-1.0
RF	-5	603	32	Smith, Reggie^	0.307	0.427	0.576	17%	45%	54	1	0	50	5.1
2B,RF	0	180	29	Lacy, Lee	0.266	0.306	0.414	6%	40%	-1	1	-2	-2	-0.2
CF	0	175	24	Burke, Glenn	0.254	0.280	0.320	3%	47%	-8	1	-7	-14	-1.4
C	3	171	31	Oates, Johnny*	0.269	0.314	0.353	6%	38%	-3	0	-1	-1	-0.1
2B,SS	2	143	29	Martinez, Ted	0.299	0.309	0.380	1%	55%	-2	0	-3	-3	-0.3
RF,OF	-3	124	23	Hale, John*	0.241	0.331	0.352	12%	28%	-1	0	4	0	0.0
LF	0	50	39	Mota, Manny	0.395	0.521	0.500	20%	0%	5	-1	0	4	0.4
	-7	757		Others	0.198	0.247	0.246	6%	23%	-57	-3	-8	-75	-7.5
	0		29.4	Team Total	0.266	0.336	0.418	9.3%	45%	58	6	11	75	7.6
				League Average	0.262	0.328	0.396	8.7%	45%					
				% Lg Avg	101	102	105	107	99					
				League Rank	5	3	3	3	7		4	6		

GS	GR	IP	Age	Name	W–L	GmSc	K/9	BB/9	HR/9	FIP	ERA	RA/9	RAA	WAA
33	0	240	32	Sutton, Don	14–8	57.5	5.6	2.6	0.86	3.73	3.18	3.48	23	2.3
31	1	223	27	Hooton, Burt	12–7	60.0	6.2	2.4	0.56	3.09	2.62	2.98	34	3.4
31	0	220	34	John, Tommy*	20–7	55.7	5.0	2.0	0.49	3.14	2.78	3.35	24	2.4
31	0	216	24	Rhoden, Rick	16–10	51.9	5.1	2.6	0.83	3.82	3.74	4.08	6	0.6
32	0	212	28	Rau, Doug*	14–8	52.4	5.3	2.1	0.64	3.34	3.43	3.69	15	1.5
1	69	127	29	Hough, Charlie	6–12	67.0	7.4	4.9	0.71	3.91	3.32	3.75	8	0.8
0	44	64	27	Sosa, Elias	2–2	—	6.6	1.7	0.99	3.29	1.98	2.12	16	1.6
0	49	63	27	Garman, Mike	4–4	—	4.2	3.2	1.01	4.30	2.73	2.87	10	1.0
0	25	32	26	Wall, Stan*	2–3	—	6.2	3.7	0.84	3.83	5.34	5.63	-5	-0.5
0	25	21	24	Rautzhan, Lance*	4–1	—	5.7	3.0	0.00	2.48	4.35	4.35	0	0.0
3	25	56		Others	4–2	—	6.4	3.7	1.28	4.51	4.79	4.79	-3	-0.3
162	238		27.8	Team Total		55	5.67	2.67	0.73	3.54	3.22	3.55	128	12.9
				League Average		49	5.39	3.33	0.84	3.91	3.91	4.40		
				% Lg Avg		112	105	125	115	111	121	124		
				League Rank		1	2	1	4	1	1			

1978 Los Angeles Dodgers

The Dodgers edged the Reds to repeat as winners of the NL West but lost again to the Yankees in 6 games in the Series. The Dodgers led the NL in runs scored and fewest runs allowed. Forster was signed as a free agent and had his best season as the closer and North was obtained from the A's to shore up the CF position.

Strengths: (1) hitting for average and power led by Smith (27 2B, 29 HR), MVP runner-up Garvey (36 2B, 9 3B, 21 HR, 319 TB, 202 H), Cey (32 2B, 23 HR), and Lopes (25 2B, 17 HR), (2) drawing walks featuring Cey (96 BB), Lopes (71 BB), and Smith (70 BB), (3) baserunning especially from Lopes (45 SB, 4 CS, 35% RS) and North (27 SB, 8 CS, 39% RS, 4 GIDP), (4) fielding led by C Yeager (3.18 ERA, 47% CS) and LF Baker (101 Rng+, 13 assists, 106 Held+), and (5) pitching anchored by Cy Young runner-up Hooton (78% QS), rookie Welch (77% QS), and closer Forster (22/26/85% Sv, 32/40/80% IR stranded, 1.965 Lv).

Weaknesses: (1) hitting from Yeager, (2) baserunning from Ferguson (9 GIDP, 17% RS), (3) fielding from CF Monday (86 Rng+) and RF Smith (93 Rng+), and (4) CS% from Grote (19 SB, 2 CS, 10%).

Mgr	Tommy Lasorda	
Rk	35	105
Gm	162	
Place	1	
GA	2.5	
Rival	9–9 vs Reds, 80 RS, 76 RA; 7–5 vs Phillies, 48 RS, 55 RA	

	W	*L*	*Win%*
Regular Season	95	67	0.586
Runs Record	100	62	0.618
1 Run	28	28	0.500
Extra Innings	11	5	0.688
Blowout	23	9	0.719

	Team	*LgAvg*	*%Avg*	*LgRk*
BABIP	0.275	0.280	102	4
E	140	140	100	7
sOBP	0.306	0.316	103	3
rOBP	0.312	0.331	106	2
R/G	4.49	3.99	113	1
RA/G	3.54	3.99	113	1

	Tm	*LgAvg*	*>Avg*
RS	727	645	82
RA	573	645	72
DP	138	141	-3

	R/G	*HR*	*BB*	*BB*	*SB*	*CS*	*SB%*	*OPS*
Team Offense	4.49	149	818	610	137	52	72%	0.740
Team Defense	3.54	107	800	440	105	56	65%	0.662
Difference	0.95	42	-18	170	32			112%

Pos	*Rpos*	*PA*	*Age*	*Name*	*BA*	*OBP*	*SLG*	*BB%*	*XBT*	*Bat R>Avg*	*BR R>Avg*	*Fld R>Avg*	*RAA*	*WAA*
C	5	266	29	Yeager, Steve	0.193	0.301	0.276	14%	21%	-8	0	12	9	0.9
1B	-9	689	29	Garvey, Steve	0.316	0.353	0.499	6%	46%	34	-1	3	27	2.9
2B	5	665	33	Lopes, Davey	0.278	0.355	0.421	11%	54%	18	9	-2	30	3.2
3B	4	667	30	Cey, Ron	0.270	0.380	0.452	14%	41%	32	-1	1	36	3.8
SS	10	672	29	Russell, Bill	0.286	0.320	0.365	4%	74%	-3	3	2	12	1.3
LF	-6	579	29	Baker, Dusty	0.262	0.325	0.375	8%	41%	2	2	8	6	0.6
CF	0	377	30	North, Bill^	0.234	0.371	0.266	17%	51%	-1	3	2	4	0.4
RF	-5	531	33	Smith, Reggie^	0.295	0.382	0.559	13%	48%	42	2	-6	33	3.4
CF,RF	-2	397	32	Monday, Rick*	0.254	0.348	0.468	12%	47%	15	-1	-5	7	0.7
RF,2B	-1	276	30	Lacy, Lee	0.261	0.335	0.518	10%	50%	13	-2	-2	8	0.8
C	4	235	31	Ferguson, Joe	0.237	0.350	0.399	14%	26%	5	-5	-1	3	0.3
C	2	83	35	Grote, Jerry	0.271	0.354	0.343	12%	30%	1	0	-4	-1	-0.1
RF,OF	0	81	41	Davalillo, Vic*	0.312	0.333	0.390	4%	47%	1	1	1	3	0.3
C	1	80	32	Oates, Johnny*	0.307	0.350	0.320	6%	20%	0	0	-1	0	0.0
	-8	627		Others	0.178	0.219	0.207	4%	32%	-51	1	-4	-62	-6.6
	0			Team Total	0.264	0.338	0.402	9.8%	46%	98	11	4	113	12.0
				League Average	0.254	0.320	0.372	8.6%	43%					
				% Lg Avg	104	105	108	114	107					
				League Rank	1	1	1	2	3		2	3		

GS	*GR*	*IP*	*Age*	*Name*	*W–L*	*GmSc*	*K/9*	*BB/9*	*HR/9*	*FIP*	*ERA*	*RA/9*	*RAA*	*WAA*
34	0	238	33	Sutton, Don	15–11	54.8	5.8	2.0	1.10	3.71	3.55	4.12	-3	-0.3
32	0	236	28	Hooton, Burt	19–10	58.8	4.0	2.3	0.65	3.55	2.71	2.82	31	3.3
30	3	213	35	John, Tommy*	17–10	51.8	5.2	2.2	0.46	2.99	3.30	4.01	0	-0.1
30	0	199	29	Rau, Doug*	15–9	51.3	4.3	3.1	0.77	3.90	3.26	3.71	6	0.7
23	7	165	25	Rhoden, Rick	10–8	51.6	4.3	2.8	0.71	3.82	3.66	4.21	-4	-0.4
13	10	111	21	Welch, Bob	7–4	59.8	5.3	2.1	0.49	2.96	2.02	2.26	21	2.3
0	47	65	26	Forster, Terry*	5–4	—	6.3	3.2	0.28	2.63	1.93	2.62	10	1.1
0	55	93	30	Hough, Charlie	5–5	—	6.4	4.6	0.58	3.77	3.28	3.67	3	0.4
0	43	61	25	Rautzhan, Lance*	2–1	—	3.7	2.8	0.15	3.00	2.94	3.23	5	0.5
0	18	34	23	Castillo, Bobby	0–4	—	7.9	8.7	0.53	4.06	3.97	5.03	-4	-0.4

GS	GR	IP	Age	Name	W–L	GmSc	K/9	BB/9	HR/9	FIP	ERA	RA/9	RAA	WAA
0	15	24		Others	0–1	—	4.1	1.5	1.12	4.10	3.73	3.73	1	0.1
162	198			Team Total		54	5.00	2.75	0.67	3.50	3.12	3.58	66	7.0
				League Average		52	5.14	3.26	0.66	3.58	3.57	4.02		
				% Lg Avg		104	97	119	99	102	114	112		
				League Rank		3	8	2	8	6	1			

1979 BALTIMORE ORIOLES

The 1979 season featured a terrific Oriole team who won the AL East by 8 games leading the AL in fewest runs allowed and run differentiation. The Orioles were the class of the AL in 1979 spending most of the season comfortably in front of the AL East. However, the O's lost the World Series to the Pirates in 7 games.

Strengths: (1) hitting led by MVP runner-up Singleton (29 2B, 35 HR), Murray (30 2B, 25 HR), and Roenicke (25 HR), (2) drawing walks featuring Singleton (109 BB) and Murray (72 BB), (3) fielding from C Dempsey (48% CS, 3.15 ERA), 2B/3B Dauer (93 Rng+ at 2B, 94 Rng+ at 3B), 3B DeCinces (97 Rng+), SS Belanger (96 Rng+), and CF Bumbry (96 Rng+), and (4) pitching from Cy Young winner Flanagan (71% QS, 190 K), McGregor (48% QS), Stoddard (5 Holds, 14/28/50% IR stranded, 1.372 Lv) and Stanhouse (21/27/78% Sv, 29/51/57% IR stranded, 2.258 Lv). The baserunning leader was Bumbry (37 SB, 12 CS, 36% RS, 6 GIDP).

Weaknesses: (1) hitting for average and contact, (2) hitting from the SS position (Garcia & Belanger), Dauer, and Dempsey, (3) fielding from RF Singleton (84 Rng+, 92 Held+) and C Skaggs (25% CS), and (4) % IR stranded.

				W	L	Win%
Mgr	Earl Weaver		**Regular Season**	102	57	0.642
Rk	24	73	**Runs Record**	100	59	0.632
Gm	159		**1 Run**	32	20	0.615
Place	1		**Extra Innings**	11	5	0.688
GA	8.0		**Blowout**	24	9	0.727
Rival	8–5 vs Brewers, 66 RS, 59 RA; 8–5 vs Red Sox, 72 RS, 53 RA					

	Team	LgAvg	%Avg	LgRk
BABIP	0.258	0.286	111	1
E	125	140	112	3
sOBP	0.298	0.331	111	1
rOBP	0.313	0.343	110	2
R/G	4.76	4.67	102	6
RA/G	3.66	4.67	127	1

	Tm	LgAvg	>Avg
RS	757	752	5
RA	582	752	170
DP	161	166	-5

	R/G	HR	K	BB	SB	CS	SB%	OPS
Team Offense	4.76	181	847	608	99	49	67%	0.755
Team Defense	3.66	133	786	467	88	58	60%	0.667
Difference	1.10	48	-61	141	11			113%

	Held+
LF	106
CF	103
RF	94

Pos	Rpos	PA	Age	Name	BA	OBP	SLG	BB%	XBT	Bat R>Avg	BR R>Avg	Fld R>Avg	RAA	WAA
C	8	413	29	Dempsey, Rick	0.239	0.307	0.351	9%	29%	-11	0	12	9	0.8
1B	-9	687	23	Murray, Eddie^	0.295	0.369	0.475	10%	42%	23	-2	8	20	2.0
2B,3B	4	528	26	Dauer, Rich	0.257	0.305	0.355	7%	46%	-14	0	14	4	0.4
3B	3	484	28	DeCinces, Doug	0.230	0.318	0.412	11%	47%	-2	0	9	10	0.9
SS,2B	8	457	25	Garcia, Kiko	0.247	0.303	0.362	7%	61%	-13	-2	3	-4	-0.4
LF,CF	-6	453	24	Roenicke, Gary	0.261	0.378	0.508	13%	48%	21	-1	8	22	2.1
CF	0	621	32	Bumbry, Al*	0.285	0.336	0.376	7%	57%	-6	5	7	6	0.6
RF,DH	-7	688	32	Singleton, Ken^	0.295	0.405	0.533	16%	41%	44	1	-4	34	3.4
DH	0	491	36	May, Lee	0.254	0.297	0.412	6%	40%	-8	-2	0	-10	-1.0
SS	4	242	35	Belanger, Mark	0.167	0.273	0.217	12%	54%	-18	1	8	-5	-0.4
LF,RF	-4	232	32	Lowenstein, John*	0.254	0.351	0.482	13%	39%	7	1	7	11	1.0
2B	2	214	25	Smith, Billy^	0.249	0.309	0.434	7%	41%	-1	1	4	6	0.6
LF,DH	-3	177	34	Kelly, Pat*	0.288	0.367	0.536	11%	47%	9	-1	-1	4	0.4
C	3	152	28	Skaggs, Dave	0.248	0.313	0.328	9%	13%	-5	-2	-4	-8	-0.8
LF,DH	-2	94	28	Ayala, Bennie	0.256	0.298	0.523	6%	29%	2	0	3	3	0.3
DH	0	78	32	Crowley, Terry*	0.317	0.449	0.476	18%	50%	5	0	0	5	0.5
	-1	95		Others	0.200	0.269	0.224	8%	30%	-8	1	0	-8	-0.7
	0		29.3	Team Total	0.261	0.336	0.419	10.0%	44%	25	0	74	99	9.7
				League Average	0.270	0.334	0.408	8.6%	46%					

Pos	Rpos	PA	Age	Name	BA	OBP	SLG	BB%	XBT	Bat R>Avg	BR R>Avg	Fld R>Avg	RAA	WAA
				% Lg Avg	97	101	103	116	96					
				League Rank	11	8	5	2	10		7	1		

GS	GR	IP	Age	Name	W–L	GmSc	K/9	BB/9	HR/9	FIP	ERA	RA/9	RAA	WAA
39	1	292	24	Martinez, Dennis	15–16	54.0	4.1	2.4	0.86	3.99	3.66	3.97	9	0.8
38	1	266	27	Flanagan, Mike*	23–9	58.0	6.4	2.4	0.78	3.36	3.08	3.62	19	1.9
32	0	186	31	Stone, Steve	11–7	51.0	4.6	3.5	1.50	5.16	3.77	4.40	-3	-0.3
23	4	175	25	McGregor, Scott*	13–6	54.0	4.2	1.2	0.98	3.77	3.35	3.61	12	1.2
22	1	156	33	Palmer, Jim	10–6	54.0	3.9	2.5	0.69	3.82	3.30	3.82	7	0.7
2	7	30	22	Ford, Dave	2–1	54.0	2.1	2.1	0.60	3.95	2.10	2.10	7	0.7
0	52	73	28	Stanhouse, Don	7–3	0.0	4.2	6.3	0.50	4.49	2.85	2.97	11	1.0
3	28	118	24	Stewart, Sammy	8–5	67.0	5.4	5.4	0.84	4.69	3.52	3.59	9	0.9
0	39	78	29	Martinez, Tippy*	10–3	0.0	7.0	3.6	0.00	2.36	2.88	3.35	8	0.8
0	29	58	26	Stoddard, Tim	3–1	0.0	7.3	2.9	0.47	2.78	1.71	1.86	16	1.5
0	5	4		Others	0–0	0.0	0.0	2.5	0.00	3.67	0.00	0.00	2	0.2
			26.9	Team Total		54	4.93	2.93	0.83	3.92	3.28	3.65	97	9.5
				League Average		49	4.54	3.33	0.90	4.23	4.22	4.72		
				% Lg Avg		110	109	114	108	108	129	129		
				League Rank		1	3	5	6	2	1			

1985 Toronto Blue Jays

In 1985, both the Blue Jays and Yankees had an impressive run differentiation of 1.1 per game and fought each other in a two team race until the last weekend of the season for the AL East divisional crown. The Yankees led the AL in runs scored while the Blue Jays led the AL in fewest runs allowed. Caudill, Henke, and Lavelle were obtained in the offseason to shore up the relief staff. Both the Yankees and the Blue Jays each won 10 more games than they had won in 1984. The Blue Jays captured their first divisional title since the franchise was formed in 1977. In the postseason, this team lost to the Royals in the ALCS in 7 games.

Strengths: (1) hitting for average & power led by Barfield (34 2B, 9 3B, 27 HR), Mulliniks (26 2B), Bell (28 2B, 28 HR), Upshaw (31 2B), and Moseby (30 2B), (2) fielding led by SS Fernandez (104 Rng+, 109 DP) and RF Barfield (112 Rng+, 22 assists, 8 DP), (3) Held+ from LF Bell (112), (4) CS% from Martinez (37%), (5) pitching anchored by the top 3 starters: Stieb (75% QS, 167 K), Key (56% QS), and Alexander (61% QS), and 6% IR stranded.

Weaknesses: (1) 2B position, (2) hitting from 2B Garcia and reserves Matuszek, Martinez, and Oliver, (3) pitching from Leal (29% QS, 11.0 H/9), and (4) Held+ from CF Moseby (90).

Mgr	Bobby Cox	
Rk	26	76
Gm	161	
Place	1	
GA	2.0	
Rival	7–6 vs Yankees, 47 RS, 49 RA; 5–7 vs Royals, 46 RS, 41 RA	

	W	L	Win%
Regular Season	99	62	0.615
Runs Record	101	60	0.628
1 Run	26	21	0.553
Extra Innings	12	5	0.706
Blowout	30	10	0.750

	Team	LgAvg	%Avg	LgRk
BABIP	0.260	0.281	108	1
E	125	129	103	6
sOBP	0.302	0.328	109	1
rOBP	0.315	0.326	103	4
R/G	4.71	4.56	103	4
RA/G	3.65	4.56	125	1

	Tm	LgAvg	>Avg
RS	759	737	22
RA	588	737	149
DP	164	159	5

	R/G	HR	K	BB	SB	CS	SB%	OPS	Held+	
Team Offense	4.71	158	807	503	144	77	65%	0.756	**LF**	115
Team Defense	3.65	147	823	484	83	44	65%	0.681	**CF**	86
Difference	1.06	11	16	19	61			111%	**RF**	101

Pos	Rpos	PA	Age	Name	BA	OBP	SLG	BB%	XBT	Bat R>Avg	BR R>Avg	Fld R>Avg	RAA	WAA
C	7	465	33	Whitt, Ernie*	0.245	0.323	0.444	10%	36%	4	-2	4	13	1.3
1B	-8	557	28	Upshaw, Willie*	0.275	0.342	0.447	9%	51%	10	0	8	10	1.0
2B	4	627	28	Garcia, Damaso	0.282	0.302	0.377	2%	46%	-13	-1	3	-7	-0.7

Pos	Rpos	PA	Age	Name	BA	OBP	SLG	BB%	XBT	Bat R>Avg	BR R>Avg	Fld R>Avg	RAA	WAA
3B	1	427	29	Mulliniks, Rance*	0.295	0.383	0.454	13%	51%	16	0	3	20	2.0
SS	10	618	23	Fernandez, Tony^	0.289	0.340	0.390	7%	63%	0	0	12	22	2.2
LF	-6	666	25	Bell, George	0.275	0.327	0.479	6%	55%	14	6	4	18	1.8
CF	1	670	25	Moseby, Lloyd*	0.259	0.345	0.426	11%	52%	9	0	3	13	1.3
RF,CF	-6	612	25	Barfield, Jesse	0.289	0.369	0.536	11%	53%	33	1	23	51	5.0
DH	0	227	34	Burroughs, Jeff	0.257	0.366	0.429	15%	25%	6	-2	0	4	0.3
3B	2	312	30	Iorg, Garth	0.313	0.358	0.469	7%	38%	9	-3	1	9	0.9
DH	0	195	38	Oliver, Al*	0.251	0.282	0.374	4%	30%	-6	0	0	-6	-0.6
DH	0	166	30	Matuszek, Len*	0.212	0.259	0.318	7%	87%	-9	1	1	-7	-0.7
C	2	113	36	Martinez, Buck	0.162	0.239	0.313	9%	17%	-7	0	1	-4	-0.4
1B	-1	81	21	Fielder, Cecil	0.311	0.358	0.527	7%	50%	4	0	2	5	0.5
	-6	371		Others	0.208	0.254	0.260	6%	48%	-28	0	6	-28	-2.7
	0		28.9	Team Total	0.269	0.331	0.425	8.2%	50%	43	0	71	114	11.3
				League Average	0.261	0.327	0.406	8.6%	44%					
				% Lg Avg	103	101	105	95	113					
				League Rank	2	5	4	10	2		7	1		

GS	GR	IP	Age	Name	W–L	GmSc	K/9	BB/9	HR/9	FIP	ERA	RA/9	RAA	WAA
36	0	265	27	Stieb, Dave	14–13	60.1	5.7	3.3	0.75	3.80	2.48	3.02	34	3.4
36	0	261	34	Alexander, Doyle	17–10	53.6	4.9	2.3	0.97	3.97	3.45	3.63	15	1.5
32	3	213	24	Key, Jimmy*	14–6	54.4	3.6	2.1	0.93	4.09	3.00	3.26	21	2.1
23	0	129	29	Clancy, Jim	9–6	51.5	4.6	2.6	1.05	4.18	3.78	3.78	5	0.5
14	1	67	28	Leal, Luis	3–6	43.0	4.4	3.2	1.74	5.42	5.75	6.15	-15	-1.5
9	2	49	28	Filer, Tom	7–0	52.4	4.4	3.3	1.11	4.55	3.88	3.88	2	0.2
0	67	69	28	Caudill, Bill	4–6	—	6.0	4.5	1.17	4.53	2.99	3.38	6	0.6
1	52	106	32	Lamp, Dennis	11–0	54.0	5.8	2.3	0.60	3.08	3.32	3.58	7	0.7
0	61	86	26	Acker, Jim	7–2	—	4.4	4.5	0.73	4.47	3.23	3.65	5	0.5
0	69	73	36	Lavelle, Gary*	5–7	—	6.2	4.5	0.62	3.62	3.10	3.72	4	0.4
0	28	40	27	Henke, Tom	3–3	—	9.5	1.8	0.90	2.47	2.03	2.70	7	0.7
10	33	91		Others	5–3	—	5.7	4.3	0.89	4.22	4.25	5.04	-9	-0.9
161	316		29.0	Team Total		54.0	5.12	3.01	0.91	4.01	3.31	3.65	81	8.0
				League Average		49.0	5.25	3.33	0.97	4.15	4.15	4.60		
				% Lg Avg		110	97	111	106	103	125	126		
				League Rank		1	8	3	3	5	1			

1985 St. Louis Cardinals

The 1985 Cardinals used their tremendous speed to help win 24 more games than they had won in 1984 to capture the divisional crown by 3 games over a tough Met team that won 98 games by leading the league in fewest runs allowed. The Cardinals, who led the NL in runs scored, were able to conquer the Dodgers in 6 games in the NLCS, but lost to the overachieving Royals in 7 games in the World Series. The 1985 Cardinals were one of only two teams since 1912 to steal over 300 bases. Before the season, Tudor was obtained from the Pirates in a trade for George Hendrick and Clark was obtained in a trade with the Giants. Cedeno came over from the Reds in late August.

Strengths: (1) hitting led by MVP McGee (26 2B, 18 3B, 216 Hits, 308 TB), Clark (26 2B, 22 HR), Herr (38 2B), Cedeno, and Van Slyke (25 2B), (2) drawing walks featuring Clark (83 BB) and Herr (80 BB), (3) baserunning featuring RoY Coleman (110 SB, 25 CS, 3 GIDP, 48% RS), McGee (56 SB, 16 CS, 3 GIDP, 43% RS), Van Slyke (34 SB, 6 CS, 7 GIDP), Herr (31 SB, 3 CS, 6 GIDP), and Smith (31 SB, 8 CS), (4) fielding led by SS Smith (106 Rng+. 111 DP), 3B Pendleton (121 Rng+, 26 DP), RF Van Slyke (103 Rng+, 114 Held+, 13 assists), LF Coleman (111 Rng+, 109 Held+, 16 assists), and CF McGee (103 Rng+, 11 assists), and (5) pitching anchored by Cy Young runner-up Tudor (75% QS), Cox (74% QS), and Lahti (19/20/95% Sv).

Weaknesses: (1) C position, (2) power, (3) Pendleton's hitting, (4) fielding from 1B Clark and C Nieto (19% CS), and (5) Kepshire's pitching (45% QS).

Mgr	Whitey Herzog	
Rk	42	120
Gm	162	
Place	1	
GA	3.0	
Rival	10–8 vs Mets, RS 70, RA 53; 5–7 vs Dodgers, 35 RS, 39 RA	

	W	*L*	*Win%*
Regular Season	101	61	0.623
Runs Record	99	63	0.613
1 Run	28	19	0.596
Extra Innings	9	11	0.450
Blowout	38	15	0.717

	Team	*LgAvg*	*%Avg*	*LgRk*
BABIP	0.270	0.280	104	2
E	108	135	125	1
sOBP	0.302	0.315	104	3
rOBP	0.311	0.327	105	2
R/G	4.61	4.07	113	1
RA/G	3.53	4.07	115	2

	Tm	*LgAvg*	*>Avg*
RS	747	658	89
RA	572	658	86
DP	166	150	16

	R/G	*HR*	*K*	*BB*	*SB*	*CS*	*SB%*	*OPS*
Team Offense	4.61	87	853	586	314	96	77%	0.714
Team Defense	3.53	98	798	453	104	37	74%	0.659
Difference	1.08	-11	-55	133	210			108%

Held+	
LF	100
CF	103
RF	113

Pos	*Rpos*	*PA*	*Age*	*Name*	*BA*	*OBP*	*SLG*	*BB%*	*XBT*	*Bat R>Avg*	*BR R>Avg*	*Fld R>Avg*	*RAA*	*WAA*
C	5	288	24	Nieto, Tom	0.225	0.305	0.281	9%	28%	-9	-3	-5	-12	-1.3
1B	-7	532	29	Clark, Jack	0.281	0.393	0.502	16%	31%	35	-3	-10	15	1.6
2B	5	696	29	Herr, Tom^	0.302	0.379	0.416	11%	53%	27	5	-5	32	3.3
3B	2	602	24	Pendleton, Terry^	0.240	0.285	0.306	6%	61%	-21	-1	24	4	0.5
SS	10	615	30	Smith, Ozzie^	0.276	0.355	0.361	11%	62%	7	5	20	42	4.4
LF,OF	-6	692	23	Coleman, Vince^	0.267	0.320	0.335	7%	46%	-8	12	7	5	0.5
CF	1	652	26	McGee, Willie^	0.353	0.384	0.503	5%	60%	41	9	5	56	5.9
RF,CF	-5	475	24	Van Slyke, Andy*	0.259	0.335	0.439	10%	51%	12	4	9	20	2.1
C	4	284	33	Porter, Darrell*	0.221	0.335	0.413	14%	37%	5	2	3	14	1.5
1B	-1	82	34	Cedeno, Cesar	0.434	0.463	0.750	6%	25%	14	0	-3	10	1.0
1B	-2	146	36	Jorgensen, Mike*	0.196	0.375	0.250	21%	23%	0	0	-2	-4	-0.5
LF	-1	115	29	Smith, Lonnie	0.260	0.377	0.323	13%	57%	1	0	0	0	0.0
RF	-2	181	30	Landrum, Tito	0.280	0.356	0.429	10%	45%	5	-2	4	5	0.6
RF,LF	0	79	37	Braun, Steve*	0.239	0.342	0.343	13%	20%	0	1	0	1	0.1
	-3	743		Others	0.172	0.222	0.229	6%	29%	-58	2	3	-56	-5.9
	0		29.1	Team Total	0.264	0.335	0.379	9.5%	47%	52	31	50	133	14.0
				League Average	0.252	0.319	0.374	8.6%	43%					
				% Lg Avg	105	105	101	110	109					
				League Rank	1	1	6	1	3		1	1		

GS	*GR*	*IP*	*Age*	*Name*	*W–L*	*GmSc*	*K/9*	*BB/9*	*HR/9*	*FIP*	*ERA*	*RA/9*	*RAA*	*WAA*
36	0	275	31	Tudor, John*	21–8	64.8	5.5	1.6	0.46	2.73	1.93	2.23	47	5.0
35	0	241	25	Cox, Danny	18–9	55.9	4.9	2.4	0.71	3.46	2.88	3.40	10	1.0
38	0	270	32	Andujar, Joaquin	21–12	53.0	3.7	2.7	0.50	3.55	3.40	3.77	-1	-0.1
19	15	136	35	Forsch, Bob	9–6	50.6	3.2	3.1	0.73	4.09	3.90	4.17	-6	-0.7
29	3	153	25	Kepshire, Kurt	10–9	47.3	3.9	4.2	0.94	4.57	4.76	5.23	-25	-2.7
0	52	68	28	Lahti, Jeff	5–2	—	5.4	3.4	0.40	2.83	1.84	1.98	14	1.4
0	6	12	26	Perry, Pat*	1–0	—	4.4	2.2	0.00	2.26	0.00	0.00	5	0.5
0	17	22	25	Worrell, Todd	3–0	—	7.1	2.9	0.83	3.08	2.90	2.90	2	0.2
0	57	65	26	Dayley, Ken*	4–4	—	8.5	2.5	0.28	1.67	2.76	3.31	4	0.4
0	50	64	36	Campbell, Bill	5–3	—	5.7	2.9	0.70	3.14	3.50	4.48	-5	-0.5
3	46	90	25	Horton, Ricky*	3–2	50.7	5.9	3.4	0.50	2.96	2.91	3.01	8	0.8
2	50	67		Others	1–6	—	6.0	4.1	0.80	3.69	4.27	5.34	-12	-1.2
162	296		28.5	Team Total		54.0	4.91	2.78	0.60	3.35	3.10	3.52	40	4.2
				League Average		52.0	5.50	3.28	0.73	3.60	3.59	4.07		
				% Lg Avg		104	89	118	122	107	116	116		
				League Rank		3	10	2	1	3	2			

1986 Mets

The 1986 Mets won 10 more games in 1986 compared to what they won in 1985 to have their best regular season record in franchise history. The Mets led the league in runs scored and led the NL East division in fewest runs allowed running away with their division. The Mets beat the Astros in an exciting 6 game NLCS and then beat the Red Sox in the World Series when Buckner made an error on a groundball in the seventh game of the World Series beginning a Met rally. Prior to the season, Ojeda came over from the Red Sox. This team featured 5 pitchers with 14 or more wins.

Strengths: (1) hitting led by Hernandez (34 2B), Strawberry (27 HR), Dykstra (27 2B), Carter (24 HR), Knight (24 2B), and Mitchell (22 2B), (2) drawing walks from Hernandez (94 BB) and Strawberry (72 BB), (3) baserunning from Wilson (25 SB, 7 CS, 39% RS, 5 GIDP), Dykstra (31 SB, 7 CS, 39% RS, 4 GIDP), and Backman (42% RS, 3 GIDP), (4) fielding from SS Santana (104 Rng+) and 1B Hernandez (149 assists), and (5) pitching anchored by Ojeda (70% QS), Darling (76% QS), Gooden (67% QS, 200 K, 7.6 IP/S), Fernandez (61% QS, 200 K), McDowell (22/28/79% Sv, 28/32/87% IR stranded), and Orosco (21/29/72% Sv, 31/40/78% IR stranded).

Weaknesses: (1) hitting from Santana, (2) fielding from 2B Teufel (83 Rng+), RF Strawberry (92 Rng+), and 3B Knight (85 Rng+), (3) CS% from Hearn (21%, 3.53 ERA) and Carter (28%), (4) Held+ from Wilson (85 in LF and 84 in CF), and (5) pitching from Aguilera.

					W	L	Win%		Team	LgAvg	%Avg	LgRk
Mgr	Davey Johnson			**Regular Season**	108	54	0.667	**BABIP**	0.274	0.285	104	4
Rk	27	81		**Runs Record**	101	61	0.624	**E**	138	139	101	7
Gm	162			**1 Run**	29	20	0.592	**sOBP**	0.294	0.319	109	2
Place	1			**Extra Innings**	13	10	0.565	**rOBP**	0.325	0.328	101	6
GA	21.5			**Blowout**	27	9	0.750	**R/G**	4.83	4.18	116	1
Rival	8–10 vs Phillies, 84 RS, 83 RA; 7–5 vs Astros, 54 RS, 40 RA							**RA/G**	3.57	4.18	117	2

	Tm	LgAvg	>Avg		R/G	HR	K	BB	SB	CS	SB%	OPS	Held+	
RS	783	675	108	**Team Offense**	4.83	148	968	631	118	48	71%	0.740	**LF**	94
RA	578	675	97	**Team Defense**	3.57	103	1083	509	159	55	74%	0.644	**CF**	103
DP	145	145	0	**Difference**	1.27	45	115	122	-41			115%	**RF**	106

Pos	Rpos	PA	Age	Name	BA	OBP	SLG	BB%	XBT	Bat R>Avg	BR R>Avg	Fld R>Avg	RAA	WAA
C,1B	7	573	32	Carter, Gary	0.255	0.337	0.439	11%	47%	15	-1	1	15	1.5
1B	-8	652	32	Hernandez, Keith*	0.310	0.413	0.446	14%	34%	37	-4	9	42	4.4
2B	3	440	26	Backman, Wally^	0.320	0.376	0.385	8%	65%	10	3	3	16	1.7
3B	2	541	33	Knight, Ray	0.298	0.351	0.424	7%	33%	14	-3	-5	6	0.6
SS	8	436	28	Santana, Rafael	0.218	0.285	0.254	8%	46%	-22	0	9	-13	-1.4
LF	-2	256	37	Foster, George	0.227	0.289	0.429	8%	41%	0	-1	-3	-4	-0.4
CF	1	498	23	Dykstra, Lenny*	0.295	0.377	0.445	12%	57%	20	5	4	29	3.0
RF	-5	562	24	Strawberry, Darryl*	0.259	0.358	0.507	13%	61%	29	0	-6	23	2.4
CF,LF	-3	415	30	Wilson, Mookie^	0.289	0.345	0.430	8%	64%	9	6	6	21	2.2
OF,SS	-1	364	24	Mitchell, Kevin	0.277	0.344	0.466	9%	60%	12	-1	4	15	1.6
2B	2	318	27	Teufel, Tim	0.247	0.324	0.369	10%	34%	0	-3	-7	-10	-1.1
3B,SS	3	253	25	Johnson, Howard^	0.245	0.341	0.445	12%	65%	7	2	-3	6	0.6
LF,RF	-2	227	28	Heep, Danny*	0.282	0.379	0.421	13%	43%	8	-2	-3	3	0.3
C	2	151	25	Hearn, Ed	0.265	0.322	0.390	8%	39%	0	-2	-4	-6	-0.6
	-7	663		Others	0.163	0.225	0.222	6%	34%	-54	-3	3	-54	-5.6
	0		28.1	Team Total	0.263	0.339	0.401	9.9%	48%	84	-4	8	88	9.1
				League Average	0.253	0.322	0.380	8.9%	45%					
				% Lg Avg	104	105	106	112	108					
				League Rank	1	2	1	1	2		7	5		

GS	GR	IP	Age	Name	W–L	GmSc	K/9	BB/9	HR/9	FIP	ERA	RA/9	RAA	WAA
33	0	250	21	Gooden, Dwight	17–6	61.2	7.2	2.9	0.61	3.14	2.84	3.31	23	2.3
34	0	237	25	Darling, Ron	15–6	58.5	7.0	3.1	0.80	3.52	2.81	3.19	25	2.6
30	2	217	28	Ojeda, Bobby*	18–5	59.6	6.1	2.2	0.62	3.12	2.57	2.98	28	2.9
31	1	204	23	Fernandez, Sid*	16–6	56.8	8.8	4.0	0.57	3.10	3.52	3.61	12	1.2
20	8	142	24	Aguilera, Rick	10–7	51.5	6.6	2.3	0.95	3.68	3.88	4.45	-5	-0.5
5	10	50	29	Anderson, Rick	2–1	56.0	3.8	2.0	0.54	3.31	2.72	3.08	6	0.6
0	75	128	25	McDowell, Roger	14–9	—	4.6	3.0	0.28	3.21	3.02	3.38	11	1.1
0	58	81	29	Orosco, Jesse*	8–6	—	6.9	3.9	0.67	3.61	2.33	2.56	14	1.5
0	41	71	28	Sisk, Doug	4–2	—	3.9	3.9	0.00	3.32	3.06	3.95	1	0.1
1	30	36	30	Niemann, Randy*	2–3	58.0	4.5	3.0	0.50	3.44	3.78	4.29	-1	-0.1
8	27	69		Others	2–3	—	6.6	5.0	0.92	4.46	5.11	5.51	-11	-1.1
162	252		26.2	Team Total		57.0	6.57	3.09	0.62	3.36	3.11	3.51	102	10.6
				League Average		51.0	6.00	3.38	0.78	3.73	3.72	4.17		
				% Lg Avg		112	109	109	126	111	119	119		
				League Rank		2	2	3	1	1	1			

1987 Toronto Blue Jays

The 1987 Blue Jays were in first place as late as Oct 2, but then an elbow injury struck SS Fernandez in the last week of the season. The Blue Jays lost 3 straight games in October to the Tigers who would win the division championship by 2 games. The Tigers led the majors in offense with 5.5 runs scored per game while the Blue Jays led the majors in fewest runs allowed. The Blue Jay team was one of the two best teams in the majors in 1987, but was stuck in the same division as the other best team, the Tigers.

Strengths: (1) hitting for average and power led by Bell (32 2B, 47 HR), Moseby (27 2B, 26 HR, 70 BB), rookie McGriff (20 HR, 60 BB), Mulliniks (28 2B), and Fernandez (29 2B, 8 3B), (2) baserunning featuring Moseby (39 SB, 7 CS, 38% RS), Fernandez (32 SB, 12 CS, 36% RS), and rookie Liriano (13 SB, 2 CS, 3 GIDP, 52% RS), (3) fielding especially from RF Barfield (112 Rng+, 17 assists), SS Fernandez (108 Rng+), 1B Upshaw (127 assists), and C Whitt (36% CS, 3.70 ERA), (4) Held+ from RF Barfield (125) and CF Moseby (110), and (5) pitching anchored by Cy Young runner-up Key (75% QS, 7.3 IP/S), Clancy (65% QS), Henke (34/42/81% Sv, 36/58/62% IR stranded, 1.829 Lv), and Eichhorn (70/97/72% IR stranded, 1.033 Lv).

Weaknesses: (1) hitting from infielders Iorg, Gruber, and Upshaw, (2) fielding from CF Moseby (77 Rng+) and C Moore (19% CS, 4.25 ERA), and (3) pitching from back of the rotation starter Joe Johnson (21% QS, 10.4 H/9) and starter/reliever Nunez (22% QS).

				W	L	Win%		Team	LgAvg	LgRk	%Avg
Mgr	Jimy Williams		**Regular Season**	96	66	0.593	**BABIP**	0.275	0.288	105	2
Rk	37	108	**Runs Record**	100	62	0.618	**E**	111	124	112	4
Gm	162		**1 Run**	27	24	0.529	**sOBP**	0.313	0.331	106	1
Place	2		**Extra Innings**	10	7	0.588	**rOBP**	0.323	0.339	105	1
GB	2.0		**Blowout**	29	12	0.707	**R/G**	5.22	4.90	106	3
Rival	6–7 vs Tigers, 50 RS, 46 RA; 9–3 vs Twins, 81 RS, 47 RA						**RA/G**	4.04	4.90	121	1

	Tm	LgAvg	>Avg		R/G	HR	K	BB	SB	CS	SB%	OPS	Held+	
RS	845	794	51	**Team Offense**	5.22	215	970	555	126	50	72%	0.782	**LF**	103
RA	655	794	139	**Team Defense**	4.04	158	1064	567	123	59	68%	0.712	**CF**	114
DP	148	151	-3	**Difference**	1.17	57	94	-12	3			110%	**RF**	121

Pos	Rpos	PA	Age	Name	BA	OBP	SLG	BB%	XBT	Bat R>Avg	BR R>Avg	Fld R>Avg	RAA	WAA
C	7	494	35	Whitt, Ernie*	0.269	0.334	0.455	9%	28%	4	-5	7	13	1.2
1B	-8	577	30	Upshaw, Willie*	0.244	0.324	0.391	10%	45%	-8	-1	14	-3	-0.3
2B,3B	3	342	32	Iorg, Garth	0.210	0.262	0.284	6%	52%	-24	0	4	-17	-1.7
3B,SS	3	368	25	Gruber, Kelly	0.235	0.283	0.399	5%	48%	-11	2	2	-4	-0.4
SS	8	642	25	Fernandez, Tony^	0.322	0.379	0.426	8%	55%	13	4	6	31	2.9
LF	-7	665	27	Bell, George	0.308	0.352	0.605	6%	47%	40	1	1	35	3.3
CF	1	670	27	Moseby, Lloyd*	0.282	0.358	0.473	10%	53%	16	5	-7	15	1.4
RF,CF	-6	654	27	Barfield, Jesse	0.263	0.331	0.458	9%	49%	5	-1	25	23	2.2
DH,1B	0	356	23	McGriff, Fred*	0.247	0.376	0.505	17%	39%	14	1	-2	13	1.3
3B,DH	-1	372	31	Mulliniks, Rance*	0.310	0.371	0.500	9%	38%	14	-3	3	13	1.2
RF,DH	-5	224	30	Leach, Rick*	0.282	0.371	0.405	11%	43%	2	0	2	-1	-0.1
DH,1B	0	197	23	Fielder, Cecil	0.269	0.345	0.560	10%	14%	8	-1	-1	6	0.6
2B	1	176	23	Liriano, Nelson^	0.241	0.310	0.342	9%	47%	-6	3	3	1	0.1
2B,SS	2	129	22	Lee, Manuel^	0.270	0.303	0.365	5%	62%	-4	2	2	2	0.2
C	2	125	34	Moore, Charlie	0.213	0.303	0.352	10%	33%	-4	0	-7	-9	-0.9
	0	304		Others	0.211	0.275	0.342	8%	56%	-15	0	-2	-17	-1.6
	0		27.6	Team Total	0.269	0.336	0.446	8.8%	46%	42	7	50	99	9.5
				League Average	0.265	0.333	0.425	8.9%	45%					
				% Lg Avg	101	101	105	99	102					
				League Rank	5	4	2	8	7		6	2		

GS	GR	IP	Age	Name	W–L	GmSc	K/9	BB/9	HR/9	FIP	ERA	RA/9	RAA	WAA
36	0	261	26	Key, Jimmy*	17–8	59.4	5.6	2.3	0.83	3.62	2.76	3.21	42	4.0
37	0	241	31	Clancy, Jim	15–11	53.8	6.7	3.0	0.90	3.69	3.54	3.84	21	2.0
31	2	185	29	Stieb, Dave	13–9	50.4	5.6	4.2	0.78	4.29	4.09	4.48	3	0.3

GS	GR	IP	Age	Name	W–L	GmSc	K/9	BB/9	HR/9	FIP	ERA	RA/9	RAA	WAA
14	0	67	25	Johnson, Joe	3–5	44.4	3.6	2.4	1.35	4.99	5.13	5.94	-10	-1.0
21	23	151	27	Cerutti, John*	11–4	48.2	5.5	3.5	1.78	5.40	4.40	4.46	3	0.3
7	0	49	35	Flanagan, Mike*	3–2	59.4	7.8	2.7	0.55	2.73	2.37	2.74	10	1.0
0	72	94	29	Henke, Tom	0–6	—	12.3	2.4	0.96	2.31	2.49	2.59	22	2.1
0	89	128	26	Eichhorn, Mark	10–6	—	6.8	3.7	0.99	3.93	3.17	3.31	19	1.8
9	28	97	23	Nunez, Jose	5–2	45.6	9.2	5.4	1.11	4.06	5.01	5.29	-7	-0.6
1	67	89	24	Musselman, Jeff*	12–5	54.0	5.5	5.5	0.71	4.27	4.15	4.35	3	0.3
6	44	92		Others	7–8	—	6.8	5.2	0.79	4.12	5.40	5.79	-12	-1.1
162	325		27.5	Team Total		52	6.59	3.51	0.98	3.98	3.74	4.05	95	9.1
				League Average		49	5.99	3.48	1.17	4.47	4.46	4.95		
				% Lg Avg		106	110	99	120	112	119	122		
				League Rank		3	2	11	3	2	1			

1988 NEW YORK METS

The 1988 Mets won the division by double digits, led the NL in most runs scored, and led the majors in fewest runs allowed. The 1988 Mets were the best team in the majors in 1988. Unfortunately, they lost an exciting 7 game NLCS playoff series to a hot Dodger team who the Mets had consistently beaten during the regular season. Dykstra and Wilson platooned in CF and Backman and Teufel platooned at 2B.

Strengths: (1) hitting for average, contact, and power led by MVP runner-up Strawberry (39 HR), McReynolds (30 2B, 27 HR), and Johnson (24 HR), (2) drawing walks featuring Johnson (86 BB) and Strawberry (85 BB), (3) baserunning especially from Dykstra (30 SB, 8 CS, 35% RS, 3 GIDP), McReynolds (21 SB, 0 CS), and Johnson (23 SB, 7 CS), (4) Held+ by RF Strawberry (110), (5) pitching from all 5 starters: Cone (79% QS, 7.6 IP/S, 213 K), Fernandez (55% QS), Gooden (71% QS), Darling (76% QS), and Ojeda (66% QS), and (6) relief pitching from Myers (26/29/90% Sv, 44/54/81% IR stranded, 1.921 Lv), McDowell (7 Holds, 16/20/80% Sv, 29/33/88% IR stranded, 1.656 Lv), and Leach (22/29/76% IR stranded, 0.761 Lv).

Weaknesses: (1) C position, (2) hitting from SS Elster, (3) baserunning from Carter (20% RS) and Magadan (26% RS), (4) CS% from Carter (19%) and Sasser (22%), and (5) fielding from LF McReynolds (89 Rng+), RF Strawberry, and CF Wilson (86 Rng+).

Mgr	Davey Johnson	
Rk	68	93
Gm	160	
Place	1	
GA	15.0	
Rival	12–6 vs Pirates, 65 RS, 46 RA; 10–1 vs Dodgers, 49 RS, 18 RA	

	W	L	Win%
Regular Season	100	60	0.625
Runs Record	100	60	0.624
1 Run	31	21	0.596
Extra Innings	9	5	0.643
Blowout	23	7	0.767

	Team	LgAvg	%Avg	LgRk
BABIP	0.279	0.279	100	8
E	115	132	115	1
sOBP	0.286	0.307	107	1
rOBP	0.306	0.319	104	2
R/G	4.39	3.88	113	1
RA/G	3.33	3.88	117	1

	Tm	LgAvg	>Avg
RS	703	627	76
RA	532	627	95
DP	127	134	-7

	R/G	HR	K	BB	SB	CS	SB%	OPS
Team Offense	4.39	152	842	544	140	51	73%	0.721
Team Defense	3.33	78	1100	404	204	52	80%	0.620
Difference	1.07	74	258	140	-64			116%

Held+	
LF	94
CF	101
RF	109

Pos	Rpos	PA	Age	Name	BA	OBP	SLG	BB%	XBT	Bat R>Avg	BR R>Avg	Fld R>Avg	RAA	WAA
C,1B	7	503	34	Carter, Gary	0.242	0.301	0.358	7%	30%	-2	-5	-10	-10	-1.1
1B	-5	384	34	Hernandez, Keith*	0.276	0.333	0.417	8%	61%	9	0	2	6	0.7
2B	3	347	28	Backman, Wally^	0.303	0.388	0.344	12%	55%	9	-2	4	14	1.5
3B,SS	5	594	27	Johnson, Howard^	0.230	0.343	0.422	14%	52%	19	4	-7	21	2.2
SS	8	450	23	Elster, Kevin	0.214	0.282	0.313	8%	60%	-12	2	1	-1	-0.1
LF	-6	600	28	McReynolds, Kevin	0.288	0.336	0.496	6%	56%	29	5	-8	20	2.1
CF	1	466	25	Dykstra, Lenny*	0.270	0.321	0.385	6%	61%	4	6	3	14	1.6
RF	-6	640	26	Strawberry, Darryl*	0.269	0.366	0.545	13%	46%	47	1	-6	36	3.8
CF,OF	-1	410	32	Wilson, Mookie^	0.296	0.345	0.431	7%	67%	13	1	-5	8	0.9

Pos	Rpos	PA	Age	Name	BA	OBP	SLG	BB%	XBT	Bat R>Avg	BR R>Avg	Fld R>Avg	RAA	WAA
1B,3B	-3	380	25	Magadan, Dave*	0.277	0.393	0.334	16%	34%	11	-5	2	5	0.5
2B	2	309	29	Teufel, Tim	0.234	0.306	0.352	9%	63%	-1	2	8	11	1.2
C	2	131	25	Sasser, Mackey*	0.285	0.313	0.407	5%	44%	2	-1	-4	-1	-0.1
3B,2B	1	118	20	Jefferies, Gregg^	0.321	0.364	0.596	7%	23%	10	0	-2	9	1.0
1B,LF	-1	132	33	Mazzilli, Lee	0.147	0.227	0.164	9%	60%	-11	1	-1	-12	-1.3
	-7	641		Others	0.209	0.238	0.286	3%	37%	-32	-3	-11	-53	-5.7
	0		27.8	Team Total	0.256	0.325	0.396	8.9%	51%	95	6	-34	67	7.2
				League Average	0.248	0.310	0.363	7.9%	45%					
				% Lg Avg	103	105	109	113	112					
				League Rank	2	1	1	2	1		4	9		

IP	GS	GR	Age	Name	W–L	GmSc	K/9	BB/9	HR/9	FIP	ERA	RA/9	RAA	WAA
248	34	0	23	Gooden, Dwight	18–9	56.7	6.3	2.1	0.29	2.56	3.19	3.55	15	1.6
241	34	0	27	Darling, Ron	17–9	56.6	6.0	2.2	0.90	3.58	3.25	3.63	12	1.3
231	28	7	25	Cone, David	20–3	64.9	8.3	3.1	0.39	2.56	2.22	2.61	38	4.0
190	29	0	30	Ojeda, Bobby*	10–13	58.2	6.3	1.6	0.28	2.40	2.88	3.50	12	1.3
187	31	0	25	Fernandez, Sid*	12–10	59.5	9.1	3.4	0.72	3.06	3.03	3.32	15	1.6
25	3	8	26	Aguilera, Rick	0–4	31.7	5.8	3.6	0.73	3.69	6.92	7.29	-9	-0.9
68	0	55	25	Myers, Randy*	7–3	—	9.1	2.3	0.66	2.52	1.72	1.99	16	1.7
92	0	52	34	Leach, Terry	7–2	—	5.0	2.3	0.49	3.19	2.54	3.13	10	1.1
89	0	62	27	McDowell, Roger	5–5	—	4.7	3.1	0.10	2.86	2.63	3.13	10	1.0
19	0	12	25	Innis, Jeff	1–1	—	6.6	0.9	0.00	1.52	1.89	2.84	3	0.3
49	1	45		Others	3–1	54.0	6.1	3.7	0.37	3.25	3.88	4.25	-1	-0.1
	160	241	26.7	Team Total		58.0	6.88	2.53	0.49	2.86	2.91	3.33	121	13.1
				League Average		53.0	5.68	2.98	0.66	3.45	3.45	3.87		
				% Lg Avg		109	121	118	135	121	119	116		
				League Rank		1	1	1	2	1	1			

1993 Atlanta Braves

The NL expanded to 14 teams in 1993 with the addition of the Colorado Rockies and the Florida Marlins. In the NL West, the Braves, who led the majors in fewest runs allowed, edged out the Giants who led the division in runs scored. The Giants won 31 more games than they won in 1992 and became the poster child for the proposal to have a wild card playoff format which was put into effect in 1994 along with the creation of the three division format. The Braves had a wonderful 54–19 record since the All-Star break. This team outscored every team during the regular season. The already strong starting pitching staff became one of the best ever with the addition of free agent Greg Maddux. In the postseason, the Braves lost to the Phillies in 6 games in the NLCS.

Strengths: (1) isolated power led by Blauser (29 2B), Justice (40 HR), Gant (27 2B, 36 HR), and McGriff (18 2B, 19 HR) obtained in a mid-season trade with the Padres, (2) drawing walks featuring Blauser (85 BB) and Justice (78 BB), (3) fielding from 2B Lemke (103 Rng+, 100 DP) and the outfielders, and (4) pitching anchored by Cy Young winner Maddux (81% QS, 197 K), Avery (71% QS), Glavine (78% QS), McMichael (12 Holds, 19/21/90% Sv, 16/22/73% IR stranded, 1.337 Lv), Bedrosian (20/36/56% IR stranded), and Howell (7 Holds, 14/25/56% IR stranded). The stolen base leader was Nixon (47).

Weaknesses: (1) C position, (2) hitting from Olson, Berryhill, Nixon, and Lemke, (3) baserunning from Lemke (21 GIDP, 25% RS), (4) %IR stranded, and (5) pitching control from Stanton (5.0 BB/9, 27/33/82% Sv, 15/25/60% IR stranded, 1.782 Lv).

Mgr	Bobby Cox	
Rk	46	68
Gm	162	
Place	1	
GA	1.0	
Rival	7–6 vs Giants, 63 RS, 50 RA; 6–6 vs Phillies, 65 RS, 64 RA	

	W	L	Win%
Regular Season	104	58	0.642
Runs Record	102	60	0.631
1 Run	37	22	0.627
Extra Innings	7	6	0.538
Blowout	27	10	0.730

	Team	LgAvg	%Avg	LgRk
BABIP	0.278	0.294	105	1
E	108	134	124	3
sOBP	0.304	0.326	107	1
rOBP	0.300	0.330	110	1
R/G	4.73	4.49	105	3
RA/G	3.45	4.49	130	1

	Tm	LgAvg	>Avg
RS	767	728	39
RA	559	728	169
DP	146	145	1

	R/G	HR	K	BB	SB	CS	SB%	OPS		Held+
Team Offense	4.73	169	946	560	125	48	72%	0.739	LF	100
Team Defense	3.45	101	1036	480	121	53	70%	0.652	CF	91
Difference	1.28	68	90	80	4			113%	RF	95

Pos	Rpos	PA	Age	Name	BA	OBP	SLG	BB%	XBT	Bat R>Avg	BR R>Avg	Fld R>Avg	RAA	WAA
C	5	363	29	Berryhill, Damon^	0.245	0.291	0.382	6%	52%	-8	-1	2	-2	-0.2
1B	-4	311	32	Bream, Sid*	0.260	0.332	0.415	10%	26%	2	-1	4	1	0.1
2B	4	569	27	Lemke, Mark^	0.252	0.335	0.341	11%	27%	-6	-5	17	10	1.0
3B	2	682	32	Pendleton, Terry^	0.272	0.311	0.408	5%	44%	-3	3	2	4	0.4
SS	9	710	27	Blauser, Jeff	0.305	0.401	0.436	12%	51%	30	1	-5	35	3.5
LF	-6	682	28	Gant, Ron	0.274	0.345	0.510	10%	58%	26	3	18	41	4.1
CF	2	532	34	Nixon, Otis^	0.269	0.351	0.315	11%	40%	-6	4	12	12	1.2
RF	-6	670	27	Justice, Dave*	0.270	0.357	0.515	12%	36%	30	-2	14	36	3.6
C	4	295	32	Olson, Gregg	0.225	0.304	0.309	10%	40%	-10	-4	-3	-13	-1.3
CF,LF	1	294	25	Sanders, Deion*	0.276	0.321	0.452	5%	52%	3	2	3	9	0.9
1B	-4	291	29	McGriff, Fred*	0.310	0.392	0.612	12%	53%	25	1	2	24	2.4
SS,2B	3	89	31	Belliard, Rafael	0.228	0.291	0.291	4%	0%	-4	0	8	7	0.7
1B	0	91	26	Cabrera, Francisco	0.241	0.308	0.422	9%	38%	0	0	0	0	0.0
3B	0	65	33	Pecota, Bill	0.323	0.344	0.387	3%	47%	0	-1	0	-1	-0.1
	-10	590		Others	0.181	0.217	0.237	4%	26%	-52	-1	8	-55	-5.5
	0		29.4	Team Total	0.262	0.331	0.408	9.0%	43%	26	-1	82	107	10.7
				League Average	0.264	0.327	0.399	8.2%	41%					
				% Lg Avg	99	101	102	110	104					
				League Rank	9	5	6	3	5		6	1		

GS	GR	IP	Age	Name	W–L	GmSc	K/9	BB/9	HR/9	FIP	ERA	RA/9	RAA	WAA
36	0	267	27	Maddux, Greg	20–10	61.7	6.6	1.8	0.47	2.86	2.36	2.87	34	3.4
35	0	244	26	Smoltz, John	15–11	56.1	7.7	3.7	0.85	3.76	3.62	3.84	5	0.5
36	0	239	27	Glavine, Tom*	22–6	53.3	4.5	3.4	0.60	4.02	3.20	3.42	14	1.4
35	0	223	23	Avery, Steve*	18–6	55.2	5.0	1.7	0.56	3.29	2.94	3.26	18	1.8
14	6	91	27	Smith, Pete	4–8	47.4	5.3	3.6	1.49	5.22	4.37	4.47	-5	-0.5
0	63	52	26	Stanton, Mike*	4–6	—	7.4	5.0	0.69	3.70	4.67	6.06	-12	-1.2
0	74	92	26	McMichael, Greg	2–3	—	8.7	2.8	0.29	2.39	2.06	2.16	19	1.9
0	54	58	37	Howell, Jay	3–3	—	5.7	2.5	0.46	3.10	2.32	2.47	10	1.0
0	49	50	35	Bedrosian, Steve	5–2	—	6.0	2.5	0.72	3.65	1.63	1.99	11	1.1
0	46	48	23	Wohlers, Mark	6–2	—	8.4	4.1	0.38	3.00	4.50	4.69	-3	-0.3
6	37	66	25	Mercker, Kent*	3–1	54.5	8.0	4.9	0.27	3.28	2.86	3.27	6	0.6
0	24	25		Others	2–0	—	9.6	4.6	0.36	2.89	7.11	7.11	-9	-0.9
162	353		27.5	Team Total		56	6.41	2.97	0.62	3.48	3.14	3.46	90	9.0
				League Average		50	5.93	3.15	0.87	4.05	4.04	4.52		
				% Lg Avg		112	108	106	139	116	129	131		
				League Rank		1	3	7	2	1	1			

1994 Chicago White Sox

The 1994 season featured six close divisional races but was unfortunately shortened by a strike on August 10 because of the owners' insistence of a salary cap to improve team profits. This was the first baseball season with 3 divisions in each league and the first season without any postseason games since 1904. The 1994 White Sox was the best AL team in the strike-shortened 1994 season and the second best White Sox team since the Dead-ball Era.

Strengths: (1) hitting for average and contact led by MVP Frank Thomas (34 2B, 38 HR in 99 games played) and Julio Franco (20 HR), (2) drawing walks featuring Thomas (109 BB), (3) fielding from 3B Ventura (94 Rng+), SS Guillen (85 Rng+), and CF Johnson (115 Rng+, 107 Held+), and (4) pitching anchored by McDowell (64% QS, 7.2 IP/S), Alvarez (71% QS), Bere (50% QS), Fernandez (58% QS), and DeLeon (22/32/69% IR stranded, 0.792 Lv). The baserunning leaders on this team were Johnson (26 SB, 6 CS, 38% RS, 14 3B) and Raines (13 SB, 0 CS, 45% RS).

Weaknesses: (1) hitting for power especially from Guillen and Johnson, (2) fielding from 1B Thomas and 2B Cora (93 Rng+), (3) Held+ from LF Raines (90) and RF Jackson (87), and (4) CS% from LaValliere (29%).

				W	L	Win%		Team	LgAvg	%Avg	LgRk
Mgr	Gene Lamont		**Regular Season**	67	46	0.593	**BABIP**	0.282	0.299	106	1
Rk	29	86	**Runs Record**	71	42	0.626	**E**	79	83	105	4
Gm	113		**1 Run**	16	12	0.571	**sOBP**	0.316	0.343	109	1
Place	1		**Extra Innings**	5	4	0.556	**rOBP**	0.323	0.349	108	1
GA	1.0		**Blowout**	25	7	0.781	**R/G**	5.60	5.23	107	4
Rival	7–5 vs Indians, 63 RS, 50 RA; 4–2 vs Yankees, 31 RS, 31 RA						**RA/G**	4.41	5.23	119	1

	Tm	LgAvg	>Avg		R/G	HR	K	BB	SB	CS	SB%	OPS	Held+	
RS	633	595	38	**Team Offense**	5.60	121	568	497	77	27	74%	0.810	**LF**	91
RA	498	595	97	**Team Defense**	4.41	115	754	377	81	30	73%	0.708	**CF**	111
DP	91	108	-17	**Difference**	1.19	6	186	120	-4			114%	**RF**	90

Pos	Rpos	PA	Age	Name	BA	OBP	SLG	BB%	XBT	Bat R>Avg	BR R>Avg	Fld R>Avg	RAA	WAA
C	4	248	30	Karkovice, Ron	0.213	0.325	0.425	15%	29%	-2	-1	3	4	0.3
1B,DH	-7	517	26	Thomas, Frank	0.353	0.487	0.729	21%	40%	71	-5	-8	51	4.7
2B,DH	2	368	29	Cora, Joey^	0.276	0.353	0.362	10%	46%	-5	-1	-5	-9	-0.9
3B	1	474	26	Ventura, Robin*	0.282	0.373	0.459	13%	32%	10	0	7	18	1.7
SS	6	390	30	Guillen, Ozzie*	0.288	0.311	0.348	4%	59%	-16	0	5	-5	-0.5
LF	-4	453	34	Raines, Tim^	0.266	0.365	0.409	13%	55%	1	4	1	2	0.2
CF	2	443	30	Johnson, Lance*	0.277	0.321	0.393	6%	66%	-10	6	3	1	0.0
RF,CF	-3	403	31	Jackson, Darrin	0.312	0.362	0.455	7%	42%	5	1	9	12	1.1
DH,1B	-2	505	35	Franco, Julio	0.319	0.406	0.510	12%	44%	25	1	-2	22	2.0
C	3	172	33	LaValliere, Mike*	0.281	0.368	0.331	12%	0%	-2	-3	1	-1	-0.1
2B,SS	1	145	27	Martin, Norberto	0.275	0.317	0.366	6%	54%	-5	0	0	-4	-0.3
RF	-1	118	29	Newson, Warren*	0.255	0.345	0.363	12%	39%	-2	0	-1	-4	-0.4
2B,SS	1	113	29	Grebeck, Craig	0.309	0.391	0.361	11%	47%	0	0	4	5	0.5
	-3	207		Others	0.230	0.264	0.377	4%	41%	-11	1	-4	-17	-1.6
	0		29.9	Team Total	0.287	0.366	0.444	10.9%	44%	58	3	13	74	6.8
				League Average	0.273	0.345	0.434	9.5%	44%					
				% Lg Avg	105	106	102	115	101					
				League Rank	3	2	5	3	8		6	4		

GS	GR	IP	Age	Name	W–L	GmSc	K/9	BB/9	HR/9	FIP	ERA	RA/9	RAA	WAA
25	0	181	28	McDowell, Jack	10–9	54.1	6.3	2.1	0.60	3.50	3.73	4.08	22	2.0
24	0	170	24	Fernandez, Alex	11–7	53.8	6.4	2.6	1.32	4.59	3.86	4.39	14	1.3
24	0	162	24	Alvarez, Wilson*	12–8	54.1	6.0	3.5	0.89	4.37	3.45	4.01	21	1.9
24	0	142	23	Bere, Jason	12–2	53.1	8.1	5.1	1.08	4.77	3.81	4.13	16	1.5
14	4	92	37	Sanderson, Scott	8–4	46.0	3.5	1.2	1.96	5.76	5.09	5.58	-5	-0.4
0	45	48	29	Hernandez, Roberto	4–4	—	9.4	3.6	0.94	3.75	4.91	5.48	-2	-0.2
0	42	67	33	DeLeon, Jose	3–2	—	9.0	4.2	0.67	3.69	3.36	3.76	10	1.0
0	40	53	33	McCaskill, Kirk	1–4	—	6.3	3.8	1.03	4.39	3.42	3.76	8	0.8
0	38	33	31	Cook, Dennis*	3–1	—	7.1	3.8	1.09	4.29	3.55	4.64	2	0.2
0	44	33	33	Assenmacher, Paul*	1–2	—	7.9	3.5	0.55	3.41	3.55	3.55	6	0.5
2	26	31		Others	2–3	—	7.2	9.2	0.86	5.91	7.48	8.63	-12	-1.1
			29.5	Team Total		52	6.71	3.35	1.02	4.38	3.96	4.43	81	7.5
				League Average		47	6.08	3.76	1.12	4.81	4.80	5.27		
				% Lg Avg		111	110	112	110	110	121	119		
				League Rank		1	3	3	4	2	1			

1994 Montreal Expos

The NL featured the resurgent Expos and Reds with the Reds leading the NL in runs scored per game while the Braves edged out the Expos to lead the league in fewest runs allowed. The Expos led the NL with a 1.1 run per game differentiation. The 1994 Expos were by far the best ever Expo team with the best MLB record in 1994 becoming the only Expo team to finish first in its division.

Strengths: (1) hitting for average, contact, and power led by Alou (31 2B, 22 HR), Walker (44 2B, 19 HR), and Cordero (30 2B, 15 HR), (2) baserunning especially from Grissom (36 SB, 6 CS, 51% RS, 13 ROE) and Cordero (16 SB, 3 CS, 11 ROE, 8 GIDP), (3) fielding featuring CF Grissom (115 Rng+), 2B/3B Lansing (92 Rng+ at 2B, 129 Rng+ at 3B), LF/RF Alou (86 Rng+ in LF, 116 Rng+ in RF), and RF Walker (98 Rng+), (4) Held+ from CF Grissom (115), LF/RF Alou (114 in LF and 131 in RF), and RF Walker (110), and (5) pitching depth with 9 pitchers better than league average anchored by Henry (53% QS), Cy Young runner-up Ken Hill (70% QS), Pedro Martinez (61% QS), Fassero (71% QS), and Wetteland (25/35/71% Sv, 20/29/69% IR stranded, 2.070 Lv).

Weaknesses: (1) hitting from 2B Lansing and LF reserve Frazier, (2) fielding from SS Cordero (90 Rng+) and 3B Berry (92 Rng+), (3) turning DP, (4) CS% from Fletcher (23%) and Webster (28%), and (5) pitching from Rueter (25% QS, 4.6 IP/S, 10.3 H/9).

Mgr	Felipe Alou	
Rk	20	67
Gm	114	
Place	1	
GA	6.0	
Rival	5–4 vs Braves, 31 RS, 33 RA; 2–4 vs Reds, 25 RS, 39 RA	

	W	*L*	*Win%*
Regular Season	74	40	0.649
Runs Record	72	42	0.631
1 Run	21	14	0.600
Extra Innings	6	8	0.429
Blowout	24	12	0.667

	Team	*LgAvg*	*%Avg*	*LgRk*
BABIP	0.285	0.300	105	2
E	94	86	91	11
sOBP	0.304	0.328	108	2
rOBP	0.300	0.341	114	1
R/G	5.13	4.62	111	3
RA/G	3.98	4.62	116	2

	Tm	*LgAvg*	*>Avg*
RS	585	530	55
RA	454	530	76
DP	90	105	-15

	R/G	*HR*	*K*	*BB*	*SB*	*CS*	*SB%*	*OPS*
Team Offense	5.13	108	669	379	137	36	79%	0.778
Team Defense	3.98	100	805	288	99	32	76%	0.683
Difference	1.15	8	136	91	38			114%

Held+	
LF	104
CF	112
RF	117

Pos	*Rpos*	*PA*	*Age*	*Name*	*BA*	*OBP*	*SLG*	*BB%*	*XBT*	*Bat R>Avg*	*BR R>Avg*	*Fld R>Avg*	*RAA*	*WAA*
C	4	325	27	Fletcher, Darrin*	0.260	0.314	0.435	8%	26%	1	0	-1	4	0.3
1B,LF	-6	366	21	Floyd, Cliff*	0.281	0.332	0.398	7%	38%	-2	2	0	-6	-0.6
2B,3B	3	435	26	Lansing, Mike	0.266	0.328	0.368	7%	42%	-7	-3	11	4	0.4
3B	1	359	28	Berry, Sean	0.278	0.347	0.453	9%	23%	6	2	-8	1	0.1
SS	7	467	22	Cordero, Will	0.294	0.363	0.489	9%	36%	16	4	-11	16	1.6
LF,RF	-4	471	27	Alou, Moises	0.339	0.397	0.592	9%	44%	37	0	8	41	4.0
CF	2	521	27	Grissom, Marquis	0.288	0.344	0.427	8%	46%	4	9	19	34	3.4
RF,1B	-5	452	27	Walker, Larry*	0.322	0.394	0.587	10%	47%	34	3	6	38	3.7
C	2	166	29	Webster, Lenny	0.273	0.370	0.448	10%	29%	4	-1	-1	4	0.4
LF	-1	160	29	Frazier, Lou^	0.271	0.358	0.307	11%	41%	-3	3	2	1	0.1
2B	1	114	26	Bell, Juan	0.278	0.372	0.381	13%	33%	1	2	1	5	0.5
LF	-1	109	22	White, Rondell	0.278	0.358	0.464	8%	59%	3	0	-1	1	0.1
1B	-1	98	32	Milligan, Randy	0.232	0.337	0.329	14%	36%	-2	1	1	-1	-0.1
	-2	471		Others	0.175	0.224	0.224	5%	20%	-44	-1	-3	-50	-5.0
	0		26.4	Team Total	0.278	0.343	0.435	8.4%	38%	47	21	23	91	9.0
				League Average	0.267	0.333	0.415	8.4%	43%					
				% Lg Avg	104	103	105	100	88					
				League Rank	3	3	4	6	13		1	7		

GS	*GR*	*IP*	*Age*	*Name*	*W–L*	*GmSc*	*K/9*	*BB/9*	*HR/9*	*FIP*	*ERA*	*RA/9*	*RAA*	*WAA*
23	0	155	28	Hill, Ken	16–5	54.3	4.9	2.6	0.70	3.93	3.32	3.55	15	1.5
23	1	145	22	Martinez, Pedro	11–5	57.7	8.8	2.8	0.68	3.31	3.42	3.61	14	1.4
21	0	139	31	Fassero, Jeff*	8–6	57.3	7.7	2.6	0.84	3.49	2.98	3.50	15	1.5
15	9	107	25	Henry, Butch*	8–3	56.3	5.9	1.7	0.84	3.68	2.43	2.52	23	2.3
20	0	92	23	Rueter, Kirk*	7–3	45.2	4.9	2.2	1.07	4.43	5.17	5.85	-15	-1.4
0	52	64	27	Wetteland, John	4–6	—	9.6	3.0	0.71	3.01	2.83	3.11	10	1.0
0	58	84	27	Rojas, Mel	3–2	—	9.0	2.3	1.18	3.78	3.32	3.75	7	0.7
3	36	75	28	Heredia, Gil	6–3	59.7	7.4	1.6	0.84	3.22	3.47	4.06	3	0.3
0	46	67	27	Shaw, Jeff	5–2	—	6.3	2.0	1.07	4.00	3.88	4.28	1	0.1
0	40	53	27	Scott, Tim	5–2	—	6.2	3.0	0.00	2.75	2.70	2.87	9	0.9
9	17	55		Others	1–3	—	6.7	4.5	1.95	6.20	7.31	8.29	-24	-2.3
114	259		26.5	Team Total		53	6.99	2.50	0.87	3.75	3.56	3.94	59	5.8
				League Average		49	6.36	3.26	0.96	4.22	4.21	4.65		
				% Lg Avg		108	110	130	111	113	118	118		
				League Rank		2	3	1	5	2	1			

1995 Cleveland Indians

The 1995 season began late and was shortened to 154 games due to labor issues. The Cleveland Indians featured all-stars at every position and dominated the AL Central division by 30 games and won both AL playoff series to reach the World Series for the first time since 1954 but lost in 6 games to the Braves. The Indians easily led the AL in runs scored and fewest runs allowed. Pitching ruled in the World Series as the Braves allowed an average of only about 3 runs per game to win it all in 6 games.

Strengths: (1) hitting led by Belle (52 2B, 50 HR), Thome (29 2B, 25 HR), Ramirez (26 2B, 31 HR), and Murray (21 2B, 21 HR) and (2) pitching anchored by Dennis Martinez (75% QS), Mesa (46/48/96% Sv, 9/12/75% IR stranded, 2.211 Lv), Ogea (64% QS), Tavarez (19 Holds, 29/36/81% IR stranded, 1.297 Lv), Hersheiser (62% QS), Plunk (10 Holds, 21/26/81% IR stranded, 1.303 Lv), Assenmacher (9 Holds, 25/28/89% IR stranded, 1.087 Lv), and Poole (6 Holds, 23/27/85% IR stranded, 0.818 Lv). Baserunning leaders were Lofton (54 SB, 15 CS, 13 3B, 47% RS) and Baerga (11 SB, 2 CS, 36% RS). Fielding leaders were CF Lofton (11 assists, 114 Held+) and CF/RF Kirby (1 error in 97 chances).

Weaknesses: (1) hitting from Kirby, Espinoza, and Pena, (2) CS% from Pena (21%) and Alomar (28%), (3) baserunning from Ramirez (6 SB, 6 CS, 27% RS, 2 ROE), and (4) fielding from RF Ramirez (87 Rng+), 1B Sorrento, and 2B Baerga (102 Rng+, 99 DP).

				W	L	Win%
Mgr	Mike Hargrove		**Regular Season**	100	44	0.694
Rk	5	23	**Runs Record**	95	49	0.662
Gm	144		**1 Run**	28	14	0.667
Place	1		**Extra Innings**	13	0	1.000
GA	30.0		**Blowout**	29	11	0.725
Rival	11–1 vs Royals, 76 RS, 28 RA; 7–6 vs Red Sox, 71 RS, 69 RA					

	Team	LgAvg	%Avg	LgRk
BABIP	0.287	0.298	104	2
E	101	98	97	8
sOBP	0.325	0.343	106	2
rOBP	0.308	0.346	112	1
R/G	5.83	5.06	115	1
RA/G	4.22	5.06	120	1

	Tm	LgAvg	>Avg
RS	840	730	110
RA	607	730	123
DP	142	142	0

	R/G	HR	K	BB	SB	CS	SB%	OPS		Held+
Team Offense	5.83	207	766	542	132	53	71%	0.839	**LF**	94
Team Defense	4.22	135	926	445	117	38	75%	0.718	**CF**	111
Difference	1.62	72	160	97	15			117%	**RF**	100

Pos	Rpos	PA	Age	Name	BA	OBP	SLG	BB%	XBT	Bat R>Avg	BR R>Avg	Fld R>Avg	RAA	WAA
C	5	279	38	Pena, Tony	0.262	0.302	0.376	5%	27%	-10	-2	-3	-10	-0.9
1B,DH	-6	378	29	Sorrento, Paul*	0.235	0.336	0.511	13%	40%	7	1	-8	-6	-0.5
2B	3	600	26	Baerga, Carlos^	0.314	0.355	0.452	6%	53%	7	2	-8	4	0.4
3B	2	557	24	Thome, Jim*	0.314	0.438	0.558	17%	44%	42	0	0	44	4.2
SS	8	622	28	Vizquel, Omar^	0.266	0.333	0.351	9%	46%	-15	2	1	-4	-0.4
LF	-6	629	28	Belle, Albert	0.317	0.401	0.690	12%	55%	61	-1	-1	53	4.9
CF	2	529	28	Lofton, Kenny*	0.310	0.362	0.453	8%	56%	8	7	8	25	2.3
RF	-6	571	23	Ramirez, Manny	0.308	0.402	0.558	13%	42%	35	-4	-12	13	1.2
DH,1B	-2	480	39	Murray, Eddie^	0.323	0.375	0.516	8%	36%	19	-2	4	19	1.8
C	3	218	29	Alomar, Sandy	0.300	0.332	0.478	3%	19%	2	-1	0	4	0.3
CF,RF	-1	205	31	Kirby, Wayne*	0.207	0.260	0.298	6%	55%	-15	3	7	-6	-0.6
1B	-3	184	25	Perry, Herbert	0.315	0.376	0.463	7%	50%	4	-3	3	1	0.1
3B,2B	2	150	33	Espinoza, Alvaro	0.252	0.264	0.322	1%	33%	-10	-1	0	-9	-0.9
DH	0	130	43	Winfield, Dave	0.191	0.285	0.287	11%	58%	-9	-1	0	-10	-0.9
	-1	154		Others	0.256	0.318	0.391	6%	42%	-3	-3	2	-5	-0.5
	0		30.3	Team Total	0.291	0.361	0.479	9.5%	45%	122	-3	-7	112	10.5
				League Average	0.270	0.344	0.427	9.6%	44%					
				% Lg Avg	108	105	112	99	103					
				League Rank	1	1	1	9	6		6	10		

GS	GR	IP	Age	Name	W–L	GmSc	K/9	BB/9	HR/9	FIP	ERA	RA/9	RAA	WAA
28	0	187	40	Martinez, Dennis	12–5	55.4	4.8	2.2	0.82	4.24	3.08	3.42	36	3.4
29	0	178	28	Nagy, Charles	16–6	49.2	7.0	3.1	1.01	4.25	4.55	4.80	7	0.7
26	0	167	36	HershIser, Orel	16–6	53.5	6.0	2.7	1.13	4.51	3.87	4.09	20	1.9
21	1	125	27	Clark, Mark	9–7	44.4	4.9	3.0	0.94	4.59	5.27	5.56	-5	-0.5

GS	GR	IP	Age	Name	W–L	GmSc	K/9	BB/9	HR/9	FIP	ERA	RA/9	RAA	WAA
14	6	106	24	Ogea, Chad	8–3	52.2	4.8	2.5	0.93	4.34	3.05	3.22	23	2.2
11	1	75	29	Hill, Ken	4–1	50.2	5.8	3.9	0.60	4.13	3.98	4.34	7	0.6
0	62	64	29	Mesa, Jose	3–0	—	8.2	2.4	0.42	2.72	1.13	1.27	28	2.6
0	57	85	22	Tavarez, Julian	10–2	—	7.2	2.2	0.74	3.54	2.44	3.81	13	1.2
0	56	64	31	Plunk, Eric	6–2	—	10.0	3.8	0.70	3.38	2.67	2.67	18	1.7
0	42	50	29	Poole, Jim*	3–3	—	7.3	3.0	1.25	4.53	3.76	3.94	7	0.6
0	47	38	34	Assenmacher, Paul*	6–2	—	9.4	2.8	0.70	3.09	2.82	3.05	9	0.8
15	63	161		Others	7–7	—	7.0	5.0	1.28	5.15	5.74	6.41	-22	-2.1
144	335		29.9	Team Total		50	6.41	3.08	0.93	4.24	3.83	4.20	140	13.1
				League Average		47	6.07	3.79	1.08	4.72	4.71	5.12		
				% Lg Avg			106	123	116	111	123	122		
				League Rank		2	3	1	2	1	1			

1997 New York Yankees

The Yankees led the AL in run differentiation but finished in second place to a less talented O's team primarily due to their 4–8 W–L record in their head-to-head matchups despite outscoring them by 8 runs. In the postseason, they lost 3 games to 2 to the Indians.

Strengths: (1) hitting led by Williams (35 2B, 21 HR), Martinez (31 2B, 44 HR), O'Neill (42 2B, 21 HR), and Jeter (31 2B), (2) Held+ from LF Whitten (128), CF Williams (112), and RF O'Neill (121), and (3) pitching from Pettitte (69% QS), Cone (72% QS, 222 K), Wells (53% QS), Rivera (43/52/83% Sv, 13/17/76% IR stranded, 2.223 Lv), Stanton (26 Holds, 36/49/73% IR stranded, 1.632 Lv), Nelson (22 Holds, 42/53/79% IR stranded), Mendoza (47% QS), and Boehringer (22/30/73% IR).

Weaknesses: (1) C, 2B, & LF positions, (2) power from Duncan & Girardi, (3) baserunning from O'Neill (16 GIDP, 29% RS) & Fielder (14 GIDP, 19% RS), (4) fielding from RF O'Neill (97 Rng+), LF/CF Curtis (86 Rng+ in LF, 85 Rng+ in CF), LF Raines (78 Rng+), CF Williams (80 Rng+), C Posada (20% CS, 8 PB, 4.71 ERA), and 2B Sojo (102 Rng+), and (5) pitching from Rogers (18% QS).

Mgr	Joe Torre	
Rk	38	111
Gm	162	
Place	2	
GB	2.0	
Rival	4–8 vs O's; 82 RS, 74 RA	

	W	L	Win%
Regular Season	96	66	0.593
Runs Record	100	62	0.619
1 Run	23	16	0.590
Extra Innings	9	9	0.500
Blowout	39	13	0.750

	Team	LgAvg	%Avg	LgRk
BABIP	0.303	0.303	100	8
E	104	111	107	6
sOBP	0.329	0.340	103	5
rOBP	0.322	0.342	106	3
R/G	5.50	4.93	112	2
RA/G	4.25	4.94	116	2

	Tm	LgAvg	>Avg
RS	891	797	94
RA	688	798	110
DP	156	156	0

	R/G	HR	BB	BB	SB	CS	SB%	OPS	Held+	
Team Offense	5.50	161	954	676	99	58	63%	0.798	**LF**	107
Team Defense	4.25	144	1165	532	111	47	70%	0.721	**CF**	109
Difference	1.25	17	211	144	-12			111%	**RF**	117

Pos	Rpos	PA	Age	Name	BA	OBP	SLG	BB%	XBT	Bat R>Avg	BR R>Avg	Fld R>Avg	RAA	WAA
C	7	433	32	Girardi, Joe	0.282	0.331	0.358	6%	29%	-10	-4	0	-7	-0.7
1B	-9	685	29	Martinez, Tino*	0.297	0.371	0.578	11%	31%	38	-2	4	31	3.0
2B	1	239	32	Sojo, Luis	0.301	0.349	0.365	7%	25%	-3	2	-6	-6	-0.6
3B	1	398	32	Hayes, Charlie	0.277	0.353	0.426	10%	25%	2	-3	0	0	0.0
SS	10	748	23	Jeter, Derek	0.314	0.397	0.438	10%	45%	19	3	-3	29	2.8
LF,DH	-4	318	37	Raines, Tim^	0.306	0.387	0.433	13%	56%	8	2	-9	-3	-0.3
CF	3	591	28	Williams, Bernie^	0.332	0.412	0.551	12%	49%	39	5	-7	40	3.8
RF	-6	637	34	O'Neill, Paul*	0.333	0.409	0.529	12%	29%	37	-6	-18	7	0.6
DH,1B	-4	425	33	Fielder, Cecil	0.287	0.388	0.451	12%	11%	11	-5	1	3	0.3
3B,DH	1	407	39	Boggs, Wade*	0.283	0.363	0.385	12%	29%	0	0	4	5	0.4
LF,CF	-2	372	28	Curtis, Chad	0.295	0.367	0.483	10%	44%	11	-1	-10	-2	-0.2
C	3	224	25	Posada, Jorge^	0.254	0.364	0.416	13%	41%	2	-1	-6	-2	-0.2

Pos	Rpos	PA	Age	Name	BA	OBP	SLG	BB%	XBT	Bat R>Avg	BR R>Avg	Fld R>Avg	RAA	WAA
LF	-3	248	30	Whiten, Mark	0.265	0.360	0.386	12%	54%	-1	0	-4	-8	-0.7
2B	1	179	34	Duncan, Mariano	0.244	0.270	0.308	3%	40%	-12	1	-5	-15	-1.5
2B	1	150	29	Sanchez, Rey	0.312	0.338	0.420	3%	41%	-1	0	-2	-2	-0.2
	0	473		Others	0.231	0.313	0.322	11%	42%	-20	3	-2	-19	-1.8
	0		31	Team Total	0.287	0.362	0.436	10.4%	37%	80	-6	-63	11	4.8
				League Average	0.271	0.340	0.428	9.0%	42%					
				% Lg Avg	106	106	102	115	88					
				League Rank	2	1	5	1	14		10	13		

GS	GR	IP	Age	Name	W–L	GmSc	K/9	BB/9	HR/9	FIP	ERA	RA/9	RAA	WAA
35	0	240	25	Pettitte, Andy*	18–7	56.5	6.2	2.4	0.26	3.07	2.88	3.22	58	5.5
32	0	218	34	Wells, David*	16–10	51.2	6.4	1.9	0.99	3.93	4.21	4.50	22	2.0
29	0	195	34	Cone, David	12–6	60.8	10.2	4.0	0.78	3.44	2.82	3.09	48	4.5
22	9	145	32	Rogers, Kenny*	6–7	41.3	4.8	3.8	1.12	5.17	5.65	6.21	-13	-1.2
19	1	106	32	Gooden, Dwight	9–5	46.2	5.6	4.5	1.18	5.36	4.91	5.16	3	0.3
15	24	134	25	Mendoza, Ramiro	8–6	45.3	5.5	1.9	1.01	4.15	4.24	4.51	13	1.3
0	66	72	27	Rivera, Mariano	6–4	—	8.5	2.5	0.63	2.82	1.88	2.13	26	2.4
0	77	79	30	Nelson, Jeff	3–7	—	9.3	4.2	0.80	3.43	2.86	3.66	14	1.4
0	64	67	30	Stanton, Mike*	6–1	—	9.4	4.6	0.40	3.29	2.56	2.56	20	1.9
0	46	49	30	Lloyd, Graeme*	1–1	—	4.8	3.7	1.10	4.61	3.31	4.41	5	0.5
0	34	48	28	Boehringer, Brian	3–2	—	9.9	6.0	0.75	3.73	2.63	3.00	12	1.2
10	47	115		Others	8–10	—	7.6	3.9	1.87	5.63	6.48	7.02	-21	-2.0
162	368		29.7	Team Total		51	7.14	3.26	0.88	4.01	3.84	4.22	187	17.8
				League Average		47	6.43	3.50	1.10	4.57	4.56	4.98		
				% Lg Avg		109	111	107	125	114	119	118		
				League Rank		2	3	4	2	1	1			

1997 Atlanta Braves

The Braves were easily the best team in the majors in 1997 leading the NL in run differentiation. However, their Achilles heel was the Marlin team during the season and the playoffs losing in 6 games in the NLCS.

Strengths: (1) SP, 3B, SS, CF, and RF positions, (2) hitting from Blauser (31 2B, 17 HR), Chipper Jones (41 2B, 21 HR), Lofton (20 2B), and Lopez (28 2B, 23 HR), (3) drawing walks from C Jones (76 BB) and Blauser (70 BB), (4) Held+ from CF Lofton (119), (5) fielding led by OF Andruw Jones (123 Rng+ in RF, 131 Rng+ in CF), CF Lofton (105 Rng+), and 2B Lemke (104 Rng+), and (6) pitching from Cy Young runner-up Maddux (82% QS), Glavine (79% QS), Smoltz (71% QS, 241 K), and Neagle (79% QS).

Weaknesses: (1) 1B position, (2) hitting from Lemke and Perez, (3) team baserunning especially from McGriff (22 GIDP), and (4) fielding from 1B McGriff and 3B Chipper Jones (83 Rng+).

Mgr	Bobby Cox	
Rk	13	52
Gm	162	
Place	1	
GA	9.0	
Rival	4–8 vs Marlins, 34 RS, 50 RA	

	W	L	Win%
Regular Season	101	61	0.623
Runs Record	103	59	0.637
1 Run	33	20	0.623
Extra Innings	10	10	0.500
Blowout	32	10	0.762

	Team	LgAvg	%Avg	LgRk
BABIP	0.288	0.300	104	2
E	114	120	105	5
sOBP	0.291	0.328	113	1
rOBP	0.328	0.343	105	4
R/G	4.88	4.60	106	3
RA/G	3.59	4.60	128	1

	Tm	LgAvg	>Avg
RS	791	746	45
RA	581	745	164
DP	136	148	-12

	R/G	HR	K	BB	SB	CS	SB%	OPS	Held+	
Team Offense	4.88	174	1160	597	108	58	65%	0.741	**LF**	98
Team Defense	3.59	111	1196	450	124	54	70%	0.718	**CF**	116
Difference	1.30	63	36	147	-16			103%	**RF**	99

Pos	Rpos	PA	Age	Name	BA	OBP	SLG	BB%	XBT	Bat R>Avg	BR R>Avg	Fld R>Avg	RAA	WAA
C	7	464	26	Lopez, Javy	0.295	0.361	0.534	9%	36%	21	-1	0	20	2.0

Pos	Rpos	PA	Age	Name	BA	OBP	SLG	BB%	XBT	Bat R>Avg	BR R>Avg	Fld R>Avg	RAA	WAA
1B	-9	641	33	McGriff, Fred*	0.277	0.356	0.441	11%	25%	12	-6	-7	-1	-0.1
2B	1	397	31	Lemke, Mark^	0.245	0.306	0.316	8%	38%	-15	-1	16	0	0.0
3B	1	679	25	Jones, Chipper^	0.295	0.371	0.479	11%	60%	24	3	-6	21	2.1
SS	8	623	31	Blauser, Jeff	0.308	0.405	0.482	11%	41%	32	0	-2	30	3.0
LF	-6	522	26	Klesko, Ryan*	0.261	0.334	0.490	9%	42%	11	-4	-4	3	0.3
CF	2	564	30	Lofton, Kenny*	0.333	0.409	0.428	11%	60%	21	-3	18	36	3.6
RF,LF	-6	554	26	Tucker, Michael*	0.283	0.347	0.445	8%	57%	8	2	12	22	2.2
RF,CF	-2	467	20	Jones, Andruw	0.231	0.329	0.416	12%	67%	0	-2	28	26	2.6
2B	1	221	25	Graffanino, Tony	0.258	0.344	0.446	12%	48%	4	-1	6	9	0.9
C	3	206	29	Perez, Eddie	0.215	0.259	0.335	5%	25%	-11	-2	-1	-14	-1.4
2B,3B	0	169	32	Lockhart, Keith*	0.279	0.337	0.476	8%	37%	4	-1	2	5	0.5
LF,RF	-1	112	25	Bautista, Danny	0.243	0.282	0.398	4%	63%	-3	1	6	4	0.4
	1	693		Others	0.194	0.250	0.253	6%	29%	-54	-3	1	-56	-5.5
	0		27.6	Team Total	0.270	0.343	0.426	9.5%	45%	56	-18	69	107	10.5
				League Average	0.263	0.333	0.410	8.8%	43%					
				% Lg Avg	103	103	104	107	105					
				League Rank	3	4	2	4	4		14	1		

GS	GR	IP	Age	Name	W–L	GmSc	K/9	BB/9	HR/9	FIP	ERA	RA/9	RAA	WAA
35	0	256	30	Smoltz, John	15–12	59.8	8.5	2.2	0.74	2.99	3.02	3.41	23	2.3
33	0	240	31	Glavine, Tom*	14–7	58.6	5.7	3.0	0.75	3.91	2.96	3.23	26	2.6
34	0	233	28	Neagle, Denny*	20–5	58.0	6.6	1.9	0.69	3.34	2.97	3.36	22	2.1
33	0	233	31	Maddux, Greg	19–4	62.9	6.8	0.8	0.35	2.40	2.20	2.24	51	5.0
8	4	51	22	Millwood, Kevin	5–3	50.2	7.4	3.7	0.18	3.07	4.03	4.56	-2	-0.2
0	71	69	27	Wohlers, Mark	5–7	—	11.9	4.9	0.52	2.91	3.50	3.76	4	0.4
0	50	57	37	Bielecki, Mike	3–7	—	9.4	3.3	1.41	4.11	4.08	5.18	-6	-0.6
0	51	48	26	Clontz, Brad	5–1	—	7.9	3.4	0.56	3.23	3.75	4.50	-2	-0.2
0	66	46	27	Embree, Alan*	3–1	—	8.8	3.9	0.20	2.80	2.54	2.54	9	0.9
0	35	38	26	Cather, Mike	2–4	—	6.9	4.5	0.24	3.32	2.39	2.39	8	0.8
19	97	194		Others	10–10	—	6.7	4.7	1.11	4.74	4.64	5.47	-28	-2.7
162	374		28.5	Team Total		58	7.34	2.76	0.68	3.39	3.18	3.57	104	10.3
				League Average		50	6.89	3.47	0.97	4.21	4.20	4.63		
				% Lg Avg		116	107	126	142	124	132			
				League Rank		1	4	1	1	1	1			

1998 New York Yankees

The 1998 season featured 3 all-time great teams: the Yankees, Braves, and Astros. Two expansion teams were added: Tampa Bay Devil Rays and Colorado Rockies. The Brewers were moved to the NL who now had 16 teams. The 1998 Yankees were a terrific team with no real weaknesses plus strength and depth at every position winning 11 out of 13 postseason games including sweeping the Padres in the World Series. Eight players hit at least 17 home runs during the regular season.

Strengths: (1) hitting led by Williams (30 2B, 26 HR), O'Neill (40 2B, 24 HR), Jeter (25 2B, 19 HR), Martinez (33 2B, 28 HR), Brosius (34 2B, 19 HR), and Strawberry (24 HR), (2) walks from Knoblauch (76), Curtis (75), and Williams (75), (3) fielding from 3B Brosius (108 Rng+, 29 DP), RF O'Neill (99 Rng+, 11 assists), LF Curtis (112 Rng+), and C Posada (40% CS), and (4) pitching depth from Wells (63% QS, 7.1 IP/S, 5 shutouts), Cone (61% QS, 209 K), Hernandez (67% QS), Mendoza (50% QS, 14/24/58% IR stranded, 1.070 Lv), and Rivera (36/41/88% Sv, 20/24/83% IR stranded, 1.999 Lv). Derek Jeter had a terrific base-running season (21 ROE, 30 SB, 6 CS, and 44% RS).

Weaknesses: (1) power from Raines, Curtis, and Girardi, (2) fielding from CF Williams (92 Rng+), LF Raines (80 Rng+), and an erratic arm from Knoblauch (99 Rng+), and (3) HR/9 from Irabu and Stanton.

Mgr	Joe Torre	
Rk	3	18

	W	L	Win%
Regular Season	114	48	0.704
Runs Record	108	54	0.668

	Team	LgAvg	%Avg	LgRk
BABIP	0.280	0.301	108	1
E	98	114	116	3

Gm	162
Place	1
GA	22.0
Rival	7–5 vs Red Sox; 73 RS, 53 RA

	W	L	Win%
1 Run	21	10	0.677
Extra Innings	9	2	0.818
Blowout	42	13	0.764

	Team	LgAvg	%Avg	LgRk
sOBP	0.309	0.340	110	1
rOBP	0.320	0.337	105	2
R/G	5.96	5.01	119	1
RA/G	4.05	5.01	124	1

	Tm	LgAvg	>Avg
RS	965	797	168
RA	656	798	142
DP	146	149	-3

	R/G	HR	K	BB	SB	CS	SB%	OPS		Held+
Team Offense	5.96	207	1025	653	153	63	71%	0.825	**LF**	95
Team Defense	4.05	156	1080	466	102	51	67%	0.699	**CF**	99
Difference	1.91	51	55	187	51			118%	**RF**	106

Pos	Rpos	PA	Age	Name	BA	OBP	SLG	BB%	XBT	Bat R>Avg	BR R>Avg	Fld R>Avg	RAA	WAA
C,DH	5	409	26	Posada, Jorge^	0.268	0.350	0.475	11%	36%	7	-2	7	12	1.1
1B	-8	608	30	Martinez, Tino*	0.281	0.355	0.505	10%	34%	17	-3	4	18	1.7
2B	4	706	29	Knoblauch, Chuck	0.265	0.361	0.405	11%	54%	2	-2	-4	-4	-0.4
3B	2	603	31	Brosius, Scott	0.300	0.371	0.472	9%	49%	15	1	12	28	2.6
SS	8	694	24	Jeter, Derek	0.324	0.384	0.481	8%	52%	23	6	2	31	2.9
LF,CF	-4	545	29	Curtis, Chad	0.243	0.355	0.360	14%	47%	-6	1	8	3	0.3
CF	2	578	29	Williams, Bernie^	0.339	0.422	0.575	13%	47%	44	-1	-14	29	2.7
RF	-6	672	35	O'Neill, Paul*	0.317	0.372	0.510	8%	47%	25	1	11	37	3.5
DH,LF	-2	345	36	Strawberry, Darryl*	0.247	0.354	0.542	13%	29%	12	0	-2	10	1.0
LF,DH	-3	382	38	Raines, Tim^	0.290	0.395	0.383	14%	41%	5	1	-6	0	0.0
C	5	279	33	Girardi, Joe	0.276	0.317	0.386	5%	34%	-7	0	0	-7	-0.6
2B,DH	2	78	25	Bush, Homer	0.380	0.421	0.465	6%	56%	3	2	1	6	0.6
LF,RF	-1	73	26	Spencer, Shane	0.373	0.411	0.910	7%	29%	12	-1	-1	10	1.0
	-4	472		Others	0.230	0.276	0.307	6%	35%	-30	-3	10	-23	-2.2
	0		30.1	Team Total	0.288	0.364	0.460	10.1%	45%	123	0	28	151	14.3
				League Average	0.271	0.340	0.432	8.8%	43%					
				% Lg Avg	106	107	107	115	104					
				League Rank	2	1	4	1	4		7	5		

GS	GR	IP	Age	Name	W–L	GmSc	K/9	BB/9	HR/9	FIP	ERA	RA/9	RAA	WAA
32	1	216	26	Pettitte, Andy*	16–11	49.8	6.1	3.6	0.83	4.41	4.24	4.58	7	0.7
30	0	214	35	Wells, David*	18–4	57.8	6.8	1.2	1.22	3.94	3.49	3.61	30	2.9
31	0	208	35	Cone, David	20–7	57.0	9.1	2.6	0.87	3.58	3.55	3.86	24	2.3
28	1	173	29	Irabu, Hideki	13–9	53.3	6.6	4.0	1.40	5.31	4.06	4.11	15	1.4
21	0	141	32	Hernandez, Orlando	12–4	58.8	8.4	3.3	0.70	3.65	3.13	3.38	24	2.2
14	27	130	26	Mendoza, Ramiro	10–2	51.0	3.9	2.1	0.62	4.08	3.25	3.45	20	1.9
0	54	61	28	Rivera, Mariano	3–0	—-	5.3	2.5	0.44	3.58	1.91	1.91	20	1.9
0	67	79	31	Stanton, Mike*	4–1	—-	7.9	3.0	1.48	4.78	5.47	5.81	-8	-0.8
0	45	40	31	Nelson, Jeff	5–3	—-	7.8	4.9	0.22	3.81	3.79	4.02	4	0.4
0	50	38	31	Lloyd, Graeme*	3–0	—-	4.8	1.4	0.72	3.74	1.67	2.39	11	1.0
6	89	156		Others	10–7	—-	5.1	3.6	1.16	5.01	5.38	5.61	-13	-1.3
162	334		30.4	Team Total		54	6.67	2.88	0.96	4.24	3.82	4.05	135	12.7
				League Average		47	6.39	3.43	1.10	4.66	4.65	5.06		
				% Lg Avg		115	104	119	115	110	122	125		
				League Rank		1	4	2	2	1	1			

1998 Atlanta Braves

The 1998 Braves was the best Brave team in their long franchise history including the great Milwaukee Brave teams in the 1950's and other great Atlanta Brave teams in the 1990's. The Cy Young winner was Atlanta pitcher Tom Glavine. The Braves were upset in the NLCS by the Padres in 6 games.

Strengths: (1) SP, C, 1B, 3B, SS, LF, and CF positions, (2) hitting for average and power led by Galarraga (27 2B, 41 HR), Chipper Jones (29 2B, 34 HR), Lopez (21 2B, 34 HR), and Andruw Jones (33 2B, 31 HR), (3) fielding led by CF Andruw Jones (20 assists, 113 Rng+, 110 Held+) and RF Gerald Williams (120 Rng+), and (4) pitching led by Maddux (79% QS, 204 K, 7.4 IP/S), Cy Young winner Glavine (79% QS), Smoltz (65% QS), and Ligtenberg (11 Holds, 30/34/88% Sv, 23/31/65% IR stranded).

Weaknesses: (1) RP and 2B position, (2) hitting from 2B & SS positions, (3) GIDP from Lopez (22), (4) fielding from 1B Galarraga, and (5) pitching from Martinez (10.8 H/9).

Mgr	Bobby Cox	
Rk	4	19
Gm	162	
Place	1	
GA	18.0	
Rival	9–3 vs Mets, 59 RS, 30 RA; 4–5 vs Astros, 29 RS, 30 RA	

	W	*L*	*Win%*
Regular Season	106	56	0.654
Runs Record	108	54	0.665
1 Run	23	21	0.523
Extra Innings	2	4	0.333
Blowout	35	8	0.814

	Team	*LgAvg*	*%Avg*	*LgRk*
BABIP	0.289	0.299	103	3
E	91	116	127	1
sOBP	0.297	0.331	111	1
rOBP	0.321	0.333	104	4
R/G	5.10	4.60	111	3
RA/G	3.59	4.60	128	1

	Tm	*LgAvg*	*>Avg*
RS	826	746	80
RA	581	746	165
DP	139	151	-12

	R/G	*HR*	*K*	*BB*	*SB*	*CS*	*SB%*	*OPS*
Team Offense	5.10	215	1062	548	98	43	70%	0.795
Team Defense	3.59	117	1232	467	85	40	68%	0.657
Difference	1.51	98	170	81	13			121%

	Held+
LF	99
CF	111
RF	106

Pos	*Rpos*	*PA*	*Age*	*Name*	*BA*	*OBP*	*SLG*	*BB%*	*XBT*	*Bat R>Avg*	*BR R>Avg*	*Fld R>Avg*	*RAA*	*WAA*
C	8	534	27	Lopez, Javy	0.284	0.328	0.540	6%	31%	19	-5	-1	21	2.1
1B	-10	648	37	Galarraga, Andres	0.305	0.397	0.595	10%	34%	51	2	-5	38	3.7
2B	1	401	33	Lockhart, Keith*	0.257	0.311	0.388	7%	47%	-6	1	6	2	0.2
3B	2	707	26	Jones, Chipper^	0.313	0.404	0.547	14%	44%	49	1	3	55	5.4
SS	5	424	34	Weiss, Walt^	0.280	0.386	0.343	14%	42%	3	1	8	17	1.7
LF	-5	490	27	Klesko, Ryan*	0.274	0.359	0.473	11%	35%	15	1	7	18	1.7
CF	3	631	21	Jones, Andruw	0.271	0.321	0.515	6%	55%	16	4	35	58	5.7
RF	-5	469	27	Tucker, Michael*	0.244	0.327	0.418	10%	45%	0	3	1	-1	-0.1
2B	1	317	26	Graffanino, Tony	0.211	0.275	0.318	8%	60%	-16	-3	5	-13	-1.3
SS	4	295	34	Guillen, Ozzie*	0.264	0.325	0.336	8%	57%	-7	2	1	0	0.0
RF,OF	-3	289	31	Williams, Gerald	0.305	0.352	0.504	6%	55%	10	1	11	19	1.9
C	2	167	30	Perez, Eddie	0.336	0.404	0.537	9%	29%	11	-1	2	14	1.4
LF	-2	156	26	Bautista, Danny	0.250	0.281	0.389	4%	47%	-4	-1	6	-1	-0.1
	-1	687		Others	0.209	0.264	0.283	6%	39%	-43	0	5	-39	-3.8
	0		29.2	Team Total	**0.272**	0.342	0.453	8.8%	43%	102	6	84	192	18.5
				League Average	**0.262**	0.331	0.410	8.7%	42%					
				% Lg Avg	104	103	110	101	102					
				League Rank	4	4	2	2	6		4	1		

GS	*GR*	*IP*	*Age*	*Name*	*W–L*	*GmSc*	*K/9*	*BB/9*	*HR/9*	*FIP*	*ERA*	*RA/9*	*RAA*	*WAA*
34	0	251	32	Maddux, Greg	18–9	64.0	7.3	1.6	0.47	2.70	2.22	2.69	39	3.9
33	0	229	32	Glavine, Tom*	20–6	59.0	6.2	2.9	0.51	3.49	2.47	2.63	37	3.6
31	1	210	29	Neagle, Denny*	16–11	55.0	7.1	2.6	1.07	4.02	3.55	3.89	5	0.5
29	2	174	23	Millwood, Kevin	17–8	52.0	8.4	2.9	0.93	3.59	4.08	4.44	-7	-0.7
26	0	168	31	Smoltz, John	17–3	60.0	9.3	2.4	0.54	2.68	2.90	3.11	19	1.9
0	75	73	27	Ligtenberg, Kerry	3–2	0.0	9.7	3.0	0.74	3.00	2.71	2.96	10	1.0
5	48	91	43	Martinez, Dennis	4–6	40.0	6.1	1.9	0.79	3.49	4.45	5.24	-12	-1.2
0	36	41	27	Cather, Mike	2–2	0.0	7.2	2.6	1.52	4.70	3.92	4.57	-2	-0.2
0	47	38	23	Rocker, John*	1–3	0.0	9.9	5.2	0.95	3.97	2.13	2.37	8	0.8
0	34	36	29	Seanez, Rudy	4–1	0.0	12.5	4.0	0.50	2.51	2.75	3.25	4	0.4
4	111	128		Others	4–5	49.0	7.3	6.7	0.78	4.83	5.22	5.85	-25	-2.5
162	354		29.6	Team Total		57.0	7.70	2.92	0.73	3.46	3.25	3.63	75	7.4
				League Average		49.0	6.80	3.39	1.00	4.24	4.23	4.63		
				% Lg Avg		116	113	116	137	122	130	127		
				League Rank		1	1	2	1	1	1			

1998 HOUSTON ASTROS

The 1998 Astros were an incredible team of all-star hitters and pitchers having some of their best seasons. This team also lost to the upstart giant killer Padres in the NLDS 3 games to 1.

Strengths: (1) SP, RP, 1B, 2B, 3B, LF, CF, and RF positions, (1) hitting from Alou (34 2B, 38 HR, 84 BB), Bagwell (33 2B, 34 HR, 109 BB), Biggio (51 2B, 20 HR), Bell (41 2B, 22 HR), Everett (34 2B, 15 HR), and Berry, (2) baserunning featuring Biggio (50 SB, 8 CS) and Spiers (41% RS), (3) Held+ from RF Bell (110), CF Hidalgo (130), and LF Alou (115), and (4) pitching from mid-season pick-up Randy Johnson (91% QS, 7.7 IP/S), Reynolds (74% QS), Lima (73% QS, 7.1 IP/S), Hampton (69% QS), Wagner (30/35/86% Sv, 2.234 Lv), and Henry (11 Holds, 41/52/73% IR stranded, 1.359 Lv).

Weaknesses: (1) slugging at the SS position (Guiterrez, Bogar), (2) GIDP from Guiterrez (20) and Ausmus (18), and (3) fielding from SS Guiterrez (108 Rng+, 82 DP) and 3B Spiers (101 Rng+, only 9 DP).

				W	*L*	*Win%*		*Team*	*LgAvg*	*%Avg*	*LgRk*
Mgr	Larry Dierker		**Regular Season**	102	60	0.630	**BABIP**	0.298	0.299	100	9
Rk	6	24	**Runs Record**	107	55	0.662	**E**	108	116	107	8
Gm	162		**1 Run**	30	18	0.625	**sOBP**	0.316	0.331	105	3
Place	1		**Extra Innings**	10	12	0.455	**rOBP**	0.312	0.333	107	1
GA	12.5		**Blowout**	35	9	0.795	**R/G**	5.40	4.60	117	1
Rival	7–4 vs Cubs, 65 RS, 36 RA; 5–4 vs Braves, 30 RS, 29 RA						**RA/G**	3.83	4.60	120	2

	Tm	*LgAvg*	*>Avg*		*R/G*	*HR*	*K*	*BB*	*SB*	*CS*	*SB%*	*OPS*	*Held+*	
RS	874	746	128	**Team Offense**	5.40	166	1122	548	155	51	75%	0.792	**LF**	113
RA	620	746	126	**Team Defense**	3.83	147	1187	467	75	42	64%	0.709	**CF**	103
DP	144	151	-7	**Difference**	1.57	19	65	81	80			112	**RF**	108

Pos	*Rpos*	*PA*	*Age*	*Name*	*BA*	*OBP*	*SLG*	*BB%*	*XBT*	*Bat R>Avg*	*BR R>Avg*	*Fld R>Avg*	*RAA*	*WAA*
C	8	472	29	Ausmus, Brad	0.269	0.356	0.357	11%	52%	-2	-1	4	9	0.9
1B	-10	661	30	Bagwell, Jeff	0.304	0.424	0.557	16%	46%	53	3	4	50	4.9
2B	2	738	32	Biggio, Craig	0.325	0.403	0.503	9%	53%	42	10	-7	47	4.7
3B,2B	1	437	32	Spiers, Billy*	0.273	0.356	0.396	10%	53%	3	7	-10	1	0.1
SS	8	561	28	Guiterrez, Ricky	0.261	0.337	0.334	10%	52%	-9	-5	-17	-23	-2.3
LF	-7	679	31	Alou, Moises	0.312	0.399	0.582	12%	34%	52	0	4	49	4.9
CF	2	519	27	Everett. Carl^	0.296	0.359	0.482	8%	51%	16	-1	4	21	2.1
RF	-7	695	29	Bell, Derek	0.314	0.364	0.490	7%	39%	26	2	16	37	3.7
3B	1	342	32	Berry, Sean	0.314	0.387	0.508	9%	35%	18	-1	-1	17	1.7
CF	0	234	23	Hidalgo, Richard	0.303	0.355	0.474	7%	34%	7	-1	8	14	1.4
C	3	203	31	Eusebio, Tony	0.253	0.320	0.313	9%	29%	-6	1	-1	-3	-0.3
SS	2	169	31	Bogar, Tim	0.154	0.208	0.212	5%	45%	-19	0	3	-14	-1.3
RF,LF	-1	146	35	Clark, Dave*	0.206	0.288	0.260	10%	56%	-9	0	-4	-14	-1.4
	-2	585		Others	0.171	0.219	0.234	5%	41%	-55	-1	-3	-61	-6.0
	0		30.0	Team Total	0.280	0.356	0.436	9.6%	45%	119	13	0	132	13.0
				League Average	0.261	0.330	0.409	8.7%	42%					
				% Lg Avg	107	108	106	111	107					
				League Rank	2	1	4	5	2			11		

GS	*GR*	*IP*	*Age*	*Name*	*W–L*	*GmScA*	*K/9*	*BB/9*	*HR/9*	*FIP*	*ERA*	*RA/9*	*RAA*	*WAA*
35	0	233	30	Reynolds, Shane	19–8	54.1	8.1	2.0	0.96	3.44	3.51	3.82	21	2.1
33	0	233	25	Lima, Jose	16–8	55.5	6.5	1.2	1.31	4.10	3.70	3.86	20	2.0
32	0	212	25	Hampton, Mike*	11–7	51.7	5.8	3.4	0.77	4.18	3.36	3.91	17	1.7
27	4	172	28	Bergman, Sean	12–9	50.3	5.2	2.2	1.05	4.28	3.72	4.24	7	0.7
11	0	84	34	Johnson, Randy*	10–1	73.7	12.4	2.8	0.43	2.02	1.28	1.28	31	3.1
15	0	80	29	Schourek, Pete*	7–6	48.5	6.6	4.1	1.13	4.81	4.50	4.84	-2	-0.2
0	58	60	26	Wagner, Billy*	4–3	—	14.6	3.8	0.90	2.43	2.70	2.85	12	1.2
0	59	71	34	Henry, Doug	8–2	—	7.5	4.4	1.14	4.42	3.04	3.17	11	1.1
0	43	60	25	Nitkowski, C.J.*	3–3	—	6.6	3.5	0.60	3.92	3.77	4.07	4	0.4
0	29	34	26	Powell, Jay	3–3	—	10.1	4.0	0.26	2.46	2.38	2.38	8	0.8
9	147	232		Others	9–10	—	6.2	3.8	0.62	3.98	4.15	4.38	6	0.6
162	340		28.2	Team Total		54	7.26	2.84	0.90	3.83	3.50	3.79	136	13.4
				League Average		49	6.80	3.39	1.00	4.25	4.23	4.63		
				% Lg Avg		110	107	119	111	111	121	122		
				League Rank		2	4	1	7	3	2			

1999 Arizona Diamondbacks

The 1999 Diamondbacks shocked the baseball world by winning their division in their second year of existence by: (1) outstanding seasons from Jay Bell, Cy Young award winner Randy Johnson, Matt Williams, Luis Gonzalez, Steve Finley, and Omar Daal, (2) favorable trades such as the acquisitions of Gonzalez from the Tigers for Karim Garcia and Tony Womack from the Pirates, and (3) the free agent signings of Johnson and Finley. This team had the highest run differentiation in the majors. Their postseason terminated early losing to the Mets 3 games to 1 in the NLDS.

Strengths: (1) hitting and scoring a franchise best 908 runs led by Gonzalez (45 2B, 26 HR), Bell (32 2B, 38 HR, 82 BB), Williams (37 2B, 35 HR), Finley (32 2B, 10 3B, 34 HR), and Durazo (11 HR), (3) baserunning led by Womack (72 SB, 13 CS, 49% RS, 4 GIDP) and Finley (4 GIDP), (4) fielding from LF Gonzalez (105 Held+, 96 Rng+), CF Finley (108 Held+, 103 Rng+), and 3B Williams (104 Rng+), and (5) pitching from Cy Young winner Johnson (83% QS, 7.8 IP/S, 364 K), Daal (66% QS), and Swindell (19 Holds, 37/46/76% IR stranded, 1.159 Lv).

Weaknesses: (1) 1B, SS, and RF positions, (2) slugging from Womack and Lee, (3) Held+ from RF Womack (88), (4) turning DPs, and (5) pitching from Benes (50% QS, 9.8 H/9).

				W	L	Win%
Mgr	Buck Showalter		**Regular Season**	100	62	0.617
Rk	21	68	**Runs Record**	102	60	0.629
Gm	162		**1 Run**	24	24	0.500
Place	1		**Extra Innings**	11	10	0.524
GA	14.0		**Blowout**	32	9	0.780
Rival	9–3 vs Giants, 99 RS, 47 RA; 4–5 vs Braves, 38 RS, 44 RA					

	Team	LgAvg	%Avg	LgRk
BABIP	0.287	0.300	105	3
E	104	120	115	3
sOBP	0.315	0.339	108	2
rOBP	0.332	0.346	104	5
R/G	5.60	5.00	0.60	1
RA/G	4.17	4.95	0.78	3

	Tm	LgAvg	>Avg
RS	908	810	98
RA	676	802	126
DP	132	150	-18

	R/G	HR	K	BB	SB	CS	SB%	OPS
Team Offense	5.60	216	1045	588	137	39	78%	0.805
Team Defense	4.17	176	1198	543	138	66	68%	0.722
Difference	1.43	40	153	45	-1			112%

	Held+
LF	106
CF	109
RF	89

Pos	Rpos	PA	Age	Name	BA	OBP	SLG	BB%	XBT	Bat R>Avg	BR R>Avg	Fld R>Avg	RAA	WAA
C	5	320	29	Miller, Damian	0.270	0.316	0.446	6%	40%	-2	-1	3	5	0.4
1B	-6	436	24	Lee, Travis*	0.237	0.337	0.363	13%	56%	-9	4	0	-11	-1.0
2B	4	688	33	Bell, Jay	0.289	0.374	0.557	12%	48%	34	0	0	38	3.6
3B	2	678	33	Williams, Matt	0.303	0.344	0.536	6%	41%	21	0	7	30	2.9
SS,3B	5	320	28	Fox, Andy*	0.255	0.351	0.380	10%	52%	-3	0	-3	-1	-0.1
LF	-7	693	31	Gonzalez, Luis*	0.336	0.403	0.549	10%	38%	42	1	18	54	5.1
CF	3	663	34	Finley, Steve*	0.264	0.336	0.525	10%	50%	16	5	17	41	3.9
RF,SS	-4	684	29	Womack, Tony*	0.277	0.332	0.370	8%	58%	-14	11	2	-5	-0.5
C	5	317	29	Stinnett, Kelly	0.232	0.302	0.426	8%	34%	-6	-1	4	2	0.2
RF,LF	-2	241	32	Gilkey, Bernard	0.294	0.379	0.500	12%	38%	9	-2	1	6	0.6
1B	-2	185	25	Durazo, Erubiel*	0.329	0.422	0.594	14%	33%	15	-1	1	13	1.2
SS	2	164	25	Batista, Tony	0.257	0.335	0.396	10%	45%	-2	1	0	1	0.1
RF,OF	-1	123	25	Dellucci, David*	0.394	0.463	0.505	9%	29%	9	-2	-2	4	0.4
1B	-2	153	29	Colbrunn, Greg	0.326	0.392	0.519	8%	41%	7	-2	-3	0	0.0
	-2	750		Others	0.207	0.271	0.290	7%	35%	-51	2	-3	-54	-5.2
	0		29.0	Team Total	0.277	0.347	0.459	9.2%	44%	66	15	42	123	11.6
				League Average	0.268	0.342	0.429	9.5%	43%					
				% Lg Avg	103	101	107	97	102					
				League Rank	3	7	2	10	8		1	3		

GS	GR	IP	Age	Name	W–L	GmSc	K/9	BB/9	HR/9	FIP	ERA	RA/9	RAA	WAA
35	0	272	35	Johnson, Randy*	17–9	68.0	12.1	2.3	0.99	2.76	2.48	2.85	59	5.6
32	0	215	27	Daal, Omar*	16–9	54.0	6.2	3.3	0.88	4.21	3.65	3.86	21	2.0
32	1	198	31	Benes, Andy	13–12	47.0	6.4	3.7	1.54	5.22	4.81	5.31	-13	-1.2
27	4	167	33	Reynoso, Armando	10–6	48.0	4.3	3.6	1.08	4.96	4.37	4.85	-3	-0.3
19	12	130	27	Anderson, Brian*	8–2	49.0	5.2	1.9	1.25	4.41	4.57	4.78	-1	-0.1
17	0	101	34	Stottlemyre, Todd	6–3	50.0	6.6	3.6	1.07	4.57	4.09	4.53	2	0.2
0	30	29	25	Mantei, Matt	0–1	0.0	15.2	5.9	0.31	2.51	2.79	3.10	6	0.5
0	63	65	34	Swindell, Greg*	4–0	0.0	7.1	2.9	1.11	4.17	2.50	2.64	15	1.4

GS	GR	IP	Age	Name	W–L	GmSc	K/9	BB/9	HR/9	FIP	ERA	RA/9	RAA	WAA
0	61	61	32	Olson, Gregg	9–4	0.0	6.7	3.7	1.33	4.84	3.71	4.15	4	0.4
0	44	49	33	Holmes, Darren	4–3	0.0	6.5	4.6	0.55	3.63	3.70	3.88	5	0.4
0	32	40	27	Chouinard, Bobby	5–2	0.0	5.1	2.7	0.67	3.73	2.68	3.57	5	0.5
0	135	141		Others	8–11	0.0	7.3	4.8	1.09	4.58	4.48	4.93	-3	-0.3
162	382		30.7	Team Total		54	7.35	3.33	1.08	4.20	3.77	4.15	96	9.1
				League Average		48	6.69	3.73	1.13	4.57	4.56	4.99		
				% Lg Avg		113	110	112	105	109	121	120		
				League Rank		1	3	4	8	3	2			

2001 Seattle Mariners

The 2001 season featured two dominant teams in the AL, the Mariners and A's. Unfortunately for the Mariners, the post-season was highlighted by an inspired Yankee team who came within a game of winning the world championship despite having a less talented team than all 3 of their postseason opponents. The AL MVP and RoY was Ichiro Suzuki of the Mariners. The Mariners set the AL record winning 116 regular season games.

Strengths: (1) hitting for led by Boone (37 2B, 37 HR), Edgar Martinez (40 2B, 23 HR), Ichiro (34 2B, 8 3B), and Olerud (32 2B, 21 HR), (2) drawing walks from Olerud (94) and Martinez (93), (4) baserunning especially from Ichiro (56 SB, 14 CS, 3 GIDP, 13 ROE, 44% RS) and Cameron (34 SB, 5 CS, 37% RS), (5) fielding from 3B Bell (101 Rng+, 14 E), RF Ichiro (113 Rng+, 111 Held+), 2B Boone (94 Rng+, 90 DP,), CF Cameron (110 Rng+), SS Guillen (90 Rng+, 10 errors in 510 chances), and LF Javier (103 Rng+, 110 Held+), and (6) pitching from Garcia (71% QS), Rhodes (31 Holds, 48/58/83% IR stranded), Pineiro (55% QS), Moyer (61% QS), Nelson (26 Holds, 33/38/87% IR stranded), and closer Sasaki (45/52/87% Sv).

Weaknesses: (1) hitting from Lampkin, Wilson, Bell, and Martin, (2) baserunning from Martinez (26% RS), Wilson, and Olerud (21 GIDP), (3) Held+ from CF Cameron (92), (4) 28% CS from both Wilson and Lampkin, and (5) pitching from Halama (35% QS).

				W	L	Win%
Mgr	Lou Piniella		**Regular Season**	116	46	0.716
Rk	2	9	**Runs Record**	110	52	0.679
Gm	162		**1 Run**	26	12	0.684
Place	1		**Extra Innings**	9	4	0.692
GA	14.0		**Blowout**	34	10	0.773
Rival	10–9 vs A's, 93 RS, 94 RA; 6–3 vs Yankees, 55 RS, 43 RA					

	Team	LgAvg	%Avg	LgRk
BABIP	0.262	0.297	113	1
E	83	114	137	1
sOBP	0.308	0.336	109	1
rOBP	0.284	0.330	116	1
R/G	5.72	4.86	0.86	1
RA/G	3.87	4.86	0.99	1

	Tm	LgAvg	>Avg
RS	927	787	140
RA	627	787	160
DP	137	150	-13

	R/G	HR	K	BB	SB	CS	SB%	OPS
Team Offense	5.72	169	989	614	174	42	81%	0.805
Team Defense	3.87	160	1051	465	73		100%	0.679
Difference	1.85	9	62	149	101			119%

	Held+
LF	102
CF	92
RF	115

Pos	Rpos	PA	Age	Name	BA	OBP	SLG	BB%	XBT	Bat R>Avg	BR R>Avg	Fld R>Avg	RAA	WAA
C	6	408	32	Wilson, Dan	0.265	0.305	0.403	5%	28%	-9	-3	6	0	0.0
1B	-9	679	32	Olerud, John*	0.302	0.401	0.472	14%	29%	29	-3	7	24	2.3
2B	4	690	32	Boone, Bret	0.331	0.372	0.578	6%	47%	42	4	12	62	5.9
3B	2	510	28	Bell, David	0.260	0.303	0.415	5%	43%	-9	-2	19	10	1.0
SS	7	523	25	Guillen, Carlos^	0.259	0.333	0.355	10%	49%	-10	3	10	10	1.0
LF,DH	-5	324	33	Martin, Al*	0.240	0.330	0.382	11%	53%	-4	1	6	-2	-0.2
CF	3	633	28	Cameron, Mike	0.267	0.353	0.480	11%	64%	16	6	11	36	3.4
RF	-7	738	27	Suzuki, Ichiro*	0.350	0.381	0.457	4%	46%	21	15	15	44	4.2
3B,SS	0	487	36	McLemore, Mark^	0.286	0.384	0.406	14%	53%	9	2	3	14	1.3
LF,OF	-3	323	37	Javier, Stan^	0.292	0.375	0.391	11%	49%	3	4	10	14	1.3
DH,1B	0	581	38	Martinez, Edgar	0.306	0.423	0.543	16%	33%	41	-4	0	37	3.6
C	3	231	37	Lampkin, Tom*	0.225	0.309	0.348	8%	48%	-8	2	1	-2	-0.2
3B,LF	-2	107	33	Sprague, Ed	0.298	0.374	0.436	10%	50%	2	-2	1	-1	-0.1

Pos	Rpos	PA	Age	Name	BA	OBP	SLG	BB%	XBT	Bat R>Avg	BR R>Avg	Fld R>Avg	RAA	WAA
	1	240		Others	0.225	0.287	0.311	7%	34%	-12	2	3	-6	-0.6
	0		32.2	Team Total	0.288	0.360	0.445	9.5%	44%	110	25	104	239	22.9
				League Average	0.267	0.334	0.428	8.3%	42%					
				% Lg Avg	108	108	104	115	105					
				League Rank	1	1	4	2	4		1	1		

GS	GR	IP	Age	Name	W–L	GmSc	K/9	BB/9	HR/9	FIP	ERA	RA/9	RAA	WAA
34	0	239	26	Garcia, Freddy	18–6	57.9	6.1	2.6	0.60	3.54	3.05	3.32	25	2.4
33	1	215	31	Sele, Aaron	15–5	52.1	4.8	2.1	1.05	4.41	3.60	3.89	7	0.7
33	0	210	38	Moyer, Jamie*	20–6	54.6	5.1	1.9	1.03	4.24	3.43	3.61	15	1.4
27	1	163	33	Abbott, Paul	17–4	50.5	6.5	4.8	1.16	5.04	4.25	4.36	-2	-0.2
17	14	110	29	Halama, John*	10–7	41.5	4.1	2.1	1.47	5.26	4.73	5.63	-18	-1.7
11	6	75	22	Pineiro, Joel	6–2	56.9	6.7	2.5	0.24	2.99	2.03	2.87	12	1.2
0	69	67	33	Sasaki, Kazuhiro	0–4	—	8.4	1.5	0.81	3.07	3.24	3.24	8	0.8
0	71	68	31	Rhodes, Arthur*	8–0	—	11.0	1.6	0.66	2.26	1.72	1.85	19	1.8
0	60	66	27	Paniagua, Jose	4–3	—	6.3	5.2	0.95	4.98	4.36	4.77	-4	-0.4
0	69	65	34	Nelson, Jeff	4–3	—	12.1	6.1	0.41	3.33	2.76	2.89	11	1.1
7	100	187		Others	14–6	—	7.3	3.0	1.59	4.92	4.24	4.62	-7	-0.7
162	391		30.4	Team Total		52	6.5	2.9	0.98	4.19	3.54	3.85	67	6.4
				League Average		48	6.4	3.2	1.11	4.48	4.47	4.90		
				% Lg Avg		108	100	113	112	107	126	127		
				League Rank		3	5	4	5	5	1			

2001 OAKLAND ATHLETICS

The 2001 A's had perhaps their best team since the franchise moved to Oakland. However, the Mariners chose 2001 to also have their best season winning the division by 14 games. The A's and Mariners were easily the two best teams in the majors in 2001. However, the A's lost to the Yankees in the ALDS 3 games to 2.

Strengths: (1) SP, RP 1B, 3B, and SS position, (2) hitting for contact and power led by MVP runner-up Jason Giambi (47 2B, 38 HR), Chavez (43 2B, 32 HR), Jeremy Giambi (26 2B), and Dye, (3) drawing walks led by Jason Giambi (129) and Menechino (79), (4) baserunning from Damon (7 GIDP, 27 SB, 12 CS, 45% RS), (5) fielding from 3B Chavez (106 Rng+, 12 errors in 433 chances), CF/LF Damon (121 Held+, 85 Held+ in LF), 2B Menechino (105 Rng+), and C Hernandez, and (6) pitching from Cy Young runner-up Mulder (65% QS, 3.0 K/BB), Hudson (71% QS), Zito (69% QS, 205 K), Lidle (59% QS), and closer Isringhausen (34/43/79% Sv, 1.929 Lv, 3.2 K/BB).

Weaknesses: (1) hitting from Damon and Saenz, (2) baserunning from Hernandez (28% RS) and Jeremy Giambi (13 GIDP), (3) fielding from RF Jeremy Giambi (71 Held+, 63 Rng+), and (4) pitching from Heredia (44% QS, 11.8 H/9).

Mgr	Art Howe	
Rk	25	74
Gm	162	
Place	2	
GB	14.0	
Rival	9–10 vs Mariners, 94 RS, 93 RA	

	W	L	Win%
Regular Season	102	60	0.630
Runs Record	101	61	0.626
1 Run	21	19	0.525
Extra Innings	7	7	0.500
Blowout	31	9	0.775

	Team	LgAvg	%Avg	LgRk
BABIP	0.285	0.297	104	2
E	125	114	91	11
sOBP	0.309	0.336	109	2
rOBP	0.306	0.330	108	2
R/G	5.46	4.86	0.60	4
RA/G	3.98	4.86	0.88	2

	Tm	LgAvg	>Avg
RS	884	787	97
RA	645	787	142
DP	151	150	1

	R/G	HR	K	BB	SB	CS	SB%	OPS	Held+	
Team Offense	5.46	199	1021	640	68	29	70%	0.784	**LF**	90
Team Defense	3.98	153	1117	440	124	55	69%	0.688	**CF**	114
Difference	1.48	46	96	200	-56			114%	**RF**	107

Pos	Rpos	PA	Age	Name	BA	OBP	SLG	BB%	XBT	Bat R>Avg	BR R>Avg	Fld R>Avg	RAA	WAA
C	8	509	25	Hernandez, Ramon	0.254	0.316	0.408	7%	33%	-7	-4	6	3	0.3

Pos	Rpos	PA	Age	Name	BA	OBP	SLG	BB%	XBT	Bat R>Avg	BR R>Avg	Fld R>Avg	RAA	WAA
1B,DH	-7	671	30	Giambi, Jason*	0.342	0.477	0.660	19%	26%	82	-2	4	77	7.4
2B	3	578	30	Menechino, Frank	0.242	0.369	0.374	14%	28%	2	-2	7	10	1.0
3B	3	604	23	Chavez, Eric*	0.288	0.338	0.540	7%	56%	20	3	12	38	3.7
SS	9	683	27	Tejada, Miguel	0.267	0.326	0.476	6%	45%	6	1	-1	15	1.5
CF,OF	-2	687	25	Long, Terrence*	0.283	0.335	0.412	8%	46%	-3	1	1	-3	-0.3
CF,LF	-1	719	27	Damon, Johnny*	0.256	0.324	0.363	8%	53%	-16	4	8	-5	-0.5
RF	-2	265	27	Dye, Jermaine	0.297	0.366	0.547	10%	46%	13	1	-1	11	1.0
DH,RF	-4	443	26	Giambi, Jeremy*	0.283	0.391	0.450	14%	37%	14	-3	-10	-3	-0.3
DH,1B	-2	341	30	Saenz, Olmedo	0.220	0.291	0.384	6%	36%	-11	1	2	-10	-0.9
C	1	100	35	Myers, Greg*	0.184	0.290	0.437	13%	50%	-2	0	2	1	0.1
DH,LF	-1	93	36	Gant, Ron	0.259	0.344	0.420	12%	50%	0	1	-3	-3	-0.3
	0	-5	692	Others	0.191	0.277	0.281	9%	34%	-44	0	-8	-57	-5.5
	0			Team Total	0.264	0.345	0.439	10.0%	40%	55	1	19	75	7.2
			28.4	League Average	0.267	0.334	0.428	8.3%	41%					
				% Lg Avg	99	104	102	121	97					
				League Rank	9	3	5	1	11		10	5		

GS	GR	IP	Age	Name	W–L	GmSc	K/9	BB/9	HR/9	FIP	ERA	RA/9	RAA	WAA
35	0	235	25	Hudson, Tim	18–9	55.5	6.9	2.7	0.77	3.66	3.37	3.83	25	2.4
34	0	229	23	Mulder, Mark*	21–8	55.3	6.0	2.0	0.63	3.43	3.45	3.61	30	2.9
35	0	214	23	Zito, Barry*	17–8	55.7	8.6	3.4	0.76	3.66	3.49	3.86	22	2.1
29	0	188	29	Lidle, Cory	13–6	54.0	5.6	2.3	1.10	4.31	3.59	4.02	16	1.5
18	6	110	35	Heredia, Gil	7–8	40.1	3.9	2.4	2.22	6.27	5.58	6.15	-17	-1.6
11	5	66	28	Hiljus, Erik	5–0	50.8	9.1	2.9	0.95	3.43	3.41	3.95	6	0.6
0	65	71	28	Isringhausen, Jason	4–3	0.0	9.3	2.9	0.63	2.77	2.65	3.03	14	1.3
0	70	75	30	Tam, Jeff	2–4	0.0	5.3	3.5	0.36	3.44	3.01	3.25	13	1.2
0	54	63	31	Mecir, Jim	2–8	0.0	8.7	3.7	0.57	3.02	3.43	3.57	9	0.8
0	65	55	36	Magnante, Mike*	3–1	0.0	3.7	2.1	1.14	4.59	2.77	3.74	6	0.6
0	54	52	35	Guthrie, Mark*	6–2	0.0	8.9	3.4	1.20	4.25	4.47	4.99	-1	-0.1
0	97	104		Others	4–3	0.0	7.8	2.6	1.38	4.20	3.71	3.88	11	1.0
162	416		29.4	Team Total		53	6.87	2.71	0.94	3.90	3.59	3.97	133	12.8
				League Average		48	6.44	3.24	1.11	4.48	4.47	4.90		
				% Lg Avg		110	107	120	117	115	125	124		
				League Rank		1	4	1	1	2	2			

2002 Anaheim Angels

The 2002 season had two dominant NL teams and four dominant AL teams all with run differentiations of 0.9 or higher culminating with two Wild Card teams, the Angels and Giants, competing in the World Series. The 2002 Angels got hot at the right time winning 3 straight postseason series to take the world championship. Their head-to-head 9–11 W–L record against the A's was the primary reason for their second place division finish.

Strengths: (1) hitting for average and contact led by Salmon (37 2B, 22 HR, 71 BB), Anderson (56 2B, 29 HR), Fullmer (35 2B, 19 HR, 15 HBP), Spiezio (34 2B) and Glaus (24 2B, 30 HR, 88 BB), (2) baserunning featuring Erstad (45% RS, 23 SB, 3 CS), Eckstein (7 GIDP, 41% RS), and Kennedy (5 GIDP, 17 SB, 4 CS), (3) fielding led by CF Erstad (11 assists, 122 Rng+, 111 Held+), LF/CF Anderson (2 errors out of 311 chances, 96 Rng+ in LF, 141 Rng+ in CF), 2B Kennedy (105 Rng+, 90 DP), and C Bengie Molina (45% CS), and (4) pitching led by starter Washburn (72% QS) and relievers Donnelly (13 Holds, 32/37/84% IR stranded), Percival (40/44/91% Sv), Shields (12/13/92% IR stranded), and Weber (18 Holds).

Weaknesses: (1) C position, (2) hitting for power, (3) hitting and baserunning from Molina (24% RS), (4) drawing walks, and (5) pitching from Sele (42% QS, 10.7 H/9) and Schoeneweis.

				W	L	Win%		Team	LgAvg	%Avg	LgRk
Mgr	Mike Scioscia		**Regular Season**	99	63	0.611	**BABIP**	0.271	0.292	108	1
Rk	36	106	**Runs Record**	100	62	0.620	**E**	87	106	122	2
Gm	162		**1 Run**	31	22	0.585	**sOBP**	0.318	0.330	104	5

Place	2
GB	4.0
Rival	9–11 vs A's; 81 RS, 82 RA

	W	*L*	*Win%*
Extra Innings	10	5	0.667
Blowout	30	12	0.714

	Team	*LgAvg*	*%Avg*	*LgRk*
rOBP	0.303	0.335	111	1
R/G	5.25	4.81	0.44	4
RA/G	3.98	4.80	0.82	1

	Tm	*LgAvg*	*>Avg*
RS	851	778	73
RA	644	776	132
DP	151	149	2

	R/G	*HR*	*K*	*BB*	*SB*	*CS*	*SB%*	*OPS*	*Held+*	
Team Offense	5.25	152	805	462	117	51	70%	0.773	**LF**	101
Team Defense	3.98	169	999	509	78	51	60%	0.706	**CF**	116
Difference	1.28	-17	194	-47	39			110%	**RF**	99

Pos	*Rpos*	*PA*	*Age*	*Name*	*BA*	*OBP*	*SLG*	*BB%*	*XBT*	*Bat R>Avg*	*BR R>Avg*	*Fld R>Avg*	*RAA*	*WAA*
C	7	459	27	Molina, Bengie	0.245	0.274	0.322	3%	25%	-25	-6	10	-14	-1.3
1B,3B	-8	571	29	Spiezio, Scott^	0.285	0.371	0.436	12%	38%	12	-4	5	5	0.5
2B	3	509	26	Kennedy, Adam*	0.312	0.345	0.449	4%	41%	6	4	12	25	2.4
3B	3	671	25	Glaus, Troy	0.250	0.352	0.453	13%	48%	12	1	7	23	2.2
SS	8	702	27	Eckstein, David	0.293	0.363	0.388	6%	47%	3	5	10	26	2.5
LF,CF	-6	678	30	Anderson, Garret*	0.306	0.332	0.539	4%	32%	23	-1	12	28	2.7
CF	2	663	28	Erstad, Darin*	0.283	0.313	0.389	4%	46%	-13	10	39	38	3.7
RF,DH	-6	568	33	Salmon, Tim	0.286	0.380	0.503	13%	33%	25	-1	0	18	1.7
DH,1B	-1	479	27	Fullmer, Brad*	0.289	0.357	0.531	7%	55%	20	3	-1	21	2.0
RF,OF	-4	300	33	Palmeiro, Orlando*	0.300	0.368	0.354	10%	38%	-1	1	2	-2	-0.2
2B,SS	0	139	29	Gil, Benji	0.285	0.307	0.431	4%	33%	-1	-1	6	4	0.4
DH,1B	-1	121	29	Wooten, Shawn	0.292	0.331	0.442	5%	21%	1	0	1	1	0.1
RF,LF	-1	75	30	Ochoa, Alex	0.277	0.373	0.477	13%	50%	2	-2	-1	-2	-0.2
	4	392		Others	0.246	0.280	0.301	4%	24%	-23	3	-4	-20	-1.9
	0		28.7	Team Total	0.282	0.341	0.433	7.3%	39%	42	12	98	152	14.6
				League Average	0.264	0.331	0.424	8.4%	40%					
				% Lg Avg	107	103	102	87	98					
				League Rank	1	4	6	13	8		2	1		

GS	*GR*	*IP*	*Age*	*Name*	*W–L*	*GmSc*	*K/9*	*BB/9*	*HR/9*	*FIP*	*ERA*	*RA/9*	*RAA*	*WAA*
32	0	217	29	Ortiz, Ramon	15–9	55.3	6.7	2.8	1.66	5.04	3.77	4.02	6	0.6
32	0	206	27	Washburn, Jarrod*	18–6	55.8	6.1	2.6	0.83	3.87	3.15	3.28	22	2.1
32	0	188	34	Appier, Kevin	14–12	50.9	6.3	3.1	1.10	4.42	3.92	4.25	0	0.0
26	0	160	32	Sele, Aaron	8–9	45.3	4.6	2.8	1.18	4.83	4.89	5.18	-18	-1.7
18	0	108	23	Lackey, John	9–4	50.6	5.7	2.7	0.83	4.09	3.66	4.32	-2	-0.1
0	58	56	32	Percival, Troy	4–1	—	10.9	4.0	0.80	3.15	1.92	1.92	15	1.5
15	39	118	28	Schoeneweis, Scott*	9–8	44.7	5.0	3.7	1.30	5.18	4.88	5.19	-13	-1.2
0	63	78	32	Weber, Ben	7–2	—	5.0	2.5	0.46	3.54	2.54	2.88	12	1.1
0	52	64	34	Levine, Alan	4–4	—	5.7	4.8	1.13	5.06	4.24	4.95	-5	-0.5
0	46	50	30	Donnelly, Brendan	1–1	—	9.8	3.4	0.36	2.57	2.17	2.35	11	1.1
1	28	49	26	Shields, Scot	5–3	43.0	5.5	3.9	0.73	4.26	2.20	2.39	10	1.0
6	114	158		Others	5–4	—	6.6	3.8	0.91	4.36	3.82	4.17	2	0.2
162	400		29.7	Team Total		51	6.19	3.15	1.05	4.37	3.69	3.99	40	3.9
				League Average		49	6.26	3.25	1.10	4.47	4.46	4.85		
				% Lg Avg		104	99	103	105	102	121	121		
				League Rank		4	8	7	6	7	2			

2002 New York Yankees

Exceptional hitting and consistent pitching powered the 2002 Yankees to 103 wins with help from free agent signees Giambi, Wells, and White. However, the Yankees lost their postseason series losing 3 games to 1 to the Angels in the ALDS.

Strengths: (1) hitting led by Giambi (34 2B, 41 HR), Soriano (51 2B, 39 HR), Posada (40 2B, 20 HR), Ventura (27 HR), Jeter (26 2B, 18 HR), and Williams (37 2B, 19 HR), (2) drawing walks featuring Giambi (109), Ventura (90), Williams (83), and Posada (81), (3) baserunning from Jeter (32 SB, 3 CS, 42% RS) and Soriano (41 SB, 13 CS, 8 GIDP, 43% RS), (4) fielding from LF White (110 Rng+), (5) Held+ from RF Mondesi (115), and (6) pitching from Mussina (55% QS), Hernandez (59% QS), Wells (58% QS), Pettitte (50% QS), Clemens (55% QS, 192 K),

Rivera (24/28/88% Sv), Stanton (17 Holds, 42/60/70% IR stranded), Karsay (14 Holds, 12/16/75% Sv, 39/54/72% IR stranded), and Mendoza (12 Holds, 34/52/65% IR).

Weaknesses: (1) LF and RF positions, (2) hitting from White and Wilson, (3) GIDP especially from Posada (23), and (4) fielding from CF Williams (86 Rng+, 89 Held+), SS Jeter (84 Rng+, 69 DP), 2B Soriano (93 Rng+, 86 DP), and RF Mondesi (84 Rng+).

			W	L	Win%
Mgr	Joe Torre	**Regular Season**	103	58	0.640
Rk	30 88	**Runs Record**	101	60	0.624
Gm	161	**1 Run**	21	21	0.500
Place	1	**Extra Innings**	6	7	0.462
GA	10.5	**Blowout**	35	13	0.729
Rival	10–9 vs Red Sox, 100 RS, 80 RA; 4–3 vs Angels, 28 RS, 24 RA				

	Team	LgAvg	%Avg	LgRk
BABIP	0.295	0.292	99	8
E	87	106	122	2
sOBP	0.305	0.330	108	2
rOBP	0.319	0.335	105	4
R/G	5.57	4.81	0.76	1
RA/G	4.33	4.80	0.47	5

	Tm	LgAvg	>Avg
RS	897	778	119
RA	697	776	79
DP	117	149	-32

	R/G	HR	K	BB	SB	CS	SB%	OPS
Team Offense	5.57	223	1171	640	100	38	72%	0.809
Team Defense	4.33	144	1135	403	92	39	70%	0.705
Difference	1.24	79	-36	237	8			115%

	Held+
LF	102
CF	91
RF	109

Pos	Rpos	PA	Age	Name	BA	OBP	SLG	BB%	XBT	Bat R>Avg	BR R>Avg	Fld R>Avg	RAA	WAA
C	8	598	30	Posada, Jorge^	0.268	0.370	0.468	14%	40%	17	-2	-4	19	1.9
1B,DH	-5	689	31	Giambi, Jason*	0.314	0.435	0.598	16%	29%	63	-3	1	56	5.4
2B	4	741	26	Soriano, Alfonso	0.300	0.332	0.547	3%	70%	27	6	-13	24	2.3
3B+	2	562	34	Ventura, Robin*	0.247	0.368	0.458	16%	37%	15	0	3	20	1.9
SS	8	730	28	Jeter, Derek	0.297	0.373	0.421	10%	50%	12	8	-18	10	1.0
LF,DH	-6	494	30	White, Rondell	0.240	0.288	0.378	5%	57%	-16	2	10	-10	-1.0
CF	2	699	33	Williams, Bernie^	0.333	0.415	0.493	12%	43%	39	3	-22	22	2.1
RF,CF	-2	302	31	Mondesi, Raul	0.241	0.315	0.430	9%	55%	-2	2	-9	-11	-1.0
1B,DH	-4	441	23	Johnson, Nick*	0.243	0.347	0.402	11%	33%	0	-2	4	-2	-0.2
RF,LF	-4	329	30	Spencer, Shane	0.247	0.324	0.375	9%	48%	-5	-1	0	-10	-1.0
RF,DH	-3	245	36	Vander Wal, John*	0.260	0.327	0.429	9%	35%	0	-2	0	-5	-0.5
3B,DH	0	156	35	Coomer, Ron	0.264	0.290	0.372	4%	27%	-5	-2	-3	-10	-1.0
3B,2B	1	119	28	Wilson, Enrique^	0.181	0.239	0.295	7%	24%	-9	-1	-2	-11	-1.1
LF,RF	-1	91	23	Rivera, Juan	0.265	0.311	0.361	7%	50%	-2	-1	0	-4	-0.4
C	1	68	31	Widger, Chris	0.297	0.338	0.375	3%	43%	-1	0	-1	-1	-0.1
	-1	113		Others	0.146	0.176	0.233	4%	41%	-14	1	-2	-16	-1.5
	0		29.9	Team Total	0.275	0.354	0.455	10.0%	44%	119	8	-56	71	6.8
				League Average	0.264	0.331	0.424	8.4%	41%					
				% Lg Avg	104	107	107	119	108					
				League Rank	3	1	1	1	3		5	14		

GS	GR	IP	Age	Name	W–L	GmSc	K/9	BB/9	HR/9	FIP	ERA	RA/9	RAA	WAA
33	0	216	33	Mussina, Mike	18–10	53.8	7.6	2.0	1.13	3.80	4.05	4.30	21	2.0
31	0	206	39	Wells, David*	19–7	52.5	6.0	2.0	0.92	3.83	3.75	4.36	20	1.9
29	0	180	39	Clemens, Roger	13–6	52.9	9.6	3.2	0.90	3.37	4.35	4.70	9	0.9
22	2	146	36	Hernandez, Orlando	8–5	54.8	7.0	2.2	1.05	3.96	3.64	3.88	21	2.0
22	0	135	30	Pettitte, Andy*	13–5	52.8	6.5	2.1	0.40	3.03	3.27	3.88	20	1.9
11	5	77	26	Lilly, Ted*	3–6	56.3	6.9	2.8	1.17	4.31	3.40	3.64	13	1.3
8	7	78	25	Weaver, Jeff	5–3	51.1	6.6	1.7	1.38	4.25	4.04	4.38	7	0.7
0	45	46	32	Rivera, Mariano	1–4	0.0	8.0	2.2	0.59	2.92	2.74	3.13	10	1.0
0	62	92	30	Mendoza, Ramiro	8–4	0.0	6.0	1.6	0.79	3.46	3.44	4.22	10	1.0
0	78	88	30	Karsay, Steve	6–4	0.0	6.6	3.1	0.71	3.30	3.26	3.36	18	1.7
0	79	78	35	Stanton, Mike*	7–1	0.0	5.1	3.2	0.46	3.63	3.00	3.35	16	1.6
5	56	111		Other	2–3	0.0	7.1	4.5	0.90	4.37	6.18	7.24	-25	-2.4
161	334		32.3	Team Total		52	7.04	2.50	0.89	3.70	3.87	4.32	141	13.6
				League Average		49	6.26	3.25	1.10	4.47	4.46	4.85		
				% Lg Avg		106	112	130	123	121	115	112		
				League Rank		3	2	1	3	1	4			

2002 Boston Red Sox

The 2002 Red Sox had a strong team but the 2002 Yankees were a bit stronger and much luckier winning the AL East by a comfortable 10.5 game margin. The Red Sox also lost out on the Wild Card spot as the Angels had an even more impressive season. The Curse of the Babino was still going strong in Boston.

Strengths: (1) hitting for average, contact, and power especially from Ramirez (31 2B, 33 HR), Garciaparra (56 2B, 24 HR), and Damon (34 2B, 11 3B, 14 HR), (2) baserunning from Damon (4 GIDP, 31 SB, 6 CS, 44% RS), (3) fielding from SS Garciaparra (101 Rng+, 92 DP), 2B Sanchez (95 Rng+), RF Nixon (98 Rng+), and 3B Hillenbrand (94 Rng+), and (4) pitching from Lowe (75% QS), Cy Young runner-up Pedro Martinez (70% QS, 239 K), and Wakefield (73% QS).

Weaknesses: (1) RP and 1B positions, (2) hitting from Clark, Sanchez, and Offerman, (3) baserunning from Daubach (27% RS), (4) winning games decided by 1 run, and (5) pitching from Castillo (48% QS, 9.6 H/9).

					W	L	Win%		Team	LgAvg	%Avg	LgRk
Mgr	Grady Little			**Regular Season**	93	69	0.574	**BABIP**	0.284	0.292	103	4
Rk	41	119		**Runs Record**	100	62	0.617	**E**	104	106	102	2
Gm	162			**1 Run**	13	23	0.361	**sOBP**	0.300	0.330	110	1
Place	2			**Extra Innings**	3	5	0.375	**rOBP**	0.323	0.335	104	7
GB	10.5			**Blowout**	34	19	0.642	**R/G**	5.30	4.81	0.49	2
Rival	9–10 vs Yankees, 80 RS, 100 RA; 4–3 vs Angels, 29 RS, 26 RA							**RA/G**	4.10	4.80	0.69	3

	Tm	LgAvg	>Avg		R/G	HR	K	BB	SB	CS	SB%	OPS		Held+
RS	859	778	81	**Team Offense**	5.30	177	944	545	80	28	74%	0.789	**LF**	89
RA	665	776	111	**Team Defense**	4.10	146	1157	430	118	50	70%	0.693	**CF**	94
DP	140	149	-9	**Difference**	1.20	31	213	115	-38			114%	**RF**	84

Pos	Rpos	PA	Age	Name	BA	OBP	SLG	BB%	XBT	Bat R>Avg	BR R>Avg	Fld R>Avg	RAA	WAA
C	7	519	30	Varitek, Jason^	0.266	0.332	0.392	8%	36%	-5	0	4	6	0.6
1B	-4	298	30	Clark, Tony^	0.207	0.265	0.291	7%	19%	-20	-1	3	-22	-2.2
2B	3	386	34	Sanchez, Rey	0.286	0.318	0.345	4%	42%	-11	1	8	1	0.1
3B	3	676	26	Hillenbrand, Shea	0.293	0.330	0.459	4%	40%	6	0	6	15	1.4
SS	8	693	28	Garciaparra, Nomar	0.310	0.352	0.528	6%	45%	27	-2	16	49	4.7
LF,DH	-7	518	30	Ramirez, Manny	0.349	0.450	0.647	14%	27%	57	-3	1	48	4.7
CF	3	702	28	Damon, Johnny*	0.286	0.356	0.443	9%	42%	11	11	3	28	2.7
RF	-6	612	28	Nixon, Trot*	0.256	0.338	0.470	11%	40%	10	2	6	12	1.2
DH,2B	0	194	33	Baerga, Carlos^	0.286	0.316	0.379	4%	37%	-4	1	0	-3	-0.3
1B,DH	-3	506	30	Daubach, Brian*	0.266	0.348	0.464	10%	29%	9	-4	3	5	0.5
1B,DH	-2	275	33	Offerman, Jose^	0.232	0.325	0.325	12%	58%	-8	-1	4	-7	-0.7
2B	2	222	31	Merloni, Lou	0.247	0.332	0.392	9%	21%	-2	-1	6	5	0.5
LF	-2	222	43	Henderson, Rickey	0.223	0.369	0.352	17%	50%	0	0	-1	-3	-0.3
LF,DH	-2	190	29	Floyd, Cliff*	0.316	0.374	0.561	8%	28%	11	2	-2	9	0.9
C	2	173	31	Mirabelli, Jason	0.225	0.312	0.411	10%	19%	-2	-1	2	1	0.1
	-2	146		Others	0.220	0.314	0.293	11%	40%	-6	1	3	-4	-0.4
	0		30.9	Team Total	0.277	0.345	0.444	8.6%	37%	74	5	62	141	13.6
				League Average	0.264	0.331	0.424	8.4%	40%					
				% Lg Avg	105	104	105	102	93					
				League Rank	2	3	4	7	14		6	2		

GS	GR	IP	Age	Name	W–L	GmSc	K/9	BB/9	HR/9	FIP	ERA	RA/9	RAA	WAA
32	0	220	29	Lowe, Derek	21–8	60.3	5.2	2.0	0.49	3.51	2.58	2.66	44	4.2
30	0	199	30	Martinez, Pedro	20–4	64.8	10.8	1.8	0.59	2.40	2.26	2.80	38	3.7
29	0	173	37	Burkett, John	13–8	48.3	6.5	2.6	1.30	4.50	4.53	4.84	-8	-0.8
23	13	163	33	Castillo, Frank	6–15	46.6	6.2	3.2	1.05	4.36	5.07	5.57	-21	-2.0
15	30	163	35	Wakefield, Tim	11–5	61.3	7.4	2.8	0.83	3.75	2.81	3.14	24	2.3
12	31	107	24	Fossum, Casey*	5–4	49.7	8.5	2.5	1.01	3.66	3.46	4.72	-3	-0.3
9	5	58	31	Oliver, Darren*	4–5	45.6	5.0	4.2	1.09	5.31	4.66	4.66	-1	-0.1
0	61	60	28	Urbina, Ugueth	1–6	0.0	10.7	3.0	1.20	3.25	3.00	3.15	9	0.9
8	21	81	33	Arrojo, Rolando	4–3	47.1	5.6	3.0	0.77	4.18	4.98	5.20	-7	-0.7
0	32	33	32	Embree, Alan*	1–2	0.0	11.6	3.0	1.08	3.10	2.97	3.24	5	0.5

GS	GR	IP	Age	Name	W–L	GmSc	K/9	BB/9	HR/9	FIP	ERA	RA/9	RAA	WAA
0	29	39	33	Banks, Willie	2–1	0.0	6.0	3.2	1.15	4.78	3.23	3.46	4	0.4
4	116	149		Others	5–8	0.0	5.9	3.3	1.15	4.68	5.98	6.40	-33	-3.2
162	338		31.4	Team Total		55	7.20	2.68	0.91	3.85	3.75	4.14	52	5.0
				League Average		49	6.26	3.25	1.10	4.47	4.46	4.85		
				% Lg Avg		112	115	122	121	116	119	117		
				League Rank		1	1	4	4	2	3			

2002 San Francisco Giants

The 2002 Giants were the best of the Giant teams since the team relocated from New York to San Francisco. Barry Bonds repeated as the NL MVP award winner. This team went all the way to the seventh game of the World Series before losing to the Angels.

Strengths: (1) hitting for average and power led by MVP Bonds (major league record 198 BB, 68 IBB, 31 2B, 41 HR) and Kent (42 2B, 37 HR), (2) home run differentiation, (3) fielding especially RF Sanders (116 Rng+, 12 assists), CF Shinjo (122 Rng+, 10 assists), 3B Bell (94 Rng+, only 9 errors in 331 chances), and CF Lofton (112 Rng+), and (4) pitching anchored by Rueter (58% QS), Ortiz (73% QS), Schmidt (52% QS, 196 K, 2.7 K/BB), closer Nen (43/51/84% Sv, 18/26/69% IR stranded, 4.0 K/BB, 2.241 Lv), and Worrell (23 holds, 28/42/67% IR stranded, 1.149 Lv).

Weaknesses: (1) 1B position, (2) hitting from CF Shinjo and Snow, (3) Held+ from CF Shinjo (92), and (4) pitching from Jensen (43% QS, 9.6 H/9) and Hernandez (58% QS, 9.7 H/9).

				W	L	Win%		Team	LgAvg	%Avg	LgRk
Mgr	Dusty Baker		**Regular Season**	95	66	0.590	**BABIP**	0.286	0.293	103	4
Rk	33	100	**Runs Record**	100	61	0.621	**E**	90	109	121	4
Gm	161		**1 Run**	28	22	0.560	**sOBP**	0.323	0.332	103	5
Place	2		**Extra Innings**	8	1	0.889	**rOBP**	0.308	0.329	107	3
GB	2.5		**Blowout**	31	11	0.738	**R/G**	4.86	4.45	0.41	3
Rival	11–8 vs Diamondbacks, 79 RS, 70 RA; 3–3 vs Braves, 24 RS, 23 RA							**RA/G**	3.83	4.46	0.64
2											

	Tm	LgAvg	>Avg		R/G	HR	K	BB	SB	CS	SB%	OPS	Held+	
RS	783	720	63	**Team Offense**	4.86	198	961	616	74	21	78%	0.786	**LF**	98
RA	616	722	106	**Team Defense**	3.83	116	992	523	87	36	71%	0.691	**CF**	87
DP	166	155	11	**Difference**	1.04	82	31	93	-13			114%	**RF**	101

Pos	Rpos	PA	Age	Name	BA	OBP	SLG	BB%	XBT	Bat R>Avg	BR R>Avg	Fld R>Avg	RAA	WAA
C	7	517	37	Santiago, Benito	0.278	0.315	0.450	5%	40%	2	-1	0	8	0.8
1B	-6	494	34	Snow, J.T.*	0.246	0.344	0.360	12%	22%	-3	-3	-3	-15	-1.5
2B,1B	3	682	34	Kent, Jeff	0.313	0.368	0.565	8%	46%	40	-1	3	45	4.5
3B,2B	3	628	29	Bell, David	0.261	0.333	0.429	9%	44%	4	-2	9	14	1.4
SS	7	589	30	Aurilia, Rich	0.257	0.305	0.413	6%	36%	-6	-4	-4	-7	-0.7
LF	-6	612	37	Bonds, Barry*	0.370	0.582	0.799	32%	27%	118	-2	0	110	11.0
CF	2	398	30	Shinjo, Tsuyoshi	0.238	0.294	0.370	6%	50%	-11	0	12	3	0.3
RF	-5	571	34	Sanders, Reggie	0.250	0.324	0.455	8%	49%	6	2	14	17	1.7
CF	1	205	35	Lofton, Kenny*	0.267	0.353	0.406	11%	46%	2	2	6	11	1.1
1B	-2	201	28	Minor, Damon*	0.237	0.333	0.445	12%	20%	2	0	0	0	0.0
SS,2B	2	200	29	Martinez, Ramon	0.271	0.335	0.414	7%	63%	0	1	-2	1	0.1
CF,LF	-1	171	33	Goodwin, Tom*	0.260	0.321	0.338	8%	52%	-4	3	6	4	0.4
C	3	155	23	Torrealba, Yorvit	0.279	0.355	0.397	9%	25%	1	0	2	6	0.6
	-8	875		Others	0.220	0.248	0.296	3%	36%	-59	2	-5	-70	-7.0
	0		31.8	Team Total	0.267	0.344	0.442	9.8%	38%	92	-3	38	127	12.7
				League Average	0.259	0.331	0.410	9.0%	41%					
				% Lg Avg	103	104	108	109	93					
				League Rank	3	2	1	3	15		9	4		

GS	GR	IP	Age	Name	W–L	GmSc	K/9	BB/9	HR/9	FIP	ERA	RA/9	RAA	WAA
33	0	216	27	Hernandez, Livan	12–16	49.4	5.6	3.0	0.79	3.88	4.38	4.71	-11	-1.1
33	0	214	28	Ortiz, Russ	14–10	53.5	5.8	3.9	0.63	3.93	3.61	3.74	12	1.2
33	0	204	31	Rueter, Kirk*	14–8	51.6	3.4	2.4	0.97	4.37	3.23	3.67	13	1.3
29	0	185	29	Schmidt, Jason	13–8	57.8	9.5	3.5	0.73	3.14	3.45	3.79	10	1.0
30	2	172	26	Jensen, Ryan	13–8	46.7	5.5	3.5	1.10	4.54	4.51	4.87	-12	-1.2
0	68	74	32	Nen, Robb	6–2	—	9.9	2.4	0.24	1.69	2.20	2.32	16	1.6
0	80	72	34	Worrell, Tim	8–2	—	6.9	3.8	0.38	3.18	2.25	2.63	13	1.3
0	71	69	29	Rodriguez, Felix	8–6	—	7.6	3.8	0.65	3.65	4.17	4.30	0	0.0
0	44	68	29	Witasick, Jay	1–0	—	7.1	2.8	0.40	2.96	2.37	2.50	13	1.3
0	50	56	30	Zerbe, Chad*	2–0	—	4.2	3.4	0.48	4.00	3.04	3.52	5	0.5
4	102	107		Others	4–6	—	5.9	3.7	0.67	3.93	3.36	3.87	5	0.5
162	417		29.5	Team Total		52	6.21	3.27	0.73	3.75	3.54	3.86	64	6.4
				League Average		50	6.77	3.49	1.01	4.11	4.11	4.50		
				% Lg Avg		104	92	107	140	110	116	117		
				League Rank		5	13	3	1	2	2			

2004 St. Louis Cardinals

The 2004 Cardinals had the highest run differentiation in the majors leading the NL in both runs scored and runs allowed. The two best teams in each league squared off against each other in the World Series. The Red Sox, coming back from the brink of elimination by the Yankees in the ALCS, won seven straight playoff games to win their first world championship since 1918 breaking the Curse of the Bambino.

Strengths: (1) hitting for average and power led by Pujols (51 2B, 46 HR, 84 BB), Edmonds (38 2B, 42 HR, 101 BB), Rolen (32 2B, 34 HR), Walker, and Mabry (13 HR), (2) team baserunning especially from Womack (26 SB, 5 CS, 6 GIDP, 42% RS), (3) fielding from 3B Rolen (10 E in 428 chances, 111 Rng+), 2B Womack (99 Rng+), and 1B Pujols (114 assists), (4) Held+ from LF Lankford (110), CF Edmonds (113), and RF Sanders (111), and (5) pitching from Carpenter (64% QS), Marquis (59% QS), Kline (15 Holds, 28/38/74% IR stranded, 1.274 Lv), King (32 Holds, 34/44/77% IR stranded, 1.093 Lv), Tavarez (19 Holds, 32/43/74% IR stranded, 1.138 Lv), and closer Isringhausen (47/54/87% Sv, 16/23/70% IR stranded, 1.768 Lv).

Weaknesses: (1) C and LF position, (2) hitting from Matheny and Anderson, (3) fielding from LF/3B Mabry (104 Rng+ in LF, 99 Rng+ at 3B), and (4) pitching from Morris (50% QS, 9.1 H/9).

				W	L	Win%
Mgr	Tony LaRussa		**Regular Season**	105	57	0.648
Rk	32	96	**Runs Record**	100	62	0.620
Gm	162		**1 Run**	29	20	0.592
Place	1		**Extra Innings**	9	4	0.692
GA	13.0		**Blowout**	32	13	0.711
Rival	8–10 vs Astros, 78 RS, 92 RA; 4–2 vs Braves, 36 RS, 23 RA					

	Team	LgAvg	%Avg	LgRk
BABIP	0.280	0.296	106	1
E	97	103	106	6
sOBP	0.321	0.333	104	5
rOBP	0.294	0.333	113	1
R/G	5.28	4.64	0.64	1
RA/G	4.07	4.66	0.59	1

	Tm	LgAvg	>Avg
RS	855	751	104
RA	659	754	95
DP	154	149	5

	R/G	HR	K	BB	SB	CS	SB%	OPS
Team Offense	5.28	214	1085	548	111	47	70%	0.804
Team Defense	4.07	169	1041	440	53	29	65%	0.715
Difference	1.21	45	-44	108	58			112%

	Held+
LF	104
CF	110
RF	108

Pos	Rpos	PA	Age	Name	BA	OBP	SLG	BB%	XBT	Bat R>Avg	BR R>Avg	Fld R>Avg	RAA	WAA
C	7	419	33	Matheny, Mike	0.247	0.292	0.348	5%	29%	-17	-3	-2	-15	-1.4
1B	-9	692	24	Pujols, Albert	0.331	0.415	0.657	12%	56%	69	0	7	67	6.6
2B	3	606	34	Womack, Tony*	0.307	0.349	0.385	6%	60%	-2	9	8	18	1.7
3B	2	593	29	Rolen, Scott	0.314	0.409	0.598	12%	56%	48	2	30	82	8.0
SS	7	642	27	Renteria, Edgar	0.287	0.327	0.401	6%	48%	-5	-1	3	4	0.4
LF	-2	235	37	Lankford, Ray*	0.255	0.349	0.425	12%	33%	2	-2	-1	-3	-0.3
CF	3	612	34	Edmonds, Jim*	0.301	0.418	0.643	17%	31%	58	-2	2	61	6.0
RF,LF	-5	487	36	Sanders, Reggie	0.260	0.315	0.482	7%	43%	4	2	3	4	0.4

Pos	Rpos	PA	Age	Name	BA	OBP	SLG	BB%	XBT	Bat R>Avg	BR R>Avg	Fld R>Avg	RAA	WAA
LF,3B	-3	275	33	Mabry, John*	0.296	0.363	0.504	9%	32%	10	-2	-10	-5	-0.5
2B,LF	-1	271	30	Anderson, Marlon*	0.237	0.269	0.379	4%	35%	-11	-1	-2	-15	-1.4
C	3	151	21	Molina, Yadier	0.267	0.329	0.356	9%	36%	-3	0	2	2	0.2
CF,LF	-3	206	34	Taguchi, So	0.291	0.337	0.419	6%	56%	0	0	-2	-5	-0.5
RF	-2	178	37	Walker, Larry*	0.280	0.393	0.560	13%	44%	11	0	-5	4	0.4
	0	930		Others	0.215	0.256	0.285	5%	41%	-67	2	-2	-67	-6.5
	0		31.5	Team Total	0.278	0.344	0.460	8.7%	45%	98	4	31	133	13.1
				League Average	0.263	0.333	0.423	8.7%	41%					
				% Lg Avg	106	103	109	100	109					
				League Rank	1	4	1	9	2		3	4		

GS	GR	IP	Age	Name	W–L	GmSc	K/9	BB/9	HR/9	FIP	ERA	RA/9	RAA	WAA
32	0	202	29	Morris, Matt	15–10	50.0	5.8	2.5	1.56	4.93	4.72	5.17	-15	-1.5
32	0	201	25	Marquis, Jason	15–7	51.0	6.2	3.1	1.16	4.59	3.71	4.02	10	1.0
31	0	190	37	Williams, Woody	11–8	51.0	6.2	2.8	0.95	4.10	4.18	4.41	2	0.2
31	0	188	29	Suppan, Jeff	16–9	49.0	5.3	3.1	1.20	4.81	4.16	4.69	-4	-0.4
28	0	182	29	Carpenter, Chris	15–5	56.0	7.5	1.9	1.19	3.87	3.46	3.71	16	1.6
0	74	75	31	Isringhausen, Jason	4–2	0.0	8.5	2.7	0.60	2.91	2.87	3.23	11	1.1
0	52	67	36	Eldred, Cal	4–2	0.0	7.3	2.3	1.48	4.38	3.76	4.16	3	0.2
0	77	64	31	Tavarez, Julian	7–4	0.0	6.7	2.7	0.14	2.98	2.38	2.94	11	1.1
0	86	62	30	King, Ray*	5–2	0.0	5.8	3.5	0.15	3.33	2.61	2.76	12	1.2
0	67	50	31	Kline, Steve*	2–2	0.0	6.3	3.0	0.54	3.50	1.79	2.15	13	1.3
0	41	45	29	Calero, Kiko	3–1	0.0	9.3	2.0	0.99	3.12	2.78	2.78	9	0.9
8	72	126		Others	8–5	0.0	6.0	3.1	0.93	4.25	4.27	4.49	0	0.0
162	469		30.6	Team Total		51	6.45	2.72	1.05	4.18	3.75	4.08	67	6.6
				League Average		49	6.74	3.38	1.11	4.35	4.30	4.69		
				% Lg Avg		104	96	124	106	104	115	115		
				League Rank		3	10	2	5	6	2			

2007 Boston Red Sox

The 2007 season featured strong seasons from both the Red Sox and Yankees. The 2007 Red Sox repeated as world champions by having the major league best seasons at the starting pitching, relief pitching, and DH positions as measured by Wins Above Average in baseball-reference.com. The Rockies won 7 straight playoff games to start the postseason but then were swept themselves by the Red Sox in the World Series.

Strengths: (1) hitting led by Ortiz (52 2B, 35 HR), Lowell (37 2B, 21 HR), Ramirez (33 2B, 20 HR), Youklis (35 2B, 16 HR), and Roy Pedroia (39 2B, 8 HR), (2) drawing walks especially from Ortiz (111), Drew (79), Youklis (77), Varitek (71), and Ramirez (71), (3) baserunning from Crisp (28 SB, 6 CS, 42% RS), (4) fielding from CF Crisp (114 Rng+, 105 Held+) and 1B Youklis (0 E in 1080 chances), and (5) pitching from Cy Young runner-up Beckett (67% QS, 4.9 K/BB, 194 K), Schilling (58% QS, 4.4 K/BB), Papelbon (37/40/93% Sv, 14/19/74% IR stranded, 5.6 K/BB), and Okajima (27 Holds, 24/28/86% IR).

Weaknesses: (1) SS and LF positions, (2) hitting from Lugo, (3) baserunning from Ramirez (21 GIDP, 0 SB, 0 CS), (4) fielding from LF Ramirez (81 Rng+, 93 Held+), (5) CS% from Varitek (24%) and Mirabelli (22%), and (6) pitching from Tavarez (30% QS, 10.1 H/9).

Mgr	Terry Francona	
Rk	14	53
Gm	162	
Place	1	
GA	2.0	
Rival	8–10 vs Yankees, 99 RS, 93 RA	

	W	L	Win%
Regular Season	96	66	0.593
Runs Record	103	59	0.635
1 Run	22	28	0.440
Extra Innings	2	5	0.286
Blowout	36	17	0.679

	Team	LgAvg	%Avg	LgRk
BABIP	0.286	0.304	106	2
E	81	98	121	2
sOBP	0.317	0.336	106	2
rOBP	0.306	0.336	110	1
R/G	5.35	4.90	0.45	3
RA/G	4.06	4.82	0.77	1

	Tm	LgAvg	>Avg
RS	867	794	73

	R/G	HR	K	BB	SB	CS	SB%	OPS		Held+
Team Offense	5.35	166	1042	689	96	24	80%	0.806	**LF**	91

	Tm	*LgAvg*	*>Avg*
RA	657	781	124
DP	145	160	-15

	R/G	*HR*	*K*	*BB*	*SB*	*CS*	*SB%*	*OPS*	*Held+*	
Team Defense	4.06	151	1149	482	107	32	77%	0.705	**CF**	104
Difference	1.30	15	107	207	-11			114%	**RF**	107

Pos	*Rpos*	*PA*	*Age*	*Name*	*BA*	*OBP*	*SLG*	*BB%*	*XBT*	*Bat R>Avg*	*BR R>Avg*	*Fld R>Avg*	*RAA*	*WAA*
C	8	518	35	Varitek, Jason^	0.255	0.367	0.421	14%	15%	7	-2	-1	12	1.1
1B,3B	-8	625	28	Youklis, Kevin	0.288	0.390	0.453	12%	39%	20	2	11	25	2.4
2B	3	581	23	Pedroia, Dustin	0.317	0.380	0.442	8%	37%	14	2	2	21	2.0
3B	3	653	33	Lowell, Mike	0.324	0.378	0.501	8%	35%	26	-3	5	31	3.0
SS	7	630	31	Lugo, Julio	0.237	0.294	0.349	8%	36%	-25	3	0	-15	-1.5
LF	-6	569	35	Ramirez, Manny	0.296	0.388	0.493	12%	25%	24	-6	-14	-2	-0.2
CF	3	591	27	Crisp, Coco^	0.268	0.330	0.382	8%	48%	-9	8	15	17	1.7
RF	-5	552	31	Drew, J.D.*	0.270	0.373	0.423	14%	34%	9	2	-3	3	0.3
DH,1B	-1	667	31	Ortiz, David*	0.332	0.445	0.621	17%	33%	66	-2	-1	62	6.0
2B,SS	2	232	31	Cora, Alex*	0.246	0.298	0.386	3%	35%	-6	0	5	1	0.1
1B,LF	-4	218	29	Hinske, Eric*	0.204	0.317	0.398	13%	32%	-3	-1	-1	-9	-0.9
RF,OF	-2	172	25	Pena, Wily Mo	0.218	0.291	0.385	8%	31%	-6	1	-7	-14	-1.3
LF,CF	-1	127	23	Ellsbury, Jacoby*	0.353	0.394	0.509	6%	50%	6	2	-5	2	0.2
C	2	127	36	Mirabelli, Doug	0.202	0.278	0.360	9%	11%	-6	-2	-1	-7	-0.6
	-1	164		Others	0.194	0.268	0.306	9%	13%	-10	-3	5	-9	-0.9
	0		29.9	Team Total	0.279	0.362	0.444	10.7%	34%	108	1	10	119	11.4
				League Average	0.271	0.338	0.423	8.5%	40%					
				% Lg Avg	103	107	105	125	84					
				League Rank	5	2	3	1	14		8	6		

GS	*GR*	*IP*	*Age*	*Name*	*W–L*	*GmSc*	*K/9*	*BB/9*	*HR/9*	*FIP*	*ERA*	*RA/9*	*RAA*	*WAA*
32	0	205	26	Matsuzaka, Dice-K	15–12	53.2	8.8	3.5	1.10	4.36	4.40	4.40	10	0.9
30	0	201	27	Beckett, Josh	20–7	57.8	8.7	1.8	0.76	3.23	3.27	3.41	31	3.0
31	0	189	40	Wakefield, Tim	17–12	48.4	5.2	3.0	1.05	4.80	4.76	4.95	-3	-0.3
24	0	151	40	Schilling, Curt	9–8	51.7	6.0	1.4	1.25	4.34	3.87	4.05	13	1.2
23	11	135	34	Tavarez, Julian	7–11	44.4	5.1	3.4	0.94	4.80	5.15	5.95	-17	-1.6
11	1	63	23	Lester, Jon*	4–0	48.2	7.1	4.4	1.43	5.39	4.57	4.71	1	0.1
0	59	58	26	Papelbon, Jonathan	1–3	0.0	13.0	2.3	0.77	2.60	1.85	1.85	19	1.9
0	66	69	31	Okajima, Hideki*	3–2	0.0	8.2	2.2	0.78	3.39	2.22	2.22	20	1.9
0	50	55	41	Timlin, Mike	2–1	0.0	5.0	2.3	1.14	4.67	3.42	3.74	7	0.6
0	44	44	25	Delcarmen, Manny	0–0	0.0	8.4	3.5	0.82	3.94	2.05	2.25	13	1.2
0	61	41	29	Lopez, Javier*	2–1	0.0	5.8	4.0	0.44	4.23	3.10	3.54	6	0.6
0	46	54	29	Snyder, Kyle	2–3	0.0	6.8	5.3	1.16	5.54	3.81	4.80	0	0.0
11	113	174		Others	0–0	0.0	6.7	4.1	0.57	4.22	3.83	4.09	14	1.3
162	451		30.9	Team Total		51	7.19	3.02	0.94	4.25	3.87	4.11	113	10.8
				League Average		48	6.64	3.32	1.01	4.52	4.50	4.88		
				% Lg Avg		106	108	110	107	106	117	119		
				League Rank		2	3	5	5	3	1			

2008 CHICAGO CUBS

The Cubs were the best team in the majors in 2008 but were embarrassingly swept in the NLDS by the Dodgers in 3 games.

Strengths: (1) hitting from Aramis Ramirez (44 2B, 27 HR), DeRosa (30 2B, 21 HR), RoY Soto (35 2B, 23 HR), Soriano (27 2B, 29 HR), Lee (41 2B, 20 HR), Edmonds (17 2B, 19 HR), and Fontenot (21 2B, 9 HR), (2) drawing walks led by Fukedome (81) and Ramirez (74), and (3) pitching from Dempster (64% QS), Harden (50% QS, 3.0 K/BB), Zambrano (57% QS), Lilly (62% QS), Marmol (30 Holds, 7/9/78% Sv, 37/47/79% IR stranded, 1.459 Lv), and primary closer Kerry Wood (34/40/85% Sv, 10/12/83% IR stranded, 4.7 K/BB, 1.988 Lv).

Weaknesses: (1) RF position, (2) 2B DeRosa's fielding (92 Rng+, 32 DP) and CF Edmonds (98 Rng+), (3) making DP, and (4) GIDP.

				W	L	Win%		Team	LgAvg	%Avg	LgRk
Mgr	Lou Piniella		**Regular Season**	97	64	0.602	**BABIP**	0.284	0.300	106	1
Rk	39	112	**Runs Record**	99	62	0.616	**E**	99	99	100	8
Gm	161		**1 Run**	24	22	0.522	**sOBP**	0.312	0.333	107	1
Place	1		**Extra Innings**	10	6	0.625	**rOBP**	0.323	0.334	103	3
GA	7.5		**Blowout**	33	14	0.702	**R/G**	5.31	4.54	0.77	1
Rival	9–7 vs Brewers, 94 RS, 72 RA; 3–4 vs Phillies, 24 RS, 33 RA						**RA/G**	4.17	4.63	0.46	2

	Tm	LgAvg	>Avg
RS	855	734	121
RA	671	749	78
DP	118	145	-27

	R/G	HR	K	BB	SB	CS	SB%	OPS	Held+	
Team Offense	5.31	184	1186	636	87	34	72%	0.797	**LF**	103
Team Defense	4.17	160	1264	548	87	36	71%	0.711	**CF**	95
Difference	1.14	24	78	88	0			112%	**RF**	106

Pos	Rpos	PA	Age	Name	BA	OBP	SLG	BB%	XBT	Bat R>Avg	BR R>Avg	Fld R>Avg	RAA	WAA
C	8	563	25	Soto, Geovany	0.285	0.364	0.504	11%	23%	22	-2	-2	26	2.6
1B	-9	698	32	Lee, Derrek	0.291	0.361	0.462	10%	34%	19	-4	6	12	1.1
2B,OF	0	593	33	DeRosa, Mark	0.285	0.376	0.481	12%	33%	23	4	-18	9	0.9
3B	3	645	30	Ramirez, Aramis	0.289	0.380	0.518	11%	30%	33	-3	-9	24	2.3
SS	7	661	28	Theriot, Ryan	0.307	0.387	0.359	11%	49%	6	-1	2	14	1.4
LF	-4	503	32	Soriano, Alfonso	0.280	0.344	0.532	9%	36%	20	-1	2	17	1.6
CF	2	298	38	Edmonds, Jim*	0.256	0.369	0.568	15%	45%	17	0	-10	9	0.9
RF	-5	590	31	Fukedome, Kosuke*	0.257	0.359	0.379	14%	48%	3	4	0	2	0.2
CF,LF	0	374	31	Johnson, Reed	0.303	0.358	0.420	5%	50%	5	1	-2	4	0.4
2B	2	284	28	Fontenot, Mike*	0.305	0.395	0.514	12%	38%	16	4	7	29	2.8
2B,SS	3	236	25	Cedeno, Ronny	0.269	0.328	0.352	8%	34%	-5	1	-4	-5	-0.5
C	2	128	36	Blanco, Henry	0.292	0.325	0.392	5%	17%	-1	-1	1	1	0.1
1B	-1	119	33	Ward, Daryle*	0.216	0.319	0.402	13%	13%	-1	-1	-1	-4	-0.4
1B,OF	-1	80	28	Hoffpauir, Micah*	0.342	0.400	0.534	8%	20%	5	0	-2	2	0.2
P	0	85	27	Zambrano, Carlos^	0.337	0.337	0.554	0%	14%	4	0	0	4	0.4
	-7	527		Others	0.186	0.222	0.247	4%	39%	-47	-2	5	-51	-5.0
	0		30.5	Team Total	0.278	0.354	0.443	10.0%	37%	118	-1	-25	92	9.0
				League Average	0.260	0.331	0.413	8.8%	39%					
				% Lg Avg	107	107	107	113	95					
				League Rank	2	1	1	1	11		9	10		

GS	GR	IP	Age	Name	W–L	GmSc	K/9	BB/9	HR/9	FIP	ERA	RA/9	RAA	WAA
33	0	207	31	Dempster, Ryan	17–6	57.4	8.1	3.3	0.61	3.47	2.96	3.27	35	3.5
34	0	205	32	Lilly, Ted*	17–9	53.5	8.1	2.8	1.41	4.45	4.09	4.22	13	1.3
30	0	189	27	Zambrano, Carlos	14–6	52.7	6.2	3.4	0.86	4.30	3.91	4.05	16	1.6
28	1	167	29	Marquis, Jason	11–9	48.1	4.9	3.8	0.81	4.58	4.53	4.69	3	0.3
12	0	71	26	Harden, Rich	5–1	64.7	11.3	3.8	0.76	3.11	1.77	2.15	21	2.0
10	2	59	22	Gallagher, Sean	3–4	49.9	7.5	3.4	0.92	4.15	4.45	4.76	0	0.0
0	65	66	31	Wood, Kerry	5–4	—	11.4	2.4	0.41	2.21	3.26	3.26	11	1.1
0	82	87	25	Marmol, Carlos	2–4	—	11.7	4.2	1.03	3.60	2.68	3.09	16	1.6
0	72	71	34	Howry, Bob	7–5	—	7.5	1.7	1.66	4.35	5.35	5.60	-6	-0.6
0	45	45	29	Wuertz, Michael	1–1	—	6.0	4.0	0.81	4.24	3.63	4.63	1	0.1
0	50	36	28	Cotts, Neal*	0–2	—	10.8	3.3	1.77	4.36	4.29	4.54	1	0.1
7	27	65	25	Marshall, Sean*	3–5	51.9	8.0	3.2	1.24	4.28	3.86	3.86	7	0.7
0	26	28	23	Samardzija, Jeff	1–0	—	8.1	4.9	0.00	2.92	2.28	3.90	3	0.3
7	108	156		Others	11–8	—	7.0	4.1	1.32	4.92	5.30	5.81	-17	-1.7
161	478		27.8	Team Total		54	7.84	3.40	0.99	4.07	3.87	4.16	105	10.3
				League Average		49	6.99	3.45	1.02	4.30	4.29	4.66		
				% Lg Avg		110	112	101	103	105	111	112		
				League Rank		1	1	7	11	3	3			

2009 Los Angeles Dodgers

The 2009 season featured two strong teams with a run differentiation of 1.0 per game from each side of the country, the LA Dodgers and the eventual World Series winner New York Yankees. The Dodgers had a great first half and cruised into the playoffs leading every day of the season after the first 10 games. Ramirez was suspended 50 games by MLB for testing positive for a banned substance. The Dodgers went down to the Phillies in five games in the NLCS.

Strengths: (1) hitting led by Ramirez (24 2B, 19 HR), Ethier (42 2B, 31 HR), Kemp (25 2B, 26 HR), and Blake (25 2B, 18 HR), (2) baserunning from Hudson (8 SB, 1 CS), Kemp (34 SB, 8 CS), and Furcal (38% RS), (3) fielding from Blake (109 Rng+, 32 DP, 10 E in 372 chances), (4) Held+ from CF Kemp (110), and (5) pitching from Kershaw (53% QS, 185 K), Wolf (71% QS), Broxton (36/42/86% Sv, 14/19/74% IR stranded, 1.824 Lv), Belisario (12 Holds, 26/36/72% IR stranded, 1.171 Lv), Sherrill (11 Holds, 10/13/77% IR stranded, 1.651 Lv), and Troncoso (6/7/86% Sv, 27/32/84% IR stranded, 1.369 Lv).

Weaknesses: (1) fielding from LF Ramirez (81 Rng+) and RF Ethier (90 Rng+, 93 Held+), (2) converting double plays, and (3) GIDP.

Mgr	Joe Torre	
Rk	40	118
Gm	162	
Place	1	
GA	3.0	
Rival	14–4 vs Rockies, 105 RS, 63 RA	

	W	*L*	*Win%*
Regular Season	95	67	0.586
Runs Record	100	62	0.615
1 Run	28	22	0.560
Extra Innings	12	9	0.571
Blowout	30	13	0.698

	Team	*LgAvg*	*%Avg*	*LgRk*
BABIP	0.280	0.298	107	1
E	83	96	116	4
sOBP	0.312	0.330	106	2
rOBP	0.312	0.335	107	1
R/G	4.81	4.43	109	4
RA/G	3.77	4.49	119	2

	Tm	*LgAvg*	*>Avg*
RS	780	718	62
RA	611	727	116
DP	134	147	-13

	R/G	*HR*	*K*	*BB*	*SB*	*CS*	*SB%*	*OPS*
Team Offense	4.81	145	1068	607	116	48	71%	0.757
Team Defense	3.77	127	1272	584	89	39	70%	0.673
Difference	1.04	18	204	23	27			112%

	Held+
LF	98
CF	106
RF	95

Pos	*Rpos*	*PA*	*Age*	*Name*	*BA*	*OBP*	*SLG*	*BB%*	*XBT*	*Bat R>Avg*	*BR R>Avg*	*Fld R>Avg*	*RAA*	*WAA*
C	9	588	26	Martin, Russell	0.250	0.352	0.329	12%	47%	-7	-3	7	6	0.6
1B	-9	651	25	Loney, James*	0.281	0.357	0.399	11%	37%	6	-3	5	-1	-0.1
2B	3	631	31	Hudson, Orlando^	0.283	0.357	0.417	10%	55%	9	5	6	23	2.3
3B+	2	565	35	Blake, Casey	0.280	0.363	0.468	11%	42%	18	1	9	30	3.0
SS	7	680	31	Furcal, Rafael^	0.269	0.335	0.375	9%	39%	-6	4	7	12	1.2
LF	-4	431	37	Ramirez, Manny	0.290	0.418	0.531	16%	40%	30	-1	-12	13	1.3
CF	3	667	24	Kemp, Matt	0.297	0.352	0.490	8%	52%	21	4	-3	25	2.5
RF	-6	685	27	Ethier, Andre*	0.272	0.361	0.508	11%	40%	28	-2	-8	12	1.2
LF,CF	-3	425	31	Pierre, Juan*	0.308	0.365	0.392	6%	53%	4	3	-4	0	0.0
3B,1B	-1	204	37	Loretta, Mark	0.232	0.309	0.276	10%	33%	-9	-1	3	-8	-0.8
SS,2B	2	121	37	Castro, Juan	0.277	0.311	0.339	5%	25%	-4	0	2	0	0.0
C	2	107	40	Ausmus, Brad	0.295	0.343	0.368	5%	75%	-1	0	0	1	0.1
2B,3B	0	83	34	Belliard, Ronnie	0.351	0.398	0.636	7%	60%	8	1	-1	8	0.8
	-5	547		Others	0.166	0.214	0.239	4%	28%	-50	-6	3	-58	-5.8
	0		31.9	Team Total	0.270	0.346	0.412	9.5%	43%	47	2	14	63	6.3
				League Average	0.259	0.331	0.409	9.0%	39%					
				% Lg Avg	104	105	101	106	111					
				League Rank	1	1	7	4	2		7	5		

GS	*GR*	*IP*	*Age*	*Name*	*W–L*	*GmSc*	*K/9*	*BB/9*	*HR/9*	*FIP*	*ERA*	*RA/9*	*RAA*	*WAA*
34	0	214	32	Wolf, Randy*	11–7	56.6	6.7	2.4	1.01	4.00	3.23	3.40	25	2.5
32	1	196	24	Billingsley, Chad	12–11	53.7	8.2	3.9	0.78	3.77	4.03	4.31	3	0.3
30	1	171	21	Kershaw, Clayton*	8–8	58.0	9.7	4.8	0.37	3.07	2.79	2.89	30	3.0
20	1	117	34	Kuroda, Hiroki	8–7	52.9	6.7	1.8	0.92	3.62	3.76	4.53	-1	-0.1
10	0	50	29	Stults, Eric*	4–3	46.9	5.9	4.7	0.54	4.30	4.86	4.86	-2	-0.2
7	21	79	32	Weaver, Jeff	6–4	50.6	7.3	3.8	0.80	3.79	3.65	3.87	5	0.5
0	73	76	25	Broxton, Jonathan	7–2	0.0	13.5	3.4	0.47	1.99	2.61	2.84	14	1.4
0	73	83	26	Troncoso, Ramon	5–4	0.0	6.0	3.7	0.33	3.32	2.72	3.27	11	1.1
0	69	71	26	Belisario, Ronald	4–3	0.0	8.2	3.7	0.51	3.27	2.04	2.67	14	1.4
0	61	65	35	Mota, Guillermo	3–4	0.0	5.4	3.3	0.83	4.12	3.44	3.44	7	0.7
4	41	63	24	McDonald, James	5–5	39.5	7.7	4.9	0.86	4.30	4.00	4.86	-3	-0.3
0	30	28	32	Sherrill, George*	1–0	0.0	7.2	3.6	0.33	3.01	0.65	0.65	12	1.2
0	35	30	27	Kuo, Hong-Chih*	2–0	0.0	9.6	3.9	0.60	3.19	3.00	3.00	5	0.5
25	120	230		Others	19–9	0.0	7.2	3.6	1.21	4.52	4.07	4.50	-2	-0.2

GS	GR	IP	Age	Name	W–L	GmSc	K/9	BB/9	HR/9	FIP	ERA	RA/9	RAA	WAA
162	526			Team Total		54	7.77	3.57	0.78	3.72	3.41	3.73	117	11.6
			28.2	League Average		50	7.09	3.52	0.99	4.20	4.19	4.53		
				% Lg Avg		108	110	99	128	113	123	121		
				League Rank		3	3	11	3	2	1			

2011 Philadelphia Phillies

The 2011 season featured great seasons from the Phillies, Rangers, and Yankees. The 2011 Phillies were easily the best Philly team since the 1970's. Unfortunately, they ran into a hot postseason experienced Cardinal team who beat them 3 games to 2 during the NLDS in a close series. The Cardinals surprised everyone in the playoffs winning the World Series as a wild card team.

Strengths: (1) hitting from Victorino (27 2B, 16 3B, 17 HR), Howard (30 2B, 33 HR, 75 BB), Pence (12 2B, 11 HR), and Mayberry (17 2B, 15 HR), (2) baserunning from Utley (14 SB, 0 CS, 3 GIDP) and Victorino (19 SB, 3 CS, 4 GIDP, 41% RS), (3) fielding from 3B Polanco (115 Rng+) and 2B Utley (103 Rng+), (4) Held+ from CF Victorino (108) and RF Pence (136), and (5) pitching from Cy Young runner-up Halladay (78% QS, 6.3 K/BB, 220 K), Lee (78% QS, 5.7 K/BB, 238 K), Hamels (77% QS, 4.4 K/BB, 194 K), Worley (57% QS), Oswalt (61% QS), closer Madson (32/34/94% Sv), and Bastardo (28/32/87% IR).

Weaknesses: (1) LF position, (2) hitting from Martinez & Schneider, (3) fielding from LF Ibanez (86 Rng+), 1B Howard (70 assists), 2B/3B Valdez (104 Rng+ at 2B, 84 Rng+ at 3B), RF Francisco (88 Rng+, 93 Held+), and RF Brown (77 Rng+), and (4) CS% from Ruiz (23%) and Schneider (13%).

Mgr	Charlie Manuel	
Rk	17	60
Gm	162	
Place	1	
GA	13.0	
Rival	12–6 s Braves, 82 RS, 48 RA	

	W	L	Win%
Regular Season	102	60	0.630
Runs Record	102	60	0.629
1 Run	28	19	0.596
Extra Innings	9	10	0.474
Blowout	30	10	0.750

	Team	LgAvg	%Avg	LgRk
BABIP	0.292	0.296	102	6
E	74	101	136	1
sOBP	0.284	0.320	113	1
rOBP	0.325	0.320	98	13
R/G	4.40	4.13	0.27	7
RA/G	3.27	4.16	0.89	1

	Tm	LgAvg	>Avg
RS	713	668	45
RA	529	673	144
DP	135	138	-3

	R/G	HR	K	BB	SB	CS	SB%	OPS
Team Offense	4.40	153	1024	539	96	24	80%	0.717
Team Defense	3.27	120	1299	404	106	29	79%	0.657
Difference	1.14	33	275	135	-10			109%

Held+	
LF	100
CF	110
RF	107

Pos	Rpos	PA	Age	Name	BA	OBP	SLG	BB%	XBT	Bat R>Avg	BR R>Avg	Fld R>Avg	RAA	WAA
C	8	472	32	Ruiz, Carlos	0.283	0.371	0.383	10%	37%	9	-3	0	14	1.5
1B	-9	644	31	Howard, Ryan*	0.253	0.346	0.488	12%	20%	25	-3	-13	0	0.0
2B	2	454	32	Utley, Chase*	0.259	0.344	0.425	9%	73%	9	8	7	26	2.7
3B	2	523	35	Polanco, Placido	0.277	0.335	0.339	8%	44%	-3	-1	9	7	0.7
SS	7	631	32	Rollins, Jimmy^	0.268	0.338	0.399	9%	50%	6	4	-7	10	1.1
LF	-6	575	39	Ibanez, Raul*	0.245	0.289	0.419	6%	29%	-3	-1	-23	-33	-3.4
CF	3	586	30	Victorino, Shane^	0.279	0.355	0.491	9%	55%	25	8	2	38	3.9
RF	-2	236	28	Pence, Hunter	0.324	0.394	0.560	11%	55%	19	0	0	17	1.7
2B,3B	3	300	33	Valdez, Wilson	0.249	0.294	0.341	6%	53%	-8	3	-10	-12	-1.2
CF,LF	-2	296	27	Mayberry, John	0.273	0.341	0.513	9%	44%	13	1	-3	9	0.9
RF,LF	-3	293	29	Francisco, Ben	0.244	0.340	0.364	11%	35%	1	-2	-9	-13	-1.4
RF	-2	210	23	Brown, Domonic*	0.245	0.333	0.391	12%	53%	1	1	-9	-9	-0.9
3B	2	234	28	Martinez, Michael	0.196	0.258	0.282	8%	67%	-13	2	0	-9	-0.9
C	2	139	34	Schneider, Brian*	0.176	0.246	0.256	8%	17%	-9	-1	-3	-11	-1.2
1B,RF	0	118	35	Gload, Ross*	0.252	0.271	0.322	3%	33%	-5	0	0	-5	-0.5
	-5	568		Others	0.171	0.221	0.208	5%	25%	-51	1	2	-53	-5.5
	0		31.2	Team Total	0.252	0.322	0.395	8.6%	42%	16	17	-57	-24	-2.5
				League Average	0.253	0.319	0.391	8.1%	41%					

Pos	Rpos	PA	Age	Name	BA	OBP	SLG	BB%	XBT	Bat R>Avg	BR R>Avg	Fld R>Avg	RAA	WAA
				% Lg Avg	100	101	101	106	101					
				League Rank	9	6	7	6	8			1	14	

GS	GR	IP	Age	Name	W–L	GmSc	K/9	BB/9	HR/9	FIP	ERA	RA/9	RAA	WAA
32	0	234	34	Halladay, Roy	19–6	63.3	8.5	1.3	0.39	2.22	2.35	2.50	52	5.4
32	0	233	32	Lee, Cliff*	17–8	64.1	9.2	1.6	0.70	2.68	2.40	2.55	50	5.2
31	1	216	27	Hamels, Cole*	14–9	62.1	8.1	1.8	0.79	3.10	2.79	2.83	40	4.2
23	0	139	33	Oswalt, Roy	9–10	51.4	6.0	2.1	0.65	3.47	3.69	3.88	11	1.1
21	4	132	23	Worley, Vance	11–3	56.4	8.1	3.1	0.68	3.35	3.01	3.21	19	2.0
15	19	115	26	Kendrick, Kyle	8–6	52.5	4.6	2.4	1.10	4.50	3.22	3.92	8	0.8
0	62	61	30	Madson, Ryan	4–2	0.0	9.2	2.4	0.30	1.93	2.37	2.37	14	1.5
0	57	62	24	Stutes, Michael	6–2	0.0	8.4	4.1	1.02	4.05	3.63	3.63	6	0.6
0	64	58	25	Bastardo, Antonio*	6–1	0.0	10.9	4.0	0.93	3.38	2.64	2.64	12	1.2
0	45	57	25	Herndon, David*	1–4	0.0	6.2	3.8	1.42	4.78	3.32	4.11	3	0.3
0	25	19	34	Lidge, Brad	0–2	0.0	10.7	6.1	0.00	2.43	1.40	1.40	7	0.7
8	117	152		Others	7–7	0.0	7.3	4.0	0.89	4.17	4.79	5.08	-9	-1.0
162	394		28.5	Team Total		59	7.92	2.46	0.73	3.23	3.02	3.22	212	22.1
				League Average		52	7.29	3.12	0.90	3.83	3.81	4.17		
				% Lg Avg		113	109	127	123	118	126	129		
				League Rank		1	4	1	2	1	1			

2013 BOSTON RED SOX

The 2013 season featured two excellent AL teams, the Tigers and Red Sox, and one rather lucky NL team, the Cardinals. The Cardinals had a team major league record 0.330 batting average with runners in scoring position (RISP) contributing to this team easily leading the NL in runs scored. The Red Sox were able to come from last in the division in 2012 to the world championship in 2013 with excellent hitting and solid defense beating the Cardinals in 6 games in the World Series.

Strengths: (1) hitting for average and power led by Ortiz (38 2B, 30 HR), Napoli (38 2B, 23 HR), Nava (29 2B, 12 HR, 15 HBP), Pedroia (42 2B), Carp (18 2B, 9 HR), Victorino (26 2B, 15 HR, 18 HBP), Ellsbury (31 2B, 8 3B), and Saltalamacchia (40 2B, 14 HR), (2) drawing walks led by Ortiz (76), Napoli (73), and Pedroia (73), (3) baserunning from Ellsbury (52 SB, 4 CS, 39% RS) and Victorino (21 SB, 3 CS, 5 GIDP, 40% RS), (4) fielding from RF Victorino (130 Rng+, 9 assists), 2B Pedroia (95 Rng+, 5 E in 688 chances, 102 DP), CF Ellsbury (100 Rng+, 109 Held+), and 1B Napoli (87 assists), and (5) pitching from Buchholtz (81% QS, 2.7 K/BB), Uehara (11.2 K/BB, 21/24/88% Sv, 16/23/70% IR stranded, 1.288 Lv), and Breslow.

Weaknesses: (1) 3B position, (2) hitting for contact, (3) fielding from 3B Middlebrooks (94 Rng+), (4) CS% from Saltalamacchia (21%) and Lavarnway (19%), and (5) pitching from Dempster (48% QS, 8.9 H/9).

Mgr	John Farrell	
Rk	31	90
Gm	162	
Place	1	
GA	5.5	
Rival	12–7 vs Rays, 71 RS, 57 RA; 3–4 vs Tigers, 43 RS, 35 RA	

	W	L	Win%
Regular Season	97	65	0.599
Runs Record	100	62	0.620
1 Run	21	21	0.500
Extra Innings	10	6	0.625
Blowout	33	13	0.717

	Team	LgAvg	%Avg	LgRk
BABIP	0.295	0.298	101	6
E	80	89	111	5
sOBP	0.314	0.322	103	5
rOBP	0.320	0.316	99	9
R/G	5.27	4.33	0.94	1
RA/G	4.05	4.29	0.24	6

	Tm	LgAvg	>Avg
RS	853	702	151
RA	656	696	40
DP	142	146	-4

	R/G	HR	K	BB	SB	CS	SB%	OPS
Team Offense	5.27	178	1308	581	123	19	87%	0.795
Team Defense	4.05	156	1294	524	133	43	76%	0.710
Difference	1.22	22	-14	57	-10			112%

	Held+
LF	100
CF	108
RF	100

Pos	Rpos	PA	Age	Name	BA	OBP	SLG	BB%	XBT	Bat R>Avg	BR R>Avg	Fld R>Avg	RAA	WAA
C	7	470	28	Saltalamacchia, Jarrod^	0.273	0.338	0.466	9%	36%	12	0	-6	13	1.3
1B,DH	-8	578	31	Napoli, Mike	0.259	0.360	0.482	13%	43%	22	-1	10	23	2.3

Pos	Rpos	PA	Age	Name	BA	OBP	SLG	BB%	XBT	Bat R>Avg	BR R>Avg	Fld R>Avg	RAA	WAA
2B	4	724	29	Pedroia, Dustin	0.301	0.372	0.415	10%	40%	18	1	15	38	3.9
3B	2	374	24	Middlebrooks, Will	0.227	0.271	0.425	5%	36%	-6	0	-7	-11	-1.1
SS	6	501	30	Drew, Stephen*	0.253	0.333	0.443	11%	42%	8	1	-2	13	1.4
LF,DH	-4	366	32	Gomes, Jonny	0.247	0.344	0.426	12%	46%	7	0	0	3	0.3
CF	3	636	29	Ellsbury, Jacoby*	0.296	0.353	0.423	7%	42%	12	8	13	36	3.7
RF,CF	-4	532	32	Victorino, Shane	0.294	0.351	0.451	5%	41%	13	3	23	35	3.6
DH,1B	-1	600	37	Ortiz, David*	0.309	0.395	0.564	13%	23%	45	0	-1	43	4.4
LF,RF	-7	536	30	Nava, Daniel^	0.303	0.385	0.445	10%	37%	22	-1	-6	8	0.8
LF,1B	-4	243	27	Carp, Mike*	0.296	0.362	0.523	9%	38%	13	0	-4	5	0.5
3B,SS	2	234	23	Iglesias, Jose	0.330	0.376	0.409	5%	48%	6	0	-1	7	0.7
C	2	116	36	Ross, David	0.216	0.298	0.382	9%	57%	-2	0	3	3	0.3
CF,LF	0	107	23	Bradley, Jackie*	0.189	0.280	0.337	9%	47%	-4	0	-3	-7	-0.7
C	1	82	25	Lavarnway, Ryan	0.299	0.329	0.429	2%	11%	1	0	-1	1	0.1
	1	283		Others	0.204	0.264	0.312	7%	41%	-13	1	-11	-22	-2.3
	0		29.1	Team Total	0.277	0.349	0.446	9.1%	39%	153	12	22	187	19.1
				League Average	0.256	0.320	0.404	8.1%	39%					
				% Lg Avg	108	109	110	112	100					
				League Rank	2	1	1	3	9		2	3		

GS	GR	IP	Age	Name	W–L	GmSc	K/9	BB/9	HR/9	FIP	ERA	RA/9	RAA	WAA
33	0	213	29	Lester, Jon*	15–8	53.6	7.5	2.8	0.80	3.67	3.75	3.97	5	0.5
29	0	189	34	Lackey, John	10–13	55.6	7.7	1.9	1.24	3.95	3.52	3.80	8	0.8
29	3	171	36	Dempster, Ryan	8–9	49.4	8.2	4.1	1.37	4.74	4.57	5.10	-18	-1.8
27	2	162	25	Doubront, Felix*	11–6	51.9	7.7	3.9	0.72	3.87	4.32	4.66	-9	-0.9
16	0	108	28	Buchholz, Clay	12–1	64.6	8.0	3.0	0.33	2.86	1.74	1.91	27	2.8
10	0	65	32	Peavy, Jake	4–1	54.0	6.3	2.6	0.84	3.87	4.04	4.04	1	0.1
0	73	74	38	Uehara, Koji	4–1	—	12.2	1.1	0.61	1.61	1.09	1.21	25	2.5
0	71	68	27	Tazawa, Junichi	5–4	—	9.5	1.6	1.19	3.26	3.16	3.29	7	0.7
0	61	60	32	Breslow, Craig*	5–2	—	5.0	2.7	0.45	3.69	1.81	2.41	12	1.2
0	37	31	28	Miller, Andrew*	1–2	—	14.1	5.0	0.88	3.13	2.64	3.52	2	0.2
0	30	29	29	Bailey, Andrew	3–1	—	12.2	3.8	2.20	4.84	3.77	3.77	1	0.1
18	173	283		Others	19–17	—	7.2	4.6	1.11	4.76	5.37	5.53	-43	-4.4
162	450		30.7	Team Total		53	8.01	3.24	0.97	3.90	3.79	4.06	18	1.8
				League Average		51	7.65	3.06	1.04	3.99	3.99	4.31		
				% Lg Avg		104	105	94	107	102	105	106		
				League Rank		2	6	12	8	7	6			

PART II

4. Rankings

Table 1
Best Teams of All-Time (1–50)

Overall	*Year*	*Team*	*Games*	*Hitting R>Avg*	*BR R>Avg*	*Fielding R>Avg*	*Pitching R>Avg*	*Total R>Avg*	*Pythag W%*
1	1927	New York Yankees	155	235	-2	41	124	398	0.7294
2	1939	New York Yankees	152	134	3	88	150	375	0.7273
3	1906	Chicago Cubs	155	84	9	83	97	273	0.7205
4	1902	Pittsburgh Pirates	142	152	1	52	77	282	0.7130
5	1905	New York Giants	155	143	10	44	86	283	0.6924
6	1969	Baltimore Orioles	162	135	-3	114	39	285	0.6909
7	1948	Cleveland Indians	156	112	-4	80	103	291	0.6887
8	1910	Philadelphia A's	155	105	1	48	88	242	0.6844
9	2001	Seattle Mariners	162	110	25	104	67	306	0.6828
10	1936	New York Yankees	155	162	2	25	142	331	0.6820
11	1942	New York Yankees	154	104	7	70	78	259	0.6808
12	1904	New York Giants	158	87	10	60	88	245	0.6798
13	1943	St. Louis Cardinals	157	93	0	53	96	242	0.6789
14	1942	St. Louis Cardinals	156	109	-1	20	112	240	0.6767
15	1954	Cleveland Indians	156	76	10	33	128	247	0.6762
16	1911	New York Giants	154	109	22	9	127	267	0.6760
17	1909	Philadelphia A's	153	91	2	28	90	210	0.6697
18	1998	New York Yankees	162	123	0	28	135	286	0.6683
19	1998	Atlanta Braves	162	102	6	84	74	266	0.6674
20	1909	Pittsburgh Pirates	154	100	-4	42	79	217	0.6673
21	1953	New York Yankees	151	113	6	35	95	249	0.6659
22	1929	Philadelphia A's	151	110	6	11	136	263	0.6640
23	1995	Cleveland Indians	144	122	-3	-7	140	252	0.6638
24	1998	Houston Astros	162	116	14	0	136	266	0.6637
25	1909	Chicago Cubs	155	7	0	33	150	190	0.6628
26	1937	New York Yankees	157	113	1	21	137	271	0.6614
27	1906	Cleveland Naps	157	111	-3	71	32	211	0.6600
28	1912	New York Giants	154	89	15	20	116	241	0.6588
29	1976	Cincinnati Reds	162	214	27	7	12	260	0.6585
30	1931	Philadelphia A's	153	93	4	54	107	257	0.6585
31	1922	St. Louis Browns	154	148	7	39	63	256	0.6583
32	1912	Boston Red Sox	154	104	-15	15	126	230	0.6564
33	1931	New York Yankees	155	220	8	-9	62	280	0.6551
34	1908	New York Giants	157	138	-7	8	60	198	0.6540
35	1932	New York Yankees	156	172	-4	-18	117	267	0.6528
36	1905	Chicago Cubs	155	-30	9	64	146	189	0.6527
37	1901	Pittsburgh Pirates	140	99	0	42	72	213	0.6523
38	1975	Cincinnati Reds	162	128	24	61	23	236	0.6520
39	1953	Brooklyn Dodgers	155	188	16	50	5	259	0.6519
40	1907	Chicago Cubs	155	25	6	85	57	173	0.6511
41	1974	Los Angeles Dodgers	162	103	8	37	78	226	0.6507
42	1971	Baltimore Orioles	158	133	2	54	28	217	0.6488
43	1941	Brooklyn Dodgers	157	128	0	56	37	221	0.6479
44	1935	Chicago Cubs	154	81	-2	55	88	222	0.6465

Overall	Year	Team	Games	Hitting R>Avg	BR R>Avg	Fielding R>Avg	Pitching R>Avg	Total R>Avg	Pythag W%
45	1970	Baltimore Orioles	162	101	4	59	54	218	0.6454
46	1910	Chicago Cubs	154	81	-7	23	101	198	0.6447
47	1928	Philadelphia A's	153	114	-3	11	104	226	0.6440
48	1957	New York Yankees	154	75	9	46	73	204	0.6436
49	1973	Baltimore Orioles	162	61	9	119	19	208	0.6405
50	1913	New York Giants	156	43	6	17	125	191	0.6404

TABLE 2
BEST TEAMS OF ALL-TIME (51–100)

Overall	Year	Team	Games	Hitting R>Avg	BR R>Avg	Fielding R>Avg	Pitching R>Avg	Total R>Avg	Pythag W%
51	1948	Boston Braves	154	94	2	21	91	208	0.6402
52	1997	Atlanta Braves	162	56	-18	69	104	211	0.6402
53	2007	Boston Red Sox	162	108	1	10	113	231	0.6394
54	1955	New York Yankees	154	71	21	72	42	206	0.6391
55	1911	Philadelphia A's	152	108	-5	-3	112	212	0.6391
56	1919	Cincinnati Reds	140	43	-4	43	71	153	0.6378
57	1915	Chicago White Sox	155	83	-8	14	97	186	0.6371
58	1961	New York Yankees	163	82	6	73	53	214	0.6365
59	1977	Los Angeles Dodgers	162	58	6	11	128	203	0.6351
60	2011	Philadelphia Phillies	162	17	17	-57	212	189	0.6351
61	1955	Brooklyn Dodgers	154	142	24	66	-16	216	0.6346
62	1993	Atlanta Braves	162	26	-1	82	90	197	0.6343
63	1912	Pittsburgh Pirates	152	44	-1	56	94	193	0.6341
64	1954	New York Giants	154	17	14	50	109	191	0.6340
65	1972	Pittsburgh Pirates	155	74	7	17	83	181	0.6335
66	1938	New York Yankees	157	77	11	21	115	224	0.6333
67	1994	Montreal Expos	114	47	21	23	59	150	0.6329
68	1999	Arizona Diamondbacks	162	66	15	42	96	219	0.6322
69	1954	New York Yankees	155	101	9	18	65	193	0.6321
70	1988	New York Mets	160	95	6	-34	121	188	0.6317
71	1949	Boston Red Sox	155	147	6	24	36	213	0.6310
72	1976	Philadelphia Phillies	162	106	-5	29	61	191	0.6309
73	1979	Baltimore Orioles	159	25	0	74	97	196	0.6308
74	2001	Oakland A's	162	55	1	19	133	208	0.6303
75	1903	Boston Americans	141	91	-2	37	41	167	0.6299
76	1985	Toronto Blue Jays	161	43	0	71	81	195	0.6296
77	1942	Brooklyn Dodgers	155	79	-1	40	55	174	0.6294
78	1954	Chicago White Sox	155	51	0	72	55	178	0.6289
79	1920	Cleveland Indians	154	123	-7	25	63	205	0.6288
80	1922	New York Giants	156	77	3	65	61	206	0.6287
81	1986	New York Mets	162	84	-4	8	102	190	0.6287
82	1935	Detroit Tigers	152	96	0	41	71	208	0.6286
83	1909	Detroit Tigers	158	98	12	37	20	167	0.6282
84	1918	Chicago Cubs	131	48	-2	0	87	133	0.6279
85	1968	Detroit Tigers	164	102	-7	63	11	169	0.6278
86	1994	Chicago White Sox	113	58	3	13	81	155	0.6276
87	1947	New York Yankees	155	110	3	22	50	185	0.6264
88	2002	New York Yankees	161	119	8	-56	141	212	0.6259
89	1921	New York Yankees	153	138	3	33	39	213	0.6257
90	2013	Boston Red Sox	162	154	10	22	18	204	0.6252
91	1952	New York Yankees	154	88	7	57	27	180	0.6245
92	1934	New York Yankees	154	71	-2	38	92	199	0.6242
93	1949	Brooklyn Dodgers	156	103	27	41	25	196	0.6241
94	1948	New York Yankees	154	99	2	11	82	194	0.6239
95	1930	Washington Senators	154	57	-2	64	85	204	0.6238
96	2004	St. Louis Cardinals	162	98	4	31	67	201	0.6236
97	1940	Cincinnati Reds	155	6	1	99	61	168	0.6232

Overall	Year	Team	Games	Hitting R>Avg	BR R>Avg	Fielding R>Avg	Pitching R>Avg	Total R>Avg	Pythag W%
98	1917	New York Giants	158	50	1	59	43	153	0.6231
99	1932	Philadelphia A's	154	150	6	28	31	214	0.6229
100	2002	San Francisco Giants	162	92	-3	38	64	192	0.6228

Table 3
Best Teams of All-Time (101–150)

Overall	Year	Team	Games	Hitting R>Avg	BR R>Avg	Fielding R>Avg	Pitching R>Avg	Total R>Avg	Pythag W%
101	1958	New York Yankees	155	88	23	58	10	179	0.6226
102	1924	New York Giants	154	124	10	38	20	192	0.6222
103	1977	New York Yankees	162	104	8	44	39	195	0.6214
104	1942	Boston Red Sox	152	132	-5	32	22	181	0.6214
105	1978	Los Angeles Dodgers	162	98	11	4	66	179	0.6212
106	2002	Anaheim Angels	162	42	12	98	40	193	0.6212
107	1956	New York Yankees	154	80	17	29	61	187	0.6208
108	1987	Toronto Blue Jays	162	42	7	50	95	194	0.6208
109	1910	New York Giants	155	106	9	-21	81	174	0.6207
110	1946	Boston Red Sox	156	136	1	25	17	179	0.6206
111	1997	New York Yankees	162	80	-6	-63	187	199	0.6203
112	2008	Chicago Cubs	161	118	-1	-25	105	197	0.6201
113	1917	Chicago White Sox	156	36	2	-4	115	149	0.6201
114	1923	New York Yankees	152	73	-4	56	59	183	0.6201
115	1934	Detroit Tigers	154	111	5	23	62	201	0.6200
116	1915	Boston Red Sox	155	46	-8	33	87	158	0.6199
117	1905	Chicago White Sox	158	0	0	71	71	142	0.6192
118	2009	Los Angeles Dodgers	162	48	2	14	117	180	0.6190
119	2002	Boston Red Sox	162	74	5	62	52	193	0.6188
120	1985	St. Louis Cardinals	162	52	31	50	40	173	0.6180
121	1928	St. Louis Cardinals	154	73	1	17	87	178	0.6172
122	1955	Chicago White Sox	155	31	6	39	90	166	0.6171
123	1985	New York Yankees	161	82	31	27	49	189	0.6169
124	1939	St. Louis Cardinals	155	122	-1	16	42	180	0.6168
125	1921	Cleveland Indians	154	114	5	-15	92	195	0.6166
126	2005	Cleveland Indians	162	62	0	51	71	184	0.6166
127	1999	New York Yankees	162	81	2	-19	138	202	0.6165
128	1969	Minnesota Twins	162	118	-5	18	45	176	0.6162
129	1964	Chicago White Sox	162	-32	24	96	66	155	0.6161
130	1941	New York Yankees	156	64	2	64	48	179	0.6159
131	1971	Pittsburgh Pirates	162	121	17	15	21	175	0.6158
132	1984	Detroit Tigers	162	103	-2	52	29	182	0.6157
133	1928	New York Yankees	154	143	-4	-16	65	189	0.6157
134	2013	Detroit Tigers	162	123	-20	-45	121	179	0.6156
135	1914	Philadelphia A's	158	112	0	14	32	159	0.6152
136	1901	Chicago White Sox	137	41	11	28	88	168	0.6146
137	1950	New York Yankees	155	92	4	19	73	188	0.6145
138	1996	Cleveland Indians	161	109	-10	-13	119	205	0.6145
139	1915	Detroit Tigers	156	131	8	10	19	168	0.6143
140	1905	Philadelphia A's	152	60	5	6	76	147	0.6142
141	1990	Oakland A's	162	31	1	107	26	165	0.6141
142	2011	Texas Rangers	162	136	16	17	19	188	0.6141
143	2003	New York Yankees	163	111	-1	-43	127	193	0.6139
144	1925	Pittsburgh Pirates	153	116	17	26	32	191	0.6139
145	2011	New York Yankees	162	122	-4	4	61	182	0.6138
146	1994	New York Yankees	113	97	-19	-2	65	141	0.6134
147	1977	Philadelphia Phillies	162	143	-2	62	-19	184	0.6130
148	1952	Brooklyn Dodgers	155	107	8	17	34	167	0.6130
149	1994	Cincinnati Reds	115	78	7	-1	48	132	0.6127
150	1906	Pittsburgh Pirates	154	55	-1	22	63	139	0.6123

TABLE 4
BEST TEAMS OF THE DEAD BALL ERA (1901–1919)

Era	*Overall*	*Year*	*Team*	*Games*	*Hitting R>Avg*	*BR R>Avg*	*Fielding R>Avg*	*Pitching R>Avg*	*Total R>Avg*	*Pythag W%*
1	3	1906	Chicago Cubs	155	84	9	83	97	273	0.7205
2	4	1902	Pittsburgh Pirates	142	152	1	52	77	282	0.7130
3	5	1905	New York Giants	155	143	10	44	86	283	0.6924
4	8	1910	Philadelphia A's	155	105	1	48	88	242	0.6844
5	12	1904	New York Giants	158	87	10	60	88	245	0.6798
6	16	1911	New York Giants	154	109	22	9	127	267	0.6760
7	17	1909	Philadelphia A's	153	91	2	28	90	210	0.6697
8	20	1909	Pittsburgh Pirates	154	100	-4	42	79	217	0.6673
9	25	1909	Chicago Cubs	155	7	0	33	150	190	0.6628
10	27	1906	Cleveland Naps	157	111	-3	71	32	211	0.6600
11	28	1912	New York Giants	154	89	15	20	116	241	0.6588
12	32	1912	Boston Red Sox	154	104	-15	15	126	230	0.6564
13	34	1908	New York Giants	157	138	-7	8	60	198	0.6540
14	36	1905	Chicago Cubs	155	-30	9	64	146	189	0.6527
15	37	1901	Pittsburgh Pirates	140	99	0	42	72	213	0.6523
16	40	1907	Chicago Cubs	155	25	6	85	57	173	0.6511
17	46	1910	Chicago Cubs	154	81	-7	23	101	198	0.6447
18	50	1913	New York Giants	156	43	6	17	125	191	0.6404
19	55	1911	Philadelphia A's	152	108	-5	-3	112	212	0.6391
20	56	1919	Cincinnati Reds	140	43	-4	43	71	153	0.6378
21	57	1915	Chicago White Sox	155	83	-8	14	97	186	0.6371
22	63	1912	Pittsburgh Pirates	152	44	-1	56	94	193	0.6341
23	75	1903	Boston Americans	141	91	-2	37	41	167	0.6299
24	83	1909	Detroit Tigers	158	98	12	37	20	167	0.6282
25	84	1918	Chicago Cubs	131	48	-2	0	87	133	0.6279
26	98	1917	New York Giants	158	50	1	59	43	153	0.6231
27	109	1910	New York Giants	155	106	9	-21	81	174	0.6207
28	113	1917	Chicago White Sox	156	36	2	-4	115	149	0.6201
29	116	1915	Boston Red Sox	155	46	-8	33	87	158	0.6199
30	117	1905	Chicago White Sox	158	0	0	71	71	142	0.6192
31	135	1914	Philadelphia A's	158	112	0	14	32	159	0.6152
32	136	1901	Chicago White Sox	137	41	11	28	88	168	0.6146
33	139	1915	Detroit Tigers	156	131	8	10	19	168	0.6143
34	140	1905	Philadelphia A's	152	60	5	6	76	147	0.6142
35	150	1906	Pittsburgh Pirates	154	55	-1	22	63	139	0.6123
36	164	1904	Boston Americans	157	42	-3	26	70	136	0.6097
37	165	1904	Cleveland Naps	154	78	3	0	61	141	0.6094
38	184	1903	Pittsburgh Pirates	141	89	-2	43	22	152	0.6053
39	191	1911	Pittsburgh Pirates	155	28	-8	55	71	146	0.6039
40	196	1901	Boston Americans	138	9	-4	56	84	144	0.6021
41	209	1916	Brooklyn Robins	156	46	1	17	58	123	0.6001

TABLE 5
BEST TEAMS OF THE LIVE BALL ERA (1920–1960)

Era	*Overall*	*Year*	*Team*	*Games*	*Hitting R>Avg*	*BR R>Avg*	*Fielding R>Avg*	*Pitching R>Avg*	*Total R>Avg*	*Pythag W%*
1	1	1927	New York Yankees	155	235	-2	41	124	398	0.7294
2	2	1939	New York Yankees	152	134	3	88	150	375	0.7273
3	7	1948	Cleveland Indians	156	112	-4	80	103	291	0.6887
4	10	1936	New York Yankees	155	162	2	25	142	331	0.6820
5	11	1942	New York Yankees	154	104	7	70	78	259	0.6808
6	13	1943	St. Louis Cardinals	157	93	0	53	96	242	0.6789
7	14	1942	St. Louis Cardinals	156	109	-1	20	112	240	0.6767

Era	Overall	Year	Team	Games	Hitting R>Avg	BR R>Avg	Fielding R>Avg	Pitching R>Avg	Total R>Avg	Pythag W%
8	15	1954	Cleveland Indians	156	76	10	33	128	247	0.6762
9	21	1953	New York Yankees	151	113	6	35	95	249	0.6659
10	22	1929	Philadelphia A's	151	110	6	11	136	263	0.6640
11	26	1937	New York Yankees	157	113	1	21	137	271	0.6614
12	30	1931	Philadelphia A's	153	93	4	54	107	257	0.6585
13	31	1922	St. Louis Browns	154	148	7	39	63	256	0.6583
14	33	1931	New York Yankees	155	220	8	-9	62	280	0.6551
15	35	1932	New York Yankees	156	172	-4	-18	117	267	0.6528
16	39	1953	Brooklyn Dodgers	155	188	16	50	5	259	0.6519
17	43	1941	Brooklyn Dodgers	157	128	0	56	37	221	0.6479
18	44	1935	Chicago Cubs	154	81	-2	55	88	222	0.6465
19	47	1928	Philadelphia A's	153	114	-3	11	104	226	0.6440
20	48	1957	New York Yankees	154	75	9	46	73	204	0.6436
21	51	1948	Boston Braves	154	94	2	21	91	208	0.6402
22	54	1955	New York Yankees	154	71	21	72	42	206	0.6391
23	61	1955	Brooklyn Dodgers	154	142	24	66	-16	216	0.6346
24	64	1954	New York Giants	154	17	14	50	109	191	0.6340
25	66	1938	New York Yankees	157	77	11	21	115	224	0.6333
26	69	1954	New York Yankees	155	101	9	18	65	193	0.6321
27	71	1949	Boston Red Sox	155	147	6	24	36	213	0.6310
28	77	1942	Brooklyn Dodgers	155	79	-1	40	55	174	0.6294
29	78	1954	Chicago White Sox	155	51	0	72	55	178	0.6289
30	79	1920	Cleveland Indians	154	123	-7	25	63	205	0.6288
31	80	1922	New York Giants	156	77	3	65	61	206	0.6287
32	82	1935	Detroit Tigers	152	96	0	41	71	208	0.6286
33	87	1947	New York Yankees	155	110	3	22	50	185	0.6264
34	89	1921	New York Yankees	153	138	3	33	39	213	0.6257
35	91	1952	New York Yankees	154	88	7	57	27	180	0.6245
36	92	1934	New York Yankees	154	71	-2	38	92	199	0.6242
37	93	1949	Brooklyn Dodgers	156	103	27	41	25	196	0.6241
38	94	1948	New York Yankees	154	99	2	11	82	194	0.6239
39	95	1930	Washington Senators	154	57	-2	64	85	204	0.6238
40	97	1940	Cincinnati Reds	155	6	1	99	61	168	0.6232
41	99	1932	Philadelphia A's	154	150	6	28	31	214	0.6229
42	101	1958	New York Yankees	155	88	23	58	10	179	0.6226
43	102	1924	New York Giants	154	124	10	38	20	192	0.6222
44	104	1942	Boston Red Sox	152	132	-5	32	22	181	0.6214
45	107	1956	New York Yankees	154	80	17	29	61	187	0.6208
46	110	1946	Boston Red Sox	156	136	1	25	17	179	0.6206
47	114	1923	New York Yankees	152	73	-4	56	59	183	0.6201
48	115	1934	Detroit Tigers	154	111	5	23	62	201	0.6200
49	121	1928	St. Louis Cardinals	154	73	1	17	87	178	0.6172
50	122	1955	Chicago White Sox	155	31	6	39	90	166	0.6171

Table 6
Best Teams of the Expansion Era (1961–2014)

Era	Overall	Year	Team	Games	Hitting R>Avg	BR R>Avg	Fielding R>Avg	Pitching R>Avg	Total R>Avg	Pythag W%
1	6	1969	Baltimore Orioles	162	135	-3	114	39	285	0.6909
2	9	2001	Seattle Mariners	162	110	25	104	67	306	0.6828
3	18	1998	New York Yankees	162	123	0	28	135	286	0.6683
4	19	1998	Atlanta Braves	162	102	6	84	74	266	0.6674
5	23	1995	Cleveland Indians	144	122	-3	-7	140	252	0.6638
6	24	1998	Houston Astros	162	116	14	0	136	266	0.6637
7	29	1976	Cincinnati Reds	162	214	27	7	12	260	0.6585
8	38	1975	Cincinnati Reds	162	128	24	61	23	236	0.6520
9	41	1974	Los Angeles Dodgers	162	103	8	37	78	226	0.6507

Era	Overall	Year	Team	Games	Hitting R>Avg	BR R>Avg	Fielding R>Avg	Pitching R>Avg	Total R>Avg	Pythag W%
10	42	1971	Baltimore Orioles	158	133	2	54	28	217	0.6488
11	45	1970	Baltimore Orioles	162	101	4	59	54	218	0.6454
12	49	1973	Baltimore Orioles	162	61	9	119	19	208	0.6405
13	52	1997	Atlanta Braves	162	56	-18	69	104	211	0.6402
14	53	2007	Boston Red Sox	162	108	1	10	113	231	0.6394
15	58	1961	New York Yankees	163	82	6	73	53	214	0.6365
16	59	1977	Los Angeles Dodgers	162	58	6	11	128	203	0.6351
17	60	2011	Philadelphia Phillies	162	17	17	-57	212	189	0.6351
18	62	1993	Atlanta Braves	162	26	-1	82	90	197	0.6343
19	65	1972	Pittsburgh Pirates	155	74	7	17	83	181	0.6335
20	67	1994	Montreal Expos	114	47	21	23	59	150	0.6329
21	68	1999	Arizona Diamondbacks	162	66	15	42	96	219	0.6322
22	70	1988	New York Mets	160	95	6	-34	121	188	0.6317
23	72	1976	Philadelphia Phillies	162	106	-5	29	61	191	0.6309
24	73	1979	Baltimore Orioles	159	25	0	74	97	196	0.6308
25	74	2001	Oakland A's	162	55	1	19	133	208	0.6303
26	76	1985	Toronto Blue Jays	161	43	0	71	81	195	0.6296
27	81	1986	New York Mets	162	84	-4	8	102	190	0.6287
28	85	1968	Detroit Tigers	164	102	-7	63	11	169	0.6278
29	86	1994	Chicago White Sox	113	58	3	13	81	155	0.6276
30	88	2002	New York Yankees	161	119	8	-56	141	212	0.6259
31	90	2013	Boston Red Sox	162	154	10	22	18	204	0.6252
32	96	2004	St. Louis Cardinals	162	98	4	31	67	201	0.6236
33	100	2002	San Francisco Giants	162	92	-3	38	64	192	0.6228
34	103	1977	New York Yankees	162	104	8	44	39	195	0.6214
35	105	1978	Los Angeles Dodgers	162	98	11	4	66	179	0.6212
36	106	2002	Anaheim Angels	162	42	12	98	40	193	0.6212
37	108	1987	Toronto Blue Jays	162	42	7	50	95	194	0.6208
38	111	1997	New York Yankees	162	80	-6	-63	187	199	0.6203
39	112	2008	Chicago Cubs	161	118	-1	-25	105	197	0.6201
40	118	2009	Los Angeles Dodgers	162	48	2	14	117	180	0.6190
41	119	2002	Boston Red Sox	162	74	5	62	52	193	0.6188
42	120	1985	St. Louis Cardinals	162	52	31	50	40	173	0.6180
43	123	1985	New York Yankees	161	82	31	27	49	189	0.6169
44	126	2005	Cleveland Indians	162	62	0	51	71	184	0.6166
45	127	1999	New York Yankees	162	81	2	-19	138	202	0.6165
46	128	1969	Minnesota Twins	162	118	-5	18	45	176	0.6162
47	129	1964	Chicago White Sox	162	-32	24	96	66	155	0.6161
48	131	1971	Pittsburgh Pirates	162	121	17	15	21	175	0.6158
49	132	1984	Detroit Tigers	162	103	-2	52	29	182	0.6157
50	134	2013	Detroit Tigers	162	123	-20	-45	121	179	0.6156

TABLE 7
BEST WORLD CHAMPIONSHIP TEAMS (1901–2014)

Rank	Overall	Year	Team	Pythag W%	Post Season Results
1	1	1927	New York Yankees	0.7294	Won World Series 4–0 over Pirates
2	2	1939	New York Yankees	0.7273	Won World Series 4–0 over Reds
3	4	1902	Pittsburgh Pirates	0.7130	Won NL Pennant; no World Series
4	5	1905	New York Giants	0.6924	Won World Series 4–1 over A's
5	7	1948	Cleveland Indians	0.6887	Won World Series 4–2 over Braves
6	8	1910	Philadelphia A's	0.6844	Won World Series 4–1 to Cubs
7	10	1936	New York Yankees	0.6820	Won World Series 4–2 over Giants
8	12	1904	New York Giants	0.6798	Won NL Pennant; no World Series
9	14	1942	St. Louis Cardinals	0.6767	Won World Series 4–1 over Yankees
10	18	1998	New York Yankees	0.6683	Won World Series 4–0 over Padres
11	20	1909	Pittsburgh Pirates	0.6673	Won World Series 4–3 over Tigers
12	21	1953	New York Yankees	0.6659	Won World Series 4–2 over Dodgers

Rank	Overall	Year	Team	Pythag W%	Post Season Results
13	22	1929	Philadelphia A's	0.6640	Won World Series 4–1 over Cubs
14	26	1937	New York Yankees	0.6614	Won World Series 4–1 over Giants
15	29	1976	Cincinnati Reds	0.6585	Won World Series 4–0 over Yankees
16	32	1912	Boston Red Sox	0.6564	Won World Series 4–3–1 over Giants
17	35	1932	New York Yankees	0.6528	Won World Series 4–0 over Cubs
18	38	1975	Cincinnati Reds	0.6520	Won World Series 4–3 over Red Sox
19	40	1907	Chicago Cubs	0.6511	Won World Series 4–0 over Tigers
20	45	1970	Baltimore Orioles	0.6454	Won World Series 4–1 over Reds
21	53	2007	Boston Red Sox	0.6394	Won World Series 4–0 over Rockies
22	55	1911	Philadelphia A's	0.6391	Won World Series 4–2 over Giants
23	56	1919	Cincinnati Reds	0.6378	Won World Series 5–3 over White Sox
24	58	1961	New York Yankees	0.6365	Won World Series 4–1 over Reds
25	61	1955	Brooklyn Dodgers	0.6346	Won World Series 4–3 over Yankees
26	64	1954	New York Giants	0.6340	Won World Series 4–0 over Indians
27	66	1938	New York Yankees	0.6333	Won World Series 4–0 over Cubs
28	75	1903	Boston Americans	0.6299	Won World Series 5–3 over Pirates
29	79	1920	Cleveland Indians	0.6288	Won World Series 5–2 over Dodgers
30	80	1922	New York Giants	0.6287	Won World Series 4–0–1 over Yankees
31	81	1986	New York Mets	0.6287	Won World Series 4–3 over Red Sox
32	82	1935	Detroit Tigers	0.6286	Won World Series 4–2 over Cubs
33	85	1968	Detroit Tigers	0.6278	Won World Series 4–3 over Cardinals
34	87	1947	New York Yankees	0.6264	Won World Series 4–3 over Dodgers
35	90	2013	Boston Red Sox	0.6252	Won World Series 4–2 over Cardinals
36	91	1952	New York Yankees	0.6245	Won World Series 4–3 over Dodgers
37	97	1940	Cincinnati Reds	0.6232	Won World Series 4–3 over Tigers
38	101	1958	New York Yankees	0.6226	Won World Series 4–3 over Braves
39	103	1977	New York Yankees	0.6214	Won World Series 4–2 over Dodgers
40	106	2002	Anaheim Angels	0.6212	Won World Series 4–3 over Giants
41	107	1956	New York Yankees	0.6208	Won World Series 4–3 over Dodgers
42	113	1917	Chicago White Sox	0.6201	Won World Series 4–2 over Giants
43	114	1923	New York Yankees	0.6201	Won World Series 4–2 over Giants
44	116	1915	Boston Red Sox	0.6199	Won World Series 4–1 over Phillies
45	127	1999	New York Yankees	0.6165	Won World Series 4–0 over Braves
46	130	1941	New York Yankees	0.6159	Won World Series 4–1 over Dodgers
47	131	1971	Pittsburgh Pirates	0.6158	Won World Series 4–3 over Orioles
48	132	1984	Detroit Tigers	0.6157	Won World Series 4–1 over Padres
49	133	1928	New York Yankees	0.6157	Won World Series 4–0 over Cardinals
50	137	1950	New York Yankees	0.6145	Won World Series 4–0 over Phillies

Table 8
Worst World Championship Teams (1901–2014)

Rank	Overall	Year	Team	Pythag W%	Post Season Results
1	534	1987	Minnesota Twins	0.4811	Won World Series 4–3 vs Cardinals
2	529	2006	St. Louis Cardinals	0.5255	Won World Series 4–1 vs Tigers
3	527	2014	San Francisco Giants	0.5281	Won World Series 4–3 vs Royals
4	525	1959	Los Angeles Dodgers	0.5332	Won World Series 4–2 over White Sox
5	521	2012	San Francisco Giants	0.5386	Won World Series 4–0 over Tigers
6	518	2003	Florida Marlins	0.5396	Won World Series 4–2 vs Yankees
7	515	1988	Los Angeles Dodgers	0.5417	Won World Series 4–1 over A's
8	511	1985	Kansas City Royals	0.5452	Won World Series 4–3 over Cardinals
9	508	1964	St. Louis Cardinals	0.5469	Won World Series 4–3 over Yankees
10	488	2011	St. Louis Cardinals	0.5544	Won World Series 4–3 over Rangers
11	487	1997	Florida Marlins	0.5547	Won World Series 4–3 over Indians
12	486	1980	Philadelphia Phillies	0.5554	Won World Series 4–2 over Royals
13	485	1906	Chicago White Sox	0.5557	Won World Series 4–2 over Cubs
14	481	1969	New York Mets	0.5562	Won World Series 4–1 over Orioles
15	479	1992	Toronto Blue Jays	0.5567	Won World Series 4–2 over Braves
16	478	1996	New York Yankees	0.5569	Won World Series 4–2 over Braves

Rank	Overall	Year	Team	Pythag W%	Post Season Results
17	475	1914	Boston Braves	0.5570	Won World Series 4–0 over A's
18	466	1982	St. Louis Cardinals	0.5605	Won World Series 4–3 over Brewers
19	463	1916	Boston Red Sox	0.5608	Won World Series 4–1 over Dodgers
20	460	1963	Los Angeles Dodgers	0.5609	Won World Series 4–0 over Yankees
21	409	2005	Chicago White Sox	0.5706	Won World Series 4–0 over Astros
22	407	1993	Toronto Blue Jays	0.5708	Won World Series 4–2 over Phillies
23	393	1926	St. Louis Cardinals	0.5727	Won World Series 4–3 over Yankees
24	392	1965	Los Angeles Dodgers	0.5728	Won World Series 4–3 over Twins
25	383	1918	Boston Red Sox	0.5742	Won World Series 4–2 over Cubs
26	356	1974	Oakland A's	0.5791	Won World Series 4–1 over Dodgers
27	355	1973	Oakland A's	0.5791	Won World Series 4–3 over Mets
28	350	1933	New York Giants	0.5795	Won World Series 4–1 over Senators
29	335	1962	New York Yankees	0.5815	Won World Series 4–3 over Giants
30	310	2008	Philadelphia Phillies	0.5852	Won World Series 4–1 over Rays
31	285	1995	Atlanta Braves	0.5877	Won World Series 4–2 over Indians
32	283	1983	Baltimore Orioles	0.5880	Won World Series 4–1 over Phillies
33	269	2010	San Francisco Giants	0.5905	Won World Series over Rangers 4–1
34	265	1934	St. Louis Cardinals	0.5910	Won World Series 4–3 over Tigers
35	255	1990	Cincinnati Reds	0.5939	Won World Series 4–0 over A's
36	254	1913	Philadelphia A's	0.5939	Won World Series 4–1 over Giants
37	253	1978	New York Yankees	0.5940	Won World Series 4–2 over Dodgers
38	252	1991	Minnesota Twins	0.5942	Won World Series 4–3 over Braves
39	250	1967	St. Louis Cardinals	0.5943	Won World Series 4–3 over Red Sox
40	244	1960	Pittsburgh Pirates	0.5950	Won World Series 4–3 over Yankees
41	242	1946	St. Louis Cardinals	0.5951	Won World Series 4–3 over Red Sox
42	236	1989	Oakland A's	0.5965	Won World Series 4–0 over Giants
43	232	2001	Arizona Diamondbacks	0.5972	Won World Series 4–3 over Yankees
44	227	1979	Pittsburgh Pirates	0.5978	Won World Series 4–3 over Orioles
45	220	1908	Chicago Cubs	0.5990	Won World Series 4–1 over Tigers
46	215	1949	New York Yankees	0.5994	Won World Series 4–1 over Dodgers

TABLE 9
BEST POSTSEASON LOSING TEAMS

Rank	Year	Team	Pythag W%	Post Season Results
1	1906	Chicago Cubs	0.7205	Lost World Series 2–4 to White Sox
2	1969	Baltimore Orioles	0.6909	Lost World Series 1–4 to Mets
3	2001	Seattle Mariners	0.6828	Lost ALCS 1–4 to Yankees
4	1942	New York Yankees	0.6808	Lost World Series 1–4 to Cardinals
5	1943	St. Louis Cardinals	0.6789	Lost World Series 1–4 to Yankees
6	1954	Cleveland Indians	0.6762	Lost World Series 0–4 to Giants
7	1911	New York Giants	0.6760	Lost World Series 2–4 to A's
8	1998	Atlanta Braves	0.6674	Lost NLCS 2–4 to Padres
9	1995	Cleveland Indians	0.6638	Lost World Series 2–4 to Braves
10	1998	Houston Astros	0.6637	Lost NLDS 1–3 to Padres
11	1912	New York Giants	0.6588	Lost World Series 3–4–1 to Red Sox
12	1931	Philadelphia A's	0.6585	Lost World Series 3–4 to Cardinals
13	1953	Brooklyn Dodgers	0.6519	Lost World Series 2–4 to Yankees
14	1974	Los Angeles Dodgers	0.6507	Lost World Series 1–4 to A's
15	1971	Baltimore Orioles	0.6488	Lost World Series 3–4 to Pirates
16	1941	Brooklyn Dodgers	0.6479	Lost World Series 1–4 to Yankees
17	1935	Chicago Cubs	0.6465	Lost World Series 2–4 to Tigers
18	1910	Chicago Cubs	0.6447	Lost World Series 1–4 to A's
19	1957	New York Yankees	0.6436	Lost World Series 3–4 to Braves
20	1973	Baltimore Orioles	0.6405	Lost ALCS 2–3 to A's
21	1913	New York Giants	0.6404	Lost World Series 1–4 to A's
22	1948	Boston Braves	0.6402	Lost World Series 2–4 to Indians
23	1997	Atlanta Braves	0.6402	Lost NLCS 2–4 to Marlins
24	1955	New York Yankees	0.6391	Lost World Series 3–4 to Dodgers
25	1977	Los Angeles Dodgers	0.6351	Lost World Series 2–4 to Yankees

Table 10
Biggest World Series Upsets

Era	*Overall*	*Year*	*Team*	*Pythag W%*	*Post Season Results*
71	485	1906	Chicago White Sox	0.5557	Won World Series 4–2 over Cubs
1	3	1906	Chicago Cubs	0.7205	Lost World Series 2–4 to White Sox
249	481	1969	New York Mets	0.5562	Won World Series 4–1 over Orioles
1	6	1969	Baltimore Orioles	0.6909	Lost World Series 1–4 to Mets
129	285	1995	Atlanta Braves	0.5877	Won World Series 4–2 over Indians
5	23	1995	Cleveland Indians	0.6638	Lost World Series 2–4 to Braves
277	518	2003	Florida Marlins	0.5396	Won World Series 4–2 vs Yankees
54	143	2003	New York Yankees	0.6139	Lost World Series 2–4 to Marlins
72	511	1985	Kansas City Royals	0.5452	Won World Series 4–3 over Cardinals
42	120	1985	St. Louis Cardinals	0.6180	Lost World Series 3–4 to Royals
166	356	1974	Oakland A's	0.5791	Won World Series 4–1 over Dodgers
9	41	1974	Los Angeles Dodgers	0.6507	Lost World Series 1–4 to A's
64	162	1943	New York Yankees	0.6101	Won World Series 4–1 over Cardinals
6	13	1943	St. Louis Cardinals	0.6789	Lost World Series 1–4 to Yankees
275	515	1988	Los Angeles Dodgers	0.5417	Won World Series 4–1 over A's
65	167	1988	Oakland A's	0.6093	Lost World Series 1–4 to Dodgers
254	488	2011	St. Louis Cardinals	0.5544	Won World Series 4–3 over Rangers
53	142	2011	Texas Rangers	0.6141	Lost World Series 3–4 to Cardinals
70	475	1914	Boston Braves	0.5570	Won World Series 4–0 over A's
31	135	1914	Philadelphia A's	0.6152	Lost World Series 0–4 to Braves
84	209	1931	St. Louis Cardinals	0.6005	Won World Series 4–3 over A's
12	30	1931	Philadelphia A's	0.6585	Lost World Series 3–4 to Cardinals
59	383	1918	Boston Red Sox	0.5742	Won World Series 4–2 over Cubs
25	84	1918	Chicago Cubs	0.6279	Lost World Series 2–4 to Red Sox

Table 11
Best Teams That Never Made the Postseason

Rank	*Overall*	*Year*	*Team*	*Pythag W%*	*Post Season Results*
1	17	1909	Philadelphia A's	0.6697	2nd AL
2	25	1909	Chicago Cubs	0.6628	2nd NL
3	27	1906	Cleveland Naps	0.6600	3rd AL
4	31	1922	St. Louis Browns	0.6583	2nd AL
5	33	1931	New York Yankees	0.6551	2nd AL
6	34	1908	New York Giants	0.6540	2nd NL
7	36	1905	Chicago Cubs	0.6527	3rd NL
8	47	1928	Philadelphia A's	0.6440	2nd AL
9	57	1915	Chicago White Sox	0.6371	3rd AL
10	63	1912	Pittsburgh Pirates	0.6341	2nd NL
11	69	1954	New York Yankees	0.6321	2nd AL
12	71	1949	Boston Red Sox	0.6310	2nd AL
13	77	1942	Brooklyn Dodgers	0.6294	2nd NL
14	78	1954	Chicago White Sox	0.6289	3rd AL
15	92	1934	New York Yankees	0.6242	2nd AL
16	94	1948	New York Yankees	0.6239	3rd AL
17	95	1930	Washington Senators	0.6238	2nd AL
18	99	1932	Philadelphia A's	0.6229	2nd AL
19	104	1942	Boston Red Sox	0.6214	2nd AL
20	108	1987	Toronto Blue Jays	0.6208	2nd AL East
21	109	1910	New York Giants	0.6207	2nd NL
22	117	1905	Chicago White Sox	0.6192	2nd AL
23	119	2002	Boston Red Sox	0.6188	2nd AL East
24	122	1955	Chicago White Sox	0.6171	3rd AL
25	123	1985	New York Yankees	0.6169	2nd AL East
26	124	1939	St. Louis Cardinals	0.6168	2nd NL

Rank	Overall	Year	Team	Pythag W%	Post Season Results
27	125	1921	Cleveland Indians	0.6166	2nd AL
28	126	2005	Cleveland Indians	0.6166	2nd AL Central
29	129	1964	Chicago White Sox	0.6161	2nd AL
30	139	1915	Detroit Tigers	0.6143	2nd AL
31	150	1906	Pittsburgh Pirates	0.6123	3rd NL
32	151	1993	San Francisco Giants	0.6122	2nd NL West
33	153	1950	Cleveland Indians	0.6118	4th AL
34	156	1957	Chicago White Sox	0.6111	2nd AL
35	157	1949	St. Louis Cardinals	0.6108	2nd NL
36	160	1963	Minnesota Twins	0.6105	3rd AL
37	161	1936	Chicago Cubs	0.6104	2nd NL
38	166	1904	Cleveland Naps	0.6094	4th AL
39	171	1935	New York Yankees	0.6084	2nd AL
40	174	1961	Detroit Tigers	0.6077	2nd AL
41	178	1951	Brooklyn Dodgers	0.6070	Lost 3 game play-off to Giants
42	187	1934	New York Giants	0.6050	2nd NL
43	191	1920	New York Yankees	0.6042	3rd AL
44	192	1911	Pittsburgh Pirates	0.6039	3rd NL
45	195	1931	New York Giants	0.6025	2nd NL
46	197	1901	Boston Americans	0.6021	2nd AL
47	199	1975	Los Angeles Dodgers	0.6020	2nd NL West
48	200	1952	Cleveland Indians	0.6019	2nd AL
49	201	1955	Cleveland Indians	0.6019	2nd AL
50	204	1941	St. Louis Cardinals	0.6017	2nd in NL to Dodgers

TABLE 12
MOST DOMINANT HITTING TEAMS

Rank	Era	Overall	Year	Team	Bat R>Avg
1	1	1	1927	New York Yankees	235
2	14	33	1931	New York Yankees	220
3	7	29	1976	Cincinnati Reds	214
4	77	190	2003	Boston Red Sox	192
5	16	39	1953	Brooklyn Dodgers	188
6	15	35	1932	New York Yankees	172
7	60	154	2009	New York Yankees	162
8	4	10	1936	New York Yankees	162
9	31	90	2013	Boston Red Sox	154
10	74	184	2007	New York Yankees	154
11	2	4	1902	Pittsburgh Pirates	152
12	41	99	1932	Philadelphia A's	150
13	13	31	1922	St. Louis Browns	148
14	27	71	1949	Boston Red Sox	147
15	54	133	1928	New York Yankees	143
16	3	5	1905	New York Giants	143
17	57	147	1977	Philadelphia Phillies	143
18	23	61	1955	Brooklyn Dodgers	142
19	34	89	1921	New York Yankees	138
20	13	34	1908	New York Giants	138
21	80	198	2004	Boston Red Sox	137
22	53	142	2011	Texas Rangers	136
23	46	110	1946	Boston Red Sox	136
24	48	254	1913	Philadelphia A's	135
25	1	6	1969	Baltimore Orioles	135
26	2	2	1939	New York Yankees	134
27	10	42	1971	Baltimore Orioles	133
28	44	104	1942	Boston Red Sox	132
29	33	139	1915	Detroit Tigers	131

Rank	Era	Overall	Year	Team	Bat R>Avg
30	68	172	2000	San Francisco Giants	130
31	72	178	1951	Brooklyn Dodgers	130
32	17	43	1941	Brooklyn Dodgers	128
33	8	38	1975	Cincinnati Reds	128
34	66	168	1940	Detroit Tigers	124
35	43	102	1924	New York Giants	124
36	30	79	1920	Cleveland Indians	123
37	3	18	1998	New York Yankees	123
38	50	134	2013	Detroit Tigers	123
39	71	181	1962	San Francisco Giants	123
40	51	124	1939	St. Louis Cardinals	122
41	5	23	1995	Cleveland Indians	122
42	55	145	2011	New York Yankees	122
43	48	131	1971	Pittsburgh Pirates	121
44	30	88	2002	New York Yankees	119
45	46	128	1969	Minnesota Twins	118
46	39	112	2008	Chicago Cubs	118
47	63	160	1963	Minnesota Twins	116
48	56	144	1925	Pittsburgh Pirates	116
49	6	24	1998	Houston Astros	116
50	254	488	2011	St. Louis Cardinals	116

Table 13
Most Dominant Baserunning Teams

Rank	Era	Overall	Year	Team	BR R>Avg
1	42	120	1985	St. Louis Cardinals	31
2	43	123	1985	New York Yankees	31
3	61	156	1957	Chicago White Sox	28
4	7	29	1976	Cincinnati Reds	27
5	37	93	1949	Brooklyn Dodgers	27
6	2	9	2001	Seattle Mariners	25
7	74	184	2007	New York Yankees	25
8	8	38	1975	Cincinnati Reds	24
9	23	61	1955	Brooklyn Dodgers	24
10	47	129	1964	Chicago White Sox	24
11	42	101	1958	New York Yankees	23
12	95	227	1979	Pittsburgh Pirates	23
13	6	16	1911	New York Giants	22
14	22	54	1955	New York Yankees	21
15	20	67	1994	Montreal Expos	21
16	141	310	2008	Philadelphia Phillies	19
17	72	182	1976	New York Yankees	18
18	17	60	2011	Philadelphia Phillies	17
19	45	107	1956	New York Yankees	17
20	48	131	1971	Pittsburgh Pirates	17
21	56	144	1925	Pittsburgh Pirates	17
22	16	39	1953	Brooklyn Dodgers	16
23	53	142	2011	Texas Rangers	16
24	191	392	1965	Los Angeles Dodgers	16
25	11	28	1912	New York Giants	15
26	21	68	1999	Arizona Diamondbacks	15
27	60	155	1957	Milwaukee Braves	15
28	111	255	1990	Cincinnati Reds	15
29	197	407	1993	Toronto Blue Jays	15
30	6	24	1998	Houston Astros	14
31	24	64	1954	New York Giants	14
32	110	253	1978	New York Yankees	14

Rank	Era	Overall	Year	Team	BR R>Avg
33	280	521	2012	San Francisco Giants	14
34	64	163	2014	Washington Nationals	13
35	248	479	1992	Toronto Blue Jays	13
36	285	528	2006	St. Louis Cardinals	13
37	24	83	1909	Detroit Tigers	12
38	36	106	2002	Anaheim Angels	12
39	71	177	1951	New York Giants	12
40	108	250	1967	St. Louis Cardinals	12
41	269	508	1964	St. Louis Cardinals	12
42	25	66	1938	New York Yankees	11
43	35	105	1978	Los Angeles Dodgers	11
44	32	136	1901	Chicago White Sox	11
45	60	154	2009	New York Yankees	11
46	78	193	1975	Pittsburgh Pirates	11
47	3	5	1905	New York Giants	10
48	5	12	1904	New York Giants	10
49	8	15	1954	Cleveland Indians	10
50	31	90	2013	Boston Red Sox	10
51	43	102	1924	New York Giants	10
52	236	460	1963	Los Angeles Dodgers	10

Table 14
Most Dominant Fielding Teams

Rank	Era	Overall	Year	Team	Fielding R>Avg
1	12	49	1973	Baltimore Orioles	119
2	1	6	1969	Baltimore Orioles	114
3	52	141	1990	Oakland A's	107
4	2	9	2001	Seattle Mariners	104
5	40	97	1940	Cincinnati Reds	99
6	36	106	2002	Anaheim Angels	98
7	47	129	1964	Chicago White Sox	96
8	72	182	1976	New York Yankees	96
9	2	2	1939	New York Yankees	88
10	16	40	1907	Chicago Cubs	85
11	4	19	1998	Atlanta Braves	84
12	165	355	1973	Oakland A's	84
13	1	3	1906	Chicago Cubs	83
14	81	199	1975	Los Angeles Dodgers	83
15	18	62	1993	Atlanta Braves	82
16	3	7	1948	Cleveland Indians	80
17	62	159	2002	Atlanta Braves	77
18	280	521	2012	San Francisco Giants	76
19	24	73	1979	Baltimore Orioles	74
20	141	310	2008	Philadelphia Phillies	74
21	15	58	1961	New York Yankees	73
22	22	54	1955	New York Yankees	72
23	29	78	1954	Chicago White Sox	72
24	133	350	1933	New York Giants	72
25	10	27	1906	Cleveland Naps	71
26	26	76	1985	Toronto Blue Jays	71
27	30	117	1905	Chicago White Sox	71
28	5	11	1942	New York Yankees	70
29	13	52	1997	Atlanta Braves	69
30	23	61	1955	Brooklyn Dodgers	66
31	31	80	1922	New York Giants	65
32	65	164	1958	Milwaukee Braves	65
33	14	36	1905	Chicago Cubs	64

Rank	Era	Overall	Year	Team	Fielding R>Avg
34	39	95	1930	Washington Senators	64
35	53	130	1941	New York Yankees	64
36	28	85	1968	Detroit Tigers	63
37	41	119	2002	Boston Red Sox	62
38	57	147	1977	Philadelphia Phillies	62
39	8	38	1975	Cincinnati Reds	61
40	61	156	1957	Chicago White Sox	61
41	5	12	1904	New York Giants	60
42	68	173	1939	Cincinnati Reds	60
43	69	174	1961	Detroit Tigers	60
44	73	180	1921	New York Giants	60
45	191	392	1965	Los Angeles Dodgers	60
46	11	45	1970	Baltimore Orioles	59
47	26	98	1917	New York Giants	59
48	42	101	1958	New York Yankees	58
49	74	187	1934	New York Giants	58
50	35	91	1952	New York Yankees	57

Table 15
Most Dominant Pitching Teams

Rank	Era	Overall	Year	Team	RAA
1	17	60	2011	Philadelphia Phillies	212
2	38	111	1997	New York Yankees	187
3	75	186	1966	Los Angeles Dodgers	187
4	9	25	1909	Chicago Cubs	150
5	2	2	1939	New York Yankees	150
6	14	36	1905	Chicago Cubs	146
7	4	10	1936	New York Yankees	142
8	30	88	2002	New York Yankees	141
9	5	23	1995	Cleveland Indians	140
10	45	127	1999	New York Yankees	138
11	11	26	1937	New York Yankees	137
12	10	22	1929	Philadelphia A's	136
13	6	24	1998	Houston Astros	136
14	3	18	1998	New York Yankees	135
15	70	179	2002	Oakland A's	134
16	25	74	2001	Oakland A's	133
17	8	15	1954	Cleveland Indians	128
18	16	59	1977	Los Angeles Dodgers	128
19	6	16	1911	New York Giants	127
20	54	143	2003	New York Yankees	127
21	12	32	1912	Boston Red Sox	126
22	247	478	1996	New York Yankees	125
23	18	50	1913	New York Giants	125
24	1	1	1927	New York Yankees	124
25	22	70	1988	New York Mets	121
26	50	134	2013	Detroit Tigers	121
27	51	138	1996	Cleveland Indians	119
28	15	35	1932	New York Yankees	117
29	40	118	2009	Los Angeles Dodgers	117
30	11	28	1912	New York Giants	116
31	28	113	1917	Chicago White Sox	115
32	25	66	1938	New York Yankees	115
33	14	53	2007	Boston Red Sox	113
34	7	14	1942	St. Louis Cardinals	112
35	66	169	1999	Atlanta Braves	112
36	19	55	1911	Philadelphia A's	112

Rank	Era	Overall	Year	Team	RAA
37	272	511	1985	Kansas City Royals	112
38	24	64	1954	New York Giants	109
39	129	285	1995	Atlanta Braves	108
40	59	153	1950	Cleveland Indians	108
41	69	175	1924	Washington Senators	108
42	12	30	1931	Philadelphia A's	107
43	39	112	2008	Chicago Cubs	105
44	111	255	1990	Cincinnati Reds	105
45	13	52	1997	Atlanta Braves	104
46	19	47	1928	Philadelphia A's	104
47	100	236	1989	Oakland A's	103
48	3	7	1948	Cleveland Indians	103
49	236	460	1963	Los Angeles Dodgers	102
50	27	81	1986	New York Mets	102
51	118	269	2010	San Francisco Giants	101
52	17	46	1910	Chicago Cubs	101

TABLE 16
BEST BASEBALL DYNASTIES (AT LEAST 3 CONSECUTIVE IMPRESSIVE SEASONS)

Era	Overall	Year	Team	Pythag W%	Post Season Results
4	10	1936	New York Yankees	0.6820	Won World Series 4–2 over Giants
11	26	1937	New York Yankees	0.6614	Won World Series 4–1 over Giants
25	66	1938	New York Yankees	0.6333	Won World Series 4–0 over Cubs
2	2	1939	New York Yankees	0.7273	Won World Series 4–0 over Reds
14	36	1905	Chicago Cubs	0.6527	3rd NL
1	3	1906	Chicago Cubs	0.7205	Lost World Series 2–4 to White Sox
16	40	1907	Chicago Cubs	0.6511	Won World Series 4–0 over Tigers
7	17	1909	Philadelphia A's	0.6697	2nd AL
4	8	1910	Philadelphia A's	0.6844	Won World Series 4–1 to Cubs
19	55	1911	Philadelphia A's	0.6391	Won World Series 4–2 over Giants
1	6	1969	Baltimore Orioles	0.6909	Lost World Series 1–4 to Mets
11	45	1970	Baltimore Orioles	0.6454	Won World Series 4–1 over Reds
10	42	1971	Baltimore Orioles	0.6488	Lost World Series 3–4 to Pirates
6	16	1911	New York Giants	0.6760	Lost World Series 2–4 to A's
11	28	1912	New York Giants	0.6588	Lost World Series 3–4–1 to Red Sox
18	50	1913	New York Giants	0.6404	Lost World Series 1–4 to A's
5	12	1904	New York Giants	0.6798	Won NL Pennant; no World Series
3	5	1905	New York Giants	0.6924	Won World Series 4–1 over A's
43	219	1906	New York Giants	0.5991	2nd NL
15	37	1901	Pittsburgh Pirates	0.6523	Won NL Pennant; no World Series
2	4	1902	Pittsburgh Pirates	0.7130	Won NL Pennant; no World Series
38	185	1903	Pittsburgh Pirates	0.6053	Lost World Series 3–5 to Red Sox
83	204	1941	St. Louis Cardinals	0.6017	2nd in NL to Dodgers
7	14	1942	St. Louis Cardinals	0.6767	Won World Series 4–1 over Yankees
6	13	1943	St. Louis Cardinals	0.6789	Lost World Series 1–4 to Yankees
19	47	1928	Philadelphia A's	0.6440	2nd AL
10	22	1929	Philadelphia A's	0.6640	Won World Series 4–1 over Cubs
58	152	1930	Philadelphia A's	0.6120	Won World Series 4–2 over Cardinals
12	30	1931	Philadelphia A's	0.6585	Lost World Series 3–4 to Cardinals
41	99	1932	Philadelphia A's	0.6229	2nd AL
13	52	1997	Atlanta Braves	0.6402	Lost NLCS 2–4 to Marlins
4	19	1998	Atlanta Braves	0.6674	Lost NLCS 2–4 to Padres
66	169	1999	Atlanta Braves	0.6087	Lost World Series 0–4 to Yankees

Era	*Overall*	*Year*	*Team*	*Pythag W%*	*Post Season Results*
90	217	1974	Cincinnati Reds	0.5992	2nd NL West
8	38	1975	Cincinnati Reds	0.6520	Won World Series 4–3 over Red Sox
7	29	1976	Cincinnati Reds	0.6585	Won World Series 4–0 over Yankees
53	130	1941	New York Yankees	0.6159	Won World Series 4–1 over Dodgers
5	11	1942	New York Yankees	0.6808	Lost World Series 1–4 to Cardinals
64	162	1943	New York Yankees	0.6101	Won World Series 4–1 over Cardinals
44	220	1908	Chicago Cubs	0.5990	Won World Series 4–1 over Tigers
9	25	1909	Chicago Cubs	0.6628	2nd NL
17	46	1910	Chicago Cubs	0.6447	Lost World Series 1–4 to A's
38	111	1997	New York Yankees	0.6203	Lost ALDS 2–3 to Indians
3	18	1998	New York Yankees	0.6683	Won World Series 4–0 over Padres
45	127	1999	New York Yankees	0.6165	Won World Series 4–0 over Braves
55	137	1950	New York Yankees	0.6145	Won World Series 4–0 over Phillies
78	196	1951	New York Yankees	0.6022	Won World Series 4–2 over Giants
35	91	1952	New York Yankees	0.6245	Won World Series 4–3 over Dodgers
9	21	1953	New York Yankees	0.6659	Won World Series 4–2 over Dodgers
26	69	1954	New York Yankees	0.6321	2nd AL
22	54	1955	New York Yankees	0.6391	Lost World Series 3–4 to Dodgers
45	107	1956	New York Yankees	0.6208	Won World Series 4–3 over Dodgers
20	48	1957	New York Yankees	0.6436	Lost World Series 3–4 to Braves
42	101	1958	New York Yankees	0.6226	Won World Series 4–3 over Braves
96	251	1953	Cleveland Indians	0.5943	2nd AL
8	15	1954	Cleveland Indians	0.6762	Lost World Series 0–4 to Giants
80	201	1955	Cleveland Indians	0.6019	2nd AL
72	178	1951	Brooklyn Dodgers	0.6070	Lost 1 game play-off to Giants
57	148	1952	Brooklyn Dodgers	0.6130	Lost World Series 3–4 to Yankees
16	39	1953	Brooklyn Dodgers	0.6519	Lost World Series 2–4 to Yankees
114	260	1994	Cleveland Indians	0.5925	2nd AL Central
5	23	1995	Cleveland Indians	0.6638	Lost World Series 2–4 to Braves
51	138	1996	Cleveland Indians	0.6145	Lost ALDS 1–3 to Orioles
33	87	1947	New York Yankees	0.6264	Won World Series 4–3 over Dodgers
38	94	1948	New York Yankees	0.6239	3rd AL
85	215	1949	New York Yankees	0.5994	Won World Series 4–1 over Dodgers
34	89	1921	New York Yankees	0.6257	Lost World Series 3–5 to Giants
81	202	1922	New York Yankees	0.6019	Lost World Series 0–4–1 to Giants
47	114	1923	New York Yankees	0.6201	Won World Series 4–2 over Giants
18	44	1935	Chicago Cubs	0.6465	Lost World Series 2–4 to Tigers
63	161	1936	Chicago Cubs	0.6104	2nd NL
110	293	1937	Chicago Cubs	0.5875	2nd NL
29	78	1954	Chicago White Sox	0.6289	3rd AL
50	122	1955	Chicago White Sox	0.6171	3rd AL
100	263	1956	Chicago White Sox	0.5915	3rd AL
61	156	1957	Chicago White Sox	0.6111	2nd AL
73	180	1921	New York Giants	0.6062	Won World Series 5–3 over Yankees
31	80	1922	New York Giants	0.6287	Won World Series 4–0–1 over Yankees
103	268	1923	New York Giants	0.5907	Lost World Series 2–4 to Yankees
43	102	1924	New York Giants	0.6222	Lost World Series 3–4 to Senators
54	304	1919	Cleveland Indians	0.5860	2nd AL
30	79	1920	Cleveland Indians	0.6288	Won World Series 5–2 over Dodgers
52	125	1921	Cleveland Indians	0.6166	2nd AL
41	119	2002	Boston Red Sox	0.6188	2nd AL East
77	190	2003	Boston Red Sox	0.6044	Lost ALCS 3–4 to Yankees
80	198	2004	Boston Red Sox	0.6020	Won World Series 4–0 over Cardinals
72	182	1976	New York Yankees	0.6058	Lost World Series 0–4 to Reds
34	103	1977	New York Yankees	0.6214	Won World Series 4–2 over Dodgers
110	253	1978	New York Yankees	0.5940	Won World Series 4–2 over Dodgers
65	167	1988	Oakland A's	0.6093	Lost World Series 1–4 to Dodgers
100	236	1989	Oakland A's	0.5965	Won World Series 4–0 over Giants
52	141	1990	Oakland A's	0.6141	Lost World Series 0–4 to Reds

Era	*Overall*	*Year*	*Team*	*Pythag W%*	*Post Season Results*
21	57	1915	Chicago White Sox	0.6371	3rd AL
55	345	1916	Chicago White Sox	0.5801	2nd AL
28	113	1917	Chicago White Sox	0.6201	Won World Series 4–2 over Giants
14	53	2007	Boston Red Sox	0.6394	Won World Series 4–0 over Rockies
73	183	2008	Boston Red Sox	0.6056	Lost ALCS 3–4 to Rays
184	382	2009	Boston Red Sox	0.5742	Lost ALDS 3–0 to Angels
87	228	1956	Milwaukee Braves	0.5977	2nd AL
60	155	1957	Milwaukee Braves	0.6112	Won World Series 4–3 over Yankees
65	164	1958	Milwaukee Braves	0.6099	Lost World Series 3–4 to Yankees
60	154	2009	New York Yankees	0.6115	Won World Series 4–2 over Phillies
119	271	2010	New York Yankees	0.5901	Lost ALCS 2–4 to Rangers
55	145	2011	New York Yankees	0.6138	Lost ALDS 2–3 to Tigers

TABLE 17
LUCKIEST (MOST OVERACHIEVING) GREAT TEAM SEASONS

Rank	*Era*	*Overall*	*Year*	*Team*	*Pythag W%*	*Proj W*	*Proj L*	*Actual Win*	*Actual Loss*	*Actual Win%*	*W% Diff*
1	249	481	1969	New York Mets	0.5562	90	72	100	62	0.6173	-0.0610
2	71	485	1906	Chicago White Sox	0.5557	84	67	93	58	0.6159	-0.0602
3	274	513	1961	Cincinnati Reds	0.5438	84	70	93	61	0.6039	-0.0601
4	70	475	1914	Boston Braves	0.5570	85	68	94	59	0.6144	-0.0574
5	8	20	1909	Pittsburgh Pirates	0.6673	101	51	110	42	0.7237	-0.0564
6	84	209	1931	St. Louis Cardinals	0.6005	92	62	101	53	0.6558	-0.0553
7	46	110	1946	Boston Red Sox	0.6206	96	58	104	50	0.6753	-0.0547
8	268	507	2004	New York Yankees	0.5469	92	76	101	67	0.6012	-0.0543
9	16	40	1907	Chicago Cubs	0.6511	99	53	107	45	0.7039	-0.0529
10	77	531	1911	Detroit Tigers	0.5253	81	73	89	65	0.5779	-0.0526
11	58	152	1930	Philadelphia A's	0.6120	94	60	102	52	0.6623	-0.0504
12	236	460	1963	Los Angeles Dodgers	0.5609	91	71	99	63	0.6111	-0.0502
13	287	532	1969	Atlanta Braves	0.5242	85	77	93	69	0.5741	-0.0498
14	82	203	1933	Washington Senators	0.6018	91	61	99	53	0.6513	-0.0495
15	29	116	1915	Boston Red Sox	0.6199	94	57	101	50	0.6689	-0.0490
16	281	523	1987	St. Louis Cardinals	0.5382	87	75	95	67	0.5864	-0.0483
17	20	56	1919	Cincinnati Reds	0.6378	89	51	96	44	0.6857	-0.0480
18	258	495	2009	LA Angels of Anaheim	0.5511	89	73	97	65	0.5988	-0.0476
19	56	346	1905	Pittsburgh Pirates	0.5800	89	64	96	57	0.6275	-0.0474
20	50	275	1908	Pittsburgh Pirates	0.5891	91	63	98	56	0.6364	-0.0473
21	261	498	1984	Chicago Cubs	0.5496	88	73	96	65	0.5963	-0.0466
22	28	77	1942	Brooklyn Dodgers	0.6294	97	57	104	50	0.6753	-0.0459
23	12	30	1931	Philadelphia A's	0.6585	100	52	107	45	0.7039	-0.0454
24	62	426	1907	Detroit Tigers	0.5679	85	65	92	58	0.6133	-0.0454
25	65	442	1902	Philadelphia A's	0.5651	77	59	83	53	0.6103	-0.0452
26	38	185	1903	Pittsburgh Pirates	0.6053	85	55	91	49	0.6500	-0.0447
27	8	15	1954	Cleveland Indians	0.6762	104	50	111	43	0.7208	-0.0446
28	264	501	1975	Boston Red Sox	0.5494	88	72	95	65	0.5938	-0.0443
29	44	220	1908	Chicago Cubs	0.5990	92	62	99	55	0.6429	-0.0439
30	289	534	1987	Minnesota Twins	0.4811	78	84	85	77	0.5247	-0.0435
31	79	194	1963	New York Yankees	0.6027	97	64	104	57	0.6460	-0.0433
32	152	429	1947	Brooklyn Dodgers	0.5671	87	67	94	60	0.6104	-0.0433
33	160	473	1927	St. Louis Cardinals	0.5581	85	68	92	61	0.6013	-0.0432
34	182	377	1962	Los Angeles Dodgers	0.5753	95	70	102	63	0.6182	-0.0429
35	1	3	1906	Chicago Cubs	0.7205	110	42	116	36	0.7632	-0.0427
36	107	286	1960	New York Yankees	0.5877	91	63	97	57	0.6299	-0.0421
37	275	515	1988	Los Angeles Dodgers	0.5417	87	74	94	67	0.5839	-0.0421
38	140	308	1971	Oakland A's	0.5853	94	67	101	60	0.6273	-0.0420

Rank	Era	Overall	Year	Team	Pythag W%	Proj W	Proj L	Actual Win	Actual Loss	Actual Win%	W% Diff
39	288	533	1998	Chicago Cubs	0.5101	83	80	90	73	0.5521	-0.0420
40	15	35	1932	New York Yankees	0.6528	101	53	107	47	0.6948	-0.0420
41	52	296	1919	Chicago White Sox	0.5870	82	58	88	52	0.6286	-0.0416
42	124	330	1920	Chicago White Sox	0.5821	90	64	96	58	0.6234	-0.0413
43	161	344	2003	San Francisco Giants	0.5801	93	68	100	61	0.6211	-0.0410
44	122	274	1970	Cincinnati Reds	0.5891	95	67	102	60	0.6296	-0.0405
45	199	409	2005	Chicago White Sox	0.5706	92	70	99	63	0.6111	-0.0405
46	276	517	2011	Arizona Diamondbacks	0.5399	87	75	94	68	0.5802	-0.0403
47	54	133	1928	New York Yankees	0.6157	95	59	101	53	0.6558	-0.0402
48	155	453	1932	Washington Senators	0.5639	87	67	93	61	0.6039	-0.0399
49	53	130	1941	New York Yankees	0.6159	95	59	101	53	0.6558	-0.0399
50	270	509	2005	Boston Red Sox	0.5466	89	73	95	67	0.5864	-0.0398

Table 18
Unluckiest (Most Underachieving) Great Team Seasons

Rank	Era	Overall	Year	Team	Pythag W%	Proj W	Proj L	Actual Win	Actual Loss	Actual Win%	W% Diff
1	10	27	1906	Cleveland Naps	0.6600	101	52	89	64	0.5817	0.0783
2	3	7	1948	Cleveland Indians	0.6887	107	48	97	58	0.6258	0.0629
3	81	199	1975	Los Angeles Dodgers	0.6020	98	64	88	74	0.5432	0.0588
4	172	364	1997	Houston Astros	0.5771	93	69	84	78	0.5185	0.0586
5	13	31	1922	St. Louis Browns	0.6583	101	53	93	61	0.6039	0.0544
6	39	192	1911	Pittsburgh Pirates	0.6039	93	61	85	69	0.5519	0.0520
7	150	324	1980	Milwaukee Brewers	0.5828	94	68	86	76	0.5309	0.0519
8	153	443	1955	Detroit Tigers	0.5649	87	67	79	75	0.5130	0.0519
9	14	36	1905	Chicago Cubs	0.6527	100	53	92	61	0.6013	0.0514
10	214	425	1970	Chicago Cubs	0.5680	92	70	84	78	0.5185	0.0495
11	7	17	1909	Philadelphia A's	0.6697	102	51	95	58	0.6209	0.0488
12	14	53	2007	Boston Red Sox	0.6394	104	58	96	66	0.5926	0.0468
13	231	451	1962	St. Louis Cardinals	0.5643	91	71	84	78	0.5185	0.0458
14	63	161	1936	Chicago Cubs	0.6104	94	60	87	67	0.5649	0.0455
15	21	51	1948	Boston Braves	0.6402	98	55	91	62	0.5948	0.0454
16	63	160	1963	Minnesota Twins	0.6105	98	63	91	70	0.5652	0.0453
17	41	119	2002	Boston Red Sox	0.6188	100	62	93	69	0.5741	0.0447
18	86	211	2012	New York Yankees	0.6001	97	65	90	72	0.5556	0.0445
19	44	126	2005	Cleveland Indians	0.6166	100	62	93	69	0.5741	0.0425
20	12	49	1973	Baltimore Orioles	0.6405	104	58	97	65	0.5988	0.0418
21	50	134	2013	Detroit Tigers	0.6156	100	62	93	69	0.5741	0.0415
22	14	33	1931	New York Yankees	0.6551	100	53	94	59	0.6144	0.0407
23	101	239	2012	Washington Nationals	0.5961	97	65	90	72	0.5556	0.0405
24	37	166	1904	Cleveland Naps	0.6094	92	59	86	65	0.5695	0.0398
25	100	263	1956	Chicago White Sox	0.5915	91	63	85	69	0.5519	0.0395
26	202	412	1990	Toronto Blue Jays	0.5704	92	70	86	76	0.5309	0.0395
27	90	235	1930	Brooklyn Robins	0.5968	92	62	86	68	0.5584	0.0384
28	137	303	1972	Chicago Cubs	0.5860	91	64	85	70	0.5484	0.0376
29	121	325	1955	Boston Red Sox	0.5827	90	64	84	70	0.5455	0.0373
30	136	300	2004	Chicago Cubs	0.5866	95	67	89	73	0.5494	0.0372
31	146	401	1923	Cleveland Indians	0.5720	88	65	82	71	0.5359	0.0361
32	217	432	2009	Atlanta Braves	0.5666	92	70	86	76	0.5309	0.0358
33	35	105	1978	Los Angeles Dodgers	0.6212	101	61	95	67	0.5864	0.0348
34	29	86	1994	Chicago White Sox	0.6276	71	42	67	46	0.5929	0.0347
35	6	24	1998	Houston Astros	0.6637	108	54	102	60	0.6296	0.0341
36	58	149	1994	Cincinnati Reds	0.6127	70	44	66	48	0.5789	0.0338
37	200	410	2003	Houston Astros	0.5706	92	70	87	75	0.5370	0.0336
38	232	452	2010	St. Louis Cardinals	0.5643	91	71	86	76	0.5309	0.0334

Rank	Era	Overall	Year	Team	Pythag W%	Proj W	Proj L	Actual Win	Actual Loss	Actual Win%	W% Diff
39	21	57	1915	Chicago White Sox	0.6371	98	56	93	61	0.6039	0.0332
40	64	438	1903	Cincinnati Reds	0.5654	79	60	74	65	0.5324	0.0330
41	33	100	2002	San Francisco Giants	0.6228	100	61	95	66	0.5901	0.0328
42	40	118	2009	Los Angeles Dodgers	0.6190	100	62	95	67	0.5864	0.0326
43	154	332	1988	Boston Red Sox	0.5818	94	68	89	73	0.5494	0.0325
44	128	284	1996	Texas Rangers	0.5879	95	67	90	72	0.5556	0.0323
45	78	193	1975	Pittsburgh Pirates	0.6036	97	64	92	69	0.5714	0.0322
46	111	255	1990	Cincinnati Reds	0.5939	96	66	91	71	0.5617	0.0322
47	159	342	1965	Cincinnati Reds	0.5805	94	68	89	73	0.5494	0.0311
48	76	189	1982	California Angels	0.6047	98	64	93	69	0.5741	0.0306
49	104	276	1933	Chicago Cubs	0.5889	91	63	86	68	0.5584	0.0305
50	187	387	2014	Oakland A's	0.5734	93	69	88	74	0.5432	0.0302

5. Great Teams by Franchise

Anaheim/California/LA Angels

Year	Franchise Rank	Era Rank	Overall Rank	Pythag Win %	Hitting RAA	BR RAA	Fielding RAA	Pitching RAA	Total RAA	Post Season Results
2002	1	36	106	0.6212	42	12	98	40	193	Won World Series
1982	2	76	189	0.6047	108	-2	50	12	168	Lost ALCS
2005	3	234	457	0.5615	-43	7	43	84	91	Lost ALCS
1995	4	242	469	0.5592	51	6	17	17	91	2nd AL West
2004	5	257	494	0.5522	-1	7	-11	90	85	Lost ALDS
2009	6	258	495	0.5511	64	9	71	-59	85	Lost ALCS

Arizona Diamondbacks

Year	Franchise Rank	Era Rank	Overall Rank	Pythag Win %	Hitting RAA	BR RAA	Fielding RAA	Pitching RAA	Total RAA	Post Season Results
1999	1	21	68	0.6322	66	15	42	96	219	Lost NLDS 1–3
2001	2	98	232	0.5972	54	7	49	45	155	Won World Series
2002	3	205	415	0.5699	65	-5	-4	53	109	Lost NLDS
2011	4	276	517	0.5399	46	7	51	-44	60	Lost NLDS

Colorado Rockies

Year	Franchise Rank	Era Rank	Overall Rank	Pythag Win %	Hitting RAA	BR RAA	Fielding RAA	Pitching RAA	Total RAA	Post Season Results
2007	1	210	421	0.5683	84	5	14	12	115	Lost World Series
2009	2	241	467	0.5603	91	-2	7	2	98	Lost NLDS

Florida/Miami Marlins

Year	Franchise Rank	Era Rank	Overall Rank	Pythag Win %	Hitting RAA	BR RAA	Fielding RAA	Pitching RAA	Total RAA	Post Season Results
1997	1	253	487	0.5547	11	-3	-5	81	84	Won World Series
2003	2	277	518	0.5396	8	0	-16	69	61	Won World Series

Houston Astros

Year	Franchise Rank	Era Rank	Overall Rank	Pythag Win %	Hitting RAA	BR RAA	Fielding RAA	Pitching RAA	Total RAA	Post Season Results
1998	1	6	24	0.6637	116	14	0	136	266	Lost NLDS
1999	2	91	218	0.5991	24	0	31	103	159	Lost NLDS
1994	3	115	262	0.5919	66	12	26	3	108	2nd NL Central
1997	4	172	364	0.5771	20	8	64	27	119	Lost NLDS
1986	5	176	371	0.5761	3	-2	29	77	106	Lost NLCS
2003	6	200	410	0.5706	36	4	64	7	111	2nd NL Central
2004	7	233	454	0.5636	49	-1	31	23	102	Lost NLCS
1995	8	282	524	0.5381	43	4	-47	55	55	2nd NL Central

New York Mets

Year	Franchise Rank	Era Rank	Overall Rank	Pythag Win %	Hitting RAA	BR RAA	Fielding RAA	Pitching RAA	Total RAA	Post Season Results
1988	1	22	70	0.6317	95	6	-34	121	188	Lost NLCS
1986	2	27	81	0.6287	84	-4	8	102	190	Won World Series
1999	3	96	230	0.5974	71	-6	22	75	162	Lost NLCS
1985	4	112	256	0.5936	31	-5	2	103	131	2nd NL East
1990	5	146	319	0.5835	48	12	-36	100	125	2nd NL East
1987	6	160	343	0.5804	81	13	-22	58	130	2nd NL East
2006	7	223	439	0.5654	32	13	34	28	107	Lost NLCS
1969	8	249	481	0.5562	-52	0	53	72	74	Won World Series

Kansas City Royals

Year	Franchise Rank	Era Rank	Overall Rank	Pythag Win %	Hitting RAA	BR RAA	Fielding RAA	Pitching RAA	Total RAA	Post Season Results
1977	1	61	158	0.6108	82	4	31	58	175	Lost ALCS
1980	2	169	359	0.5787	62	26	22	16	126	Lost World Series
1978	3	213	424	0.5682	34	24	54	-9	102	Lost ALCS 3–1
1985	4	272	511	0.5452	-47	5	-4	112	66	Won World Series

San Diego Padres

Year	Franchise Rank	Era Rank	Overall Rank	Pythag Win %	Hitting RAA	BR RAA	Fielding RAA	Pitching RAA	Total RAA	Post Season Results
1998	1	177	372	0.5760	-4	6	-52	165	115	Lost World Series
2010	2	263	500	0.5496	-62	0	64	67	68	2nd NL West

Seattle Mariners

Year	Franchise Rank	Era Rank	Overall Rank	Pythag Win %	Hitting RAA	BR RAA	Fielding RAA	Pitching RAA	Total RAA	Post Season Results
2001	1	2	9	0.6828	110	25	104	67	306	Lost ALCS
2003	2	92	223	0.5986	0	2	35	116	153	2nd AL West

Year	Franchise Rank	Era Rank	Overall Rank	Pythag Win %	Hitting RAA	BR RAA	Fielding RAA	Pitching RAA	Total RAA	Post Season Results
2002	3	149	323	0.5829	48	7	5	75	134	3rd AL West
2000	4	225	441	0.5652	37	0	29	46	112	Lost ALCS
1995	5	271	510	0.5454	45	-1	10	15	69	Lost ALCS
1996	6	273	512	0.5442	117	-1	50	-83	83	2nd NL West

Tampa Bay Rays

Year	Franchise Rank	Era Rank	Overall Rank	Pythag Win %	Hitting RAA	BR RAA	Fielding RAA	Pitching RAA	Total RAA	Post Season Results
2008	1	178	373	0.5759	19	6	23	71	118	Lost World Series
2010	2	186	385	0.5737	13	27	53	19	112	Lost ALDS
2012	3	204	414	0.5700	-34	-9	12	129	98	2nd NL
2011	4	209	420	0.5685	-11	8	82	21	100	Lost ALDS

Texas Rangers

Year	Franchise Rank	Era Rank	Overall Rank	Pythag Win %	Hitting RAA	BR RAA	Fielding RAA	Pitching RAA	Total RAA	Post Season Results
2011	1	53	142	0.6141	136	16	17	19	188	Lost World Series
1996	2	128	284	0.5879	67	17	22	52	158	Lost ALDS
1977	3	135	299	0.5866	34	10	62	27	133	2nd AL West
2010	4	220	435	0.5656	50	18	-8	43	103	Lost World Series
2012	5	251	484	0.5557	98	-11	-3	5	89	Lost AL Wild Card

Toronto Blue Jays

Year	Franchise Rank	Era Rank	Overall Rank	Pythag Win %	Hitting RAA	BR RAA	Fielding RAA	Pitching RAA	Total RAA	Post Season Results
1985	1	26	76	0.6296	43	0	71	81	195	Lost ALCS
1987	2	37	108	0.6208	42	7	50	95	194	2nd AL East
1993	3	197	407	0.5708	85	15	10	9	119	Won World Series
1990	4	202	412	0.5704	56	11	28	13	108	2nd AL East
1992	5	248	479	0.5567	63	13	32	-19	89	Won World Series

Montreal Expos

Year	Franchise Rank	Era Rank	Overall Rank	Pythag Win %	Hitting RAA	BR RAA	Fielding RAA	Pitching RAA	Total RAA	Post Season Results
1994	1	20	67	0.6329	47	21	23	59	150	1st NL East
1979	2	168	358	0.5789	23	-10	30	69	112	2nd NL East
1980	3	267	504	0.5491	36	13	-8	31	72	2nd NL East

Washington Nationals

Year	Franchise Rank	Era Rank	Overall Rank	Pythag Win %	Hitting RAA	BR RAA	Fielding RAA	Pitching RAA	Total RAA	Post Season Results
2014	1	64	163	0.6100	43	13	5	95	155	Lost NLDS
2012	2	101	239	0.5961	57	-3	-12	98	140	Lost NLDS

Washington Senators

Year	Franchise Rank	Era Rank	Overall Rank	Pythag Win %	Hitting RAA	BR RAA	Fielding RAA	Pitching RAA	Total RAA	Post Season Results
1930	1	39	95	0.6238	57	-2	64	85	204	2nd AL
1924	2	69	175	0.6072	-5	0	56	108	159	Won World Series
1925	3	75	188	0.6048	44	1	38	84	167	Lost World Series
1933	4	82	203	0.6018	47	1	42	68	158	Lost World Series
1931	5	139	369	0.5762	11	-5	33	80	119	3rd AL
1912	6	61	418	0.5688	-32	16	38	73	95	2nd AL
1932	7	155	453	0.5639	8	2	44	48	102	3rd AL

Minnesota Twins

Year	Franchise Rank	Era Rank	Overall Rank	Pythag Win %	Hitting RAA	BR RAA	Fielding RAA	Pitching RAA	Total RAA	Post Season Results
1969	1	46	128	0.6162	118	-5	18	45	176	Lost ALCS
1963	2	63	160	0.6105	116	-3	36	18	167	3rd AL
1965	3	97	231	0.5972	84	20	70	-30	144	Lost World Series
1991	4	109	252	0.5942	82	-5	35	36	148	Won World Series
1970	5	190	391	0.5729	50	-12	53	15	106	Lost ALCS
2006	6	208	419	0.5688	0	2	12	95	108	Lost ALDS
2010	7	230	449	0.5646	62	-12	-16	65	100	Lost ALDS
1962	8	266	503	0.5492	67	0	26	-15	78	2nd AL
1987	9	289	534	0.4811	-8	-3	12	-33	-31	Won World Series

Boston Braves

Year	Franchise Rank	Era Rank	Overall Rank	Pythag Win %	Hitting RAA	BR RAA	Fielding RAA	Pitching RAA	Total RAA	Post Season Results
1948	1	21	51	0.6402	94	2	21	91	208	Lost World Series
1914	2	70	475	0.5570	17	-4	43	19	75	Won World Series

Milwaukee Brewers

Year	Franchise Rank	Era Rank	Overall Rank	Pythag Win %	Hitting RAA	BR RAA	Fielding RAA	Pitching RAA	Total RAA	Post Season Results
1978	1	105	245	**0.5950**	**114**	**8**	**24**	**3**	149	3rd AL East
1979	2	130	287	**0.5877**	**95**	**17**	**6**	**28**	146	2nd AL East
1980	3	150	324	**0.5828**	**78**	**9**	**25**	**21**	133	3rd AL East
1982	4	158	341	**0.58054**	**109**	**7**	**16**	**0**	132	Lost World Series

Year	Franchise Rank	Era Rank	Overall Rank	Pythag Win %	Hitting RAA	BR RAA	Fielding RAA	Pitching RAA	Total RAA	Post Season Results
1992	5	201	411	**0.5705**	**-10**	**14**	**12**	**87**	102	2nd AL East
2011	6	212	423	**0.5682**	**73**	**0**	**12**	**18**	103	Lost NLCS

Milwaukee Braves

Year	Franchise Rank	Era Rank	Overall Rank	Pythag Win %	Hitting RAA	BR RAA	Fielding RAA	Pitching RAA	Total RAA	Post Season Results
1957	1	60	155	0.6112	82	15	36	34	167	Won World Series
1958	2	65	164	0.6099	14	3	65	70	152	Lost World Series
1956	3	87	228	0.5977	38	4	58	37	137	2nd AL
1953	4	92	238	0.5964	-22	2	12	147	138	2nd NL
1954	5	98	259	0.5931	-33	4	15	141	127	3rd NL
1959	6	144	396	0.5724	32	4	-21	91	105	2nd NL

Atlanta Braves

Year	Franchise Rank	Era Rank	Overall Rank	Pythag Win %	Hitting RAA	BR RAA	Fielding RAA	Pitching RAA	Total RAA	Post Season Results
1998	1	4	19	0.6674	102	6	84	74	266	Lost NLCS
1997	2	13	52	0.6402	56	-18	69	104	211	Lost NLCS
1993	3	18	62	0.6343	26	-1	82	90	197	Lost NLCS
2002	4	62	159	0.6106	0	-11	77	91	157	Lost NLDS
1999	5	66	169	0.6087	9	8	43	112	172	Lost World Series
1996	6	85	208	0.6008	49	-13	38	83	157	Lost World Series
2013	7	87	212	0.5998	40	-4	30	74	140	Lost ALDS
2003	8	88	213	0.5998	150	10	35	-24	171	Lost NLDS
1995	9	129	285	0.5877	-10	-2	19	108	115	Won World Series
2004	10	133	291	0.5875	48	3	43	45	138	Lost NLDS
1994	11	148	322	0.5833	25	-18	25	58	89	2nd NL East
2010	12	181	376	0.5755	44	-5	11	63	113	Lost NLDS
2000	13	196	405	0.5712	8	11	36	62	116	Lost NLDS
2005	14	215	428	0.5675	42	4	58	1	105	Lost ALDS
1983	15	216	431	0.5668	91	-9	-16	35	101	2nd NL West
2009	16	217	432	0.5666	17	-13	-11	106	99	3rd NL East
1992	17	218	433	0.5666	34	-2	39	21	92	Lost World Series
1991	18	228	447	0.5647	65	12	-98	119	97	Lost World Series
2012	19	259	496	0.5505	-12	14	76	-6	72	Lost NL Wild Card
2011	20	286	530	0.5255	-36	-10	12	69	35	2nd NL East
1969	21	287	532	0.5242	20	-10	50	-25	35	Lost NLCS

St. Louis Browns

Year	Franchise Rank	Era Rank	Overall Rank	Pythag Win %	Hitting RAA	BR RAA	Fielding RAA	Pitching RAA	Total RAA	Post Season Results
1922	1	13	31	0.6583	148	7	39	63	256	2nd AL

Baltimore Orioles

Year	Franchise Rank	Era Rank	Overall Rank	Pythag Win %	Hitting RAA	BR RAA	Fielding RAA	Pitching RAA	Total RAA	Post Season Results
1969	1	1	6	0.6909	135	-3	114	39	285	Lost World Series
1971	2	10	42	0.6488	133	2	54	28	217	Lost World Series
1970	3	11	45	0.6454	101	4	59	54	218	Won World Series
1973	4	12	49	0.6405	61	9	119	19	208	Lost ALCS
1979	5	24	73	0.6308	25	0	74	97	196	Lost World Series
1966	6	83	206	0.6010	114	1	19	15	149	Won World Series
1975	7	103	241	0.5953	-14	3	80	63	132	2nd AL East
1980	8	106	246	0.5950	52	2	28	65	146	2nd AL East
1994	9	116	264	0.5911	13	7	56	31	107	2nd AL East
1983	10	127	283	0.5880	70	-10	6	71	137	Won World Series
1997	11	145	318	0.5836	6	-1	14	113	132	Lost ALCS
1964	12	153	331	0.5820	14	9	75	17	116	3rd AL
2014	13	180	375	0.5756	41	-14	51	30	108	Lost ALCS

Cincinnati Reds

Year	Franchise Rank	Era Rank	Overall Rank	Pythag Win %	Hitting RAA	BR RAA	Fielding RAA	Pitching RAA	Total RAA	Post Season Results
1976	1	7	29	0.6585	214	27	7	12	260	Won World Series
1975	2	8	38	0.6520	128	24	61	23	236	Won World Series
1919	3	20	56	0.6378	43	-4	43	71	153	Won World Series
1940	4	40	97	0.6232	6	1	99	61	168	Won World Series
1994	5	58	149	0.6127	78	7	-1	48	132	1st NL Central
1939	6	68	173	0.6082	51	0	60	46	156	Lost World Series
1974	7	90	217	0.5992	95	12	59	-14	152	2nd NL West
1972	8	102	240	0.5958	67	11	53	1	132	Lost World Series
1904	9	47	249	0.5945	56	-3	12	63	128	3rd NL
1990	10	111	255	0.5939	35	15	-17	105	138	Won World Series
1970	11	122	274	0.5891	94	3	29	18	144	Lost World Series
1999	12	126	282	0.5881	34	11	96	4	145	2nd NL Central
1995	13	147	321	0.5834	77	1	27	16	121	Lost NLCS
1965	14	159	342	0.5805	188	-5	-26	-25	132	4th NL
1926	15	132	349	0.5796	52	-2	52	17	119	2nd NL
2010	16	163	352	0.5794	103	-2	32	-7	126	Lost NLDS
1973	17	170	361	0.5780	43	14	46	12	115	Lost NLCS
2013	18	171	363	0.5772	40	-4	23	50	110	Lost NL Wild Card
1962	19	185	384	0.5738	54	14	-10	59	117	3rd NL
1956	20	149	404	0.5716	103	1	15	-11	109	3rd AL
1964	21	207	417	0.5690	-10	13	20	72	95	2nd NL
1903	22	64	438	0.5654	95	-8	-19	28	96	4th NL
1977	23	229	448	0.5646	115	15	-1	-22	107	2nd NL West
1961	24	274	513	0.5438	19	3	35	8	65	Lost World Series

Cleveland Indians/Naps

Year	Franchise Rank	Era Rank	Overall Rank	Pythag Win %	Hitting RAA	BR RAA	Fielding RAA	Pitching RAA	Total RAA	Post Season Results
1948	1	3	7	0.6887	112	-4	80	103	291	Won World Series
1954	2	8	15	0.6762	76	10	33	128	247	Lost World Series
1995	3	5	23	0.6638	122	-3	-7	140	252	Lost World Series
1906	4	10	27	0.6600	111	-3	71	32	211	3rd AL
1920	5	30	79	0.6288	123	-7	25	63	205	Won World Series

Year	Franchise Rank	Era Rank	Overall Rank	Pythag Win %	Hitting RAA	BR RAA	Fielding RAA	Pitching RAA	Total RAA	Post Season Results
1921	6	52	125	0.6166	114	5	-15	92	195	2nd AL
2005	7	44	126	0.6166	62	0	51	71	184	2nd AL Central
1996	8	51	138	0.6145	109	-10	-13	119	205	Lost ALDS
1950	9	59	153	0.6118	39	4	24	108	176	4th AL
1904	10	37	166	0.6094	78	3	0	61	141	4th AL
1952	11	79	200	0.6019	95	8	1	46	150	2nd AL
1955	12	80	201	0.6019	60	0	-51	140	149	2nd AL
1951	13	95	248	0.5945	0	11	10	115	136	2nd AL
1953	14	96	251	0.5943	76	9	33	24	143	2nd AL
1994	15	114	260	0.5925	73	9	-5	39	117	2nd AL Central
1908	16	53	298	0.5868	14	0	31	58	103	2nd AL
1919	17	54	304	0.5860	78	1	-1	34	112	2nd AL
1949	18	122	326	0.5826	-30	-12	61	95	114	3rd AL
2000	19	157	340	0.5807	103	3	-14	54	146	2nd AL Central
1956	20	131	348	0.5797	-35	6	7	134	112	2nd AL
1926	21	135	360	0.5783	-17	10	40	80	113	2nd AL
2007	22	193	397	0.5724	26	1	1	88	116	Lost ALCS
1923	23	146	401	0.5720	134	-4	-14	3	119	3rd AL
1999	24	198	408	0.5708	130	4	33	-37	131	Lost ALDS
1940	25	156	455	0.5626	-43	1	35	99	92	2nd AL

Detroit Tigers

Year	Franchise Rank	Era Rank	Overall Rank	Pythag Win %	Hitting RAA	BR RAA	Fielding RAA	Pitching RAA	Total RAA	Post Season Results
1935	1	32	82	0.6286	96	0	41	71	208	Won World Series
1909	2	24	83	0.6282	98	12	37	20	167	Lost World Series
1968	3	28	85	0.6278	102	-7	63	11	169	Won World Series
1934	4	48	115	0.6200	111	5	23	62	201	Lost World Series
1984	5	49	132	0.6157	103	-2	52	29	182	Won World Series
2013	6	50	134	0.6156	123	-20	-45	121	179	Lost ALCS
1915	7	33	139	0.6143	131	8	10	19	168	2nd AL
1940	8	66	168	0.6093	124	3	-29	84	183	Lost World Series
1961	9	69	174	0.6077	96	6	60	12	174	2nd AL
1987	10	94	226	0.5981	91	9	9	57	167	Lost ALCS
1950	11	113	302	0.5860	60	-12	32	58	138	2nd AL
1946	12	114	305	0.5859	43	4	7	64	118	2nd AL
1983	13	151	327	0.5823	67	15	80	-31	131	2nd AL East
1907	14	62	426	0.5679	63	0	-28	54	89	Lost World Series
2006	15	224	440	0.5652	-12	-6	39	81	101	Lost World Series
1955	16	153	443	0.5649	46	23	-1	30	98	5th AL
1908	17	68	468	0.5593	102	1	-38	14	79	Lost World Series
1910	18	72	490	0.5542	96	7	5	-32	76	3rd AL
1923	19	164	491	0.5538	91	5	0	-8	88	2nd AL
2011	20	265	502	0.5493	91	-14	16	-15	79	Lost ALCS
1916	21	74	514	0.5434	78	2	-5	-15	60	3rd AL
1911	22	77	531	0.5253	91	10	-36	-24	41	2nd AL

Boston Red Sox/Americans

Year	Franchise Rank	Era Rank	Overall Rank	Pythag Win %	Hitting RAA	BR RAA	Fielding RAA	Pitching RAA	Total RAA	Post Season Results
1912	1	12	32	0.6564	104	-15	15	126	230	Won World Series
2007	2	14	53	0.6394	108	1	10	113	231	Won World Series

Year	Franchise Rank	Era Rank	Overall Rank	Pythag Win %	Hitting RAA	BR RAA	Fielding RAA	Pitching RAA	Total RAA	Post Season Results
1949	3	27	71	0.6310	147	6	24	36	213	2nd AL
1903	4	23	75	0.6299	91	-2	37	41	167	Won World Series
2013	5	31	90	0.6252	154	10	22	18	204	Won World Series
1942	6	44	104	0.6214	132	-5	32	22	181	2nd AL
1946	7	46	110	0.6206	136	1	25	17	179	Lost World Series
1915	8	29	116	0.6199	46	-8	33	87	158	Won World Series
2002	9	41	119	0.6188	74	5	62	52	193	2nd AL East
1904	10	36	165	0.6097	42	-3	26	70	136	1st AL; no World Series
2008	11	73	183	0.6056	114	-4	21	44	175	Lost ALCS
2003	12	77	190	0.6044	192	6	-23	15	190	Lost ALCS
1901	13	40	197	0.6021	9	-4	56	84	144	2nd AL
2004	14	80	198	0.6020	137	0	-15	58	180	Won World Series
1977	15	99	233	0.5971	144	8	19	-7	163	2nd AL East
1979	16	121	273	0.5893	108	-1	37	3	147	3rd AL East
1999	17	125	280	0.5884	25	-8	48	82	147	Lost ALCS
1950	18	108	288	0.5876	185	-2	-9	-18	156	3rd AL
1978	19	134	295	0.5871	96	1	10	28	134	Lost playoff to Yankees
1948	20	119	314	0.5844	115	9	28	-14	138	Lost play-off to Indians
2011	21	142	315	0.5843	167	-9	33	-49	142	3rd AL East
1998	22	143	316	0.5840	77	-14	62	16	141	Lost ALDS
1955	23	121	325	0.5827	77	11	40	-3	126	4th AL
1988	24	154	332	0.5818	140	-15	5	3	133	Lost ALCS
1938	25	134	353	0.5792	87	-8	1	54	134	2nd AL
2009	26	184	382	0.5742	93	-1	-18	51	124	Lost ALDS
1918	27	59	383	0.5742	6	0	43	26	74	Won World Series
1995	28	194	398	0.5723	76	-2	79	-42	112	Lost ALDS
1967	29	195	400	0.5721	118	3	37	-52	106	Lost World Series
1941	30	151	427	0.5678	136	-3	-19	-1	114	2nd AL
1916	31	67	463	0.5608	-20	-1	24	71	74	Won World Series
2010	32	255	489	0.5543	110	1	27	-49	89	3rd AL East
1986	33	256	493	0.5532	59	-18	-2	45	84	Lost World Series
1975	34	264	501	0.5494	108	-9	67	-87	78	Lost World Series
2005	35	270	509	0.5466	132	3	-22	-31	81	Lost ALDS

BROOKLYN DODGERS/ROBINS/SUPERBAS

Year	Franchise Rank	Era Rank	Overall Rank	Pythag Win %	Hitting RAA	BR RAA	Fielding RAA	Pitching RAA	Total RAA	Post Season Results
1953	1	16	39	0.6519	188	16	50	5	259	Lost World Series
1941	2	17	43	0.6479	128	0	56	37	221	Lost World Series
1955	3	23	61	0.6346	142	24	66	-16	216	Won World Series
1942	4	28	77	0.6294	79	-1	40	55	174	2nd NL
1949	5	37	93	0.6241	103	27	41	25	196	Lost World Series
1952	6	57	148	0.6130	107	8	17	34	167	Lost World Series
1951	7	72	178	0.6070	130	3	42	-6	170	Lost play-off to Giants
1916	8	41	210	0.6001	46	1	17	58	123	Lost World Series
1930	9	90	235	0.5968	21	0	59	83	163	4th NL
1956	10	111	297	0.5869	81	-6	87	-35	127	Lost World Series
1946	11	115	309	0.5853	61	1	11	45	118	2nd NL
1920	12	117	312	0.5845	19	-1	1	91	110	Lost World Series
1950	13	143	394	0.5725	107	7	28	-25	117	2nd NL
1947	14	152	429	0.5671	62	-1	39	2	103	Lost World Series
1901	15	63	430	0.5669	64	-2	-1	33	93	3rd NL
1957	16	158	459	0.5612	-11	11	38	48	85	3rd NL

Los Angeles Dodgers

Year	Franchise Rank	Era Rank	Overall Rank	Pythag Win %	Hitting RAA	BR RAA	Fielding RAA	Pitching RAA	Total RAA	Post Season Results
1974	1	9	41	0.6507	103	8	37	78	226	Lost World Series
1977	2	16	59	0.6351	58	6	11	128	203	Lost World Series
1978	3	35	105	0.6212	98	11	4	66	179	Lost World Series
2009	4	40	118	0.6190	48	2	14	117	180	Lost NLCS
1966	5	75	186	0.6053	-37	0	-13	187	137	Lost World Series
1975	6	81	199	0.6020	-10	8	83	58	139	2nd NL West
1981	7	82	205	0.6017	16	0	-5	80	92	Won World Series
1985	8	117	266	0.5908	38	9	12	71	130	Lost NLCS
1973	9	124	279	0.5886	-5	5	58	65	123	2nd NL West
2014	10	138	306	0.5858	95	-2	16	19	128	Lost NLDS
1962	11	182	377	0.5753	41	28	-14	65	120	Lost play-off to Giants
2013	12	183	381	0.5744	43	-7	44	26	106	Lost NLCS
1991	13	189	389	0.5732	1	-2	-26	128	101	2nd NL West
1965	14	191	392	0.5728	-61	16	60	80	95	Won World Series
1963	15	236	460	0.5609	-3	10	-28	102	82	Won World Series
1988	16	275	515	0.5417	-32	1	12	74	55	Won World Series
1959	17	167	525	0.5332	17	4	-2	30	49	Won World Series

Chicago Cubs

Year	Franchise Rank	Era Rank	Overall Rank	Pythag Win %	Hitting RAA	BR RAA	Fielding RAA	Pitching RAA	Total RAA	Post Season Results
1906	1	1	3	0.7205	84	9	83	97	273	Lost World Series
1909	2	9	25	0.6628	7	0	33	150	190	2nd NL
1905	3	14	36	0.6527	-30	9	64	146	189	3rd NL
1907	4	16	40	0.6511	25	6	85	57	173	Won World Series
1935	5	18	44	0.6465	81	-2	55	88	222	Lost World Series
1910	6	17	46	0.6447	81	-7	23	101	198	Lost World Series
1918	7	25	84	0.6279	48	-2	0	87	133	Lost World Series
2008	8	39	112	0.6201	118	-1	-25	105	197	Lost NLDS
1936	9	63	161	0.6104	44	-1	40	82	166	2nd NL
1929	10	70	176	0.6072	92	5	36	51	184	Lost World Series
1908	11	44	220	0.5990	49	0	40	30	119	Won World Series
1911	12	49	270	0.5902	44	-5	39	53	131	2nd NL
1933	13	104	276	0.5889	47	-1	41	32	120	3rd NL
1937	14	110	293	0.5875	117	1	11	9	137	2nd NL
2004	15	136	300	0.5866	48	-11	-16	114	135	3rd NL Central
1972	16	137	303	0.5860	74	8	-24	62	120	2nd NL East
1928	17	123	329	0.5823	11	3	50	56	120	3rd NL
1938	18	126	334	0.5818	25	-1	24	67	115	Lost World Series
1930	19	130	347	0.5798	110	6	4	27	146	2nd NL
1931	20	140	379	0.5747	131	-1	1	-11	120	3rd NL
1903	21	60	386	0.5735	19	7	15	60	101	3rd NL
1970	22	214	425	0.5680	49	15	-10	54	108	2nd NL East
1932	23	161	476	0.5570	0	0	33	49	83	Lost World Series
1969	24	246	477	0.5570	37	-4	-11	60	82	2nd NL East
1984	25	261	498	0.5496	78	6	-18	10	76	Lost NLCS
1998	26	288	533	0.5101	58	-8	-16	-17	17	Lost NLDS

CHICAGO WHITE SOX

Year	*Franchise Rank*	*Era Rank*	*Overall Rank*	*Pythag Win %*	*Hitting RAA*	*BR RAA*	*Fielding RAA*	*Pitching RAA*	*Total RAA*	*Post Season Results*
1915	1	21	57	0.6371	83	-8	14	97	186	3rd AL
1954	2	29	78	0.6289	51	0	72	55	178	3rd AL
1994	3	29	86	0.6276	58	3	13	81	155	1st AL Central
1917	4	28	113	0.6201	36	2	-4	115	149	Won World Series
1905	5	30	117	0.6192	0	0	71	71	142	2nd AL
1955	6	50	122	0.6171	31	6	39	90	166	3rd AL
1964	7	47	129	0.6161	-32	24	96	66	155	2nd AL
1901	8	32	136	0.6146	41	11	28	88	168	1st AL; no World Series
1957	9	61	156	0.6111	39	28	61	29	158	2nd AL
1963	10	113	258	0.5933	4	2	42	80	128	2nd AL
1956	11	100	263	0.5915	30	17	13	78	137	3rd AL
1919	12	52	296	0.5870	69	-1	11	33	112	Lost World Series
1920	13	124	330	0.5821	50	1	12	63	126	2nd AL
1916	14	55	345	0.5801	18	6	30	47	101	2nd AL
1993	15	162	351	0.5794	11	9	61	42	124	Lost ALCS
1960	16	136	362	0.5775	57	-1	44	14	114	3rd AL
1983	17	175	370	0.5761	26	16	44	31	117	Lost ALCS
1959	18	141	390	0.5731	-20	13	79	28	101	Lost World Series
2005	19	199	409	0.5706	-20	-6	42	89	105	Won World Series
1904	20	66	450	0.5644	4	5	71	-1	79	3rd AL
1953	21	159	465	0.5606	-18	-6	32	76	84	3rd AL
2000	22	245	472	0.5581	69	14	6	15	104	Lost ALDS
1906	23	71	485	0.5557	-47	1	46	64	64	Won World Series
1907	24	73	492	0.5538	-37	-3	42	61	63	3rd AL

PITTSBURGH PIRATES

Year	*Franchise Rank*	*Era Rank*	*Overall Rank*	*Pythag Win %*	*Hitting RAA*	*BR RAA*	*Fielding RAA*	*Pitching RAA*	*Total RAA*	*Post Season Results*
1902	1	2	4	0.7130	152	1	52	77	282	1st NL; no World Series
1909	2	8	20	0.6673	100	-4	42	79	217	Won World Series
1901	3	15	37	0.6523	99	0	42	72	213	1st NL; no World Series
1912	4	22	63	0.6341	44	-1	56	94	193	2nd NL
1972	5	19	65	0.6335	74	7	17	83	181	Lost NLCS
1971	6	48	131	0.6158	121	17	15	21	175	Won World Series
1925	7	56	144	0.6139	116	17	26	32	191	Won World Series
1906	8	35	150	0.6123	55	-1	22	63	139	3rd NL
1903	9	38	185	0.6053	89	-2	43	22	152	Lost World Series
1911	10	39	192	0.6039	28	-8	55	71	146	3rd NL
1975	11	78	193	0.6036	44	11	34	61	150	Lost NLCS
1924	12	86	222	0.5987	11	15	81	34	141	3rd NL
1991	13	93	225	0.5984	104	13	-13	47	151	Lost NLCS
1979	14	95	227	0.5978	68	23	6	52	149	Won World Series
1927	15	91	237	0.5965	99	-1	14	39	150	Lost World Series
1960	16	94	244	0.5950	72	-3	38	30	137	Won World Series
1966	17	107	247	0.5950	117	5	11	14	147	3rd NL
1908	18	50	275	0.5891	63	1	19	27	109	2nd NL
1990	19	152	328	0.5823	64	-2	18	43	123	Lost NLCS
1905	20	56	346	0.5800	38	2	42	29	111	2nd NL
1907	21	57	378	0.5751	62	13	-10	31	95	2nd NL
1922	22	145	399	0.5723	56	20	-49	92	119	3rd NL
1992	23	219	434	0.5661	48	3	0	42	93	Lost NLCS
2013	24	238	462	0.5608	8	-8	61	23	84	Lost NLDS

Year	Franchise Rank	Era Rank	Overall Rank	Pythag Win %	Hitting RAA	BR RAA	Fielding RAA	Pitching RAA	Total RAA	Post Season Results
1923	25	162	480	0.5565	26	14	25	23	88	3rd NL
1928	26	163	482	0.5558	89	-4	0	3	88	4th NL
1929	27	166	506	0.5480	28	-3	0	55	80	2nd NL

Philadelphia Phillies

Year	Franchise Rank	Era Rank	Overall Rank	Pythag Win %	Hitting RAA	BR RAA	Fielding RAA	Pitching RAA	Total RAA	Post Season Results
2011	1	17	60	0.6351	17	17	-57	212	189	Lost NLDS
1976	2	23	72	0.6309	106	-5	29	61	191	Lost NLCS
1977	3	57	147	0.6130	143	-2	62	-19	184	Lost NLCS
1915	4	42	216	0.5994	31	-2	33	61	123	Lost World Series
1901	5	46	224	0.5984	29	-4	27	79	131	2nd NL
2010	6	120	272	0.5894	47	18	-6	78	137	Lost NLCS
1952	7	105	277	0.5888	25	-1	22	75	121	4th NL
2008	8	141	310	0.5852	47	19	74	-4	136	Won World Series
1993	9	144	317	0.5838	117	24	-49	49	140	Lost World Series
1978	10	173	365	0.5770	49	6	78	-22	111	Lost NLCS
1950	11	147	402	0.5717	-14	6	29	83	104	Lost World Series
2009	12	211	422	0.5683	76	10	17	7	110	Lost World Series
1980	13	252	486	0.5554	61	-3	4	20	82	Won World Series
2007	14	260	497	0.5498	122	10	40	-84	88	Lost NLDS
1905	15	75	516	0.5407	13	-2	5	40	56	4th NL
1964	16	278	519	0.5395	41	-7	-12	36	57	2nd NL
1983	17	285	528	0.5269	17	-12	-59	93	39	Lost World Series

Philadelphia A's

Year	Franchise Rank	Era Rank	Overall Rank	Pythag Win %	Hitting RAA	BR RAA	Fielding RAA	Pitching RAA	Total RAA	Post Season Results
1910	1	4	8	0.6844	105	1	48	88	242	Won World Series
1909	2	7	17	0.6697	91	2	28	90	210	2nd AL
1929	3	10	22	0.6640	110	6	11	136	263	Won World Series
1931	4	12	30	0.6585	93	4	54	107	257	Lost World Series
1928	5	19	47	0.6440	114	-3	11	104	226	2nd AL
1911	6	19	55	0.6391	108	-5	-3	112	212	Won World Series
1932	7	41	99	0.6229	150	6	28	31	214	2nd AL
1914	8	31	135	0.6152	112	0	14	32	159	Lost World Series
1905	9	34	140	0.6142	60	5	6	76	147	Lost World Series
1930	10	58	152	0.6120	102	5	14	72	193	Won World Series
1913	11	48	254	0.5939	135	-1	28	-25	137	Won World Series
1925	12	102	267	0.5908	54	1	10	83	148	2nd AL
1926	13	129	339	0.5809	-37	2	9	138	113	3rd AL
1927	14	138	367	0.5764	82	1	0	42	124	2nd AL
1912	15	58	380	0.5744	83	7	41	-17	114	2nd AL
1902	16	65	442	0.5651	50	4	-19	58	93	Won AL Pennant

Oakland A's

Year	Franchise Rank	Era Rank	Overall Rank	Pythag Win %	Hitting RAA	BR RAA	Fielding RAA	Pitching RAA	Total RAA	Post Season Results
2001	1	25	74	0.6303	55	1	19	133	208	Lost ALDS
1990	2	52	141	0.6141	31	1	107	26	165	Lost World Series

Year	Franchise Rank	Era Rank	Overall Rank	Pythag Win %	Hitting RAA	BR RAA	Fielding RAA	Pitching RAA	Total RAA	Post Season Results
1988	3	65	167	0.6093	50	7	15	92	164	Lost World Series
1972	4	67	170	0.6087	37	3	52	39	131	Won World Series
2002	5	70	179	0.6063	35	5	-6	134	168	Lost ALDS
1989	6	100	236	0.5965	12	4	19	103	139	Won World Series
1975	7	104	243	0.5951	34	19	42	46	141	Lost ALCS
1971	8	140	308	0.5853	42	5	46	25	118	Lost ALCS
1973	9	165	355	0.5791	28	7	84	-3	117	Won World Series
1974	10	166	356	0.5791	1	1	38	69	109	Won World Series
2003	11	179	374	0.5758	-36	6	4	141	116	Lost ALDS
2014	12	187	387	0.5734	-4	3	32	71	102	Lost Wild Card
2013	13	188	388	0.5733	43	-4	-41	111	109	Lost ALDS
2012	14	239	464	0.5607	-38	16	19	90	87	Lost ALDS
2005	15	250	483	0.5557	-31	10	39	66	84	2nd AL West
2000	16	262	499	0.5496	57	-9	-46	85	87	Lost ALDS

NEW YORK GIANTS

Year	Franchise Rank	Era Rank	Overall Rank	Pythag Win %	Hitting RAA	BR RAA	Fielding RAA	Pitching RAA	Total RAA	Post Season Results
1905	1	3	5	0.6924	143	10	44	86	283	Won World Series
1904	2	5	12	0.6798	87	10	60	88	245	1st NL; no World Series
1911	3	6	16	0.6760	109	22	9	127	267	Lost World Series
1912	4	11	28	0.6588	89	15	20	116	241	Lost World Series
1908	5	13	34	0.6540	138	-7	8	60	198	2nd NL
1913	6	18	50	0.6404	43	6	17	125	191	Lost World Series
1954	7	24	64	0.6340	17	14	50	109	191	Won World Series
1922	8	31	80	0.6287	77	3	65	61	206	Won World Series
1917	9	26	98	0.6231	50	1	59	43	153	Lost World Series
1924	10	43	102	0.6222	124	10	38	20	192	Lost World Series
1910	11	27	109	0.6207	106	9	-21	81	174	2nd NL
1951	12	71	177	0.6072	91	12	32	30	165	Lost World Series
1921	13	73	180	0.6062	94	1	60	8	163	Won World Series
1934	14	74	187	0.6050	8	3	58	80	150	2nd NL
1931	15	77	195	0.6025	61	-3	36	56	150	2nd NL
1906	16	43	219	0.5991	91	8	16	15	131	2nd NL
1903	17	45	221	0.5987	9	5	-4	123	133	2nd NL
1928	18	99	261	0.5924	68	-2	50	25	141	2nd NL
1923	19	103	268	0.5907	72	6	40	26	144	Lost World Series
1937	20	106	281	0.5883	40	-1	51	39	128	Lost World Series
1919	21	51	294	0.5874	64	2	46	-8	104	2nd NL
1929	22	118	313	0.5845	18	-3	40	81	136	3rd NL
1936	23	128	338	0.5809	19	2	63	36	121	Lost World Series
1933	24	133	350	0.5795	-14	2	72	41	101	Won World Series
1920	25	148	403	0.5716	23	1	59	12	95	2nd NL
1930	26	150	406	0.5710	67	-2	49	12	125	3rd NL
1927	27	157	456	0.5623	113	-3	22	-32	100	3rd NL

SAN FRANCISCO GIANTS

Year	Franchise Rank	Era Rank	Overall Rank	Pythag Win %	Hitting RAA	BR RAA	Fielding RAA	Pitching RAA	Total RAA	Post Season Results
2002	1	33	100	0.6228	92	-3	38	64	192	Lost World Series
1993	2	59	151	0.6122	82	-2	37	59	175	2nd NL West
2000	3	68	172	0.6083	130	-8	6	61	189	Lost NLDS

Year	Franchise Rank	Era Rank	Overall Rank	Pythag Win %	Hitting RAA	BR RAA	Fielding RAA	Pitching RAA	Total RAA	Post Season Results
1962	4	71	181	0.6059	123	8	30	14	175	Lost World Series
2010	5	118	269	0.5905	8	-9	30	101	129	Won World Series
2003	6	161	344	0.5801	31	-12	35	68	122	Lost NLDS
1989	7	221	436	0.5656	50	7	39	-1	94	Lost World Series
1963	8	222	437	0.5655	111	4	-35	18	98	3rd NL
1965	9	226	445	0.5648	24	5	-4	67	92	2nd NL
1998	10	227	446	0.5648	84	3	13	7	107	2nd NL West
2001	11	237	461	0.5609	93	-17	6	19	101	2nd NL West
1987	12	243	470	0.5588	33	-17	14	59	90	Lost NLCS
1961	13	244	471	0.5587	35	3	20	30	88	3rd NL
1971	14	279	520	0.5392	57	12	-1	-10	58	Lost NLCS
2012	15	280	521	0.5386	20	14	76	-53	57	Won World Series
2014	16	284	527	0.5281	7	2	-7	38	40	Won World Series

St. Louis Cardinals

Year	Franchise Rank	Era Rank	Overall Rank	Pythag Win %	Hitting RAA	BR RAA	Fielding RAA	Pitching RAA	Total RAA	Post Season Results
1943	1	6	13	0.6789	**93**	**0**	**53**	**96**	242	Lost World Series
1942	2	7	14	0.6767	**109**	**-1**	**20**	**112**	240	Won World Series
2004	3	32	96	0.6236	**98**	**4**	**31**	**67**	201	Lost World Series
1985	4	42	120	0.6180	**52**	**31**	**50**	**40**	173	Lost World Series
1928	5	49	121	0.6172	**73**	**1**	**17**	**87**	178	Lost World Series
1939	6	51	124	0.6168	**122**	**-1**	**16**	**42**	180	2nd NL
1949	7	62	157	0.6108	**61**	**4**	**17**	**84**	166	2nd NL
1941	8	83	204	0.6017	**62**	**1**	**44**	**39**	146	2nd NL
1931	9	84	209	0.6005	**61**	**2**	**23**	**63**	149	Won World Series
2005	10	89	214	0.5995	**37**	**16**	**61**	**39**	153	Lost NLCS 2–4
1930	11	88	229	0.5975	**72**	**-3**	**3**	**99**	171	Lost World Series
1935	12	89	234	0.5969	**33**	**3**	**14**	**95**	144	2nd NL
1946	13	93	242	0.5951	**54**	**1**	**17**	**58**	129	Won World Series
1967	14	108	250	0.5943	**52**	**12**	**8**	**60**	132	Won World Series
1934	15	101	265	0.5910	**63**	**1**	**6**	**68**	138	Won World Series
1963	16	123	278	0.5888	**119**	**22**	**28**	**-35**	134	2nd NL
1968	17	132	290	0.5875	**2**	**16**	**-3**	**93**	108	Lost World Series
1947	18	109	292	0.5875	**41**	**1**	**0**	**88**	130	2nd AL
1921	19	112	301	0.5861	**114**	**0**	**9**	**13**	136	3rd AL
2013	20	156	337	0.5811	**67**	**-9**	**-35**	**95**	118	Lost World Series
2002	21	164	354	0.5791	**44**	**3**	**49**	**26**	121	Lost NLCS
2001	22	167	357	0.5790	**48**	**5**	**61**	**13**	127	Lost NLDS
2012	23	174	368	0.5762	**89**	**-3**	**-2**	**32**	116	Lost NLCS
1926	24	142	393	0.5727	**76**	**-1**	**42**	**-5**	112	Won World Series
2009	25	203	413	0.5702	**14**	**7**	**23**	**62**	106	Lost NLDS
2000	26	206	416	0.5696	**83**	**0**	**43**	**-6**	120	Lost NLCS
1962	27	231	451	0.5643	**22**	**6**	**62**	**9**	99	6th NL
2010	28	232	452	0.5643	**25**	**2**	**32**	**37**	96	2nd NL Central
1982	29	240	466	0.5605	**24**	**9**	**53**	**2**	87	Won World Series
1927	30	160	473	0.5581	**47**	**3**	**54**	**-16**	88	2nd NL
2011	31	254	488	0.5544	**116**	**-16**	**-32**	**18**	85	Won World Series
1948	32	165	505	0.5481	**29**	**4**	**-7**	**45**	71	2nd AL
1964	33	269	508	0.5469	**62**	**12**	**19**	**-22**	70	Won World Series
1901	34	76	522	0.5384	**87**	**-2**	**28**	**-56**	56	4th NL
1987	35	281	523	0.5382	**-9**	**21**	**11**	**36**	59	Lost World Series
2006	36	285	528	0.5255	**15**	**13**	**34**	**-20**	42	Won World Series

NEW YORK YANKEES

Year	Franchise Rank	Era Rank	Overall Rank	Pythag Win %	Hitting RAA	BR RAA	Fielding RAA	Pitching RAA	Total RAA	Post Season Results
1927	1	1	1	0.7294	235	-2	41	124	398	Won World Series
1939	2	2	2	0.7273	134	3	88	150	375	Won World Series
1936	3	4	10	0.6820	162	2	25	142	331	Won World Series
1942	4	5	11	0.6808	104	7	70	78	259	Lost World Series
1998	5	3	18	0.6683	123	0	28	135	286	Won World Series
1953	6	9	21	0.6659	113	6	35	95	249	Won World Series
1937	7	11	26	0.6614	113	1	21	137	271	Won World Series
1931	8	14	33	0.6551	220	8	-9	62	280	2nd AL
1932	9	15	35	0.6528	172	-4	-18	117	267	Won World Series
1957	10	20	48	0.6436	75	9	46	73	204	Lost World Series
1955	11	22	54	0.6391	71	21	72	42	206	Lost World Series
1961	12	15	58	0.6365	82	6	73	53	214	Won World Series
1938	13	25	66	0.6333	77	11	21	115	224	Won World Series
1954	14	26	69	0.6321	101	9	18	65	193	2nd AL
1947	15	33	87	0.6264	110	3	22	50	185	Won World Series
2002	16	30	88	0.6259	119	8	-56	141	212	Lost ALDS
1921	17	34	89	0.6257	138	3	33	39	213	Lost World Series
1952	18	35	91	0.6245	88	7	57	27	180	Won World Series
1934	19	36	92	0.6242	71	-2	38	92	199	2nd AL
1948	20	38	94	0.6239	99	2	11	82	194	3rd AL
1958	21	42	101	0.6226	88	23	58	10	179	Won World Series
1977	22	34	103	0.6214	104	8	44	39	195	Won World Series
1956	23	45	107	0.6208	80	17	29	61	187	Won World Series
1997	24	38	111	0.6203	80	-6	-63	187	199	Lost ALDS
1923	25	47	114	0.6201	73	-4	56	59	183	Won World Series
1985	26	43	123	0.6169	82	31	27	49	189	2nd AL East
1999	27	45	127	0.6165	81	2	-19	138	202	Won World Series
1941	28	53	130	0.6159	64	2	64	48	179	Won World Series
1928	29	54	133	0.6157	143	-4	-16	65	189	Won World Series
1950	30	55	137	0.6145	92	4	19	73	188	Won World Series
2003	31	54	143	0.6139	111	-1	-43	127	193	Lost World Series
2011	32	55	145	0.6138	122	-4	4	61	182	Lost ALDS
1994	33	56	146	0.6134	97	-19	-2	65	141	1st AL East
2009	34	60	154	0.6115	162	11	-24	47	196	Won World Series
1943	35	64	162	0.6101	97	-8	31	32	151	Won World Series
1935	36	67	171	0.6084	42	-1	46	80	168	2nd AL
1976	37	72	182	0.6058	64	18	96	-25	153	Lost World Series
2007	38	74	184	0.6053	154	25	-15	24	188	Lost ALDS
1920	39	76	191	0.6042	69	-4	31	65	160	3rd AL
1963	40	79	194	0.6027	27	7	53	57	144	Lost World Series
1951	41	78	196	0.6022	61	8	28	58	155	Won World Series
1922	42	81	202	0.6019	35	-2	51	68	152	Lost World Series
1980	43	84	207	0.6008	79	8	-14	87	160	Lost ALCS
2012	44	86	211	0.6001	120	-2	-8	51	161	Lost ALCS
1949	45	85	215	0.5994	58	7	32	55	152	Won World Series
1978	46	110	253	0.5940	14	14	47	60	135	Won World Series
1946	47	97	257	0.5934	54	2	48	25	129	3rd AL
2010	48	119	271	0.5901	114	10	44	-22	147	Lost ALCS
1960	49	107	286	0.5877	63	11	76	-20	130	Lost World Series
1964	50	131	289	0.5876	13	5	49	55	123	Lost World Series
2006	51	139	307	0.5854	112	11	-55	80	148	Lost ALDS
1926	52	116	311	0.5848	123	-1	-16	32	138	Lost World Series
1933	53	120	320	0.5835	155	-1	-38	26	143	2nd AL
1924	54	125	333	0.5818	35	-2	6	88	127	2nd AL
1962	55	155	335	0.5815	87	-6	35	13	129	Won World Series
1940	56	127	336	0.5812	25	2	41	58	126	3rd AL

Appendix A: Team Valuations

Teams are ranked by their calculated winning percentage based on their calculated offensive runs scored and calculated defensive runs allowed. Below is an illustration of how the winning percentage of the 1961 New York Yankees is calculated based on the team's calculated offensive runs scored and defensive runs allowed.

Calculating the value of an out

Value of an out = ((0.47*1B) + (0.78*2B) + (1.09*3B) + (1.4*HR) + 0.31*(BB + HBP)) / (At Bats—Hits)

Calculating the value of an out for the 1961 American League

League outs = 54,904—14,037 = 40,867

Numerator = (9873 singles * 0.47) + (2,226 doubles * 0.78) + (404 triples * 1.09) + (1,534 homeruns * 1.40) +(5,902 walks * 0.31) + (319 * 0.31) = 10,893

Value of a league out = 10,893 / 40,867 = 0.2665

Calculating team batting runs

(0.47*1B) + (0.78*2B) + (1.09*3B) + (1.4*HR) + 0.31*(BB + HBP)—(Value of an Out *(At Bats—Hits))

Calculating batting runs for the 1961 Yankees

Team singles = 987
Team doubles = 194
Team triples = 40
Team homeruns = 240
Team walks = 543
Team HBP = 35
Team at bats = 5559
Team hits = 1461

(0.47*987) + (0.78*194) + (1.09*40) + (1.4*240) + 0.31*(543 + 35)—(0.2665 *(5559–1461)) = 82

Calculating team offensive runs

a. Add the Baserunning runs (extracted from baseball-reference.com) above league average to the hitting runs above league average to calculate offensive runs above league average
b. Divide the total league runs scored by the number of league teams to calculate average runs scored per team
c. Add the offensive runs above average to the average runs scored per team to calculate offensive runs

Calculating offensive runs for the 1961 Yankees

82 batting runs above average + 6 baserunning runs above average = 88 offensive runs above average

League runs scored = 7342 runs / 10 teams = 734 average team runs scored

88 + 734 = 822 estimated offensive runs scored

Calculating runs allowed

a. Divide league runs allowed by league innings pitched to calculate league runs allowed per inning pitched (A)

b. Multiply A by team innings pitched to obtain the number of runs allowed if this was a league average pitching team (B)
c. Subtract the team's actual runs allowed from B (C)
d. Divide the total league runs allowed divided by the number of teams to calculate the average team runs allowed (D)
e. Subtract C from D to estimate the team's runs allowed

Calculating runs allowed for the 1961 Yankees team

a. League runs allowed in 1961 AL = 7,342
League innings pitched in 1961 AL = 14,427
League runs allowed per inning pitched 1961 AL = 7,342 / 14,427 = 0.51
b. 1961 Yankees innings pitched = 1,451
1451 * 0.51 = 738
c. 1961 Yankees actual runs allowed = 612
738–612 = 126
d. Total league runs allowed = 7,342
Total league number of teams = 10
Average team runs allowed = 734
e. 734–126 = 608 estimated runs allowed

Calculating the team winning percentage

The Pythagenpat Winning Percentage (PythagW%) formula is used to calculate a team's winning percentage which is how teams are ranked in this book. The PythagW% formula is below:

Offensive Runs Scored^X / (Offensive Runs Scored^X + Defensive Runs Allowed^X)

The exponent X used in the above formula is calculated using the following formula:

((Offensive Runs Scored + Defensive Runs Allowed) / games played)^0.285

Calculating the 1961 Yankee team winning percentage (Pythag W%)

1961 Yankees calculated offensive runs scored = 822

1961 Yankees calculated defensive runs allowed = 608

1961 Yankee games played = 163

((822 + 608) / 163) ^ 0.285 = 1.86

(822^1.86) / ((822^1.86) + (608^1.86)) = 0.6365 Pythagenpat Winning Percentage

Calculating luck

Luck, as defined in this book, is the difference between the Pythagenpat Winning Percentage (PythagW%) and the actual Winning Percentage (Win%). If the actual Win% is higher than the PythagW%, then the team is considered lucky. If the actual Win% is lower than the Pythag%, then the team is considered unlucky. Tables 17 and 18 contain a list of the luckiest and unluckiest teams of the 534 teams that are ranked in this book.

Appendix B: Player Valuations

Positional Players

a. Calculating the value of batting runs above/below league average for the player using the below formula:

(0.47*1B) + (0.78*2B) + (1.09*3B) + (1.4*HR) + 0.31*(BB + HBP)—(Value of an Out *(At Bats—Hits))

Calculating the value of batting runs above/below league average for Mickey Mantle of the 1961 Yankees

Singles = 87	Walks = 126	Value of an out = 0.2665 (see Appendix 1 for calculation)
Doubles = 16	HBP = 0	
Triples = 6	At Bats = 514	
Homeruns = 54	Hits = 163	

(0.47*87+ (0.78*16) + (1.09*6) + (1.4*54) + 0.31*(126 + 0)—(0.2665 *(514–163)) = 81

b. Add the Baserunning runs above league average (extracted from baseball-reference.com)

c. Add the Fielding runs above league average (extracted from baseball-reference.com)

d. Add the Positional runs (extracted from baseball-reference.com)

Calculating the total player value for Mickey Mantle of the 1961 Yankees measured in runs above league average

Hitting runs above league average = 81

Baserunning runs above league average = 8

Fielding runs above league average = 1

Position runs (CF) = -1

Total runs above league average = 81 + 8 + 1 + -1 = 89

e. Converting runs above league average to wins above league average using the below formula:

Square Root of (League Runs / (League Innings Pitched/2)) * 10 = Runs required per Win

The value of Runs Required per Win in most seasons in nearly all seasons is between 9 and 11 converging around 10.

Calculating the total player value for Mickey Mantle of the 1961 Yankees measured in wins above league average

SQRT(7342 / (14,427/2)) * 10 = 10.09 Runs required per Win

89 / 10.09 = 8.8 Wins above league average

Pitchers

Calculating individual pitcher values measured in runs above league average

a. Divide league runs allowed by league innings pitched to calculate league runs allowed per inning pitched (A)

b. Multiply A by the pitcher's innings pitched to obtain the number of runs allowed if this was a league average pitcher (B)
c. Subtract the pitcher's actual runs allowed from B to obtain un-adjusted pitcher runs better than league average (C)
d. Adjust (C) by subtracting the team fielding runs above average multiplied by the percentage of Balls in Play (BIP) that the pitcher allowed

Calculating the player value for Whitey Ford of the 1961 Yankees measured in runs above league average

a. 7,342 League runs allowed / 14,426.7 League Innings Pitched = 0.51 League Runs per Innings Pitched
b. 0.51 League Runs per Innings Pitched * 283 Innings Pitched = 144 Runs Allowed if pitcher is league average
c. 144 Runs Allowed if pitcher is league average—108 Actual Runs Allowed = 36 Runs Allowed better than league average
d. Fielding Runs above league average for the 1961 Yankees is 73; Ford had 827 BIP out of 4,417 team BIP; 36 Runs allowed better than league average (un-adjusted)—73 * (827 / 4,417) = 22.4 Runs Allowed better than league average (adjusted for fielding)

Converting runs above league average to wins above league average

Use the below formula to convert runs above league average to wins above league average:
Square Root of (League Runs / (League Innings Pitched/2)) * 10 = Runs required per Win
The value of Runs Required per Win in most seasons in nearly all seasons is between 9 and 11 usually around 10.

Calculating the pitching value for Whitey Ford of the 1961 Yankees measured in wins above league average

(1) SQRT(7342 / (14,427/2)) * 10 = 10.09 Runs required per Win
(2) 22.4 / 10.09 = 2.2 Wins above league average

Index